This requires a very special and unique approach to component selection and system design along with a hig\ specialised production environment. We \ always been cautious of market fashions and believe in being honest with our customers.

P9-CRK-539

Consistent top quality musical performance, safety and unsurpassed reliability are highly prized here in Salisbury. Naim users across the globe, including numerous musicians, are our most discerning critics. They demand the very best and we have enjoyed responding to the challenge of bringing them closer to the music. To this end, we have also created our own recording label, our intention being to faithfully reproduce original music on to Compact Disc, with the emotion, musicality and ambience intact.

With the Millennium fast approaching this is an exciting time and we are confident that as long as people have a need for music in their lives, Naim Audio has the answer.

Naim Audio Limited

Southampton Road   Salisbury   England SP1 2LN
Tel 01722 332266   Fax 01722 412034
Web Site http://www.naim-audio.com

DAWN UPSHAW

"The voice of the century ...on the most bewitching path."
Diapason

Two-time Grammy Award winner Dawn Upshaw returns with 'THE WORLD SO WIDE a collection of 20th century repertoire from Bernstein to Weill

Release Date: 13.4.98

Cat No: 7559 794582

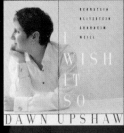

Cat No: 7559 793452

Cat No: 7559 794062

Gramophone

MUSICALS

GOOD CD GUIDE

In association with Naim Audio

© **Gramophone Publications Limited 1998**

UK ISBN 0 902470 98 1

USA ISBN 1 902274 01 6

Sales and distribution

North America

Music Sales Corporation
257 Park Avenue South,
New York, NY 10010, USA.
Telephone (212) 254 2100
Fax (212) 254 2013

UK and Rest of World Record trade

Gramophone Publications Limited
135 Greenford Road, Sudbury Hill, Harrow,
Middlesex HA1 3YD, Great Britain.
Telephone +44 (0)181-422 4562
Fax +44 (0)181-869 8404

UK and Rest of World Book trade

Music Sales
8/9 Frith Street,
London WIV 5TZ
Telephone +44 (0)171-434 0066
Fax +44 (0)171-734 2246

Editor	**Mark Walker**
Editorial Consultant	**Michael Patrick Kennedy**
Contributors	**Rexton S. Bunnett** **Robert A. Cozens** **Robert Cushman** **Adrian Edwards** **Piers Ford** **Michael P. Kennedy** **Andrew Lamb** **Patrick O'Connor** **John Williams**
Production Manager	**Dermot Jones**
Designer	**Isabel Jagoe**
Advertisement Manager	**Paul Geoghegan**
Advertisement Co-ordinator	**Patti Alvarez**
Editorial Director	**Christopher Pollard**

Cover illustration Franklin Hammond
Printed in England by William Clowes Limited,
Beccles, Suffolk, NR34 9QE.

Specialists in Theatrical Recording

2/3 FITZROY MEWS LONDON W1P 5DQ
Telephone: 0171 383 7767   Fax: 0171 383 3020

Contents

Introduction
A year in Musicals

Michael Patrick Kennedy Editorial Consultant

When a brilliant, though eccentric, critic writes a book that sounds a death knell for the Broadway musical, while wistfully recalling the days of the feelgood show as typified by those originally produced and directed by George Abbott and his kind, there is naturally an upsurge in response from the lyric stage both on Broadway and in London. Musicals, both old and new, by established hands and by bright young talents continue to dominate the stages of London and Broadway. The latter celebrates the longevity of *Phantom of the Opera*, *Cats*, *Miss Saigon*, *Les Misérables*, to which, in London, can be added *Starlight Express*. Revivals of *Grease* continue to please and delight on both sides of the Atlantic. (Remember that the original London production of this show back in 1973, with Richard Gere toplined, was not a success.) A recent phenomenon is the screen-to-stage musical. Disney have led the way here, with stunning productions of *Beauty and the Beast* and, most recently in New York, a superbly arresting, visually stunning *Lion King*. 1998 will add stage versions of *Saturday Night Fever* and *Doctor Dolittle* to the entertainment roster here in London.

1997 was a fruitful and encouraging year for musicals in London. A stunning revival of *Chicago* headed the list. Chichester provided a welcome return for Sandy Wilson's sequel to *The Boy Friend – Divorce Me, Darling!* As always, the tiny Bridewell theatre came up trumps, notably with a brand new musical, *Dearly Beloved*, based on Evelyn Waugh's satire on Californian undertakers, and the world première of Stephen Sondheim's earliest show, *Saturday Night*. The Donmar also came up with two completely new shows, which deserved better receptions than they got – *The Fix* and *Enter the Guardsman*. The same goes for two West End shows that achieved brief runs – *The Goodbye Girl* and *Maddie*. About *Always* I'm not so sure: perhaps the subject matter – Edward and Mrs Simpson – defeated the authors. A good revival of *Damn Yankees* enjoyed a brief run. And for the first time London audiences could enjoy Kurt Weill's trailblazing *Lady in the Dark*, courtesy of the Royal National Theatre. In contrast, a celebration of Leiber and Stoller, *Smokey Joe's Cafe*, duplicated its Broadway success. 1998 has already many attractions lined up including revivals of *Bells are Ringing*, *The Pajama Game* and *Show Boat*. Following on from the brilliant Gale Edwards revival of *Jesus Christ Superstar*, Andrew Lloyd Webber has entrusted the talented Australian director with his latest show *Whistle Down the Wind*.

Broadway gave a warm welcome to the latest by Cy Coleman, *The Life*, and Maury Yeston's impressively epic *Titanic*, but Kander and Ebb's fine *Steel Pier* was overshadowed by the fizzing revival of their classic *Chicago*. Frank Wildhorn saw two of his shows finally reach Broadway – *Jekyll and Hyde* and *The Scarlet Pimpernel*. Henry Krieger was represented by a fine show about Siamese twins called *Side Show*. Mary Rodgers saw a successful revival of *Once Upon a Mattress*, Sondheim's *A Funny Thing Happened on the Way to the Forum* completed a successful revival, and Rodgers and Hammerstein's *The King and I* proved its longevity with an imaginatively staged revival by Britain's Christopher Renshaw. Ahrens and Flaherty's *Ragtime* finally reached Broadway after extensive tryouts. Sam Mendes brings his Donmar production of *Cabaret* to Broadway in 1998, and there'll be a full-scale revival of *The Sound of Music* as well.

The death of the musical? I think not. Record companies don't think so, either. Although there have been some deletions, Sony and BMG-RCA have continued to mine the riches of their back catalogues.

Pick of the year

Who'd have thought that we'd ever see *Rex* and *The Golden Apple* on CD? Although collectors will continue to pine for CD transfers of original cast recordings of *Juno*, *Applause*, *Maggie May*, *Trelawny* and many more, each year brings many first recordings, often from the smaller companies – First Night, DRG, Varèse Sarabande – and fascinating radio transcriptions from the 1940s (AEI). TER are particularly to be congratulated for their complete two-disc sets of classic musicals – *The Pajama Game*, *The King and I*, *My Fair Lady* (which won the 1997 **Gramophone** Award) and *Annie Get Your Gun* being especially fine examples. While it's sad that the Gershwin estate have stopped funding the Roxbury series of authentic recordings of Gershwin musicals, those issued already, including *Pardon My English* and *Oh, Kay!* do honour to the Gershwins and to Nonesuch who issued them. It's heartening to find new musicals being recorded from *Titanic*, *Steel Pier* and *The Life* to *The Fix* and *Always*. Equally exciting is the stream of soundtrack reissues on Rhino (in the USA) and EMI (in the UK) from MGM and Warner Bros. classics, sometimes in stereo for the first time, often including cutouts and always with extensive background music restored for the first time on record.

With such a welter of new issues each year it can be easy to overlook the fact that record companies are first and foremost commercial businesses. If the CDs don't sell they will probably be deleted – and the companies may have inhibitions about future issues. Let's hope that doesn't happen!

This year we are very pleased to publish the *Musicals Good CD Guide* in association with Naim Audio, a leading audio manufacturer with a passionate interest in all things musical.

Ten highlights, both new and old, from last year's releases

Cabin in the Sky
EMI CDODEON31
page 56

Divorce Me, Darling!
TER CDTER1245
page 206

The Fix
First Night CASTCD62
page 158

The Golden Apple
RCA Victor 09026 68934-2
page 128

The King and I
TER CDTER2 1214
page 149

The Life
Sony Broadway SK63312
page 49

The Pajama Game
TER CDTER2 1232
page 21

Ragtime
RCA Victor 09026 68629-2
page 61

Steel Pier
RCA Victor 09026 68878-2
page 90

Titanic
RCA Victor 09026 68834-2
page 208

The Best of Musical THEATRE

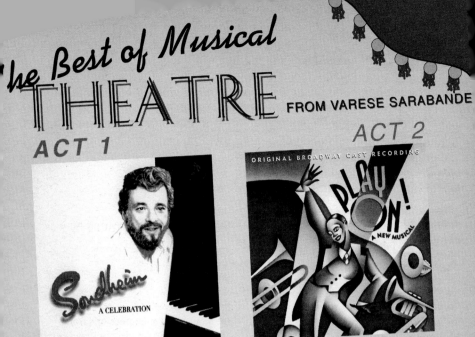

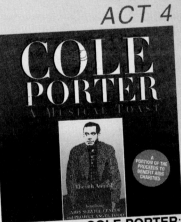

Using the Guide

The recordings reviewed in this Guide have been selected by the editor and the contributors as being, in their opinion, the best of the currently available versions of each show. In several cases, however, different recordings of the same show are reviewed side-by-side and their individual merits assessed – it is rare that any one performance can be considered as definitive when other recordings have their own particular merits: a remarkable singer in the lead role, perhaps, or the new interpretation of the score found in the film version of a stage show.

Other available recordings are listed at the end of each composer's entry.

Uniquely, this Guide gives due credit to the composers and lyricists responsible for bringing us this wealth of enduringly popular music, with biographies of all the principal figures prefacing the reviews, helping to place individual shows in the context of their creators' other work. Readers should consult the index if they wish to look up entries by show title.

Each review opens with a title heading. For individual shows the layout is

Show/Film Title Cast performance
(principal cast members);
**any named chorus or orchestra /
conductor**.
Issuing company (price code) catalogue number (disc timing: recording mode).

For collections, the layout is

Album Title Principal singers; chorus
and orchestra / conductor.
Issuing company (price code) catalogue number (disc timing: recording mode).
Show/Film Title 1. Show/Film Title 2.

Show/Film Title 3...
The price codes are given simply as

Ⓕ Full
Ⓜ Mid
Ⓑ Budget

although the cost of discs will vary from one retail outlet to another, and from country to country.

A note on availability:

Although we have endeavoured only to list currently available recordings, discs are often deleted with lightning rapidity (and no advance warning), and many albums listed here are only available as imports, as they have either been deleted in certain territories or were never released there. Although these import albums are inevitably somewhat less easy to obtain – and generally more expensive – than domestic product, they form a significant part of the available recordings. In case of difficulty, the specialist dealers and mail order companies listed at the back of the book should be able to obtain most, if not all, of the CDs mentioned in these pages. Persistence usually pays off, even in the case of deleted product.

Biographical sources:

Cordial thanks must be extended to all the numerous sources of biographical information, including the *New Grove Dictionary of American Music*, the *Oxford Companion to Popular Music*, the *Faber Companion to 20th-Century Music*, among other publications, and the many unsung writers of informative CD booklet-notes.

Musicals Top 50

A chronological selection of 50 famous musicals.

1899

Florodora (Leslie Stuart) Opal
OPALCD9835
page 183

1916

Chu Chin Chow (Frederic Norton)
EMI ZDM7 89939-2
page 130

1924

Lady, Be Good! (George Gershwin)
Nonesuch 7559-79308-2
page 69

1926

The Desert Song (Sigmund Romberg)
Pearl GEMMCD9100
page 156

1927

Show Boat (Jerome Kern)
EMI CDS7 49108-2
page 94

1929

Bitter Sweet (Noël Coward)
TER CDTER2 1160
page 52

1934

Anything Goes (Cole Porter)
EMI CDC7 49848-2
page 134

1937

Me and My Girl (Noel Gay)
EMI CDP7 46393-2
page 65

1939

The Wizard of Oz (Harold Arlen)
Rhino 71964 / EMI CDODEON7
page 25

1940

Pal Joey (Richard Rodgers/
Lorenz Hart)
DRG 94763
page 144

1943

Oklahoma! (Richard Rodgers/Oscar
Hammerstein II)
EMI CDP7 46631-2
page 151

1945

Carousel (Richard Rodgers/Oscar
Hammerstein II)
First Night OCRCD6042
page 147

1946

Annie Get Your Gun
(Irving Berlin)
TER CDTER2 1229
page 28

1947

Bless the Bride (Vivian Ellis)
AEI AEICD015
page 56

Finian's Rainbow (Burton Lane)
RCA 1057-2
page 99

Street Scene (Kurt Weill)
Columbia MK44668
page 200

1948

Kiss Me Kate (Cole Porter)
TERCDTER2 1212
page 137

1950

Guys and Dolls (Frank Loesser)
TER CDTER2 1228
page 111

1951

The King and I (Richard Rodgers/Oscar
Hammerstein II)
TER CDTER2 1214
page 149

1953

Kismet (George Forrest/
Robert Wright)
TER CDTER2 1170
page 63

The Boy Friend (Sandy Wilson)
RCA 60056-2
page 206

1954

The Pajama Game (Richard Adler)
TER CDTER2 1232
page 21

Salad Days (Julian Slade)
EMI CDC5 55200-2
page 168

Seven Brides for Seven Brothers
(Gene Vincent De Paul)
EMI CDODEON17
page 55

1956

My Fair Lady (Frederick Loewe)
TER CDTER2 1211
page 115

1957

West Side Story (Leonard Bernstein)
Columbia CK64419
page 34

The Music Man (Meredith Willson)
Warner Bros 1459-2
page 205

1958

Gigi (Frederick Loewe)
EMI CDODEON10
page 114

1959

The Sound of Music
(Richard Rodgers/Oscar
Hammerstein II)
Sony SK53537
page 153

Gypsy (Jule Styne)
Columbia CK32607
page 185

1960

Oliver! (Lionel Bart)
TER CDTER1184
page 26

The Fantasticks
(Harvey Schmidt)
TER CDTER1099
page 160

1963

Half a Sixpence
(David Heneker)
Deram 820 589-2
page 82

1964

Fiddler on the Roof (Jerry Bock)
EMI CDP7 46091-2
page 38

Hello, Dolly! (Jerry Herman)
RCA GD83814
page 83

Funny Girl (Jule Styne)
EMI ZDM7 64661-2
page 184

1966

Sweet Charity
(Cy Coleman)
Sony SMK66172
page 50

Cabaret (John Kander)
TER CDTER2 1210
page 88

1970

Jesus Christ Superstar
(Andrew Lloyd Webber)
Polydor 533 735-2
page 105

1971

Follies (Stephen Sondheim)
RCA BD87128
page 171

1975

A Chorus Line (Marvin Hamlisch)
Columbia CK33581
page 76

1978

Evita (Andrew Lloyd Webber)
Warner Brothers 9362-46346-2
page 104

1979

Sweeney Todd (Stephen Sondheim)
RCA 3379-2
page 179

1981

Cats (Andrew Lloyd Webber)
Polydor 817 810-2
page 103

1983

Blood Brothers (Willy Russell)
First Night CASTCD17
page 159

1985

Les Misérables (Claude-Michel
Schönberg)
First Night ENCORECD8
page 161

1986

Phantom of the Opera (Andrew Lloyd
Webber) Polydor 813 273-2
page 107

1992

Aladdin (Alan Menken)
Walt Disney Records WDR74260-2
page 122

1996

Passion (Stephen Sondheim)
First Night CASTCD61
page 176

Rent (Jonathan Larson)
Dreamworks DRD50003
page 100

The reviews

Richard Adler
b. 1921 USA

Jerry Ross
1926-1955 USA

A self-taught musician, Richard Adler studied playwriting at the University of North Carolina and wrote songs in his spare time. Fellow New Yorker Jerry Ross wrote songs for revues at New York University. In 1950, Adler and Ross teamed up to write for individual singers and radio shows. Aided by Frank Loesser, they had their first hit with "Rags to riches" in 1953. After having four songs used in *John Murray Anderson's Almanac* in 1953 they wrote their first show, *The Pajama Game* in 1954. This ran for 1,063 performances on Broadway (featuring a young dancer named Shirley MacLaine) and was filmed in 1957. Their second show, *Damn Yankees*, ran for 1,019 performances and was filmed in 1958 (although it was re-titled *Whatever Lola Wants* in the UK). Ross died in 1955, and afterwards, Adler, alone, wrote the television musicals *Gift of the Magi*, *Little Women* and *Olympus 7-0000*. He returned to Broadway for *Kwamina* (1961) and *His Mother's Kisses* (1968). His last Broadway show was a version of *Twelfth Night* called *Music Is* (1976).

Damn Yankees 1955 **Broadway Cast** (with Gwen Verdon, Stephen Douglass, Ray Walston, Robert Shafer and Shannon Bolin) **/ Hal Hastings**.
RCA Victor Ⓜ 3948-2 (46 minutes: ADD).
Damn Yankees 1958 **Film Cast** (with Gwen Verdon, Tab Hunter, Ray Walston, Robert Shafer and Shannon Bolin) **/ Ray Heindorf**.
RCA Ⓜ 1047-2 (38 minutes: ADD).
Damn Yankees 1994 **Broadway Cast** (with Bebe Neuwirth, Victor Garber, Jarrod Emick, Dennis Kelly, Dick Latessa and Vicki Lewis) **/ William Meade**.
Mercury Ⓕ 522 396-2 (78 minutes: DDD).

Considering the popularity of the Faust story in literary and operatic circles, it's surprising that Adler and Ross's *Damn Yankees* was the first really successful attempt to bring the plot to the musical comedy stage. It was, of course, the subject of Jack Buchanan's preposterous stage musical in the film *The Band Wagon*, before being jettisoned for a good old song-and-dance extravaganza featuring Fred Astaire and Cyd Charisse. The Adler/Ross team turned out an effervescent score. Here are three recordings of it. First – the original cast toplined by Gwen Verdon and Ray Walston, who also appeared in Stanley Donen's lively film version along with most of their stage colleagues. Stephen Douglass was replaced here by teen idol Tab Hunter, and for Britain and Australia the film was temporarily renamed after its hit tune "Whatever Lola wants". It also added a new number, "There's something about an empty chair", that did not retain its place for the 1994 revival. The soundtrack (heard here for the first time in stereo) is by far the shortest version but finds the cast in top form, led by Ray Walston's wacky devil Mr Applegate and Gwen Verdon's eternal vamp. Yet it can't be top recommendation. For the fullest impression of the score, go for either the original Broadway cast with that particular first-time-around Broadway radiance or the even more comprehensive revival cast recording. The latter uses a revised plot that robs Joe Hardy, our hero of his duet "Two lost souls" and gives it to Applegate. This, the newest recording, does include a lot of incidental music and dance routines not previously recorded, and offers fine sound and good performances. Victor Garber takes a more laid-back view of the devil than Ray Walston did, but Neuwirth and Emick have punch and charm. **MPK**

The Pajama Game 1954 **Broadway Cast** (with John Raitt, Janis Paige, Eddie Foy Jr., Carol Haney, Reta Shaw, Ralph Dunn, Stanley Prager, Jack Waldron, Marion Colby, Peter Gennaro, Buzz Miller and Thelma Pelish).
Columbia mono Ⓜ CK 32606 (52 minutes: ADD).
The Pajama Game 1957 **Film Cast** (with Doris Day, John Raitt, Eddie Foy Jr., Carol Haney and Reta Shaw).
Sony mono Ⓜ 467610-2 (49 minutes: AAD). Disc also includes songs from **Fain:** Calamity Jane 1953 **Film Cast** (with Doris Day and Howard Keel).
New review
The Pajama Game 1996 **Studio Cast** (with Judy Kaye, Ron Raines, Kim Criswell, Avery Saltzman, Brookes Almy and David Green); **National Symphony Orchestra / John Owen Edwards.**
TER Ⓕ CDTER2 1232 (two discs: 92 minutes: DDD).

From the first bars of the overture, John Owen Edwards and the National Symphony Orchestra summon up the authentic Broadway sound. TER's hugely enjoyable two-disc set in thrilling sound is not merely the first stereo recording, it's also the first absolutely complete one of Richard Adler and Jerry Ross's 1954 show. The original Broadway cast recording headlines Janis Paige's feisty heroine Babe Williams and John Raitt's masculine hero Sid; it's in mono but should be in any collection. Doris Day memorably replaced Paige for the 1957 film, which otherwise featured most of the original Broadway cast. The CD of this production, an acceptable souvenir, squeezes in songs from *Calamity Jane* at the expense of numbers from both scores.

Some members of producer John Yap's cast recreate the roles they played in the New York City Opera production of 1989: Judy Kaye brings character, charm and bags of enthusiasm to the role of Babe; Avery Saltzman's manic possessiveness as time-study man Hines is impressive; Ron Raines is strong-voiced and subtle as hero Sid; minor roles are more than capably filled by Kim Criswell, David Green and Brookes Almy. There are no weak links here. Don Walker's glowing orchestrations grace full versions (including dance music) of all the well-known songs including "Hernando's hideaway", "Hey there", "Once a year day", "Steam heat" and "Small talk". The recording also features "Think of the time I save", "Her is" and the touching "A new town is a blue town", from the original show. It even includes the "Sleep tite" commercial jingle. There are fascinating in-depth notes by Rexton Bunnett to complete the appeal of this important issue. Here is a recording that does *The Pajama Game* justice; it is the definitive recording of one of musical theatre's greatest scores from the 1950s.   **MPK**

New review
The Songs of Richard Adler Marlene VerPlanck; The Radio Big Band (London) / J. Billy VerPanck.
Varèse Sarabande Spotlight Series Ⓕ VSD5804 (64 minutes: DDD).
Songs from The Pajama Game, Damn Yankees and Kwamina. *Songs:* I'm seeing rainbows. I ask myself. Who ever invented love? If I knew then. You knew what I needed. Christmas in your heart. No soap blues. If you win you lose. Put your money on me.

As 1997's all too short-lived production of *Damn Yankees* at the Adelphi theatre reminded us, Richard Adler possesses an intuitive theatrical sense for the musical stage that was nearly terminated with the early death of his collaborator Jerry Ross in 1955. Seven years later Adler bowed out of Broadway when his adventurous score for *Kwamina*, starring his then wife Sally Ann Howes, was rejected after 32 performances. Marlene VerPlanck introduces two of its songs in her selection as well as several delightful numbers with no show association. These include a cheery opener, "I'm seeing rainbows", and the charming "Christmas in your heart", a happy addition to the seasonal repertoire. VerPlanck's artistry is put entirely at the service of Adler's songs, so that even when she introduces a delicious vocal cadenza in "I see rainbows", the numbers retain their integrity. The stylish jazz-slanted arrangements, a first-rate band under Billy VerPlanck and a recording with the right degree of intimacy should leave the composer in no doubt that listeners will like this album as much as he desires them to.   **AE**

Also available:
Kwamina (1961 Broadway Cast) EMI Angel ZDM7 64891-2

Harold Arlen   1905–1986 USA

Hyman Arluck was born in Buffalo, New York State; he gained early musical experience singing in the choir at the synagogue where his father was cantor. He formed his own jazz group, The Snappy Trio, before moving to New York City in the late 1920s where he worked as a pianist, singer and arranger. With lyricist Ted Koehler he achieved his first success as a songwriter: "Get happy" which was used in the *9:15 Revue* (1930) and became a hit for Ruth Etting. Between 1930-4, Arlen and Koehler replaced Dorothy Fields and Jimmy McHugh as songwriters for the Cotton Club revues in Harlem, producing such songs as "Between the devil and the deep blue sea", "Minnie the moocher's wedding day" and "Stormy weather", written for leading black performers like Cab Calloway and Ethel Waters. Arlen wrote the revue *Life Begins at 8:40* (1934) with Ira Gershwin and E. Y. Harburg, and with Harburg the musical *Hooray for What!* (1937), but his biggest success came with films. "It's only a paper moon" was featured in *Take a Chance* (1933), and in Hollywood he worked on over 20 films, producing such songs as "That old black magic" from *Star Spangled Rhythm* (1942) and "Ac-cent-tchu-ate the positive" from *Here Come the Waves* (1944) – both with lyricist Johnny Mercer. They also collaborated on the film *Blues in the Night* (1941) and later on the all-black Broadway musical *St Louis Woman* (1946). Arlen's most famous film, however, was *The Wizard of Oz* (1939) for which he wrote all the songs with Harburg. He wrote for Judy Garland again in *A Star is Born* (1954) and *I Could Go On Singing* (1963). Other Broadway shows were *Bloomer Girl* (1941), *House of Flowers* (1954), *Jamaica* (1957) and *Saratoga* (1959).

Bloomer Girl 1944 **Broadway Cast** (with Celeste Holm, David Brooks, Richard Huey, Joan McCracken, Dooley Wilson, Matt Briggs, Toni Hart, Mabel Taliaferro, Hubert Dilworth and Harold Arlen).
MCA mono Ⓜ MCAD10522 (48 minutes: AAD).

The massive success of Rodgers and Hammerstein's epoch-making musical *Oklahoma!* on Broadway in 1943 led many producers and songwriters to seek fresh subjects for further non-metropolitan musicals. *Bloomer Girl* was one of the most successful. It was ostensibly the story of Amelia Bloomer, an early advocate for womens' suffrage at the time of the American Civil War; she was a reformer with a strong interest in women's rights – including the divided skirt or knickerbockers, commonly known as bloomers. Although Dolly Bloomer is a character in the show, the real heroine is her niece, Evelina, a Bloomer Girl played by Celeste Holm, fresh from her personal triumph in *Oklahoma!*. There is a serious undertone, too. An escape route for freed slaves operates secretly in the area, and Evelina influences her Confederate sweetheart to free his own slave and send him down the route to freedom. The score is one of Harold Arlen's best, richest and most varied with fresh, original lyrics by E. Y. Harburg – and deserves to be in every show collection. There is only one recording – featuring the original cast – and no other is needed. The songs include "The eagle and me", "Right as the rain", "When the boys come home" and "Evelina". The strong-voiced original cast give every song its due. The sound may be dated, but the performances are imperishable. **MPK**

The Harold Arlen Songbook Julie Wilson; William Roy (pf).
DRG Ⓔ CDSL5211 (62 minutes: ADD).
Songs from Blues in the Night, Life Begins at 8:40, Hooray for What!, Rhythmania, Cotton Club Revue, The Sky's the Limit, A Star is Born, At the Circus, Out of This World, Star Spangled Rhythm, The Cotton Club Parade of 1932, House of Flowers, The Great Magoo, Jamaica, Earl Carroll's Vanities of 1932, Nellie Bly, Casbah, Here Come the Waves and St Louis Woman.

Widely regarded as one of the world's leading mature cabaret performers, Julie Wilson brings a lifetime of experience to this outstanding selection of Arlen's best-known standards and some lesser-known curiosities, many of which were the result of his long-running partnership with lyricist Johnny Mercer. Her comic touch on "Lydia, the tattooed lady" (lyrics by E. Y. Harburg, from the 1939 Marx Brothers film *At the Circus*) or Mercer's "Ac-cent-tchu-ate the positive" (from 1944's *Here Come the Waves*) is exemplary. But it is the blues numbers, here combined in a series of medleys, at which Wilson truly excels. The heartbreaking "One for my baby" (lyrics Mercer, from *The Sky's the Limit*, 1943) is meshed with the 1954 Judy Garland classic "The man that got away" (Ira Gershwin's lyric from *A Star is Born*) for four minutes of exquisite torch singing. Likewise, Harburg's "Last night when we were young": Wilson's intimate, understated interpretations and effortless phrasing are a lesson in song selling for any aspiring artist. Another medley unites Mercer's "Out of this world" with "That old black magic". Not that she dwells solely on the darker aspects of love: there's some delightful duetting with her pianist, Willam Roy – who is also responsible for these expert arrangements – on "You're a builder-upper" (Gershwin and Harburg) and "Hooray for love" (Robin). A connoisseur's treat. **PF**

New review
Jamaica 1957 **Broadway Cast** (with Lena Horne, Ricardo Montalban, Josephine Premice, Joe Adams, Ossie Davis and Adelaide Hall) **/ Lehman Engel.**
RCA Victor Ⓜ 09026 68041-2 (55 minutes: AAD).

Arlen's last-but-one Broadway show was a triumph for Lena Horne in her first Broadway appearance as a star (she'd made her professional début in the Cotton Club revues which also had music by Harold Arlen). The book is not up to much – an everyday story of island folk in the West Indies – but the score, while not absolutely top-drawer Arlen, is more than delightful, and shows, yet again, Arlen's affinity and empathy with the blues and other ethnic music forms. A cut number from *Cabin in the Sky*, "Ain't it de truth?", resurfaces to be sung by Horne, its original interpreter, who also has a ball with numbers like "Napoleon" and "Push de button". Ricardo Montalban's singing voice is pleasing enough, and the show gives good opportunities to the legendary Adelaide Hall in "Savannah's wedding day" and "For every fish", while Josephine Premice captures the subtlety of Yip Harburg's lyrics in "Little biscuit", "Yankee dollar" and "Leave de atom alone". The disc, however, belongs to Horne, whose intelligence and wit made the show the success it was. The CD issue, excellently transferred, is fuller than either the mono or stereo LPs (which contained slightly differing selections). **MPK**

The Song is ... Harold Arlen with various artists, including **Harold Arlen, Bing Crosby, Judy Garland, Benny Goodman, Ray Eberle, Glenn Miller, Eddy Duchin, Lawrence Tibbett** and **Louis Armstrong**.
ASV Living Era mono Ⓜ CDAJA5159 (78 minutes: ADD). Recorded 1930-44.
Songs from Cotton Club Paradise, 9:15 Revue, The Big Broadcast, The Cotton Club Parades of 1933 and 1934, The Great Magoo, Let's Fall in Love, Earl Carroll's Vanities of 1930 and 1932, Rhythmania, Gold Diggers of 1937, Here Come the Waves, At the Circus, Andy Hardy Meets Debutante, Blues in the Night, Out of This World, Cabin in the Sky, Star Spangled Rhythm and The Wizard of Oz.

Come Rain or Shine The Harold Arlen Songbook. **Sylvia McNair**; **André Previn** (pf); **David Finck** (db).
Philips Ⓟ 446 818-2 (75 minutes: DDD).
Songs from The Wizard of Oz, Cotton Club Paradise, Rhythmania, Casbah, Star Spangled Rhythm, House of Flowers, Here Come the Waves, Saratoga, St Louis Woman, The Great Magoo, Jamaica, Bloomer Girl, Blues in the Night, Life Begins at 8:40.

Living Era's glorious and generous anthology of Harold Arlen songs is a peach – 25 of them are performed by some of the most individual artists of the twentieth century who embrace the whole compass of popular music in which Arlen was active. The composer sets the scene with "Stormy weather" delivered in his gentle, high-pitched voice; this recording dates from 1933, three years into Arlen's career as a songwriter after he'd made several records as vocalist with the likes of trumpeter Red Nichols. "Get happy" from the *9:15 Revue* (1930) was the song that got him noticed as a composer, and though this collection ends less than 15 years later in 1944, much of his best known work had been completed by then. And what a parade it was! Bing Crosby heads the artists' listing with an inimitably relaxed, freely phrased version of "I've got the world on a string" (on the debit side his 'hamming' in black southern preacher style during "Ac-cent-tchu-ate the positive" is an enduring embarrassment!). Garland gives us a reminder of her *Andy Hardy* films with Mickey Rooney in the enchanting "Buds won't bud", and there's a sparkling performance of "Between the devil and the deep blue sea" from Benny Goodman. At the other end of the mood spectrum, the Glenn Miller Orchestra with Ray Eberle send us into a nostalgic reverie with "This time the dream's on me". Artists as diverse as Eddy Duchin, Lawrence Tibbett and Louis Armstrong are amongst others who make up this indispensible collection.

Sylvia McNair's new collection of songs is as diverse as the Living Era selection. This is a beautifully recorded CD, masterminded by André Previn, whose loving arrangements and jazz-tinged accompaniments remain as fresh as those he did for Dinah Shore and Julie London back in the early 1960s. Here they make an ideal backdrop for McNair's sun-drenched interpretations. She occasionally indulges that shiny, silky top of her range to breathtaking effect, for instance in "Ac-cent-tchu-ate the positive", but the abiding impression is of two artists working in close rapport. A perfect record to end the day. **AE**

A Star is Born 1954 **Film Cast** (with Judy Garland) / **Ray Heindorf**.
Columbia Ⓜ CK44389 (41 minutes: ADD).

A Star is Born professionally reunited Judy Garland with Harold Arlen, the composer of *The Wizard of Oz*, who in the intervening 25 years had become a close friend. It resulted in a movie musical of exceptional emotional range, unprecedented at the time, with at least one song, "The man that got away", into which Arlen poured his heart and soul, and Judy likewise. This blues-style ballad, begun and ending with the singer mingling instrumentally amongst the band, was a natural extension of the screenplay, as were the star's cheerful song and dance "Gotta have me go with you" and the film's centrepiece, "Born in a trunk", written, after Arlen had returned to Broadway to compose *House of Flowers*, by Leonard Gershe and an uncredited Roger Edens (who was under contract to MGM at the time). Their words and music frame a medley of standards arranged by Edens, Garland's closest musical associate, who surely knew first-hand from his star of the triumphs and pitfalls on the way to the top. Aside from the "Overture", played and conducted with characteristic verve by Warner Bros MD Ray Heindorf, the selections follow the original LP, but with the song cuts opened out and in stereo sound for the first time. Despite that asset it still comes across as fairly primitive, particularly in comparison with the contemporaneous MGM soundtrack reissues of *Brigadoon* and *Seven Brides for Seven Brothers*.   **AE**

The Wizard of Oz 1939 **Film Cast** (with Judy Garland, Ray Bolger, Jack Haley, Bert Lahr and Frank Morgan); **MGM Studio Chorus and Orchestra / Herbert Stothart**.
Rhino Ⓕ 71964 (two discs: 136 minutes: ADD) / EMI Ⓔ CDODEON7 (39 minutes: ADD).
The Wizard of Oz 1989 **London Cast** (with Gillian Bevan, Joyce Grant, David Glover, Paul Greenwood, Simon Green, Trevor Peacock and Bille Brown) / **John Owen Edwards**.
TER Ⓕ CDTER1165 (57 minutes: DDD).

For most collectors, the MGM soundtrack of *The Wizard of Oz* will understandably remain first choice, for here is Judy Garland singing "Over the rainbow" – the song that became indelibly identified with her – with an air of innocence allied to a maturing emotional power that was to become the trademark of her later performances. In fact, the song was nearly cut from the film on account of its length and slow tempo, the one composition in Harold Arlen's score that harked back to the langorous ballads of his Cotton Club revues at the beginning of the 1930s. His remaining melodies bubble over with an infectious humour, vividly realized by Herbert Stothart's arrangements. Rhino records in the USA have issued the complete original soundtrack in a deluxe two-disc set, which includes all the songs, plus all the incidental music and even outtakes, and is accompanied by a lavishly-produced booklet full of fascinating notes and illustrations. EMI in the UK have opted for a significantly pared-down single disc of highlights, which nevertheless includes all the principal songs and set-pieces; the magnificently restored sound is common to both.

Arlen's humorous songs are still enjoyed today in stage productions like the one first mounted by the Royal Shakespeare Company in 1987. This was subsequently recorded by TER in digital sound, so making a highly enjoyable alternative to the film soundtrack. All the performances are good and with a really splendid band under John Owen Edwards, this would now be my recommendation for this much-loved film and show   **.AE**

Also available:
St Louis Woman (1946 Broadway Cast) EMI Angel ZDM7 6466-2

Eric Lane Barnes

New review
Fairy Tales 1995 **Chicago Cast** (with Keith Anderson, Jennifer Bradley, Guy Crowell, Paul Rosenberg and Matt Shea) / **Eric Lane Barnes**.
Firefly Records Ⓕ 50957 0001-2 (59 minutes: DDD).

There is no easy way to tell you this – this CD has come out of the closet and is wearing its gayness, well, I suppose right up to the title itself. This little revue has been around: it started life in Chicago and has since been seen in New York and London. It begins with a cute harmony about our faith in fairy tales which appears to have a moral about looking ahead (I think?). There are a number of these cleverish word plays which may have a heavy moral when seeing the show, but metaphors about rain, snow and beacons of light, whilst with pleasant tunes, are difficult to understand. There are more obvious gay numbers and requests like:

"smile and say hello to any homo that you see on the street" which is friendly enough, and a difficult to take "Dear Dad" letter. However, I rather enjoyed a number called "The gay guys", in which every guy the lass gets involved with is gay, and "Illinois Fred" about a "strange-talkin' cowboy" which, again, is quite witty. The bad news is a song entitled "You're the bottom" – no it's not rude (I don't think any of the songs are, unless I missed something), it's worse than that – it's plainly unfunny. Think of a Cole Porter "Anything goes"-style song, but one in which the height of wit is to keep naming Andrew Lloyd Webber, and you'll get the idea. I enjoyed this recording more on a second hearing, but it is likely to appeal most to those in sympathy with the show's subject-matter. **RSB**

Lionel Bart

b. 1930 England

Born Lionel Begleiter in the East End of London, Lionel Bart became interested in theatre after attending St Martin's School of Art. Alongside Tommy Steele and Mike Pratt he was a member of the skiffle band The Cavemen, together they wrote several songs for Steele including "Rock with the cavemen" and "Little white bull" from the film *Tommy the Toreador* (1959). Bart also wrote "Living doll" for Cliff Richard. He joined forces with Monty Norman to write music and lyrics for *Fings Ain't Wot They Used T'Be* (1959) and with composer Laurie Johnson for *Lock Up Your Daughters* (1959), before producing his own show, *Oliver!* in 1960. *Oliver!* became the most successful British musical of its time, running for 2,618 performances – all this despite Bart's admission that he doesn't read or write music, or play an instrument. Later shows include *Blitz!* (1962), *Maggie May* (1964) and *Twang!* (1965 – a musical about Robin Hood which failed dismally). *Oliver!* was filmed in 1968, with Ron Moody reprising his stage role as Fagin and Mark Lester as Oliver; it won six Oscars including Best Picture. It has been successfully revived in the West End at the London Palladium.

Oliver! 1960 **London Cast** (with Ron Moody, Georgia Brown, Paul Whitsun-Jones, Hope Jackman, Danny Sewell, Keith Hamshere and Martin Horsey) **/ Marcus Dods**.
Deram Ⓜ 820 590-2 (58 minutes: AAD).

Oliver! 1968 **Film Cast** (with Ron Moody, Shani Wallis, Mark Lester, Jack Wild and Harry Secombe) **/ John Green**.
RCA Ⓜ ND90311 (52 minutes: ADD).

Oliver! 1991 **Studio Cast** (with Julian Forsyth, Josephine Barstow, Richard South, Stuart Kale, Sheila Hancock and Richard Van Allan); **King's College School Boys Choir, Wimbledon; National Symphony Orchestra / John Owen Edwards**.
TER Ⓕ CDTER1184 (63 minutes: DDD).

Oliver! 1994 **London Cast** (with Jonathan Pryce, Sally Dexter, Gregory Bradley, Miles Anderson and James Saxon) **/ Martin Koch**.
First Night Ⓕ CASTCD47 (71 minutes: DDD).

Lionel Bart billed his most famous musical as "freely adapted from *Oliver Twist*". He maligned his own fidelity; obviously he cut a lot of the novel but, in terms of narrative, what remains stays close to the original. The tone of course is very different; a screaming underworld nightmare has been turned into a jolly singalong. But Bart was responding to something that has always lain dormant in the novel; readers have persisted in finding the story heart-warming and the villainous Fagin endearing. From there it was a short step to making him funny: the richest character in any British musical. Bart surrenders enthusiastically to cliché (musical, lyrical and emotional) but can also be witty and inventive. The songs create atmosphere, carry plot and character along, and are very performable. It is a highly ingenious show: if not the most distinguished of the Cockney caper musicals, then certainly the most fully achieved.

The original cast version is, as usual, the best, full of guts, gusto and even intelligence. Ron Moody's Fagin ("so at my time of life I should start turning over new leaves?") is unequalled by any subsequent performance, including his own in the film. Georgia Brown, as Nancy, was Bart's ideal leading lady; like him she spoke showbiz like a native, sentimentally but honestly. He wrote "It's a fine life" for her during rehearsals, and it's the best tune, and one of the best lyrics, in the score. The celebrated big ballad, "As long as he needs me", is dire, a melodramatically mawkish lyric wedded to a grindingly monotonous tune; down the years there have been tasteful attempts to underplay it, but Brown's all-stops-out approach is probably the right one. Hope Jackman makes a fine vixen of Mrs Bumble (formerly Corney) and no Artful Dodger has ever got close to Martin Horsey's shocked delivery of the words "waht, fisticuffs?". We also get Barry Humphries as Sowerberry the undertaker giving all he has – or had in those pre-Edna Everage days – to the professional anthem "That's your funeral".

Moody returned for the fine Carol Reed film and scored the success of his career. Filmic to the point of being unearthly is Mark Lester's Oliver whose voice seems to be coming out of a different channel from everybody else's. Shani Wallis – whose career, like Moody's, failed to take off from here as it should have done – is the best of all Nancys, even squeezing in some subtlety. She takes full advantage of Reed's new concept for "Oom-pah-pah", where she doubles as traditional pub rouser and nervous decoy. The film score, as arranged and conducted by John Green, is a new and stylish animal, the Cockney pastoral transformed into an epic; only occasionally is the spaciousness too much.

1991 brought the first digital *Oliver!*, and, at that date, much the completest. John Owen Edwards's booklet-notes pay deserved tribute to the original orchestrations of Eric Rogers, as do his own arrangements and his excellent conducting; you feel safe from the first note. The glory here is Julian Forsyth's Fagin, commanding and wheedling by turns, and equally adept at both. He is the best after Moody and, in the Hebraic bits, almost equally cantorial. Megan Kelly stands out a mile in the minute role of Bet.

The newest production (an *Oliver!* for the 1990s?) is the first in which the boys have actually sounded hungry; William D. Brohn gives "Food, glorious food" a thumpingly oppressive orchestration, and Mr Bumble is really savage. "That's your funeral" is here a music-hall number scored by Kurt Weill. Gregory Bradley may be the best Oliver ever. "Consider yourself" seems to go on for ever, but most of the songs – especially "You've got to pick a pocket or two" and "It's a fine life" – are taken very fast, as if to point up the desperation behind the characters' gaiety. Jonathan Pryce's neurotic Fagin is certainly interesting – he's a magnetic actor – but it's too nervous, both in conception and execution, to be fun. Bart has written some new lyrics, though not as many as the booklet-notes would have you believe. Once he rhymed "Snodgrass" with "odd glass" (he was never what you would call a perfectionist) and now he gives us "utterly" and "gluttony". So at his time of life he should start turning over new leaves?   **RC**

Also available:
Oliver! (1962 Studio Cast) EMI Angel ZDM7 64890-2
Oliver! (1963 Broadway Cast) RCA Victor GD84113
Oliver! (1966 Studio Cast) MfP CC8253
Oliver! (1994 Studio Cast) Carlton Shows Collection PWKS4194

Alan and Marilyn Bergman

For two decades the Bergmans have been providing lyrics for songs in Hollywood films. After "In the heat of the night" for the film of the same name (1967) came "The windmills of your mind" for *The Thomas Crown Affair* (1968) to music by Michel Legrand, who also provided the music the following year for "What are you doing the rest of your life?", the theme from *The Happy Ending*. Their most famous collaboration was with Marvin Hamlisch for Barbra Streisand to sing "The way we were" for the film of the same name (1973). In 1983, a further collaboration with Michel Legrand consisted of the lyrics for Streisand's film *Yentl* (1983). James Newton Howard provided the music for another success introduced by Streisand in *The Prince of Tides* (1991) called "Places that belong to you". Working again with Hamlisch they provided the theme titles for television programmes *Alice* (1976) and *Powers That Be* (1990).

Irving Berlin   1888–1989 Russia

Born Israel Baline in Tyumen, Siberia, his family moved to the USA in 1893. Life was hard in New York and the young Israel was forced to go out and work after the death of his father in 1896. He began busking on the streets, then worked as a singing waiter in a café. His first published work was the lyric to "Marie from sunny Italy" (music by the café's pianist Nick Nicholson) in 1907 – a printer's error credited him on the cover as 'Berlin'. Working as a song-plugger he published several popular songs, and performed his own songs in the revue

Up and Down Broadway (1910), before achieving lasting commercial success with "Alexander's ragtime band" (1911) which established him as the most influential ragtime songwriter of the day. His first complete Broadway show was *Watch Your Step* (1914) and he contributed numerous songs to other Broadway productions, notably the *Ziegfeld Follies*; in addition, he formed his own music publishing company and opened the Music Box Theatre to stage revues featuring many of his songs. During the depression years he worked increasingly in Hollywood, writing songs for many leading performers such as Bing Crosby, Ethel Merman, Fred Astaire and Ginger Rogers – his films included *Top Hat* (1935), *Follow the Fleet* (1936) – which featured "Let's face the music and dance" – *On the Avenue* (1937) and *Holiday Inn* (1942) the film that introduced "White Christmas" (Crosby's recording alone sold over 25 million copies). His most popular Broadway show was *Annie Get Your Gun* (1946), written for Ethel Merman, an assignment he was offered after original composer Jerome Kern had died. After the success of *Call Me Madam* in 1950 – also written for Merman – Berlin retired from Broadway but continued to write in Hollywood, returning only once to Broadway to write the relative failure *Mr President* in 1962. He was one of America's most versatile and successful songwriters, even though he was unable to read or write music, and was only capable of playing the piano in one key (F sharp). Richard Rodgers described him as "the folk-song composer of our country". He died at the respectable age of 101.

Annie Get Your Gun 1966 **Lincoln Center Cast** (with Ethel Merman, Bruce Yarnell, Benay Venuta and Jerry Orbach) / **Franz Allers**.
RCA Victor Ⓟ 81124-2 (51 minutes: ADD).

Annie Get Your Gun 1986 **London Cast** (with Suzi Quatro, Eric Flynn and Edmund Hockridge) / **Grant Hossack**.
First Night Ⓜ OCRCD6024 (56 minutes: DDD).

Annie Get Your Gun 1990 **Studio Cast** (with Kim Criswell, Thomas Hampson, David Garrison, Jason Graae, David Healy and Rebecca Luker); **Ambrosian Chorus; London Sinfonietta / John McGlinn**.
EMI Angel Ⓟ CDC 7 54206-2 (79 minutes: DDD).

Annie Get Your Gun 1995 **Studio Cast** (with Barry Bostock, Judy Kaye, David Green, Teri Ralston and Christopher Lee); **National Symphony Orchestra / John Owen Edwards**.
TER Ⓟ CDTER2 1229 (two discs: 109 minutes: DDD).

Irving Berlin's joyous musical comedy has been uncommonly well-served on disc. These versions all have something special to offer, and now that the MGM catalogue of film soundtracks is being restored to circulation we might soon see the release of their *Annie* with Betty Hutton (who replaced Judy Garland) and Howard Keel; it would also be nice too to hear again the 1947 London Cast version with Dolores Gray and Bill Johnson. *Annie* was written in 1946 for Ethel Merman who's represented here by her second recording based on a production at Lincoln Center for which Berlin wrote a new number, "An old-fashioned wedding", one of his counterpoint duets. Twenty years on, Merman still "sparkles like a crystal" in this vibrant stereo recording, though with so many songs to sing a change of dynamic would have been welcome! The strong company are very well supported by conductor Franz Allers with refined orchestrations by Robert Russell Bennett. That RCA recording is the basis for the latest one from TER, a two-CD set. Without wishing to appear pedantic, I feel it was a mistake to perpetuate the Lincoln Center version, for, as I've suggested, a greater variety of tone colour is required in this score which that production denied us by removing two delightful songs for Tommy and Winnie. Here they are presented as bonus tracks, though on John McGlinn's EMI recording they are in context, giving us a breather from the numbers sung by Annie and Frank. TER's recording nevertheless tops anything else I've heard from them, capturing all the excitement of the performance conducted by John Owen Edwards. The set includes numerous reprises and dialogue that helps set up the numbers as well as as the inventive "Wild West Ballet".

EMI cast Kim Criswell in the title role, a younger sounding Annie than TER's heroine; her partner is Thomas Hampson, their baritone of the moment, whose magnificent voice it would be thrilling to hear in the musical theatre. As a singer he outdistances all rivals – compare "My defences are down" – but Barry Bostwick gives, as they say, as good as he gets, and makes a slightly more believable Frank Butler. My favourite Annie from all of the above discs is Suzi Quatro on First Night, a recording with some agreeable new arrangements by David Firman. Quatro's voice may be slightly fragile in the upper reaches, but she brings that surprisingly rare capacity to suggest delight in being in this show whilst losing nothing in the ability to project a lyric. To sum up I wouldn't want to be without the TER recording but at the moment I also hold the EMI one dear. **AE**

New review

Call Me Madam 1950 **Studio Cast** (with Ethel Merman, Dick Haymes, Eileen Wilson) / **Gordon Jenkins.**
MCA Ⓜ MCAD10521 (48 minutes: AAD). Also includes four songs from **Porter:** Panama Hattie.

Call Me Madam 1995 **Broadway Concert Cast** (with Tyne Daly, Peter Bartlett, Walter Charles, Lewis Cleale, Gordon Connell, Jane Connell, MacIntyre Dixon, Christopher Durang, Melissa Errico, Simon Jones and Ken Page); **Coffee Club Orchestra / Rob Fisher.**
DRG Ⓕ 94761 (56 minutes: DDD).

Because the head of her record company refused to release Ethel Merman to make the original cast album, RCA went ahead anyway, substituting Dinah Shore who recorded the role with the rest of the original cast. Meanwhile, Merman recorded her own album with 12 songs from the show, with Dick Haymes, Eileen Wilson and chorus in excellent support. While the result doesn't really feel like a cast album, Merman is unique and irreplaceable and remains essential listening. Shore and the original cast haven't made it to CD yet, but there's an excellent complete recording available. This derives from a concert revival in the New York City Center "Encores" series in 1995. I'm sorry, but you'll have to have this as well. In the role of Miss Sally Adams, the naïve but warm-hearted ambassador to 'Lichtenburg', we now have Tyne Daly (any resemblance between Sally and legendary party-giver Perle Mesta and her appointment to Luxemburg is not coincidental). The score is fine late Berlin, replete with wit and full of catchy melodies. Daly previously recorded the complete show for BBC Radio and she's in her element here: charismatic, brassily confident, yet sympathetic. Lewis Cleale is a splendid Kenneth, Melissa Erico a fine Princess and Walter Charles has the appropriate *gravitas* as Cosmo. Just wait till you hear Daly and Cleale in the contrapuntal duet "You're just in love", or Daly as "The hostess with the mostes' on the ball". Wonderful. **MPK**

Easter Parade 1948 **Film Cast** (with Judy Garland, Fred Astaire, Peter Lawford and Ann Miller); **MGM Studio Chorus and Orchestra / Johnny Green.**
EMI mono Ⓕ CDODEON4 (69 minutes: ADD).

Though *Easter Parade* has never been rated among the greatest or most inventive MGM musicals, it is one of the most pleasurable: Judy Garland and Fred Astaire, the two greatest movie musical stars, teamed for the only time, with Ann Miller thrown in for good measure, plus a parade of Irving Berlin's songs. This was one of the series of musicals inaugurated by *Alexander's Ragtime Band*, for which Berlin wrote a few new tunes to supplement a ton of his old ones. The new ones here are very good. There's Astaire's infectious speciality, "Drum crazy"; the elegantly lilting "It only happens when I dance with you" – done three times, once instrumentally and once by each of the stars, Garland's version being especially fine, full of understated yearning – "A fella with an umbrella", which gives Peter Lawford a chance to be likeable (he never aims any higher); "Steppin' out with my baby", the essence of Astaire, consciously echoing "Top hat, white tie and tails"; the wry torch-song "Better luck next time", another fine helping of Garland bitter-sweet; and of course "A couple of swells", Berlin reaching back to his vaudeville roots to provide four-and-a-half minutes of undiluted ecstasy. Nobody watching Astaire and Garland going through their tramp routine here would believe that they were not a regular team, though in truth it's more her number than his; she has never seemed more gleeful.

Garland also does some of her most pointed serio-comic singing on "I want to go back to Michigan", one of the oldies that establish the film's pre-World War I ambience as well as being fun in themselves; others are the duets "Snookey ookums" ("cut it out, cut it out, *cut it out!*") and the definitive version of "When the midnight choo-choo leaves for Alabam'". Conrad Salinger's instrumental arrangement of "Call me up some rainy afternoon" summons the very spirit of an Edwardian restaurant with potted-palm orchestra; Miller gets her chance on "Shakin' the blues away", which is from a slightly later era, but who's counting? (The title song, by the way, dates from 1933.) The lavish and meticulous packaging of this Turner series reveals that the backing vocals on several tracks are by Mel Tormé's group The Mel-Tones, though Tormé's own presence is undetectable. One out-take bonus: Garland's wickedly enjoyable rendition of "Mr Monotony", also cut from the stage shows *Miss Liberty* and *Call Me Madam* before winding up in *Jerome Robbins' Broadway*. **RC**

The Melody Lingers On The Songs of Irving Berlin. **Fred Astaire, Connee Boswell, Perry Como, Bing Crosby, Tommy Dorsey, Seger Ellis, Ruth Etting, Billie Holiday, Greta Keller, Layton and Johnstone, Peggy Lee, Vera Lynn, Cavan O'Connor, Walter Pidgeon, Dick Powell, Dinah Shore, Frank Sinatra** and **Bessie Smith.**
ASV Living Era mono Ⓜ CDAJA5245 (76 minutes: ADD). Recorded 1924-46.
Songs from Puttin' on the Ritz, As Thousands Cheer, Top Hat, Follow the Fleet, On the Avenue, Louisiana Purchase, Annie Get Your Gun, Easter Parade and Holiday Inn.

Irving Berlin had the most extensive and varied output of any of the major American songwriters. In this fascinating collection of recordings dating from a 22-year period the variety is accentuated by a wide range of performing styles. The very earliest recording is also one of the least likely – a recording of "What'll I do?" made by actor Walter Pidgeon in London in 1924. By contrast there is the jazzy sound of Bessie Smith in "Alexander's ragtime band" with a backing band that includes Coleman Hawkins and Fletcher Henderson, Ethel Waters singing "Heat wave" with Bunny Berigan and Benny Goodman, and Billie Holiday's "This year's kisses" (from the film *On the Avenue*) backed by Goodman and Lester Young. Further varying the style, there's the smooth sophistication of 1930s film singers – Fred Astaire in "Puttin' on the ritz", "Cheek to cheek" and "Let's face the music and dance", Dick Powell in "I've got my love to keep me warm". Then there are the pure dance-band renderings – the Carroll Gibbons band (with Hildegarde) in "Isn't this a lovely day!", Geraldo (with Cavan O'Connor) in "A pretty girl is like a melody", Ambrose and his Orchestra (with Vera Lynn) in "It's a lovely day tomorrow". Before the inevitable play-out of Bing Crosby's "White Christmas", we have Frank Sinatra and Perry Como in a couple of numbers from *Annie Get Your Gun* recorded in 1946. The recordings have been cleaned up remarkably well, if on occasion chopped off a shade early. Jerome Kern supposedly said that "Irving Berlin has no place in American music – he is American music". This collection demonstrates the point. **AML**

Miss Liberty 1949 **Broadway Cast** (with Eddie Albert, Allyn McLerie, Mary McCarty and Ethel Griffies) / **Jay Blackton.**
Sony Broadway mono Ⓕ SK48015 (33 minutes: ADD).

This charming show, now comparatively neglected, tells of the search for the girl who had posed for the Statue of Liberty. Coming three years after the composer's *Annie Get Your Gun* it raised high hopes for a repeat success. Unfortunately the story was too flimsy, and while the principals were charming and the songs good, it ran for a respectable but not sensational 308 performances. Although the cast album runs for a mere 33 minutes, it's packed with wonderful music. "Let's take an old-fashioned walk" is a good old-time waltz. "Paris wakes up and smiles" could be by Cole Porter. The touching "You can have him" – a subtle song with a fine twist in the tail – has become a mainstay among sophisticated singers. Only Berlin could have produced the heartfelt setting of Emma Lazarus's verses, "Give me your tired, your poor", which are inscribed at the base of the statue. The singers have that front-and-centre directness typical of the golden years of Broadway, with Allyn McLerie a bright and attractive heroine. The mono recording has transferred well to CD, while the booklet has extensive notes and many pictures. *Miss Liberty* is a treat. **MPK**

Mr President 1962 **Broadway Cast** (with Robert Ryan, Nanette Fabray and Anita Gillette) / **Jay Blackton**.
Sony Broadway Ⓕ SK48212 (46 minutes: ADD).

Had it not come from the pen of Irving Berlin, this old-fashioned musical comedy might now be a footnote in history. Yet because this was Berlin's big comeback show following a 12-year silence since *Call Me Madam*, great things were expected when it opened with an unprecedented advance ticket sale in the autumn of 1962. Rumour had it that President Kennedy was the role model for the central character fashioned by librettists Lindsay and Crouse, though this is denied in the Prologue. Their President, played by Robert Ryan, is a dry old stick who could have done with some of Kennedy's charm. Fortunately, Nanette Fabray, as the President's wife and Anita Gillette as his daughter, sparkle away to redeem his deficency. At 74, one would hardly have expected Berlin to match his past track record. Although everything here is presented with a polished Broadway sheen common to all the cast albums produced by Goddard Lieberson, one can't help noticing that the material is threadbare. Clearly Berlin had no bottom-drawer numbers for the romantic moments, though there are some good lines in "The secret service", sung by the President's daughter whilst having an affair with a Russian emissary, and in the music for the finale, "This is a great country", a piece of Berlin flag waving, where he adeptly answers his question "if this is flag waving?" with "do you know of a better flag to wave?". A loving choral treatment of the refrain by Jay Blackton and Sousa-esque orchestration by Philip J. Lang further enhance Berlin's stage farewell to his adopted country. The recording sounds newly minted in this CD transfer, but it must have been a sad moment for the composer when his last show turned out to be a failure, and ran only as long as the advance bookings held up – 265 performances. **AE**

The Song is ... Irving Berlin with various artists, including **Jimmy Messene, Sam Browne, Al Jolson, The Boswell Sisters, Al Bowlly, Dick James, Roy Fox, Geraldo, Benny Goodman, Nat Gonella, Harry Roy, Bob Farnon, Carroll Gibbons, Artie Shaw, Ray Noble** and **The Dorsey Brothers**.
ASV Living Era mono Ⓜ CDAJA5068 (64 minutes: AAD).
Songs from Ziegfeld Follies of 1919, Betsy, On the Avenue, Follow the Fleet, Blue Skies, Mammy, Music Box Revue of 1924, Top Hat, As Thousands Cheer, The Awakening and Holiday Inn.

Like others in the Living Era series, this is a set of vintage recordings, mainly of British dance bands covering the songs at the time of their first appearance on film. Roy Fox offers a smooth account of "A pretty girl is like a melody", Geraldo swings surprisingly on "Alexander's ragtime band" (and closes the discs with an anaemic "White Christmas" complete with a wordless choir), Harry Roy's boys make like gentlemanly British tars on "We saw the sea" (from *Follow the Fleet*), and an unrecognizably muscular Bob (not yet Robert) Farnon steams up the joint with "Heat wave". Farnon also backs Dick James, later very rich and fairly famous as the Beatles' publisher, on "You keep coming back like a song" which turns out to be a document in the history of crooning: James sings a Crosby song (from *Blue Skies*) in the emerging style of Sinatra. A more idiosyncratic and far more substantial crooner than James, Al Bowlly, is obliterated by a chorus of "Let yourself go", but comes through very strongly on "Marie". Best of all, Nat Gonella, London's Jewish answer to Satchmo, sings the poker-faced funny "He ain't got rhythm" (from *On the Avenue*) in his wonderfully unreconstructed Cockney. Among the Yank bands, the Dorsey Brothers play an excellent "Top hat, white tie and tails". There are also a few free-standing vocal stars: the Boswell Sisters putting all their eggs in one swinging basket; Al Jolson declaiming "Let me sing and I'm happy", one of his best numbers (and he even manages a trade-marked rolled 'r' at the end of 'popular'); cabaret perennial Hildegarde genteelly purring "This year's kisses" (also from *Avenue*); and Alice Faye "Slumming on Park Avenue" which she introduced as the film's virtual title-song. (Add it all up and *On the Avenue* emerges among Berlin's film scores as second only to *Top Hat*). One rare song: "Because I love you" played – alas, without a vocal – by Artie Shaw. **RC**

White Christmas 1954 **Film Cast** (with Bing Crosby, Danny Kaye, Peggy Lee and Trudy Stevens) **/ Joseph J. Lilley**.
MCA mono Ⓜ MCLD19191 (30 minutes: AAD).

Rosemary Clooney, referring in concert to her best-known movie, declared that though *White Christmas* goes down well with the turkey and crackers it is best avoided at other times of the year. Such candour is rare and refreshing, and makes it all the more frustrating that label conflicts back in the 1950s kept her off the official cast album. She's replaced by Peggy Lee, and though they're both comparably wonderful singers, one does miss Clooney's peculiarly elegant torching on "Love, you didn't do right by me", her greatest film moment. Lee also sounds distinctly out-of-place on "Sisters", which she duets with Trudy Stevens, the off-screen singing voice of the film's Vera-Ellen. *White Christmas* was planned as a vehicle for Bing Crosby and Fred Astaire, following *Holiday Inn* and *Blue Skies*; when Astaire dropped out they considered Donald O'Connor before settling on Danny Kaye. This probably explains why Kaye's solos "The best things happen while you're dancing" and "Choreography" are songs about dance in the Astaire manner, though Kaye remakes the latter in his own image: as a leering satire in the lineage of "Manic depressive presents". Crosby, meanwhile, has only one song on his own, "Count your blessings instead of sheep", which nobody else could get away with. Compared with most of Berlin's latter-day movie scores, this one has little from his back-catalogue; other than the title song there's only "Mandy" and "Blue skies", the latter a notably hip duet for Crosby and Kaye. Some of the new songs, though, hark back to Berlin's achievements as a creator of military extravaganzas in both world wars: "Gee, I wish I was back in the army" is the upside of "Oh how I hate to get up in the morning", while "What can you do with a General?" treats of unemployment among the formerly beribboned and plays it, weirdly, for sympathy (it worked better as comedy in "I've got my Captain working for me now"). The four principals harmonize on "Snow" ("no white Christmas with no snow" sings Bing knowingly). Berlin seldom makes the lists of great lyricists, but that can only be misplaced snobbery: his instinct for the matching of words and music was unsurpassedand infallible.   **RC**

Also available:

Annie Get Your Gun (1957 TV Cast) EMI Angel ZDM7 64765-2
Annie Get Your Gun (1995 Studio Cast) Carlton Shows Collection 30362 00122-2
Unsung Irving Berlin Varèse Sarabande VSD5770
Unsung Irving Berlin (2 CDs) Varèse Sarabande VSD2 5623

Leonard Bernstein   1918–1990 USA

Leonard Bernstein's contribution to the world of music theatre was small but highly significant. Born in Lawrence, Massachusetts, Bernstein studied at Harvard and the Curtis Institute. He conducted and recorded extensively with major orchestras around the world, and wrote many serious works for the concert hall. His first musical, *On the Town* (1944), was written with lyricists Betty Comden and Adolph Green, with whom he had played and sung at the Village Vanguard in New York; they collaborated again on *Wonderful Town* (1953). After the critically-acclaimed comic opera *Candide* (1956), Bernstein collaborated with choreographer Jerome Robbins, librettist Arthur Laurents and lyricist Stephen Sondheim to produce *West Side Story* (1957) – a contemporary reworking of *Romeo and Juliet*. (As originally conceived by Robbins, the show concerned the tragic romance between a Jewish hero and Roman Catholic heroine and was to be called *East Side Story*). It was first staged at the Winter Garden Theater in New York, and later filmed in 1961. The show's mixture of modern dance and appealing songs within a grittily realistic social setting was radical and revolutionary. Despite the huge success of *West Side Story*, Bernstein returned to music theatre only once more with *1600 Pennsylvania Avenue* (1976), which was a failure.

Candide 1956 Broadway Cast (with Max Adrian, Robert Rounseville, Barbara Cook, Irra
    Pettina, William Olvis and William Chapman) / **Samuel Krachmalnik**.
    Sony Broadway Ⓜ SK48017 (51 minutes: ADD).
Candide 1990 Studio Cast (with Jerry Hadley, June Anderson, Adolph Green, Christa
    Ludwig, Nicolai Gedda, Della Jones and Kurt Ollmann); **London Symphony Chorus and
    Orchestra / Leonard Bernstein**.
    DG Ⓕ 429 734-2 (two discs: 112 minutes: DDD).

The textual history of Leonard Bernstein's *Candide* is of Shakespearian complexity. As Andrew Porter has pointed out, the original Broadway run of 73 performances would be considered triumphant for a comic opera (which *Candide* is, artistically) but was disastrous for a musical (which *Candide* was, commercially). Among the show's host of distinguished contributors, the one who took the heaviest flak was the librettist, Lillian Hellman, who in later years expressed her disaffection for the whole project. Subsequent productions, beginning with the successful Harold Prince revival of 1973, used a radically rewritten book by Hugh Wheeler, which in turn necessitated considerable alteration in the music, and especially the lyrics. The Wheeler version was itself later amended, mainly by John Wells.

Hellman, a highly successful playwright, attempted, as far as possible, to re-design Voltaire's picaresque satire in the mould of the Broadway well-made play (or musical, post-Rodgers and Hammerstein). She begins, apocryphally, with the projected marriage of Candide and Cunegonde, celebrated in Richard Wilbur's lyric to the opening song "Best of all possible worlds". Wheeler *et seq*, hewing closer to Voltaire, resurrected a discarded lyric by John Latouche, the show's designated lyricist until his untimely death. So the Sony cast album is the only chance we have to hear Wilbur's coruscating nuptial lyric, delivered with incomparably suave breeziness by Max Adrian as Dr Pangloss. The record kept the show alive and it is fabulous, from the first strains of Broadway's greatest overture to the closing chorale, "Make our garden grow", stirringly led by Robert Rounseville, a mature but affecting hero. Hear him with Barbara Cook, trilling like Papageno and Papagena, as they go into their reunion duet "You were dead you know". Cook's Cunegonde is legendary, with an operatic range and a musical-comedy temper that queered the pitch for all her successors: nobody else has managed to make "Glitter and be gay", the gold-digger's jewel song, either as thrilling or as funny. William Olvis is comparably superb as the lecherous and avaricious Governor; Irra Pettina, notorious for participation in a string of failed operettas, has her one great role as the Old Lady, singing Bernstein's irresistible (words *and* music) "I am easily assimilated". But every track is a treasure.

DG's full-length account is excellently documented: at last we are told who wrote which lyrics (six writers are listed). Bernstein's conducting is dynamite from the first downbeat; there are colours in the "Overture" one seems never to have heard before, and it is darkly amusing when the familiar helter-skelter theme turns up again as battle music. Jerry Hadley is a perfect hero: he manages to exist on two levels, ingenuous as a character, immaculate as a singer. "Candide's lament" is lovely. Too many of his peers, though, reveal again the dangers of casting a mock-opera as if it were the real thing: June Anderson's Cunegonde is less satire than the thing satirized and nobody could guess from Nicolai Gedda's muddy diction at the wit of the Governor's songs. Christa Ludwig is a variable Old Lady: fine in the musical verve of "Assimilated", less so in the more pointed lyrical fun of "Quiet" (a great song) and the quartet finale. Adolph Green, the one showbiz person in the cast (and highly musical), doesn't have the energy for Pangloss; you feel him pushing him his way through, though he hits a beautiful falsetto in "Dear boy", his avuncular song to Candide about the philosophical advantages of venereal disease. A new and credibly Voltairean plot-line manages to accommodate almost the entire score, including deletions and a few late additions: not quite everything, because some songs now exist in duplicate. You need the Sony disc to fill in the gaps and for its unbeatable cast.   **RC**

Leonard Bernstein's New York with **Dawn Upshaw, Mandy Patinkin, Audra McDonald, Judy Blazer, Richard Muenz** and **Donna Murphy; Orchestra of St Luke's / Eric Stern**.
Nonesuch Ⓔ 7559-79400-2 (55 minutes: DDD).
Songs and instrumental pieces from On the Town, Wonderful Town, Fancy Free, On the Waterfront and West Side Story.

This is an attractive and well-planned disc that embraces songs as well as ballet and descriptive music from what the booklet writer Frank Rich describes as "New York's last unfettered golden age", a period running, from Bernstein's point-of-view, from *On the Town* in 1944 to 1957, the year of *West Side Story*. The black-and-white photographs of skyscapers on the cover and inside of Broadway at night in the rain, actually taken in 1960 (a cinema is showing Presley's *G.I. Blues*), convey the soul and tempo of the city that Bernstein matched so creatively in his musical shows. Besides such seasoned favourites as "Tonight" and "Somewhere" from *West Side Story*, this collection throws up "Story of my life" cut from *Wonderful Town* and "Ain't got no tears left", a blues from *Fancy Free* recently incorporated into Michael Tilson Thomas's DG recording of *On the Town*. Donna Murphy builds her performance of it most effectively. Eric Stern and the St Luke's orchestra have worked with several of these performers in their Gershwin/Nonesuch series, but new to their number here are Richard Muenz, a light voice heard at its best in "What a waste" from *Wonderful Town*, giving a smashing performance with Dawn Upshaw; however the tune of "A quiet girl" lies rather low for him. Audra McDonald sings that charming ballad with the gentle lilt, "A little bit in love", not quite as dreamily as she might at Eric Stern's fastish tempo. Upshaw squeezes all the emotion from "Lonely town" and "Somewhere" without any self indulgence, but it's Judy Blazer who really sets things alight with her contributions to a couple of comic ensembles ,"Come up to my place" and "Ya got me" from *On the Town*. One note of caution: I find Mandy Patinkin's indecision tiresome as to whether he sings in falsetto or his stronger natural upper register. His shining moment comes in *Wonderful Town*'s vaudeville-styled "Wrong note rag", compensation for miscasting him as Tony in the Balcony Scene from *West Side Story* where Muenz and Upshaw would have been a happier partnership as they demonstrate in "One hand, one heart".   **AE**

On the Town 1960 **Studio Cast** (with Betty Comden, Adolph Green, Nancy Walker, John Reardon, Chris Alexander, George Gaynes and Randel Striboneen) / **Leonard Bernstein**. Columbia Ⓜ CK02038 (62 minutes: ADD).

On the Town 1992 **Barbican Concert Cast** (with Frederica Von Stade, Thomas Hampson, Samuel Ramey, Cleo Laine, David Garrison, Kurt Ollmann, Evelyn Lear, Marie McLaughlin and Tyne Daly); **London Voices; London Symphony Orchestra / Michael Tilson Thomas**. DG Ⓕ 437 516-2 (75 minutes: DDD).

On the Town 1995 **Studio Cast** (with Gregg Edelman, Tim Flavin, Ethan Freeman, Kim Criswell, Judy Kaye, Valerie Masterson and Tinuke Olafimihan); **National Symphony Orchestra / John Owen Edwards**. TER Ⓕ CDTER2 1217 (two discs: 90 minutes: DDD).

There was an electric atmosphere in the Barbican during 1992 on the nights that the DG recording was produced. When Betty Comden and Adolph Green led the starry company on stage, the hall exploded with applause, partly in recognition that these two Broadway legends were very belatedly making their London début as the narrators for the evening's entertainment. A virtually fully-staged performance followed that, given the possibilities for mishap, was miraculously captured on disc. No artist disappointed. Tyne Daly very funny as the lovable man-eating Hildy inviting Thomas Hampson to "come up to my place". Hampson sang his ballads with tenderness ("Lonely town") and warm-heartedness ("Lucky to be me") and without resort to operatic vocal traditions. Von Stade by turns amusing ("Carried away") and touching ("Some other time"), and Ramey as the poker-faced Pitkin were further assets in the strong line-up. Under conductor Michael Tilson Thomas the London Symphony Orchestra play with all the spark and drive Bernstein commanded on his 1960 recording with members of the 1944 New York Cast including Comden and Green.

   With Bernstein at the helm, as so often in composer-conducted performances, there's that feeling that every performer is giving their all for a unique occasion. Balanced more in line with a mainstream Broadway show recording and with artists rooted in its tradition this 1960 recording makes a clear first choice. In any event, *On the Town*, in either version is a must for any collection. I'm now inclined to put it above *West Side Story* in the canon of Bernstein musicals, for it seems to capture the spirit of a city that can be awesome and energizing at the turn of a street corner.

   The new TER version on two CDs offers more music than the others proclaiming on its sleeve "first complete recording". Since the composer and Tilson Thomas eschew the "Overture", "Entr'acte" and "Closing music", one wonders on what authority they are included here? At a very short running time of 90 minutes, TER might have included the much-maligned songs Roger Edens wrote with Comden and Green for the film version released in 1949. However, up against the strong competition this recording ends up in third place despite vital contributions from Judy Kaye and Kim Criswell. After their convincing account of the same composer's *West Side Story*, both conductor and orchestra sound curiously uninvolved in this one, with several dodgy moments in the execution of one of Bernstein's trickiest scores. **AE**

West Side Story 1957 **Broadway Cast** (with Carol Lawrence, Larry Kert, Chita Rivera, Art Smith, Mickey Calin, Ken LeRoy, David Winters, Tony Mordente, Eddie Roll and Grover Dale) / **Max Goberman**. Columbia Ⓕ CK64419 (57 minutes: ADD).

West Side Story 1961 **Film Cast** (with Marni Nixon for Natalie Wood, Jim Bryant for Richard Beymer, Russ Tamblyn, Betty Wand for Rita Moreno and George Chakiris) / **Johnny Green**. Sony Ⓜ SK48211 (77 minutes: ADD).

West Side Story 1984 **Studio Cast** (with Kiri Te Kanawa, José Carreras, Tatiana Troyanos, Kurt Ollmann and Marilyn Horne); **Chorus and Orchestra / Leonard Bernstein**. DG Ⓕ 415 253-2 (two discs: 98 minutes: DDD). Also includes *On the Waterfront* Suite.

West Side Story 1993 **Leicester Haymarket Cast** (with Caroline O'Connor, Paul Manuel, Tinuke Olafimihan, Nicholas Warnford and Sally Burgess); **National Symphony Orchestra / John Owen Edwards**. TER Ⓕ CDTER2 1197 (two discs: 102 minutes: DDD).

Surely one of the most frequently revived shows, *West Side Story* marked a turning point in the history of musical theatre, taking the jagged realities of gang warfare on the streets of New York and working them into a thrillingly romantic modern musical. Most of the show's best numbers, thanks to Sondheim's timeless lyrics, have enjoyed independent success, passing into the great deposit bank of standards. But Bernstein's entire balletic, panoramic score, by turns discordant and lyrical, is the key to *West Side Story*'s enduring popularity, together with its infinitely moving reworking of the tragedy of Romeo and Juliet. The orchestral set-pieces don't just provide the structure for the dance numbers – which break out as manifestations of the rising tensions in the plot – they also create sweeping musical Manhattan vistas. Apart from Gershwin, what other composer could give you such a definitive sense of place?

The original Broadway cast recording retains a freshness and immediacy which few works of a similar age could boast. In the lead roles of Tony and Maria, Carol Lawrence and Larry Kert have probably never been matched for their sweet innocence, creating a fragile bubble of sanctuary with their duets "Tonight", "One hand, one heart" and "Somewhere", while tragedy moves inexorably nearer. The production made a star of Chita Rivera as a fiery Anita, leading the ensemble through an exhilarating "America" and sounding a bitter note of realistic caution with "A boy like that". The recording is also notable for Eddie Roll and Grover Dale as they lead the Jets through the show's frantic comic high spot, "Gee, Officer Krupke".

West Side Story was not filmed until 1961, when it made history for its use of real Manhattan locations – one of the first times a musical had been freed from the confines of a studio. Some of the songs were re-ordered, resulting in a stronger position for "Officer Krupke"; "America" was expanded into a larger production number. Among the performers, Russ Tamblyn as Riff ("Jet Song") and Betty Wand singing for Rita Moreno as Anita have real fire: Moreno won an Oscar for her performance. Natalie Wood gets star billing on this original soundtrack recording, but in reality, Hollywood followed its usual policy of casting a bankable non-singing star and dubbing the songs, so it is actually Marni Nixon's voice we hear.

Both the Broadway cast recording and the film soundtrack provide definitive vocal performances, but by limiting themselves largely to the songs, much of Bernstein's score is lost, together with the book's mounting dramatic tension. There are a couple of notable alternatives. In 1984 the maestro, Bernstein himself, conducted a studio recording of his score which included many of the instrumental passages. At the forefront of the now established vogue for 'classical' recordings of popular musicals featuring leading opera singers, it was, by all accounts, a tumultuous event. In this case, the overall effect is stately, even grandiose, rather than vibrant and exciting. With the best will in the world, the mature charms of Te Kanawa and Carreras are not easily allied with the youthful innocence of Maria and Tony, however beautifully they sing. Kurt Ollmann is more convincing as Riff and Marilyn Horne (as 'A Girl') delivers a sublime "Somewhere". An important work for the serious archivist's collection. However, a rather more animated proposition is a double CD inspired by the 1992 Leicester Haymarket production and featuring many of the artists from that revival. The performances are fairly standard, although Tinuke Olafimihan is exceptional as Maria, and the production quality is excellent. Its main benefits are that it includes a significant amount of dialogue to put the numbers in context, large swathes of the score, richly and fluidly played by the National Symphony Orchestra, and features the complete "Dance at the gym" and "Ballet sequence". There are also bonus tracks of the alternative versions of "Something's coming", "America", "Gee, Officer Krupke" and "Somewhere", taken from the film score. Sally Burgess makes a guest appearance (here billed as 'A Voice') singing "Somewhere". It isn't clear what she's doing there, but she sings it beautifully. **PF**

Wonderful Town 1953 **Broadway Cast** (with Rosalind Russell, George Gaynes, Edith Adams, Dort Clark, Jordan Bentley and Cris Alexander) **/ Lehman Engel**.
MCA mono Ⓜ MCAD10050 (45 minutes: AAD).

Wonderful Town 1958 **Television Cast** (with Rosalind Russell, Sydney Chaplin, Jacquelyn McKeever, Jordan Bentley and Cris Alexander) **/ Lehman Engel**.
Sony Broadway Ⓜ SK48021 (47 minutes: ADD).

Wonderful Town 1986 **London Cast** (with Maureen Lipman, Ray Lonnen, Emily Morgan and Nicolas Colicos) **/ David Steadman**.
First Night Ⓜ OCRCD6011 (49 minutes: DDD).

In *Wonderful Town* Leonard Bernstein wrote a pastiche of the 1930s pop styles as brilliant as the opera and operetta spoof of *Candide* – though pastiche seems a condescending term for a score this vibrant. Written in five weeks (after the previous composing team had been unceremoniously dumped) it sounds as if the music of the composer's youth were surging through him. "Swing!",

"Conga!" and "Wrong note rag" are jubilant distillations of their respective idioms, written with love and with a bubbling wit, but also with a tense angularity that is unmistakably Bernstein. The re-imagined era sounds poised (as historically it was) between the Jazz Age and the Age of Anxiety. The ballads "It's love" and "A little bit in love" are among his most ingratiating. Betty Comden and Adolph Green, also writing under the gun, came up with the best set of lyrics of their career: smart, conversational and very funny. It's a shame they didn't write the book as well; the show on stage always comes as a slight disappointment to those who grew up with the original cast album.

That album, now on MCA, is one of the great show records. It definitively enshrines the performance of Rosalind Russell as the elder and brainier of the two mid-Western sisters who come to New York in search of careers. Comden and Green gave her perfect material: the sadder-but-wiser "One hundred easy ways" (to lose a man – "Just tell him where his grammar errs then mark your towels hers and hers"); the desperately embarrassed sociability of "Conversation piece" ("I was reading *Moby Dick* the other night – it's about this whale"); the orgiastic birth of a hepcat in "Swing!". She may not have been a singer, but she had great rhythm. Edith (later Edie) Adams is the perfect complement, blithe and melodious, as the ingenuous sibling who melts all hearts and stiffens all libidos, from the news-desks to the police precinct. The moment when the cops' respectful salute to "My darlin' Eileen" comes out of hushed *colla voce* to show its true colours as a rollicking Irish jig remains the most joyous in the score. The supporting cast, apart from the oleaginous George Gaynes in the male lead, are absolutely on the money.

Russell repeated her role on television five years later. It's still a great performance though, as often happens, time has brought over-elaboration; her throwaways and zingers no longer have their former perfect pace. The same goes on a smaller scale for two other Broadway hold-overs: Cris Alexander as a bashful dispenser of banana splits ("that's our special, 28 cents" – those were the days) and Jordan Bentley whose original energy and precision are way down on "Pass the football", the priceless saga of a sports champ who's a scholastic chump. Jacquelyn McKeever sounds scratchy compared to Adams, but Sydney Chaplin, though an erratic vocalist, makes a far more appealing Bob Baker than Gaynes. The Sony disc has one other thing going for it: the "Overture".   **RC**

Also available:

Candide (1988 Scottish Opera Cast) TER CDTER1156
West Side Story (1993 Studio Cast) Carlton Shows Collection 30362 0032-2
Wonderful Town (1986 London Cast) First Night OCRCD6011

Richard Besoyan   1924–1970 USA

Born in Reedley, California Rick Besoyan studied at the University of California and on a scholarship at Trinity College, London before touring the USA with the Savoy Light Opera Company (he sang the role of Koko in *The Mikado* over 500 times). He gave up performing to produce and direct an off-Broadway revival of Cole Porter's *Out of This World*, and contributed a short sketch to a revue, *In Your Hat* in 1957. This sketch was later expanded into the full-length show *Little Mary Sunshine* (1959) – a minor off-Broadway production satirizing old-fashioned operettas attracting advance ticket sales totalling $8·70 – which turned into an unexpected hit. Two later shows, *The Student Gypsy* (1963) and *Babes in the Wood* (1964), failed to achieve the same success.

New review

Little Mary Sunshine 1962 London Cast (with Patricia Routledge, Bernard Cribbins, Joyce
   Blair, Terence Cooper, Gita Denise and Erik Chitty) / **Philip Martell.**
   DRG Ⓜ 13108 (46 minutes: AAD).

Rick Besoyan's fame is essentially limited to this 1959 off-Broadway show, into which he put his own extensive experience of enjoying and performing in the musical shows of old. The show makes gentle, if rather obvious, fun of various key works in the history of musicals. Listen to this recording, and you will revisit the male choruses of Sigmund Romberg, followed by take-offs of Jerome Kern's "Look for a silver lining", Sullivan's "It is not love" from *The Sorcerer*,

Friml's "Indian love call", the double sextet "Tell me, pretty maiden" from Leslie Stuart's *Florodora*, Hoschka's "Every little movement" and Johann Strauss's "I'm in love with Vienna". There are some good tunes – most particularly the title song and "Look for a sky of blue", both sung by the title character. However, there is little of the subtlety of Sandy Wilson's affectionate and clever reincarnation of a 1920s musical, *The Boy Friend*. This is very much a 'take-it-or-leave-it' show. Whereas New York was happy to take it, London was more inclined to leave it. There was also an original New York cast recording with slightly different numbers that is currently unavailable; but for British listeners this London cast recording will have a particular fascination for a number of performers who went on to achieve greater things – not just Patricia Routledge and Bernard Cribbins but others too among the chorus of young ladies of the Eastchester Finishing School and young gentlemen of the United States Forest Rangers. **AML**

Marc Blitzstein
1905-1964 USA

Originally a composer with distinctly intellectual and abstract pretensions, who had studied with Boulanger and Schoenberg in Europe, Blitzstein's increasing left-wing awareness of the function of music in society during the 1930s found expression in works for the theatre. Influenced by Kurt Weill, Hans Eisler and Bertolt Brecht, Blitzstein wrote *The Cradle Will Rock* in 1937. It was later independently staged by Orson Welles and John Houseman as a Mercury Theatre production. Later theatrical works include the opera *No for an Answer* (1941) and the show *Reuben Reuben* (1955). He also wrote numerous other works, including film scores and the *Airborne* Symphony (1946), and received critical acclaim for his translation and adaptation of Weill's *Die Dreigroschenoper*, *The Threepenny Opera* (1952).

The Cradle Will Rock 1985 **London Cast** (with Patti LuPone and John Houseman) **/ Michael Barrett**.
TER Ⓕ CDTEM2 1105 (two discs: 91 minutes: DDD).

This revival had for prologue the director, John Houseman, recalling the original 1937 production, on which he worked with Orson Welles. In the teeth of a government ban and a union lock-out, Welles, Houseman and their cast marched from their own New York theatre to a deserted one where the actors, illuminated by a single roving spotlight, performed the show from the auditorium, with the composer accompanying from an onstage piano. The first (12-minute) CD of this two-disc set is devoted to Houseman's recreation of that legendary night. The show may never have seemed so stirring since.

But it still stirs. A frank piece of agitprop, maybe the first expressionist musical, it ferociously satirizes Mister Mister, boss of Steeltown, and his coterie of sycophants – an editor, minister, a doctor, an academic, and a couple of self-proclaimed artists, all more than willing to prostitute whatever ideals they may have. Over against them stand a more innocent prostitute, Moll, and the heroic labour organizer Larry Foreman (ironic that the unions came out against this show). It may sound dated, but there is a scorching sincerity in Blitzstein's sometimes clumsy lyrics, and a startling beauty, as well as a piercing sense of parody, in much of his music. It is what it is – a more Brechtian musical than Brecht and Weill ever wrote – and in both New York and London this production showed that to be a lot. Patti LuPone is the best-known name, and as Moll she makes much of the hauntingly tough lament "Nickel under the foot". (She also does an oddly-accented turn as one of Mister Mister's awful children who share a playful attack on 1930s sentiment called "Croon/Spoon" and a spot-on Hawaiian pastiche, "Honolulu"). But what really devastates, as it did in both cities, is the climactic anger of "Joe Worker gets gypped", sung by Michele-Denise Woods. Randle Mell overdoes Larry's winsome swagger (you feel like knocking the smile off his face, or at least out of his voice), but is effective in the thunderous title-song, and the assorted victims and parasites are fine. Michael Barrett plays piano and narrates: an impromptu device that now seems built into the show. **RC**

Also available:
No for an Answer (1941 US Cast) AEI CD-031

Jerry Bock
b. 1928 USA

Sheldon Harnick
b. 1924 USA

Born Jerrold Lewis in New Haven, Connecticut, Jerry Bock wrote music for student productions at the University of Wisconsin before moving to New York and writing for television and revues. In collaboration with lyricist Larry Holofcener he had a hit with his first full-length show *Mr Wonderful* in 1956; subsequently he worked extensively with lyricist Sheldon Harnick, beginning with *The Body Beautiful* (1958), followed by the Pulitzer Prize-winning *Fiorello!* (1959). Chicago-born Harnick had previously written both music and lyrics for songs in revues such as *New Faces* (1952) and *Shangri-La* (1956). After unexpected failures with *Tenderloin* (1960), and the critically-acclaimed but commercially unsuccessful *She Loves Me* (1963 – the first show directed by Hal Prince) Bock and Harnick penned their most successful show, *Fiddler on the Roof* in 1964. Based on stories by Sholom Aleichem, and staged by Jerome Robbins, *Fiddler* ran for over 3,000 performances in New York and 2,000 in London. Originally starring Zero Mostel on Broadway, it was filmed in 1971 with the star of the first London production, Topol. Numerous productions around the world demonstrate its continuing popularity. Later Bock/Harnick shows – *The Apple Tree* (1966) and *The Rothschilds* (1970) – received good reviews but were not such big hits. Bock and Harnick parted company after a dispute over who should direct *The Rothschilds*. Harnick also wrote *Smiling the Boy Fell Dead* (1961) with David Baker, *Captain Jinks of the Horse Marines* (1975) with Jack Beeson and *Rex* (1976) with Richard Rodgers. *She Loves Me* was successfully revived on Broadway and the West End in 1994.

New review
The Apple Tree 1966 **Broadway Cast** (with Barbara Harris, Alan Alda and Larry Blyden) / **Elliot Lawrence.**
Sony Broadway ℗ SK48209 (56 minutes: ADD).

Before his successful career in films and television (notably in *M.A.S.H.*), Alan Alda was one of the three leads in Bock and Harnick's triple-decker musical *The Apple Tree*. Bock and Harnick aren't always given the credit they deserve for their clever lyrics and fine melodies, but this show with its pleasing collection of songs is typical of their output. The three mini-musicals are adaptations of Mark Twain's *The Diary of Adam and Eve*, Frank Stockton's *The Lady or the Tiger* and Jules Feiffer's *Passionella*. The show was a modest success, running for 463 performances on Broadway. From a gentle but witty biblical tale of the first man and woman on earth, through a medieval puzzle with a teasing ending, to a wish fulfilment dream of a chimney sweep cleaner who sees herself as a Hollywood star, the team's sure touch never fails them. This is the show that made Barbara Harris a Broadway star, and this cast recording shows her versatility and charm. "Gorgeous" is a delightful sample of her humour and timing. Alda and the late and much missed Larry Blyden complete the talented trio of principals in a variety of contrasting roles. *The Apple Tree* is a vintage recording from Broadway's golden years. **MPK**

Fiddler on the Roof 1964 **Broadway Cast** (with Zero Mostel, Maria Karnilova, Beatrice Arthur, Joanna Merlin, Austin Pendleton, Bert Convy, Julia Migenes, Michael Granger, Joseph Sullivan, Tanya Everett and Joe Ponazecki) / **Milton Greene.**
RCA Victor ℗ RD87060 (50 minutes: ADD).
Fiddler on the Roof 1971 **Film Cast** (with Topol, Norma Crane, Leonard Frey, Molly Picon, Paul Mann and Ruth Madoc) / **John Williams.**
EMI Ⓜ CDP7 46091-2 (61 minutes: ADD).

From the haunting fiddle solo at the start to its melancholy reprise at the end, this charming, warm, sad study of the problems faced by Jewish milkman Tevye as his family copes with change in the context of the gathering clouds of anti-Semitism in late Czarist Russia is one of the most enduring musicals of all time. Countless, regular revivals might have bred contempt. Instead, over 30 years after its arrival on Broadway, *Fiddler on the Roof* is regarded with more affection by popular musical-goers than virtually any other show. Central to this durable appeal are Jerry Bock's score, which borrows freely from the Jewish folk idiom, and Sheldon Harnick's humorous, apposite lyrics. Combined, they evoke the microcosm of Anatevka, complete with its Orthodox beliefs and traditions, facing the twin threats of modern social values and the bigotry which will eventually scatter its inhabitants across the world in a mini diaspora. The Broadway cast recording features Zero Mostel in the pivotal role of Tevye, singing the humorously acrid "If I were a rich man", a song which was written especially for him. Together, Mostel and Maria Karnilova's Golda face the bewildering onslaught of change and its impact on their five daughters with general equanimity, invention and a touch of superstition ("Sunrise, sunset" and "Do you love me?"). The ensemble pieces, which include the deeply affecting "Sabbath Prayer" and the rousing drinking song "Tradition", are delivered with great zest. Other notable voices in the cast include Beatrice Arthur as Yente the matchmaker and a youthful Julia Migenes as the second daughter, Hodel.

Despite his long association with the role on Broadway, Mostel's excellent performance has tended to be eclipsed by the rich and hearty playing of Topol, who created the role in the West End and subsequently won the film role. Not surprisingly, Topol dominates the 1971 film soundtrack. John Williams's Oscar-winning arrangements open the score out and paint the story with bolder, lusher strokes without diminishing the intimate, moving quality of many of the songs such as "Sabbath Prayer", "Do you love me?" and Hodel's lament, "Far from the home I love". "Tevye's dream", the device with which he persuades Golda that their oldest daughter Tzeitel must marry Motel, the tailor, for love rather than Lazar Wolf, the butcher, for money, is a delight. Ruth Madoc plays the butcher's vengeful dead wife Frumah Sarah with a deal of evil wailing and cackling. Led by Molly Picon's Tzeitel, the daughters are played with dignity and humour ("Matchmaker") and Norma Crane makes a more brusque Golda than Karnilova on Broadway.   **PF**

Fiorello! 1959 **Broadway Cast** (with Tom Bosley, Bob Holiday, Nathaniel Frey,
   Patricia Wilson, Howard da Silva, Pat Stanley, Ellen Hanley and Eileen Rodgers) /
   Hal Hastings.
   EMI Angel Ⓜ ZDM7 65023-2 (47 minutes: ADD).

Musicals with a political theme have regularly surfaced on Broadway: most recently Mayor Ed Koch and Gentleman Jimmy Walker have been the subject of musical comedies. In earlier times the Gershwins (twice) and Rodgers and Hart (once) had created successful political musicals. Few, however, have been as tuneful and attractive as *Fiorello!*. Bock and Harnick's Pulitzer Prize-winner which dealt with a diminutive crime-busting mayor of New York, Fiorello (Little Flower) LaGuardia and his fight against the entrenched corruption of union bosses in the New York of the period before and after the First World War. The show provided a meaty principal role that catapulted Tom Bosley into stardom (long before his long-running TV series *Happy Days*). Jerry Bock's fine score and Sheldon Harnick's witty and often tender lyrics reflect with style and sensitivity the life and times of an unconventional politician with a zeal for reform. The irridescent score ranges from charming ballads to acute comments on politics and social conditions. The original cast recording (the only one) reflects true theatrical magic – apart from a powerhouse leading performance from Bosley in "The name's LaGuardia" and "Unfair" there are affecting softer moments from Ellen Hanley in "Til tomorrow", and Patricia Wilson in "When did I fall in love?". A classic original cast album of a key show.   **MPK**

New review
The Rothschilds 1970 **Broadway Cast** (with Hal Linden, Paul Hecht, Leila Martin, Keene
   Curtis, Jill Clayburgh and Chris Sarandon) / **Milton Greene**.
   Sony Broadway Ⓔ SK30337 (51 minutes: ADD).

How can you top a great success like *Fiddler on the Roof*? You can't. But six years later, Bock and Harnick revisited their rich Jewish cultural heritage when they wrote an endearing musical version of the founding of a great European financial dynasty, the Rothschilds. As opposed to Tevye's five daughters, Meyer Rothschild had five sons. These were deployed throughout the financial centres of Europe and with wisdom and acuity set the foundations for the great banking house. Yet again, the writers came up with a richly melodic and finely-crafted score, which while lacking the universality of *Fiddler*, has many musical joys – an irresistibly jaunty "Rothschild and sons" and a deeply touching plea for peace, "In our own lifetime". The fine cast acquits itself well on Sony Broadway's CD transfer. Hal Linden contributes a towering, authoritative performance as the patriarch Meyer Rothschild, and Keene Curtis impresses in a variety of aristocratic roles. The distaff side have rather less to do than the men, but Leila Martin and Jill Clayburgh are very appealing in their few opportunities. *The Rothschilds* is a fine score that doesn't deserve its comparative neglect.   **MPK**

She Loves Me 1963 **Broadway Cast** (with Barbara Cook, Daniel Massey, Barbara Baxley, Jack Cassidy and Nathaniel Frey) / **Hal Hastings**.
Polydor Ⓕ 831 968-2 (74 minutes: AAD).

She Loves Me 1964 **London Cast** (with Anne Rogers, Gary Raymond, Rita Moreno, Gary Miller, Gregory Phillips and Peter Sallis) / **Alyn Ainsworth**.
EMI Angel Ⓜ ZDM7 28595-2 (53 minutes: AAD).

She Loves Me 1993 **Off-Broadway Cast** (with Boyd Gaines, Diane Fratantoni, Sally Mayes, Jonathan Freeman, Howard McGillin and Brad Kane) / **David Loud**.
Varèse Sarabande Spotlight Series Ⓕ VSD5464 (67 minutes: DDD).

She Loves Me 1994 **London Cast** (with John Gordon Sinclair, Ruthie Henshall, Tracie Bennett, Gerard Casey, Barry James and David de Keyser) / **Robert Scott**.
First Night Ⓕ CASTCD44 (71 minutes: DDD).

The first two issues commemorate the original production on Broadway and in London of one of the most charming and attractive musicals of the 1960s. The story that had already served for two films, *The Shop Around the Corner* (James Stewart and Margaret Sullavan) and *In the Good Old Summertime* (Judy Garland and Van Johnson) was pressed into service yet again for a stage musical. Two shop workers in a perfumery don't get on in their working life. But as pen pals, unaware of each other's identity, they do. In addition, the man is wrongly believed by the shop's owner to be carrying on an affair with the owner's wife. Jerry Bock's brilliant Central European-flavoured score has melody and style a-plenty. All four recordings do it justice. Yet there is a particularly strong case to be made for the supremacy of the original Broadway version. It has the original full Broadway orchestrations (as has the London original cast recording) – and it has Barbara Cook and Daniel Massey as the two leads, and as the icing on the cake, Jack Cassidy as a philandering sales clerk. It is also the most complete recording available. ("Tango tragique" was excised for the revivals, perhaps for reasons of taste.) The original London cast has a piquancy and charm all its own and fine performances from the three principals, as well as an alternate song "Heads I win" that replaced "I resolve". Nor is there anything wrong with either of the two recent recordings: each offers an intimate performance with old-world attractions. Ruthie Henshall in particular makes a memorable impression in "Ice cream". I wonder why it was necessary to have the performers in the recent English version adopt American accents, though.   **MPK**

Tenderloin 1960 **Broadway Cast** (with Maurice Evans, Eileen Rodgers and Lee Becker) / **Hal Hastings**.
EMI Angel Ⓜ ZDM5 65022-2 (53 minutes: ADD).

New York has been the setting for many shows, but no period has proved more lucrative than the years between the 'gay nineties' through to the First World War. *Hello, Dolly!* is the most widely known of their number, with *Tenderloin* the most deserving to be better known. It was written by Bock and Harnick in the wake of their first Broadway hit, *Fiorello!*, but audiences who'd flocked to see their portrayal of New York's charismatic Mayor of the 1920's Fiorello La Guardia, stayed away from *Tenderloin*'s Protestant Minister Doctor Brock – a straight-laced figure bent on cleaning up the district of the city known as the 'Tenderloin'. Maurice Evans, the English Shakespearian actor, is the Reverend caught betwixt pulpit and populace, with Eileen Rodgers and Lee Becker in the opposing camp bringing the house down with their brilliant duet, "Little old New York". A secondary plot involves a raffish young reporter out to woo a pretty girl in Brock's congregation with "Artifical flowers", an old-fashioned waltz that climbed into the American top ten via a recording by Bobby Darin. Irwin Kostal's evocative orchestrations deftly mirror the congregationalist fervour of Brock's camp and the brash behaviour of the street folk. Jerry Bock's delightful score, with half a dozen tunes that can be readily hummed should be investigated by all collectors and given serious consideration by those searching for something new to add to their repertoire.   **AE**

Also available:

Fiddler on the Roof (1967 London Cast) Sony West End SMK 53499
Fiddler on the Roof (1995 Studio Cast) Carlton Shows Collection 30362-0014-2
Mr Wonderful (1956 Broadway Cast) MCA MCAD10303

Jacques Brel

1929-1978 Belgium

A singer with a reputation for biting satire, his songs – most of which had music by Gérard Jouannest – were turned into a cabaret-revue in New York in 1968. *Jacques Brel is Alive and Well and Living in Paris* starred Elly Stone and ran for 1,847 performances, although by this time Brel had been forced into near-retirement by cancer. His last album, *Brel* (1977), sold over two million copies.

Jacques Brel is Alive and Well and Living in Paris 1995 London Revival Cast
(with Michael Cahill, Alison Egan, Liz Greenaway and Stuart Pendred) / **Ruth Alexander.**
TER Ⓔ CDTEM2 1231 (two discs: 91 minutes: DDD).

Twenty years after his death, the chansons of Belgian singer Jacques Brel are still regarded as a cornerstone of the post-war repertoire. His observations on the close relationship between love and hate and the many facets of the human condition are both intensely personal and universally relevant. Sometimes brilliantly witty ("Middle class"), often savage and raw, his songs provide pungent material for any performer. This cult revue based on Brel's work, with English lyrics by Eric Blau and Mort Shuman, was hugely successful off-Broadway at the end of the 1960s, but failed to shine in London until a talented although largely unknown team revived it at the Canal Café and, subsequently, the King's Head Theatre in 1995.

In keeping with TER's laudable philosophy this is the first complete recording of the show. Like the cabaret songs of Brecht and Weill, Brel's material holds a mirror up to its audience. That interaction is inevitably missing in the studio, but the commitment and passion of the cast are nicely preserved. They fall on the meat offered by these mini-dramas with obvious relish. Michael Cahill's "Bachelor's dance" has an authentic troubadour-like zest, while Stuart Pendred brings a morbid anger to "Funeral tango". The women are at their best in ensemble numbers like "The desperate ones" and "If we only have love", although Liz Greenaway's "Carousel" is a yearning, melancholy delight. Occasionally I longed for the more lived-in voice of a Marianne Faithfull or an Agnes Bernelle to generate that extra edge. But this is compelling stuff, the discreet accompaniment of the small band allowing the clarity of the lyrics to take centre-stage.   **PF**

Also available:
Jacques Brel is Alive and Well and Living in Paris (1968 Broadway Cast) Columbia CGK40817

Leslie Bricusse

b. 1931 England

Anthony Newley

b. 1931 England

Composer and lyricist Leslie Bricusse studied at Cambridge University, where his revue *Out of the Blue* was successful enough to be staged in the West End. He again wrote both music and lyrics for his first full-length show, *Lady at the Wheel* (1958) before beginning a long-standing collaboration with Anthony Newley, the writer, actor and singer who had first become known as the Artful Dodger in David Lean's 1948 film version of *Oliver Twist*. Newley had written and performed his own songs in the film *Idle on Parade* (1959) which he followed with some hit records, including "Why?" and "D-Darling", and several more film and TV appearances. Bricusse and Newley had successes with *Stop the World – I Want to Get Off* (1960) and *The Roar of the Greasepaint – The Smell of the Crowd* (1965), the latter being premièred in New York after failing in out of town try-outs in England. Their only other show together was *The Good Old Bad Old Days* (1972), although the collaboration also included songs for a variety of films such as *Willy Wonka and the Chocolate Factory* (1971) and the title song for *Goldfinger* (1964 – music by John Barry). Newley starred in the Bricusse-scored *Doctor Dolittle* (1967) for which Bricusse won an Academy Award for "Talk to the animals". Bricusse was responsible for the music and lyrics for the films *Goodbye, Mr Chips* (1969) and *Scrooge* (1970) both of which have also been seen on stage. He also wrote the stage show *Sherlock Holmes* (1989). As lyricist, Bricusse has collaborated with many leading film composers: with John Barry on *The Knack* (1965) and *You Only Live Twice* (1967), with Jerry Goldsmith on *The Sand Pebbles* (1966) and *In Like Flint* (1967), with John Williams on *How to Steal a Million* (1966), *Superman* (1978), *Home Alone*

(1990) and *Hook* (1991), and with Henry Mancini on *Victor/Victoria* (1982). He wrote the lyrics for Frank Wildhorn's version of *Jekyll and Hyde* (1990), which finally reached Broadway in 1997.

New review
Doctor Dolittle 1967 Film Cast (with Rex Harrison, Anthony Newley and Samantha Eggar) / Lionel Newman.
Philips Ⓔ 534 500-2PH (46 minutes: ADD).

A 30-year-old film that can still command a UK television audience on Christmas Eve 1996 of 2·8 million viewers "can't be reckoned altogether bad", to quote Matthew Dolittle's assistant about the man himself. Yet when this costly production was laid before Her Majesty the Queen at a Royal Première back in 1967 there were many who found more excitement in the events surrounding the making of the film, which included the damming of a stream to form a harbour in the Cotswold village of Castle Coombe, an eccentric army man who climbed the village steeple with a flag proclaiming "Go home Fox", actors bitten and defecated upon by animals, the temperamental off-screen performance of the leading man, a storm in the West Indies that nearly drowned him and the crew, and finally the abandonment of Castle Coombe owing to the vagaries of the British weather for a model set back in California. Nor did the film's musical director, long-term Fox conductor Lionel Newman, like Leslie Bricusse's songs.

Yes, it was a flawed film, pleasant enough to idle away two hours and more watching Hugh Lofting's characters under a Constable sky, but often let down by a tortoise-like pace and some indifferent songs. These were arranged by Alexander Courage, of *Star Trek* fame, who took full advantage of the large studio orchestra still on hand at the Fox studios. It is regrettable therefore that in asking full price for this reissue Philips couldn't have included more of the music from the film where Courage was given free reign. His extended arrangements of such sequences as the Academy Award-winning "Talk to the animals", culminating in a marvellous widescreen shot of Rex Harrison surrounded by a menagerie of farm life, or the film's outstanding circus song-and-dance number, "I've never seen anything like it", where Richard Attenborough appears alongside the Pushmi-Pullyu, the double-ended lama, would both have been inestimable assets if presented in full. As it is the improvement on the LP soundtrack is marginal, as was the case with *Hello, Dolly!* from the same source. With the video retailing at a similar price only the convenience of tracking down the musical numbers would weigh in favour of the CD.   **AE**

Goodbye, Mr Chips 1982 Chichester Festival Theatre Cast (with Sir John Mills, Colette Gleeson and Nigel Stock) / John Owen Edwards.
TER Ⓔ CDTER1025 (53 minutes: DDD).

Leslie Bricusse rejigged his 1969 MGM film score for an early 1980s stage production by writing additional material for Chips himself, sung by Sir John Mills, his wife, Colette Gleeson and the school-boys at his public school. Though the omitted numbers are not sorely missed, the fantastical scoring of them for the film version, like those that have been retained, certainly is! John Williams's arrangements were such an integral part of the soundtrack that what remains is penny plain in the chamber-like proportions heard on this disc. Nor do Bricusse's variable additions enhance the slim but touching tale of the school master passed over for the headship at the school where he had given long and dedicated service. Sir John gives an understated performance as the schoolmaster and his boys are a well-drilled squad, but this has to be a stop gap recommendation until the Peter O'Toole/Petula Clark disc returns hopefully in the Rhino/EMI series of MGM soundtracks.   **AE**

The Roar of the Greasepaint – The Smell of the Crowd 1965 Broadway Cast (with Anthony Newley, Cyril Ritchard, Sally Smith and Gilbert Price) / Herbert Grossman.
RCA Victor Ⓜ 60351-2 (51 minutes: ADD).

For their second collaborative show Bricusse and Newley tapped a similar formula to their initial success, *Stop the World*, casting Newley as a down-trodden man at odds with life. This time Cyril Ritchard was his co-star. It was produced on Broadway after an unsuccessful tryout in England with a different cast, where, thanks to a hugely profitable tour, its modest six-month run was adjuged a success. Once again it was with Newley in harness that Bricusse gave of his very best in the musical numbers. Their score was one of the last to boast a number of hit songs that were subsequently taken up by a bevy of artists. The era of the musical that produced the standard song was virtually over, though late in 1972 Bricusse and Newley did produce a comparable work in *The Good Old Bad Old Days*. But in 1965 it seemed that solidly built numbers like "Who can I turn to?", "A wonderful day like today" and, subsequently, "Feeling good" and "Nothing can stop me now", were being sung *ad infinitum* on radio and in cabaret. Fans of Newley and Ritchard will hear no deviation from characterizations they've offered in other shows. The one performer who does command attention is Gilbert Price who delivers the beautifully written "Feeling good" with complete command of its Arlen-like style.   **AE**

Scrooge 1992 **Birmingham Production** (with Anthony Newley, Stratford Johns, Tom Watt and
    Jon Pertwee) **/ Stuart Pedlar.**
        TER Ⓕ CDTER1194 (66 minutes: DDD).

Like *Goodbye, Mr Chips* and *Victor/Victoria*, *Scrooge* is another screen musical adapted for the stage by its author and composer Leslie Bricusse. Unlike *Mr Chips*, *Scrooge* works better within the confines of the proscenium arch where the Dickensian characters spring to life in a more convincing way. On this recording the orchestra and chorus are not so far removed in numbers from the ensemble on the 1970 film soundtrack, yet to be released on CD. Anthony Newley's ability to hold in check those extraordinary vowel sounds so closely associated with him is a further asset! The supporting cast is a strong one and the recording robust. Cordially recommended.   **AE**

New review

Sherlock Holmes – The Musical 1989 **Bristol Old Vic Cast** (with Robert Powell, Roy
    Barraclough, Louise English, Sarah Hay) **/ Stuart Pedlar.**
        TER Ⓕ CDTER1198 (72 minutes: DDD).

With Ron Moody in the title role, *Sherlock Holmes* had a brief run at London's Cambridge Theatre in 1989, before setting out on the road in the Bristol Old Vic production recorded by TER. I found it hard to raise much enthusiasm for Leslie Bricusse's score which had the hallmarks of having been composed at least a decade earlier – one number, "London is London", found its way into his movie score of *Goodbye Mr Chips* (1969). Despite my admiration for Ron Moody and the cast on the RCA Victor recording, the present company, with Stuart Pedlar's vital musical direction and recording engineer John Kurlander's exemplary musical balance, have done their best to make me believe that this is a much better score than I had remembered. And that's some feat bearing in mind lines like "without Shakespeare there would be no to be or not to be". Robert Powell's youthful Holmes forms a real partnership with his Watson, Roy Barraclough, whilst Louise English in the ungrateful role of Bella finds some common humanity that had eluded Liz Robertson on the earlier recording. But it's Sarah Hay as Holmes's house keeper Mrs Hudson who steals this recording with her solo "A lousy life". This is a fine bit of characterization that alongside "Down the apple 'n' pears" – that little masterpiece of cockney patter – gives this *Sherlock Holmes* a real lift.   **AE**

Stop the World – I Want to Get Off 1995 **Studio Cast** (with Mike Holoway and Louise
    Gold); **NSO Ensemble / Martin Yates.**
        TER Ⓕ CDTER1226 (67 minutes: DDD).

This 1961 first opus from the pens of Leslie Bricusse and Anthony Newley has resolutely refused to budge with the times. Its revival in the West End with Newley recreating his original role vanished after a few weeks back in 1989 whilst a disco version starring Sammy Davis Jr., who did so much to popularize songs like "Gonna build a mountain" and "What kind of fool am I?", likewise failed to take off. Since the show had little in the way of a storyline it would seem the much-recorded songs are better suited to presentation on disc than on stage where the anti-hero, to coin a fashionable term of the time, now comes across as a chauvinist and unpleasant little Englander. The cast assembled for this studio recording take its cue from the original Decca recording in that Mike Holoway's portrayal is evidently modelled on Newley's own, if without the creator's lung power. Louise Gold as Evie, offers charming support. The original orchestrations add a period charm to this now rather quaint entertainment.   **AE**

Also available:
Pickwick (1993 Chichester Cast) TER CDTER1205

Joe Brooks

Metropolis 1989 **London Cast** (with Brian Blessed, Judy Kuhn, Graham Bickley, Jonathan
Adams, Paul Keown and Stiffyn Parri) / **Mark Warren**.
TER Ⓕ CDTER2 1168 (two discs: 122 minutes: DDD).

On stage an overblown and cumbrous set spoiled *Metropolis*'s hopes for success, but its
recording demonstrates the potential contained within. Brooks's music covers a wide variety of
styles: rock songs, synthesized pop songs, classic ballads and impressive choral pieces. By
necessity, the work bears little relation to Fritz Lang's original 1926 movie, as is carefully
explained in lyricist Dusty Hughes's booklet note on the musical, which also constitutes a
useful accompanying essay about the movie itself. The recording is satisfying in its
completeness, lengthy dramatic sections interweaving music and dialogue with a series of
exemplary performances. Brian Blessed as the megalomaniac Freeman is in strong voice,
dealing confidently with the complex "The machines are beautiful". Graham Bickley is a little
bland in the dialogue scenes, but makes up for this in the songs, particularly the strong ballads
such as "It's only love". Judy Kuhn shines in the dual role of Maria, the spiritual leader of the
oppressed workers, and Futura, the robot created with Maria's face as a tool to continue their
subjugation. She carefully differentiates the two characters using a free, open voice to
emphasize the rebellious spirit of the former, and a chilling tone for the latter. As an
exploration of the increasingly dehumanizing nature of the modern world and the need for man
to be free from oppression, *Metropolis* paints with broad strokes, but with a fresh musical
approach, offering a positive and hopeful message. **RAC**

Jason Robert Brown

New review
Songs for a New World WPA **Theatre Cast** (with Brooks Ashmanskas, Andrea Burns,
Jessica Molaskey and Ty Taylor).
RCA Victor Ⓕ 09026 68631-2 (77 minutes: DDD).

The age of the blockbuster musical has all but stifled the art of revue which, these days, tends to
centre on the familiar: an evening with Sondheim, Porter, Coward and so on. Take your pick. Any
project which attempts to bring new material to this beleaguered format has to be worth a second
listen. In 1995, Jason Robert Brown produced this vibrant collection of songs off-Broadway,
loosely linked by 'big' themes such as arrival and departure, seminal experiences and life choices,
using New York through the ages as a backdrop. The narrative is lost on this disc but it's still a
compelling patchwork of musical styles and emotions, delivered by a very talented cast.
    There are indeed echoes of Sondheim at times, particularly in the lyrics. But there are also
good, modern rock tunes and blues numbers such as "The steam train", "The river won't flow"
and "Stars and the moon" which has more than a hint of Joni Mitchell or Suzanne Vega.
Admirers of fine pastiche will appreciate the excellent "Surubaya-Santa", a Weill-esque take on
married life as seen by Mrs Santa Claus, performed with a neurotic, throaty Dietrich-like warble
by Jessica Molaskey. It's almost too much to take in at one sitting, but Brown is clearly a lyricist
and composer of some talent, and with so much second-rate material dominating the West End
and Broadway, it's good to see RCA giving his first success a broader airing. **PF**

Nacio Herb Brown   1896–1964 USA

Born in Deming New Mexico, he was taught to play piano by his mother, but later studied
composition formally in Los Angeles. Initially Brown only wrote songs as a hobby after
achieving financial security first running a Beverly Hills menswear store and then in real estate.
Early hits arrived with "Coral sea" (1920) and "When Buddha smiles" (1921) – this last with
lyricist Arthur Freed who became Brown's regular collaborator – although it was not until 1929
that Brown decided to take up songwriting full time. With Freed he wrote the songs for MGM's
first full-length film musical, *The Broadway Melody* (1929) and followed this up with music for

The Hollywood Revue of 1929, which introduced "Singin' in the rain". The songwriting team of Freed and Brown dominated early Hollywood musicals, and they worked on numerous productions including *Sadie McKee* (1934) and *Broadway Melody of 1936* ("You are my lucky star"). Brown also worked with other lyricists, including Gus Kahn with whom he penned "You stepped out of a dream" for *Ziegfeld Girl* (1941). In the 1940s, Brown moved gradually towards retirement; Freed became increasingly involved in producing, setting up the famous 'Freed Unit' that was responsible for many of the greatest MGM film musicals, including *Singin' in the Rain* (1952) which immortalized many Brown and Freed songs.

Singin' in the Rain 1952 Film Cast (with Gene Kelly, Debbie Reynolds, and Donald O'Connor); **MGM Studio Chorus and Orchestra / Lennie Hayton**.
EMI mono/stereo Ⓟ CDODEON14 (76 minutes: ADD).

In the canon of Metro musicals, I would guess that in Britain *Singin' in the Rain* vies in the public affection for top place alongside *Seven Brides for Seven Brothers*. In France it has been admired by Truffaut and Resnais, whilst its title song sequence with Gene Kelly, co-director of the film, grinning and dancing his way across a rainwashed pavement and gutter, is universally loved. The screenplay of the film, by Betty Comden and Adolph Green, was based, like much of their Metro output, on a song catalogue, that of the film's producer Arthur Freed and composer Nacio Herb Brown, with a number of embellishments from conductor Lennie Hayton and arranger Conrad Salinger who transforms the song "Broadway melody" into a breathtaking 13-minute ballet. Listening to this disc, we become participants in an authentic musical-comedy experience as the three principals put their heart and soul into their renditions, backed by the flawless precision of the MGM Studio Orchestra. Amongst the 30 tracks, mention must be made of a short instrumental sequence, "Good night Kathy", where Gene kisses goodnight to Debbie Reynolds before strolling up the watery sidewalk. Muted strings echo his song "All I do is dream of you" and then gradually introduce the rhythm of "Singin' in the rain", leading to the song itself – so, at last, on this medium, we hear this celebrated number complete and in its rightful musical context.   **AE**

Also available:
Singin' in the Rain (1983 London Cast) First Night OCRCD6013

Irving Caesar   1895-1996 USA

Lyricist Irving Caesar was a friend of George Gershwin at school, and wrote the words to one of Gershwin's earliest hits, "Swanee". During the 1920s he contributed songs to various shows and revues including the *Greenwich Village Follies* and *George White's Scandals* series. With Vincent Youmans he penned the song "Tea for two" which appeared in *No, No, Nanette* (1924).

The Great Ones with various artists, including **Marion Harris, Louise Groody, Charles King, Little Jack Little, Annette Hanshaw, Cliff Edwards, Nick Lucas, Bing Crosby, Eddie Cantor, Alice Faye, Fats Waller, Mae Questel, Jimmy Durante** and **Al Jolson**.
Flapper mono Ⓜ PASTCD7075 (71 minutes: ADD).
Songs from No, No, Nanette, Yes, Yes, Yvette, Hit the Deck, Here's Howe, Whoopee, The Wonder Bar, The Crooner, The Kid from Spain, George White's Scandals, Curly Top and Demi-Tasse.

Irving Caesar, who died at the end of 1996 aged 101, is the lyricist who wrote "Swanee" with George Gershwin and "Tea for two" and the rest of the *No, No, Nanette* score with Vincent Youmans. They were his most distinguished collaborators, but he was both productive and promiscuous; other composers represented in this Caesarean selection are Philip Charig, Joseph Meyer, Roger Wolfe Kahn, Cliff Friend (there's a lot of him), Con Conrad, Oscar Levant, Leonello Casucci (Caesar put the English words to "Just a gigolo", hurtingly done here by the young Bing Crosby), Harry Ruby, Harry Akst, Ray Henderson, Gerald Marks, Jimmy Durante and Caesar himself ("What! no Mickey Mouse", not a deathless melody – or lyric). He also worked in harness with other lyricists: Bert Kalmar, Jack Yellen, Sammy Lerner and Ted Koehler.

Probably his best lyric was "Crazy rhythm". His most disingenuous was "Is it true what they say about Dixie?". (It isn't).

He's never been anthologized before, so this CD (the first in a "Songwriter Series") is welcome, but – since his words, though sometimes impish, are not readily distinguishable from anybody else's – it works better as the portrait of an era than of a writer. Unlike similarly-themed ASV Living Era issues, this is devoted to American recordings, all from the inter-war years, except for an invigorating bit of wartime swing ("Umbriago") from Durante. They're a starry bunch. There's a rare original cast performance of *Hit the Deck*'s "Sometimes I'm happy" by Louise Groody, who sings with a simper, and Charles King, who sings with a sneer. Alice Faye's provocative "Nasty man" (from the film *George White's Scandals*) is here and "There ought to be a law against that", a funny song of complaint ("Her other serves you with pig's feet/Your name is Cohen but you've got to eat") by the confiding crooner Little Jack Little. "Tea for two" gets a forthright but dreamy reading from the fine 1920s singer Marion Harris, and the enchanting Annette Hanshaw sings "My Blackbirds are Bluebirds now". Eddie Cantor does "What a perfect combination" and Jolson, naturally, "Swanee". Missing are the vocals by Caesar himself (an inveterate song-salesman – indeed the Sammy Cahn of his day – he recorded an "And then I wrote" album for Coral in the 1950s) and any performance of "If I forget you", his finest moment as a composer. **RC**

Mark Charlap

Peter Pan 1954 **Broadway Cast** (with Mary Martin and Cyril Ritchard).
RCA Victor mono Ⓜ 3762-2 (49 minutes: ADD).

Given its quota of hummable tunes, it is surprising that this Broadway version of James Barrie's seasonal favourite took 30-odd years to arrive in the West End (with Bonnie Langford and Joss Ackland). In the meantime, the show had returned to Broadway in 1979 when it ran a good deal longer, 551 performances, than this original production of 1954 with Mary Martin. Her mellow delivery of the Mark Charlap score, supplemented by some charming contributions by Jule Styne, makes a perfect foil to Cyril Ritchard's smarmy Captain Hook – a performance that endeared him to American audiences and subsequently gained him parts in several big Broadway shows. What makes this version of *Peter Pan* more than just a quaint period piece – 1950s rather than its Edwardian original – is the sheer tunefulness of its score that keeps bubbling up to the surface, for which reason it remains the most attractive of the many musical *Peter Pan*s produced over the years. **AE**

Also available:
Peter Pan (1994 London Cast) First Night CASTCD46

Frank Churchill 1901–1942 USA

Born in Rumford, Minnesota, Churchill became a cinema pianist after abandoning a medical career. He was put under contract at Walt Disney Studios and wrote songs and music for their animated films. *The Three Little Pigs* (1933) introduced "Who's afraid of the big bad wolf?", co-written with Ann Ronell. With lyricist Larry Morey he wrote *Snow White and the Seven Dwarfs* (1937), which included "Whistle while you work" and "Heigh-ho". "Baby mine" from *Dumbo* (1941) and "Love is a song" from *Bambi* (1942) both received Academy Award nominations.

Snow White and the Seven Dwarfs 1937 **Film Cast** (with Adriana Caselotti and Harry Stockwell) **/ Frank Churchill, Paul Smith, Leigh Harline**.
Walt Disney Records mono Ⓔ WD74540-2 (74 minutes: ADD). Additional music by Paul Smith and Leigh Harline.

The importance of this landmark score should not be underestimated. Disney's first full-length animated film became in turn the first original soundtrack album (a fact that is little-known). Listing the disc under Frank Churchill's name conceals the many additional contributions by Paul Smith and Leigh Harline. However, the provenance of the score notwithstanding, the principal songs have gone into musical history as film classics: "I'm wishing", "Whistle while you work", "Heigh-ho" and "Some day my prince will come" have been known and loved by generations of moviegoers. For this new reissue, the music has been lovingly restored by producers Randy Thornton and Michael Leon using the latest digital techniques, and the score is given a new lease of life. Especially interesting is how Leigh Harline incorporates the songs into his orchestral underscore: for example, "Heigh-ho" crops up in the cue "There's trouble a-brewing", a stylish and witty piece. Alongside the famous songs, therefore, the instrumental tracks should not be neglected.   **JW**

Douglas J. Cohen

New review

No Way to Treat a Lady 1996 **Off-Broadway Cast** (with Adam Grupper, Alix Korey, Marguerite MacIntyre and Paul Schoeffler) **/ Wendy Bobbitt.**
Varèse, Sarabande Spotlight Series Ⓔ VSD5815 (72 minutes: DDD).

This show was first seen in 1987 and since then has received a number of productions around the world and is due to be seen in London in 1998. This is a recording of New York's York Theatre Company production and it shows a maturely perfected product. Remembering the 1968 Rod Steiger movie about a serial killer seeking publicity and the policeman hunting him down I would not have thought this a likely subject for a musical – so what a pleasant surprise to find the transformation has been done with a light but sure hand and with a great sense of comedy. No *grand guignol Sweeney Todd* here – these murders are fun and the story is told with an amusingly tuneful score attached. As in all good 'whodunnit' tales it is not until the last track and after various killings that the killer is discovered. The story is very easy to follow in this well-recorded, bright-sounding album, and there is one other great discovery, a young lady called Alix Korey who plays a number of parts with more comic virtuosity than any one performer should be allowed to have. There are only three other performers and each are perfectly suited and matched and they all sing with gusto. This is an album that can be enjoyed simply for what is on offer and if it had been on vinyl I would have worried that I was wearing it out – yes it is that good. Leave the CD playing and you will hear a joke 'hidden track' and then you may well want to play it again.   **RSB**

Cy Coleman   b. 1929 USA

A precociously musical child who gave a piano recital aged six, Seymour Kaufman was born in New York and studied at the New York College of Music. He formed a nightclub trio and began writing songs, initially with lyricist Joseph McCarthy and later with Carolyn Leigh. Coleman worked in television during the 1950s, and wrote several hit songs: "Witchcraft" (lyrics by Leigh), for example, was a hit for Frank Sinatra in 1957. His first full-length show was *Wildcat* (1960) and this was followed by *Little Me* (1962) before Coleman teamed up with veteran lyricist Dorothy Fields to produce his biggest Broadway success, *Sweet Charity* in 1966; they had another success with *Seesaw* (1973). Coleman worked with writing duo Betty Comden and Adolph Green to write some songs for the revue *Straws in the Wind* (1975) before a full-scale collaboration ensued, *On the Twentieth Century* (1978). *Barnum* in 1980 (lyrics by Michael Stewart) was a big Broadway hit for leading man Jim Dale, and proved similarly successful for Michael Crawford in the London production and the subsequent 1986 film. Coleman teamed up again with Comden and Green on *The Will Rogers Follies* in 1991. *City of Angels* (1990) proved a critical success on both sides of the Atlantic but failed to find the audiences it deserved. 1997 saw *The Life* on Broadway.

Barnum 1980 **Broadway Cast** (with Jim Dale, Glenn Close, Marianne Tatum, Terri White, Leonard John Crofoot and William C. Witter) **/ Peter Howard.**
Columbia Ⓔ CK36576 (51 minutes: AAD).
Barnum 1981 **London Cast** (with Michael Crawford, Deborah Grant, William C. Witter, Sarah Payne, Jennie McGustie and Christopher Beck) **/ Michael Reed.**
Chrysalis Ⓔ CCD1348 (49 minutes: AAD).

It was inevitable that Cy Coleman, creator of some of the best of all Broadway marches should eventually choose a circus subject for a musical. The life of Phineas Taylor Barnum provided just what he was looking for. The quintessential American showman, Barnum rose to fame through a series of dubious sideshow attractions, a short political career, all culminating in his assumption of co-ownership of one of the greatest of all touring attractions – the Barnum and Bailey Circus. Coleman's brassy, confident score – including "Come follow the band", "The colours of my life" and "Join the circus" – reflects perfectly the consuming self-confidence of its subject. That makes it all the more remarkable that both the original Broadway and London Barnums were English – a tribute to the panache and professionalism of both performers, Jim Dale and Michael Crawford. In the event, there's not much to choose between the two cast recordings that they head. The Broadway cast features a pre-*Sunset Boulevard* Glenn Close as Mrs Barnum. In heading the London cast Michael Crawford gives a tremendous impression (he would go on to make a television version of the show) bringing added light and shade to a role that's drawn in broad strokes by the librettist. Crawford adds pathos and style in a more sympathetic interpretation that, for all his intelligence and professionalism, Jim Dale just fails to achieve. As the show stands or falls by the performance of its leading character, the English cast recording, therefore, is the one to have, though few will be disappointed with the Broadway original.   **MPK**

City of Angels 1990 **Broadway Cast** (with James Naughton, Gregg Edelman, Randy Graff, Dee Hoty, Kay McClelland and Rene Auberjonois) / **Gordon Lowry Harrell**. Columbia Ⓕ CK46067 (59 minutes: DDD).

City of Angels 1993 **London Cast** (with Roger Allam, Henry Goodman, Martin Smith, Haydn Gwynne, Susannah Fellows and Fiona Hendley) / **Richard Balcombe**. First Night Ⓜ OCRCD6034 (62 minutes: DDD).

City of Angels is one of the most attractive, ingenious and complex musicals of recent years. Its subject is a detective writer Stine and his creation, the gumshoe Stone. The stage is divided into two halves – reality on one side, fiction on the other, as parallel events unfold and the writer finds himself no longer in control of his own fantasies. Eventually, fact and fiction merge to bring a wonderfully satisfying conclusion in which the Hollywood studio philistines are routed and Stine and Stone reign triumphant. David Zippel's cracking lyrics match Cy Coleman's peerlessly crafted score that perfectly recreates the feeling of Warner Brothers *film noir* in the 1940s when Bacall and Bogart were the current screen stars. The songs are Coleman at his best – "With every breath I take", "Lost and found" and "Stay with me" are torchy ballads – and the score is spiced with witty point numbers: "It needs work", "You're nothing without me" and "The tennis song". As an example of the Broadway musical at its most happily sophisticated *City of Angels* would take a lot of beating. The Broadway cast, whose members have an instinctive sense of the style required, beats its London equivalent on points despite telling performances in the dual lead roles from Martin Smith, Roger Allam. Gregg Edelman and James Naughton bring that little extra authenticity to the Broadway cast, and there's a strong backup in Dee Hoty, Randy Graff and Kay McClelland as the wives, secretaries and *femmes fatales*.   **MPK**

New review

I Love My Wife 1977 **Broadway Cast** (with Lenny Baker, Joanna Gleason, Ilene Graff and James Naughton) / **John Miller**. DRG Ⓕ CDSBL6109 (48 minutes: ADD).

A microcosm of its time, *I Love My Wife* is a with-it musical postcard of the 1970s with a plot rather like that of *Bob and Carol and Ted and Alice*. Will two happily married couples try swapping partners for a night of sexual variety? Well, no, as it happens, but there's some fun and games to be enjoyed along the way. A success in Britain (where we really like Cy Coleman musicals) as well as on Broadway, there was an eerie parallel in that the comic leads, Lenny Baker in the US and Richard Beckinsale in the UK subsequently died tragically young. Coleman contributed a vibrant, jazzy score played by the four-man band and one of his irresistibly catchy Broadway march-songs in "Hey there, good times" – once heard, never forgotten. The score defines the time it was written with songs like "Love revolution", "Ev'rybody is turnin' on" and "Sexually free". But the writers can be touching too – the title tune is gentle and appealing. The original cast of four could not be bettered and DRG's transfer is excellent. **MPK**

The Life 1997 Broadway Cast (with Pamela Isaacs, Lillias White, Vernel Bagneris, Kevin Ramsey and Sam Harris) / **Gordon Lowry Harrell**.
Sony Broadway Ⓕ SK63312 (69 minutes: DDD).

As the disc starts the memory of Cy Coleman's previous venture into the seamier side of life in the cleansed *Sweet Charity* is evoked by some well-chosen words. But this is short lived. *The Life* is a raw, non-sanitized view of 'life' and Ira Gasman's lyrics are street-wise and not for the sensitive. A preview of the score had been heard in a studio star cast version but it is better served here. Cy Coleman has remained a top Broadway composer by delivering uniformly high quality scores – he does not disappoint now in this much varied jazz-to-rap score. It is set in the sordid 1980s 42nd Street before Mr Disney won it back for the family audience. Here the prostitutes live in hope of a life away from the street, but dreams seldom come true as they are ruled by pimps. The story follows the black hustler known as Queen through disillusionment to an eventual opportunity for a life somewhere else. There is no easy money and the voyage is not an easy one, and there is death in the air as pimps fight it out. Inevitably there is a tart with a heart played beautifully by Lillias White (she's been laid by over 15,000 men) who helps Queen get away. There are fine performances throughout. Pamela Isaacs as Queen is strong and touching. Sam Harris, Vernel Bagneris and Kevin Ramsey all shine with high vitality performances. This is probably the best Broadway score of the 1996/7 season but the subject-matter does not help make it an easy ride. **RSB**

Little Me 1962 Broadway Cast (with Sid Caesar, Nancy Andrews, Virginia Martin and Swen Swenson) / **Charles Sanford**.
RCA Victor Ⓜ 09026 61482-2 (40 minutes: ADD).
Little Me 1964 London Cast (with Bruce Forsyth, Avril Angers, Eileen Gourlay and Swen Swenson) / **Ed Coleman**.
DRG Ⓕ DRGCD13111 (51 minutes: ADD).

Little Me was that rare event – a Broadway musical which with Bruce Forsyth in London comfortably outran the original American production. On Broadway, Sid Caesar played the seven men featured in the memoirs of Belle Poitrine, a girl from the other side of the tracks who goes in quest of wealth and social position. The Belle of today dictates her story on stage, but we see her past played by another actress, thereby enabling the authors to come up with a good old-fashioned knock-'em-in-the-aisles duet in the title song. Amongst her other admirers a Chicago gambler, Swen Swenson in both recordings, woos her with a smooth song and dance routine, "I've got your number". Sid Caesar doesn't offer much in the way of variety in his performance. In the London company, Bruce Forsyth relishes his chances to a greater degree, compare his Mister Pinchley in "Deep down inside". It's much the same story with Avril Angers and Eileen Gourlay as the two Belles, both of them offering more distinctive characterizations than on the Broadway disc. Cy Coleman's bright and brassy score is at its sassy best in "Be a performer", where the unorthodox metre of the melody is the perfect pitch for a couple of vaudeville bookers trying to tempt our Belle into showbusiness. It's all light-hearted rowdy fun of the kind once found in Broadway shows. **AE**

On the Twentieth Century 1978 Broadway Cast (with John Cullum, Madeline Kahn, Imogene Coca, Kevin Kline, George Coe, Dean Dittman and Judy Kaye) / **Paul Gemignani**.
Sony Broadway Ⓕ SK35330 (65 minutes: ADD).

Cy Coleman took everyone by surprise when he came up with a brilliant rococo-style score for this musical set on a train journey between Chicago and New York in the 1930s. Period music is seldom alluded to – for the rest, courtesy of Hershy Kay's brilliant orchestrations, Coleman's music mirrors all the glamour and style of this "luxury liner" tearing along on its 16-hour journey. On board are an estranged theatrical couple sung by John Cullum and Madeline Kahn, her present beau, Kevin Kline, and Imogene Coca as a wealthy religious nut who finances the heroine's return to the stage in a production directed by her husband. Save for the charming duet,

"Our private world", with its Gounod-esque melody and pretty tag, "You opposite me/Opposite you/Living our private two character play", the rhythm of the train underpins the entire journey where the antics on board are charted in a series of giddy ensembles. Of the principal singers, Madeline Kahn makes the most distinctive impression from her first entry in a flash-back through to her *tour de force*, "Babette"; the quasi-operatic writing holds no bars for her as she assails the florid demands with style and conviction. The other star of the recording is conductor Paul Gemignani who keeps this train rolling along with bags of energy. The first class recording and copious notes are further assets.   **AE**

Seesaw 1973 **Broadway Cast** (with Michele Lee and Ken Howard) / **Don Pippin**.
   DRG Ⓕ CDRG6108 (48 minutes: AAD).

Seesaw may not have achieved the same degree of success of other Cy Coleman scores such as *Sweet Charity, Barnum, On the Twentieth Century* and *City of Angels*; but its music should not be altogether unfamiliar. Based on the 1950s play *Two for the Seesaw* with just two characters (played by Henry Fonda and Anne Bancroft), it underwent a great deal of tribulation and change before its musical adaptation opened on Broadway in 1973. By then the show had various subsidiary characters added to reduce the complete dependence on the two leads, played by Ken Howard and Michele Lee. As revised, the piece tells of sober, besuited provincial Jerry Ryan who comes to town and meets not only decidedly bohemian New Yorker, Gittel Mosca (with whom he falls in love) but also various characters typifying the city, including a group of Puerto Ricans producing *Hamlet*. Two numbers from Coleman's attractive score were taken up outside the show – the leading lady's "Nobody does it like me" (alias "If there's a wrong way to say it") and the showstopping chorus number "It's not where you start", led by up-and-coming choreographer Tommy Tune. As always with Coleman, there is much more that soon impresses itself on the listener. It is *Sweet Charity* that *Seesaw* most closely resembles and, if not quite up to the standard of that exceptional show, it is well worth hearing on its own account.   **AML**

Sweet Charity 1967 **London Cast** (with Juliet Prowse, Paula Kelly and Josephine Blake) / **Alyn Ainsworth**.
   Sony West End Ⓜ SMK66172 (48 minutes: ADD).

I'd forgotten that this recording is such a cracker, one which on a personal note brings back memories of a great night in the West End theatre when Bob Fosse let his dancers loose in "Rich man's frug" and "The rhythm of life". The cast, led by the late Juliet Prowse as the dance hall hostess Charity Hope Valentine, are every bit as good as their Broadway counterparts. When she and her two buddies, Josephine Blake and Paula Kelly, join up for "Big spender" the effect is electric; nor should we forget Blake and Kelly's tough-tender duet "Baby dream your dream" (dropped from the Shirley MacLaine film version) where the girls' harmonization on the phrase "life could be rose and peaches and cream" is as delicious as it sounds! Cy Coleman's score, which also contains such memorable numbers as "If my friends could see me now" and "There's gotta be something better than this", is in Broadway's brassiest tradition, one that's relished to the hilt by the ensemble and orchestra under Alyn Ainsworth's dynamic direction. The recording betrays signs of overloading as the decibels mount in a very close-up sound picture.   **AE**

Wildcat 1960 **Broadway Cast** (with Lucille Ball and Keith Andes) / **John Morris**.
   RCA Victor Ⓜ 60353-2 (44 minutes: ADD).

Cy Coleman has specialized in bright, brassy, jazzy scores, with a good number of extractable song standards. Following success in the 1950s with songs such as "Witchcraft", it was with *Wildcat* that he and lyricist Carolyn Leigh made their débuts as creators of a complete Broadway score in 1960. It also marked the Broadway début of film and television comedienne Lucille Ball in the role of Wildcat Jackson, a brash young woman who in 1912 arrives at a town on the Mexican border where oil has just been discovered. She hopes to strike it rich in order to provide for her shy, lame sister, which of course she ultimately succeeds in doing, as well as winning the love of drill-team boss Joe Dynamite. That the show was no great commercial success was due to Miss Ball having to leave the show through illness; but Coleman's score is a typically inventive one with a succession of bright, breezy, varied numbers. He lays his cards on the table early on, with Wildcat's show-stopping "Hey, look me over!", and there is much else in the same enjoyable vein, for example the leading lady's lively "What takes my fancy", the high-spirited "Give a little whistle", and the amusing dancing lesson "Tippy, tippy toes". The score more than once recalls *Annie Get Your Gun*, not only in its musical numbers but in Miss Ball's raucous contribution. **AML**

The Will Rogers Follies 1991 Broadway Cast (with Keith Carradine and Dee Hoty) / Eric Stern.
Columbia ℗ CK48606 (70 minutes: DDD).

The libretto of this hit Broadway show has the hero, Will Rogers (Keith Carradine), stepping out of the show's Ziegfeld opening number to take us back and forth on a journey through his career – a career that not only made the former cowboy into a Ziegfeld star, but a radio personality and orator to boot. His lifelong fascination for flying led to his death in a plane crash in 1935. Rogers's easy-going mid-West personality is summed up in "Never met a man I didn't like", a ballad in country style, one of several idioms found in composer Cy Coleman's attractive score. It's a joy, too, to hear him in partnership again with Betty Comden and Adolph Green. The fun is guaranteed when they are on hand as lyricists: try "The big time" to hear their inimitable way with the title words, or the duet of Mr and Mrs Rogers where, on their second attempt to get wed, she sings "Down to the altar I'll sidle/I feel twice as bridal/No shy violet/Let's middle aisle it". Dee Hoty is the sweet-voiced wife. Conductor Eric Stern directs this infectious concoction with the verve he's subsequently brought to the Nonesuch Gershwin series. It remains a puzzle why this show remains unproduced in London. **AE**

Also available:
Doing Something Right Randy Graff sings Cy Coleman. Varèse Sarabande VSD5652
The Life (1996 Studio Cast) RCA Victor 09026 68001-2
Sweet Charity (1966 Broadway Cast) Columbia CK02900
Sweet Charity (1969 Film Cast) EMI Angel CDP7 46562-2
Sweet Charity (1995 Studio Cast) Showtine SHOWCD035

Betty Comden
b. 1915 USA

Adolph Green
b. 1915 USA

The longest-lasting and best-known writing team in Broadway's history, lyricists Comden and Green met at New York University and formed a cabaret act at the Village Vanguard, along with actress Judy Holliday. It was here they met Leonard Bernstein with whom they wrote their first show, *On the Town* (1944) – which featured small acting parts for both lyricists. *Billion Dollar Baby* (1945) with music by Morton Gould followed, before the duo, at the invitation of Arthur Freed, moved to MGM to write screenplays for film musicals including *Singin' in the Rain* (1952) and *The Band Wagon* (1953). Back on Broadway their success continued, collaborating with Jule Styne on several shows including *Two on the Aisle* (1951), *Peter Pan* (1954), *Bells Are Ringing* (1956), *Subways Are for Sleeping* (1961) and *Fade Out–Fade In* (1964); with Bernstein again they wrote lyrics for *Wonderful Town* (1953); and with Cy Coleman *On the Twentieth Century* (1978) and *The Will Rogers Follies* (1991).

Noël Coward
1899–1973 England

A self-taught musician, although from a musical family, Coward was a prolific composer unhampered by his lack of formal training, as well as a writer, actor and director. Regarded as the successor to Gilbert and Sullivan, Coward was the only British theatre composer of his time whose success rivalled that of his American contemporaries. Aged ten he won a prize for singing, and wrote his first successful song, "Forbidden fruit", in 1916. In addition to writing plays, he staged revues – *On With the Dance* (1925) and *This Year of Grace* (1928) – before penning the full-length operetta *Bitter Sweet* in 1929. This was followed by further operettas *Conversation Piece* (1934) and *Operette* (1938); as well as numerous revues and musicals, including *Pacific 1860* (1946), *Ace of Clubs* (1950) and *The Girl Who Came to Supper* (1963). His ballet *London Morning* was staged in 1959. Coward is most famous for his dryly satirical songs like "Mad dogs and Englishmen", which first appeared in *Words and Music* (1932) and "The stately homes of England" from *Set to Music*

(1939); much of the impact of his songs depended on his own deadpan delivery and the talents of his acting partners who included Gertrude Lawrence, Beatrice Lillie and Jack Buchanan.

Bitter Sweet 1988 **New Sadler's Wells Cast** (with Valerie Masterson, Martin Smith and Rosemary Ashe); **New Sadler's Wells Opera Chorus and Orchestra / Michael Reed**.
TER Ⓕ CDTER2 1160 (two discs: 84 minutes: DDD).

This is – almost – the best recording one can imagine being made of Noël Coward's 1929 operetta. It has a fine chorus, also effective in their spoken lines, highly polished orchestral playing and a handsome set of new orchestrations from the conductor Michael Reed, captured in opulent sound. Valerie Masterson heads the cast with her clear strong voice heard to thrilling effect from the opening "Call of life" through to "Zigeuner", the gipsy song in Act 3, on which she lavishes a wide palette of tone colour. It's unfortunate that she is ill-matched by Martin Smith. Operetta isn't his idiom, the voice too light, his approach too 'pop' in style. Nevertheless, when sheltered by his partner in the heart-stopping "I'll see you again" and "Dear little café", the results are never less than pleasing. Rosemary Ashe makes the most of her cabaret scene, running the gamut between some pretty dubious material and the absolutely charming "If love were all". Outside the principal numbers, Coward never really managed to put his stamp on the operatic idiom – even if a score like *Phantom of the Opera* is not to everyone's taste, it is not possible to remain indifferent to it as happens in *Bitter Sweet*'s sometimes vague invocations to the past. **AE**

The Girl Who Came to Supper 1963 **Broadway Cast** (with José Ferrer, Florence Henderson, Irene Browne, Roderick Cook and Tessie O'Shea) **/ Jay Blackton**.
Sony Broadway Ⓕ SK48210 (55 minutes: ADD).
The Girl Who Came to Supper Noël Coward (sngr/pf)
DRG Ⓕ DRG5178 (55 minutes: ADD). Recorded 1963

Coward's last show was based on Terence Rattigan's play *The Sleeping Prince* (which had been filmed with Laurence Olivier and Marilyn Monroe as *The Prince and the Showgirl*). Coward only provided the songs, and his frustration at not having control of the whole production is spelled out at length in his published diaries. It only lasted for 113 performances, and seems never to have been revived, which is a great shame as the original play remains charming and strong, and Coward's songs, though they must have seemed very old-fashioned in 1963, have a great deal of his old style.

As the Prince, José Ferrer suffers from Coward-itis, trying too hard to imitate Coward's delivery, but Florence Henderson is very charming as the musical-comedy actress caught up in the 1911 Coronation. The great Tessie O'Shea stopped the show every night with her scene as a Cockney pub singer ("London is a little bit of all right", "Saturday night at the Rose and Crown" etc.).

Coward's own, piano-accompanied run-through of the score includes five numbers that were dropped: "What's the matter with a nice beef stew?", "If only Mrs Applejohn were here", "Just people", "I'm a lonely man" and "Long live the King – if he can", this last a satire on assassinations which suddenly became unperformable after President Kennedy was assassinated during the rehearsals. Like Coward's 1938 *Operette*, this show contains a small show-within-a-show, when the girl, Mary Morgan, gives the Prince a run-through of *The Coconut Girl*. Henderson does a splendid job with this on the Broadway cast album, but to hear Coward, nearing 65, tear into "Paddy MacNeil and his automobile" and "The walla walla boola" is a treat not to be missed. **PO'C**

The Master's Voice Noël Coward – His HMV Recordings 1928-1953. **Noël Coward**, with various artists.
EMI mono Ⓜ CDC7 80580-2 (four discs: 275 minutes: ADD).
Includes songs from: This Year of Grace, Operette, Bitter Sweet, Sigh No More, Ace of Clubs, Cavalcade, Private Lives, Tonight at 8.30, Pacific 1860 and The Globe Revue, among others.

This four-disc set begins with Coward's first published recording, "A room with a view" from the 1928 revue *This Year of Grace*, and includes all of his published EMI recordings, as well as three unpublished sides, up to his final 78s made in 1952. One of the latest recordings is of a medley of successes, with the Café de Paris Orchestra, at the time of his first essay into cabaret. As well as all the songs most closely associated with Coward, written for his own shows and plays, he sings some lesser-known numbers such as "Gypsy melody" from *Operette* (cut during the try-out), "The dream is over" from 1928 and "Most of ev'ry day" from 1934. Coward composed most of his material for specific performers, ranging from operatic voices like Peggy Wood (the original Sarah in *Bitter Sweet*), to blues singers, for instance Alberta Hunter for whom he wrote "I travel alone", or typical revue performers like Jessie Matthews (who created "A room with a view"), Alice Delysia (who first sang "Poor little rich girl") and Coward's close friend Graham Payn, who created "Matelot" in *Sigh No More* and "Sail away" in *Ace of Clubs*. Coward, though, takes hold of each song and makes it his own – as a performer, he had three great virtues: his diction was always crisp and clear, he seemed to have perfect pitch, even in old age there is never a hesitation. Above all he had the art of the *diseur*, mixing song and speech seamlessly, never allowing the interpretation to cloak the melody. Like so many other originals, his style has often been crudely imitated, but you only need to play Coward's original versions of such classics as "Mad dogs and Englishmen", or in serious vein, "Let's say goodbye", to hear his brilliance. Above all, he never lets any of his singing seem like a parody, even when he employs quite extraordinary falsetto effects, for instance in the waltz-song from *Cavalcade*, "Lover of my dreams".

The sound that the engineers have achieved with these recordings, the first two discs all over 60 years old, is quite remarkable. Coward's voice and the accompaniments are as clear as a bell, with no hiss or crackle; more important, there is no sense of artificial added bass or 'distancing'. All four of Coward's recordings with Gertrude Lawrence are included, the famous *Private Lives* extracts, and the three scenes from *Tonight at 8.30*, "Shadow play", "Red peppers" and "Family album". Their partnership is one of the show business legends of the twentieth century, and even to a non-expert it must immediately seem obvious why. Their timing, the sudden switches from irony to sentiment, the sense of danger, of improvisation, all confirm what one has read of this great double-act.

Coward sings a few songs by other composers, Kern ("The last time I saw Paris"), Porter ("You'd be so nice to come home to") and Rainger ("Love in bloom"), but most of the songs are his own. From his post-war shows, Coward is inimitable – or ought to be – in "I wonder what happened to him" from *Sigh No More* and "Uncle Harry" from *Pacific 1860*. The whole sequence ends with "There are bad times just around the corner", a 1952 song for *The Globe Revue*, originally sung by Dora Bryan, Ian Carmichael and Graham Payn. For Coward this was far from true, he remade himself in the 1950s as a cabaret performer, took to films and television, and continued to write new plays and songs almost to the end. **PO'C**

Sail Away 1961 Broadway Cast (with Elaine Stritch, James Hurst and Charles Braswell) **/** Peter Matz.
EMI Angel Ⓟ ZDM7 64759-2 (49 minutes: ADD).

Originally conceived as a film script, Coward's penultimate musical is set on board a cruise ship, with Elaine Stritch as the tour organizer, Mimi, who sings "Later than spring", and one of Coward's last comedy numbers, "Why do the wrong people travel?". The title song was lifted from Coward's earlier *Ace of Clubs*; the style is influenced by his later cabaret performances, and is the most 'modern' of his scores, without any of the pseudo-operetta numbers. The Broadway production did not include the duet which was such a success in London, "Bronxville Darby and Joan" (and which was included on the London cast album, also with Stritch). Coward's own description of his first version is accurate, "a brittle, stylized, sophisticated, insignificant comedy with music." The performance is dominated by Stritch, whose very modern delivery somehow fused with Coward's style perfectly. **PO'C**

The Songs of Noël Coward with various artists, including **Noël Coward** and **Gertrude Lawrence**.
Flapper mono Ⓜ PASTCD7080 (78 minutes: ADD). Recorded 1924-41.
Songs from London Calling, On With the Dance, Bitter Sweet, This Year of Grace, Conversation Piece, Tonight at 8.30, Private Lives, Operette, Cochran's 1931 Revue and Words and Music.

A good selection of vintage Coward songs, some sung by Coward himself (including "Mrs Worthington", "Any little fish" and "The party's over now"), and others by singers who created them. Alice Delysia's "Poor little rich girl" from *On With the Dance* and Ivy St Helier's "If love were all" from *Bitter Sweet* are particularly valuable. For those who have the French EMI two-disc set of Yvonne Printemps, which includes all of Printemps's numbers from *Conversation Piece*, this CD is useful for it adds the two other original cast numbers, "There's always something fishy about the French", sung by Heather Thatcher and Moya Nugent, and "Regency rakes" by George Sanders and others. Three solos by Gertrude Lawrence ("Someday I'll find you", "Mad about the boy" and "Parisian Pierrot") are from her 1932 Decca recordings, but the extracts from *Tonight at 8.30* are not presented complete, which is a bit frustrating.   **PO'C**

Joan Sutherland sings Noël Coward Joan Sutherland; chorus and orchestra / Richard Bonynge.
Belart ⑧ 450 014-2 (47 minutes: ADD). Recorded 1966.
Songs from Conversation Piece, Bitter Sweet, Operette, After the Ball and Pacific 1860.

One of Coward's last recordings, made in London in July 1966, during his final season on stage as an actor (in his own *Suite in Three Keys*). As he wrote in his diaries: "I had very little to do, I merely spoke bits of the verses of 'Secret heart' and 'Dearest love' ... to hear (Sutherland) singing my music with a big orchestra was a rare treat." Sutherland adapts her operatic soprano fairly successfully to "I'll see you again", "Zigeuner" and less famous songs such as "This is a changing world" from *Pacific 1860* and "I knew that you would be my love" from *After the Ball*, but perhaps the most enjoyable tracks are those from *Operette*. "Dearest love", in which Coward's diction and Sutherland's joyful singing are suprisingly compatible, and "Countess Mitzi" in which she does an outrageous 'mittel-Europe' accent. The orchestral arrangements are rather overblown, in the fashion of the 1960s.   **PO'C**

A Talent to Amuse The Words and Music of Noël Coward. **Peter Greenwell** (sngr/pf).
Silva Treasury ⓜ SILVAD3009 (63 minutes: DDD). Recorded at a performance in the Swan Theatre, Stratford-Upon-Avon on 9th July, 1995.

Composer Peter Greenwell was Noël Coward's last accompanist, but he came late to a solo career. This one-man show, based around many of Coward's most fondly regarded songs and some highly amusing personal anecdotes, has been a tremendous success, proving that the art of cabaret, of which Coward was the supreme exponent, is not dead. Many successful revues are recorded, but few of them are recorded with a live audience. This was, and it makes all the difference. Greenwell is a likeable, sympathetic host who obviously knows these songs inside out. Also, it makes a change to hear Coward's works stripped down to a piano and a solo performer who can really do justice to both the acerbic innuendo, the vein of acute nostalgia which runs through so many of them, and the patriotism (here embodied in a London medley consisting of "London is a little bit of all right", "What-ho, Mrs Brisket", "London at night" and "London pride"). Coward was passionate about the world of show business but hardly blind to its peccadilloes. Here, we get Greenwell's delightful readings of "Why must the show go on?" (a must for anyone tired of reading about the affectations of celebrity) and, naturally, "Mrs Worthington". There is also the wonderful, rather outrageous "That is the end of the news", first performed by Joyce Grenfell, which rubs shoulders with old favourites like "Mad dogs and Englishmen", "A room with a view", the touching "Where are the songs we sung?" and "The party's over now". Most intriguing of all is the first public performance of the original gay lyrics of "Mad about the boy" written in 1938. As Greenwell says, in many ways Coward was truly ahead of his time. A gem.   **PF**

Also available:
Cavalcade (1931 Cast, with Coward) AEI CD-033
London Pride (with Coward and Gertrude Lawrence) Happy Days CDHD216
Noël and Gertie (1986 London Cast) TER CDTER1117
Classic Recordings 1928-1938 Happy Days CHCD168

Mike Craver

Mark Hardwick

Radio Gals 1995 **Original Cast** (with Eileen Barnett, Klea Blackhurst, Mike Craver, Helen Geller, Emily Mikesell, Mark Nadler and Lenny Wolpe) / **Steven Smith**.
Varèse Sarabande Spotlight Series ⓕ VSD5604 (46 minutes: DDD).

A delightful comedy musical based on the 'mom and pop' radio stations of 1920s America. Before the Department of Commerce stepped in to regulate the airwaves, anyone with the means could set up a licensed radio transmitter and broadcast what they wished. The inspiration for this show was a (possibly) factual incident in which Aimee Semple MacPherson got herself into trouble using airspace for her Los Angeles evangelical radio station. Here the broadcast station is Miss Hazel Hunt's front parlour in Cedar Ridge, Arkansas. From here Miss Hunt (the gravel-voiced Helen Geller) accompanied by her "Hazelnuts" transmits important local information, such as the next appearance of Doc May and his Musical Goats at the Lake Kitchyboo Lodge or advertising "Hunt's Amazing Elixir of Horehound", designed for dyspepsia, flatulence and palpitations. Various friends and relatives are brought on to sing local popular songs, or about their lives. Rennabelle (Klea Blackhurst) sings of her meeting with "Dear Mr Gershwin", Gladys Fritts (Eileen Barnett) injects culture with classics such as "The tranquil boxwood" and "Fairies in my mother's flower garden", and O. B. Abbott (Lenny Wolpe) sings the popular dixie ditty "A fireside, a pipe and a pet". There are also thrills as the radio station takes the listener to exotic places, with stories of "Edna Jones, the elephant girl" and "That wicky wacky hula hula honka wonka Honolulu Hawaiian honey of mine". The whole recording is infectiously funny – cleverly put together with great humour and affection. The writers clearly adore the silliness of the concept, while all the performers throw themselves into their roles with great aplomb. Hazel says repeatedly, "I hope you've enjoyed the programme" – that's guaranteed with this fun recording. **RAC**

Gene Vincent De Paul   1919-1988 USA

New York-born De Paul performed and recorded as a pianist before moving to Hollywood to write for the musicals *Hellzapoppin* (1941), *Ride 'em Cowboy* (1942) – which introduced "I'll remember April" – *Broadway Rhythm* (1944) and *A Song is Born* (1948). His most famous screen musical, however, is MGM's *Seven Brides for Seven Brothers*, a collaboration with lyricist Johnny Mercer. It was staged in New York in 1982 and London in 1985. On Broadway, De Paul and Mercer wrote the show *L'il Abner* (1956) which ran for 693 performances. A film version was released in 1959.

Seven Brides for Seven Brothers 1954 **Film Cast** (with Jane Powell and Howard Keel);
   MGM Studio Chorus and Orchestra / Adolph Deutsch.
   EMI Ⓟ CDODEON17 (74 minutes: ADD).

It wouldn't surprise me to learn that this musical is the most loved of all the MGM titles. Its star, Howard Keel, has been held in enormous affection since he made his London stage début nearly 50 years ago as Curly in *Oklahoma!*, and this film, in which he introduced the rollicking "Bless yore beautiful hide", contains one indisputably great episode, the barn raising where the dancing and acrobatics of the incredibly agile male and female company and the music unite to produce the best square-dance ever. Now for the first time on disc we can visualize it at home – another technological wonder in this stunning parade of soundtrack transfers. The video may come cheaper, but with the CinemaScope photography compromised and the sound less clearly defined, it doesn't – if you'll forgive the pun – give the whole picture. You need this CD to truly relish the stunning playing of the MGM Studio Orchestra, guaranteed to lift you out of your seat from the very start of the "Overture". The conductor Adolph Deutsch's arrangement of the barn raising episode culminates in some deft augmentation of the "Bless yore beautiful hide" number. Nearly on a par with it is the "Lament", sung by the love-lorn brothers while chopping wood in a snowy landscape, words and music in time with their hatchet blows. All previous versions of this number have featured Bill Lee, another all-purpose Hollywood ghost voice (John Kerr in *South Pacific*, Christopher Plummer in *The Sound of Music*), but his overdubs don't survive, so now Matt Mattox, less polished than Lee but more apt in the rural idiom, takes his rightful place. Jane Powell makes an enchanting partner to Howard Keel: her solo of "Wonderful, wonderful day" sounds fresher and less plummy than I recalled from the film. The recording ends with a series of demonstration tracks sung by director Stanley Donen, composer Gene De Paul and lyricist Johnny Mercer, which includes several verses to "Goin' co'tin'", "Spring, spring, spring" and "Sobbin' women" that never made the soundtrack on account of their 'suggestive nature', and a pretty ballad, "Queen of the May" with a quintessential Mercer lyric. **AE**

Also available:
Seven Brides for Seven Brothers (1985 London Cast) First Night OCRCD6008
Seven Brides for Seven Brothers (1994 Studio Cast) Carlton Shows Collection PWKS4209

Vernon Duke

1903-1969 Russia/USA

Vladimir Dukelsky was born in the railway station of Parfianovka in Russia while his mother was *en route* to Pskov. After studying at Kiev University he and his family moved to the USA in 1921. Eventually, after spending time in Paris and London, he settled in New York where he wrote popular songs and played the piano in burlesque shows, as he had been unable to make a living writing serious music. He changed his name to Vernon Duke at the suggestion of George Gershwin. He worked both in Hollywood and on Broadway, writing shows and film musicals including *Three's a Crowd* (1930), *Americana* (1932), *Walk a Little Faster* (1932 – with lyrics by E. Y. Harburg, including "April in Paris"), *The Goldwyn Follies* (1938) and *Cabin in the Sky* (1940 – filmed 1943).

New review
Cabin in the Sky 1943 Film Cast (with Ethel Waters, Eddie 'Rochester' Anderson, Lena
Horne, Louis Armstrong, Rex Ingram and Duke Ellington); **MGM Studio Chorus and Orchestra / Georgie Stoll.**
EMI mono Ⓟ CDODEON31 (77 minutes: ADD).

Although it ran for just 156 performances in 1940, *Cabin in the Sky* was Vernon Duke's most successful Broadway show; even so, it lost half of its remarkably low production costs of $50,000. It was the first black stage musical to make its way to the screen (in 1943), and recouped the filming costs threefold, grossing over $3,000,000. Arthur Freed produced it for MGM despite apprehension within the studio. Ethel Waters repeated her role as Petunia on film, with Eddie 'Rochester' Anderson as her weak-willed husband Joe. The part of the seductive Georgia Brown was switched from a dancing to a singing role and given to Lena Horne. As composer Vernon Duke was then in the Navy on War service, Freed called on Harold Arlen and 'Yip' Harburg to provide extra songs (but not Duke Ellington's numbers). This disc offers the full film score, cut numbers and alternative takes and underscoring, and – after a rather overbright opening – sounds fine. Duke (and lyricist John Latouche) provided strongly melodic songs with plenty of bounce and, where required, pathos. The extra numbers reflect Arlen and Harburg's sensibility to black culture. Ethel Waters is deeply affecting in "Happiness is just a thing called Joe" and the title-song. She was deeply (and needlessly) jealous of Horne – which probably helped her portrayal! The latter is marvellous, her intelligence and seductive style shining through every bar. One of her cut songs, "Ain't it the truth?", later turned up in her triumphant 1957 Broadway show *Jamaica*. **MPK**

Vivian Ellis

1904–1996 England

One of the most distinguished and successful British composers of musicals, Vivian Ellis was born in London to musical parents. He began writing songs in his mid-teens. He contributed songs to shows and revues by others before scoring his first real hit with *Mr Cinders* (1929) . For Sophie Tucker he wrote the bulk of the score of *Follow a Star* (1930). *Jill Darling* (1934) consolidated his reputation. *Running Riot* (1938) and *Under Your Hat* (1938) were further pre-war successes. After the war came *Big Ben* (1946) and one of the great British post-war successes *Bless the Bride* (1947). After *Tough at the Top* (1949) and *And So to Bed* (1951) came the composer's last success *The Water Gipsies* (1955). Ellis lived to see a resurgence of interest in his music with a revival of *Bless the Bride* and in 1992 a musical revue of his output entitled *Spread a Little Happiness*.

Bless the Bride 1947 London Cast (with Lizbeth Webb, Brian Reece, Georges Guetary,
Betty Paul, Anona Winn and Joan Elvin) **/ Michael Collins.**
AEI mono Ⓟ AEICD015 (65 minutes: AAD).

Bless the Bride was Vivian Ellis's most successful show, and until recently it was not available in any substantial form in performances by the original cast. There had been a couple of 78 rpm recordings, subsequently issued on LP, that was all. The appearance of this recording, taken from a contemporary broadcast of the show and offering the majority of the score in good cleaned-up sound, came as a bolt from the blue. The show is set in 1870 and in subsequent years, and offers (as does Noël Coward's 1930s musical *Bitter Sweet*) a heroine who runs away to the Continent – immediately prior to her planned wedding to an English stuffed-shirt (with a talent for lying) – with an attractive foreigner. In this case, it is the charismatic Pierre (Georges Guetary at the launch of his international career). "Ma belle Marguerite" and "A table for two" fell to him, while he shared "This is my lovely day" and "I was never kissed before" with Lizbeth Webb. The latter's broadcast recording of "Silent heart" has not survived, but there is so much else to enjoy. Vivian Ellis is here writing at the height of his melodic powers, and A. P. Herbert's lyrics are always suitable and often rise to something greater. A word of warning – some of the dialogue between songs is unlikely to foster good relations with the French. Nevertheless, here is a valuable souvenir of one of the most successful English shows of the 1940s. **MPK**

Mr Cinders 1983 **London Cast** (with Christina Matthews, Diana Martin, Andrea Kealy, Denis Lawson, Graham Hoadly and Donald Douglas) / **Michael Reed**.
TER ⓔ CDTER1069 (49 minutes: DDD).

"There goes my index-linked old-age pension" said Vivian Ellis when he heard Sting's 1982 recording of "Spread a little happiness". The following year *Mr Cinders* was given a revival at the King's Head Theatre in Islington, an immensely lively and charming production that transferred to the West End, when this recording was made. Ellis wrote a new song, "Please Mr Cinders", over 50 years after the original production – this must surely be a record. Denis Lawson was funny and touching in the title role, and the whole cast hit off the mood of affectionate pastiche so that the show appealed both to the older generation and to young people who had never heard of Ellis or the show. Michael Reed's orchestrations are discreetly modern, and he conducts a performance that has lost nothing of its appeal in the intervening 15 years. The well-known songs, "On the Amazon", "One-man girl" as well as "Spread a little happiness" are all the more enjoyable in context with other winners such as "True to two", "Ev'ry little moment" and "Honeymoon for four". **PO'C**

Spread a Little Happiness The music and songs of Vivian Ellis. With various artists including **Binnie Hale, Bobby Howes, Louise Brown, John Mills, Norah Howard, Sophie Tucker** and **Vivian Ellis**.
Happy Days mono Ⓜ CDHD257/8 (two discs: 148 minutes: ADD). Recorded 1928-39.
Songs from Clowns in Clover, Mr Cinders, Follow a Star, Falling for You, Streamline, Jill Darling, Public Nuisance No. 1, Running Riot and Under Your Hat.
Spread a Little Happiness with various singers including **Louise Browne, John Mills, Frances Day, Leslie Hutchinson, Binnie Hale, Bobby Howes, Jack Hulbert, Cicely Courtneidge** and **Norah Howard**.
Flapper Songwriter Series mono Ⓜ PASTCD7076 (68 minutes: ADD). Recorded 1928-37.
Songs from The Fleet's Lit Up, Cochran's 1930 Revue, Mr Cinders, Falling for You, Jack's the Boy, Streamline, Hide and Seek and Clowns in Clover.

Of the three leading composers of the London musical stage in the 1930s – the others being Noël Coward and Ivor Novello – Vivian Ellis was the most eclectic. He had a much keener ear than the others for the developments coming from the USA, and like them he could turn his tunes equally to comedy or romance.

Conifer's generous selection of his songs covers a wide range, including what are perhaps his three most famous songs: "Spread a little happiness" from *Mr Cinders* (1929), sung by Binnie Hale, "She's my lovely" from *Hide and Seek* (1937) sung by Bobby Howes, and "I'm on a see-saw" the duet from *Jill Darling* (1933) sung by Louise Brown and John Mills. Ellis found his ideal librettist in A. P. Herbert, who penned the once risqué "Other people's babies" for the Cochran revue *Streamline* (1934), where it was sung by Norah Howard ("Other people's babies, that's my life/Mother to dozens and nobody's wife") as the philosophical nanny. Elsewhere, the great Sophie Tucker in her only British show, *Follow a Star* in 1930, intones "If your kisses can't hold the man you love" with all her famous 'red hot momma' verve, and Marie Burke is splendidly haughty and dramatic in "Within my heart" from *The Song of the Drum* (1931). The composer himself is heard in several selections, including a piano-solo medley from *Running Riot* (1938), the last show ever produced at the Gaiety Theatre before it fell victim first to the Blitz and then to the traffic planners.

The earliest track on the Flapper disc is "Little boy blues" from *Clowns in Clover* (1928), sung by June with a male trio, in close harmony with ukelele accompaniment and then a few chorus girls in the background. It is one of the quintessential records to sum up the mood of the dancing 1920s. Leslie Hutchinson ("Hutch") sings a beautiful, forgotten song, "The wind in the willows" from *Cochran's 1930 Revue*, and Cochran himself is heard introducing some of the songs from S*treamline*. Cicely Courtneidge contributes a hilarious bridesmaid's number, "Follow the bride" from *Hide and Seek* (1937), and her husband, Jack Hulbert, is heard in the classic "The flies crawled up the window" from the 1932 film *Jack's the Boy*. The humour *chez* Ellis is never cruel or sardonic: good-natured and charming, his songs suggest a world of optimism and warmth. The delightful Frances Day sings two lesser-known songs from *Jill Darling* (1933).   **PO'C**

Sammy Fain   1902-1989 USA

Samuel Feinberg worked as a popular songwriter from 1927, and contributed songs to the film *The Big Pond* (1930). His successes were principally from films. On Broadway, the songwriter was, without exception, unsuccessful. His shows include *Everybody's Welcome* (1931), *She Had to Say Yes* (1940), *Toplitzky of Notre Dame* (1946), and *Flahooley* (1951 – with Barbara Cook). *Ankles Away* (1955) achieved 176 performances but could not be considered a success. *Christine* (1960) continued the trend, and *Something More!* (1964) concluded it. Ironically, a stage version of the Doris Day picture *Calamity Jane* (1953, staged 1961 with several new songs) has made fitful appearances. Fain's film success was much more long-lasting, with many film scores and themes to his credit including *Footlight Parade* (1933), Disney's *Peter Pan* (1953), *April Love* (1957) and *Love is a Many-Splendored Thing* (1955).

Calamity Jane **1995 Studio Cast** (with Debbie Shapiro, Jason Howard, Graham Bickley, Susannah Fellows, Tim Flavin, Alisa Endsley, Brian Greene, Hilary Western, Nicolas Colicos and Geoffrey Dallamore); **National Symphony Orchestra / John Owen Edwards**. TER Ⓕ CDTER2 1215 (two discs: 86 minutes: DDD).

In these economy-conscious (cheap, even) times, musical production budgets rarely extend to a full orchestra and, despite the best efforts of the musicians in the pit, it's hard to escape the conclusion that a key element of the show is missing. On CD at least, it is possible to appreciate the sheer depth of the scores of the great musicals, with so many top-quality studio recordings now being made. They don't come much better, or more welcome, than this new double CD of *Calamity Jane*, originally a screen musical starring Doris Day in one of her best-loved roles. The recording uses the complete original score, rousingly played by the National Symphony Orchestra under the expert direction of John Owen Edwards, with an excellent chorus and a talented cast who are clearly enjoying themselves. Broadway star Debbie Shapiro is a splendid Jane, by turns feisty ("Men!" and "Windy city") and meltingly vulnerable ("Secret love"). Jason Howard's Bill is the perfect counterpart, his resonant tenor richly enhancing the ballad "Higher than a hawk". The experienced West End star Susannah Fellows is an appealing Katie, the aspiring actress whose feminine influence helps to smooth Jane's rough and gruff exterior ("A woman's touch"). With Graham Bickley's Danny, she sings the engaging duet "Love you dearly". But this is an ensemble piece, played at full pelt with a real sense of the book and with the richness of the chorus bringing "The black hills of Dakota" to life in the musical equivalent of widescreen format. You actually feel the "Deadwood stage" is about to come thundering by. More, please.   **PF**

Also available:
Calamity Jane (1953 Film Cast) Sony 467610-2
Calamity Jane (1996 Studio Cast) Carlton Shows Collection 30362 0030-2

John Farrar

Tim Rice

Heathcliff   **1996 London Cast** (with Sir Cliff Richard, Helen Hobson, Darryl Knock and Gordon Giltrap) / **Mike Moran.**
EMI Ⓕ CDEMD1099 (two discs: 120 minutes: DDD). Recorded live.

There have been two CD issues relating to this Cliff Richard theatrical vehicle based on the Emily Brontë classic *Wuthering Heights*. The first was released prior to the show with Olivia Newton-John singing the part of Cathy (see below) but this, a more complete 'live' recording with Helen Hobson, is the one to go for. It is a handsome double album with a beautifully produced booklet and box and the recording itself is a credit to modern recording techniques. The rather beautiful and inventive orchestrations of John Farrar's score are built on diverse contemporary sounds which range from the traditional Irish *Riverdance* and African-style beats to the more momentous themes of the modern musical. The lyrics are quality pop as only Tim Rice can write. Remember this is 'live' and when the superstar appears the delighted screams of his adoring fans fill the speakers. And why not – for Heathcliff is our Cliff. It would be unkind to linger on the fact that this is a vanity piece for star and loving fans and that Cliff is not the greatest actor in the world, but then nor does he pretend to be. So what if his accent wobbles here and there: he has a stage (and disc) presence that is hard to define – but that is what is meant by 'star quality'. Helen Hobson is a fine singer and actress, and a newcomer to listen out for is Darryl Knock who manages to get a look in now and again. But above all, it is many of the musical passages and the masterful guitar playing of Gordon Giltrap which stand out.   **RSB**

Also available:
Heathcliff (1995 Studio Cast) EMI EMD1091

Dorothy Fields   1904-1974 USA

Lyricist and librettist Dorothy Fields was born in New Jersey. She formed a successful songwriting partnership with composer Jimmy McHugh – early hits included "I can't give you anything but love" featured in both *Delmar's Revels* (1927) and *Blackbirds of 1928*, and "On the sunny side of the street" from *The International Revue* (1930). Together they moved to Hollywood where Fields began to work with Jerome Kern, notably on the Fred Astaire/Ginger Rogers films *Roberta* (1935) – "Lovely to look at" and "I won't dance" – and *Swing Time* (1936) – "The way you look tonight". On Broadway, Fields wrote the librettos of Cole Porter's *Let's Face It* (1941) and *Mexican Hayride* (1944), and Irving Berlin's biggest success, *Annie Get Your Gun* (1946). In 1966 she wrote the lyrics for Cy Coleman's *Sweet Charity*, which included the song made into a hit by Shirley Bassey, "Big spender".

William Finn   b. 1952 USA

William Finn has succeeded with three off-Broadway musicals based on the social and sexual adventures of Marvin, but no other projects have yet proved successful. The first of the three was called *In Trousers* (1979), the second *March of the Falsettos* (1981) and the third *Falsettoland* (1990). Never someone to let a good idea go to waste, Finn then combined the second and third to form one musical – *Falsetto* (1992). He attempted a subject rejected by Sondheim based on the book *Muscle*, and provided a scenario for the dance musical *Dangerous Games* (1989, the same year as a six-performance Shakespeare Festival mounting of *Romance in Hard Times*).

In Trousers   **1979 Off-Broadway Cast** (with Alison Fraser, Joanna Green, Mary Testa and Chip Zien) / **Michael Starobin.**
Original Cast Records Ⓜ OC9614 (56 minutes: AAD).

It has taken a long time for this CD transfer to appear and that is surprising as it's the recording of the first of a trilogy of musicals and the last two sections played Broadway with some success in one programme. The trilogy is about Marvin who, as composer William Finn explains, goes back to being 14 when things get too hot for him – the indication is that he is immature, but not really, it has just taken time for him to find himself and, on the way, a wife, a son and a male lover. When recorded, it was still a work in progress (which is not uncommon for Finn) and it has since changed to fit the continuing story which can be heard on the *Falsettoland* discs (see below). However, don't be put off, this CD stands up wonderfully well on its own as an intelligent look at relationships and in particular Marvin's relationships with the women in his life. The score is adventurous with voice gymnastics accompanied by a small band which succeeds in creating an intenseness which often accompanies Finn's work. Finn is an original who disappoints only because his output has been so small and he has not always lived up to the enormous promise given by scores such as this. The performances are uniformly excellent and Chip Zien excels as Marvin. One complaint – this deserved a better booklet-note with a plot line even though this sung-through piece is basically complete. One bonus track gives a song added in a later incarnation. **RSB**

March of the Falsettos 1981 **Broadway Cast** (with Michael Rupert, Stephen Bogardus, Chip Zien, James Kushner and Alison Fraser) **/ Michael Starobin**.
Falsettoland 1990 **Broadway Cast** (with Michael Rupert, Stephen Bogardus, Chip Zien, Danny Gerard, Faith Prince, Heather MacRae and Janet Metz) **/ Michael Starobin**.
DRG Ⓕ 22600 (two discs, also available separately: 120 minutes: ADD).
CDSBL12581 – March of the Falsettos. *CDSBL12601* – Falsettoland.

Parts 2 and 3 of William Finn's challenging trilogy of one-act musicals about dysfunctional Jewish family life, homosexuality and the onset of the AIDS crisis – combined under the title *Falsettos* – were presented on Broadway in 1990. They tell the story of Marvin, who has left his wife and family for a homosexual relationship, while his analyst moves in on the ex-wife, confusing all their relationships, not least Marvin's young son. Far from easy to listen to, but deeply rewarding, Finn is unafraid to tackle subjects head-on. His characters are all highly intelligent and sing of their frustrations and psychoses with amazing self-examination and knowledge, while displaying the inability to express and handle basic emotions. The songs do not stand in isolation, they are deeply tied to the text and progress of the piece, and are unconventional in their rhythmic feel. Each play is recorded almost in its entirety – a necessity with this style of writing, and all the performances are exemplary. The alteration of cast members is barely noticeable in the second disc, such is the quality of the playing. Finn has written a contemporary examination of modern mores in the musical idiom that is fresh, innovative and demanding. The message is hopeful, but uncloying and never pulls any punches. These essential recordings preserve a very important piece of musical theatre which deserves a much wider audience. **RAC**

Stephen Flaherty

b. 1960 USA

Lynn Ahrens

b. 1948 USA

Lynn Ahrens and Stephen Flaherty have collaborated on musical theatre projects since 1982 when they met at a Lehman Engel BMI Theater Workshop. Their musical *Lucky Stiff* (1988) won the 1988 Richard Rodgers Production Award. *Once on This Island* (1990) had eight Tony nominations, and Broadway and London productions. In 1993 their musical version of *My Favorite Year* was produced at the Lincoln Center and the following year was mounted at Guildhall School of Music. In 1996 *Ragtime* opened in Toronto and arrived on Broadway in December 1997.

New review
Lucky Stiff 1994 **Studio Cast** (with Evan Pappas, Judy Blazer, Debbie Gravitte and Jason Graae) **/ Jeffrey Saver.**
Varèse Sarabande Spotlight Series Ⓕ VSD5461 (49 minutes: DDD).

It's sheer bad luck that the well-received British première of this show in 1997 didn't make its way onto CD as planned. Its timing was wrong, as it had the great misfortune to open at the time of a national tragedy, when a bright musical about a corpse being taken for a last fling to Monte Carlo seemed a bit of an irrelevance. The show, the first American success from one of the brightest of new writing teams, has the unique distinction of having as its hero a nerdish shoe salesman from East Grinstead, who has to accompany his late uncle on a Mediterranean gambling trip. If he fails to fulfil all the conditions he loses a six million dollar inheritance to a dogs' home, whose representative is always on hand to try to trip him up. The music and lyrics show the great promise that would lead to *Once On This Island* and *Ragtime*. The songs are resolutely plot based and the attractive cast perform them with relish, accompanied by a small five-piece band. It's good to have this early Flaherty-Ahrens show on record.   **MPK**

New review

My Favorite Year 1992 **Broadway Cast** (with Evan Pappas, Tim Curry, Andrea Martin, Josh
Mostel and Lainie Kazan) **/ Ted Spurling.**
RCA Victor ℗ 09026 6167-2 (65 minutes DDD)

Based on the film of the same name, *My Favorite Year* the musical is an agreeable romp with the creative staff of an American television programme of the 1950s, based on the (thinly disguised) *Sid Caesar Show*, which has also proved a rich mine of comedy for Neil Simon and others. Benjamin Stone, a lowly team member, has been given the nigh-impossible task of looking after former film swashbuckler Alan Swann (probably based on Errol Flynn), keeping him sober and presenting him up for a live sketch on the weekly show. The show finds Ahrens and Flaherty coping expertly with the demands of a big Broadway production, their third work in five years. Evan Pappas is an attractive hero, and there's expert comedy from Andrea Martin and Lainie Kazan. Tim Curry makes a much stronger impression as the film star on disc than he did in the theatre (where he didn't seem egocentric and selfish enough). The cunning writers saved their best song till last – and it's the title song that has all the charm and warmth you could wish for.   **MPK**

Once on This Island 1990 **Broadway Cast** (with Jerry Dixon, Andrea Frierson, Sheila
Gibbs, La Chanze, Ellis E. Williams and Kecia Lewis-Evans) **/ Steve Marzullo.**
RCA Victor ℗ 60595-2 (71 minutes: DDD).
Once on This Island 1994 **London Cast** (with P. P. Arnold, Clive Rowe, Shezwae Powell,
Lorna Brown and Sharon Dee Clarke) **/ Richard Balcome.**
TER ℗ CDTER1224 (76 minutes: DDD).

Although not their first musical, *Once on This Island* was the first commercial success for the team of Stephen Flaherty and Lynn Ahrens. It's set on a tropic island in the Caribbean, in the French Antilles, and consists of a tale told by peasants in song and dance as they endure a violent storm. A young peasant girl has her love tested by the gods – tested to the ultimate, losing her life at the end of the show. Yet when the storm is ended, there's no sadness – the peasants have survived another potential calamity. Perhaps their storytelling has helped, too – it has certainly passed the time pleasurably. But then, it's difficult to remain sombre for long in the Caribbean.The exotic locale has enabled Flaherty to come up with a variety of vivid and varied musical rhythms and attractive melodies which are skilfully matched by Ahrens's adroit lyrics. The whole show has a beautiful simplicity and the Broadway cast capture the spirit perfectly. It works well on record, too. The richly melodious score includes some real gems – "Waiting for life", "Ti Moune", "Mama will provide", "The human heart" and "Forever yours". RCA's finely detailed recording is led by La Chanze as the girl Ti Moune, Sheila Gibbs as Mama Euralie and Ellis E. Williams as Tonton Julian. The British cast has more authentic Caribbean accents and a cast which includes some highly experienced performers – P. P. Arnold, Clive Rowe, Shezwae Powell amongst them. In the end the choice must be personal preference.   **MPK**

New review

Ragtime 1996 **Studio Cast** (with Brian Stokes Mitchell, Peter Friedman, Marin Mazzie,
Audra McDonald, Mark Jacobi and Lynnette Perry) **/ Ted Sperling.**
RCA Victor ℗ 09026 68629-2 (61 minutes: DDD).

The most recent Lynn Ahrens/Stephen Flaherty collaboration is a musical patchwork which admirably serves E. L. Doctorow's potent novel. Painting on the broad canvas of America at the turn of the century, it's a powerful mixture of the influences (immigration, revolution, social and industrial progress) which exposed the turbulent reality beneath the surface of the land of opportunity. Key figures from the age are woven into the tragic tales of three New York families, with Henry Ford, Evelyn Nesbit, Emma Goldman and Harry Houdini all putting in appearances. As Marty Bell's entertaining booklet-notes suggest, musicals are never actually finished. They simply open and continue to evolve. The implication is that, in this format, *Ragtime* should still be seen as a work in progress. But there are no rough edges. It's a lush, polished, epic score which – thanks to the seamless joining of ragtime tunes, Irish lullabies and soaring ballads – is accessible and often deeply moving. As the ragtime pianist Coalhouse Walker, Brian Stokes Mitchell has the pivotal singing role. His duet with Audra McDonald's Sarah, "Wheels of a dream", is a touching confirmation of their faith in the golden opportunities represented by a new Model T car. McDonald shines, too, in an impassioned plea for understanding, "Your daddy's son". As Evelyn Nesbit, Lynnette Perry does a fine vaudeville turn in a scandalous trial scene. Despite the underlying theme of violence and the inevitable tragedy at the conclusion, Flaherty's score retains an essential thread of hope which is, ultimately, inspirational. **PF**

Also available:
Ragtime – selections. Varèse Sarabande Spotlight Series VSD5880

Nancy Ford
b. 1935 USA

I'm Getting My Act Together and Taking It on the Road 1981 **London Cast** (with Diane Langton, Ben Cross, Nicky Croydon, Megg Nicol and Greg Martin) **/ Stuart Pedlar**. TER Ⓕ CDTER1006 (35 minutes: ADD).

It is a rare occurrence for the book, lyrics and music of a show to be written by women. *I'm Getting My Act Together* is rather unfairly viewed as a typical piece of late-1970s feminism, for it manages to make its points without becoming over strident, and sees failings on both sides of the battle of the sexes. It is a short score consisting of a series of pop songs performed by a cabaret singer and her band that illustrate and comment on her life as she approaches her 39th birthday. There are two sets of songs: those derived from her new act, which have a stronger pop flavour and are more political lyrically, reflecting Heather's increasing awareness. The remainder are from her old repertoire, which she has now abandoned: these are designed as ironic comments, the sort of song that would appeal to 'middle America'. But it is these latter that offer the most pleasing aspect of the score, and are its best songs. "In a simple way I love you" may be a formulaic piece, but its gentle tenderness is quite delightful. The finest number is "Old friend", which has subsequently become an oft-recorded modern classic, but Diane Langton's interpretation is heartfelt and moving and has rarely been bettered. Indeed, it is as a showcase of Langton's formidable talents that the recording works most successfully as she effortlessly glides from rock songs to romantic ballads. **RAC**

George Forrest
b. 1915 USA

Robert Wright
b. 1914 USA

Brooklyn-born George Forrest and Robert Wright who hails from Daytona Beach, Florida attended the same high school and the University of Miami. They have worked exclusively together as a lyricist and composer team who specialize in the adaptation of classical music for Broadway shows. The duo had their first hit with "The donkey serenade", an adaptation of Friml's "Chansonette" for the movie *The Firefly* in 1937. Their first Broadway hit was *Song of Norway* (1944) for which they adapted the music of Grieg; *Gypsy Lady* (1946) was based on Victor Herbert's music, whilst *Magdalena* (1948) had a score by Villa-Lobos. Their biggest success came in 1953 with *Kismet* which freely adapted themes from Borodin, winning the Russian composer a posthumous Tony Award for best composer. *Kismet* was filmed in 1955 with Howard Keel in the leading role. *Anya* (1965) drew on the music of Rachmaninov, and *The Great Waltz* (1970) adapted Johann Strauss. Shows with original music are *Kean* (1961) and *Grand Hotel* (1989 – a new collaboration with Maury Yeston which updated their earlier failure, *At the Grand* of 1956).

Grand Hotel 1992 Broadway Cast (with Brent Barrett, John Whylie, David Jackson, Danny Strayhorn, Hal Robinson, Jane Krakowski, Michael Jeter, Karen Akers and Liliane Montevecchi) **/ Jack Lee**.
RCA Victor Ⓕ 09026 61327-2 (65 minutes: DDD).

Vicki Baum's Art Deco soap opera of a novel was turned into a classic film in 1932 and, on the face of it, should have formed the basis for an absorbing, extravagant musical. Many consider that this treatment from Forrest and Maury Yeston, which premièred on Broadway in 1989, more than fitted the bill. It's certainly sumptuous, but the multiple strands of the plot make for a rather unwieldy whole and there were criticisms that some of the numbers failed to live up to the show's grandiose premise. Still, it was a huge success on Broadway, although the London production lasted a sad three months. Perhaps the score's major achievement is the manner in which it evokes the constant, busy activity of a glamorous Berlin hotel at the end of the 1920s, just as Nazism was making its presence felt. In fact, this cast recording was not made until 1992, by which time David Carroll, who played the Baron, had died of AIDs. His place was taken by Brent Barrett but as a tribute to Carroll, the CD includes a live, cabaret performance of his big ballad, "Love can't happen". This song is one of the few real show-stoppers in the score, together with the vibrant "Maybe my baby loves me" (David Jackson and Danny Strayhorn as the two Johnnys) and "Who couldn't dance with you?" (Jane Krakowski, Barrett and Michael Jeter). Liliane Montevecchi makes much of the neurotic Garbo role, Grushinskaya the ballerina ("Fire and ice") and Karen Akers is deeply affecting as her maid Raffaela ("How can I tell her?"). But best of all is Jane Krakowski's pragmatic, opportunistic typist, Flaemmchen ("I want to go to Hollywood"). All of human life is encapsulated in the swirling score, punctuated by moments of high drama, and the recording more than does justice to the show's expansive, romantic quality, avoiding the trap of sounding too studio-bound.   **PF**

Kismet 1953 Broadway Cast (with Alfred Drake, Doretta Morrow and Richard Kiley) **/ Louis Adrian**.
Columbia mono Ⓜ CK32605 (54 minutes AAD).
Kismet 1989 Studio Cast (with Valerie Masterson, Donald Maxwell, David Rendall, Richard Van Allan and Judy Kaye); **Philharmonia Orchestra / John Owen Edwards**.
TER Ⓕ CDTER2 1170 (two discs: 97 minutes: DDD). Also includes songs from *Timbuktu* (1978).
Kismet 1992 Studio Cast (with Samuel Ramey, Julia Migenes, Jerry Hadley, Ruth Ann Swenson and Dom DeLuise); **London Symphony Orchestra / Paul Gemignani**.
Sony Ⓕ SK46438 (68 minutes:DDD).

Of all the stage musicals adapted from the works of the great composers *Kismet* remains the favourite, at least of the record companies who have bestowed on it a number of fine recordings. Those who saw Alfred Drake as the poet Hajj in the original Broadway production or at the Stoll Theatre in the Kingsway rate his performance amongst their most memorable theatrical evenings – an experience ratified by his commanding performance on the still healthy-sounding 1953 mono recording. Of the two recordings that followed one another in the late-1980s and early-1990s, the starry Sony production puts one foot wrong in casting Dom DeLuise as the Wazir; as a comedian in the Zero Mostel tradition he's vocally out of sorts in this company as his part in the quartet "And this is my beloved" testifies. Otherwise, here's a feast of magnificent singing with playing of great élan from the London Symphony Orchestra under Paul Gemignani's authoritative baton. The TER recording on two discs includes a good deal of frankly risible dialogue and some songs from *Timbuktu*, an Eartha Kitt vehicle based on the same source as *Kismet*. Yet there's a particularly endearing quality in the potentially awkward exchanges between the lovers Valerie Masterson and David Rendall which are enchanting, sounding full of freshness and wonder. With Donald Maxwell a believable Poet and Richard Van Allan a splendid Wazir, this spaciously balanced recording takes the prize for best performance.   **AE**

New review
Kismet 1955 Film Cast (with Howard Keel, Ann Blyth, Dolores Gray and Vic Damone); **MGM Studio Chorus and Orchestra / André Previn**.
EMI Ⓜ CDODEON23 (72 minutes: ADD).

Kismet 1964 **Studio Cast** (with Adele Leigh, Regina Resnik, Kenneth McKellar, Robert Merrill and Ian Wallace); **Sammes Chorus; Mantovani Orchestra / Annunzio Paolo Mantovani.**
Decca London Phase 4 Ⓜ 452 488-2LPF (52 minutes: ADD).

In his autobiography, *No Minor Chords*, André Previn described the film version of *Kismet* as "a turkey if ever there was one". Perhaps the director, Vincente Minnelli, wasn't inspired by the story or the larger-than-life characters who were more believable on stage. Nevertheless, the remastering team have done a marvellous job in resuscitating one of the poorest of the MGM soundtrack LPs. Howard Keel is his usual assured self and in support the sweet Ann Blyth, sultry Dolores Gray and the vocally assured Vic Damone are excellent. The musical credentials behind the Phase 4 reissue couldn't be more different. Here are five artists from the operatic world, each of them relishing Borodin's music in Wright and Forrest's adaptation and giving truly outstanding performances. I know of no better sung musical than this on disc. There are a couple of bumpy aural moments shown up by this transfer but no qualms over Mantovani's assured direction: clearly he'd not been musical director of *Pacific 1860* and other Coward musical shows for nothing! His cascading strings do ring through, phrased as always with a touch of rubato, but their presence is never intrusive. **AE**

New review
Song of Norway 1990 **Studio Cast** (with Valerie Masterson, Donald Maxwell, Diana Montague, David Rendall, Elizabeth Bainbridge, Jason Howard, Richard Van Allan and Yit Kin Seow); **Ambrosian Chorus; Philharmonia Orchestra / John Owen Edwards.**
TER Ⓔ CDTER2 1173 (two discs: 94 minutes: DDD).

Whether or not *Song of Norway* is for you may depend on your reaction to hearing Grieg's Piano Concerto chopped up and served up in various different forms for this 1944 operetta loosely based on Grieg's career. There is other Grieg music used as well, of course – the *Lyric Pieces* and the *Peer Gynt* music prominently included – but it's the concerto that steals the show. The arrangement was made by the same Wright and Forrest who created *Kismet* out of Borodin's music; and it must be said that they fulfilled their task with immense skill. Grieg's lyrical music makes good operetta material, and there are fine ensemble numbers (the delightful "Bon vivant" for instance) as well as impressive solos and duets that include "Hill of dreams" (based on the Piano Concerto), "I love you" (an adaptation of Grieg's most famous song) and the big hit "Strange music" which merely uses the harmonic structure of *Wedding Day at Troldhaugen*. The English stage version and the film version both made changes to the score; but the fact that Wright and Forrest themselves supervised this recording (and provided fascinating historical notes) ensures its authenticity. If the work appeals, it would certainly be difficult to imagine a more worthy performance than this. The quality is ensured by the committed musical direction of John Owen Edwards and a fine cast of opera singers headed by Donald Maxwell as Grieg, Valerie Masterson as his future wife Nina and David Rendall as Rikaard Nordraak (a poet in the show, though a fellow-composer in real life), with Yit Kin Seow as Grieg the pianist in some fairly straight extracts from the Piano Concerto. **AML**

Also available:
Kismet (1965 Broadway Cast) RCA Victor 09026 68040-2

Harold Fraser-Simson
1878-1944 England

Despite a successful business career as a ship owner, Harold Fraser-Simson published several songs during the early 1900s, leading eventually to a series of musical comedies. *The Maid of the Mountains*, which opened in Manchester in 1916, ran for over 1,000 performances after it moved to London. *Bonita* (1911), *A Southern Maid* (1917), *Our Peg* (1919), *Head Over Heels* (1923) and *Betty in Mayfair* (1925) were some of his other shows. He published six volumes of song-settings from A. A. Milne's *When We Were Very Young*, and wrote incidental music for *Toad of Toad Hall* in 1929.

A Southern Maid 1920 **London Cast** – See Collections: **Lilac Time**

Dick Gallagher

Mark Waldrop

New review
Howard Crabtree's When Pigs Fly 1996 Off-Broadway Cast (with Michael West,
  Stanley Bojarski, Keith Cromwell, John Treacy Egan, David Pevsner and Jay Rogers) /
  Dick Gallagher.
  RCA Victor ℗ 09026 68729-2 (67 minutes: DDD).

There are few original revues around these days and that is a shame for they used to be a
wonderful training-ground for show writers. However, they do pop up now and again off-
Broadway. *Howard Crabtree's Whoop-Dee-Doo!* (which did play London) was a hit and this, its
successor, has been playing for over a year. It is sad to report that Crabtree (yes, it is a real name)
died before it opened, although his zany comedy style should live on. But to the show – the
final number is "Over the top" and I doubt if any revue could be more 'over the top' than this.
There is a slight plot – Howard (Michael West) is a high school kid who visits his guidance
councillor dressed as Dream Curly (think *Oklahoma!*) in feathered chaps, sparkle vest and false
eyelashes – he wants to go into showbusiness and put on shows. She believes his chance will
come only "when pigs fly" – and it's not too long before they do. On CD we miss out on the
outrageous costumes and visual laughs – instead we can linger on the sketches and songs and
the bright and often very funny lyrics. This show is gay in every sense of the word, but there are
no heavy political issues here and everyone sends themselves up – indeed it's fun all the way
(e.g. a muscular centaur asks why he is not called Mister but Myth – well I laughed). It's good
to see a major company recognize a class act and invest in a little show like this. Leave social
significance aside and have a good time.   **RSB**

Noel Gay
1898–1954 England

Reginald Moxon Armitage was born in Wakefield, where at age 12 he became deputy organist
of Wakefield Cathedral. At 15 he won a scholarship to the Royal College of Music, and at 18
was appointed organist and musical director at St Anne's, Soho. He studied at Christ's College,
Cambridge where an interest in Gilbert and Sullivan inspired him to begin writing popular
songs. In 1925 he contributed to the revue *Stop Press*; more of his songs were included in the
Charlot Show of 1926 and *Clowns in Clover* (1927). He soon established himself as one of the
most popular British songwriters of the period, producing a string of simple, memorable songs
for revues, musicals and films. "The sun has got his hat on" (1932), "Leaning on a lamp-post"
(1937 – sung by George Formby in the film *Feather Your Nest*), "Love makes the world go
round" (1938 – used in *These Foolish Things*), and "Run, rabbit, run" (1939) are just some
examples. His musical *Me and My Girl* was staged at the Victoria Palace, London in 1937 and
ran for 1,646 performances – the most popular song from the show, "The Lambeth walk",
inspired a dance craze; it remains to this day the anthem for chirpy Cockneys everywhere. The
show was filmed in 1939 as *The Lambeth Walk*, and was successfully revived in London in 1984.
Gay formed his own publishing company in 1938, and also composed for military band.

Me and My Girl 1985 London Cast (with Robert Lindsay, Emma Thompson, Susannah
  Fellows, Robert Longden and Frank Thornton) / **Ian Hughes**.
  EMI ℗ CDP7 46393-2 (52 minutes: DDD).
Me and My Girl 1986 Broadway Cast (with Robert Lindsay and Maryann Plunkett) / **Stanley
  Lebowsky**.
  TER ℗ CDTER 1145 (54 minutes: DDD).
Me and My Girl Studio Cast (with David Kernan and Jacqui Scott).
  Carlton Shows Collection ® PWKS4143 (34 minutes: DDD).

Noel Gay, one of the most successful British song writers of the inter-war years, composed this
still popular musical comedy in 1937 when it ran for 1,646 performances at the Victoria Palace
Theatre. The show starred Lupino Lane as a Cockney who turns out to be a long-lost nobleman
who gave up the high-life to return to his sweetheart and his roots in Lambeth – the London

district that lent its name to the hit song in the score, "The Lambeth walk". In 1985 Gay's son, Richard Armitage, revived his father's show and with a new book by Stephen Fry it outran the original production making stars of Emma Thompson and Robert Lindsay. The latter also appeared in the Broadway production. The choice between these two recordings will likely hinge on the casting of the heroine in her principal song, "Once you lose your heart", where Emma Thompson makes for a more vulnerable figure than her strident counterpart; on the other hand Stanley Lebowsky's arrangements on the American recording offer Lindsay a greater chance to display his dancing steps. In the bargain basement department, Carlton's studio recording comes into the reckoning with Jacqui Scott as the prettiest sounding of all heroines, a fresh-voiced ensemble and David Kernan in non-Cockney though supremely relaxed form, backed by an excellent small band. At its budget price, this is more than worth the asking price. **AE**

Also available:
The Song is ... Noel Gay. ASV Living Era CDAJA5081

Sir Edward German

Sir Edward German Jones (the composer lopped-off his real surname) made his name as creator of incidental music for various Shakespeare plays. On the death of Sir Arthur Sullivan, German completed the score for *The Emerald Isle*. Its success at the Savoy Theatre led to the commissioning (with Basil Hood as lyricist) of *Merrie England* (1902) and *A Princess of Kensington* (1903) for the D'Oyly Carte Company. In 1907 came *Tom Jones*, but an ill-judged setting of a Gilbert libretto, *Fallen Fairies* (1909), put an end to German's career in musical comedy. From then on, the composer largely withdrew from composition altogether.

Merrie England 1960 Studio Cast (with William McAlpine, June Bronhill, Peter Glossop, Monica Sinclair and Patricia Kern); **Rita Williams Singers; Orchestra / Michael Collins**. Classics for Pleasure ® CD-CFPSD4796 (two discs: 97 minutes: ADD).

Gilbert and Sullivan were not the beginning and end of British comic opera, and Edward German was the composer who came closest to assuming Sullivan's crown. His *Merrie England* is based on a supposed rivalry between Queen Elizabeth I and her lady-in-waiting Bessie Throckmorton for the attentions of Sir Walter Raleigh. The piece was long popular, and this 1960 studio recording was inspired by a full-scale revival of the time by Sadler's Wells Opera. Most of the singers were associated with that company, and they give a strong performance of a score that, whilst lacking the fluency of Sullivan, contains some justly popular numbers. June Bronhill delivers the lovely waltz "Who shall say that love is cruel?" with brilliance and clarity, William McAlpine wrings the charm out of the beautiful ballad "The English rose", Peter Glossop sings "The yeomen of England" with imposing power, and Monica Sinclair caresses her song "O peaceful England" with regal tone. The ensemble numbers are an important part of the work's appeal and are given their full weight. A slight lack of theatricality is increased by the way the minor singers are switched between roles, but their comic numbers are delivered with appropriate lightness and sparkle. **AML**

George Gershwin

Ira Gershwin

Born in Brooklyn, George and Ira Gershwin were the sons of Russian Jewish immigrants. Although neither parent was particularly musical, the family owned a phonograph through which opera and Gilbert and Sullivan operettas were frequently heard. Whilst Ira was an attentive student and an avid reader, young George spent much of his time absent from school roller-skating and picking up early musical experience listening to player pianos on Seventh Street. When the family acquired their first piano, it was a reluctant Ira who was originally chosen to have lessons, but George unexpectedly demonstrated an aptitude and supplanted his older brother at the keys. In 1912 he became a pupil of Charles Hambitzer who was quick to discern his natural ability and introduced his student to the classics. In 1914, George dropped out of school and took his first job working as a song-plugger for a Tin Pan Alley music publisher, where he began writing songs, although not encouraged to do so by his employer. In 1917 he moved to Broadway – initially as a rehearsal pianist on Jerome Kern's *Miss 1917* – where his songwriting talent was soon recognized; he was retained by music publisher T. B. Harms for $35 a week.

Ira, meanwhile, had continued his education at New York's City College and submitted light verses to newspapers and other periodicals. George encouraged him to write song lyrics; their first collaboration, "The real American folk song", was sung by Nora Bayes in *Ladies First* (1918), although Ira was at first unwilling to trade on his brother's growing reputation so adopted the pseudonym Arthur Francis. In 1919, George wrote his first Broadway show, *La La Lucille*, and had a hit with Al Jolson's rendition of "Swanee", which earned him $10,000 in royalties. He contributed to *George White's Scandals* from 1920-24. In 1924, George and Ira wrote their first full-length musical together, *Lady, Be Good!*. Ira's witty lyrics proved to be the perfect foil for George's dazzlingly inventive music. 1924 was also the year *Rhapsody in Blue* was premièred at the Aeolian Hall: George was no longer just a songwriter, but had become an important bridge between the previously separate worlds of jazz and classical music.

The Gershwins continued their prolific and successful Broadway collaboration throughout the 1920s and 1930s, winning along the way a Pulitzer Prize for *Of Thee I Sing* in 1931, and conquering Hollywood with their songs for *Shall We Dance?* (1937), *A Damsel in Distress* (1937) and *The Goldwyn Follies* (1938). In 1935, their most ambitious work to date, the opera *Porgy and Bess*, was greeted with only a lukewarm response. Whilst working on a ballet sequence for *The Goldwyn Follies*, George began to experience dizziness and depression; he was given emergency surgery after falling into a coma, but died unexpectedly on July 11th at the age of 38. Ira continued to write for other composers after his brother's death, including Kurt Weill (*Lady in the Dark*, 1941), Jerome Kern (*Cover Girl*, 1944), Harry Warren (*The Barkleys of Broadway*, 1949) and Harold Arlen (*A Star is Born*, 1954). He lived to see the confirmation of George's reputation as one of America's greatest composers.

An American in Paris 1951 Film Cast (with Gene Kelly, Georges Guetary and Oscar Levant); **MGM Studio Chorus and Orchestra / Johnny Green**.
EMI mono/stereo Ⓕ CDODEON20 (two discs: 114 minutes: ADD).

These two discs consist of 47 cues ranging from the first release of the uncut "An American in Paris" ballet recorded before small revisions were made, to a series of off-the-record improvisations by pianist Oscar Levant, some running for less than a minute. The set also offers Benny Carter's delectable 'little band' arrangements of some Gershwin standards, recorded as background for a nightclub scene, now restored with one number, "Do, do, do" in stereo, and some joyous swing arrangements by Skip Martin, dazzlingly executed by the MGM Studio Orchestra.

For the ballet, the orchestra, whose personnel are listed in the 43-page booklet, was increased from 50 to 72 players. In a long interview the film's co-musical supervisor, Saul Chaplin, offers the salutary reminder that it was through his arrangement of the ballet that a whole generation grew up thinking that this was Gershwin's definitive score, only to learn subsequently that it was an adaptation and had never been intended as a dance piece! Listening to it again confirms the ultra-sophisticated nature of the string playing and the riotous trumpet contribution of Uan Rasey, a class apart from any other version. If the ballet dominates, the songs are no less intoxicating: "I got rhythm", Kelly's song and dance with kids from the street, "'S wonderful" with Kelly and Georges Guetary ending in an exhilarating high-angle shot of them united in song, and "Love is here to stay", unknown in 1951, sung by Kelly to Leslie Caron by the Seine in shadowy-blue light.

Michael Feinstein and his fellow producers have carried out their restoration work with evident love and care. Conductor Johnny Green puts his individual stamp on the "Main Title", taking his orchestra and the listener through the opening of the ballet via a breathtaking segue into "'S wonderful". **AE**

Crazy for You 1992 Broadway Cast (with Harry Groener, Jodi Benson, John Hillner, Michelle Pawk, Bruce Adler, Ronn Carroll, Jane Connell, Beth Leavel, Stephen Temperley, Amelia White, Stacey Logan and The Manhattan Rhythm Kings) / **Paul Gemignani**.
EMI Ⓕ CDC7 54618-2 (71 minutes: DDD).
Crazy for You 1993 London Cast (with Kirby Ward, Ruthie Henshall, Helen Way, Chris Langham. Avril Angers, Don Fellows, Shaun Scott, Vanessa Leagh-Hicks, Amanda Prior, Robert Austin and Paula Tinker) / **Jae Alexander**.
First Night Ⓕ CASTCD37 (66 minutes: DDD).

There's nothing like creating one musical from bits of others. Gershwin had been already anthologized in *My One and Only*. Now here's *Crazy for You*, which uses as its barest skeleton the basic plot of the Gershwin's 1930 musical *Girl Crazy*, and some of the songs, adding to them a sheaf of extra songs from *A Damsel in Distress* and other stage and film successes written by George and Ira. In the show the playboy and potential show producer, Bobby, leaves New York for the more basic delights of the West where he tries to create a a show that might interest his New York producer. In so doing he falls in love with a local girl. Purists may frown as great Gershwin hit follows great Gershwin hit almost with without pause, but the overall effect is well-nigh irresistible. The cast zizz happily through 21 numbers including some rarities. This is an instant Gershwin songbook and includes "Shall we dance?", "Someone to watch over me" "Embraceable you", "I got rhythm", "They can't take that away from me", "But not for me" among its delights. Both recordings are fine, but the London cast led by American Kirby Ward and Ruthie Henshall from England is slightly more pointed, with more characterization of the individual songs. Although it misses out the song "K-ra-zy for you" which helps to give the show its title, the London cast recording is the current recommendation – but there's very little in it – either will give much pleasure.   **MPK**

New review

George and Ira Gershwin in Hollywood Original Film Casts.
EMI mono/stereo Ⓟ CDODEON29 (two discs: 152 minutes: ADD).
Songs from Girl Crazy (1932 and 1943 versions), Shall We Dance, A Damsel in Distress, The Goldwyn Follies, Artie Shaw's Symphony in Swing, Strike Up the Band, Broadway Rhythm, Rhapsody in Blue, Ziegfeld Follies, The Man I Love, The Shocking Miss Pilgrim, The Barkleys of Broadway, An American in Paris, Give a Girl a Break, Funny Face and But Not for Me.

Girl Crazy 1943 Film Cast (with Judy Garland, Mickey Rooney, Tommy Dorsey and his orchestra) / Georgie Stoll.
EMI mono/stereo Ⓟ CDODEON30 (57 minutes: ADD).

It's hard to imagine a more joyous way to celebrate the Gershwin centenary than with these discs, packed with a treasure-trove of performance and booklet-note documentation that are models of authority and expertise. "George and Ira Gershwin in Hollywood" includes some very rare key performances drawn from all the Hollywood studios where a Gershwin credit rolled. Included are Dick Haymes and Betty Grable in charming performances of two duets from Gershwin's posthumous score, *The Shocking Miss Pilgrim* (1947), Astaire in "He loves and she loves" from *Funny Face* (1957) – produced at Paramount 20 years after the composer's death and 30 years after the show's Broadway première – and a heady mixture of numbers from the Gershwin biopic *Rhapsody in Blue* (1945), that begins with a ten-minute "Overture" orchestrated and conducted by Ray Heindorf. Also from *Rhapsody* are "135th Street blues", a quasi-operatic number and prototype for such pop ephemera as "Tenement Symphony"; a magnificently sung "Summertime" from Anne Brown, the original Bess in *Porgy and Bess*; Al Jolson recreating "Swanee", Gershwin's first hit song; and the title-song of *Delicious*, an early Fox musical that brought the Gershwin brothers to Hollywood in 1931 – its subsequent box office failure kept them away for five years until they returned to write a collection of classic scores for Astaire and Rogers at RKO. Though Astaire came to be known as every songwriter's favourite singer, he and Rogers share the vocal honours in an effervescent account of "Let's call the whole thing off" from *Shall We Dance* (1937). Ira without George is represented by Astaire singing "You'd be hard to replace" from *The Barkleys of Broadway* (1949), where the inclusion of the verse makes a much stronger case for Harry Warren's melody, and "In our United State" from *Give a Girl a Break* (1953), where a young Bob Fosse sings and hoofs to Burton Lane's melody.

Both albums contain brilliantly executed big band performances, with Artie Shaw and his orchestra letting their hair down in "Oh lady be good" from the Warner Bros short *Artie Shaw's Symphony in Swing* (1939), and Tommy Dorsey with arrangers Sy Oliver and Axel Stordahl contributing greatly to the success of the 1943 remake of *Girl Crazy*, a soundtrack that contains much more of the original 1930 Broadway score (familiar from *Crazy for You*) than one might expect. In this, the fourth of the Garland/Rooney pictures produced by Arthur Freed, both stars are on top form in a brilliantly lit and full-bodied CD transfer enriched with vocal arrangements by Hugh Martin and Ralph Blane and orchestrations by Conrad Salinger. No expense seems to have been spared bringing out these discs, and surely no one can quibble at the full price asked.   **AE**

Girl Crazy 1990 Studio Cast (with Lorna Luft, David Carroll, Judy Blazer, Frank Gorshin, David Garrison, Vicki Lewis, Eddie Korbich, Stan Chandler, David Engel, Larry Raben and Guy Stroman) / **John Mauceri**.
Nonesuch Ⓟ 7559-79259-2 (73 minutes: DDD).

Faced with the recent success of the pastiche *Crazy for You*, a few historians and other malcontents hinted that they would rather have seen a revival of *Girl Crazy*, the 1930 Gershwin Wild West musical on which it was distantly based. There isn't much to choose between the books of the shows – each has the kind of inconsequentiality favoured by its period – but an organic original score is in theory preferable to a cobbled collection of greatest hits.

Girl Crazy has one of the legendary Broadway scores: three of its songs ("Embraceable you", "I got rhythm" and "But not for me") are undeniable standards, and five more have claims (all but one turned up in *Crazy for You*). The obscurer numbers, however, turn out to be proficient but not very exciting: the most fun is probably "Barbary coast". This disc was the first in the (sadly aborted) Roxbury project to record complete authentic recreations of all the George and Ira Gershwin scores, so it uses Robert Russell Bennett's original orchestrations which are crisp but sedate, as are most of the performers. These choristers are meant to be cowboys and showgirls?

Best is Judy Blazer, whose "Could you use me?" and "But not for me" have something of a Garland tone; as, for more obvious reasons, does Lorna Luft, the-daughter-who's-not-Liza, in the Ethel Merman role. Her "I got rhythm" is pretty terrific: with a hot piano solo by Dick Hyman, one of the many top-flight session men in the band, it's the only number that cuts loose. Richard M. Sudhalter theorizes in the accompanying booklet that it was scored by bandleader (and original MD) Red Nichols rather than Bennett, and he's probably right. There's also a charming close-harmony quartet for "Bidin' my time". This recording is a huge improvement on the only previous version (on Columbia, with no style and Mary Martin hogging all the famous songs) but it's to be nibbled rather than devoured. **RC**

Lady, Be Good! 1992 Studio Cast (with Lara Teeter, Ann Morrison, Jason Alexander, Michael Maguire, John Pizzarelli, Ivy Austin, Michelle Nicastro, Robin Langford and Carol Swarbrick) / **Eric Stern**.
Nonesuch Ⓟ 7559-79308-2 (70 minutes: DDD).

The Gershwin siblings had their first joint Broadway success with *Lady, Be Good!*, written for the Astaire siblings; and the show, first staged in 1924, remains one of their freshest. Its frothily frivolous book still works in revival, and its score – starting with the tuneful, jaunty overture here arranged by Larry Wilcox – makes this recording a delight. Nearly every song, sweet or sassy, is a jewel.

Porgy and Bess apart, the Gershwins may have done their best work – certainly their most characteristic – in the 1920s; they had mixed influences and in this show the lingering sound of Gilbert and Sullivan ("End of a string" for a collection of gilded youths at a house-party) rubs against the emerging spirit of the Jazz Age. This disc contains a "Fascinating rhythm" (orchestrated by Russell Warner) that builds to a shattering series of climaxes, after starting with a very cool vocal by John Pizzarelli. His adopted style of hip is two or three decades younger than that of the original's Cliff Edwards, alias Ukelele Ike, but it doesn't matter. Pizzarelli plays the uke like a guitar (his accustomed instrument), and both here and on his solo, the delightful "Little jazz bird", he proves the liner-notes' contention that this is a show built for specialists. (For the original sound of the original cast try – if you can find it – a historical reconstruction released by the Smithsonian).

Lara Teeter doesn't have Fred Astaire's wit, or his shyly authoritative vocal style (who does?), but he furnishes an obliging pair of feet for the taps on "The half of it, dearie, blues". Ann Morrison makes a pert stand-in for sister Adele, while the endearingly crooked lawyer is played by the magnificent Jason Alexander who, if he weren't tied up with films and TV, could be the biggest musical star on Broadway. His grip on the dialogue ("she's doing ten years in Canto Canto – that's Mexican for Sing Sing") is unshakeable, and his singing grand: he gets the title song, which is not a romantic number but an overture to fraud and seduction. The very Gershwinian two-piano sound (Steven Blier and John Musto) sparkles in "I'd rather Charleston", inserted for the 1920s London production. Desmond Carter wrote the lyric, which has Ira Gershwin's pedagogic stance but not his slyness. It's an archetypal squabbling brother and sister lyric to balance the sibling togetherness of the sweet opening song, "Hang on to me". One puzzle: not only is "The man I love" – the most celebrated cut-out song of all time – not included, it isn't even mentioned in the notes (but see under *Strike Up the Band*) . **RC**

Oh, Kay! 1994 Studio Cast (with Dawn Upshaw, Kurt Ollmann, Patrick Cassidy, Adam Arkin, Robert Westenberg, Liz Larsen, Stacey A. Logan, Susan Lucci and Fritz Weaver); **Orchestra of St Luke's / Eric Stern**.
Nonesuch Ⓟ 7559-79361-2 (65 minutes: DDD).

There has been no shortage of *Oh Kay!* records: a Smithsonian "historical reconstruction" with Gertrude Lawrence and cohorts from 1926, a negligible doctored 1960s revival, and a splendid, seemingly complete mid-1950s studio recording on Columbia. But this Roxbury disc (which seems, alas, to be the last of the line – how can we live without hearing *Tip-Toes* and *Funny Face* in their entireties?) more than justifies its existence. in fact, it supersedes all others.

First, it restores some songs unheard in the original production: among them the buoyant "The moon is on the sea" and the wonderful "Ain't it romantic?" which combines a far-out tune with a comedy lyric. Then, it has Dawn Upshaw in the title role (yes, there really is a Kay) and she is a revelation, surpassing even Frederica von Stade in the crossover lists. She subdues her voice beautifully to musical-comedy tone and phrasing, her rhythm is supple, and she has humour: only a few dialogue jokes defeat her. She even manages to make "Someone to watch over me", one of the most over-recorded of all songs, seem fresh – and she sings it very simply. Kurt Ollmann also has the right idea, though his sound is a little heavy. Eric Stern seems a far more idiomatic Gershwin conductor than his Roxbury predecessor John Mauceri, and the overall feel of the performance is delightful. The disc uses new period-sounding orchestrations by Russell Warner (were all the originals lost? Tommy Krasker, the series' meticulous "restorer" is silent on the subject). The overture begins like Sullivan in Japanese mode, then resolves into recognizable Gershwin, delicate and incorporating a lovely treatment of "Someone". George and Ira get joint credit for both music and lyrics: an attempt to prolong the copyright by rewriting history?   **RC**

Pardon My English 1993 Studio Cast (with William Katt, John Cullum, Arnetia Walker and Michelle Nicastro) **/ Eric Stern**.
Nonesuch Ⓟ 7559-79338-2 (68 minutes: DDD).

Pardon My English was the biggest disaster of the Gershwin brothers' joint career. It had a plot about mistaken identity (a product of schizophrenia, cued by repeated blows to the head of the accident-prone hero) that is impossible to follow even now, with eyes glued to the synopsis. It suffered wholesale re-writings and re-castings on the road. It was a farce about law-breaking German nightclubs and lovably incompetent German troops that opened in, of all years, 1933.

It also had a truly terrific score that the Gershwins, for all their protestations, must have enjoyed writing and that this Roxbury cast obviously love performing. Given an abundance of discarded songs and variant lyrics, researcher-editor-producer Tommy Krasker had a field day. Here are the complete conversational lyrics, set to a magically conversational tune, of "Isn't it a pity?" (Mel Tormé once called it far-and-away his favourite Gershwin ballad); here is a previously unheard second chorus of "The Lorelei". Here are obscurities like the raucous "I've got to be there", and total rediscoveries like "Luckiest man in the world", a suave, teasing tune for two lovers with pasts, and a "Tonight" that's nothing like *West Side Story*'s. There are plenty of Ira's peculiarly chaste and distanced sex jokes and bookish romanticism, and a barrelful of George's energy and unexpectedness: both oom-pah and waltz are up for irreverent grabs.

William Katt takes the brunt in the dual role of raffish Golo and innocent Michael (in which he sounds appropriately like Feinstein – or is that just the sound that's going around?). John Cullum plays a German Clouseau in the ripe tones of an ex-matineé idol, though the role was written for a dialect comic. Michelle Nicastro does the spirited heroine thing, and Arnetia Walker the smoky *chanteuse* bit. The chorus can never have had such fun, whether playing Polizei out of some Teutonic-American *Pirates of Penzance* or chorines who prefigure *Cabaret*: Katt's MC turn at the beginning of "Lorelei" clearly has the parallel in mind. Despite the modern (or post-modern) tone of the whole thing, many of the spikiest orchestrations are originals by Gershwin's closest musical counsellor, William Daly. The overture unites the talents of Daly and Robert Russell Bennett (old) and Russell Warner (new), and is an intriguing piece of work, alternately dainty and edgy.   **RC**

The Song is ... George Gershwin with **Elisabeth Welch, Fred Astaire, Cliff Edwards, Fats Waller, Gertrude Lawrence, Irene Audrey, Charles Hart, Jack Smith, Al Jolson, Lawrence Tibbett, Zelma O'Neal, Fats Waller, Benny Carter, Jack Hylton, Al Goodman, Carroll Gibbons, Fred Waring, Ben Selvin, Arthur Wood, Marius B. Winter, Paul Whiteman** and **Alexander Smallens**.
ASV Living Era mono Ⓜ CDAJA5048 (50 minutes: ADD).
Songs from Girl Crazy, Lady, Be Good!, Show Girl, Funny Face, George White's Scandals of 1922, Nifties of 1923, Tip-Toes, Oh, Kay! and Porgy and Bess.

Sticking strictly to songs from stage shows (no movies) this collection includes some classic performances. Some are even original cast: Gertrude Lawrence's Roedean-inflected "Someone to watch over me" (with variant lyrics), Cliff Edwards's pioneer scatting on "Fascinating rhythm", Paul Whiteman's "I'll build a stairway to paradise" *sans* vocal, Fred Astaire singing and dancing "The half of it, dearie, blues" with piano accompaniment and encouragement by George Gershwin; they genuinely sound, as was presumably intended, like two guys fooling around in someone's apartment. There are two Gershwin piano solos – a tumbling "My one and only" and a humdrum "When do we dance?" – and Alexander Smallens, first conductor of *Porgy and Bess*, officiates for Lawrence Tibbett, not of the cast, in "I got plenty o' nuttin'". Al Jolson does his semi-official rendition of "Liza" – he wasn't in *Show Girl* where it originated but he used to rise from the audience and serenade his wife Ruby Keeler whose number it was supposed to be; reports of her reaction differ.

Outsiders include Fats Waller with the most rhythmic "I got rhythm" ever, certainly the most joyous; and Elisabeth Welch singing "The man I love" with her customary unstrained sensitivity. Whispering Jack Smith half-sings "Funny face", sounding like an old-style radio uncle. Broadway flapper Zelma O'Neal, cheerfully flat, does what she does to "Do what you do". There is none of the steam that later, slower singers have found in the song but the record does have some period charm; she was a star for a few minutes. A London hotel orchestra's "'S wonderful" shows just how bad band vocals could be. How low Gershwin himself could sink is shown by "I found a four leaf clover", unmitigated hackwork from the *1922 Scandals*. But he was very young. The pre-electric recording and atrocious singing between them obliterate Buddy de Sylva's lyric, which may be as well. Other words are by Ira, some with Gus Kahn.   **RC**

Strike Up the Band 1990 **Studio Cast** (with Brent Barrett, Don Chastain, Rebecca Luker, Jason Graae, Beth Fowler, Charles Goff, Juliet Lambert, Jeff Lyons, Dale Sandish and James Rocco) **/ John Mauceri**.
Nonesuch Ⓟ 7559-79273-2 (two discs: 111 minutes: DDD).

Strike Up the Band, a whimsical satire on war and the first of the Gershwin comic operas on political themes, exists in two forms. The first folded out of town in 1927, the second, sweetened version was a Broadway success in 1930. The Roxbury project recorded both of them but so far only the first has been issued.

The savagery even of the initial attempt is open to question. In synopsis – America declares war on Switzerland to protect its own supremacy in the cheese market – it sounds wonderful, and George S. Kaufman's script, to judge from what's heard here, is full of great wisecracks. George Gershwin's music is always vivacious, sometimes tart, and occasionally beautiful: "Meadow serenade" (its verse was lost but Burton Lane, at least as good a melodist, wrote a new one) is a gem, as is the lilting "17 and 21", with the lines "You've made me gay and fresher/You gave me high blood pressure". Ira Gershwin's particular brand of wit is, however, the undoing of the tougher narrative numbers; his polysyllabic rhymes turn everything into a game. The blandness that pervaded *Girl Crazy* afflicts this disc as well. It's been cast more for voice than personality. For the romantic leads (Brent Barrett and Rebecca Luker) this may be acceptable; but Don Chastain does a very tame job on the cheese-paring cheesemonger, the show's capitalist villain, and Jeff Lyons, in a role written for a vaudeville comic, just sounds quaint. The band strike up well, though, and "The man I love" – transferred to this show after its eviction from *Lady, Be Good!* – has never sounded lovelier than in the overture. After serving as the Act 1 romantic duet it reappears in Act 2 as "The girl I love", heart-stoppingly sung by Dale Sandish as a homesick soldier and cutting, as was intended, right through the frivolity.

The non-appearance of the 1930 score is mitigated by the inclusion of an appendix that includes nearly all of its songs that weren't merely rewrites of their predecessors. They're a knockout bunch, including the standard "Soon", gracefully done by Barrett and Luker. Players underserved in the original come to the fore, with juveniles Jason Graae and Juliet Lambert tearing the place up in a trio of duets (including an authentic fast dance treatment of "I've got a crush on you") and Charles Goff as a lecherous senator who sings "If I became the President" and a tuneful roof-raiser "Mademoiselle for New Rochelle". It's heretical to say so but the commercialized score is actually the better: Gershwin swings. **RC**

Also available:
A Musical Celebration MCA MCAD2-10865
Funny Face (1956 Film Cast) Verve 531 231-2
The Glory of Gershwin. Mercury 522 727-2
Of Thee I Sing (1952 Broadway Cast) EMI Angel ZDM5 65025-2
Our Love is Here to Stay Happy Days 75605 52249-2

Dan Goggin

Nunsense 1986 **Off-Broadway Cast** (with Christine Anderson, Semina de Laurentis, Marilyn Farina, Edwina Lewis and Suzi Winson) / **Michael Rice**.
DRG ⓕ CDSBL12589 (47 minutes: ADD).
Nunsense 1987 **London Cast** (with Honor Blackman, Anna Sharkey, Pip Hinton, Louise Gold and Bronwen Stanway) / **Barrie Bignold**.
TER ⓕ CDTER1132 (51 minutes: DDD).
Nunsense II: The Second Coming ... 1993 **Broadway Cast** (with Christine Anderson, Semina de Laurentis, Mary Gillis, Kathy Robinson and Lyn Vaux) / **Michael Rice**.
DRG ⓕ 12608 (48 minutes: AAD).

A wild and silly show, *Nunsense* is utterly delightful and hysterically funny. Forced to raise funds in order to bury four of their order (you have to read the liner-notes to discover why this is necessary), the five remaining nuns of the Little Sisters of Hoboken stage a talent show, of which this is a recording. The sisters are under the tutelage of Reverend Mother Sister Mary Cardelia (Marilyn Farina) who decides who should perform and who should not. Sister Robert Anne (Christine Anderson), consigned to the role of understudy, complains bitterly of "Playing second fiddle", although in the second half she is given her chance to shine in "I just want to be a star". Among the other nuns there is the talented Sister Mary Hubert (Edwina Lewis), who leads the nuns in a tap routine "Tackle that temptation with a time step", and later offers advice on how to become a saint in "Holier than thou"; and Sister Mary Amnesia (Semina de Laurentis), who explains the convent life in the superb "So you want to be a nun". With her name, the latter character naturally has no idea who she is until the end of the evening when a dramatic revelation takes place that brings on a happy ending. Dan Goggin's music is performed by a small band – the tunes are simple and unexceptional, but accompanied by his wonderfully funny lyrics, and of course it is the situation itself that brings on much of the humour. The entire cast is infectiously funny – not one of them would find a place in *The Sound of Music* but one cannot help but warm to their delirious silliness. Goggin has created a minor comic masterpiece that has become, after *The Fantasticks*, the longest-running off-Broadway show in history. This is not in the least surprising, and the original cast recording is just as funny on repeat hearings.

The London production features a wonderful cast in a slightly extended recording. Anna Sharkey is excellent as the struggling Sister Robert Anne, and Honor Blackman sounds far too sexy to be a Reverend Mother, while Louise Gold nearly steals the show as a wonderful Sister Mary Amnesia. There are no liner-notes accompanying the recording which is a little disappointing because the basic joke of the show is not set up, but even so it is a fine complement to the original.

In *Nunsense II* the Little Sisters of Hoboken return to thank all the people who supported their last variety show, by presenting another one. Christine Anderson and Semina de Laurentis reprise their roles as Sisters Robert Anne and Mary Amnesia respectively, while excellent newcomers perform the other three roles. Although not quite as funny as the original – the joke is not as fresh – this is still highly entertaining and enjoyable. The original show had declared, in a bad pun, that *Nunsense* is habit-forming, under Goggin's expert care, the statement is probably true as this is a must for those who enjoyed the first in the series. **RAC**

Billy Goldenberg
b. 1936 USA

Ballroom 1978 **Broadway Cast** (with Dorothy Loudon, Vincent Gardenia, Lynne Roberts and
Bernie Knee) **/ Don Jennings**.
Sony Broadway Ⓕ SK35762 (47 minutes: ADD).

The bittersweet story of lonely middle-aged people meeting at a dance-hall was an unlikely
follow-up to *A Chorus Line* for director/choreographer Michael Bennett. *Ballroom*, adapted
from the TV movie *The Queen of the Stardust Ballroom*, did not find favour with critics or
audiences and closed after 116 performances. Billy Goldenberg's score (with lyrics by Alan and
Marilyn Bergman) points out the essential problem of the show – it is predominantly a series
of pleasant but unmemorable dance band numbers (nicely sung by Roberts and Knee),
interspersed with a few character songs for Loudon. And it is the magnificent Loudon who
brings the recording to life: her brittle, raw voice is perfect for the lonely widow, at first nervous
of standing on her own two feet ("A terrific band and a real nice crowd"), growing confident
("Somebody did all right for herself") and finding new love ("I love to dance"). This last, sadly,
is the only piece that involves Vincent Gardenia. In the classic eleven o'clock number, "Fifty
per cent", Loudon surpasses herself, delivering a definitive, shattering performance
accepting that "any per cent" of her married lover is better than "all of anybody else at all".
The effect of this piece is dampened by the pretty but banal "I wish you a waltz" which ends the
selection. **RAC**

Howard Goodall
b. 1958 UK

Howard Goodall was a choirboy at New College Oxford, returning as an adult to study
music at Christ Church College. An early collaboration at university with Rowan Atkinson
and Richard Curtis led to Goodall's writing music for *Not the Nine O'Clock News*
and *Blackadder* for television. He has also composed for Wayne Sleep's dance shows *Dash*
and for *The Hot Shoe Show*. An opera *Der Glockner von Notre-Dame* was mounted in
Zurich in 1983. *The Hired Man* (1984) was his first musical. In 1987 came *Girlfriends* about life
in the WRAF during the Second World War and 1991 saw *Days of Hope*, set in the
Spanish Civil War. 1998 sees a new musical collaboration with the National Youth Musical
Theatre.

New review
Days of Hope 1991 **London Cast** (with Una Stubbs, John Turner, Carla Mendonça, Nicholas
Caunter, Phyllida Hancock, Darryl Knock, Danny Cerqueira) **/ Paul Smith**.
TER Ⓕ CDTER1183 (50 minutes: DDD).

Howard Goodall's *Days of Hope* is recognizably by the composer of *The Hired Man*, with strong,
surging melodies deeply embedded in the European folk music tradition. It is set in the Spanish
Civil War, on Valentine's Day 1939. An Englishman is about to be married to the daughter of a
fishing family. But General Franco's troops are advancing and the family are making
preparations to leave, to journey to France and thence to England. In the event, the mother and
her husband give up their place on the boat, to await their fate at the hands of the incoming
troops. Goodall's score, while encompassing a variety of Iberian rhythms and melodic styles,
remains his own. There's even a charming version of the English folk song "Parsley, Sage,
Rosemary and Thyme" (better known as *Scarborough Fair* in the version made popular by Simon
and Garfunkel). Judging by the recording the show merits a revival; the singers, led by John
Turner, are firm, strong and convincing. Those who only remember Una Stubbs as a bubbly
teenage dancer in Cliff Richard musicals or in *Till Death Us Do Part* will be delighted by her
mature performance here. There's a bonus of two tracks not performed in the show excellently
sung by the composer, Howard Goodall. **MPK**

New review
The Hired Man 1992 **Concert Cast** (with Julia Hills, Paul Clarkson, Richard Walsh, Billy
Harman, Gerald Doyle, Claire Burt and Philip Schofield) **/ Kate Young**.
TER Ⓕ CDTER2 1189 (two discs: 92 minutes: DDD).

Smaller companies tend to keep their show recordings in the catalogue for longer than the giants – indeed the latter, with the honourable exceptions of Sony and RCA, seem largely determined to ignore their valuable back catalogue of recordings. While Polydor never issued their original recording of *The Hired Man* on Compact Disc, TER have recorded (in more complete form) a concert version of Howard Goodall's score that features many members of the original company. As with Willy Russell's *Blood Brothers* the music here is deeply influenced by the English folk-song tradition. Melvyn Bragg's novel about a Northumbrian rural community – the miners and agricultural workers in the years up to and through the First World War – hopes, dreams, achievements, infidelities and disappointments. The focus is on John and Emily – a typical working class hero and heroine touchingly portrayed by Paul Clarkson and Julia Hills (yes, the maneater neighbour from TV's *Two Point Four Children*) and the dashing Jackson (Richard Walsh) who dallies with Emily. At the end John and Emily are back together, strengthened by tragedy and John once again hires himself out for a season of agricultural labour. The music is varied, heartstirring and frequently uplifting, grounded in the English choral tradition and sounds even better than memory suggests. The narration is apposite and comparatively unobtrusive. *The Hired Man* is a rare example of a comparatively recent and very enjoyable British musical recorded in its virtual entirety. **MPK**

Ron Grainer
1922-1981 Australia

Australian-born Ron Grainer made his name with television themes: *Steptoe and Son* and *Dr Who* being typical examples. After contributing two songs to *Cindy-Ella* (1962) he provided the full score for the finest post-war British operetta-cum-musical comedy, *Robert and Elizabeth* (1964), a full-blooded exploration of the elopement of Elizabeth Barrett with Robert Browning. A contemporary musical, *On the Level* (1966), was not as successful. Two further shows, *Sing a Rude Song* (1970), about music-hall star Marie Lloyd, and *Nickleby and Me* about the Crummles theatricals followed, but could not achieve the same success. Grainer then retired to Portugal.

Robert and Elizabeth 1964 **London Cast** (with John Clements, June Bronhill, Keith Michell, Jeremy Lloyd, Rod McLennan, Stella Moray and Angela Richards) **/ Alexander Faris**. EMI Angel Ⓜ ZDM7 65069-2 (52 minutes: ADD).

Robert and Elizabeth 1987 **Chichester Cast** (with Gaynor Miles, Mark Wynter, John Savident, Alexander Hanson, Karen Ascoe and Geoffrey Abbott) **/ Alexander Faris**. First Night Ⓜ OCRCD6032 (62 minutes: DDD).

Robert and Elizabeth was a welcome dip into the past: the romance of Elizabeth Barrett with fellow poet Robert Browning and her eventual escape from a semi-permanent sick-bed to a new healthy life in Italy, thus releasing her from the suffocating affection of her martinet father. Ron Grainer provided a captivating score full of melodic plums, including a deeply affecting setting of Browning's poem "Escape me never". The varied, appealing score encompasses such joyfully vigorous numbers as "The moon in my pocket", "Pass the Eau de Cologne" and passionate Victorian ballads which include "I know now" and "Woman and man". The show was successfully revived 20 years after the original production, and included some new material, performed by the Chichester cast. Yet the power and passion of the original 1964 version glows fresh-minted in EMI's fine digital transfer. June Bronhill is a fiery invalid, gradually awakening to the strength of her feelings for Keith Michell's dashingly ardent poet. The strong supporting cast includes the always reliable Angela Richards, who introduces one of the show's best and most affecting songs "You only to love me", and who would graduate to a leading role in Grainer's next musical, *On the Level*. By contrast there is often a sense of strain underlying the performances of the revival cast as they cope with the often taxing music. While one would like to own both recordings, the original 1964 recording is the one to start with. **MPK**

Larry Grossman

Snoopy!!! 1975 **San Francisco Cast** (with Pamela Myers, Roxanne Pyle, Carla Manning, Jimmy Dodge, James Gleason and Don Potter) **/ Jon Olson**. DRG Ⓟ CDSBL6103 (41 minutes: AAD).

Snoopy 1983 London Cast (with Teddy Kempner, Susie Blake, Zoe Bright, Nicky Croydon, Mark Hadfield and Robert Locke) / **Stuart Pedlar**.
TER Ⓕ CDTER1073 (57 minutes: ADD).

The talented Larry Grossman has had his biggest hit with this most modest show. The second musical to be based on the *Peanuts* comic-strip, *Snoopy!!!* is less charming than Clark Gesner's *You're a Good Man, Charlie Brown* but wittier. The opening "The world according to Snoopy" is a bit icky in the manner of small winsome American musicals; so (although more acceptably, because a prettier tune) is the closing "Just one person". But in between, Grossman furnishes a cunningly unassuming and catchy miniature of a Broadway score to which Hal Hackady, his regular collaborator at the time, has affixed some zippy, gently sardonic if sometimes overloaded lyrics. The show, like the strip, is really about disillusion: the adult variety filtered through the child's growing-up process. The boys, and the dog, are the vulnerable idealists, the girls the puncturing realists ("I know now that you can't trust a daisy/They blab, every chance they get"). Charlie Brown bashfully dreams of a future wife who will call him "Poor sweet baby"; Peppermint Patty sings him a touching threnody with just that title, then snaps, "forget it! it'll never happen".

Pamela Myers, the performer for whom Stephen Sondheim wrote "Another hundred people", sings Patty on the San Francisco cast recording in the cast-iron tones of an Ethel Merbaby. The other females, Sally and the fearsome Lucy, get less chance; but James Gleason is a touchingly wistful Charlie Brown, Jimmy Dodge a sharply neurotic Linus keeping his Christmas vigil for the non-appearing Great Pumpkin ("Santa Clause", he loyally shrieks, "just gets more publicity"), and Don Potter is a tangy-voiced Snoopy. A dog's life in this musical is a rewarding one, with numbers ranging from the country-flavoured reminiscence "Daisy Hill" to the eleven o'clock "The big bow-wow" which might be subtitled "Snoopy's strut".

The London beagle, Teddy Kempner, romps home with his disc's honours, having less bite than the American mutt but a more infectious bark. *Snoopy* here has lost its triple exclamation mark but gained several songs, among them "Mother's day", a bit of Jolsonian bravura for the dog himself; a good company number, "When do the good things start"; and another solo for Patty, "Hurry up face", which like most of the disc has a pop sound in place of the US cast's traditional theatrics. On both, the number that most summons up the image of the comic is "The great writer", with Snoopy, perched at the typewriter on top of his dog-house, weaving the narrative strands of his *magnum opus*, "Meanwhile on a small farm in Kansas...": the music to this passing phrase strikingly anticipates the main strain of Andrew Lloyd Webber's "Memory" (unless, of course, there's a common source). **RC**

Adam Guettel

Floyd Collins 1996 Off-Broadway Cast (with Christopher Innvar, Martin Moran, Theresa McCarthy, Jason Danieley, Cass Morgan and Don Chastain) / **Ted Sperling**.
Nonesuch Ⓕ 7559-79434-2 (68 minutes: DDD).

Floyd Collins was a young man who, after becoming trapped in a cave in 1925, became the centre of a media circus with an estimated 20,000 people above ground at the height of the drama. They disappeared all too quickly when it was announced that, despite several rescue attempts, he was dead. So no happy endings here and no conventional Broadway sound either. The tale is told above and below ground and explores the characters involved, the efforts to free the lad and the emptiness which follows. It is an intelligent piece of theatre which focuses upon the intimate turmoil of the family and the cynical circus who see no more than a story – a storyline which is timeless. *Floyd Collins* is a fascinating, intricate musical piece with an original score which is basically of country style (fitting the Kentucky locale). The small orchestra is made up of violins, guitars and other string instruments, a keyboard and a harmonica – it creates an astonishingly atmospheric country sound which is an essential part of the whole. But, it is more – one moment melodious, the next layered in raw sounds and at times a folk opera of great depth. Anyone interested in the evolution of the popular musical form will find this intriguing, but it's not for those wanting a comfortable ride in a more conventional format, for this is no lightweight whimsy. Adam Guettel is the son of Mary Rodgers, the daughter of Richard Rodgers. A family tree to follow and enough reason for many to give this a try. **RSB**

Carol Hall

The Best Little Whorehouse in Texas 1978 **Broadway Cast** (with Carlyn Glynn, Henderson Forsythe, Pamela Blair, Jay Garner, Clint Allmon, Delores Hall and Susan Mansur) / **Robert Billig.**
MCA Ⓜ MCAD11683 (53 minutes: ADD).

It has taken almost 20 years for this hit Broadway show to arrive on CD – it was worth the wait. On the way it has been filmed (with unsatisfactory score changes), had a London showing (not a success) and a flop sequel (both of which managed CD releases). The subject-matter makes this an adult musical but don't expect to be shocked – the treatment of this story (which is based on fact) is as wholesome as the energetic young men who learn about 'life' with a visit to what was warmly called the chicken ranch. But the story is more a comment on dual standards and political spin-doctors who see the existence of a long-established and locally accepted, almost respectable home of fun (and it is also a home for the girls) as an ideal place to attack for political gain. Unfortunately, the notoriety it attracts brings its closure and the end to a beautiful relationship between the local sheriff and the madam. This is a top-notch score by Carol Hall in her own Country and Western idiom, and it's strong on often intelligent and clever lyrics which help the listener follow the storyline – again adding to the listening enjoyment. Much is infectious stuff and may encourage you to take up line dancing! The show was choreographed by Tommy Tune, close your eyes and you can almost see the football team perform one of Broadway's greatest choreographic treats. One of those rare recordings which has an almost three-dimensional quality – recommended. **RSB**

Also available:
The Best Little Whorehouse Goes Public (1994 Broadway Cast) Varèse Sarabande VSD5542

Marvin Hamlisch

b. 1944 USA

Born in New York of Austrian Jewish stock (his parents emigrated to the USA in 1937), Hamlisch became the youngest student to be admitted to the Juilliard School (aged seven). He later studied at Queen's College, during which time his songs were already reaching a wide audience: schoolfriend Liza Minnelli recorded his song "Travellin' man", and in 1965 he had his first hit with "Sunshine, lollipops and rainbows". He worked on Broadway as a rehearsal pianist and arranger, wrote cabaret songs for Ann-Margret and Liza Minnelli, and toured with Groucho Marx in the early 1970s. Film producer Sam Spiegel engaged him to write for films, and he composed scores for several movies including *The Swimmer* (1968), *Take the Money and Run* (1969) and *The Sting* (1973) – the latter winning an Academy Award for best adapted score. In the same year he also picked up another two Academy Awards for the Barbra Streisand film *The Way We Were* (best original score and song). On Broadway he had a great success with *A Chorus Line* in 1975 – 6,238 performances in 15 years, nine Tony Awards and a Pulitzer Prize – which was filmed in 1985. *They're Playing Our Song* followed in 1979. Later shows such as *The Goodbye Girl* (1993) were not successes. He had another movie hit with "Nobody does it better" from the James Bond film *The Spy Who Loved Me* (1977), written with his then girlfriend, lyricist Carole Bayer Sager.

A Chorus Line 1975 **Broadway Cast** (with Scott Allen, Rene Baughman, Carole Bishop, Pamela Blair, Wayne Cilento, Chuck Cissell, Clive Clerk and Kay Cole) / **Don Pippin**.
Columbia Ⓔ CK33581 (49 minutes: AAD).
A Chorus Line 1985 **Film Cast** (with Michael Blevins, Yamil Borges, Jan Gan Boyd, Sharon Brown, Greg Burge and Michael Douglas) / **Ralph Burns**.
Casablanca Ⓜ 826 655-2 (38 minutes: DDD).

The arrival of the non-linear musical enabled creative talents to dispense with strict storylines and concentrate on other aspects. Both *A Chorus Line* and its supplanter as longest-running show on Broadway, *Cats*, are unconventional shows, lacking a plot line, but concentrating on revealing character points. Each leads to a centrally-important event. In *A Chorus Line* the audience eavesdrops on an elimination process to choose dancers to form a dancing chorus for a new

Broadway show. The director/choreographer probes the lives of the candidates standing before him before making his choice on a combination of dancing ability and, presumably, character. The original cast recording is already a classic . Offering strong and definitive performances of "I can do that", "The music and the mirror", "One", "Hello twelve", "Dance: ten, looks three" and "Nothing" it deserves a place in every collection of classic Broadway cast albums. The howls of protest when an English director was chosen to direct the film (after many previous attempts came to grief) were as nothing to the dismay of Broadway buffs when they discovered that Richard Attenborough had reworked the show for film – it was no front-and-centre reproduction of the original. There were some fine new songs, some terrific singer/dancers, and for the first time "What I did for love" made proper sense when placed in a new position in the action. While not supplanting the original cast, the film recording has many virtues, some previously overlooked. **MPK**

New review
The Goodbye Girl 1993 Broadway Cast (with Bernadette Peters, Martin Short, Carol Woods and Tammy Minoff) **/ Jack Everly.**
Columbia Ⓟ CK53761 (63 minutes: DDD).

Based on the film hit of the same title this sounded like a good idea for a musical. It has a nice predictable ending with the guy getting a ready-made family and the talent brought together pointed to success. But, it did not work and it stayed on Broadway for less than 200 performances. It still seemed like a good idea when lyricist Don Black was brought in to assist with writing new lyrics to Marvin Hamlisch's tunes for a London showing – lightning struck quicker the second time. So here it is, a show that looks as though it's not going anywhere further and will remain just a memory on disc. Well that's the bad news. There is good. If you like Bernadette Peters then here she is, albeit sounding a little tired at times, playing the unlucky-in-love mother, warbling with some more than serviceable songs. The surprise, however, is Martin Short who gives a powerful performance and has the ability to be funny, warm and generous. He plays the actor forced into an unconventional production of *Richard III* and has to share an apartment with Miss Peters (and daughter) – neither situation is perfect and this comes over clearly on disc. It's one of those serviceable scores which is up and down and not totally a whole, making it less than a perfect listen. There are the neighbour's kids and a blues-singing apartment house attendant which take away some of the Short shine.

The London production inspired a four-track, three-song single, with Gary Wilmot and Ann Crumb performing new songs (First Night SCORECD44). It is a different sound, a more up-to-date, intense feel that is a long way from the Broadway version and is heavy on drama, so losing the lighter touch. Although not perfect, I preferred the Broadway sound both on stage and off. **RSB**

Also available:
They're Playing Our Song (1979 Broadway Cast) Casablanca 826 240-2
They're Playing Our Song (1980 London Cast) TER CDTER1035

Oscar Hammerstein II

1895-1960 USA

The grandson of opera impresario Oscar Hammerstein and son of theatre manager William, Oscar II always seemed destined to pursue a theatrical career, despite studying law at Columbia University. He took a job as stage manager with his Uncle Arthur Hammerstein, and wrote the libretto and lyrics for his first musical, *Always You*, in 1920 to music by Herbert Stothart. Hammerstein, often collaborating with lyricist Otto Harbach, was responsible for a succession of popular Broadway shows during the 1920s, including Friml's *Rose-Marie* (1924) and Romberg's *The Desert Song* (1926). An early landmark arrived with his libretto for Jerome Kern's *Show Boat* (1927) which, unlike most shows of the period, drew inspiration from uniquely American history and traditions. He worked with Kern again on *Sweet Adeleine* (1929), *Music in the Air* (1932) and *Very Warm for May* (1939), and also wrote extensively for films. In 1943 he began a long-standing partnership with composer Richard Rodgers; their first musical together was *Oklahoma!* which, like *Show Boat*, took place in a recognizably American setting. The partnership flourished with *Carousel* (1945), *South Pacific* (1949), *The King and I* (1951) and *The Sound of Music* (1959). *Carmen Jones*, Hammerstein's adaptation of Bizet's *Carmen*, was staged with an all-black cast in 1943. It ran for 502 performances and was filmed in 1954.

Carmen Jones 1952 **Film Cast** (with Marilyn Horne, La Vern Hutcherson, Pearl Bailey, Olga James, Brock Peters, Marvin Hayes, Diahann Carroll and Roy Glenn) **/ Herschel Burke Gilbert.** RCA Victor Ⓜ GD81881 (46 minutes: AAD).

Carmen Jones 1991 **London Cast** (with Wilhelmenia Fernandez, Sharon Benson, Damon Evans, Michael Austin, Gregg Baker, Karen Parks, José Garcia, Clive Rowe, Danny John Jules, Carolyn Sebrion and Wendy Brown) **/ Henry Lewis.** EMI Ⓕ CDC 754351-2 (63 minutes DDD) .

One of the most surprising and successful adaptations of opera, *Carmen Jones* takes the music of Bizet's *Carmen* and, while retaining the characterizations and story of the original, moves the location from nineteenth-century Spain to the deep South of America during the Second World War. Carmen is no longer a cigarette girl but a worker in a parachute factory. Her lover Joe (Don José) is still a soldier, but her subsequent love, bullfighter Escamillo, is now a prize fighter Husky Miller. Oscar Hammerstein's book and lyrics have zest, confidence and dynamism: all the more remarkable considering that he had been responsible for *Oklahoma!* just nine months before. The film starred singers Dorothy Dandridge and Harry Belafonte, who were not permitted to sing (but were dubbed by the young Marilyn Horne and La Vern Hutcherson respectively) and Pearl Bailey, who was. The CD, in slightly glaring sound, is a fine souvenir of the film, but in the absence of the original 1943 cast recording with Muriel Smith that does not seem to have found its way onto disc, the fine original London cast recording of just a few years back will more than suffice. Simon Callow's convincing Old Vic production had alternate principals as Carmen and Joe, and both pairs can be found on EMI's finely produced and well recorded issue. Wilhelmenia Fernandez and Damon Evans, the more operatic sounding pairing, appear in the first and fourth acts, Sharon Benson and Michael Austin take over for the second act, and Benson in Act 3 (in which Joe doesn't sing). Henry Lewis conducts with zest and the well-drilled cast are extremely effective. While the politically correct may look askance at some of the spelling, there's no doubt of the strength of the lyrics – "Dere's a cafe on de corner", "Whizzin' away along de track" fit the music like a glove, and "De cards don' lie" can still produce a chill in the listener. **MPK**

Otto Harbach   1873-1963 USA

Born in Salt Lake City, Otto Harbach was an English teacher, journalist and copywriter before his friendship with composer Karl Hoschna tempted him to try his hand as a lyricist. Their first collaboration, *Three Twins* (1908), was conspicuously successful, and they worked together until Hoschna's death in 1911. Harbach penned *The Firefly* (1912) with composer Rudolf Friml, and often collaborated with Oscar Hammerstein II, on Friml's *Rose-Marie* (1924), for example, for which they wrote "Indian love call". Harbach later wrote the words for Jerome Kern's *Roberta* (1932) which included "Smoke gets in your eyes".

E. Y. Harburg   1898-1981 USA

Born Isidore Hochberg in New York, Edgar 'Yip' Harburg attended City College along with fellow would-be lyricist Ira Gershwin. After his electrical business went bankrupt during the Depression, Harburg wrote his first lyrics for *Earl Carroll's Sketch Book* (1929 – music by Jay Gorney). Also with Gorney he penned "Brother, can you spare a dime?" for the revue *Americana* (1932). Harburg worked with composers Vernon Duke – *Walk a Little Faster* (1932) – and Burton Lane – *Hold on to Your Hats* (1940), *Finian's Rainbow* (1947) – but his most successful partnership was with Harold Arlen. On Broadway they wrote *Hooray for What!* (1937), *Bloomer Girl* (1944) and *Jamaica* (1957), and in Hollywood created a series of musical films beginning with *Gold Diggers of 1937* and including *The Wizard of Oz* (1939). Harburg's last Broadway show, *Darling of the Day* (1968), had music by Jule Styne.

Yip sings Harburg Edgar 'Yip' Harburg (sngr/pf); [a]Sammy Fain, [b]Earl Robinson, [c]Jay Gorney (pfs).

Koch International Classics mono Ⓟ 37386-2 (68 minutes: AAD). Texts included. Recorded at performances in New York and Martha's Vineyard between 1939-80.
Songs from **H. Arlen:** The Wizard of Oz. A Day at the Circus. Life Begins at 8:40. Bloomer Girl. Jamaica. The Great Magoo. **Duke:** Walk a Little Faster. Ziegfeld Follies of 1934. **B. Lane:** Finian's Rainbow. **Fain:** Flahooley[a]. **E. Robinson:** The same boat, brother[b]. **Gorney:** Americana[c].

'Yip' Harburg has an assured place in the pantheon of twentieth-century lyricists as author of, among others, "April in Paris", "Lydia the tattooed lady" and *The Wizard of Oz* score. After being rescued from the Wall Street crash by Jay Gorney, with whom he wrote "Brother, can you spare a dime?", he formed a long but intermittent partnership with Harold Arlen, teamed up with Burton Lane for *Finian's Rainbow* (1947), then fell foul of the un-American activities committee, an experience which fuelled his satire on American capitalism, *Flahooley* (1951), the Broadway show in which Barbara Cook made her début. As late as 1968, when the writing was on the wall for many of his colleagues, he and Jule Styne composed *Darling of the Day*, a charming score, although unrepresented in this collection.

Most of his performances on this CD emanate from the "Lyrics and Lyricists Series", 1970-80, given before a New York audience who reserve their biggest cheer for "When I'm not near the girl I love", that joyous number from *Finian's Rainbow*, sung in the show by a randy leprechaun. Other recordings have been caught on the wing or from a distance, such as a private recording from 1951 of "Something sort of grandish". What we have, then, is a warts-and-all presentation of his art ranging from gems like "It's only a paper moon" to the embarrassing "Monkey in the mango tree". Although a fascinating document for the collector, for the general listener I would recommend the recent Sylvia McNair/André Previn disc, "Come Rain or Come Shine" (see separate review under Arlen) where the two performers recreate with much affection many of the Harburg/Arlen titles given here. **AE**

Leigh Harline

1907-1969 USA

Born in Salt Lake City, Harline studied at the University of Utah and with J. Spencer Cornwall, conductor of the Mormon Tabernacle Choir. In 1928 he relocated to Los Angeles where, from 1932-42, he was on the staff at Walt Disney Studios, composing for the Silly Symphony series and Disney's first two full-length animated features, *Snow White and the Seven Dwarfs* (1937, in collaboration with Frank Churchill and Paul Smith) and *Pinocchio* (1940, also with Smith). The score and the song "When you wish upon a star" from the latter film won him Academy Awards. After leaving Disney, Harline wrote prolifically for other studios, principally RKO and 20th Century-Fox, producing scores for dozens of films.

Pinocchio 1940 **Film Cast** (with Cliff Edwards, Dickie Jones and Walter Catlett) **/ Leigh Harline, Paul J. Smith**.
Walt Disney Records Ⓟ WDR75430-2 (62 minutes: ADD).

Another superbly restored treasure from the Disney archives. Selections from this and other Disney classics have been available over the years in a variety of formats, but never with such clarity, which yields new insights into this magical score. For this CD reissue the original master tapes have been cleaned up by restorer Michael Leon and his team, and the music now sparkles with a vivacity that lives up to the cliché of its timelessness. "When you wish upon a star" has become Disney's unofficial anthem, while "Give a little whistle", "I've got no strings" and "Hi-diddle-dee-dee" have all been heard so many times in different guises that it is quite easy to forget their actual source. The remarkable and insightful scoring of Leigh Harline is a revelation, although when one considers how much effort Walt Disney lavished on the animation, it should come as no surprise to realize that the same care and attention was given to the music, resulting in a score with a style and inventiveness all of its own. **JW**

Ray Henderson
1896-1970 USA

Buddy De Sylva
1895-1950 USA

Lew Brown
1893-1958 USA

The songwriting team of De Sylva, Brown and Henderson was formed in 1925. Composer Ray Henderson, born Raymond Brost, had studied at the Chicago Conservatory of Music and worked as a pianist and song-plugger in New York. He had his first hit with "Georgette" from the *Greenwich Village Follies of 1922*. He wrote "Alabamy bound" (1925) with Bud Green and Buddy De Sylva. De Sylva was raised in Los Angeles, the son of a vaudeville artist. With composer Gus Kahn he had written "I'll say she does" (1918) for Al Jolson. He also wrote lyrics for George Gershwin ("Nobody but you", 1920) and Jerome Kern ("Look for the silver lining", 1920). Lew Brown, born Louis Browstein, had written "Give me the moonlight, give me the girl" (1917) which was adopted by Frankie Vaughan as his signature tune. De Sylva, Brown and Henderson first collaborated on *George White's Scandals of 1925* – a flop – and then on the 1926 *Scandals*, which was a great success, enabling them in 1927 to produce their first show, *Good News!*. They followed this with other comedies in a similar vein, including *Hold Everything!* (1928), *Following Thru'* (1929) and *Flying High* (1930). The trio established their own publishing house, giving them creative control over their own songs. Their first film musical, *Sunny Side Up* (1929), was a success, but *Just Imagine* (1930) failed, causing De Sylva to leave the team for a career as a film producer. Henderson and Brown continued writing songs for shows, including *George White's Scandals of 1931*, which was the first show to have its hit songs released as a 12-inch 78rpm album, sung by Bing Crosby and the Boswell Sisters. When Brown also moved to Hollywood, Henderson teamed up with Ted Koehler and Irving Caesar to write "Animal crackers in my soup" for Shirley Temple in the movie *Curly Top* (1935). A biopic about the songwriting team, *The Best Things in Life are Free*, was made in 1956.

Good News! 1995 Studio Cast (with Kim Huber, Ann Morrison, Linda Michele, Michael Gruber, Hal Davis, Jessica Boevers, Michael McCormick and Mark Madama); **Chorus; National Symphony Orchestra / Craig Barna**.
TER Ⓕ CDTER1230 (52 minutes: DDD).

Gerald Boardman described *Good News!*, a college football show of the 1920s, as "the quintessential musical comedy of the era of wonderful nonsense ... mirrored in a hilarious melody-packed evening". Five of its songs became standards, of which "The varsity drag" and "The best things in life are free" are still fondly remembered. With the enchanting "Lucky in love" and "Just imagine" amongst that group, it would hardly seem necessary to bolster the score with other De Sylva, Brown and Henderson songs, but that's what this recording offers us, taking as its cue a short-lived Broadway revival of 1974 that underwent a complete revision for a production at the Music Theater of Wichita in 1993. The additional songs are perfectly in keeping with the spirit of the piece and are delightfully performed by a relatively unknown yet very attractive ensemble, with immaculate orchestral playing under conductor Craig Barna. Save for a hint of strain in the opening choral ensemble, this unexpected addition to the show music catalogue, in excellent sound, is heartily welcome.   **AE**

New review
The Best Things in Life are Free The Songs of Ray Henderson. With **Jack Hylton, Frank Crumit, Nathan Glantz, Howard Lannin, The California Ramblers, Gene Austin, Annette Hanshaw, Layton and Johnstone, Johnny Marvin, Zelma O'Neal, Al Jolson, Ruth Etting, The High Hatters, Johnny Hamps, Rudy Vallée, Paul Robeson, Hutch, Cliff "Ukelele Ike" Edwards, Shirley Temple, Bing Crosby, Jack Teagarden, Dick Haymes, Helen Forrest** and **Harry Roy.**
ASV Living Era mono Ⓜ CDAJA5207 (77 minutes: ADD). Recorded 1925-44.

Ray Henderson was the purveyor of some of the most potent melodies of the 1920s, including "Black bottom", "The varsity drag", "You're the cream in my coffee" and "Birth of the blues", all of them from Broadway shows. In Hollywood he composed the score for *Sunnyside Up* (1929), an early and innovative 20th Century-Fox musical, as well as numbers for Al Jolson ("Sonny boy" from *The Singing Fool*, 1929) and Shirley Temple ("Animal crackers in my soup" from *Curly*

Top, 1935), both of which are sung here by the original artists. Other highlights include Jack Hylton's renditions of "The best things in life are free" from *Good News!* (1927) and "If I had a talking picture of you" (*Sunnyside Up*) – both inventive in performance and full-bodied in recording – and the distinctive timbres and charms of Layton and Johnstone in "Bye bye, Blackbird", Hutch in "Life is just a bowl of cherries" and Ruth Etting in "Button up your overcoat". Potent melodies, yes, but there is nothing cheap about these performances. Peter Dempsey's booklet-note is an additional attraction to this entry in ASV's ongoing series.   **AE**

David Heneker b. 1906 England

Born into an army family, Heneker was educated at Wellington College and Sandhurst, and was a serving army officer until 1948. Afterwards, he began writing for the stage and scored hits in 1958 with *Expresso Bongo* and the English adaptation of Marguerite Monnot's *Irma la Douce*, which were both collaborations with Monty Norman (later composer of the "James Bond" theme"). *Bongo* was filmed in 1959 starring Cliff Richard. Amongst others, Heneker has also written *Half a Sixpence* (1963) for Tommy Steele, *Charlie Girl* (1965), *The Biograph Girl* (1980) and *Peg* (1982).

The Biograph Girl 1980 **London Cast** (with Sheila White, Bruce Barry, Ron Berglas, Philip Griffiths, Jane Hardy, Richard Kates, Tano Rea, Kate Revill and Guy Siner) **/ Michael Reed**. TER Ⓕ CDTER1003 (48 minutes: ADD).

David Heneker's homage to the silent movie era enjoyed an all too brief run in London in 1980. Fortunately, it lasted long enough for the cast to lay down this recording which preserves the show's naïve charm and delicate nostalgia. Ironically, those qualities may have contributed to box office failure at a time when audience appetite for spectacle was already anticipating the high-tech blockbusters of the decade to come. *Mack and Mabel*, which covered similar territory on a grander scale, died a death on Broadway almost as soon as it opened in 1974 and wasn't seen in London until the mid-1990s. Nevertheless, *The Biograph Girl* is fondly remembered by those who did get to see it. Heneker's witty score has a bit of everything: furiously jangling pianos, Dixieland jazz, a tango and a couple of plangent ballads. Warner Brown's book manages to cram in the decline and fall of D. W. Griffith, the scandal which surrounded the release of his masterwork *Birth of a Nation* and biographies of major early film stars Mary Pickford, Lillian Gish and Mack Sennett. Sheila White is outstanding as Pickford, conveying the steely business sense of the private woman ("I like to be the way I am in my own front parlour") which lay beneath the baby-voiced public persona ("Working in flickers"). Bruce Barry is a dignified, earnest Griffith, resigned to the advent of the talkies which will make him yesterday's man ("One of the pioneers"), and Kate Revill is a touching Gish, in thrall to Griffith's artistry ("More than a man"). A poignant, unsophisticated little treat.   **PF**

Charlie Girl 1986 **London Cast** (with Paul Nicholas, Cyd Charisse, Dora Bryan, Nicholas Parsons, Mark Wynter and Lisa Hull) **/ Ian McMillan**. First Night Ⓜ OCRCD6009 (57 minutes: DDD).

Depending on your point of view, *Charlie Girl* is either a quaint 1960s period piece in which the upper classes get to slum it with "Fish 'n' chips", and the chirpy Cockney hero and his aristocratic sweetheart bridge the social divide with love; or a tawdry bauble which encapsulates everything mediocre in post-war British musical theatre. Whichever camp you belong to, it is hard to ignore *Charlie Girl*'s historic five-and-a-half-year run of 2,202 performances in the West End. However, the 1986 revival, of which this is the recording, only lasted for six months, in spite of a revised score. Today, this sort of show is probably best viewed as good old-fashioned entertainment. This recording is notable for the valiant efforts of a noble bunch of troupers who bring a touch of class to some rather ordinary numbers. Lisa Hull certainly makes a clear-voiced impression in the title role ("Bells will ring" and "Like love") and Paul Nicholas as Joe has ample opportunity to indulge his popular appeal as the jovial Cockney chap made good ("Charlie Girl", "My favourite occupation" – one of the best songs in the score, "I 'ates money" and the aforementioned "Fish 'n' chips"). Hollywood legend Cyd Charisse adds a touch of glamour as Charlie's mother, Lady Hadwell, although she was better known for her dancing than her singing (check out her *diseuse* treatment of "When I hear music I dance", complete with an angelic chorus). As her old comrade in arms, Kay Connor, Dora Bryan offers an irresistible "Party of a lifetime". Undemanding stuff with a good old-fashioned happy ending, and remembered with affection by some.

PF

Half a Sixpence 1963 **London Cast** (with Tommy Steele, Marti Webb, Cheryl Kennedy, Anthony Valentine, Sheila Reid, Arthur Brough and James Grout) / **Kenneth Alwyn**. Deram Ⓜ 820 589-2 (46 minutes: AAD).

This fresh and invigorating musical version of H. G. Wells's *Kipps* provided versatile teenage pop star Tommy Steele with the part of a lifetime: one he was to repeat on Broadway and also in the subsequent film. Beverley Cross's succinct libretto and David Heneker's excellent music and lyrics gave the show's star and a fine supporting cast much to work with – and they did extremely well. Steele and company made the most of the showstopper, the rumbustious "Flash, bang, wallop" set in a photographer's studio (Heneker would write a similar number, "Fish 'n' chips" for *Charlie Girl*). The only version currently available on CD features the original (London) cast. It also features more of the score than any other version (both film and Broadway added additional songs, but dropped much more of the original). I'd be sorry to lose "The oak and the ash", a really authentic-sounding new folk song. Marti Webb is affecting as Kipps's sweetheart – her version of "I know what I am" is very appealing, and she joins in duets with Tommy Steele with a sweet appeal – "Long ago" and "Half a sixpence" are typical. The show, nevertheless, belongs to Steele who has the lion's share of the numbers and delivers them with a vivid commitment and panache that marked him out as a natural star of musical comedy.

MPK

Peg 1984 **London Cast** (with Sian Phillips, Edward Duke, John Hewer, Patricia Michael, Julia Sutton, David McAlister, Martin Smith and Ann Morrison) / **Kevin Amos**. TER Ⓔ CDTER1024 (56 minutes: DDD).

Based on J. Hartley Manners's Edwardian play *Peg o' My Heart*, David Heneker's charming little musical didn't last long in the West End when it opened in April 1984. Perhaps it was a victim of musical-goers' increasingly ravenous appetite for spectacle and extravagance but, like Heneker's other early 1980s work *The Biograph Girl*, of which some of the score is highly reminiscent, it deserved a longer run than it achieved. As the homesick American heiress, Ann Morrison turns in a winning performance. By turns wistful as she remembers her late father ("That's my father") or longs to return home ("The steamers go by"), and feisty as she battles with her paid guardian Mrs Chichester ("There's a devil in me"), she makes an appealing heroine. Martin Smith, as her suitor Jerry, gets to sing the Fred Fisher/Alfred Bryan standard "Peg o' my heart" with great tenderness. Sian Phillips, an actress of considerable style, came late to musicals but has impressed in a range of shows from *Pal Joey* to *A Little Night Music*. Here, as the enterprising Mrs Chichester, who agrees to 'finish' Peg for a sum of money which will solve the family's financial problems, she is imperious with a kind heart. "Fishing fleet", a rollicking music-hall number in which she recalls her own search for a husband, is one of the best songs in the score. *Peg*'s time may come again, once country house musicals with cheerful servants, perky songs like "How would you like me?" and simple romance come back into fashion.

PF

Also available:

Charlie Girl (1965 London Cast) Sony West End SMK66174

Jerry Herman

b. 1932 USA

New Yorker Jerry Herman taught himself to play the piano, despite his mother being a music teacher. He later studied drama at Miami University before returning to New York where he worked briefly as a nightclub pianist and began writing for television. *I Feel Wonderful*, his first revue, was staged off-Broadway in 1954; he followed this with *Nightcap* (1958) and *Parade* (1960). *Milk and Honey* (1961), his first Broadway show, won a Tony Award for the composer/lyricist and spawned the hit "Shalom". After a failure with *Mighty Aphrodite* (1961) he had his biggest hit to date with *Hello, Dolly!* in 1964, a show originally written for Ethel

Merman but which became a huge success for Carol Channing instead. When it finally closed in 1970 (by then belatedly starring Merman), it was Broadway's longest-running show with 2,844 performances (a record broken shortly afterwards by *Fiddler on the Roof*). *Dolly!* scooped an unprecedented ten Tony awards, and was filmed in 1969 with Barbra Streisand in the lead role. Louis Armstrong's rendition of the title song reached No. 1 in 1964 and was adopted by the Democratic Party's 1964 presidential campaign as "Hello, Lyndon!". *Mame* in 1966, starring Angela Lansbury, received another Tony and ran for 1,508 performances (with a further 443 in London) but subsequent shows *Dear World* (1969 – also with Lansbury), *Mack and Mabel* (1974) and *The Grand Tour* (1979) were all relatively unsuccessful. Herman had to wait until 1983 before scoring another big hit with *La Cage aux Folles*, the first Broadway show to deal overtly with homosexuality. In 1996 he wrote a successful TV musical, *Mrs Santa Clause*, for Angela Lansbury.

La Cage aux Folles 1983 **Broadway Cast** (with Gene Barry, George Hearn and John Weiner) **/ Donald Pippin**.
RCA Ⓕ BD84824 (54 minutes: DDD).

It looks as if Jerry Herman has taken early retirement from the Broadway stage with this, his most recent score, now 12 years old. In 1994, the West End finally caught up with *Mack and Mabel*, undoubtedly his most distinctive score but here we have his most succinct offering, presenting for the first time, a gay love affair to a mainstream Broadway audience. Those familar with the movie will recall the subject being handled with such humour and honesty that the specific nature of the relationship is transcended. This musical takes the same line. Conservative and reassuring, it only once challenges us to accept Albin as he is – "I am what I am". There are nine numbers in the score, each one sitting snugly into the plot and all of them exuding a robust tunefulness that has become Herman's hallmark. One number, "Song on the sand", a ballad of romantic devotion sung by Georges to his lover is one of Herman's simplest yet most touching creations. Gene Barry and George Hearn are the stars and they perform well together, yet I remember Hearn and Denis Quilley exuding more fun in the unrecorded London Palladium production. Donald Pippin conducts an outstanding ensemble in RCA's recording that captures the glitter and slightly tawdry air of the nightclub to a tee.　　　　　　**AE**

New review
Hello, Dolly! 1964 **Broadway Cast** (with Carol Channing, David Burns, Charles Nelson Reilly, Eileen Brennan, Sondra Lee and Jerry Dodge) **/ Shepard Coleman**.
RCA Victor Ⓜ GD83814 (43 minutes: ADD).
Hello, Dolly! 1967 **Broadway Cast** (with Pearl Bailey and Cab Calloway) **/ Saul Schechtman**.
RCA Victor Ⓜ GD81147 (46 minutes: ADD).
Hello, Dolly! 1969 **Film Cast** (with Barbra Streisand, Walter Matthau, Michael Crawford and Louis Armstrong) **/ Lennie Hayton, Lionel Newman.**
Philips Ⓜ 810 368-2 (50 minutes: ADD).
Hello, Dolly! 1994 **American Cast** (with Carol Channing, Jay Garner and Florence Lacey) **/ Tim Stella**.
Varèse Sarabande Spotlight Series Ⓕ VSD5557 (56 minutes: DDD).

The ultimate star-comes-down-a-staircase musical, *Hello, Dolly!* is an old-fashioned show and proud of it. It's been Carol Channing's calling card for over 30 years, and indeed her original cast recording has imperishable splendour with the star competing in growliness with her co-star David Burns. The score is simply gorgeous – catchy, highly appropriate for the time in which the show is set, and extremely effective. "Elegance" (actually by Bob Merrill) is indeed elegant, and "Before the parade passes by" is both wistful and triumphant. And then there's the title-song ... irresistible. Well worth investigating is Pearl Bailey's version with Cab Calloway – it's surprisingly successful (and my own personal favourite). It has a wonderful Mrs Molloy in Emily Yancey. Unless you really must have the "Waiters' Gallop", ignore Channing's 1994 remake – her voice had become a parody of itself by then. Her fellow artistes are first class, though. Much more tempting is the Barbra Streisand film soundtrack. The obvious age difference between hero and heroine doesn't matter on record, and you get two fine additional songs, "Just leave everything to me" and "Love is only love", and even if Streisand plays the matchmaker as Dolly Levi Gallagher rather than Dolly Gallagher Levi, who cares? Hers is a totally committed performance, and she sings with intelligence, authority and conviction. Where else will you find Walter Matthau singing at his curmudgeonly best? It's at least the equal of Lee Marvin in *Paint Your Wagon*. The sound is wonderfully widescreen and a fine bonus is the luxury casting of Louis Armstrong who sidles on for the title-tune. **MPK**

New review
The Jerry Herman Songbook Michael Feinstein; Jerry Herman (pf).
Nonesuch Ⓟ 7559-79315-2 (58 minutes: DDD).
Songs from A Day in Hollywood/A Night in the Ukraine, Milk and Honey, Hello Dolly!, Dear World, La Cage Aux Folles, The Grand Tour, Mame, Ben Franklin in Paris, Mack and Mabel.

"I've been accused of being old fashioned all my life. What people don't realize is that I take it as the greatest compliment." Jerry Herman's own words sum up his position in the musical theatre as the final custodian of the Rodgers and Hammerstein tradition. In preparing this recording, he and Feinstein were keen to include rarer numbers alongside the *Dollys* and *Mames*. One of them is a little masterpiece: "Penny in my pocket" describes how Horace Vandergelder made his first half-million. Unfortunately, it came too late in *Hello, Dolly!* for the audience to care, so it was cut. The song encapsulates Herman's virtues as a song craftsman with a strong visual sense coming through in the lyric. Not everyone takes to Feinstein's stylized way with a ballad, several of which are scattered throughout this CD, but even they would find it hard to resist his interpretations of the lightly tripping "Just go to the movies", "With you on my arm" or "Mame", where Herman joins him on vocals and piano for a blockbuster rendition. As ever in this series the balance between voices and the exceptionally fine piano, is a model of its kind. **AE**

Jerry's Girls 1984 American Cast (with Carol Channing, Leslie Uggams and Andrea McArdle) / Janet Glazener.
TER Ⓟ CDTER2 1093 (two discs: 97 minutes: DDD).

At the beginning of his career, Jerry Herman wrote a nightclub revue called *Nightcap* (1958) whose highlight was "Show tune in 2/4", a tribute to (and example of) the traditional Broadway rouser. Some years later he reworked the melody as "It's today", the best of the (mostly interchangeable) cheer-up songs in *Mame*. The tune appears in *Jerry's Girls* in both these incarnations, plus a third during the title song, paying tribute to the leading ladies who have appeared as Herman's heroines, especially the indestructible Dolly and Mame, down the decades. Between them the three numbers say a lot about Herman's talent and his appeal. He offers, for the most part, divas in showstoppers, and this anthology – which toured America before landing briefly in New York – is a faithful reflection of that. It isn't an exhaustive representation of Herman's range; it excludes *The Grand Tour* (1979) which is about a couple of guys, but it admits *La Cage aux Folles* (1983) which is also about a couple of guys, one of whom happens to be a female impersonator. In so doing it points up – maybe inadvertently – the kinship of diva-worship and drag.

In the all-female cast of nine, only the three stars get solos; and they all, in varying degrees, deliver (the show should have been recorded live; applause is its *raison d'etre*). Carol Channing, the original Jerry's Girl, takes very well to the gleeful heartlessness of *Mack and Mabel*'s "Tap your troubles away", sportingly and screechingly sends up "Hello, Dolly!", goes riotously Yiddish in "Take it all off", which is a burlesque of burlesque (source undisclosed), and enjoys herself hatcheting Dietrich in the title song from *La Cage*. Andrea McArdle, a few years on from creating the title role in *Annie*, makes quite a good comic fist of "Gooch's song" from *Mame* but otherwise functions as an efficient but anonymous young trouper. The revelation is Leslie Uggams, her burnished, clarion voice stripped of mannerisms and excess, taking over "Movies were movies" and finding real emotion in "I won't send roses" and in two songs from *Dear World*: "I don't want to know" and the beautiful, unfamiliar "Kiss her now." The composer himself appears at the end for "Jerry's turn": a medley of "My best girl" (now pluralized), "Hundreds of girls", and his two trademark title songs; you're left wondering whether this was part of the show on a nightly basis. **RC**

Mack and Mabel 1974 Broadway Cast (with Robert Preston, Bernadette Peters and Lisa Kirk) / Donald Pippin.
MCA Ⓜ MCLD19089 (46 minutes: AAD).

Mack and Mabel 1995 **London Cast** (with Howard McGillin, Caroline O'Connor and Kathryn Evans) / **Julian Kelly**.
EMI ℗ CDEMC3734 (66 minutes: DDD).

The first vocal cut on the original cast *Mack and Mabel* is "Movies were movies", Mack Sennett's rollicking remembrance of his days as the king of silent comedy, delivered with incomparable panache and authority by Robert Preston, who of all stars turned ebullience into art. Then, in flashback, comes "Look what happened to Mabel", one of Jerry Herman's most delectable tunes graced with some of his nimblest lyrics; Bernadette Peters is bewitchingly bewildered as Mabel Normand, raised from deli assistant to movie queen. These are two terrific list-songs, even if they repeat themselves when they should really go on inventing. Next, Lisa Kirk, who had one of the most attractive of Broadway's belting voices and didn't get to use it often enough, leads the ensemble in "Big time", whose joyful *schadenfreude* ("This time we won't say 'those lucky bastards'/This time those lucky bastards are us") makes it one of the toughest showbiz songs extant; this isn't one of those self-consciously 'dark' musicals but there seems to be an iron fist inside Herman's customary velvet glove. Then the two stars take turns on "I won't send roses", a piercing if short-breathed anti-love song. Few shows have sported a more attractive clutch of opening numbers. The middle of the score doesn't maintain the same level, but things pick up again on the last lap with the bracingly poignant "Time heals everything" for Peters; "Tap your troubles away", another acrid celebration for Kirk; and Preston's defiantly bitter-sweet "I promise you a happy ending".

The show flopped; it had book trouble, which the dip in the score reflects. Nevertheless, over the years it became a favourite with Radio 2 (not to mention Torvill and Dean), and an eventual London production was inevitable. This substituted a genuine happy ending for the original's make-believe, thus ruining the wishful-thinking closing number. There is little wrong with the ensemble, and Caroline O'Connor is all right as Mabel, but Howard McGillin – excellent on Broadway in *Anything Goes*, *Kiss of the Spider Woman* and *She Loves Me* – is disastrously miscast as Mack, lacking gusto, machismo, and even humour; when he sings "I wanna make the world laugh" he sounds in need of career-counselling. His voice – technically far better than Preston's – serves him well on "Hundreds of girls", but when he flourishes his top notes at the climax of "I won't send roses" he appears not so much self-obsessed, as narcissistic. The score remains Herman's best, and there is more of it than on the American release, but on that – perfunctorily produced and packaged though it is – you get definitive performance: the brightest of Broadway's current leading ladies partnering Broadway's best ever leading man. **RC**

Mame 1966 **Broadway Cast** (with Angela Lansbury, Beatrice Arthur, Jane Connell, Willard Waterman and Frankie Michaels) / **Donald Pippin**.
Columbia Ⓜ CK03000 (50 minutes: AAD).

The emergence of Angela Lansbury as a major Broadway singing star may have been something of a surprise to some (her singing voice was usually dubbed in her early MGM films in which she never played the lead), but she has become a major star – and television's highest-paid actress. In her musical career she has been particularly identified with two composers: Stephen Sondheim, and as here, Jerry Herman (who recently wrote for her the first original US TV musical for decades, *Mrs Santa Claus*). Herman's witty, melodically resplendent version of the play *Auntie Mame* finds the actress in winning form, pointing up all the happy felicities of one of the composer's finest scores (which some prefer to his *Hello, Dolly!*), including "It's today", "If he walked into my life" and "That's how young I feel". Beatrice Arthur as the wisecracking but warmhearted friend Vera adds extra spice to "Bosom buddies" and "The man in the moon". Jane Connell, another accomplished *farceur*, has another high spot in "Gooch's song". Some spirited chorus work in the title song sets the seal on one of producer Goddard Lieberson's happiest Broadway cast albums. *Mame* is a must. **MPK**

Also available:
Dear World (1969 Broadway Cast) Sony Broadway SK48220
Hello, Dolly! (1969 Film Cast) Philips 810 368-2
Hello, Dolly! (Studio Cast) Carlton Shows Collection 30362 0025-2
Mack and Mabel (1988 UK Cast) First Night OCRCD6015
Milk and Honey (1961 Broadway Cast) RCA Victor 09026 61997-2
Mrs Santa Claus (1996 TV Cast) RCA Victor 09026 68665-2

Keith Herrmann

Romance, Romance 1988 **Broadway Cast** (with Scott Bakula, Alison Fraser, Deborah Graham and Robert Hoshour) **/ Kathy Sommer**.
TER Ⓕ CDTER1161 (68 minutes: DDD).

One of the most delightful musical surprises of the 1980s, *Romance, Romance* was that potentially dangerous evening made up of two separate and discrete musicals. The first is a bitter-sweet adventure set in the 1890s in which two high-born Viennese go slumming in disguise, fall for each other, but then become bored with the assumed poverty and revert to their more opulent selves. In the second, based on a contemporary French story, but updated to the present, two couples share a beach house and one of each decide to have an affair with each other, but think better of it before going too far. Keith Herrmann shows his versatility by exhibiting complete mastery of both nineteenth-century Viennese romantic and contemporary American idioms. He's matched with great vocal dexterity by lyricist Barry Harman. In the first part, *The Little Comedy* look out for "It's not too late" and "Yes it's love", while the second, *Summer Share*, is notable for "Words he didn't say", the moving title song and the witty "So glad I married her." There are 26 songs, none of which outstay their welcome. *Romance, Romance* is a delight. **MPK**

Also available:
Prom Queens Unchained (1997 Studio Cast) Original Cast Records OC9629

Bart Howard

b. 1916 USA

Born Howard Gustafsson, in Iowa, Bart Howard grew up in the era of Prohibition when he claimed his father was the town bootlegger and piano-player. Howard dropped out of school aged 16, then went on the road, playing in dance and hotel bands, in vaudeville, until he went to New York where he played in some famous night-clubs, such as Tony's, Spivy's Roof and for eight years at the Blue Angel. Mabel Mercer engaged him to be her pianist, and many other great musical stars featured his songs.

New review
In Other Words The Songs of Bart Howard. **KT Sullivan**, with **William Roy** (pf), **John Loehrke** (bass), **Jimmie Young** (drums), **Mia Wu** (violin).
DRG Ⓕ 91449 (61 minutes DDD). Recorded at a performance in July 1996.

Bart Howard's most famous song, "Fly me to the moon", was first sung by Felicia Sanders, when the title was still "In other words". When Peggy Lee took it up she had the title changed to the version that became world famous, and guaranteed Howard's income for the rest of his life. His songs seem to sum up the whole mood of old-style New York cabaret, bittersweet, knowing and intimate in a way that will add to the feeling of being in the right place at the right time. "If you leave Paris", the song that first brought him the attention of Mabel Mercer, and such ditties as "You are not my first love", "It was worth it!" and "Man in the looking glass" are all given the authentic treatment by KT Sullivan. Howard writes all his own lyrics, and he joins her for one number in this concert which was recorded for his 80th birthday in July 1996. **PO'C**

Jim Jacobs

Warren Casey

Grease 1978 **Film Cast** (with John Travolta, Olivia Newton-John, Stockard Channing and Frankie Avalon).
Polydor Ⓕ 817 998-2 (64 minutes: AAD).
Grease 1994 **Broadway Cast** (with Rosie O'Donnell, Ricky Paull Gildin, Susan Wood, Jason Opsahl and Sam Harris) **/ John McDaniel**.
RCA Victor Ⓕ 09026 62703 2 (59 minutes: DDD).
Grease 1994 **Studio Cast** (with John Barrowman and Shona Lindsay); **NSO Ensemble / Martin Yates**.
TER Ⓕ CDTER1220 (54 minutes: DDD).

The film soundtrack of *Grease*, with John Travolta and Olivia Newton-John, will probably remain first choice for a single recording of this early 1970s Broadway show. The on-screen chemistry between its stars, and the addition of several new numbers by other hands, turned a stage show that had had little international success – in London it ran just six months – into a monster hit. Since then there have been new productions of *Grease* on the London and Broadway stages, both still running. The London one which includes the film's hits "You're the one that I want", "Hoplesssly devoted to you" and "Grease" might seem the one to go for, but it turns out to be outclassed in all respects by RCA's Broadway recording, a really smooth production with some spot on idiomatic solo performances, a slick *a capella* group and a great band. Moreover by going back to and sticking with the original score and late 1950s storyline, this recording really gives you the 'shoo-be-do' 'wham-bam-boom' teenage idiom of the time. On TER, John Barrowman leads a company in a very good alternative to the 1993 London company recording with one star, Mark Wynter, representative of the period itself. This recording gives us the clearest words and there are some attractive arrangements by conductor Martin Yates. **AE**

Also available:
Grease (1972 Broadway Cast) Polydor 827 548-2
Grease (1993 London Cast) Epic 474632-2
Grease (1993 Studio Cast) Carlton Shows Collection PWKS4176

John Kander
b. 1927 USA

Fred Ebb
b. 1932 USA

Born in Kansas City and educated at Oberlin College and Columbia University, John Kander began working on Broadway as a rehearsal pianist, then a conductor and arranger. He wrote his first show, *The Family Affair*, in 1962, but it was not until joining forces with lyricist Fred Ebb that he had a hit with *Flora, the Red Menace* (1965), incidentally providing Liza Minnelli with her first starring role. Like Kander, Ebb had also studied at Columbia University before contributing to Broadway revues such as *From A to Z* (1960), writing the book for *Morning Sun* (1963) and working on the satirical TV series *That Was the Week That Was*. Kander and Ebb followed *Flora* with *Cabaret* in 1966, which ran for 1,166 performances (326 in London) and won Tony and Drama Critics' awards. *Cabaret* was filmed in 1972 with Minnelli as its star. Kander and Ebb's other shows include *The Happy Time* (1968), *70, Girls, 70* (1971), *Chicago* (1975) and *Woman of the Year* (1981). They contributed songs to various films: "How lucky can you get" for Barbra Streisand in *Funny Lady* (1975) and "New York, New York", once again for Liza Minnelli from the 1977 film of the same name. In 1992 they had another hit with *Kiss of the Spider Woman*, based on Manuel Puig's novel and the subsequent film, which unusually opened in Toronto and London before finally moving to Broadway. 1996 saw a revival of *Chicago* (which came to London in 1997) and the sadly short-lived new show *Steel Pier*.

New review
The Act 1977 Broadway Cast (with Liza Minnelli, Roger Minami and Gayle Crofoot).
DRG Ⓜ CDRG6101 (48 minutes: AAD).

The Act stands and falls on Liza Minnelli. On Broadway it stood when she performed with the full flood of her vivacious, barnstorming self. It likewise fell when she tired of the nightly grind and, after first seeking to get by with pre-recorded tapes, finally bowed out of the show altogether. In truth it is not so much a stage musical, as a Las Vegas cabaret act transported to Broadway. There is very little at all for the supporting characters in a story (such as it is) featuring Minnelli as faded ex-film star Michelle Craig making her come-back as a nightclub singer at the Miramar Hotel. Kander and Ebb, who had supplied her with various hits over the years, do their stuff here with brassy numbers such as "Shine it on", "Bobo's", "The money tree" and "City lights", all of which Minnelli delivers with her usual style and aplomb. This should really be regarded as a Minnelli album, with not quite the best of Kander and Ebb, but material tailor-made for the star performer. **AML**

Cabaret 1968 **London Cast** (with Judi Dench, Lila Kedrova, Peter Sallis, Kevin Colson and Barry Dennen) **/ Gareth Davies.**
Sony West End Ⓜ SMK53494 (65 minutes: ADD).

Cabaret 1986 **London Cast** (with Wayne Sleep, Oscar Quitak, Peter Land, Rodney Cottam, Grazina Frame, Vivienne Martin and Kelly Hunter) **/ Gareth Valentine.**
First Night Ⓜ OCRCD6010 (53 minutes: ADD).

New review
Cabaret 1997 **Studio Cast** (with Jonathan Pryce, Judi Dench, Fred Ebb, Gregg Edelman, Maria Friedman, John Mark Ainsley); **National Symphony Orchestra / John Owen Edwards.**
TER Ⓔ CDTER2 1210 (two discs: 110 minutes: DDD).

Harold Prince's production of *Cabaret* at the Palace Theatre in 1968 is for me the most memorable of his considerable list of credits, and this recording in Sony's West End series proves to be a happy memento, dominated by Judi Dench's portrayal of Sally Bowles the naughty but nice girl "having a marvellous time" in 1930s Berlin. The one drawback is the really unpleasantly claustrophobic recording reminiscent of Sony's contemporary release, Cy Coleman's *Sweet Charity*. So the reissue of the recording of the second London production where things are immeasurably better on that count is very welcome. Here, every performer offers something distinctive under Gareth Valentine's sensitive musical direction. Both recordings, of course, give us the complete score with which the film version played truant. The First Night disc also offers "Maybe this time", a song written some years earlier but now regarded as an integral part of *Cabaret*, and the revised money song.

One of the many virtues of TER's new recording of Kander and Ebb's first Broadway hit is how well the songs that develop character and storyline stand up outside of the cabaret itself. These, you may recall, were the ones that Bob Fosse cut from his renowned screen treatment of *Cabaret*. Given how musically and dramatically illuminating they are, one wonders, in the light of these performances, whether a remake of that film isn't in order! Songs like Sally and Cliff's "Perfectly marvellous" aren't easy to sing, but Friedman and Edelman make it sound effortless. Notice that when he enters, the conductor adopts a fractionally slower tempo allowing the romantic moment to flourish before building up to an exhilarating finish, turning a potentially awkward number into a great show duet. We find such a transformation, too, in Fraulein Schneider's songs sung by Dame Judi Dench. She knows this score well having sung Sally Bowles in the original London production of 1968. Her haunting account of "What would you do?", where she peers into a bleak future, raises a grim spectre of the world on its dark side. In this new recording Maria Friedman's Sally is refreshing, vivacious, and vulnerable. There are few singer-actresses today who could make a listener forget all the many versions of *Cabaret*'s title-song and come through with a terrifically exciting finish, the tone broadening out on the last word, the orchestra playing full tilt. The dialogue scenes between her and Greg Edelman's Cliff are beautifully produced. It was an innovative stroke to cast Fred Ebb, *Cabaret*'s lyricist, as Fraulein Schneider's admirer, but for me, the casting doesn't quite come off, maybe because I still treasure Peter Sallis in this key role on that Sony disc. Jonathan Pryce as the MC eschews Joel Grey's master of the sleaze routine seemingly for something more ordinary, yet it's that very quality that makes his portrayal so scary – his performance is the most convincing of the several musical roles he's now recorded. Any qualms about the open acoustic of his first number, "Wilkommen", are quickly forgotten as the drama unfolds. John Mark Ainsley introduces the round, "Tomorrow belongs to me" in a golden tone, a vocal replica of the Aryan youth he represents. Don Walker's imaginative orchestrations sound marvellous, especially when played as well as they are here under John Owen Edwards. This is another hit for the TER team. **AE**

New review
Chicago 1996 **Broadway Cast** (with Ann Reinking, Bebe Neuwirth, James Naughton and Joel Grey) **/ Rob Fisher.**
RCA Victor Ⓔ 09026 68727-2 (74 minutes: DDD).

"Ladies and Gentlemen, you are about to see a story of murder, greed, corruption, violence, exploitation, adultery and treachery – all the things we hold near and dear to our hearts": the stage is set even before the opening of *Chicago*. The memorable original cast recording (now deleted), featuring Gwen Verdon, Chita Rivera and Jerry Orbach, ran for 55 minutes. The new recording is some 20 minutes longer, with four new tracks. Ann Reinking sounds uncannily like

Verdon; Bebe Neuwirth (Lilith from TV's *Frasier* and Chita Rivera's takeover in the London edition of Kander and Ebb's *Kiss of the Spiderwoman*) is just as positive but is no Rivera soundalike. The main new items are "I know a girl" for Neuwirth and the band's "Hot honey rag". In the 22 years since it premièred on Broadway the show has lost none of its electricity, and this new recording is definitive. As luxury casting, Joel Grey (the original MC from the same team's *Cabaret*) takes a minor role and sings "Mr Cellophane" with pathos. James Naughton is an oh-so-smooth corrupt lawyer. But the show belongs to the women: Reinking's Roxie and Neuwirth's Velma charge through such delights as "All that jazz" and "My own best friend" as if their lives depended on it – as, in the show, they do. There's an alert band under Rob Fisher and superb recording to match. Full lyrics are enclosed. **MPK**

Flora, the Red Menace 1965 Broadway Cast (with Liza Minnelli, Bob Dishy, Mary Louise
    Wilson, Cathryn Damon, Robert Kaye, Joe E. Marks, Stephanie Hill, James Cresson and
    Dortha Duckworth) / **Hal Hastings**.
    RCA Victor ⑩ 09026 60821-2 (47 minutes: ADD).

Flora, the Red Menace 1987 Off-Broadway Cast (with Veanne Cox, Ray DeMattis, Peter
    Frechette, Maggy Gorrill, Lyn Greene, B. J. Jeffferson, Eddie Korbich, Dirk Lumbard and
    David Ossian) / **David Pogue**.
    TER Ⓕ CDTER1159 (67 minutes: DDD).

The long-running team of John Kander and Fred Ebb inaugurated their theatrical partnership with *Flora, the Red Menace*, set in Depression New York and concerning a girl lured by love and naïvete into a brief flirtation with Communism. It was a short-lived show but an auspicious début, both for young leading lady Liza Minnelli, who was to work many more times with Kander and Ebb, and for the composers themselves. There are a couple of dud songs, but nothing embarrassing; and the peaks glisten. "Sign here" is a funny if protracted patter-number in which Flora's stuttering boy-friend Harry, played terrifically by Bob Dishy, persuades her that her conscience and her future lie with the party; to hear Dishy demand "Do you want to make cannon-fodder of our youth?" is to appreciate the full force of the term 'rhetorical question'. Mary Louise Wilson as an equally dedicated comrade has an equally devastating number, "The flame". Minnelli gets, among much else, the lovely "A quiet thing", generally regarded as a song about finding love though it's actually about finding a job, and the desperately defiant "Sing happy"; she does both superbly. She is also the centrepiece of "You are you", one of the best in Kander and Ebb's rather extensive repertoire of philosophical self-affirmation songs. This is a flop that sounds like a hit.

    The usual explanation for its failure is that it didn't take its subject or its setting seriously enough. The miniature off-Broadway revival was far more politicized; the presence of the composer at the piano, and the addition of spoken Brechtian scene-headings, give it something of the air of Blitzstein's *The Cradle Will Rock*. It isn't propagandist – both Harry's commitment and Flora's honest lack of it are given their due – but a new song for Harry, "The joke", has a social anger for which Ebb has often reached before but that has generally sounded forced; this time it burns. There are other new songs (at least one of them, "The kid herself", a cut-out from the original) and a few excisions, only one of which is to be regretted: "Hello waves" in which Harry, his mouth full of pebbles, tries making like Demosthenes. Peter Frechette, if not as explosively funny as Dishy, is still excellent; and Veanne Cox, though lacking Minnelli's star-power, is a good Flora. Lyn Greene plays her rival, making far more than her predecessor of the vampy "Express yourself"; and the three share a fine new jealousy-trio called "Where did everybody go?" There is also – something this period show never had before – a pastiche number, "Keepin' it hot", for which Kander wrote a syncopated dance-tune that's somewhat George Gershwin, and Ebb a mock-precocious lyric that's decidedly Ira. This revised *Flora* may well be the better show, but the original – with its cast and its size, not to mention Don Walker's orchestrations – is unchallengeably the more enjoyable disc. **RC**

Kiss of the Spider Woman 1992 London Cast Recording (with Chita Rivera, Brent
    Carver and Anthony Crivello) / **Gareth Valentine**.
    First Night ⑩ OCRCD6030 (73 minutes: DDD).

This was an ambitious attempt to stage Manuel Puig's novel after it had become a hit film. It was a mixed success, with the dark storyline less conducive to musical treatment than the screen: the fantasies of an imprisoned window dresser sharing a cell and a relationship with another inmate, not to mention the spider woman herself who finally relieves his torture with a kiss of death – heady stuff! Chita Rivera is the Spider Woman who gets to sing the spell-binding title song. On a par with it is Molina's "Dressing them up" in which he (Brent Carver) describes his former profession, dressing window models, to his cell mate. Here, composer John Kander is at the top of his form – his music has a lightness of touch and rhythmic sleight of hand one can search for in vain in many recent musicals. Less convincing to my ear are the derivative sequences between the prisoners and their loved ones, and Valentin's song of freedom, "Day after day". However, the chilling "Morphine tango" hits home in the manner of this team's *Chicago* score; and the disc ends with "Only in the movies", a quintessential upbeat number in the team's *New York, New York* manner, signifying the final release for Molina from his imprisonment. **AE**

New review

The Rink 1984 **Broadway Cast** (with Chita Rivera and Liza Minnelli) **/ Tom Fay.**
    TER Ⓕ CDTER1091 (59 minutes: DDD).
The Rink 1988 **London Cast** (with Diane Langton and Josephine Blake) **/ David Beer.**
    TER Ⓕ CDTER1155 (72 minutes: DDD).

TER have cornered the market with their two recordings of Kander and Ebb's unusual but rewarding 1984 musical *The Rink* – the other roller skates musical of our time. For once, the setting is roughly contemporary. Mother and daughter are reconciled in Atlantic City at the roller skating rink owned by the family. Mother Anna and daughter Angel don't really get on, but Angel is tired of wandering and wants to come home. Anna has plans to sell the rink and move back to Italy. Angel won't hear of it. They quarrel and in flashbacks revisit their troubled past. All the other parts (male and female) are played by the six-man wrecking crew. Kander and Ebb have come up with a rousing honky-tonk score that fits the fairground background like a glove. There's an amusing duet, "The apple doesn't fall", a catchy title-song, a mystical and curiously touching memory of a purchase, "Blue crystal", and many rousing up-tempo toe-tappers that are typical of their creators. The Broadway cast starts with the advantage of two terrific original stars, Chita Rivera and Liza Minnelli, who bring dash and verve to their songs. The London cast happily matches them for zip and pizazz throughout. You also get an extra 13 minutes of dance music here for your money, and a better synopsis of the action. Perhaps the American wreckers sound slightly more authentic, and if you are enamoured of Liza Minnelli then this is the recording for you, but neither will disappoint – there are many good songs, well performed on both versions. **MPK**

New review

Steel Pier 1997 **Broadway Cast** (with Gregory Harrison, Karen Ziemba, Daniel McDonald and Debra Monk) **/ David Loud.**
    RCA Victor Ⓕ 09026 68878-2 (74 minutes: DDD).

It was sheer bad luck that Kander and Ebb's new show, *Steel Pier*, should find itself up against a fizzing revival of their amoral masterpiece *Chicago* on Broadway. The familiar won out over the new in awards and audiences. Yet this show finds its creators at the peak of their powers. *Steel Pier* is set in Atlantic City during 1933. Mick Hamilton is running a fixed dance marathon contest that his secret wife, Rita Racine, will win. Her partner is a stunt pilot, Bill Kelly, whom we realize is a ghost. Rita has been promised that this marathon will be Mick's last scam, but he doesn't mean it. By the end of the show, Rita has, with Bill's encouragement, summoned up the courage to leave Mick for good. The score is full of life and invention. A Gershwinesque overture is a trailer for many good jazzy/bluesy numbers that follow. Touching ballads like "The last girl" and "Somebody older" contrast beautifully with peppy numbers like "Everybody's girl" and "Everybody dance". Karen Ziemba is magnificent in her first major Broadway role; Gregory Harrison's Mick and Daniel McDonald's Bill provide firm support. The booklet includes all the lyrics; the show as recorded is a total delight. **MPK**

New review

Woman of the Year 1981 **Broadway Cast** (with Lauren Bacall, Harry Guardino, Roderick Cook and Marilyn Cooper) **/ Donald Pippin.**
    Razor & Tie Ⓕ RAZCD2146 (53 minutes: ADD).

A good old-fashioned star vehicle which makes a welcome return on CD after its original issue on Bay Cities disappeared when that company went under. The only difference is the issuing company logo and, unfortunately, a skimpy booklet with no background details or plot – even the cast list does not detail characters played which is unforgivable. But to the recording itself – well Fred Ebb has put wonderful words into Bacall's deliciously gutsy, smoky deep (singing) voice and John Kander has composed well within her (limited) range and has come up with some winners. Listen out for the voice of Fred Ebb on "So what else is new" for he, like all the rest of the cast, gives great support. "One of the boys" is a lesson in writing a song for a star and, as we expect in the lighter Kander and Ebb shows, there is a knock-out comedy song in "The grass is always greener" in which Bacall sits down with her past husband's homemaking wife (Tony – winning Marilyn Cooper) to compare lives. Not exactly one of this pair's superior scores – but then we expect so much of them.   **RSB**

Zorba 1968 **Broadway Cast** (with Herschel Bernardi, Maria Karnilova, John Cunningham, Carmen Alvarez, Lorraine Serabian and Alex Petrides) / **Harold Hastings**.
  EMI Angel Ⓜ ZDM7 64665-2 (50 minutes: ADD).
Zorba 1984 **Broadway Cast** (with Anthony Quinn, Lila Kedrova, Robert Westenberg, Taro Meyer, Frank de Sal, John Mineo and Suzanne Costallos) / **Paul Gemignani**.
  RCA Victor Ⓜ 09026 68377-2 (57 minutes: ADD).

John Kander and Fred Ebb's remarkably successful stage adaptation of *Zorba the Greek* has all the dark intensity of the same team's *Chicago* and *Cabaret*. They have thoroughly immersed themselves in Greek musical idioms and the result is that *Zorba*, a powerful and moving musical, has made two appearances on Broadway. The original cast was led by Herschel Bernardi, a former Broadway Tevye, with Maria Karnilova (the originator of the role of his wife in *Fiddler on the Roof*) and Lorraine Serabian. Zorba came over as an elemental life force able to experience triumph and surmount tragedy with equal aplomb, and Bernardi succeeds in making him entirely believable. Maria Karnilova brings pathos to her role as aging courtesan Hortense, gently wooed by Zorba. Lorraine Serabian makes a strong Leader, Carmen Alvarez a gentle widow. The score includes the rousing clarion call "Life is" as well as contrasting moments of gentleness – "Only love" and "Why can't I speak?".

  Whereas the original recording offers much light and shade, by the time Anthony Quinn headed the revival, his interpretion had coarsened and offered a broader view with only approximate accuracy to the vocal lines. There are incidental pleasures of course – the contributions of Lila Kedrova, Robert Westenberg and Taro Meyer, but you'll be acquiring *Zorba* for the performance of the main character – and that means choosing the original cast recording with Herschel Bernardi .   **MPK**

New review
70, Girls, 70 1991 **London Cast** (with Dora Bryan, James Gavin, Brian Greene, Pip Hinton, Len Howe, Shezwae Powell, Joan Savage, Buster Skeggs, Stephanie Voss) / **Jo Stewart**.
  TER Ⓕ CDTER1186 (52 minutes: DDD).

Between *Cabaret* in 1966 and *Chicago* in 1975, Kander and Ebb wrote several musical shows, of which the least successful, playing for just 35 performances, was *70, Girls, 70*. It was based on a West End comedy *Breath of Spring* that was filmed as *Make Mine Mink*, starring the much-missed Terry Thomas. In the musical adaptation the setting was changed from Knightsbridge to New York where the characters, a bunch of senior citizens, embark on a shoplifting spree to save their residential home. Their antics inspired Kander and Ebb to compose an intricate plot number, "Well laid plans", in which one of the cast explains in meticulous detail his plans for their initial raid. Other numbers celebrate ageism in a comical and affirmative manner without condescension to the characters or embarrassment to the audience. The London cast, led by the effervescent Dora Bryan, relish Kander's nifty melodies and Ebb's deft lyrics to the hilt, keeping this jolly caper rattling along in a very entertaining manner.   **AE**

Also available:
And the World Goes Round (1991 Off-Broadway Cast) RCA Victor 09026 60904-2
Cabaret (1966 Broadway Cast) Columbia CK03040
The Happy Time (1968 Broadway Cast) RCA Victor 09026 61016-2

Kiss of the Spider Woman (1992 Broadway Cast) Mercury 526 526-2
New York, New York (1977 Film Cast) EMI Liberty CDP7 46090-2
70, Girls, 70 (1971 Broadway Cast) Sony Broadway SK30589

Jerome Kern

1885-1945 USA

The composer often credited as the father of American musical theatre, Jerome Kern was born in New York where he studied at the New York College of Music. Although expected to work in his father's piano-selling business, Kern went to Germany for further musical studies in Heidleberg where his first composition, a piano piece called "At the casino", was published in 1902. Back in New York he worked as a rehearsal pianist and song-plugger, becoming involved in adapting imported British shows and European operettas for Broadway. His interpolated songs, such as "How'd you like to spoon with me?" from *The Earl and the Girl* (1905) often proved the highpoint of the show. During frequent visits to London he married Eva Leale, the daughter of the landlord of his favourite pub, the Swan Hotel, Walton-on-Thames. Kern's first Broadway show was *The Red Petticoat* (1912); although he continued to have more success with his interpolated songs before teaming up with librettist Guy Bolton for a series of shows originally based at the Princess Theater, beginning with *Nobody Home* and *Very Good Eddie* (1915). P. G. Wodehouse joined the partnership as lyric-writer in 1917, and together they scored a string of hits in quick succession: *Have a Heart, Oh, Boy!, Leave it to Jane* (all 1917), *Oh, Lady! Lady!* (1918) and *Sitting Pretty* (1924). *Sally* (1920) was Kern's first transatlantic success. *Show Boat* (1927), with lyrics by Oscar Hammerstein II, profoundly influenced the course of the Broadway musical: its realistic American setting was a revolutionary departure from the normal European-style operetta format and its songs were integral to the plot, not merely interpolations. In the 1930s Kern turned increasingly towards Hollywood, writing for many top stars including Irene Dunne and Deanna Durbin; Fred Astaire and Ginger Rogers starred in Roberta (1935 – the film version of the 1933 show) and *Swing Time* (1936). "The last time I saw Paris" interpolated in the film of Gershwin's *Lady, Be Good!* (1941) won an Academy Award. In 1945, Kern returned to New York to begin work on a musical featuring Ethel Merman based on the life of Annie Oakley; but he died suddenly of a heart attack on 11th November, leaving *Annie Get Your Gun* to be written by Irving Berlin. A biopic of his life, *Till the Clouds Roll By* was made by MGM in 1946.

Jerome Kern Treasury with **George Dvorsky, Thomas Hampson, Jeanne Lehman, Rebecca Luker, Lydia Milà, Hugh Panaro; London Sinfonietta Chorus; London Sinfonietta / John McGlinn**.
EMI Angel ℗ CDC7 54883-2 (79 minutes: DDD).
Songs from The Red Petticoat, Very Good Eddie, Love o' Mike, Have a Heart, Oh, Boy!, Zip Goes a Million, She's a Good Fellow, Dear Sir, The Cat and the Fiddle, Men of the Sky, Music in the Air, Roberta, High, Wide and Handsome and Very Warm for May.

Although this anthology of Kern songs and duets includes a handful of famous numbers, most of the material will be unfamiliar even to the most avid Broadway collector. A wonderful opening to the record is "The ragtime restaurant" from Kern's first show, *The Red Petticoat* (1912), sung with great verve by Hugh Panaro and Rebecca Luker. This is from Kern's early period, when most of his songs were written to be inserted into other people's shows. *The Red Petticoat* lasted only 61 nights, but as John McGlinn proves with his delicious selection covering nearly 30 years – up to Kern's final show, *Very Warm for May* (1939) – some of his less successful shows contain gems.

The heart of the record is the long (12-minute) scene from *Dear Sir*, which only lasted 15 nights in 1924, but contains a duet "I want to be there" which is surely a contender for any list of Kern's best tunes. Among the well-known songs, Thomas Hampson sings "The folks who live on the hill" and "The last time I saw Paris" with all his Lieder-singer's skill, and Jeanne Lehman proves equal to "She didn't say yes" from *The Cat and the Fiddle* (1931) as well as the more operetta-ish "In Egern on the Tegern See" from *Music in the Air* (1932). This is one of the most important of the various records that John McGlinn has made since his trail-blazing *Show Boat* (see below). It is both an introduction to Kern the songwriter and a revelation of the quality of so much music that remains unknown. **PO'C**

Just Kern **Andrea Marcovicci**, with various artists including **Michael Feinstein** and **Helen Marcovicci Carroll / Glenn Mehrbach**.
Elba Cabaret Ⓕ CACD5005-2 (59 minutes: DDD).
Songs from The Stepping Stones, Roberta, The Earl and the Girl, Show Boat, The Girl from Utah, Very Warm for May, Miss 1917, Centennial Summer, Sweet Adeline, One Night in the Tropics, High, Wide and Handsome, You Were Never Lovelier, Swing Time and Sally.

Andrea Marcovicci is one of the premier cabaret artists in New York, noted for a fierce intelligence, intimate knowledge of her subject and an attention to the lyric which is second to none amongst modern performers. Her mother was a torch singer in the 1940s and Marcovicci grew up hearing "Stormy weather" as a lullaby! Her love of the music of Jerome Kern is evident in this inventive compilation that mixes familiar classics such as "Bill" and "Smoke gets in your eyes", with lesser-known pieces – "Raggedy Ann", "In love in vain" and "You never knew about me". Marcovicci has an unconventional voice – there is a tendency toward flatness, but her acting talents sweep over this problem and allow her to enunciate lyrics in such a way that they sound fresh and full of new meaning. She can be playful ("How'd you like to spoon with me?") and delightfully romantic ("You were never lovelier/The way you look tonight", a triumphant medley). But it is the dramatic that suits her best. Her delivery of "Don't ever leave me/Why was I born?" is harrowing in its quiet intensity. The duet with Michael Feinstein is a little disappointing, their voices and styles do not appear to blend especially well. But the pairing with her mother on "Look for the silver lining" is a beautiful ending to this fine recording that offers a modern perspective on one of the greatest of music theatre composers. Glenn Mehrbach's arrangements pay homage to Kern's music whilst complementing Marcovicci's vocal range perfectly – together they are a great combination.   **RAC**

Kiri sings Kern **Dame Kiri Te Kanawa**; **London Sinfonietta / Jonathan Tunick**.
EMI Ⓕ CDC7 54527-2 (45 minutes: DDD).
Songs from High, Wide and Handsome, You Were Never Lovelier, Swing Time, Music in the Air, Roberta, Centennial Summer, Very Warm for May, Show Boat and Sally.

A representative selection of some of Kern's greatest songs, sung without any condescension by one of the great voices of our time. Dame Kiri finds a midway path between operatic vocalism and a jazzy feel, which works very well indeed. The orchestrations are by Jonathan Tunick, who says in the booklet that Kern is the master of "the mainstay of this music – modulation". Gloria Swanson starred in the film version of *Music in the Air* – Dame Kiri's voice is much darker than Swanson's (or Irene Dunne's) but she gives us really beautiful versions of "The folks who live on the hill", "The song is you" and "Smoke gets in your eyes". As a recital it's a bit bland to listen to all the way through, but individual tracks are splendid, including a sensual "Can't help lovin' dat man".   **PO'C**

New review
Music in the Air **Studio Cast** (with Nancy Carr, Marion Claire, Thomas L. Thomas, Everett Clark, Lois Gentile and Muriel Montel) **/ Henry Webber**.
AEI mono Ⓕ AEICD024 (56 minutes: AAD).

An unconventional show, in that its heroine does not succeed in becoming a musical star, but returns to her small village in the Bavarian Alps, *Music in the Air* was a success on both sides of the Atlantic (the disc includes as a bonus Mary Ellis's original London cast recordings – "I've told ev'ry little star", "I'm alone" and "The song is you"). These are sung in the show by the great diva who rightly supplants her small town rival who was not ready for professional stardom. The show was filmed with Gloria Swanson and John Boles. A comparatively recent performance of the show in concert during a "Discover the Lost Musicals" series in London proved the show to be a delight with "There's a hill beyond the hill" revealed as a very funny comic song. But the show's permanence lies in the stream of lovely ballads graced with Oscar Hammerstein's adroit lyrics – including "And love was born". The performances are in authentic operetta style. The undated recording, on aural evidence, probably derives from a mid-1940s radio performance. It features some narration and contains a certain amount of spoken dialogue.   **MPK**

Show Boat 1928 London Cast (with Edith Day, Marie Burke, Howett Worster and Paul Robeson); **Drury Lane Concert Orchestra / Herman Finck**.

Sunny 1926 London Cast (with Binnie Hale, Elsie Randolph, Jack Buchanan and Claude Hulbert); **Novelty Orchestra / Percival Mackay**.

Pearl mono Ⓜ GEMMCD9105 (72 minutes: ADD). Disc also includes extracts from **Rodgers:** Lido Lady **1927 London Cast**.

Show Boat 1987 Studio Cast (with Frederica Von Stade, Teresa Stratas, Karla Burns, Jerry Hadley and Bruce Hubbard); **Ambrosian Chorus; London Sinfonietta / John McGlinn**.

EMI Ⓟ CDS7 49108-2 (three discs: 222 minutes: DDD).

Show Boat 1993 Studio Cast (with Janis Kelly, Sally Burgess, Shezwae Powell, Jason Howard and Willard White); **National Symphony Chorus and Orchestra / John Owen Edwards**.

TER Ⓟ CDTER2 1199 (two discs: 95 minutes: DDD).

With *Show Boat*, Edith Day completed a never-before achieved hat-trick, starring in three Drury Lane musicals in a row: her Magnolia in *Show Boat* followed her roles in *Rose Marie* (1925) and *The Desert Song* (1927). Her rich voice, with a dark, almost contralto quality to it, and on the Pearl disc featuring the 1928 London cast, her vivid personality comes straight across nearly 70 years with undiminished power. She sings "Dance away the night", a song specially composed for the London production, and her duets with Howett Worster are models of poised, operetta singing with just enough of the vaudeville-feel. Marie Burke too has an imperious style, much more haughty as Julie than Helen Morgan, but clearly a star. Paul Robeson created a sensation as Joe singing "Ol' man river", the role he later repeated at the 1932 Broadway revival (it is his recording with Paul Whiteman that is included here, in 1928 from New York) and later in the 1936 film. Jules Bledsoe, who sang in the Broadway première, recorded the number in 1931, and that is here too. His voice is much lighter than Robeson's, but his interpretation has its own importance as the first of this famous lament.

Sunny was written as a vehicle for Marilyn Miller, who created it on Broadway in 1925. The following year it was given in London with the vivacious and strong-voiced Binnie Hale, with a starry supporting cast including the matinée-idol of the day, Jack Buchanan. Their rendition of "Who?" is a lesson in timing and the sense of relaxation. This CD also includes the 1927 London cast of Rodgers and Hart's *Lido Lady* with the Edwardian beauty Phyllis Dare attempting to swing it in "Atlantic blues" and Cicely Courtneidge and Harold French in the classic "A tiny flat near Soho Square".

The most ambitious of all the recent studio reconstructions of classic Broadway shows, EMI's 1987 *Show Boat* is more than complete, in that it also includes an appendix of songs that were cut from the original 1927 production, as well as others that Kern and Hammerstein later wrote for the 1936 film, and one each for the first London staging and the 1946 Broadway revival. The original orchestrations by Robert Russell Bennett are conducted with affection but not reverence by John McGlinn, and the opera singers adapt well to this most operatic of musicals. The slightly tentative quality that Von Stade brings to Magnolia is contrasted with the cynical, almost bitter Julie of Teresa Stratas. Jerry Hadley's smiling, swaggering Ravenal and the vaudevillian couple, Frank and Ellie, sung by David Garrison and Paige O'Hara, make up the young performers aboard the "Cotton Blossom". In the key roles of Queenie and Joe, the long-suffering black cook and boatman, Karla Burns and Bruce Hubbard sing all their solos as well as the duet "I still suits me" from the 1936 film. Lillian Gish, Margaret Tyzack and John McGlinn himself make guest appearances in non-singing roles. This set has become something of a classic already, and must be the standard recommendation for this work. All the famous numbers gain from being heard in context with dialogue and under-scoring, and from the rediscovered material there are a couple of winning songs, "Out there in an orchard", sung by Stratas in character as the older Julie, and "It's getting hotter in the North", a solo for Kim (daughter of the hero and heroine, who only appears as an adult in the penultimate scene). This last song, insists McGlinn, is essential to the completion of the story: "It should come as a great shock to hear Kim belt out a jazz number ... this is the very essence of the evening, life goes on."

TER's recording of the 1946 version of Kern's show, using Robert Russell Bennett's later orchestrations, and various alterations that Kern made to the score, but not including his final song "Nobody else but me" (included in the McGlinn recording), was "inspired by" the 1989 Opera North staging of the show. As on stage, it is Sally Burgess's Julie that stands out, her singing of "Bill" banishes the memory of every other interpreter. The attempts by the British cast to affect American accents of one kind or another are, as usual, only partly successful. Both Janis Kelly and Jason Howard are blessed with excellent diction, and Willard White's Joe contributes a fine "Ol' man river". The obvious comparision with this recording is not the full EMI version, but extracts recorded by the 1946 Broadway cast, conducted with spirit by Edwin McArthur, which included the excellent Charles Fredericks, one of the best Ravenals, and Kenneth Spencer as a dignified Joe, although Helen Dowdy stole the show as Queenie in the "Can't help lovin' dat man" ensemble. **PO'C**

Show Boat – excerpts. **1932 Studio Cast** (with Paul Robeson, James Melton, Helen Morgan, Olga Albani, Frank Munn and Elisabeth Welch); **Show Boat Chorus; Brunswick Concert Orchestra / Victor Young.**
ASV Living Era mono Ⓜ CDAJA5198 (73 minutes: ADD). Disc also includes **Rodgers: Oklahoma! – excerpts. 1943 Broadway Cast** (with Alfred Drake, Lee Dixon, Celeste Holm, Joan Roberts and Howard Da Silva) **/ Jay Blackton.**

This selection from *Show Boat* brings together two cast members from the original productions: Paul Robeson singing Joe from the Drury Lane company of 1928, and Helen Morgan's unforgettable Julie from the Broadway one of a year earlier. After hearing her heartfelt rendition of "Can't help lovin' dat man", it's no wonder that Kern had to find a spot for "Bill", a song he'd discarded from an earlier show. "Ol' man river" is preceded by a rather unsuitable 'home sweet home' introduction which sounds as if it taxed Paul Robeson's patience as well as ours because he rushes into the refrain before the orchestra have time to take a breath! The other singers on this 1932 set of recordings had no connection with either original company. "You are love" and "Why do I love you?" both conclude with some period decoration, as in arranger-conductor Victor Young's overture of melodies from the score, a tradition swept away with John McGlinn's refurbishment of *Show Boat* for EMI. Robeson also sings "Lonesome road" – interpolated into the first screen version of *Show Boat* which, though not by Kern, matches his vision rather well – and "I still suits me", a cheerful duet with Elisabeth Welch written for the second screen *Show Boat*, in which Robeson starred alongside Allan Jones and Irene Dunne.

As for *Oklahoma!*, well, I was bowled over yet again by the freshness of it all – even in these truncated recordings – 10-inch 78 originals this time. The foundation for the success of this 1943 Broadway Cast recording lies in the exemplary musical direction of Jay Blackton, also conductor of the celebrated film soundtrack, who alerts us to the pioneering spirit of Rodgers's magnificent score from the moment the overture starts through to the final rousing choral arrangement of the title song. It's good to be reminded too of Hammerstein's abilities as a writer of comedy songs – we never did know in the film that Kansas City boasted a stripper, for the rhyme "but later in the second act when she began to peel" was rewritten. Yet the film's Curly and Laurie, Gordon MacRae and Shirley Jones, remain the ideal Rodgers and Hammerstein pairing, with Alfred Drake, fine as he is, a trifle too suave for the hero and Joan Roberts, a bit square as heroine. Yet as a recorded memento of a great moment in musical theatre history – possibly its greatest – this reissue will be welcome news.

There is one audible sign, where the chorus disappear into the middle distance in the *Oklahoma!* number, that the ASV people may have had a problem with the original source material, but this is a minor point in what I hope may be the first of many reissues from the MCA show music catalogue. **AE**

Sitting Pretty **1989 Studio Cast** (with Judy Blazer, Paige O'Hara, Beverly Lambert, Roberta Peters, Davis Gaines, Jason Graae, Merwin Goldsmith, Paul V. Ames and Richard Woods); **Princess Theater Ensemble / John McGlinn.**
New World Ⓟ NW80387-2 (two discs: 105 minutes: DDD).

Even by musical comedy standards, the story of *Sitting Pretty* is fairly ridiculous, and it isn't surprising that at the height of the Charleston-crazy roaring twenties, it wasn't a success, only lasting 95 performances in the summer of 1924. A mixed-up story about a pair of identical twins, who are orphans living next door to an eccentric millionaire, it nevertheless has its fair share of good Kern melodies and lyrics by P. G. Wodehouse and Guy Bolton. "There isn't one girl", sung by Davis Gaines, as the hero Bill, "Bongo on the Congo", one of the many 'African' numbers from 1920s musicals, and "Tulip time in Sing-Sing", a song by an old jailbird who wants to get back inside are all worth hearing. Roberta Peters makes her guest-star appearance as a guest at the fancy-dress ball in Act 2, singing as the Empress Eugenie, "In days gone by", and both acts have elaborate finales that point the way towards what Kern would later achieve in *Show Boat* and *Sweet Adeline*.

McGlinn and his team give it all they've got, and it isn't their fault that the show fails to make much of an impact even on devotees. A recording of special historical and scholarly interest, nevertheless.   **PO'C**

The Song is ... Jerome Kern with various artists, including **Bing Crosby, Mary Ellis, Marilyn Miller, Helen Morgan** and **Paul Robeson**.
ASV Living Era mono Ⓜ CDAJA5036 (50 minutes: ADD). Recorded 1926-34.
Songs from Music in the Air, Roberta, Show Boat, The Three Sisters, The Cat and the Fiddle, Sunny and The Girl from Utah.

Kern's career embraced four separate eras of popular music and shows, from his Edwardian successes in New York and London, with songs like "How'd you like to spoon with me?" and others, through his early musicals like *90 in the Shade* (1915), culminating with a series of hit shows on Broadway. Then in the 1920s came the large-scale works, *Show Boat, Sweet Adeline* and *The Cat and the Fiddle*. Finally there was his Hollywood period, with songs for Astaire and Rogers and Irene Dunne. Most of his songs on this CD are from the third era, with some rarities like Marilyn Miller's film version of "Look for the silver lining" from *Sally*, Helen Morgan's earlier, 1928, recording of her two songs from *Show Boat*, and the incomparable Mary Ellis in "I've told ev'ry little star" from the London production of *Music in the Air*.

Dance bands led by Paul Whiteman, Claude Hopkins, Ambrose, Henry Hall and Lew Stone provide quick-step versions of several other songs, including "Hand in hand" from *The Three Sisters* (nothing to do with Chekhov), and "They didn't believe me", originally from the Broadway production of *The Girl from Utah* (where it was sung by Julia Sanderson, whose 1941 recording of it was reissued on "The Great Stage Musicals, Vol. 2", an extraordinary piece of nostalgia, her voice suggesting many layers of experience and regret).   **PO'C**

Very Good Eddie 1975 **Broadway Cast** (with Cynthia Wells, Travis Hudson, Spring Fairbank, Virginia Seidel, David Christmas, Charles Repole, Hal Shane and Nicholas Wyman).
DRG Ⓔ CDDRG6100 (44 minutes: ADD).

This revival of *Very Good Eddie* (1915), one of Kern's most successful earlier shows, began its life at the Goodspeed Opera House, East Haddam. It transferred to Broadway and also inspired a London production. The first of the Princess Theater shows, in which Kern collaborated with Guy Bolton (and later P. G. Wodehouse), it is a typical farce in which various married couples find misunderstandings leading to a game of change-partners. The best-known song, "Some sort of somebody" boasts lyrics by Elsie Janis and, like some of the other numbers, had started life in another Kern show of 1915, *Miss Information*.

The performance has a good deal of vitality, and the cast all provide excellent diction. Travis Hudson and the boys do well by a very catchy, forgotten number "Moon of love", and Viginia Seidel and Charles Repole sing "Babes in the wood" without any sense of extra parody. This was the duet that led to the formation of the Kern-Wodehouse-Bolton triumvirate, when Kern first heard the lyrics ("Give me your hand/You'll understand/We're off to slumberland") and at the first night was persuaded to engage Wodehouse (two of his songs from the later Princess shows also turn up here, "Honeymoon Inn" and "Bungalow in Quogue").   **PO'C**

New review
Very Warm for May 1939 **Broadway Cast** (with Hollace Shaw, Ralph Stuart, Eve Arden, Frances Mercer, Grace McDonald, Richard Quine and Hiram Sherman) **/ Matty Malneck**.
AEI mono Ⓔ AEICD008 (44 minutes: AAD).

This is a really valuable historical document, as well as containing some of Kern's finest music from his most mature period. The show had book trouble from the start, trouble that it never overcame, and the production expired after a mere 51 performances. Incidentally, the May of the title is our heroine, not the month. The original scenario had her mixed up with gangsters. Many of the songs would later turn up in a short sequence of the film *Broadway Rhythm*, but here they are in their original context. The sound is rather hollow and boomy at times, probably deriving from an uncredited radio broadcast, but your ear adjusts quite quickly as the glorious parade of songs unfolds, beginning with "All the things you are", featuring the gorgeous high soprano of Hollace Shaw. The unmistakable tones of Eve Arden grace a short scene, and further delights include "Heaven in your arms", "All in fun" and "That lucky fellow". The featured orchestra is the great swing band of Matty Malneck. The booklet doesn't identify whether "In the heart of the dark" is sung by Jack Whiting or his replacement Guy Robertson. It doesn't matter either way. Two bonuses are Jerome Kern accompanying Tony Martin on piano in "All the things you are" and the one commercial cast recording issued – of Shaw in the same song. **MPK**

Also available:
A Tribute to Jerome Kern MfP CDDL1290
Jerome Kern Goes to Hollywood (1985 London Cast) First Night OCRCD6014
Show Boat (1993 Studio Cast) Carlton Shows Collection PWKS4161
Show Boat (1951 Film Cast) EMI CDODEON5

Henry Krieger

b. 1945 USA

After working off- and off-off-Broadway, Henry Krieger leapt into the big time with his resplendent score for *Dreamgirls* (1981) which was quickly followed two years later by another success *The Tap Dance Kid* (1983). There followed an out of town collaboration with his partner in *Dreamgirls*, Tom Eyen, *Dangerous Music* (1988) and a children's musical for Leicester, *Fat Pig* (1988). In 1997 he produced *Side Show*.

Dreamgirls 1981 **Broadway Cast** (with Obba Babatunde, Cleavant Derricks, Loretta Devine, Ben Harney, Jennifer Holliday and Sheryl Lee Ralph) **/ Yolanda Segovia**.
Geffen ℗ 2007-2 (47 minutes: DDD).

Director Michael Bennett's second massive success after *A Chorus Line* tells the story of a trio of black women singers who rise to stardom only to find the pressures of their new-found fame destroy their friendship. Although strenuously denied, the parallels with Diana Ross and the Supremes were obvious. Unusually for an American musical of this time, the piece was almost entirely through-sung, but the Geffen issue has more in common with a pop album than a cast recording. Given the nature of the material this is perhaps excusable, but considering the enormous success of the show it is frustrating that a full recording was not also issued. That aside, what is preserved here is an exuberant and talented cast in a series of powerhouse numbers, ranging from lush soul, pastiche of classic Motown, through to rap and blues. Songs such as "Cadillac car" and "Family" effectively convey the excitement of growing stardom and the cruel truths lurking behind its façade. Best of all is Jennifer Holliday in her Tony Award-winning performance as Effie, who is edged out of the group because she does not fit the image, despite having the best voice. Her definitive rendition of the desperate "And I'm telling you I'm not going" sends chills down the spine at every hearing. **RAC**

Also available:
The Tap Dance Kid (1983 Broadway Cast) TER CDTER1096

Michael John LaChiusa

Hello Again 1994 **Original Cast** (with Judy Blazer, Carolee Carmello, John Dossett, Malcolm Gets, John Cameron Mitchell, Donna Murphy, Michael Park, Dennis Parlatto, Michele Pawk and David White) **/ David Evans**.
RCA Victor ℗ 09026 62680-2 (61 minutes: DDD).

Designed by choreographer-director Graciela Daniele in collaboration with composer-lyricist Michael John LaChiusa, *Hello Again* was a simply staged but breathtakingly clever adaptation of Arthur Schnitzler's classic tale of sexual immorality and partnerships *La Ronde*. Following the same pattern as the play, a series of stock unnamed characters, known simply by a description – The Whore, The Nurse, The Soldier – come together in a series of involvements that comment on society and sexuality in sharp and often unusual ways. LaChuisa's score suits the idea admirably – it is far from easy listening, but very rewarding on repeat hearings, highly intelligent and full of insight. LaChuisa tends towards the spare, and Michael Starobin's excellent orchestrations help to flesh out his music. The production itself was a model of elegant simplicity and thus the music is eminently fitting. The cast is an extraordinary ensemble. Donna Murphy may have gone on to become the best-known name, but the remainder of the cast is equally strong. Murphy's success, though, is unsurprising after one hears her sensual and bitter performance as The Whore – she has a remarkable intensity and the quality of her voice lingers on in the mind. Also fine are Michele Pawk as The Actress, Judy Blazer as The Nurse and Malcolm Gets as The Writer, but all contribute to the piece. The recording, accompanied by a well-written introduction by Ira Weitzman, Director of Musical Theatre at Lincoln Center, who sponsored the original production, is nicely presented using the play-like structure of the piece as a series of scenes, rather than individual songs. Rather like Sondheim's works, of which this is somewhat reminiscent, several listens will reap rich rewards. **RAC**

Marvin Laird

Ruthless! The Musical 1993 **Los Angeles Cast** (with Joanne Baum, Loren Freeman, Nancy Linari, Rita McKenzie, Lindsay Ridgeway and Joan Ryan) / **Nick Venden**.
Varèse Sarabande Spotlight Series Ⓔ VSD5476 (46 minutes: DDD).

Gypsy meets *All About Eve* in this wildly funny show as ambitious child prodigy Tina Denmark (superbly sung by the tiny anti-Annie Lindsay Ridgeway) spirals towards stardom and is prepared to commit murder to achieve it. But little does she know that her dreams are to be wrecked by her own mother (Joan Ryan) who suddenly finds her own voice and climbs over her daughter's shoulders by telling the police about the murder. The catalyst for all this is talent agent Sylvia St Croix (the gravel-voiced Loren Freeman) who is determined to make Tina a star – to feed her own need for fulfilment. Along the way we meet Tina's teacher (a failed actress now stuck "Teaching third grade") and Tina's grandmother, a theatre critic with a loathing for musicals ("The story is moving chock full of suspense ... Then someone sings a song like this!/It doesn't make sense"). The latter is played by Rita McKenzie who sounds an awful lot like Merman, and makes the most of her one song opportunity. Joel Paley's lyrics are a joy for all music theatre and film buffs, full of references to other shows and to the follies of showbusiness people. His work is complemented by Laird's music – very off-Broadway in feel (especially as the band consists of just two pianos, bass and percussion), but again using asides and themes that are recognizable from other shows. The small cast (who double up throughout) clearly relish the whole experience and create a wealth of caricatures that are funny, but recognizably human. **RAC**

Burton Lane

1912-1997 USA

Burton Levy was born in New York where he joined the Remick Publishing Company as a pianist and staff writer aged 15. George Gershwin encouraged him to study music with Simon Bucharoff and he began to write songs for Broadway revues, including *Three's a Crowd* (1930), *Earl Carroll's Vanities* (1931) and *Americana* (1932). He moved to California in 1933 where he wrote songs for films, such as "You took the words right out of my mouth" from *Folies Bergère* (1935), "Swing high, swing low" from the film of the same name (1937) and "How about you?" from *Babes on Broadway* (1941). He remained in California until 1954, returning to Broadway on only three occasions, for *Hold on to Your Hats* (1940), *Laffing Room Only* (1944) and *Finian's Rainbow* (1947). This latter, a collaboration with E. Y. Harburg which includes the songs "How are things in Glocca Morra?" and "Old devil moon", ran for 725 performances, but only lasted 55 in London. It was filmed in 1968 with Fred Astaire, Tommy Steele and Petula Clark. Lane's only two subsequent shows, *On a Clear Day You Can See Forever* (1965) and *Carmelina* (1979) were both collaborations with lyricist Alan Jay Lerner.

The Burton Lane Songbook, Volumes 1 and 2. **Michael Feinstein**; **Burton Lane** (pf).
Nonesuch Ⓟ 7559-79243/79285-2 (two discs, only available separately: 57 and 66 minutes: DDD).
7559-79243-2 – Songs from Give a Girl a Break, Dancing on a Dime, Babes on Broadway, Royal Wedding, College Swing and Carmelina. *7559-79285-2 – Songs from* Some Like it Hot, Carmelina, Dancing Lady, Dancing on a Dime, Give a Girl a Break, Hold on to Your Hats, Kid Millions, Love on Toast, On a Clear Day You Can See Forever, Royal Wedding and Ship Ahoy.

Burton Lane was the most senior figure of those American songwriters whose output was treated to a chapter in Alec Wilder's book, "The Great Innovators 1900-1950". Wilder deals with a number of Lane's songs on this pair of CDs, including the little known but enchanting "Dancing on a dime" from the 1941 Hollywood musical, and "Don't let it get you down" from *Hold on to Your Hats*, a Broadway show of the same period which gets short shrift from Wilder but a delicious performance from Feinstein and Lane, both of them relishing the felicitous rhymes in 'Yip' Harburg's lyric. Lane divided his time between these two meccas of entertainment, composing one of his finest scores, *On a Clear Day You Can See Forever* in 1965, well outside the time factor of Wilder's book. I well remember the thrill on hearing its elegantly fashioned title song and subsequently getting to know the remainder of the score which, alongside *Finian's Rainbow* (1947), contains Lane's best known stage songs. Save for one film, *Royal Wedding* (1951), with Fred Astaire and Jane Powell, it remains a mystery why Lane composed so little in the intervening years. *Royal Wedding* has some of Alan Jay Lerner's most romantic verses and Lane matches him with some charming melodies including the haunting "Too late now". Feinstein relishes each song as though it were newly composed and with Lane on piano, clearly delineating his path, shares his joy with us. **AE**

Finian's Rainbow 1947 **Broadway Cast** (with David Wayne, Ella Logan, Sonny Terry, Eddie Bruce, Tom McElhany, Alan Gilbert, Robert Eric Carlson and Anita Alvarez) **/ Ray Charles**.
Columbia mono Ⓜ CK04062 (39 minutes: AAD).
Finian's Rainbow 1960 **BroadwayCast** (with Jeannie Carson, Howard Morris, Biff McGuire, Carol Brice, Sorrell Booke, Bobby Howes and Tiger Haynes) **/ Max Meth**.
RCA Victor Ⓜ 1057-2 (44 minutes: ADD).

Satire is a dangerous medium for musical comedy. Yet *Finian's Rainbow* has proved a durable Broadway hit, due in part to a wonderful score by Burton Lane with pointed and memorable lyrics by E. Y. Harburg. "Old devil moon", "How are things in Glocca Morra?", "Look to the rainbow", "If this isn't love", "When I'm not near the girl I love" are already Broadway standards. Here they are set in a delightful fantasy about a leprechaun come to return a crock of gold to Ireland. It's been stolen by an adventurer who plans to plant it at Fort Knox, like potatoes. Add a deeply bigoted Southern senator who gets a chance to see life – and racial prejudice – from the other side and you have just the sort of situation that brings out the best and most impish from the socially committed lyricist. The original 1947 recording is a classic, of course, but the fine RCA 1960 version offers even greater delights – notably the great Bobby Howes as Finian and Jeannie Carson as his daughter. Biff McGuire has similar charm as Og the leprechaun. **MPK**

On a Clear Day You Can See Forever 1969 **Film Cast** (with Barbra Streisand and Yves Montand) **/ Nelson Riddle**.
Sony Columbia Ⓜ 474907-2 (31 minutes: ADD).

"I'm just a victim of time" sings Barbra Streisand, whose powers of extra-sensory perception get her entangled between past and present when she realizes that the man she loves is in love with her *alter ego*. Such a fascinating concept would seem an ideal prospect for a genre that hovers so often between reality and fantasy. Alas, as the film testifies, librettist Alan Jay Lerner soon forgot about the ESP angle and got bogged down in foolishness about reincarnation and the heroine's tiresome 'shrink'. Just as the 1965 Broadway show had only the briefest of runs, 280 performances, so the film wound up on the cutting room floor, an incomprehensible mess even before it was shown to an audience. But there was one redeeming factor – Lerner was a much better lyricist than librettist, and in Burton Lane he found a composer, much overlooked at that time, who clothed his words in a series of charming and graceful melodies. Many of these didn't survive on screen, though Streisand gets to sing two new numbers, neither of them a patch on what was left out. Streisand seemed the ideal choice when Lerner produced his movie in 1969, but even by that stage she was inclined to over indulge her vocal mannerisms and break up the line of a song to its detriment. Nelson Riddle provides some plush arrangements for her and Yves Montand singing "Come back to me" from the top of the former Pan Am skyscraper in New York provides us with the film's one imaginatively staged number. The recording has come up well in its digital transfer (those who saw the film at London's Dominion cinema may recall being fobbed off with a dim soundtrack). **AE**

Also available:
On a Clear Day You Can See Forever (1965 Broadway Cast) RCA Victor 09026 60820-2

Jonathan Larson

1960-1996 USA

Larson wrote songs for the children's television series *Sesame Street* as well as for a number of shows and revues that never reached Broadway: *Superbia*, *"tick...tick...BOOM!"*, *J. P. Morgan Saves the Nation* and *Sitting on the Edge of the Future*. His big break came with a modern-day version of *La Bohème*, with both lyrics and music by Larson. Unhappily, the composer died ten days before his 36th birthday and just before the show, *Rent*, the major Broadway hit of 1996, opened

Rent 1996 Broadway Cast (with Adam Pascal, Anthony Rapp, Jesse L. Martin, Wilson Jermaine Heredia, Daphne Rubin-Vega, Taye Diggs, Fredi Walker and Idina Menzel) / **Tim Weil.** Dreamworks Ⓕ DRD50003 (two discs: 127 minutes: DDD).

Jonathan Larson's contemporary treatment of the *La Bohème* story, transplanted to Greenwich Village, began life off-Broadway. Shortly before the show transferred to the Great White Way, where it became the biggest hit of the 1996 season, Larson died of AIDS at the age of 36. Clearly this added a poignancy to the whole production as many of his Bohemian characters are living with HIV and the subject is tackled head-on throughout the piece. Larson has created a rock-opera that is far removed from the lush dramas of Lloyd Webber and Boublil and Schönberg. The musical influences are varied, much derived from contemporary rock and pop, with the occasional sweeping bow to the traditional musical format. The recording, supervised by pop producer Arif Mardin, is excellent. Using a small band, away from the over-miked theatrical production, the lyrics and nuances of Larson's work are more apparent, always a difficult achievement with the pop-rock form. The ensemble cast is superb – Adam Pascal is exceptional as Roger, the songwriter and ex-junkie, who falls in love with Mimi. His rendition of "One song glory", a desperate plea for artistic inspiration and for life, is moving and memorable. Elsewhere, Daphne Rubin-Vega's Mimi is strong-voiced and effective, while Wilson Jermaine Heredia reprises his Tony-winning performance as the drag queen Angel. The arrival of *Rent* in the 1990s has been compared to that of *Hair* in the late 1960s – bringing new audiences to Broadway theatre and offering a new direction for the musical. But the difficulty such shows face is whether they can survive outside of the specific time for which they were written (*Hair* seems very dated nowadays). Whether *Rent* will become one of the enduring classics of musical theatre remains to be seen, but it contains a number of songs that will help this process, especially "Seasons of love", of which a pop version by Stevie Wonder and the cast of *Rent* is included at the end of disc two. The message of the show is one of hope and inspiration amidst the most difficult of circumstances – the characters banding together to provide each other with support and love. Traditionalists may find the music too contemporary, but this is an important score that should be investigated. **RAC**

Michel Legrand

b. 1932 France

Michel Legrand was born in Paris and studied at the Conservatoire National de Musique. He became an accompanist, conductor and songwriter for artists such as Maurice Chevalier and

Jacques Brel. The 1964 film *Les Parapluies de Cherbourg* brought him international success. Several of his songs became international hits, including "I will wait for you" (English lyrics by Norman Gimbel) from *Parapluies*, "Watch what happens" from *Lola* (1960) also with Gimbel, as well as "You must believe in spring" from 1967's *Les Demoiselles de Rochefort* and "What are you doing the rest of your life?" from *The Happy Ending* (1969) – both with lyrics by Alan and Marilyn Bergman. Legrand moved to Hollywood in 1968 and had further success with *The Thomas Crown Affair* ("The windmills of your mind"). He won an Academy Award for *Summer of '42* (1971). He has also recorded several jazz albums, and scored the 1991 film *Dingo* with Miles Davis.

New review

Les Parapluies de Cherbourg 1964 Film Cast (with Danielle Licari, Jose Bartel, Christiane Legrand, Georges Blanes, Claudine Meunier, Claire Leclerc, Michel Legrand, Jacques Demy) / **Michel Legrand.**
Sony Classical Ⓜ SM2K 62678 (two discs: 117 minutes: ADD). Bonus tracks with Tony Bennett, Michel Legrand Trio, Herve Meschinet.

Composer Michel Legrand and Jacques Demy, the writer and director, won the Palme d'Or at Cannes in 1964 for their enchanting film musical *Les Parapluies de Cherbourg*. Two of Legrand's melodies with lyrics by Norman Gimbel were translated into popular hits ("Watch what happens" and "I will wait for you"), and then in 1980 Gimbel and Sheldon Harnick adapted the score for the London stage where, sadly, it folded after just 12 performances. In 1996 *Parapluies* returned to the big screen in a new print which has subsequently been shown on TV. Legrand's score is through-sung, and on the screen as in opera, the story unfolds in three acts. In Act 1, Genevieve, a very attractive golden-tressed girl, becomes pregnant by her boyfriend, the handsome garage mechanic Guy, just before he goes off for military service. In Act 2 she is persuaded by her ambitious mother, who runs a boutique in Cherbourg, to marry a good-looking aristocratic diamond merchant. In the third sequence, Guy returns – and forgets his jilted bitterness through a happy marriage to Madeleine, who has long been devoted to him. When at the end he and Genevieve meet again by chance, she is more wistfully nostalgic than he. The four leading players, including Catherine Deneuve, were all chosen for their looks and acting talent: as the above credits reveal they were all dubbed, with equal satisfaction. Legrand's score flows along through a series of tender, ardent and melancholy recitatives, duets and arias, offering a whole range of human passions, affections and imperfections including the spectre of family bereavement and a sharp unsentimental look at making a pile. Legrand went on to compose many a title song and another movie musical, *Les Demoiselles de Rochefort*, but it's this work that remains his most endearing and enduring testament. The CD transfer has some moments of distortion that were on the original LP pressing. **AE**

Mitch Leigh
b. 1928 USA

Irwin Mitchnick was born in Brooklyn and studied music at Yale University with Hindemith. After working as a jazz musician he began writing music for radio and television commercials and formed his own company to produce them. He composed incidental music for the theatre before writing the musical play *Man of La Mancha* in 1965. This adaptation of Cervantes' *Don Quixote* was originally intended for television, the book was written by Dale Wasserman with lyrics by Joe Darion. The show ran for 2,328 performances (253 in London) and was named best musical of the year. It remains Leigh's biggest Broadway hit and was filmed, starring Peter O'Toole, in 1972. Subsequent shows – *Chu Chem* (1966), *Cry for Us All* (1970), *Odyssey* (1974), *Home Sweet Homer* (1976) and *Sarava* (1978) – were less successful.

Man of La Mancha 1990 Studio Cast (with Plácido Domingo, Mandy Patinkin, Julia Migenes, Carolann Page, Jerry Hadley, Rosalind Elias, Robert White, Samuel Ramey, Plácido Domingo Jr. and Alvaro Domingo); **Concert Chorale of New York; American Theatre Orchestra / Paul Gemignani.**
Sony Classical Ⓟ SK46436 (50 minutes: DDD).

It seems strange that it took Sony six years to issue this recording, made in 1990, given the starry cast they assembled for this big Broadway hit of the 1960s. Perhaps they had second thoughts about casting Plácido Domingo in the baritone role of Don Quixote whose knightly virtues of dignity and virility are better expressed by a darker voice. For these reasons Domingo comes across as too lightweight a character, though he does of course give us some fine singing, notably in the concluding "Psalm". As his henchman Sancho Panza, Mandy Patinkin turns on a peculiar whine with which his role has been blessed or cursed since the original Broadway cast recording. Beside both of them Julia Migenes as Aldonza sounds over-parted.

This recording really shines in the minor roles. Jerry Hadley and Samuel Ramey are predictably excellent as Padre and Innkeeper and Carolann Page and Rosalind Elias join Hadley to make a highlight out of the score's most enjoyable number, "I'm only thinking of him". Alvaro Domingo and Plácido Junior, the former sounding remarkably like his father, are a little too well-groomed as the Muleteers who mock Aldonza over her affection for the knight. The wind band, conducted by Paul Gemignani, adds its own distinctive colours to a pretty score that seems over the years to have lost some of the lustre which it was once accorded. **AE**

Also available:
Man of La Mancha (1965 Broadway Cast) MCA MCAD31065

Alan Jay Lerner
1918-1986 USA

For biography see entry under Loewe, Frederick.

New review
Julie Andrews sings Alan Jay Lerner
Julie Andrews; Ambrosian Singers; London Musicians Orchestra / Ian Fraser.
Philips Ⓕ 448 219-2PH (71 minutes: DDD).
Songs from **Lane:** On a Clear Day You Can See Forever, Carmelina. **Loewe:** Brigadoon, The Day Before Spring, Paint Your Wagon, My Fair Lady, Camelot. **Weill:** Love Life. **Previn:** Coco. **Bernstein:** 1600 Pennsylvania Avenue. **Strouse:** Dance a Little Closer.

Following on from her successful showcase of Richard Rodgers songs (see separate entry) Julie Andrews released this equally lush tribute to the lyrics of Alan Jay Lerner. The collection is built around four lengthy medleys from *Brigadoon*, *Paint Your Wagon* and, of course, *My Fair Lady* and *Camelot*, the two Broadway shows which confirmed Andrews as a superstar before she was even 25 years old. But she is too canny an artist to settle for an easy trip down memory lane. In some respects her decision to revisit the roles of Eliza Dolittle and Guinevere, if only on CD, was a brave one. Her voice, in its prime a marvellous soprano instrument, has endured much unjustified mockery for the crystal clarity of its delivery. Maturity has brought an inevitable decline but, equally, has introduced a pleasing variety of texture. There are times here when she sounds slightly beleaguered by a growling tendency in the lower register – particularly in the opening track "On a clear day ..." – but she puts it to good effect in "My love is a married man". Certainly, Andrews rolls back the years with "Wouldn't it be loverly", "The rain in Spain", "Just you wait", "Show me" and of course a triumphant "I could have danced all night", with excellent support from the orchestra. But the most touching moments are the lesser-known numbers which typify her skill as a singer of poignant, lyrical songs: "Here I'll stay" from *Love Life*, the sublimely touching item from *Carmelina*, "One more walk around the garden", Bernstein's moving prayer from *1600 Pennsylvania Avenue* and, lastly, "There's always one you can't forget" from the ill-fated *Dance a Little Closer*. **PF**

Sir Andrew Lloyd Webber
b. 1948 England

Britain's most commercially successful contemporary composer, Andrew Lloyd Webber was born in London, son of composer Dr William Lloyd Webber (1914-1982), and attended Westminster School. Early musical memories include attending Ralph Vaughan Williams's memorial service and the first London performance of Benjamin Britten's *War Requiem* in nearby Westminster Abbey. He wrote his first composition aged six, and a piano suite was published when he was nine. He studied at the Guildhall School of Music and the Royal College of Music, although his father tried to ensure that his natural melodic ability would not be eroded by overly formal training. In 1965 he began collaborating with lyricist Tim Rice, and they wrote their first show, *The Likes of Us*, which was never produced. In 1968, *Joseph and the Amazing Technicolor Dreamcoat* was written for Colet Court, the junior wing of St Paul's School, London. It was originally published for school use, but was expanded somewhat for the subsequent recording by Decca, then revised and expanded again when staged at the Edinburgh Festival in 1972, and went on to successful runs in London and New York. The initial success of *Joseph* on record led to the creation of *Jesus Christ Superstar* which was developed from the principal song, "Superstar", and issued on LP in 1969; after a slow start the album sold well, and the show opened on Broadway in 1971 and London in 1972 (at the Palace Theatre – which Lloyd Webber later bought) where it ran for 3,358 performances, closing in 1980. With Alan Ayckbourn, Lloyd Webber wrote the unsuccessful show *Jeeves* (1975 – revived in 1996 as *By Jeeves!*) before teaming up with Rice again for *Evita* (1976), once more first released as an LP; after scoring a No. 1 hit with "Don't cry for me, Argentina", the show opened in 1978. *Evita* was Rice and Lloyd Webber's final collaboration, and was filmed in 1996 with Madonna in the title role. The composer based his next work, the unusual but phenomenally successful *Cats* (1981), on T. S. Eliot's poems. Subsequently, he teamed up with Don Black for *Song and Dance* (1982), and Richard Stilgoe for both *Starlight Express* (1984) and *Phantom of the Opera* (1986). He worked with Don Black again on *Aspects of Love* (1989) and *Sunset Boulevard* (1993). In 1998 *Whistle Down the Wind* is due to open in London, with lyrics by Jim Steinman.

New review

By Jeeves **1996 London Cast** (with Malcolm Sinclair, Steven Pacey and Diana Morrison) **/ Kate Young.**
Polydor Ⓔ 533 187-2 (60 minutes: DDD).

Long before cats, trains and a phantom invaded London and New York, Andrew Lloyd Webber had a flop show called *Jeeves* based on P. G. Wodehouse's Jeeves stories. It sported an original cast recording which soon became a collector's item and was never transferred to CD. The failure of the show was due more to book problems than the score, but in its original overblown state this was hard to recognize. How pleasant, therefore, to find a thoughtful pocket-sized revisit some 20 years later back on the London stage playing an acceptable, if not overlong, run. The songs have changed a little on its way back (some of the original melodies having reappeared elsewhere) and it remains the most traditionalist British musical comedy score by this composer. Following a limited issue 'live' recording of the pre-London presentation at Scarborough, this studio-recorded version tells the story as it introduces its dozen or so songs. The wit of Alan Ayckbourn sits comfortably alongside that of Wodehouse in both lyric and a glorious 'thicker than mulligatawny' storyline involving Wooster's mistaken identity and the aiding and abetting of Jeeves – all punctuated by a set of top-notch songs. This beautifully produced CD includes the song "Half a moment", which is one of Lloyd Webber's best. After a few hearings try playing just the songs – it is well worth the effort. (The American issue has a few minor changes to an otherwise identical recording.)   **RSB**

Cats **1981 London Cast** (with Wayne Sleep, Paul Nicholas, Brian Blessed, Elaine Paige, Myra Sands and Bonnie Langford) **/ David Firman**.
Polydor Ⓔ 817 810-2 (two discs: 95 minutes: AAD).

Perhaps the most unexpected success in the history of the musical theatre was Andrew Lloyd Webber's first work away from his collaboration with Tim Rice. The idea that a classic work of twentieth-century poetry could provide the lyrics for a musical seemed extraordinary, even more so when that work was T. S. Eliot's *Old Possum's Book of Practical Cats*. But working with Trevor Nunn and Richard Stilgoe, who wrote a few additional lyrics, he created what has become the longest-running musical in the West End, and could well achieve that feat on Broadway as well. Considering that it is essentially a song and dance revue and has no plot, it is an exceptional achievement. Much has to be attributed to Lloyd Webber's uncanny ability to write music that holds an audience's attention and remains fixed in the mind. He also seems to judge the mood of a piece perfectly. *Cats* is an evocative and often joyous work that constantly enthrals with its varied mix of styles and rhythms, all using Eliot's rich verse as a firm foundation. Certainly from the performers' point of view, it is the brilliance of the language that helps to enrich their work. Brian Blessed's wonderful rendition of "The ad-dressing of Cats" is an obvious example of an actor thriving on language as well as music. Paul Nicholas is charmingly enthusiastic, making the most of the story of "Mr Mistoffelees". Wayne Sleep is not the greatest of singers but copes with the demands of the score well enough. The major song from the show "Memory" (ironically the one furthest from Eliot's own work) was originally intended for Judi Dench as Grizabella, but is here performed by Elaine Paige, who replaced Dench during rehearsals when the latter broke her ankle. Paige, now the acknowledged queen of British musical theatre, demonstrates all the qualities that won her that position, singing with immense power, style and perfect diction. There could be little better record of one of the astounding successes of modern musical theatre.　　　**RAC**

Evita 1976 **Studio Cast** (with Julie Covington, Paul Jones, C. T. Wilkinson, Tony Christie and Barbara Dickson) **/ Anthony Bowles**.
　　MCA Ⓕ DMCX503 (two discs: 104 minutes: ADD).
Evita 1978 **London Cast** (with Elaine Paige, David Essex, Joss Ackland, Siobhan McCarthy and Mark Ryan) **/ Anthony Bowles**.
　　MCA Ⓕ DMCG3527 (52 minutes: ADD).
Evita 1979 **Broadway Cast** (with Patti LuPone, Mandy Patinkin, Bob Gunton, Mark Syers and Jane Ohringer) **/ Rene Wiegert**.
　　MCA Ⓕ MCAD2-11007 (two discs: 101 minutes: ADD).
Evita 1996 **Film Cast** (with Madonna, Jonathan Pryce, Antonio Banderas and Jimmy Nail) **/ John Mauceri, David Caddick, Mike Dixon**.
　　Warner Bros Ⓕ 9362-46432-2 (77 minutes: DDD); 9362-46346-2 (two discs: 109 minutes: DDD).

The third of the Lloyd Webber/Rice collaborations is probably their strongest and one of Lloyd Webber's best scores. Rice may provide a somehat sanitized and undoubtedly skewed view of history (Che Guevara and Eva Perón never met, indeed Guevara was little more than a child when Eva died), but the musical theatre has always taken liberties with reality. As with *Jesus Christ Superstar*, before the musical was staged there was the concept album – in this case a hugely successful project that spawned a number one hit for Julie Covington ("Don't cry for me, Argentina") and laid the foundation for long runs in London, on Broadway and around the world. Lloyd Webber uses insistent Latin influences throughout and the recitative is generally more interesting than in some of his other work. Rice's lyrics are fine, despite a few raw lapses, and he manages to convey a great deal with some simple phrasing. Covington, although denied the opportunity to play the role on stage, is a stunning Eva – coy and girlish, but obviously ambitious in the early years, growing through a wanton youth and tyrannical grasp of power in maturity, before realizing that it is all to be taken from her. Covington's performance remains definitive, especially of the balcony scene in which she is supreme. Paul Jones is fine in the difficult role of Perón, inevitably overshadowed by Covington. Colm Wilkinson (in those days known as C. T.) is marvellous as Che, his gruff voice perfectly conveying the sarcasm and dismay as he sees his principles betrayed. Barbara Dickson is moving as the abandoned mistress in "Another suitcase in another hall" which also became a commercial pop hit. There were a number of rewrites for the stage version, but the studio album is powerful and well-crafted, with a series of stellar performances, especially from Covington whose career has disappointingly not flourished in live musical theatre.

A highlights version of the original stage cast appeared in 1978 – no full recording was issued. Elaine Paige's career as the leading lady of British musical theatre began with 'overnight stardom' in the role of Eva. Her inexperience tells in certain places and she struggles with some of the nuances of the character – it is not as sensitive a performance as Covington. But already the future star qualities are evident – the voice is powerful and insistent and there is a real presence in her singing. David Essex is a little too charming as Che, although his undoubted pop charisma carries weight. Joss Ackland is excellent as Perón, more authoritative than Paul Jones, and offering more light and shade to the role. As a truncated version this offers a fine alternative to having to work through a two-disc set, with high quality performances.

The Broadway cast album is the most complete recording of the stage show in English. Patti LuPone, like Elaine Paige, made her name with this role, and she carries it well, offering an Eva that is defiant and strong throughout, failing to capture the youthful eagerness, but triumphing in the mature scenes. Her arrogance in "Rainbow high" is particularly striking and successful. Mandy Patinkin is an overactive Che, delivering a showy performance that threatens to overshadow Eva herself. It is to LuPone's credit that she manages to stave off this disaster. But against these two remarkable forces none of the other characters have a chance to take on any life or presence. This is an impressive recording for its two star performances and for its length, but the accompanying booklet is disappointing, not offering a libretto or much detail of the production.

Despite widespread reservations about the casting of Madonna for the film version, the recording confirms that she was an ideal choice. Her singing is strong and confident, and she manages to present Eva as a many-faceted rather than one-dimensional character. But it is the rewriting of this version that is most fascinating. In keeping with her star name, Madonna is now the only major female performer, having usurped "Another suitcase in another hall" for the character of Eva. This offers a sympathetic angle to the young Eva, which was lacking in the previous version. Also, Tim Rice was prevailed upon to heal a long-standing rift with Lloyd Webber, and provide lyrics for a new song written specially for the film. "You must love me" proves to be a tender and well-crafted ballad for Eva to sing as she realizes her health is failing. Madonna demonstrates a genuine feel for this moment and makes the most of the first new Lloyd Webber/Rice song in 20 years. Of the other performers, Banderas nicely underplays Che (now simply a commentator, no longer Che Guevara), Pryce is reliable and Jimmy Nail is an excellent Magaldi. The accompanying booklet is filled with stunning shots from the film, although nothing in the way of text. The orchestra and choir are outstanding and the sound and presentation of the piece is magnificent. **RAC**

The Greatest Songs with **Lesley Garrett, Meredith Braun, Samuel Burkey, Keith Burns, Sharon Campbell, Mary Carewe, Gerard Casey, Anita Louise Combe, Chris Corcoran, Michele Hooper, Christopher Howard, Deborah Steel; Royal Philharmonic Orchestra, Concert Orchestra and Pops Orchestra; Philharmonia Orchestra / Paul Bateman**.
Silva Screen Ⓕ SONGCD911 (two discs: 121 minutes: DDD).
Songs from Jesus Christ Superstar, Joseph and the Amazing Technicolor Dreamcoat, Evita, Tell Me on a Sunday, Song and Dance, Cats, Starlight Express, Requiem, Phantom of the Opera, Aspects of Love and Sunset Boulevard.

A comprehensive tour of the Lloyd Webber canon from an expert collection of singers, revealing that for his ability to write lush, romantic ballads which stretch the talents of the finest artists, he has no rival. The star of this two-disc set is surely Lesley Garrett who, as the blossoming opera singer Christine, brings depth and credibility to the *Phantom of the Opera* selections "Wishing you were somehow here again" and "All I ask of you". She is joined by Dave Willetts, Michael Crawford's much-praised successor in the title role, who delivers a grand, soaring "Music of the night". Garrett's renderings of "Memory" (*Cats*) and "Pie Jesu" from Lloyd Webber's *Requiem* are also a delight. The original stage Mary Magdalene, Sharon Campbell, dominates the selections from *Jesus Christ Superstar*, with a definitive "I don't know how to love him". *Starlight Express* is a mammoth stage spectacle, but the score has never really joined the ranks of Lloyd Webber's musical classics. It's good, then, to hear three numbers on this set, including the duet "Next time you fall in love" performed by Campbell and Keith Burns. Among other Lloyd Webber standards, "Love changes everything" from *Aspects of Love* is stirringly sung by Chris Corcoran. Last, but hardly least, we also have Norma Desmond's towering ballads from *Sunset Boulevard* which have, over a relatively short period of time, become standard numbers by which we judge the best female singers in music theatre. Here, concert artist Mary Carewe joins their ranks with expert readings of "With one look" and "As if we never said goodbye". In all, a top quality review of Lloyd Webber's greatest hits so far. **PF**

Jesus Christ Superstar 1970 Studio Cast (with Murray Head, Ian Gillan, Yvonne Elliman, Mike d'Abo and Barry Dennen) **/ Andrew Lloyd Webber**.
MCA Ⓕ DMCX501 (two discs: 87 minutes: ADD).
Jesus Christ Superstar 1973 Film Cast (with Ted Neeley, Carl Anderson, Yvonne Elliman, Joshua Mostel and Barry Dennen) **/ André Previn**.
MCA Ⓕ MCAD2-11000 (two discs: 97 minutes: ADD).
Jesus Christ Superstar 1995 Studio Cast (with Dave Willetts, Clive Rowe, Issy van Randwyck, Christopher Biggins and Ethan Freeman) **/ Martin Yates**.
TER Ⓕ CDTER2 9026 (two discs: 94 minutes: DDD).
Jesus Christ Superstar 1996 Studio/London Cast (with Steve Balsamo, Zubin Varla, Joanna Ampil, David Burt and Alice Cooper) **/ Mike Dixon**.
Polydor Ⓕ 533 735-2 (two discs: 92 minutes: DDD).

When funding could not be found for a staged production of their second collaboration, Andrew Lloyd Webber and Tim Rice decided to invest in a studio concept recording of the work. The 1970 recording of *Jesus Christ Superstar* became an enormously successful album, especially in the United

States, where a tour production was mounted that eventually went to Broadway. A film followed as well as a long-running London production, all of which laid the foundations of the Lloyd Webber empire. The release of the studio album was perfectly timed – music theatre was entering a new era with the success of shows such as *Company* and *Hair* that aimed at a younger audience by incorporating contemporary musical influences. *Jesus Christ Superstar* offered a through-sung score with strong influences from the worlds of rock music and opera (which inspires much of the structure of the work). The presence of rock band Deep Purple's singer Ian Gillan as Christ helped immeasurably with the success of the album. It is undoubtedly an impressive piece – Lloyd Webber's music is powerful and attractive, and Tim Rice's lyrics add a contemporary (and often witty) angle to the story of Christ. Murray Head's Judas (who acts as the narrator of the story – just as Che would do for *Evita*) is excellent – bitingly savage in his condemnations, but clearly loving Christ at the same time. Gillan is surprisingly good, while Yvonne Elliman is delightful as Mary Magdalene with the recording's major hit "I don't know how to love him". Mike d'Abo turns in a good comic performance as Herod, an odd piece of camp in the midst of the dramatic second disc. Although later recordings may surpass this in terms of quality of reproduction and orchestration there is no doubt that it is a classic of modern music theatre even though it is not a production recording.

Lloyd Webber and Rice soon lost faith in Norman Jewison's 1973 film interpretation of *Jesus Christ Superstar*, but the recording is very fine, with André Previn conducting a strong orchestra that offers a far meatier sound than the original studio recording. The cast is also excellent, especially Carl Anderson's Judas, a magnificent portrayal of a man torn between two loyalties. Ted Neeley is a rather soft Jesus, while Yvonne Elliman repeats her success from the original. Joshua Mostel is a suitably camp Herod. Additional songs not on the original recording are "Then we are decided" for Caiaphas and Annas, and the impassioned "Could we start again, please?" for Mary, Peter and the Apostles. Overall one of the best recordings of this score – intense and dramatic with strong performances.

TER's new studio recording of the complete stage score includes "Could we start again, please?" as a bonus track. This is generally a good, but far from faultless version. Much of the problem resides with Dave Willetts's Jesus, which does not find focus and is difficult to listen to. Clive Rowe is a strong Judas and Issy van Randwyck a well-cast Mary. Ethan Freeman is highly effective as Pilate, turning a role which is often neglected into something of a *tour de force*. Christopher Biggins finally gets the opportunity to play Herod, having been rejected for the original London production – as expected he throws himself into the role with all his considerable personality and just about succeeds. The orchestra is really the star of this recording – almost overpowering the singers at times.

Released to coincide with the 25th anniversary revival production that opened the newly-refurbished Lyceum Theatre, the latest recording combines the leading performers from that production with a number of studio singers. Unlike the TER recording "Could we start again, please?" is included within the scope of the score, rather than as a bonus track. Steve Balsamo is an extraordinary Jesus, far superior to any of the previous, managing to emphasize the human side as well as the spiritual, combined with a superb singing voice. Zubin Varla does not quite succeed as Judas, being a little too lightweight, but Joanna Ampil is tremendous as Mary. Alice Cooper is a rather unfortunate choice for Herod not gelling well with the other performers (although his song always sits strangely in Act 2). David Burt does well with the role of Pilate and overall this is perhaps the most successful of the recordings. **RAC**

Joseph and the Amazing Technicolor Dreamcoat 1973 Studio Cast (with Gary Bond, Peter Reeves, Gordon Waller, Maynard Williams and Roger Watson).
MCA Ⓜ MCLD19023 (51 minutes: AAD).
Joseph and the Amazing Technicolor Dreamcoat 1993 Studio Cast (with Robin Cousins, Jacqui Scott, Bobby Crush, Steve Butler, Nick Curtis, Joan Baxter, Sheila Gott) / **Gordon Lorenz**.
Carlton Shows Collection Ⓑ PWKS 4163 (37 minutes: DDD).

Few hit musicals have had such a long genesis as *Joseph*. Anyone who grew up in the late 1960s or early 1970s is almost certain to have encountered the early Lloyd Webber/Rice cantata either at a concert, on a record or through performing it themselves in their own school halls. By 1973, with the word spreading, the writers had expanded it to over an hour in length and it made its début on the West End stage. Its appeal, helped by a diverse range of pop pastiche numbers, from rock and roll to country and western, has proved irresistible. After two decades as part of the staple diet of school musical life, *Joseph* finally blossomed as a full scale production at the Palladium, helped considerably by the marketing clout of soap star Jason Donovan in the lead role. Inevitably, that production was light years away from the first full-length recording, this 1973 studio version in which many of the numbers have the familiarity of well-loved nursery rhymes rather than chart-topping pop hits. Gary Bond was the first West End Joseph and, more gifted vocally than Donovan, his "Any dream will do" is considerably more resonant than the latter's. Later productions have introduced a female narrator to keep the action driving along, which has added some much needed texture to the score. The 1993 Carlton studio recording adheres to this tradition, with Jacqui Scott's bell-like clarity on numbers like "Joseph's coat" making this a most attractive budget offering. As Joseph, Robin Cousins has the right combination of sincerity and innocence which are the two keystones of this musical. As the first significant milestone in Lloyd Webber's career, it's all a far cry from the opulence of *Sunset Boulevard* or *Phantom of the Opera*.   **PF**

The Phantom of the Opera   1986 **London Cast** (with Michael Crawford, Sarah Brightman, Steve Barton, John Savident, Rosemary Ashe, David Firth, Mary Millar and John Aron) **/ Michael Reed**.
   Polydor Ⓟ 813 273-2 (two discs: 105 minutes: DDD).

The Phantom of the Opera 1993 **Studio Cast** (with Graham Bickley, Claire Moore, John Barrowman, Sandra Douglas, Megan Kelly, Mark Wynter, Michael Bauer, Ramon Remedios and Gay Soper); **Munich Symphony Orchestra / John Owen Edwards; National Symphony Orchestra / Martin Yates**.
   TER Ⓜ CDTEM1207 (43 minutes: DDD).

Lloyd Webber's work has been criticized for being derivative and certainly, for those who are looking, *The Phantom of the Opera* contains echoes of just about every notable Romantic composer. But this is a compelling tale, irresistibly told, which proved the ideal vehicle to show off Lloyd Webber's particular gifts for composing sweeping, soaring, accessible scores on a grand scale. Many consider it his finest effort so far. Romance is the *leitmotif*, not just between Christine and Raoul but, more unsettling, between Christine and the Phantom himself. And Lloyd Webber pays ample tribute to the tale's inseparable association with the genre of the horror film, so there is a thrilling undercurrent of the supernatural running through the score, with sinister organ cadences announcing the Phantom's presence (shades of Sondheim's factory whistle in *Sweeney Todd*) and, best of all, the Phantom's own throbbing, driven signature tune which will have you looking uncomfortably over your shoulder for lurking demons.

   The London cast recording contains much of the operatic dialogue (the full libretto is supplied) and was produced by Lloyd Webber himself. Michael Crawford scored an immense personal triumph as the Phantom, and remains perhaps the most touching and human of them all, suggesting the tortured soul, pathos and passion ("The music of the night") beneath the mask. Better singers have certainly succeeded Sarah Brightman in the role of Christine (Claire Moore, who is heard on the TER recording, for one), but there is no denying that her vocals, while on the shrill side, suggest the vulnerability and delicacy ("Wishing you were somehow here again") over which the Phantom and Steve Barton's Raoul must fight their ultimate battle of wills. Brightman and Barton make a fine duet of one of the show's most popular hits, "All I ask of you", while the rich exuberance of the Act 2 opening ensemble, "Masquerade", sets expectations which are more than met by the dénouement. A fine, atmospheric recording that avoids sounding studio-bound absolutely nails the lie that this show is basically a spectacle with no heart. For the economically-minded, the TER offering presents a decent selection of songs from the show. While there is little sense of the drama of the book, these are excellent vocal performances. Claire Moore is a fine Christine, bringing her delicate, controlled soprano to "Angel of music", "All I ask of you", "Wishing you were somehow here again" and "Point of no return". She is well-matched by Graham Bickley's Phantom and John Barrowman (who succeeded Steve Barton in the West End production) as Raoul.   **PF**

Song and Dance   1982 **London Cast** (with Marti Webb in *Tell Me on a Sunday*, also the music for *Theme and Variations* as danced by Wayne Sleep and company) **/ Kenny Clayton**.
   Polydor Ⓟ 843 619-2 (two discs: 102 minutes: AAD).

Song and Dance 1985 **Broadway Cast** (with Bernadette Peters in *Tell Me on a Sunday*).
   RCA Victor Ⓟ 09026 68264-2 (64 minutes: AAD).

Perhaps only Andrew Lloyd Webber could conceive London and Broadway success for an evening made up of a solo song-cycle together with a dance piece. Yet *Song and Dance* is just such a success.

It combined a one-woman concert for television, written by Lloyd Webber with Don Black for Marti Webb, *Tell Me on a Sunday* (see below) with a separate three-quarter of an hour display dance piece for the brilliant dancer Wayne Sleep and a troupe of dancers, choreographed by Anthony van Laast. It subsequently emerged on Broadway with Bernadette Peters assuming the solo role, and an entirely different choreographic setting of the *Theme and Variations*, this time by Peter Martins.

In the original show, Marti Webb returned at the end of the dance to sing "When you want to fall in love" (based on one of the *Paganini Variations*). On Broadway the lyric was changed, retitled "Unexpected song", and placed earlier in the show. The songs find both Andrew Lloyd Webber and master lyricist Don Black on top form – "Tell me on a Sunday" is a wonderful song on any level – and it's just one of many. As the English girl in New York fearing the end of a passionate relationship, Bernadette Peters is touching and effective, but the show was written for Marti Webb and her assumption of the role that was written for her, captured in a completely successful live recording on the occasion of the first night at London's Palace Theatre, is thrilling and moving – and the addition of the music for Lloyd Webber's *Variations on a Theme by Paganini* is a powerful plus. Both employ the heightened, more passionate ending to "Tell me on a Sunday" rewritten by the composer at the behest of the original director rather than that featured on the original television version.   **MPK**

Starlight Express **1984 London Cast** (with Stephanie Lawrence, Ray Shell, Lon Satton, Frances Ruffelle and Jeff Shankley) / **David Caddick**.
Polydor Ⓕ 821 597-2 (two discs: 99 minutes: AAD).
The New Starlight Express **1993 London Cast** (with Tara Wilkinson, Debbie Blackett, Greg Ellis, John Partridge, Reva Rice, Lon Satton and Maynard Williams) / **Phil Edwards**.
Polydor Ⓕ 519 041-2 (70 minutes: AAD).

Andrew Lloyd Webber's trains musical *Starlight Express* exists (or existed) in two versions. Both London and New York versions featured a set of elimination races between a number of varied locomotives. This being a British show, naturally the least advanced and powerful one, a steam engine called Rusty, won. The original, mounted in London featured a devious guards van or caboose called CB which did everything it could to thwart him – and a number of others. He was given a fine song called "There's me" but that didn't save him. The character and song were eliminated for New York and subsequently from the British production when it was revised in 1993 to parallel the Broadway one. At the same time a new song "Next time you fall in love" (lyric by Don Black) was added plus four others with alterations to a number of other lyrics, and the plot anchored to a framework of a child playing with his train set. The score has a fine eclectic mix of catchy numbers reflecting the composer's deep love of American popular music idioms – rap, gospel, country and western and rock 'n' roll predominating; this is a score for youngsters. This also happens to be a show where you really need to buy both recordings – the two-disc original offering fine performances from Frances Ruffelle, Jeff Shankley and Ray Shell with veteran Lon Satton as Papa, made in 1984, and the newer revised version offering Greg Ellis, Reva Rice – and Lon Satton in his original part.   **MPK**

Sunset Boulevard **1993 London Cast** (with Patti LuPone, Kevin Anderson, Meredith Braun and Daniel Benzali) / **David Caddick**.
Polydor Ⓕ 519 767-2 (two discs: 96 minutes: DDD).
Sunset Boulevard **1993 Los Angeles Cast** (with Glenn Close, Alan Campbell, Judy Kuhn and George Hearn) / **Paul Bogaev**.
Polydor Ⓕ 523 507 2 (two discs: 123 minutes: DDD).

The world première recording of *Sunset Boulevard* was made just after the première of the London production, before the show was closed for over a month to make adjustments to the staging and content following its disappointing reception. These changes have been incorporated into the American recording which, as its timing indicates, gives us much more of the story than the London version as well as the more authoritative performances of Glenn Close as Norma Desmond and Alan Campbell as Joe the reporter who penetrates her decaying mansion on Sunset Boulevard. Lloyd Webber has composed some of his most memorable tunes for this show, including "With one look", "The perfect year" and "As if we never said goodbye", sung by Close in three key scenes marking her journey back to the studio after 20 years absence. The rest of the score, save for a lyrical second act duet for Joe and his girl friend, veers uneasily between over-familiar Lloyd Webber trademarks and the lush orchestral compositions of the old school of Hollywood composers, fertile ground for David

Cullen's orchestrations. Though the idea of a through-sung musical has always been an exciting prospect, I still need to be convinced of its superiority over the traditional book, music and lyrics formula – especially when in this instance the words are never more than workmanlike. **AE**

Tell Me on a Sunday 1980 **Studio Cast** (with Marti Webb).
  Polydor Ⓟ 833 447-2 (41minutes: AAD).

Lloyd Webber's song cycle is built around the romantic entanglements of a young English woman who has moved to America, starting in New York and ending in California, with dry, poignant lyrics by Don Black. Later developed as the first half of the immensely successful *Song and Dance* (see above), *Tell Me on a Sunday* started out as a modest one-woman show at the Sydmonton Festival in 1979, taking British television audiences by storm when it was transmitted as a concert by the BBC. The show was a tremendous personal success for Marti Webb, a perrenial of the British musical stage who succeeded Elaine Paige as Evita and Grizabella. She seized this material for her own, interpreting the lyrics with a clever mixture of vulnerabililty, North London toughness transplanted to Manhattan and the basic optimism of the character through a series of doomed relationships. Apart from some soliloquies ("Let me finish" and "Letter home to England", for example), *Tell Me on a Sunday* is essentially a collection of fine, modern pop songs which rate among Lloyd Webber's best work. "Take that look off your face" was the show's biggest hit, a loud, up-tempo ballad directed at the bitchy friend who blows the cover of the first errant lover. Other notable numbers include "You made me think you were in love" and "I'm very you, you're very me" and the beautiful "Nothing like you've ever known", a well-crafted mistress's torch song. There is also plenty of humour in the vampish "Sheldon Bloom" and "Capped teeth and Caesar salad", a droll summary of first impressions of Californian high life. **PF**

Frank Loesser   1910-1969 USA

Born in New York, the product of a musical family with distinctly highbrow inclinations – his half-brother, Arthur, became a successful pianist and music scholar – Frank was more interested in pop than classical. He worked in various jobs after attending City College, including journalism, performing in a vaudeville act and writing lyrics for Tin Pan Alley. "In love with a memory of you", his first published song written with composer William Schuman, appeared in 1931. His lyrics for *The Illustrator's Show* (1936) resulted in a contract from Universal Pictures in Hollywood where he wrote lyrics for over 20 film musicals, with individual songs contributed to some 40 others. During the war he started writing his own music for Army shows: *Skirts* (1944) *About Face* (1944) and *OK, USA* (1945). Then in 1948 he wrote the music and lyrics for his first Broadway show, *Where's Charley?*, adapted from Brandon Thomas's farce *Charley's Aunt* by George Abbott (who also directed). This was followed by the even more successful *Guys and Dolls* (1950; filmed in 1955 with Frank Sinatra, Jean Simmons and Marlon Brando). *The Most Happy Fella* (1956) followed, another hit running for 676 performances, but *Greenwillow* (1960) was commercially unsuccessful. *How to Succeed in Business without Really Trying* (1961) ran longer than any of his other shows (1,417 performances; 520 in London) and became only the fourth musical to win a Pullitzer Prize. His last show, however, *Pleasures and Palaces* (1965), failed to even reach Broadway. The Danny Kaye film, *Hans Christian Andersen* (1952), is his best known Hollywood score: it was adapted for the London stage in 1974 with Tommy Steele in the lead.

Frank sings Loesser Frank Loesser, with **Lynn Loesser, William Schuman, Abe Burrows, Shorty Long** (sngrs); **Milton DeLugg Quartet; Mitch Miller Chorus and Orchestra**.
Koch International mono Ⓟ 37241-2 (49 minutes: AAD). Recorded 1930-60.
Songs from Where's Charley?, Variety Girl and Hans Christian Andersen. *Songs by* Loesser, Meyer, Schuman and McHugh.

Frank Loesser has a secure place in the pages of twentieth-century music theatre as the composer and lyricist of *Guys and Dolls*. This collection includes only a couple of songs from Loesser's Broadway output, the cute "Once in love with Amy" and the charming "Make a miracle" from *Where's Charley?*. This is a shame, for what we would not have given to hear him in "Luck be a lady" or "More I cannot wish you" from *Guys and Dolls*. As it is, we hear most of his score for the Danny Kaye film, *Hans Christian Andersen* and that little comedy gem, "Baby, it's cold outside" which caused Richard Rodgers to jump out of his seat in an emotional response and ring Loesser to congratulate him on "a valid work of art". Frank, with his wife Lynn – whom Broadway folklore dubbed 'the evil of two Loessers' – give it just the right touch of insouciance. Loesser himself was an outspoken man, a chain smoker (you catch that as he clears his throat at one point), who died too young at 59. He was the first to admit that he was an indifferent singer but collections of this nature never fail to throw up curiosities, as his duets with fellow composer William Schuman, recorded onto a 'speak-o-machine' in a Broadway storefront, testify. Like all Broadway songwriters he relishes his words as much as the music, bringing to such familiar songs as "Wonderful Copenhagen" ("'neath her tavern light/On this merry night/Let us clink and drink one down") a woozy charm that Danny Kaye never suggested. The transfers are tactfully managed and the fulsome notes come with a loving introduction from Susan Loesser (whose sister Emily appears on TER's *Guys and Dolls*) to her father. **AE**

Greenwillow 1960 **Broadway Cast** (with Anthony Perkins, Cecil Kellaway, Pert Kelton, Ellen McKown, William Chapman and Grover Dale) **/ Abba Bogin**.
DRG Ⓟ 19006 (44 minutes: AAD).

Greenwillow is a musical about a mythical village in which everyone talks and most behave like Ned Flanders, the goody-goody neighbour from *The Simpsons*. The first word of the first song ("A day borrowed from Heaven") is "twill"; which, coming from that smartest of lyricists Frank Loesser, sounds even quainter than intended. Mind you, within a couple of lines Loesser's old self perks up: "I turned my neck and the crick was gone ... Slept on my left side and lived the night". It's still sweetness and light but wittily specific in its details. And that grows: one of the peaks of high comic irony in the Broadway musical is "What a blessing" in which Cecil Kellaway, as a complacently benevolent minister named Reverend Birdsong, muses on the advantages of original sin; a man's backslidings are always Satan's fault and – note the clinching internal rhyme – "a liar is merely the innocent buyer of lies from the liar-in-chief". "What a blessing to know there's a devil, or we'd all simply die of shame": what a mercy, too, that Loesser couldn't help being of his party.

Not that the whimsy is all unbearable; the book may have been (Loesser co-wrote it), but the disc gives us only the score, and it contains some of his best and most original melodies. Anthony Perkins, in his only Broadway musical, brings a true if sulky voice to the near-standard "Never will I marry" and the surging, racing "Summertime love." Ellen McCown, as the object of his attention, returns the compliment with an especially graceful ballad called "Faraway boy." And just as Rodgers and

Hammerstein shaded their idyllic *Oklahoma!* with the sardonic humours of "Pore Jud is daid", so Loesser provides his own departed villain with an elegy even more blandly double-edged: "How nice for the widow in her widowhood/The comfort of knowing – he died good." **RC**

Guys and Dolls 1950 **Broadway Cast** (with Robert Alda, Vivian Blane, Stubby Kaye and Isabel Bigley) / **Irving Actman**.
MCA mono Ⓜ MCLD10301 (41 minutes: AAD).

Guys and Dolls 1992 **Broadway Cast** (with Walter Bobbie, John Carpenter, Steve Ryan, Ernie Sabella, Herschel Sparber and Ruth Williamson) / **Edward Strauss**.
RCA Victor Ⓕ 09026 61317-2 (59 minutes: DDD).

Guys and Dolls 1995 **Studio Cast** (with Lynn Loesser, Gregg Edelman, Tim Flavin and Kim Criswell); **National Symphony Orchestra** / **John Owen Edwards**.
TER Ⓕ CDTER2 1228 (two discs: 97 minutes: DDD).

Members of the original cast put their individual stamp so firmly on Damon Runyon's characters that for 40 years and more we've returned to Stubby Kaye for "Sit down you're rockin' the boat", Vivian Blane for "Adelaide's lament" and Isabel Bigley for "If I were a bell". Frank Sinatra and his chums had a crack at this show in the 1955 film version, and the 1982 National Theatre's vocally undernourished revival was also recorded. But in addition to the still worthy original, the last few years have seen the release of both a very good single CD selection of highlights from the recent Broadway production and a two-disc studio recording that gives us all of Frank Loesser's score, plus the songs he composed for the film version.

The new TER set, superbly conducted and played, features the treasurable Emily Loesser, the composer's daughter, in the role of the Salvation Army lass, Sarah Brown. Her voice is of the kind Broadway no longer seems to produce – it carries sweetness and lung power in equal measure. Gregg Edelman as Sky Masterson has the measure of his role too. All their scenes together are a joy: their opening meeting, their duet "I'll know", their evening out at the Havana bistro where he primes Sarah with Bacardi milk shakes before her tipsy carolling of "If I were a bell". Then comes his idyll to the Manhattan dawn, "My time of day", and their ecstatic duet, "I've never been in love before" – wonderful writing blessed with singing that captures all the rapture of love at first sight. Nor is there a weak link amongst the rest of the cast: Kim Criswell is a very funny Miss Adelaide, and Brian Greene is effective as the missionary who befriends Sarah in his gentle song "More I cannot wish you". The choral work, notably the tricky syncopated contributions of "Luck be a lady" and "Sit down you're rockin' the boat" complements the immaculate playing of the orchestra; the original orchestrations are conducted with loving care by John Owen Edwards. Though one may not wish to sit through the Havana bistro music on each playing, there's no doubt that this is the *Guys and Dolls* that can stand comparison with the original and, who knows, lead the selection for the next 40 years? **AE**

Hans Christian Andersen 1952 **Film Cast** (with Danny Kaye) / **Gordon Jenkins**.
Varèse Sarabande mono Ⓕ VSD5498 (56 minutes: ADD). Disc also includes **Sylvia Fine**: The Court Jester 1956 **Film Cast** (with Danny Kaye) / **Vic Schoen**.

Hearing Danny Kaye performing songs like "The ugly duckling", "Thumbelina" and "The king's new clothes" will bring back memories for anyone like me who was brought up on Derek McCulloch's *Children's Favourites* on the BBC's Light Programme. Throughout the 1950s, the requests for songs from *Hans Christian Andersen* alternated weekly on the Saturday morning programme, despite the fact that the film was never a popular favourite like *The Court Jester*. The other Danny Kaye film on this CD received less attention on the radio, but was much more fun than *Hans Andersen*, with Kaye bringing his inimitable touch to the tongue-twisting "chalice from the palace" routine. Amongst the cheerful ditties in *The Court Jester* was "Life could not better be", music by Mrs Kaye, Sylvia Fine, which became the signature tune of his subsequent television series. But it's each number in *Hans Andersen*, whether in romantic or story telling vein, that still creates a spell in Kaye's straight-as-an-arrow yet affectionate performances. **AE**

How to Succeed in Business Without Really Trying 1961 **Broadway Cast** (with Robert Morse, Rudy Vallee, Bonnie Scott and Virginia Martin) / **Elliot Lawrence**.
RCA Victor Ⓜ 60352-2 (49 minutes: ADD).

How to Succeed in Business Without Really Trying 1995 Broadway Cast (with
Matthew Broderick and Walter Kronkite).
RCA Victor ℗ 09026 68197-2 (60 minutes: DDD).

The differences in the running times of these two recordings is chiefly accounted for by the voice of the narrator, Walter Kronkite, linking together the musical numbers from this satirical musical on the theme of businessmen on the make. The original book, written way back in 1952 by Shepherd Mead, remains as pertinent as ever in our money-led culture, and Frank Loesser's songs have lost nothing in their sharply observed satirical digs at office manners. The opening chorus sets the tone as the office staff work themselves into a frenzy over their coffee break. Romance comes in the same style, "I'd be happy to keep his dinner warm", sings an infatuated girl, whilst the innocent hero isn't addressing a pretty secretary in "I believe in you" but himself in a shaving mirror! Choice between the two recordings, 34 years apart but hardly noticeable, will likely turn on the more distinctive and assured performances given by Robert Morse and Rudy Vallee in the original 1961 recording to that of Matthew Broderick and the ensemble in the latest one. As the original orchestrations are a shade more faithful to the spirit of the songs I'd be inclined to stick with the earlier of the two.   **AE**

The Most Happy Fella 1956 Broadway Cast (with Robert Weede, Jo Sullivan, Art Lund,
Susan Johnson, Short Long, Mona Paulee and Lee Cass) **/ Herbert Greene**.
Sony Broadway mono ℗ S2K48010 (two discs: 130 minutes: ADD).
The Most Happy Fella 1991 Broadway Cast (with Spiro Malas, Sophie Hayden, Claudia
Catania, Buddy Crutchfield, Tad Ingram and Liz Larsen) **/ Tom Stella**.
RCA Victor ℗ 09026 61294-2 (74 minutes: DDD).

Frank Loesser's rural semi-operatic masterpiece, *The Most Happy Fella*, is a great musical achievement packed with heart-warming songs such as "My heart is so full of you", "Somebody somewhere", "Warm all over" and rousing concerted numbers which include "Big D" and "Standing on the corner". The tale of Tony, the simple farmer who sends off for a mail-order bride with a photo of his handsome farm hand, inspired the composer of *Guys and Dolls* to create his longest and most elaborate score. As for the recordings, a glance at the timings of the two available performances tells it all. The choice is between a virtually complete recording with full Broadway orchestrations, and highlights from an intimate small-scale revival with reduced orchestration (four musicians). Both Spiro Malas and Robert Weede are excellent as Tony, and Jo Sullivan (later to become wife of the composer) and Sophie Hayden make the bride, Rosabella, both appealing and charming . Completists will insist on the Sony recording. The RCA is a useful pendant, in glowing stereo.   **MPK**

Where's Charley? 1958 London Cast (with Norman Wisdom, Pip Hinton, Marion
Grimaldi, Felix Felton, Jerry Desmonde, Terence Cooper and Barry Kent) **/ Michael
Collins**.
EMI Angel Ⓜ ZDM7 65071-2 (40 minutes: ADD).

Ten years after it appeared on Broadway in 1948, Frank Loesser's first Broadway musical turned up in the West End with Norman Wisdom as Charlie Wykeham the undergraduate who doubles as Charley's Aunt. This was EMI's first stereo recording of a West End show, though it was issued at the time only in mono. Norman Newell's production sounds remarkably fit in Vic Lanza's digital transfer which brings back memories for me of a Christmas outing to this show in the school holidays. Norman Wisdom was the biggest home-grown star of the time and he gets to sing that soft-shoe show-stopper, "Once in love with Amy" as well as the intricate "Make a miracle", a classic bit of Loesser versifying in which he's joined by Pip Hinton, a bright engaging soprano. Hinton and Marion Grimaldi, singing the pretty "Lovelier than ever" somewhat outflank the male company on this recording, although Felix Felton is not to be missed in the Gilbertian "Serenade with asides". The large orchestra, very cleanly focussed in the stereo image, was conducted with élan by Michael Collins, a distinguished name in the pantheon of light music conductors. Warmly recommended.   **AE**

Also available:
Anywhere I Wander (Liz Callaway) Varèse Sarabande VSD5434

Guys and Dolls (1982 National Theatre Cast) MfP CD-MFP5978
Guys and Dolls (1995 Studio Cast) Carlton Shows Collection 30362 0013-2
Hans Christian Andersen (1974 London Cast) DRG DRGCD13116

Frederick Loewe
1901-1988 Germany

Alan Jay Lerner
1918-1986 USA

Berlin-born Frederick Loewe was taught piano by Busoni and d'Albert and studied composition with Reznicek. He emigrated to the USA in 1924. Some of his songs appeared in Broadway productions in the 1930s before he produced his first show, *Great Lady*, in 1938. Songs featured in *Salute to Spring* (1937) were reused in *Life of the Party* (1942) which had a book by Alan Jay Lerner. Born in New York, Lerner had studied at the Institute of Musical Art and Harvard before working as a radio scriptwriter. After meeting Loewe in 1942 he wrote the lyrics for all of the composer's subsequent shows, beginning with *What's Up?* (1943). Their first success together was *Brigadoon* (1947), an original story by Lerner, which ran for 581 performances on Broadway and 685 in London and was filmed in 1954. This was followed by *Paint Your Wagon* (1951), their only distinctively American show: unlike Rodgers and Hammerstein, Lerner and Loewe specialized in European operetta-style shows. The 1969 film adaptation contains Lee Marvin's gravelly rendition of "Wand'rin' star" which was an unexpected hit. *My Fair Lady* (1956) was the team's biggest success. Loewe tailored his music to fit star Rex Harrison's recitative-like half-spoken half-sung delivery, a ploy he repeated both for Louis Jourdan in the film *Gigi* (1958) and Richard Burton in *Camelot* (1960). *Gigi*, directed by Vincente Minnelli, was the first Hollywood musical to be filmed almost entirely in Paris and won nine Academy Awards, including Best Film; unusually it was a film first and only adapted for the stage in 1973. After *Camelot* (filmed in 1967), Lerner and Loewe collaborated only one more time, on the film *The Little Prince* (1974). Lerner also worked with composers Kurt Weill (*Love Life*, 1948), Burton Lane (*On a Clear Day You Can See Forever*, 1965 and *Carmelina*, 1979), André Previn (*Coco*, 1969), Leonard Bernstein (*1600 Pennsylvania Avenue*, 1976) and Charles Strouse (*Dance a Little Closer*, 1983).

Brigadoon **1954 Film Cast** (with Gene Kelly, Van Johnson and Carol Richards for Cyd Charisse); **MGM Studio Chorus and Orchestra / Johnny Green**.
EMI Ⓔ CDODEON16 (69 minutes: ADD).
Brigadoon **1991 Studio Cast** (with Brent Barrett, Rebecca Luker, Judy Kaye and John Mark Ainsley); **Ambrosian Chorus; London Sinfonietta / John McGlinn**.
EMI Angel Ⓔ CDC7 54481-2 (79 minutes: DDD).

The film of *Brigadoon* (1954) has unfortunately long been remembered for its giant cardboard sets constructed on the MGM backlot after the studio decided against Gene Kelly's desire to have it filmed in Scotland. Loewe's score suffered too when some numbers that were originally recorded were later deleted because they slowed down the pace of the narrative. Others became victims of the Hollywood production code, so were never recorded. Whilst it remains a continuing regret that Meg's racy numbers aren't here, we do have "Come to me, bend to me" and the other ballads reinstated in their rightful position in this lovingly restored, magnificently played and arranged soundtrack. It may well be felt that the orchestral contribution is its highlight – not least in the unfolding of the glorious "Heather on the hill" melody in the luscious arrangement by Conrad Salinger. Cyd Charisse's vocals were dubbed by Carol Richards, who before Marni Nixon came along had already performed the same duty for Vera-Ellen in *Call Me Madam*. The bulk of the singing fell to Gene Kelly who worked hard to master Loewe's demanding vocal lines. His singing of "Almost like being in love", the score's one ballad with an American slant, is put over with great panache, heeding both the exultant message of the refrain and its poetic verse: "Maybe the sun gave me the pow'r/For I could swim Loch Lomond and be home in half an hour".

John McGlinn conducted *Brigadoon* for his EMI series when plans for an *Oklahoma!* recording collapsed. The result was by no means a stop-gap, but arguably the finest recording he has given us in his now complete series. With the sole reservation that Judy Kaye tries too hard to sell Meg's comic songs this is a faultless issue in all departments, not least in the lilting and pointed orchestral playing of the London Sinfonietta. In this recording, *Brigadoon* emerges as fine a piece as the same composer's *My Fair Lady*, indeed placed by some commentators as its equal. An outstanding issue. **AE**

Camelot 1961 **Broadway Cast** (with Richard Burton, Julie Andrews, Robert Goulet and Roddy McDowall) / **Franz Allers**.
Columbia Ⓜ CK32602 (52 minutes: AAD).

Camelot 1982 **London Cast** (with Richard Harris, Fiona Fullerton, Robert Meadmore, Robin Bailey and Michael Howe) / **Gerry Allison**.
TER Ⓕ CDTER1030 (60 minutes: DDD).

Camelot is one of the most uneven of musicals, and one of the most moving. It takes the intractable material of Arthurian legend and goes some way towards making a tragedy out of it: a tragedy of – in order of appearance – trust, disillusion and hope. Its basic strengths, as well as some of its glaring incidental weaknesses, lie in Alan Jay Lerner's book. So, more than any other musical in the glorious Columbia/Sony catalogue, it suffers on its original cast album from producer Goddard Lieberson's distrust of spoken dialogue. The great ending, in which Arthur dispatches the boy who presumably will grow up to be Sir Thomas Malory, to flee the battle and hand on the story, is reduced to a simple reprise of the title song. It's a tribute to Richard Burton's performance, as well as to the power of the situation and the cunning of Lerner's lyric and Loewe's music, that this still retains considerable effect. A song that started as a jingle becomes an invocation. Elsewhere Burton, in what was almost his last notable stage performance, works a sombre bardic magic, sometimes speaking his songs, sometimes singing them, and most often intoning them in a Celtic register all his own; it's a fine noise, whichever it is, and it conveys both Arthur's boyishness and his majesty. Julie Andrews has probably her best role as Guenevere, wistfully flirtatious in "The simple joys of maidenhood", and Robert Goulet certainly has his as Lancelot.

The TER disc preserves a revival designed to exploit Richard Harris's association with the show via the 1967 movie. Fiona Fullerton's giggly rendition of "The merry month of May" is even less bearable than Andrews's, and the Lancelot of Robert Meadmore bleats his way through a role that depends on pure voice. "Then you may take me to the fair", one of the score's more amusing numbers, has been cut, and "Fie on goodness", the only outright funny one, much diminished, possibly in the interests of political correctness. "Guenevere", a desperate attempt to cram half-an-hour's worth of story into three minutes, works far better on TER than on Columbia, since it's fleshed-out with speech. And this is the making of the album; significantly one of the strongest impressions is made by William Squire as Merlin, who doesn't sing (years before Squire, another Welshman, was Burton's Broadway replacement as Arthur). Harris is allowed the full version of the finale, and it pricks the eyes as surely as ever; he even gets "Resolution", the wholly spoken section in which Arthur agonizingly outlines what Mordred gleefully calls his "magnificent dilemma". The record lets us know what the show is about; and it's rewarding knowledge; and Harris, however comatose he may have been on stage, is fine on disc. He doesn't have Burton's haunting vocal contours, but he is lucid and sensitive, and actually sings more of the notes. Particularly effective is "How to handle a woman"; Harris talks the verse (omitted on Columbia) like Professor Higgins – which is how it's written – and then flows gently and touchingly into the chorus. It's how to handle a lyric. **RC**

Gigi 1958 **Film Cast** (with Maurice Chevalier, Louis Jourdan, Betty Wand for Leslie Caron and Hermione Gingold); **MGM Studio Chorus and Orchestra / André Previn**.
EMI Ⓕ CDODEON10 (75 minutes: ADD).

Though not quite the grand finale, MGM's *Gigi* was the last of its movie musicals to gain both critical acclaim and a popular appeal that has lasted to this day. Written and composed by Lerner and Loewe in the wake of their triumphant success with *My Fair Lady*, it boasted a number of likeable scenes and songs, amongst them the cheerfully impromptu "The night they invented champagne" rendered by Leslie Caron (dubbed by Betty Wand), Hermione Gingold and Louis Jourdan; the bittersweet duet between Gingold and Maurice Chevalier, "I remember it well"; Jourdan's two soliloquies, "She's not thinking of me" and "Gigi", and Caron's brief bedroom solo, "Say a prayer for me tonight". Add Chevalier's "Thank heaven for little girls" and his show-stopping "I'm glad I'm not young anymore" and you have one of the last original scores created for the screen of that era. *Gigi* was very poorly served by the MGM sound engineers on its initial appearance in 1959, but with this issue the sound editing department have performed nothing short of a miracle. The hemmed-in sound of the original recording has been opened up to reveal the MGM Studio Orchestra in all its glory, with many rich underscoring cues appearing for the first time in their full-length versions. There are 42 cues in all, including Leslie Caron's original versions of Gigi's songs, with the film's musical director André Previn at the piano. Caron had been determined to sing herself, but in this instance wise counsel prevailed and all her songs were performed by Betty Wand. Significantly Lerner and Loewe threw out the original orchestrations for the film which they felt were too steeped in the Hollywood idiom. The crisp incisive playing under Previn, more akin to a Broadway band was, according to the author's wishes, making this recording the finest memento I've heard of one of the peaks of movie musical production.   **AE**

My Fair Lady 1964 Film Cast (with Rex Harrison, Marni Nixon for Audrey Hepburn, Stanley Holloway, Bill Shirley for Jeremy Brett and Wilfred Hyde-White) / **André Previn**.
Sony Classical Ⓕ SK66711 (76 minutes: ADD).

My Fair Lady 1994 Studio Cast (with Tinuke Olafimihan, Alec McCowen, Bob Hoskins, Michael Denison, Henry Wickham, Dulcie Gray, Barrie James, Michael Bauer and Jill Pert) **Chorus; National Symphony Orchestra / John Owen Edwards**.
TER Ⓕ CDTER2 1211 (two discs: 101 minutes: DDD).

'Philips Masterworks' stated the surround of the red label of the original UK issue of the Broadway cast album of *My Fair Lady*, (available in the USA on Columbia) and I can remember the excitement as the release date approached in April 1958, the month the show opened at Drury Lane Theatre. Many visitors to America had already smuggled back their own copies of the LP on which there was a strict play ban, but it didn't stop Philips Records charging an unprecedented two pounds for their product. The original artists, Rex Harrison, Julie Andrews and Stanley Holloway left such a strong imprint on the score that, aside from the film soundtrack with two of the same performers, no top price *My Fair Lady* was recorded until Decca issued their version with Dame Kiri Te Kanawa and Jeremy Irons over 30 years later!.

Warren Mitchell's lovable portrayal of Alfred Doolittle was the highlight of that erratic production; conversely the same role is the one disappointing feature of this new TER set, where Bob Hoskins's vocal limitations allow for little humour to come across. That apart, and the overture which sounds under-rehearsed, this *My Fair Lady* takes a grip on the listener in a way that's rare outside the theatre. This is partly due to the two-disc format that gives us incidental music and passages of dialogue hitherto unavailable, so enhancing the already considerable stature of this musical. The casting of Higgins, Eliza and Freddie Eynsford-Hill is also spot-on. Alec McCowen's Higgins is the most musical performance so far on disc. It isn't just that he sings more of Loewe's music than Harrison, but rather that he invests it with such an appreciation of the English language that one forgets all about his predecessor in this role – and that's no mean feat. His Professor has a genuine desire to make his protegé not only an English lady but a girl for whom he could find a place in his heart, as Lerner and Loewe's ending suggests. Tinuke Olafimihan sings "I could have danced all night" magnificently and her Cockney scenes are no less convincing. Though not possessed with a power-house voice, Henry Wickham brings a winning charm to "On the street where you live" as well as an innate sense of Freddie's background. The listener in Freddie's words, drinks in the street where she (Eliza) lives during his exchanges at the door with Mrs Pearce, Jill Pert, who gives a touching cameo as Higgins's housekeeper. Elocution may now be out of fashion but he and McCowen are both advocates for its revival, so beautifully do they deliver their mother tongue. The chorus deserve a special mention for their splendid contribution to this *Gramophone* Award-winning recording. As with their recording of *Street Scene*, TER have added some wild track background effects for local colour to certain scenes. Did I detect the same hob nail boots on Covent Garden's cobble stones coming round again?

The soundtrack album contains material never before available and sounds all the better for it. There are certain things like Robert Tucker's Hollywood-style vocal setting of "Get me to the church on time" that make me wince each time I hear it but it remains a fine memento of a film musical where the polish and virtuosity of the orchestral playing under André Previn is a special treat.   **AE**

Paint Your Wagon 1951 Broadway Cast (with James Barton, Olga San Juan and Tony Bavaar) / **Franz Allers**.
RCA Victor mono Ⓜ 60243-2 (42 minutes: ADD)
Paint Your Wagon 1969 Film Cast (with Clint Eastwood, Lee Marvin, Harve Presnell, Anita Gordon and Alan Dexter) / **Nelson Riddle**.
MCA Ⓜ MCLD19310 (47 minutes: AAD).

Paint Your Wagon, set in the California gold fields, was not the most successful of the Alan Jay Lerner-Frederick Loewe musicals, but it competes with *Brigadoon* as the repository of Loewe's best tunes. (*My Fair Lady* obviously has Lerner's best lyrics). Its first number "I'm on my way", a wonderful scene- and mood-setter showing gold rushing to the heads of a converging band of prospective prospectors, is as stirring an opening as a musical can ever have had. "There's a coach comin' in", the first-half finale, runs a close second in the arousal stakes, and "Hand me down that can o' beans", which starts Act 2, comes in a distant but respectable third. Loewe, generally thought of as a European operetta man, has the American sound and the American vitality down amazingly well (it probably helps that it's period American). Then there are the ballads, "I talk to the trees" and "They call the wind Maria", familiar but still fresh. James Barton, a veteran song-and-dancer who was the original cast's senior gold-digger, gets three choice solos: "I still see Elisa", recalling his late wife; "In between", modestly courting a new one; and the now-classic "Wand'rin' star". Olga San Juan, as the heroine, has Lerner's most original contribution, the yearning "How can I wait?" sung to her beloved's laundry ("I wish his legs was in these pants"); and the hero, Tony Bavaar, gets a slice of the truly haunting "Another autumn." It's a sobering thought that in the 1950s audiences probably took all this for granted. Another good show, more new hits on the airwaves, and what happens next week?

What happened next decade was a film, supervised by Lerner, that supplied a new story, ditched several of the original songs (too modest and graceful, perhaps) and supplied some new ones with tunes – mostly dull – by André Previn. The film has an evil reputation but the soundtrack CD, though it begins with rapacious spectral voices intoning "Gold!", makes surprisingly painless listening (Nelson Riddle did the arrangements). Eastwood comes off as a nice amateur crooner, though he seems to be singing "I talk to the trees" in two alternating keys, one that he can manage and one that he can't. The register in which Marvin growls the middle eight of his celebrated "Wan'drin' star" may be his own discovery; the main theme he sings comparatively conventionally – and with perfect competence. He also does well by "The first thing you know", the best of the new songs and a vehicle for Lerner's social and ecological conscience. The third star, Jean Seberg, makes no impression; her one throroughly disposable song "A million miles away behind the door" was dubbed by Anita Gordon. "They call the wind Maria" was assigned to a real singer, Harve Presnell, and he rather spoils you for everything else. **RC**

Also available:
Brigadoon (1947 Broadway Cast) RCA 81001-2
Brigadoon (1988 London Cast) First Night OCRCD6022
Camelot (1967 Film Cast) Warner Bros 7599-27325-2
Gigi (1985 London Cast) First Night OCRCD6007
Gigi (1973 Broadway Cast) RCA 09026 68070-2
My Fair Lady (1956 Broadway Cast) Columbia SK66128
My Fair Lady (1958 London Cast) Columbia CK02015
My Fair Lady (1987 Studio Cast) Decca 421 200-2
My Fair Lady (1994 Studio Cast) Carlton Shows Collection PWKS4174

Amanda McBroom

Heartbeats 1994 Los Angeles Cast (with Amanda McBroom, George Ball, Michele Maika, Kevin Bailey, William Falk and Sharon McKnight) / **Ann-Carol Pence**.
Varèse Sarabande Spotlight Series Ⓕ VSD5527 (60 minutes: DDD). Additional music by Gerald Sternbach, Michele Brourman, Tom Snow and Craig Safan.

Amanda McBroom is best known as the composer of "The Rose", the title song from the 1979 Bette Midler movie. That song is included in this themed revue of her work, along with many other examples of her songwriting talents, as well as displaying her abilities as a performer. McBroom is Annie, a married woman with two children, about to 'celebrate' her fortieth birthday and taking the opportunity to reassess her life. Her husband, Steve, is played by George Ball and the remaining performers take on a variety of roles, with Michele Maika and William Falk playing the young Annie and Steve. McBroom writes strong lyrics with a contemporary often humorous feel, concerning herself with the predicaments of modern life, of ageing and the loss of one's illusions. In "Putting things away" she uses the mundane task of tidying up to illustrate how life forces one to abandon dreams. "Dance" is a stunning, bittersweet ballad about the loss of romance within a marriage, while "Ship in a bottle" (which has achieved fame as part of Barbara Cook's repertoire) is a magnificent song about the need for love to set the spirit free, here performed with real feeling by Michele Maika. Performing her own songs, McBroom is clearly in her element – these are the subjects and themes that matter to her. Her voice is warm and strong with a genuine dramatic flair. As one listens to her wondering whether to have an affair in "Somebody" or whether she should tell her husband in "Anything but the truth" one is struck by the honesty of her emotions. At the end there is reconciliation, but it is far from sentimental. *Heartbeats* is a contemporary musical, engagingly told from a woman's point of view, with the rare distinction of having a woman as book and lyric writer and the main composer. **RAC**

Galt MacDermot

b. 1928 Canada

Born in Montreal, Galt MacDermot achieved fame and not a little notoriety with his "tribal love-rock musical" *Hair* when it was first staged in October 1967 at the New York Shakespeare Festival Public Theater. The book and lyrics were by Gerome Ragni and James Rado. The show arrived in London in September 1968, where it took advantage of the recent liberalization of the theatre to run for 1,998 performances. It was filmed in 1979. MacDermot's later shows were *Isabel's a Jezebel* (1970), *Two Gentlemen of Verona* (1971) – a successful fusion of Shakespeare and rock music – *Dude* and *Via Galactica* (both 1972).

Hair 1968 Broadway Cast (with Ronald Dyson, Gerome Ragni, Steve Curry, Lamont Washington, James Rado, Melba Moore, Sally Eaton, Shelley Plimpton, Jonathan Kramer, Lynn Kellogg and Paul Jabara); **Galt MacDermot** (electric pf) and other musicians.
RCA Victor Ⓕ BD89667 (67 minutes: ADD).

Hair 1979 Film Cast (with John Savage, Treat Williams, Beverly D'Angelo, Annie Golden, Dorsey Wright, Don Dacus, Cheryl Barnes and Melba Moore) / **Galt MacDermot**.
RCA Victor Ⓜ 74321 28985-2 (two discs: 79 minutes: ADD).

Hair 1995 Studio Cast (with Carl Wayne, Nicola Dawn, John Howard and Bobby Crush) /
Gordon Lorenz.
Carlton Shows Collection Ⓑ 30362 0015-2 (40 minutes: DDD).

In 1968, *Hair* was a radical departure in musical theatre. No book to speak of, just the vague progress of a central character, George Berger, from high school drop-out to doomed Vietnam conscript, and his eclectic group of pro-love, pro-sex, anti-establishment friends, embodying the sentiments of the hippy age. The score is a sprawling mélange of rock numbers, protest songs and pop anthems, many of which ("Aquarius" and "Let the sunshine in", for example) went on to become hits all over the world. Some of them, such as the anti-pollution song "Air", remain relevant. But that aside, those very elements which made *Hair* such a groundbreaker at the time have also consigned it to a late-1960s time capsule. As a stage show, its time is long past, as the producers of occasional revivals have found to their cost. Its nudity, its focus on the drug culture (which today seems downright naïve) and the constant questioning of society by and self-analysis of the characters (which certainly was revolutionary in a musical back then, courtesy of the lyrics by Gerome Ragni and James Rado) are simply anachronistic.

Nevertheless, it stands alone in the history of the musical as the first show to tackle so many social, racial and sexual issues head-on in a totally contemporary context, and there could be no better record of this achievement than the 1968 Broadway cast recording. Vibrant and raw (despite the re-processing for CD, many of the numbers sound as if they were recorded in a shoe box), it is still possible to see why the show had the power to shock and surprise. In an outstanding cast of rock singers, Gerome Ragni (Berger), Shelley Plimpton (Crissy) and Melba Moore (Dionne) excel. Plimpton's "Frank Mills", the romantic lament of an American teenager, has real charm. Ageing hippies will appreciate the odes to "Hashish", LSD ("Initials") and tripping ("Walking in space"), although in truth they are badly dated. But the recording preserves the show's joyful and exuberant freedom.

The film was not made until 1979, by which time it was a struggle to prevent the score from sounding like a parody of its former self. On the plus side, the numbers were polished up with fine production values and new orchestrations from Galt MacDermot, helping to make them more accessible to an audience which might not have seen the show on stage, although purists might find the sound somewhat over-sanitized. Only Melba Moore survived from the Broadway production. As Sheila, Beverly D'Angelo makes a real impact, with a throaty, beautifully judged "Easy to be hard" and "My conviction" becomes a tongue-in-cheek aria to great effect. There is, however, an irritating lack of information in the sleeve-notes: where is the cast list?

Anyone looking for a budget-priced introduction to the show will find the Carlton selection more than adequate. Although it eschews the original show's format, the studio cast attack the numbers with real verve, particularly John Howard on "Aquarius" and Carl Wayne on "Hair". Sweet-voiced Nicola Dawn brings a delicate touch to "Frank Mills" and "Air".　　　　**PF**

Also available:

Hair (1968 London Cast) Polydor 519 973-2

The Human Comedy (Broadway Cast) Kilmarnock Records KIL9702

Henry Mancini
1924-1994 USA

Better known as the film composer responsible for *Peter Gunn* (1958) and *The Pink Panther* theme (1964), Mancini's songwriting talents were rewarded with Academy Awards for both "Moon river" from *Breakfast at Tiffany's* (1961) and the theme song from *Days of Wine and Roses* (1962) – both with lyrics by Johnny Mercer. His only musical films were *Darling Lili* (1969) and *Victor/Victoria* (1982). The latter earned the composer another Academy Award, and was adapted into a Broadway show in 1996.

Victor/Victoria　1982 **Film Cast** (with Julie Andrews, Robert Preston and Lesley Ann Warren) **/ Henry Mancini**.
GNP Ⓟ GNPD 8038 (50 minutes: AAD).

Victor/Victoria　1995 **Broadway Cast** (with Julie Andrews, Tony Roberts, Michael Nouri and Rachel York) **/ Ian Fraser**.
Philips Ⓟ 446 919-2 (79 minutes: DDD). Additional music by Frank Wildhorn.

Julie Andrews's welcome return to the Broadway stage 40 years after her first appearance in *The Boy Friend* wasn't in a new show, but a stage adaptation of a film directed by her husband, Blake Edwards, in which she appeared as a girl pretending to be a fellow. The best of the songs, "Crazy world", "Le jazz hot" and "You and me" have been retained from the film with additional numbers by the late Henry Mancini and Frank Wildhorn. These have been designed to match Andrews's voice as it is today, stronger in the middle and lower registers but still capable of rising upward as in that famous run-up the scales at the conclusion of "Le jazz hot". My first impression of the new show is that none of the new material, which includes a set-piece for Tony Roberts as the drag queen Toddy ("The shady dame from Seville" has been dropped), lingers on in the mind. When "Crazy world" appears in the overture it's like greeting a long lost friend. Whether you've seen the show in New York or not (and there now seems less likelihood of it coming to London), this CD production by Thomas Z. Shepard gives the illusion of having done so from the best seats in the Marquis Theater. The film soundtrack with Robert Preston as a very engaging Toddy doesn't have that theatrical ambience or indeed its open gay-club setting but there's a spontaneity to the whole thing that makes it just as winning.　　　　**AE**

Barry Manilow
b. 1946 USA

Barry Alan Pinkus was born in Brooklyn and studied at the New York College of Music and the Julliard School, where he wrote music for the off-Broadway show *The Drunkard* (1964). At CBS Television he worked as conductor and arranger for the Ed Sullivan Show and others, and wrote advertising jingles. He arranged and produced songs for Bette Midler before launching his own highly successful solo career, scoring hits with "Mandy" (1975), "I write the songs" (1976) and "Copacabana" (1978) – which formed the basis for his show of the same name. He released a live album in 1990 of his one-man Broadway show, and "Showstoppers" an album of hits from the musicals appeared in 1991.

Copacabana 1994 **London Cast** (with Gary Wilmot, Nicola Dawn, Richard Lyndon, Howard Attfield, Anna Nicholas and Jenny Logan) / **Andy Rumble**.
First Night Ⓕ CASTCD42 (60 minutes: DDD).

Basing a full musical on a late-1970s pop hit of somewhat dubious quality might seem a reckless thing to do, but Barry Manilow's *Copacabana* is in fact a surprisingly enjoyable romp. Wisely not taking itself too seriously it is a glitzy piece, very much in the style of the classic 1940s movie musicals. Women step off buses and become chorus girls, handsome men have mob involvements and exotic names, heroes are square-jawed and always get the girl in the end. All this is played in the mind of Tony (Gary Wilmot), a 1990s songwriter in an unhappy marriage (which of course is solved by the end of the show) who transports himself back to the glamorous nightclub world of the period. The plot line may be thin, but Manilow's music is a thorough delight – full of bounce and enthusiasm and eminently listenable. The charmingly likeable Wilmot shines bright in his major solos – the up-tempo "Dancin' fool", the gently swinging "Sweet heaven" and the big ballad "Who needs to dream?". All are in the classic Manilow easy-listening style, but fused with a real appreciation of musical theatre. The revelation of the show was newcomer Nicola Dawn in the major role of Lola. A fresh face and voice, she is a delight, performing with confidence and style as though she has been recording all her life. Her opening number "Just arrived" is an apt description of her path in show business, while hearing her breezy sexiness in "Man wanted" and strong sense of the comic in the Carmen Miranda pastiche "Ay Caramba!" marks her as a talent worth watching. Despite the fragility of the original idea *Copacabana* is an old-fashioned and pleasing show well preserved in this recording. **RAC**

Hugh Martin
b. 1914 USA

Ralph Blane
b. 1914 USA

Born in Birmingham, Alabama Hugh Martin studied at Birmingham University before moving to Broadway to sing in Harold Arlen's *Hooray for What!* (1937) where he met Ralph Blane. who was also in the cast. Blane – born Ralph Uriah Hunsecker – hailed from Broken Arrow, Oklahoma and had previously appeared on Broadway in *New Faces of 1936*. Martin and Blane began a songwriting partnership and also formed a vocal quartet, The Four Martins. Separately they arranged songs for several shows before writing their own show together, *Best Foot Forward*, in 1941. In 1943 they relocated to Hollywood to supervise the show's screen adaptation, and went on to write songs for *Thousands Cheer* (1943), *Meet Me in St Louis* (1944) and several others including *The Girl Rush* (1955) and *The Girl Most Likely* (1957). On Broadway, Martin wrote his own lyrics for *Look Ma, I'm Dancin'* (1948). Other Blane and Martin shows were *Make a Wish* (1951) and *Four Wishes for Jamie* (1952). Martin also wrote *High Spirits* (1964) with lyricist Timothy Gray.

Best Foot Forward 1963 **Off-Broadway Cast** (with Paula Wayne, Liza Minnelli, Glenn Walken, Karin Wolfe, Grant Walden, Edmund Gaynes, Kay Cole, Christopher Walken, Renee Winters, Jack Irwin, Gene Castle, Don Slaton and Paul Charles); **Buster Davis, Willam Goldenberg** (pfs).
DRG Ⓕ 15003 (47 minutes: AAD).

Though Hugh Martin and Ralph Blane are generally thought of as a team, it seems that they didn't actually collaborate. They composed separate songs, music and lyrics both, and then took joint credit for the results, Lennon and McCartney style. Nor was their output in this fashion very large; their names appear together on one stage show and a handful of films. The show was the 1941 *Best Foot Forward*, one in the long line of college musicals which presented American undergraduate life as entirely devoted to dating, football, and the dancing and musical craze of the day. In *Best Foot* it was swing, in all its manifestations, and no other musical tastes so engagingly of malted milk at the corner drugstore. Martin and Blane were group singers and vocal arrangers, and they played a crucial part in introducing the big-band sound and its jivey choral offshoots to Broadway and Hollywood. It would be good to hear this score with the original accompaniment; this off-Broadway revival could only afford twin pianos. The duo (co-producer Buster Davis, himself a noted vocal arranger, and William Goldenberg, future composer of the Michael Bennett musical *Ballroom*) play hard, but the conservatory sound isn't really appropriate.

The plot concerns the campus visit of a minor movie star ("Queen of the B's"), given a skilful and caressing performance by Paula Wayne (she was later replaced by Veronica Lake, an actual 1940s movie queen who turns up in the lyrics). But the eye-catching name now is Liza Minnelli, making her début at 19 as Ethel Hofflinger who "has been collecting [male] scalps since her first day at nursery school". Most of her numbers are bunched together at the end, culminating in a bruised and breath-taking ballad called "You are for loving". This wasn't in the original show; Martin and/or Blane concocted it in 1960 for a stage version of their most notable film *Meet Me in St Louis*. From the same source comes "A raving beauty", a love-song with an edge (and a definite flavour of Rodgers and Hart). These two numbers outclass much of the original score; numbers like "What do you think I am?" (bouncy) and "Just a little joint with a juke box" (wistful) begin arrestingly but don't quite follow through. One good song, "That's how I love the blues", has gone missing. But there is "Buckle down Winsocki" the paradigm football anthem notable for its enthusiastic brutality ("every team that they play will be carried away on a crutch"), and there's also the lovely bittersweet "Ev'ry time", sung by Karin Wolfe who, with that song, should be the real heroine. But there are more teenage romances going on here than be kept track of, even with the album's record number of dialogue lead-ins. Liza seems to be pining over Dutch, "a dancing fool, a Carmen Miranda in pants", played by another future star, Christopher Walken; the cast also includes Glenn Walken and Grant Walden, which is confusing enough in itself. *Best Foot Forward* sounds like it should be fun; maybe one day we'll have another chance to find out.   **RC**

High Spirits 1964 **Broadway Cast** (with Beatrice Lillie, Tammy Grimes, Edward Woodward and Louise Troy) **/ Fred Werner**.
     MCA ⓜ MCAD10767 (43 minutes: AAD).
High Spirits 1964 **London Cast** (with Cicely Courtneidge, Marti Stevens, Denis Quilley and Jan Waters) **/ Michael Moores**.
     DRG ⓟ CDSBL13107 (56 minutes: AAD). Includes four additional songs performed by Noël Coward.

It seems unlikely that a Noël Coward play should be musicalized by someone other than himself, but Martin and lyricist Timothy Gray were able to secure the rights to *Blithe Spirit* (after Coward wavered more than once) and The Master himself directed a troubled Broadway production. Whatever the problems of the rehearsal and production period (outlined in a fascinating and brilliant set of liner-notes by Max O. Preeo), the Broadway cast recording is an utter delight. The Martin and Gray score is far from the Coward style, but full of great songs. Louise Troy kicks off as Ruth with "Was she prettier than I?" and is joined by Woodward's Charles in "Where is the man I married?" and "If I gave you". But these two characters are overshadowed by Tammy Grimes's delicious Elvira and Bea Lillie's eccentric Madame Arcati. Grimes's husky, sensous voice is perfect for the ghost and she shines in all her songs, especially a swinging description of where she currently resides, "Home sweet heaven", and her appeal to Charles after her first appearance, "You'd better love me". Lillie, who struggled during the production due to the early signs of Alzheimer's disease, is in fine form on the recording, extolling the virtues of her chosen mode of transport in "The bicycle song" and becoming excited that her powers as a medium are bearing fruit, "Something is coming to tea". Her flair for comedy is undimmed and, as any good Arcati should, she shamelessly steals the show. Although not a success on stage (why tamper with a prodcut that is already near-perfect?) as a recording *High Spirits* offers one of the last examples of the classic form of the Broadway show before the revolution of the late 1960s.

Despite lack of success on the London stage, DRG have gamely issued the cast recording, and although it is not as strong as the Broadway version it is still of interest. Recordings of Cicely Courtneidge are rare and although Madame Arcati is far from her greatest role, it is fascinating to hear one of the legends of British theatre. Coward accused her of "vulgarizing" the role, and she certainly does not have the comic sophistication of Bea Lillie, but she does bring her forceful personality to the part. The other treat of this issue is the inclusion of four songs from the show performed by Coward himself, recorded by Pye in November 1964. To hear Coward singing songs written by other writers for a version of one of his classic plays is a chance that should not be missed. **RAC**

The Hugh Martin Songbook Michael Feinstein; Hugh Martin (pf).
Nonesuch Ⓟ 7559-79314-2 (59 minutes: DDD).
Songs from Look Ma, I'm Dancin', Best Foot Forward, The Girl Most Likely, Meet Me in St Louis, The Girl Rush, Athena, High Spirits, Make a Wish, Good News and Ziegfeld Follies.

Michael Feinstein continues his American songbook series for Nonesuch with the music of Hugh Martin, the least known so far of the song writers who have numbered Burton Lane, Jule Styne and the still comparatively youthful Jerry Herman. Martin got his break into the business from Richard Rodgers, who gave him the courtesan's trio, "Sing for your supper" from *The Boys from Syracuse* to arrange *à la* the Andrews Sisters. It proved a great hit and three years later Martin had his own musical on Broadway, where he was a presence on and off until the mid 1960s. This selection includes the joyous "You'd better love me" from the last of his shows *High Spirits*, improbably based on Coward's *Blithe Spirit*. Since then he's been silent.
    So let's raise a cheer to Feinstein's success in persuading the 81-year-old all-rounder, Hugh Martin, back to the keyboard, where the years slip away as he demonstrates a thing or two about how his songs should really go. The first track is a gem – Martin joins Feinstein in a self-deprecating duet, as they relate how they learnt their craft from the masters. In the next song, "Here come the dreamers", listen to the way Martin's eerie wrong-note accompaniment complements the lyric. In the celebrated "Girl next door", marvel as he marries a suspension device to the title's interrogative question, "How can I ignore the girl next door?". No wonder musicians love that song! In "Tiny room", he uses the same trick to breathtaking effect virtually throughout the composition. Feinstein relishes each song to the maximum. Surely no one could fail to chuckle at the good-humoured way he puts across "Pass that peace pipe" or the tenderness and searing intensity with which he underlines the conflicting emotions expressed in that Lena Horne standard, "Love". **AE**

Meet Me in St Louis 1944 Film Cast (with Judy Garland, Margaret O'Brien, Tom Drake and Lucille Bremer); MGM Studio Chorus and Orchestra / Georgie Stoll.
EMI Ⓟ CDODEON2 (58 minutes: ADD).

The MGM musical reached a new artistic high under Vincente Minnelli's direction in *Meet Me in St Louis*, released in 1944. The lyrical and poignant songs by Hugh Martin and Ralph Blane included "The boy next door", "Have yourself a merry little Christmas" and "The trolley song", this latter a driving theatrical production number opened up here to include an exhilarating start. All three songs were introduced by the young Judy Garland in definitive performances photographed adoringly by Minnelli, her husband at the time. The musical arrangements, chiefly by Conrad Salinger and Roger Edens, have the feet tapping to old favourites like "Skip to my lou" and the title song, as well as lingering over the harmonic novelties of the Martin/Blane songs. Variable sound quality is hardly a deterrent in these circumstances. **AE**

Also available:
Meet Me in St Louis (1989 Broadway Cast) DRG CDSBL19002

William May

Jason Sprague

New review
Always 1997 London Cast (with Clive Carter, Jan Hartley, Shani Wallis, Sheila Ferguson) / John Cameron.
WEA Ⓟ 3984 20283-2 (65 minutes: DDD).

Always opened and closed only weeks before the death of Princess Diana – perhaps its fate would have been different if it had opened later. Another royal love story – this one of Edward and Mrs Simpson – one's enjoyment depends upon the belief that this was the greatest love story ever told.

Whatever, the twice-divorced Wallis Simpson changed the course of history and this recording, at best, shows reverence to the subject and, at worst, is a pseudo-documentary based on some fact. "Behind this Prince there's more to me" states Edward VIII (played with a good try by Clive Carter), but we are not privy to knowing him. There is more of an attempt to build the character of Wallis, who is portrayed as an innocent with a lovely aunt and a loving husband. Jan Hartley is very strong in her songs and it is easy to see any man falling for the warm person her Wallis is. A real Wallis, the almost forgotten Shani of *Oliver!* fame, has a nice cameo part as the aunt and one of the better numbers in "The reason for life is to love", sung in an expressive and touching wavy way. What is annoying about the recording is the interruptions of the gentleman telling the story: "the strain started to show on the Simpson marriage" etc. The big number, one that exploded on stage to bring some life into the proceedings, is "Love's carousel", sung in "one particular night club" where "love blossomed". It is sung with verve by an otherwise wasted Sheila Ferguson. There is 'always' a haunting feeling that some of the frequently used phrases have come from 'somewhere' else. Not a flop to become a legend like the story it tells.   **RSB**

Alan Menken   USA

Howard Ashman   1951-1991 USA

Born in New Rochelle, New York, Alan Menken studied piano and violin informally and graduated from New York University with a degree in liberal arts. After attending a workshop on musical theatre organised by BMI he decided to pursue a career on Broadway. Lyricist Howard Ashman was born in Baltimore and began his career off-off-Broadway and met up with Alan Menken when they collaborated on the *Real Life Funnies* (1981). Ashman and Menken scored a hit with the rock musical *Little Shop of Horrors* (1982) based on the 1960 Roger Corman film of the same name. The show was filmed in 1986. The same year came their unsuccessful final Broadway collaboration, *Smile*. Menken's other Broadway shows include *God Bless You, Mr Rosewater* (1979), and *A Christmas Carol* (1995). But it is with Disney's animated features that Menken has established a worldwide reputation. Beginning with *The Little Mermaid* (1989), Menken's association with Disney has flourished, winning the composer Academy Awards for his work on *Beauty and the Beast* (1991), *Aladdin* (1992 – the Oscar-winning "A whole new world" with lyrics by Tim Rice), *Pocahontas* (1995) and *The Hunchback of Notre Dame* (1996) –– the latter two with lyricist/composer Stephen Schwartz (see separate entry). The stage version of *Disney's Beauty and the Beast* is currently playing both in London and on Broadway.

Aladdin 1992 **Film Cast** (with Bruce Adler, Brad Kane, Lea Salonga, Jonathan Freeman and Robin Williams) **/ David Friedman**.
Walt Disney Records ℗ WDR74260-2 (50 minutes: DDD).

After the tremendous success of *Beauty and the Beast*, Disney looked to the classic story of *Aladdin* for their next animated musical. The story remains a childhood staple, especially in the UK where it is a favourite subject for Christmas pantomime, but Alan Menken's treatment, along with lyricists Howard Ashman and Tim Rice, inhabits an altogether different world. Bolder, brasher and even more melodic than one would have believed possible, this big screen *Aladdin* sweeps all before it in a wave of well-nigh faultless and sympathetic scoring. "One jump ahead", dazzlingly sung by Brad Kane to Tim Rice's assured lyric, is a virtuoso song which, when reprised in a quieter and more delicate version, seems equally right in its new context. Robin Williams steals the show in many places, not least in his big number, "A friend like me" and the secondary song "Prince Ali", allowing the listener to revel in his mastery of style and pace. The Oscar-winning "A whole new world" (lyrics by Rice) now seems to have been around forever – surely the hallmark of a classic – and it is well performed here by Brad Kane and Lea Salonga (so good in the British production of *Miss Saigon*). As with *Beauty and the Beast*, this principal song is reprised as the final track, sung this time by Regina Belle and Peabo Bryson. Howard Ashman provides some pretty nifty underscore – "The battle" and "Aladdin's world", for example – but it is the infectious vitality of Menken's song melodies, coupled with Ashman and Rice's lyrics, that enchant the most. The whole musical team, including arranger David Troob, orchestrator Michael Starobin and vocal arranger/conductor David Friedman, have produced a colourful and inventive film score.   **JW**

Disney's Beauty and the Beast 1991 **Film Cast** (with Paige O'Hara, Angela Lansbury, Robby Benson, Jesse Corti, Jerry Orbach, David Ogden Stiers and Richard White) **/ David Friedman**.
Walt Disney Records Ⓕ WDR71360-2 (51 minutes: DDD).

Make no mistake, right from the opening song "Belle", winningly sung by Paige O'Hara, the listener is in for a glorious and charming Disney score that brings memories of their classic 1940s musicals right up to date. The recipe goes something like this: the best of old Disney, a tribute to Broadway musical theatre *à la* Rodgers and Hammerstein, plus some original 1990s style from Menken and Ashman. The result is pure delight. The sleeve-notes are somewhat reticent about who sings what, but the unmistakeable voice of Angela Lansbury can be heard on "Beauty and the beast". "Something there" is a stylish and skilful love song that any Broadway production would be proud to call its own. As with Menken's other Disney films, there are a number of purely orchestral cues, but he is no slouch when it comes to underscoring action. As a bonus, Celine Dion and Peabo Bryson perform a reprise of "Beauty and the beast" in a more obviously pop-orientated manner than the soundtrack version. The sound is well balanced and the voices upfront; the unnamed singers bring warmth to several expressive passages. Ashman and Menken's songs are woven into the texture of the film so seamlessly that without their contribution it would seem a lacklustre affair indeed. Quite wonderful. **JW**

New review
Disney's Beauty and the Beast 1997 **London Cast** (with Julie-Alanah Brighten and Alasdair Harvey) **/ Jae Alexander.**
Walt Disney Records Ⓕ WD608611 (74 minutes: DDD).
Disney's Beauty and the Beast 1996 **Broadway Cast** (with Susan Egan and Terence Mann) **/ Michael Kosarin.**
Walt Disney Records Ⓕ WD608612 (72 minutes: DDD).

Billed as the most expensive musical to hit London's West End (with costs exceeding £10 million) *Disney's Beauty and the Beast* comes to us in recordings by both London and Broadway casts. Both present a score expanded by eight numbers over that of the successful 1991 film which preceded them. Tim Rice has taken over from the late Howard Ashman as Alan Menken's lyricist, and a fine job he makes of it (one new number has Ashman's lyric as it was written for, but cut from, the film). Both casts contain showbusiness veterans: Tom Bosley (from *Happy Days* and *Fiorello*) as Maurice, Terence Mann (*Les Misérables*) as the Beast and Beth Fowler (*Baby*) as Mrs Potts for Broadway. London offers Norman Rossington (from the original cast of *Salad Days*) as Maurice, Mary Miller (Rose from *Keeping Up Appearances*, and the lead in *Ann Veronica*) as Mrs Potts, plus TV's Derek Griffiths and Barry James (last seen in *Sweeney Todd*). Even in its original animated film version the show played like a Broadway musical (see separate review). On stage the show glows opulently. "Be our guest" is one of the most lavish production numbers I have ever seen.
   As cast, both Maurices are venerable rather than full-voiced. Terence Mann's fine Beast is more mature than Alasdair Harvey's attractive London equivalent. The Belles are uniformly excellent: Broadway's Susan Egan, Julie-Alanah Brighten in London. As the teapot, Mary Miller (London) is marginally preferable to Beth Fowler (Broadway). Burke Moses is the swaggering Gaston on both recordings. The minor players have more character in London – Griffiths and James particularly so. The music on both issues is identical. What tips the balance is the presentation: only the London cast recording contains lyrics and photographs. **MPK**

New review
Hercules 1997 **Film Cast** (with Michael Bolton, Roger Bart, Danny DeVito and Susan Egan) **/ Danny Troob.**
Walt Disney Records Ⓕ WD60684-7 (48 minutes: DDD).

The latest of the Walt Disney animation movies shifts from the usual classic fairy tale to the world of ancient gods. Ancient the gods may be, but it's a vibrant rap sound that accompanies the Muses who tell much of the story. It's quality pop, however, and easy to see why Alan Menken has become king of this genre. "I won't say (I'm in love)" is a great number (sung by up-and-coming Susan Egan) and it's no wonder they chose "Go the distance" to push the hardest. The CD itself is a strange, but not unpleasant, mix of modern pop musical score and traditional musical film soundtrack. The film's songs come first – the first 12 tracks have the eight Menken and Zippel numbers (there are three versions of "The gospel truth" and "Go the distance" including the pop version) followed by 12 tracks of the film score themes (with heavenly voices). The first section is up-beat most of the way but includes a glorious vaudeville interlude with Danny DeVito sounding like Jimmy Durante in "One last hope". The final track of the vocal section is the pop single version of "Go the distance" sung by Michael Bolton (different lyrics) – a masterpiece of the fusion of beat, violins, arrangement and recording technique. The inclusion of the lyrics helps with some of the more up-beat numbers and be warned of the false security the pleasant film score sequence brings, for it ends with a sudden reminder of the vocal athletics of the first section of the CD. **RSB**

The Hunchback of Notre Dame 1996 **Film Cast** (with Tom Hulce, Paul Kandel, Tony Jay, Jason Alexander, Charles Kimbrough and Heidi Mollenhauer) **/ Michael Starobin**. Walt Disney Records ⓟ WD77490-2 (57 minutes: DDD).

If there is a somewhat darker side to Disney, then this must be it: *The Hunchback of Notre Dame* is, as the title suggests, a more solemn and introverted story than the usual Disney fare. Full marks then to the Disney hierarchy and their resident composer, Alan Menken, for setting their sights on Victor Hugo's novel (although with Boublil and Schönberg successfully mining Hugo's work for the musical theatre one can see the logic in their decision). Menken's music for this period tale begins with a powerful orchestral cue, "The bells of Notre Dame", brave stuff, with Latin choral singing and a wildly spiralling climax. The disc contains several cues for orchestra and choir: "Humiliation", "Hellfire" and "Paris burning" all conjure up a medieval world of tragedy and torment. In the middle of all this comes "A guy like you", a song-and-dance number that acts as a welcome respite from the darkly expressive score, but which might have seemed out of place if it were not for Michael Starobin's skilful orchestrations. Esmeralda's song, "God help the outcasts" – sung by Heidi Mollenhauer on the soundtrack – is reprised in a pop version by Bette Midler as the disc's final track. Although the film was regarded as a failure by some commentators, musically speaking this is an accomplished song score, and a brave departure for Disney. **JW**

King David 1997 **Concert Cast** (with Marcus Lovett, Roger Bart, Stephen Bogardus, Anthony Galde, Judy Kuhn, Alice Ripley, Peter Samuel and Martin Vidnovic) **/ Michael Kosarin**. Walt Disney Records ⓟ WD60944-7 (74 minutes: DDD).

This recording is of highlights of a 140-minute oratorio performed at the newly re-opened New Amsterdam Theatre on 42nd Street in New York. Presented in an impressive concert version for just a few performances it remains a work in progress. As it was presented by Walt Disney Theatre Productions there seems little doubt that a fully-staged version will some day appear. The Menken and Rice team is already a proven one and this is their most adventurous outing. Unfortunately, it is not totally satisfying. Tim Rice is back on a religious bent and his contribution is self-assured. Alan Menken, on the other hand, seems overpowered by the reverence of the piece and, in this over-orchestrated rendering, offers little variation to the relentless set of film score themes (often with heavenly chorus) he has written in the past. High-powered it is, and there is no getting away from a certain excitement as the story develops – but it is more interesting than fulfilling. There is plenty of the full-lunged singing we have come to expect with these pop operas but there are (some) quieter moments – like Judy Kuhn's rather nice "Never again" and Marcus Lovett (as David) in "Warm spring night". The libretto is printed in the booklet and following it does help get the most out of this recording. An historic event captured impressively on disc and one that is worth more than just a casual listen. But it's no *Jesus Christ Superstar*. **RSB**

Little Shop of Horrors 1982 **Off-Broadway Cast** (with Ellen Greene, Lee Wilkof, Hy Anzell, Franc Luz, Sheila Kay Davis, Leilani Jones and Jennifer Leigh Warren) **/ Robert Billig**. Geffen ⓜ GEFD2020 (43 minutes: DDD).

Little Shop of Horrors 1986 **Film Cast** (with Rick Moranis, Ellen Greene and Steve Martin) / **Robby Merkin**.
Geffen Ⓜ GFLD19289 (39 minutes: AAD).

Based on a low-budget horror film of the same name, *Little Shop of Horrors* proved to be a surprise hit as a fully-fledged off-Broadway musical with a good run in London. As the heroine Audrey, the wonderful Ellen Greene performed in New York and London and also retained the role for the film which, sadly, disappeared quite quickly. The story is a simple one. Nerdish Seymour works in a Skid Row florist. His prize is a plant he names Audrey II after his lovely blonde co-worker. But the plant has a particular need: human blood. Eventually it disposes of many of the cast, including Audrey herself, and by the end of the show, with cloned descendants, is intent on world domination. The jolly, clever, catchy rock 'n' roll score works well. A girl trio called Crystal, Ronnette and Chiffon are the chorus, and there are ample opportunities for Seymour, Audrey and a fiendish dentist – about whom Audrey sings "I know Seymour's the greatest, but I'm dating a semi-sadist". Try the stage version. It has more songs, and Ellen Greene is at her Betty Boop best. The show worked well in the claustrophobic atmosphere of the intimate theatre and this impression is carried over onto the respective cast albums. The film score gains in glitz and gloss, but the whole point of the show is that it should be tawdry (it rhymes with Audrey!) cut price schlock. So with a regretful backward glance at Steve Martin's maniacal film dentist, it's the stage version for me – and you – as we revel in "Somewhere that's green", "Feed me" and "Suddenly, Seymour". This is rock 'n' roll with wit and charm.　　**MPK**

Pocahontas 1995 **Film Cast** (with Judy Kahn, David Ogden Stiers, Jim Cummings, Bobbi Page and Mel Gibson) / **David Friedman, Danny Troob**.
Walt Disney Records Ⓔ WDR7546-2 (58 minutes: DDD).

Pocahontas sets the standard by which all other Alan Menken/Walt Disney musicals can be judged. It has the most sparkling collection of memorable tunes, sympathetic and rewarding lyrics, and a musical score that would not be out of place in a live-action adventure film. Add to this some seductive vocals by Judy Kahn as Pocahontas, who is especially effective in the film's main song "Colours of the wind", a fine arrangement by David Friedman (the song, as always, is reprised in a more 1990s pop arrangement at the end, here sung by Vanessa Williams). The love theme, first heard instrumentally in the track "Pocahontas", has Stephen Schwartz's lyrics added to become "If I never knew you". Other notable songs include a two-part "Savages", which, you will probably have gathered, is the Colonial view of Native Americans; whilst "Virginia company" is a sea shanty, big in sound and voice.

What sets this score apart from Menken's other Disney musicals is the amount of excellent orchestral music (conducted by Danny Troob), with cues such as the strident and up-tempo "Skirmish", "The warrior's arrive" and the more ethnic approach of "Getting acquainted" and "Grandmother Willow" (superb string playing here). "Farewell", the score's ultimate cue has the orchestra pulling out all the stops for a *tour de force* finale. If a newcomer to the magical world of Alan Menken wanted to know where to start their musical journey, I can think of no better place than the saga of Pocahontas.　　**JW**

Also available:
The Alan Menken Album (Debbie Shapiro Gravitte) Varèse Sarabande VSD5741
A Christmas Carol (1995 Cast) Columbia CK67048
Part of Your World (Debbie Shapiro Gravitte) Varèse Sarabande VSD5452

Johnny Mercer

1909-1976 USA

Born in Savannah, Georgia as John Herndon, Mercer travelled to New York in 1927 with an acting troupe; in his spare time he wrote lyrics. His song "Out of breath and scared to death of you" (music by Everett Miller) appeared in the *Garrick Gaities of 1930*. He had a hit in 1933 with "Lazy bones" (written with Hoagy Carmichael), and became one of the most successful and prolific lyricists of his time, contributing to several shows and films. Mercer worked with numerous composers including Harold Arlen (for example, *Blues in the Night*, 1941, and *St Louis Woman*, 1946), Hoagy Carmichael (*Walk With Music*, 1940 and *Here Comes the Groom*, 1951), Robert Emmett Dolan (*Texas, L'il Darlin'*, 1949 and *Foxy*, 1964), Jerome Kern (*You Were Never Lovelier*,

1942), Henry Mancini (*Breakfast at Tiffany's*, 1961, *Days of Wine and Roses*, 1962, and *Charade*, 1963), Gene De Paul (*Seven Brides for Seven Brothers*, 1954, and *L'il Abner*, 1956) and Harry Warren (*The Harvey Girls*, 1946). Mercer also sang with Paul Whiteman, Benny Goodman and Bob Crosby's bands, and co-founded Capitol Records in 1942. He wrote both music and lyrics for the show *Top Banana* in 1951. He won Academy Awards for the songs "On the Atchison, Topeka and the Santa Fe" (*The Harvey Girls*), "In the cool, cool, cool of the evening" (*Here Comes the Groom*), "Moon river" (*Breakfast at Tiffany's*) and "Days of wine and roses" (1962).

Top Banana 1951 **Broadway Cast** (with Phil Silvers) / **Harold Hastings**.
EMI Angel mono Ⓜ ZDM7 64772-2 (39 minutes: ADD).

Phil Silvers had been a big name in musical comedy years before television snapped him up for Sergeant Bilko. *Top Banana*, a term coined by Johnny Mercer to describe a comedian in a burlesque show, gave Silvers and his cast the chance to run through their old routines around which Mercer ran a serviceable score – at its best when Silvers was on hand dispensing his frenetic patter as in the description of the show's title. In the duet, "A word a day" only he could get away with an explanation for posterity as "what you're sitting on, wherever you are", or anagram, "always take it at the sign of a cold". Back in 1951, such quips kept this show on Broadway for most of the year. The recording with the characteristic Capitol reverberation has come up very well on CD.   **AE**

Also available:
The Old Music Master Flapper PASTCD7094

Bob Merrill
1921-1998 USA

Born in Atlantic City, Bob Merrill studied as an actor. During the 1940s he worked at Columbia Studios as dialogue director and at CBS Television as casting director. In the 1950s he was put under contract by MGM as a producer and songwriter: songs by Merrill include "If I knew you were coming I'd've baked a cake" and "How much is that doggie in the window?" (both written in 1950). He worked with composer Jule Styne on Broadway, writing lyrics for *Funny Girl* (1964) and *Sugar* (1972), and produced his own show, *Hannah ... 1939* in 1990.

New review
Carnival 1961 **Broadway Cast** (with Anna Maria Alberghetti, Jerry Orbach, Kaye Ballard, Henry Lascoe, James Mitchell and Pierre Olaf) / **Saul Schechtman**.
Polydor Ⓕ 837 195-2 (66 minutes: ADD).

A charming Paul Gallico short story, *The Man Who Hated People*, first gave birth to a 90-page novella *Love of Seven Dolls*, which subsequently became a successful film, *Lili*, starring Leslie Caron, and then a full-scale stage musical, well received in America, but not in Britain. An orphan girl visits a circus and is enchanted by the puppets, treating them as real people until she discovers she is really in love with their crippled and grouchy puppeteer. The score abounds in melody and Bob Merrill's lyrics are equally delightful. "Love makes the world go round" is the keynote song, admirably rendered in the sweet soprano of the show's heroine played by Anna Maria Alberghetti. Jerry Orbach is similarly convincing as the puppeteer, whose defences are gradually breached by the winning orphan. The comedy is supplied by James Mitchell and Kaye Ballard as a magician and his assistant. The attractive CD also includes five demo recordings by Merrill himself, and versions of some of the songs by JJ Johnson, Paul Smith, and Mel Tormé. Extensive notes with pictures complete this highly desirable issue.   **MPK**

Hannah ... 1939 1990 **Off-Broadway Cast** (with Julie Wilson) / **Stephen Milbank**.
TER Ⓕ CDTER1192 (65 minutes: DDD).

The only musical ever to take on Nazism in full flood was Jerry Herman's *The Grand Tour* (1979), set in occupied Europe, and it wasn't up to the task. Other shows – *Cabaret, The Sound of Music* – have confined themselves to the regime's beginnings in Germany and Austria; and even there the strain has told. Bob Merrill's *Hannah ... 1939* is also set in comparatively early days: in pre-war Prague just after the Germans have taken control. Hannah, the matriarchal Jewish owner of a commandeered dress factory, attempts to come to an understanding with the young lieutenant in charge, who reminds her alternately of her dead son and of a lost love. She thinks she has found some humanity in him, and to an extent she has, but of course it's in vain. At curtain-fall she is dragged off to a camp.

This is a chamber musical, with a chamber sound: flute and violin are prominent. Merrill, a Broadway veteran long unheard from, has done an honest job, eschewing fake gaiety and fake heroics. He has not steered as clear of fake sentiment, though perhaps the issue here is not so much falsity as irrelevance. It's possible to accept intellectually that Hannah and her employees would be consumed with nostalgia for their past lives, that Hannah would seek a surrogate love with the youthful officer and a surrogate friendship with his commandant's wife, but emotionally one feels that there are far more important things at stake. Maybe they are properly dealt with in the musical's book (also by Merrill) but here we only have the score. Musically and lyrically it is seldom less than competent (a tired waltz called "Someday" slips below the line) but it is seldom more, either. One song, "So good to see you", soars, and there is some bittersweet voltage in the Jew-Gentile duet "Gentle afternoon". But reality only breaks through in the performance of Hannah herself. Julie Wilson, the reigning queen of New York cabaret, has had little luck with new musicals but the abrasive dignity in her voice is as potent here, and as warming, as when he applies it to her Manhattan supper-club repertoire. She sounds like the ultimate *diseuse* but also like a real woman: a real European woman, full of worldly wisdom and generous with passion. She is, after all, the finest American singer of Kurt Weill.   **RC**

Also available:
New Girl in Town (1957 Broadway Cast) RCA 0902661996-2
Take Me Along (1959 Broadway Cast) RCA 09026 61994-2

Roger Miller   1936-1995 USA

A Country and Western singer from Fort Worth, Texas, Roger Miller had hits like "Dang me" (1963) and "King of the road" (1965) to his credit. His voice was heard in the animated Disney version of *Robin Hood* (1973) and he continued to enjoy pop chart success. In 1985, he wrote the score for his only Broadway show, *Big River,* a successful stage version of Mark Twain's *The Adventures of Huckleberry Finn* which won six Tony Awards.

Big River 1985 **Broadway Cast** (with Daniel Jenkins, John Short, John Goodman, Ron Richardson, Bob Gunton, Rene Auberjonois, Jennifer Leigh Warren and Patti Cohenour) / **Linda Twine**.
MCA Ⓜ MCAD6147 (46 minutes: DDD).

It may seem a daunting task to adapt one of the great classics of American literature, but Roger Miller's 1985 musical version of Mark Twain's *The Adventures of Huckleberry Finn* was a considerable success . Incorporating a wide variety of musical styles, Miller concentrates on Huck and Jim's journey down river – Huck to escape from his tyrannical father and find himself, Jim in search of freedom from slavery for himself and his family. Miller, best known as a writer of novelty pop songs with a Country and Western flavour, adapts to the music-theatre idiom with a refreshing sense of fun, offering a score that is firmly rooted in the traditions of American music of the deep south. The style is set by an opening number, "Do you wanna go to heaven", straight out of the Country and Western songbook. Huck's drunken father (John Goodman) sings a blues piece bewailing his treatment by the "Guv'ment". There are also Negro sprituals ("The crossing"), pure gospel (Jennifer Leigh Warren in one of the highlights of the score, "How blest we are") and even Dixieland jazz ("When the sun goes down in the south"). Miller's lyrics are steeped in the phrasings and feelings of the south, but he manages to convey universal messages with much of his writing (the simple but true "Worlds apart" for Huck and Jim being a prime example). The ensemble cast is fine, but Ron Richardson is outstanding as Jim, strong-voiced and blessed with some of the best numbers, including his plea for an end to slavery, "Free at last". Daniel Jenkins and John Short are good value as Huck and Tom, with Rene Auberjonois and Bob Gunton adding light relief as a pair of con artists. Unlike some of the sombre, over-reverent interpretations of the classics, *Big River* offers a light and enjoyable journey, with a darker undertone that is ever-present but far from dominating.   **RAC**

Lionel Monckton

1861-1924 England

Born in London and educated at Charterhouse and Oxford, Lionel Monckton studied Law, but found a talent for songwriting. His song "What will you have to drink?" appeared in the 1891 revue *Cinder Ellen* and its success persuaded him to write for the stage full-time. He wrote several shows, several of which starred Gertie Millar whom he married after she appeared in his show *The Toreador* (1901), although she left him when he did not give her a part in what became his most famous piece, *The Arcadians* (1909), which ran for 809 performances at the Shaftesbury Theatre. Monckton's other shows include *A Runaway Girl* (1898), *The Orchid* (1903), and *Good Morning, Judge* – his last show, staged in New York in 1919.

The Arcadians 1968 **Studio Cast** (with June Bronhill, Ann Howard, Andy Cole, Peter Regan, Jon Pertwee and Michael Burgess) **/ Vilem Tausky**.
EMI mono stereo Ⓜ ZDM7 650687-2 (71 minutes: ADD). Disc also includes original cast recordings made in 1909 and 1915.

Lionel Monckton was Sullivan's logical successor as the foremost musical theatre composer in Edwardian London. Alas, his librettists lacked Gilbert's genius and though his music has continued to be played, all but one of his shows – *The Arcadians* (1909) – has faded from the repertory. This late-1960s studio cast has a lot of style, with June Bronhill catching the mixture of airy-fairy innocence and musical sophistication necessary for the star role of the Arcadian maiden, Sombra, who follows the Londoner James Smith, whose aeroplane crashes into the Arcadian paradise. Ann Howard, later ENO's famous Carmen, is the "Girl with a bit of a brogue" and Jon Pertwee the unhappy jockey who sings "I've got a motter".

The main pleasure of this performance is the chance to hear this still charming old piece performed without any untoward nudging. Collectors would search for years before coming across copies of the original cast 78s, which are included as a fill-up here. Florence Smithson sings "The pipes of Pan", "Arcady is ever young" and two songs from the 1915 revival, "Light is my heart" (originally dropped in place of "Arcady is ever young") and "Come back to Arcady". She takes a *pianissimo* high E at the end that would nowadays put her centre stage on the international opera scene. Phyllis Dare and Alfred Lester are heard in their famous songs.

Lionel Monckton's co-composer on *The Arcadians* was Howard Talbot, who must have had sterling qualities as a long-suffering collaborator, he also worked with Paul Rubens, Herman Finck, Ivor Novello and others. Very little of Monckton's other music is available on CD. One day perhaps the recordings by his wife, the great Gertie Millar, star of *Our Miss Gibbs* (1909), *The Quaker Girl* (1910) and *Bric-à-Brac* (1915) will once again be made available.   **PO'C**

Jerome Moross

1913-1983 USA

Brooklyn-born Jerome Moross graduated from school four years early and finished University at 18. He studied music at New York's Juilliard School. Throughout the 1930s Moross earned a living writing theatre music and playing the piano in pit orchestras (at George Gershwin's suggestion he was the pianist for the touring production of *Porgy and Bess*). He travelled to Hollywood in 1940, working primarily as an orchestrator. Early films were mainly low-budget 'quickies' which earned him enough money to continue writing concert and theatre music back in New York. His most famous film score is *The Big Country* (1958). He composed numerous ballet scores and concert works, but *The Golden Apple* was his only full-length musical.

New review
The Golden Apple 1954 **Broadway Cast** (with Priscilla Gillette, Stephen Douglass, Kaye Ballard, Jack Whiting, Bibi Osterwald, Jonathan Lucas and Portia Nelson) **/ Hugh Ross.**
RCA Victor Ⓜ 09026 68934-2 (51 minutes: ADD).

Leonard Bernstein didn't have it all his way in the 1950s pushing out the boundaries of the Broadway musical to embrace a wider musical sophistication than was the custom at that time. Jerome Moross, whose music now enjoys a greater circulation than it ever did in his lifetime thanks to new recordings on CD of his film and concert works, brought a rhythmic vitality and flair for a memorable melodic line to this retelling (with lyricist/librettist John La Touche) of the Homeric legend of Helen and Ulysses transferred to an American town. At the turn of the last century in the state of Washington, Ulysses, an American soldier (Stephen Douglass) returns home from war to his wife Penelope (Priscilla Gillette). Helen (Kaye Ballard), a farmer's daughter, falls in love with a travelling salesman, Paris (Jonathan Lucas). Paris and Helen run off to the big city. For ten years Ulysses goes in search of Helen. In the city he succumbs to the pleasures of Siren and Circe, beats Paris in a boxing match and finally returns home to his patient Penelope. Helen's languorous melody "Lazy afternoon" has become the score's best-known number, with Penelope and Ulysses's "It's the going home" running it a close second. The score, through-composed in an era dominated by the book, music and lyrics formula, moves the story briskly along, but for this original long-playing recording much of it had to be omitted in favour of a specially-written narration. This works reasonably well, but there's no doubt that a new recording of *The Golden Apple* would serve Moross's work much better. The cast, a strong one, recalls an earlier era in Broadway vocal style, though no less charming for that; it has something of the quality of perusing an album of sepia prints. **AE**

Monty Norman
b. 1928 England

Singer and songwriter Monty Norman was one of the successful adaptors of the French musical *Irma la Douce* (1958) with Julian More and David Heneker. With the latter he also wrote a satirical musical about the pop world, *Expresso Bongo* (1958). With the latter's librettist, Wolf Mankowitz, he wrote *Make Me an Offer* (1959) about the antiques world. Also *Belle* (1961) about murderer Dr Crippen. 1967 saw a traditional Jewish musical, *Who's Pinkus, Where's Chelm?*, and in 1969, *Quick, Quick Slow* dealt with competitive ballroom dancing. *Songbook* (1979) was a clever parody musical and Norman's last score to date was written for the RSC, *Poppy* (1982), about the opium trade. Despite all this activity he is perhaps best known as the composer of the "James Bond theme", which he wrote for the first Bond film, *Dr No*, in 1962.

Songbook 1979 **London Cast** (with Anton Rodgers, Gemma Craven, Diane Langton, Andrew Wadsworth and David Healy) **/ Grant Hossack**.
DRG Ⓕ CD13177 (54 minutes: AAD).

A quite delightful musical confection that manages to tell the history of popular song in the twentieth century in an amusing and thoroughly convincing form. By creating the character of songwriter Mooney Shapiro, Norman and lyricist Julian More found a way to offer a revue show with a difference. The recording opens with his first hit song, written for the *Feldman Follies of 1926*, and covers all his major works up to the very last song he wrote, which was found stuffed in a bottom drawer after he was tragically electrocuted by his synthesizer! This is a masterpiece of pastiche, every style sent up with humour, affection and uncanny accuracy – the Hollywood musical, the Broadway show (both hit and flop), French cabaret, patriotic war songs, the Merseybeat sounds of the 1960s, right up to 1970s pop. The cast of five perform with verve, each revelling in the opportunities the score provides. Gemma Craven's strong voice lends itself to the songs of the depression and, later, to a husky Marlene Dietrich. Andrew Wadsworth becomes Frank Sinatra as well as the handsome but vacuous lead for the Hollywood movie spectaculars; Anton Rodgers is a wonderful Chevalier; David Healy the perfect incarnation of the fictitious songwriter. Diane Langton lends her great talents as an hysterical Cicely Courtneidge (leading the troops in a chorus of "Bumpity bump"!) and as the perfect French street singer in "Les Halles". Despite its limited success on stage this is a recording to be treasured – a simple idea executed with great wit and intelligence. **RAC**

Frederic Norton
1869-1946 England

A former insurance clerk, Manchester-born Frederic Norton wrote *Pixie and the Fairies* (1908) and contributed songs to various revues. All, however was dwarfed by the success of *Chu Chin Chow* (1916) – a hit that was not matched by *Pamela* (1917) or *Teddie Tail* (1920). Norton returned to writing songs for interpolation in other shows, occasionally appearing as an actor in *Chu Chin Chow*, in the comic role of Ali Baba

Chu Chin Chow 1959 **Studio Cast** (with Inia Te Wiata, Julie Bryan, Barbara Leigh, Charles Young and Ian Humphries) / **Michael Collins**.
EMIAngel mono/stereo Ⓜ ZDM7 89939-2 (67 minutes: ADD). Disc also includes excerpts from the 1916 original cast, the 1934 film and 1961 studio recordings.

Chu Chin Chow was a World War I phenomenon, running for a record five years. An Arabian Nights story, its cheerful exoticism was just what wartime audiences needed. It gave fame to its otherwise largely unsung composer, who turned out several numbers that achieved immense popularity at the time and in varying degrees have remained popular. The biggest hit was the philosophical "Cobbler's song", which has provided rewarding material for generations of basses. In this 1959 studio recording it is sung with relish and solemnity by Inia Te Wiata, who indeed takes several different roles, leading the rousing "Robbers' march" and shading his voice to encompass ringing baritone as well as sonorous bass numbers. Supporting roles are more than adequately taken, with Julie Bryan duetting effectively with Te Wiata in the lovely "Anytime's kissing time". To provide the most complete selection available, EMI have most cleverly spliced in numbers from a 1961 studio recording, as well as providing an appendix of eight numbers from the original 1916 West End and 1934 film versions. It makes a highly enjoyable reminder of a key show in British musical theatre history. **AML**

Ivor Novello
1893-1951 Wales

David Ivor Davies was born in Cardiff; his mother was a singing teacher, his father an enthusiastic amateur musician. He began to write songs as a teenager, having his first song published aged 17. In 1914 he wrote "Keep the home fires burning", which became one of the most popular songs of the First World War (it was originally called "Till the boys come home"), and made Novello rich. In 1919 he made his acting début in the film *The Call of the Blood*, and throughout the 1920s and 1930s enjoyed an acting career on both stage and screen. In addition, he wrote plays, but very few songs until 1935, when he returned to composing with *Glamorous Night*. He usually played the non-singing lead role in his musical plays, which included *Careless Rapture* (1936), *Crest of the Wave* (1937) and *The Dancing Years* (1939) – this latter, his most successful show, was filmed in 1947 and revived in 1968. *King's Rhapsody* (1949) and *Gay's the Word* (1951) were his last works

Centenary Celebration with **Davy Burnaby, Walter Crisham, Dorothy Dickson, Mary Ellis, Olive Gilbert, Dunstan Hart and Henry Leoni**; **Ivor Novello** (pf); **Drury Lane Theatre Orchestra / Charles Prentice; Gaiety Theatre Orchestra / Willy Redstone**.
Pearl mono Ⓜ GEMMCD9062 (73 minutes: AAD). Recorded 1916-39.
Songs from The Dancing Years, Glamorous Night, Careless Rapture, Crest of the Wave and Theodore and Co.

During the late-1930s, Ivor Novello's Ruritanian pieces kept London audiences supplied with shows catering for nostalgia for the romantic, escapist plots of old. Novello's melodies enchanted then, and still do so now. Here are excerpts from four of his works of the 1930s, in which the glorious tunes succeed each other in rich profusion. The vocal selection is sometimes a little odd, with hit numbers such as "Music in May", "Fold your wings" and "Shine through my dreams" missing, though some are heard in orchestral pot pourris. But one can scarcely complain at the numbers that are here – "Waltz of my heart", "I can give you the starlight", "Glamorous night", "Rose of England" and so on, sung with consummate artistry by distinguished performers such as Mary Ellis, Olive Gilbert and Dorothy Dickson. The collection is completed by two numbers in very different vein from an early ragtime-era show for which Novello provided additions to Jerome Kern's score. As usual with Pearl's issues, the listener is left to do his own filtering of surface noise. **AML**

A Tribute to Ivor Novello **Original Casts** (with Mary Ellis, Dorothy Dickson, Roma Beaumont, Ivor Novello, Olive Gilbert, Cicely Courtneidge, Vanessa Lee and Lizbeth Webb).
Music for Pleasure mono Ⓜ CDDL1242 (two discs: 149 minutes: ADD). Recorded 1936-51.
Songs from Glamorous Night, The Dancing Years, Careless Rapture, Crest of the Wave, King's Rhapsody and Gay's the Word.

Ivor Novello's career bears a certain similarity to that of Andrew Lloyd Webber in our own time. His shows were largely scoffed at by music and theatre critics, yet they attracted a huge public, and the songs entered the popular song repertory and stayed there for decades. Most of his shows were designed so that Novello could himself play the leading role. He wasn't a singer, so the romantic tenor and baritone solos had to go to other characters, often in a play-within-the-play. Before he took to composing the romantic operettas with which his name is now associated, Novello had had two successful careers, as a composer of music for many revues and musicals during and after the First World War (*Theodore and Co.*, *Who's Hooper?* and *A-Z*, from which came "And her mother came too") and as an actor on stage and screen (his greatest hit was the silent film *The Rat*). One of the most beloved figures in the British theatre, his songs still have immediate power and a great deal of charm. The voices of Mary Ellis in *Glamorous Night* (1936) and *The Dancing Years* (1939), Dorothy Dickson in *Careless Rapture* (1936) and *Crest of the Wave* (1937), and Vanessa Lee in *King's Rhapsody* (1949) are all heard to great effect in the high-flown romantic arias and duets, while comedy is in the air with Cicely Courtneidge in *Gay's the Word* (1951), Novello's final show. His own voice is heard speaking the "Muranian rhapsody" from *King's Rhapsody*, as well as with Dorothy Dickson and Olive Gilbert in the "Studio scene" from *Careless Rapture*. **PO'C**

Also available:
Marilyn Hill Smith sings Ivor Novello Chandos CHAN9142

Richard O'Brien

b. 1942 New Zealand

An ex-member of the chorus of the original London production of *Jesus Christ Superstar*, Richard O'Brien was the deviser and composer of music and lyrics for the rock 'n' roll B-movie spoof *The Rocky Horror Show* (1973) and played a principal role in it. The show was filmed as *The Rocky Horror Picture Show* in 1976, featuring Susan Sarandon, Tim Curry and Meatloaf, and has been revived on stage several times. Neither a further show *T Zee* (1976) nor a film sequel to *Rocky Horror*, *Shock Treatment* (1981) proved successful. O'Brien has since made a name for himself as a TV presenter, and in 1996 he appeared in a musical revue of his own devising.

The Rocky Horror Show 1973 **London Cast** (with Tim Curry, Richard O'Brien, Christopher Malcolm, Belinda Sinclair, Rayner Bourton, Patricia Quinn, Little Nell, Paddy O'Hagen and Jonathan Adams) **/ Richard Hartley**.
    First Night Ⓜ OCRCD6040 (37 minutes: ADD).
The Rocky Horror Show 1995 **Studio Cast** (with Kim Criswell, Anita Dobson, Tim Flavin, Aidan Bell, Howard Samuels, Issy van Randwyck, Adam Caine, Brian Greene, Brian May and Christopher Lee); **NSO Ensemble / Martin Yates**.
    TER Ⓕ CDTER1221 (56 minutes: DDD).

Richard O'Brien's trash opera achieved cult status overnight when it opened at the Royal Court Upstairs in June 1973, and it continues to occupy a place of its own in the annals of musical history. The briefest snatch of "Sweet transvestite" or "Time warp" is enough to plunge any devotee into a terminal bout of nostalgia. On the face of it, the basic components would hardly be enough to warrant such longevity. A sinister narrator relates the tale of all-American teen couple Brad and Janet and their encounter with the strange world of Frank 'n' Furter, where all manner of sexual deviations, Sci-Fi and B-movie horror film influences are on show in a series of lurid pastiche rock numbers. But the outrageous parts add up to an irresistible whole of considerable charm. One reviewer described it as a "harmless indulgence of monstrous fantasies". Taped in just 24 hours and produced by Jonathan King, the original London recording preserves the feverish commitment with which a cast of (then) unknowns delighted their audience. The role of Frank 'n' Furter gave Tim Curry a sinister, mad-eyed kind of stardom which he has never entirely shaken off. His versions of "Sweet transvestite" and "I'm going home" remain definitive. O'Brien himself plays Riff-Raff, leading the cast through "Time warp" with vigour. Patricia Quinn makes a screeching demoness of Magenta and as Brad and Janet, Christopher Malcolm and Belinda Sinclair are sufficiently vacuous to be open to the mind-blowing experiences which envelop them as the plot unfolds ("Touch-a-touch-a-touch-a-touch me" and "Hot patootie").

Inevitably, the 1995 studio recording (with a cast which includes many performers who have appeared in various productions of the show over the years) is a more polished, classy affair. As the Narrator, Christopher Lee brings a plummy *gravitas* to the show's tackier dimensions. The recording uses the original orchestrations. Other notable performances come from Queen's Brian May as Eddie ("Whatever happened to Saturday night?"), Aidan Bell as Riff-Raff, Anita Dobson as Magenta and Tim Flavin as Brad. Broadway star Kim Criswell brings a new, more robust quality to Janet ("Over at the Frankenstein place"). **PF**

Also available:
The Rocky Horror Picture Show (1975 Film Cast + 1973 London Cast) Castle Communications ROCKY1 (4 CDs)
The Rocky Horror Picture Show (1990 London Cast) Music for Pleasure CDMFP5977
The Rocky Horror Show (Studio Cast) Carlton Shows Collection 30362 0016-2

Stephen Oliver
1950-1992 England

Liverpool-born Stephen Oliver had completed his first opera at the age of 12, and this medium was his first love. *The Duchess of Malfi* (1971) was followed by a version of *Tom Jones* (1976) and a succession of operas for the Batignano Festival. For the West End stage he wrote *Nicholas Nickleby* (1982) and collaborated with Tim Rice on the witty, melodically rich *Blondel* (1983). But his heart belonged to opera, and he never returned to musical comedy during the rest of his short life.

Blondel 1983 **London Cast** (with Paul Nicholas, Sharon Lee Hill, Chris Langham, Stephen Tate, David Burt, Kevin Williams and Cantabile) **/ Martin Koch.**
MCA Ⓜ MCD11486 (two discs: 104 minutes: ADD).

Tim Rice's first venture working with a composer other than Andrew Lloyd Webber was not a commercial success, lasting a mere eight months in the West End. Stephen Oliver was known as a composer of 'serious' music, and thus their collaboration on the somewhat eccentric *Blondel* is surprising, but also innovative. Based on the legend of the medieval troubadour who discovered the captive Richard the Lionheart, *Blondel* never attempts to be true to its period. Indeed, it is deliberately modernistic, with Blondel writing pop songs and early on forming a team of backing singers, The Blondettes. Much of the commentary is made by a group of monks, sung by the Cantabile quartet. The recording is of the whole show and rather like another of Cameron Mackintosh's venture's, *Moby Dick*, is clearly a piece loved by the writers and performers. It is fun – some of the rhyming is deliberately awful, a whole song is devoted to why Blondel should not write songs dedicated to the Lionheart but rather to his evil brother John ("No rhyme for Richard"), while the Lionheart himself has a song concerning the state of the economy, the first letter of each line of which spells "Margaret Thatcher". There are two lovely ballads, "Running back for more", which is used in reprises throughout the show and "The least of my troubles". The latter is the main ballad for Blondel, played by the ever-charming Paul Nicholas. Sharon Lee Hill is his rather shrill wife Fiona, while Chris Langham is a wonderfully evil John. Not to be taken seriously by any means, *Blondel* is a thoroughly enjoyable romp, with no desire to offer any message or meaning: although it takes a few satirical swipes as it passes along its jolly way they are all harmless. **RAC**

Also available:
Nicholas Nickleby (1982 London Cast) TER CDTER1029

Cyril Ornadel
b. 1926 England

One of the finest of the West End theatre conductors, Ornadel had a distinguished career as a popular and theatre composer. *Starmaker* (1956) and *The Pied Piper* (1958) never came to the West End, but *Pickwick* (1963), starring Harry Secombe, did and was a big hit (but not on Broadway). The song "If I ruled the world" came from this show. *Ann Veronica* (1969) was not a success, but a version of *Treasure Island* (1975) worked at the Mermaid Theatre. A tour of *Great Expectations* (1975) did not reach London, nor did a version of a Ray Cooney farce *Once More, Darling*. A workshop of *A Kid for Two Farthings* (1996) had charm and deserved a further life.

Pickwick 1993 **Chichester Festival Theatre Cast** (with Sir Harry Secombe, Ruth Madoc, Glyn Houston, Roy Castle, Michael Howe and Peter Land) **/ Fraser Skeoch**.
TER Ⓕ CDTER1205 (70 minutes: DDD).

Christmas 1996 marked Sir Harry Secombe's final turn as Pickwick, a role he created back in 1963 when Philips recorded his original performance in this hit musical (694 performances at the Saville Theatre). Although not currently available, a comparison reveals that little has changed between that performance and Sir Harry's new one on TER. In fact the voice is now more fine-tuned if not quite so robust than it was all those years ago. Cyril Ornadel's score strikes a warm-hearted festive glow and it includes "If I ruled the world", Pickwick's election credo, and a group of characterful ensembles for the Pickwick club. When Pickwick stumbles unwittingly into trouble with Mrs Bardell, Ruth Madoc, the two of them join in a parlour duet "Look into your heart", that she parodies in counterpoint below the round-like melody. Leslie Bricusse once again proves himself more inventive as lyricist in partnership with other composers than for his own music.   **AE**

Polly Pen

Peggy Harmon

Goblin Market 1986 **Off-Broadway Cast** (with Terri Klausner and Ann Morrison) **/ Lawrence Yurman.**
TER Ⓕ CDTER1144 (47 minutes: DDD).

A two-person musical based on a nineteenth-century Christina Rossetti poem about two women returning to their childhood nursery where they appear to have a need to make up for a lost adolescence (why?) with a strange (imaginary?) involvement with goblins who sell (forbidden?) fruit. It is Laura who buys and eats the fruit while Lizzie is more wary and manages to stop Laura buying more – for which Laura attacks Lizzie as she (Laura) now has an almost drug-like longing. Laura becomes ill and Lizzie takes care of her, an act which appears to bring the two closer together. This is more a chamber opera sung with electric power by two expert and delightful performers. It is an intricate score with the voices of Klausner and Morrison complementing the string and partly-synthesized orchestral backing. There is no straight-forward or understandable plot line for, as the booklet-note states, "*Goblin Market* is open to many interpretations". A fairy tale, a tale with religious undertones, a display of Victorian sexual repression, or just an intriguing look at the relationship of these two sisters – it is left for you to work out. So, there are more questions than answers and that does not help make this an easy listen. But there are deep rewards for those who are attracted to such an intense musical happening.   **RSB**

David Pomeranz

Little Tramp 1992 **Studio Cast** (with Richard Harris, Petula Clark, Peter Duncan, Mel Brooks, Lea Salonga, Johnny Logan, Tim Curry, Treat Williams and Leonard Kirby) **/ David Pomeranz.**
WEA Ⓕ 4509-91387-2 (57 minutes: DDD).

A biographical musical of the life of Charlie Chaplin, with a star-studded cast and an enjoyable, melodic score. Taking as its starting point Chaplin's return to America for the 1971 Academy Awards ceremony, the musical is told in flashback, incorporating key scenes from his life. By nature a concept piece rather than a work conceived for the stage, the show is episodic and designed to show off the star performers, but Pomeranz writes engagingly and the score has several treats. Richard Harris is in excellent form as the 82-year-old Chaplin. He sings movingly of his feelings at being "In America again", and there is a lovely moment when he remembers the hardship of his youth and sings with his younger self (Leonard Kirby delivering a charming performance) the prayer "When the world stops turning". Petula Clark adds her distinct style as Chaplin's mother in a mock music-hall number to her children encouraging them to believe that they have "Something no one can ever take away". Peter Duncan works hard as Chaplin in his middle years, and there is a good comic turn by Mel Brooks as Mack Sennett. The second half includes the darker side of Chaplin's life, with Tim Curry and Treat Williams as FBI agent Tippy Gray and J. Edgar Hoover respectively. Pomeranz's writing does not have sufficient grandeur for this moment, and it fails to convey the malevolence and power with which the anti-communist lobby was able to exclude Chaplin from America (using a trumped-up paternity suit). But the composer immediately redeems himself with a beautiful ballad for Chaplin's young wife Oona (wonderful singing from Lea Salonga) who assures him of her devotion in "This is what I dreamed". Whether *Little Tramp* has a future as a stage production remains to be seen, but Pomeranz's work is charming and affecting, at its best in the ballads and pop-orientated numbers, while the cast of well-known names on the recording offers an added attraction. **RAC**

Cole Porter

1891-1964 USA

The son of a wealthy fruit farmer from Peru, Indiana, Cole Porter took violin and piano lessons at an early age. His mother encouraged his musical ambitions and paid to have his piano piece, "The Bobolink waltz", published in 1902. He wrote football songs and contributed to amateur shows at Yale University; then, after briefly studying law at Harvard (on the insistence of his parents), he took courses in harmony and counterpoint. He wrote songs for Broadway and staged his first show, *See America First*, in 1916 before moving to Paris in 1917 and joining the French Foreign Legion for a three-year stint. *Hitchy-Koo of 1919*, a revue with an all-Porter score, established him as financially independent of his family. Returning to Paris with his wealthy socialite wife, Linda Thomas, he threw fashionable parties at which he performed his own sophisticated, witty and cynically chic songs. Other shows and revues with Porter songs were staged in London and New York throughout the 1920s, and his jazz ballet *Within the Quota* (1923) was first seen in Paris. But it was not until *Paris* (1928) and *Fifty Million Frenchmen* (1929) that Porter achieved lasting popular success: "Brisk, crack-brained, smartly accoutred and modishly salacious" wrote one critic of the latter, neatly summing up the appeal of Porter's songs. *Gay Divorce* (1932), *Anything Goes* (1934) and *Red, Hot and Blue* (1936) consolidated his reputation, and all were subsequently filmed, taking such songs as "Night and day", "It's de-lovely" and "You're the top" to a worldwide audience. Porter suffered badly from a riding accident in 1937 – culminating in the amputation of his right leg in 1958 – and he spent his later years in constant pain from the injury. After a series of failures during the 1940s he triumphantly returned with *Kiss Me, Kate* (1948) but afterwards only *Can-Can* (1953) and the film *High Society* (1956) were reasonably successful. Porter's great legacy of 'standards' – "Let's do it", "Begin the beguine", "Anything goes", "Miss Otis regrets", for example – have established him as one of this century's most popular songwriters.

Anything Goes 1989 **Studio Cast** (with Kim Criswell, Cris Groenendaal, Jack Gilford and Frederica Von Stade); **Ambrosian Chorus; London Symphony Orchestra / John McGlinn**. EMI ℗ CDC7 49848-2 (74 minutes: DDD).

The cruise-ship or ocean-liner plot, in which various characters are thrown together, was one of the stand-bys of Hollywood and Broadway for decades, lasting well into the 1960s with *Ship of Fools* (1965). The opening scene of *Anything Goes*, set in a hotel bar in New York just before the ship sails, introduced the show's most famous number, just five minutes into the action: "I get a kick out of you". Here, Kim Criswell sings it in a gentle, almost demure manner, more like Jeanne Aubert, who was London's Reno Sweeney (under a different name), than the original, cyclonic Ethel Merman.

John McGlinn persuaded the surviving member of the original team, Hans Spialek, to help in the restoration of the orchestrations from the first production. They sound authentic, and are beautifully played by the LSO, but unlike some of the other shows which McGlinn has resurrected, *Anything Goes* demands a sort of brash energy that cannot be conveyed completely convincingly in a studio or concert performance. Von Stade is luxurious casting in the secondary role of Hope Harcourt: she's meant to sound refined, and she does. An appendix adds three songs cut from the original production, "There's no cure like travel", "Kate the Great" and "Waltz down the aisle". The veteran Jack Gilford, with no singing voice at all, gives an object lesson in putting over a Porter lyric in "Be like the bluebird", then Criswell finally comes into her own with a very good, accelerating "Buddie, beware". One of Porter's most successful shows, *Anything Goes* has been revived many times, so it is good to have this authentic edition to use as a comparison with the many different performing versions that come and go.   **PO'C**

Can-Can 1953 **Broadway Cast** (with Lilo, Gwen Verdon, Peter Cookson, Erik Rhodes and Hans Conried) **/ Milton Rosentstock.**
   EMI Angel mono Ⓔ ZDM7 64664-2 (39 minutes: ADD).

Cole Porter's name appears above the title of this 1953 show as it did when 20th Century-Fox filmed it seven years later. It was richly deserved in both cases, for the story on which he hung a cluster of his most memorable songs was strictly an excuse to evoke the Paris of Toulouse-Lautrec and the Moulin Rouge. Its star, Lilo, imported from Paris for the production, has a somewhat aggressive approach to her songs that include hits like "C'est magnifique" and the memorable "I love Paris", with Porter's favourite minor-major key switch. Peter Cookson, a strong baritone, provides sterling support as the Judge seeking to prosecute the can-can dancers. Of his two songs it was "I am in love", a tricky ballad, that initially attracted attention; it wasn't until Frank Sinatra sang "It's all right with me" in the movie version that the song was recognized as *Can-Can*'s finest number. Gwen Verdon, making a sensational Broadway début, brought the house down with her dancing and with her winning account of "If you loved me truly". The show rounds off with Porter's own "Can-Can", a zestful, champagne fizzing finale, that has a brassy Broadway exterior not to be compared with Offenbach's lighter touch.   **AE**

Can-Can and Jubilee – Rare and unreleased songs. **Cole Porter** (sngr/pf).
   Koch International Classics mono Ⓔ 37171-2 (59 minutes: ADD). Recorded 1935 and
   1952-3.

Cole Porter, like Noël Coward, was a dab hand at playing and singing his own compositions. He can underline the irony and bring out hidden nuances in his own lyrics. Although his voice was obviously on the small side, it's a sort of tenor-baritone-falsetto mixture, as he wrote in *Jubilee*, "I suppose I could somehow struggle through".
   Jubilee (1935) is best remembered for "Begin the beguine", but it had a dozen other good songs, some of which Porter gives here, on these recordings made as private demonstration discs. "Everybody who's anybody", a satire on Elsa Maxwell and her parties, a Tarzan send-up "When me, Mowgli, love" and one of Porter's catchiest tunes, "Me and Marie". As well as the famous songs from *Can-Can*, "I love Paris" and "C'est magnifique", Porter recorded several numbers that were dropped from the show. "Who said gay Paree?" is as sad and beautiful a song as Porter ever wrote, and "Her heart was in her work" is as suggestive as the title implies. The sound is of variable quality, but the performances are incomparable.   **PO'C**

Cole Porter in the 1930s with **Judy Garland, Billie Holiday, Mabel Mercer, Elisabeth Welch, Ethel Merman, Ella Fitzgerald, Bing Crosby, Louis Armstrong, Jessye Norman, Fred Astaire** and **Cole Porter.**
   Koch International Classics mono/stereo Ⓔ 37217/9-2 (three discs, only available separately:
   66, 71 and 67 minutes: ADD).
   37217-2 – Songs from The New Yorkers, Gay Divorce *and* Nymph Errant. *37218-2 – Songs
   from* Anything Goes, Adios, Argentina, Jubilee *and* Born to Dance, *plus* "Miss Otis
   Regrets". *37219-2 – Songs from* Red, Hot and Blue!, Rosalie, You Never Know, The Sun
   Never Sets, Leave it to Me, The Man Who Came to Dinner *and* Du Barry Was a Lady.

These three CDs concentrate on songs Porter wrote for his shows in the 1930s, but many of the recordings come from a later date. The booklet is without any details of dates, or any clue as to which records are by people who created the songs, and there is only the briefest hint as to backing. Nevertheless, despite this inadequate presentation, there are some great and rare records reissued here. Volume 1 has five songs from *The New Yorkers* (1930), the most famous of which, "Love for sale", is heard in different interpretations by Libby Holman, Ruby Braff, Ellis Larkins and the Mister Tram Associates.

Fred Astaire's original "Night and day" is juxtaposed with later versions by Billie Holiday and Art Tatum, and there are four other items from *Gay Divorce* (1932), including a beautiful "How's your romance?" from the inimitable Bobby Short, which gives the disc its subtitle. The most valuable track, though, is Cole Porter's own performance of "The Cocotte" from *Nymph Errant* (1933), an essay in high camp which has to be heard to be believed. Porter sings the title song from *Anything Goes* (1934) on Volume 2, which has three versions each of "Begin the beguine" from *Jubilee* (1935) and "Easy to love" from *Born to Dance* (1936), including James Stewart, who first sang it on screen. The weirdest solo is Cesare Siepi's "I've got you under my skin". On Volume 3, Jessye Norman's 1984 "In the still of the night" is not flattered by being juxtaposed with an authentic 1930s version from Al Bowlly with the New Mayfair Orchestra. Porter addicts will be pleased to have a brief snatch of the composer in "Well did you evah!" recorded from a 1956 television performance to round off the disc. Other rarities include Todd Duncan in "River god" from the 1938 Drury Lane show *The Sun Never Sets*, Hubbell Pierce in "What am I to do?" from *The Man Who Came to Dinner* (1939) and a radio broadcast of Mary Martin and Porter talking, as a prelude to Martin's original, great "My heart belongs to daddy" (from *Leave it to Me*, 1938). **PO'C**

Fifty Million Frenchmen   1991 **Studio Cast** (with Kim Criswell, Susan Powell, Kay McClelland, Karen Ziémba, Howard McGillin, Jason Graae , JC and The Bandits) **/ Evans Haile**.
New World Ⓕ 80417-2 (53 minutes: DDD).

Cole Porter's greatest Broadway success of the 1920s contains so many songs that have since become standards that the show itself has been forgotten, perhaps because it didn't, like *Anything Goes*, have a title song (Sophie Tucker's great hit, "Fifty million Frenchmen can't be wrong" is unconnected with the show). "You do something to me", "You've got that thing", "Find me a primitive man", and the song that proved too risqué, "The tale of the oyster", have all made their mark over the years in interpretations by jazz and cabaret singers.

The show is, in its way, the 1920s farewell to the old, romantic idea of Americans in Paris. It culminates at a Fourth of July party held at a Paris night spot, with the couples of the story united in love, and singing "Paree, what did you do to me?". The original orchestrations by several hands, including Robert Russell Bennett and Hans Spialek, were reconstructed by Tommy Krasker who made this performing edition, first given in concert in New York – appropriately – at the Alliance Française concert-hall. The whole show is a delight, performed with love and affection. Howard McGillin as the hero scores with one of Porter's loveliest songs, "You don't know Paree", and Kim Criswell tears into "Find me a primitive man" and "I'm unlucky at gambling". Peggy Cass as the heroine's mother sings a song dropped from the original, a waltz-tune lament, "The queen of Terre Haute". The 1929 Boston try-out had a ballet by Leonide Massine, *The Snake in the Grass*, which was replaced in New York by "You don't know Paree". It's the only thing missing from this otherwise delightful and valuable recording. **PO'C**

High Society   1956 **Film Cast** (with Bing Crosby, Frank Sinatra, Celeste Holm, Grace Kelly and Louis Armstrong).
Capitol Ⓕ CDP7 93787-2 (43 minutes: AAD).
High Society   1994 **Studio Cast** (with Kenny Ball and His Jazzmen, Dennis Lotis, Carl Wayne and Tracy Collier).
Carlton Shows Collection Ⓑ PWKS4193 (32 minutes: DDD).

High Society is one of Porter's most elegant scores. Filmed in 1956, it wasn't actually staged until the mid-1980s, when a so-so production, beefed-up with some imported numbers, enjoyed moderate success in the West End. The film, a musical remake of Philip Barry's *The Philadelphia Story*, lacked the wit and elegance of the original play. Even so, in Bing Crosby and Frank Sinatra, it boasted the presence of two of the finest singers in the history of popular music, who brought their unique styles to the soundtrack recording. Crosby crooned at his best on "I love you, Samantha" and "True love", a gentle ballad which was somewhat optimistically billed as a duet with Grace Kelly. In fact, Kelly was only required to contribute an undemanding bit of harmonizing to the final stanza. Sinatra's rendition of "Well did you evah" helped the song to become one of Porter's most popular standards. Other notable ballads in the score include "Little one" and "You're sensational". But for many, the high spots are Louis Armstrong's joyous, growling title track and the evergreen "Who wants to be a millionaire?", a sparkling, cynical duet between Sinatra and the husky, wry Celeste Holm. The budget-priced Carlton Shows Collection recording has Carl Wayne and Tracy Collier enjoying themselves with the same number and Dennis Lotis giving serviceable renditions of "Little one" and "I love you, Samantha". Kenny Ball makes a valiant Armstrong substitute.   **PF**

New review
Kiss Me, Kate 1948 Broadway Cast (with Alfred Drake, Patricia Morison, Lisa Kirk, Harold Lang) **/ Pembroke Davenport.**
Columbia mono ⓜ CK4140 (49 minutes: AAD).

Kiss Me, Kate 1953 Film Cast (with Kathryn Grayson, Howard Keel and Ann Miller) **/ André Previn, Saul Chaplin.**
EMI ⒻCDODEON25 (63 minutes: ADD).

Kiss Me, Kate 1990 Studio Cast (with Josephine Barstow, Thomas Hampson, Kim Criswell, George Dvorsky, Karla Burns, Damon Evans, Robert Nichols and David Garrison); **Ambrosian Chorus; London Sinfonietta / John McGlinn.**
EMI Ⓕ CDS7 54033-2 (two discs: 111 minutes: DDD).

Kiss Me, Kate 1996 Studio Cast (with Diana Montague, Thomas Allen, Diane Langton, Graham Bickley, Shezwae Powell, Paul Collis, Brian Greene and Matt Zimmerman); **Chorus; National Symphony Orchestra / John Owen Edwards.**
TER Ⓕ CDTER2 1212 (two discs: 108 minutes: DDD). Includes Overtures – *Can-Can, Jubilee* and *Out of This World.*

What riches are here – four recommendable versions of Cole Porter's finest, most ageless score. *Kiss Me Kate* tells of the travails of an out-of-town company mounting a musical based on *The Taming of the Shrew*. Recently divorced, formerly romantic stage partners Fred Graham and Lilli Valessi are battling together again as stars of the show. A sub-plot involves a gambling dancer signing Fred's name to his own IOUs. But it all comes right at the end after an evening of top-notch Porter. The cod operetta duet "Wunderbar" is wonderfully handled by all the principals as is Fred/Petruchio's rakish "Where is the life that once I led?" and Lilli/Kate's "So in love". Kim Criswell's "Always true to you in my fashion" leads the field by a short head from Ann Miller's film version. "Brush up your Shakespeare" fizzes away happily in all recordings. John McGlinn's absolutely complete EMI version emphasizes the strong choral work, contains all the dances and many cut numbers of which "We shall never be younger" is the most touching. In this recording Thomas Hampson is slightly more at ease than his partner, the operatic Josephine Barstow – but that's of little real consequence in this glorious set. TER's magnificent version omits the cut numbers, substituting some Cole Porter overtures. It is a gentler, beautifully sung production with Thomas Allen and Diana Montague in the leads. That leaves the original cast versions, each a single CD. Broadway's Alfred Drake and Patricia Morison lead a classic reading that has the feel of authenticity. It is less complete than either of the above alternatives, but still a 'must'. The glowing stereo film soundtrack also has its own glorious magic, though its text is bowdlerized, and the score less complete than any of the others (but adding "From this moment on" cut from *Out of this World*) . It boasts Howard Keel and Kathryn Grayson in top form and Ann Miller at her most vivacious. As with the rest of this series, this EMI soundtrack album also contains the background score.   **MPK**

New review
A Musical Toast 1997 Los Angeles Cast (with KT Sullivan, Mary Jo Catlett, Megan Mullally, Carole Carmello, Harry Groener, Bill Hutton, Tim stone, Gedde Watanabe, David Hyde Pierce, Marylynn Lovell Matz and Joely Fisher) **/ Ron Abel.**
Varèse Sarabande Spotlight Series Ⓕ VSD5826 (two discs: 136 minutes: DDD). Recorded at performances in Los Angeles in March 1997.

Received with whoops of enthusiasm by the audience on each night of four performances in Los Angeles in March 1997, this celebration of Porter and his songs was a charity benefit for the AIDS Service Center and Project Angel Food. It has a bit of everything, from a version of "Miss Otis regrets" in Japanese to authentically wordy and raucous versions of most of the Porter standards. There are a couple of rarities, a fine rendition of "Let's not talk about love" from the 1941 *Let's Face It*, sung by Kirby Tepper and "Is it the girl? (or is it the gown?)" from *Seven Lively Arts* sung by a quintet led by Joanna Gleason. Marylynn Lovell Matz sings an innuendo-laden "My heart belongs to daddy" and KT Sullivan belts out "Always true to you in my fashion". Most of the arrangements are by Ron Abel who also conducts. The general sound is jazzy, 1960s supper-club. Some of the arrangements iron out the tunes so much that they nearly disappear. One authentic note is provided by Gretchen Wyler, the original 'other woman' in Porter's last show, *Silk Stockings*, who sings "Stereophonic sound", the song she created in 1955. The event must have taken an enormous amount of organization – it would have been fun to be there. **PO'C**

Nymph Errant 1989 Concert Cast (with Patricia Hodge, Maureen McGovern, Alexis Smith, Fiona Fullerton, Lisa Kirk, Elisabeth Welch, Liliane Montevecchi and Patrice Munsel) / **Donald Pippin** and **David Firman**.
EMI Ⓕ CDC5 4079-2 (78 minutes: ADD).

Written in 1933, when Porter was at the height of his powers, *Nymph Errant* is based on James Laver's novel about the peripatetic exploits of an English school-leaver who takes as her motto the title of one of the most famous songs: "Experiment!". The 1930s censors insisted that, unlike in the novel, Evangeline, the girl in question, had always to escape a fate worse than death. Perhaps this overlaying prudery accounts for the obscurity into which the show was plunged for 55 years after its initial London production in 1933, when the star was Gertrude Lawrence.

This concert version is a series of cabaret star turns, each singer taking just one number. The consequent disparity of styles detracts from any feeling of continuity and a sharp division is evident between singers of the old school who can trip and tease Porter's intricate rhymes and the younger ones, striving for a firmer line at the expense of the witty inner rhythms that these songs demand. A unique survivor from the original cast, Elisabeth Welch repeats her famous "Solomon" (this was her fifth recording of it). Alexis Smith is utterly convincing as the "busted, disgusted Cocotte" (a song Porter recorded himself) and Liliane Montevecchi milks every last bit of *boîte-de-nuit* charm from "Si vous aimez les poitrines". The sense of occasion is well caught, there is lots of applause and the CD is important in itself for the inclusion of several songs dropped from the original, but resurrected for this concert, including a raucous "Casanova" from Kaye Ballard.   **PO'C**

Out of This World 1950 Broadway Cast (with Charlotte Greenwood, Priscilla Gillette, Barbara Ashley, William Eythe, William Redfield, George Jongeyans-Gaynes and David Burns) / **Pembroke Davenport**.
Sony Broadway mono Ⓕ SK48223 (48 minutes: ADD).
Out of This World 1995 Broadway Cast (with Andrea Martin, Marin Mazzie, La Chanze, Ken Page, Peter Scolari, Gregg Edelman and Ernie Sabella); **The Coffee Club Orchestra** / **Rob Fisher**.
DRG Ⓕ CDDRG94764 (64 minutes: DDD).

Loosely based on Titus Maccius Plautus's *Amphityron* (which had previously inspired Molière and Giraudoux), *Out of This World* contains some of Cole Porter's wittiest and raunchiest lyrics, and a quartet of great songs, the most famous of which, "From this moment on", was dropped from the original production (although it resurfaced to become a worldwide hit three years later in the movie of *Kiss Me, Kate*).

The Offenbach-like story of the gods, Jupiter, Juno and Mercury coming down from Olympus to get involved with mortals was not so much to the taste of audiences in 1950. The original cast is dominated by Charlotte Greenwood as Juno, her renditions of "I sleep easier now" and "Nobody's chasing me" are monuments of exquisite timing and resourceful vocalism, using about one-and-a-half notes. The 1995 revival cast give the work a good performance, and the version is slightly fuller, with more of the linking choruses and "Night music", but it's useless to pretend that any of the singers can erase the memory of the original cast. George Jongeyans-Gaynes as Jupiter does have a great way with the sophomore-chorus style "I Jupiter, I rex", with its cries of "Brek-ek, co-ek, co-ek, sex!". Eight other numbers were cut from the first production, of which "You don't remind me" is also reinstated in the 1995 recording; a typical, romantic Porter 'list' song, in which Jupiter tells his girlfriend of all the things she doesn't remind him of, ending up "You only remind me of you".   **PO'C**

Silk Stockings 1955 **Broadway Cast** (with Hildegarde Neff, Gretchen Wyler, Don Ameche, Henry Lascoe, David Opatoshu, Leon Belasco and Philip Sterling) / **Herbert Greene**. RCA Victor mono Ⓜ 1102-2 (41 minutes: ADD).

Cole Porter's last score for a stage musical (though there were two films and one TV show afterwards) was based on the classic Ernst Lubitsch movie starring Greta Garbo, *Ninotchka*. Updated from 1939 to the time of the show, 1955, it became one of a clutch of Cold War plays and films. Veteran Hollywood leading man Don Ameche got to sing the number that quickly became a Porter standard, "All of you", as well as "Paris loves lovers". Hildegarde Neff declared herself unhappy with the show, but she scored a big personal success in it, her one solo, "Without love", manages to suggest what Garbo might have been like had she consented to use her (very good) voice in song. The recording is very charming, and the show (which was filmed two years later with Fred Astaire and Cyd Charisse) might still have a future now that people are less coy about East/West relations, especially if an adventurous producer got to use the ten songs that were dropped from the original, plus the two extra numbers Porter wrote for the movie. **PO'C**

A Swell Party A Celebration of Cole Porter. **1991 London Cast** (with Angela Richards, Nicolas Grace, Anne Wood, David Kernan and Martin Smith); **Gary Hind** (pf). Silva Screen Ⓕ SONGCD905 (61 minutes: DDD).

This impressively slick, sophisticated revue of Cole Porter classics was first performed in London in 1991. Led by David Kernan (a past master of this format), the cast bring the music to life in spite of the lack of an audience, which surely would have given the recording an extra kick. In a fine group of performers, Angela Richards is outstanding, creating a gallery of female emotions with the comic numbers from *Fifty Million Frenchmen*, "I'm unlucky at gambling" and "Find me a primitive man", a torchy "Down in the depths" (*Red, Hot and Blue!*) and a fast and furious "Always true to you in my fashion" (*Kiss Me, Kate*). Richards and Nicolas Grace make a haunting duet of "You're sensational" (*High Society*). David Kernan, to the manner born, wrings every ounce of melancholy from "I've got you under my skin" (*Born to Dance*) and "Who said gay Paree?" (*Can-Can*), and camps it up on "Miss Otis regrets" (*Hi Diddle Diddle*), while Anne Wood reveals a powerhouse of a voice on "Red, hot and blue" and "Blow, Gabriel, blow" (*Anything Goes*). With Porter's lyrics set to music by Ann Hampton Callaway, "I gaze in your eyes" becomes a beautifully tender love song in the hands of Martin Smith. Their combined enthusiasm and well-practised ease with Porter's work lift this irresistible collection well beyond the ordinary. **PF**

Also available:
Aladdin (1958 TV Cast) Sony SK48205
Anything Goes (1962 Broadway Cast) Epic EK15100
Anything Goes (1987 Broadway Cast) RCA 7769-2
Anything Goes (1989 London Cast) First Night OCRCD6038
Anything Goes – Rebecca Luker sings Porter Varèse Sarabande VSD5647
Kiss Me, Kate (1958 Studio Cast) EMI Angel ZDM7 64760-2
Kiss Me, Kate (1987 RSC Cast) First Night OCRCD6020
The Song is ... Cole Porter ASV Living Era CDAJA5044

André Previn
b. 1929 Germany/USA

Pianist, composer and conductor, André Previn worked as an orchestrator at Universal film studios in Los Angeles, the city in which his family had settled after leaving Berlin in 1938. He was later one of the musical directors at MGM studios, arranging and conducting many of their musical films including *Gigi* (1958) and *My Fair Lady* (1964). Aside from his other activities as a classical conductor and jazz pianist, Previn has composed numerous concert works, film scores and the musicals *Coco* (1969 – with lyrics by Alan Jay Lerner) and *The Good Companions* (1974).

New review

Coco 1969 **Broadway Cast** (with Katharine Hepburn, Rene Auberjonois, George Rose and David Holliday) / **Robert Emmett Dolan.**
MCA Broadway Gold Ⓜ MCAD11682 (52 minutes: ADD).

In 1969 Katharine Hepburn made her Broadway musical début in *Coco* and, while she strutted her remarkable stuff, it was the hottest ticket in town. It was quite a performance and on a first hearing it is, perhaps, the only reason to own this CD, for she attacks the score as if to have battle with every note; it's a battle she wins gloriously. The story is about Coco Chanel and her winning little black dress (Chanel is said to have agreed to the show believing she was to be played by Audrey Hepburn). Alan Jay Lerner, here writing to the music of André Previn, used some of his speak/sing *My Fair Lady* technique and gave Miss Hepburn some rather good numbers to get her wonderfully unique vocal chords around. Previn's rare visit to the theatre is nothing to be ashamed of – in fact, second, third and fourth happy hearings prove it deserves more credit than it has been given. The joy, however, is at times eclipsed by a rather hateful recording. When originally issued on vinyl the first pressing was recalled after Hepburn thought it did her no justice – the remastered issue (which forms the base for this CD) is better for her but much appears to have been sung down tubes or recorded on stretched tape. A must for the adventurous and compassionate.   **RSB**

Tim Rice
b. 1944 England

Timothy Miles Bindon Rice was born in London and began working in the record industry before pursuing a brief career as a pop singer. In 1965 he joined forces with composer Andrew Lloyd Webber to write *The Likes of Us*, which was never produced. They had their first success in 1968 with *Joseph and the Amazing Technicolor Dreamcoat*, followed by *Jesus Christ Superstar* (1971) and *Evita* (1976). Rice later worked with Stephen Oliver on *Blondel* (1983) and ex-Abba songwriters Benny Andersson and Bjorn Ulvaeus for *Chess* (1988). He won Academy Awards for the songs "A whole new world" from Disney's *Aladdin* (1992, music by Alan Menken) and "Circle of life" from *The Lion King* (1994, co-written with Elton John). He was briefly reunited with Lloyd Webber to pen a new song, "You must love me", for the film version of *Evita* (1996).

The Tim Rice Collection Stage and Screen Classics. With **Rita Coolidge, Yvonne Elliman, Ian Gillan, Murray Head, David Essex, Julie Covington, Barbara Dickson, Paul Nicholas, Elaine Paige, Brad Kane, Lebo M** and **Elton John**.
Rhino Ⓕ 72509 (75 minutes: ADD).
The Tim Rice Collection with **Gemma Craven, Paul Jones, Stephanie Lawrence, Peter Skellern, Carl Wayne, Marti Webb** and **Dave Willetts**; **West End Concert Orchestra /
Matthew Freeman**.
Carlton Shows Collection Ⓑ 30362-0027-2 (72 minutes: ADD).
Songs from **Andersson/Ulvaeus:** Chess. **Batt:** A Winter's Tale. **Lloyd Webber:** Joseph and the Amazing Technicolor Dreamcoat. Jesus Christ Superstar. Evita. **John:** The Lion King. **Oliver:** Blondel. **Menken:** Aladdin.

As these compilations make abundantly clear, Tim Rice's status as one of the great modern lyricists is assured. Performers on the Rhino collection come from the premier league, as it were. The selection revisits the original cast recordings and concept albums of Rice's long association with Lloyd Webber. It's a joy, then, to hear Julie Covington's "Don't cry for me, Argentina" once more. The original studio recording confirms that vocally her interpretation remains the equal of any subsequent stage (or, now with Madonna, screen) Evitas. *Jesus Christ Superstar* dominates, with numbers from both the Broadway cast – including Yvonne Elliman's "I don't know how to love him" – and the film versions. Since they ceased working together, Rice has not enjoyed the stratospheric success of his erstwhile partner in terms of stage hits. *Chess* is represented by a couple of well-known songs, Murray Head's "One night in Bangkok" and the ubiquitous Paige/Dickson "I know him so well". There's also a token number from Stephen Oliver's minstrel musical, *Blondel*, "The least of my troubles", sung by Paul Nicholas. In 1983, Rice penned the lyric for that year's James Bond movie theme song, "All time high" (from *Octopussy* – music by John Barry), smoothly sung by Rita Coolidge. Rice's renaissance has come via a hugely successful collaboration with Disney on soundtracks for its recent blockbuster animations *Aladdin* and *The Lion King*. Elton John's intensely moving ballad, "Can you feel the love tonight?", is proof, if any were needed, that when it comes to writing accessible, emotionally engaging lyrics, Rice is second to none.

At the budget end of the market, the 1996 Carlton collection features many of the same numbers performed by a first division team of artists, including Marti Webb, a memorable successor to Elaine Paige as Evita. There's a particularly moving "Gethsemane" from Dave Willetts. Although by no means a match for the original cast performances on the Rhino disc, this nevertheless makes for a useful introduction to the Rice *oeuvre* with professional, workmanlike performances all round, marred occasionally by some leaden, synthesizer-driven arrangements. **PF**

Jimmy Roberts

Joe Dipietro

New review

I Love You, You're Perfect, Now Change 1996 Off-Broadway Cast (with Danny Burstein, Robert Roznowski, Jennifer Simard and Melissa Weil) **/ Tom Fay.**
Varèse Sarabande Spotlight Series Ⓕ VSD5771 (62 minutes: DDD).

This is a rare being – a heterosexual revue. And, it's good to report that from what is presented here it is far from becoming an extinct species. Two acts explore first the single and then the married variety and prove it's not always easy either way. This is a book revue – that is to say there is a thread of an idea to join the songs together. A prologue sets the scene and indicates what is ahead for the male and female of the species. It's on then through to the first date and the increasing maturity of finding a mate and the mistakes that can happen in so doing. The second act sees the newly-weds, the children and the ageing process leading to an epilogue and the title-song – and it's a good title. The sentiments are international and there is plenty for anyone who has been through the process of mate-finding to relate to – sometimes frighteningly so. It is mainly a humorous voyage, but not always, and when serious it can hit a vulnerable spot. It is also quite open in its content (that sex thingamajig) – so it's an adult listen that you may wish to check before it goes into the CD rack. Joe Dipietro's lyrics are fine and often intelligent and the cast of four perform them with ease and good diction (and that is so important in such a recording). A piano, violin and bass accompany. **RSB**

Mary Rodgers

New review

Once Upon a Mattress 1997 Broadway Cast (with Sarah Jessica Parker, Heath Lamberts, Jane Krakowski, Mary Lou Rosato, Lewis Cleale, Lawrence Clayton, Tom Alan Robbins, David Hibbard and David Aaron Baker) **/ Eric Stern.**
RCA Victor Ⓕ 09026 68728-2 (63 minutes: DDD).
Hey, Love The Songs of Mary Rodgers. 1997 Studio Cast (with Faith Prince, Mark Waldrop and Jason Workman) **/ Patrick Brady.**
Varèse Sarabande Spotlight Series Ⓕ VSD5772 (49 minutes: DDD).
Songs from The Mad Show, Once Upon a Mattress, Hot Spot, The Lady or the Tiger, Freaky Friday, The Courtship of Miles Standish and Member of the Wedding.

Floyd Collins, a new musical by Adam Guettel, the grandson of Richard Rodgers, is favourably reviewed elsewhere (see review under Guettel). Well, here we have two releases that plug the generation-gap by offering the songs of Mary Rodgers, daughter of Richard, mother of Adam and composer of *Once Upon a Mattress* (1959), a musical show she composed in her twenties that has been recently revived on Broadway. It's based on the fairy tale, *The Princess and the Pea*, around which Rodgers and her lyricist, Marshall Barer, devised a reasonable pantomime story about a wicked queen, a lugubrious jester and a royal pair to be plighted at the final curtain. To this basic plot they have brought a certain amount of wit and sophistication, more, for instance, than Rodgers and Hammerstein brought to the contemporary *Cinderella* (1957), but not quite entertaining enough to sustain a whole evening. This new recording has many good things going for it including numbers that were omitted from the original recording as well as Eric Stern's lively musical direction; but, alas, it doesn't have a sympathetically recorded heroine, certainly not one to erase memories of Carol Burnett on the long-deleted Broadway cast album.

Much of this score turns up on *Hey, Love*, an anthology show built around Mary Rodgers's subsequent output, including her famous reworking of Jobim's "Girl from Ipanema", "The boy from ...", featured in *The Mad Show* (1966). The amiable company guide us through one early song with Sondheim as lyricist and several from *Hot Spot* (1963) that sounds as though it should have been the perfect vehicle for Judy Holliday who starred as a scatty peace corps member spreading mayhem during the Cold War. But it is those *Mattress* songs that linger on in the mind, encouraging the thought that this show could be given a second chance on the London stage. The very close balance grows wearisome after a while.   **AE**

Richard Rodgers   1902-1979 USA

Lorenz Hart   1895-1943 USA

Born in Long Island, New York, Richard Rodgers had early piano lessons from his mother and copyrighted his first song, "My auto show girl", in 1914. At Columbia University in 1918 he met Lorenz Hart. Hart, who was then occupied in translating German plays (he was the son of German immigrants), wanted to replace the banal and clichéd lyrics of popular song with something more imaginative, a project in which Rodgers heartily concurred. Their first published song together was "Any old place with you" which appeared in *A Lonely Romeo* (1919); after writing for Columbia's varsity production, *Fly With Me* (1919), they contributed seven songs to the show *Poor Little Ritz Girl* (1920), although most of their songs were cut for the Broadway production. They despaired of achieving any commercial success – Rodgers even contemplated a sideways career move into the underwear business – until scoring an unexpected hit with *The Garrick Gaities of 1925*. Their next project, *Dearest Enemy* (1925), represented a move towards a drama with integral songs as opposed to the more usual song-and-dance format of the time. The partnership was an unusual one: Hart's increasing alcoholic tendencies and his habit of scribbling lyrics on the back of envelopes contrasting with the methodical and self-disciplined Rodgers. After an unsuccessful foray in Hollywood (1930-34) – where they wrote an early version of "Blue moon" only to have it rejected by a producer – Rodgers and Hart returned to acclaim on Broadway with *Jumbo* (1935), *On Your Toes* (1936) and *Babes in Arms* (1937). *Pal Joey* (1940) was a daring departure from standard musical comedy, with its rough and roguish characters. The partnership was dissolved when Hart turned down the offer to adapt the play *Green Grow the Lilacs*. He died shortly after the new show, *Oklahoma!*, opened to great applause.

Babes in Arms 1989 **Studio Cast** (with Judy Blazer, Gregg Edelman, Jason Graae, Adam Grupper, Judy Kaye); **New Jersey Symphony Orchestra / Evans Haile.**
New World ℗ NW386-2 (66 minutes: DDD).

"The lady is a tramp", "Where or when", "I wish I were in love again", "Johnny one-note", "My funny valentine" – these titles represent the cream of the standard music catalogue and they all come from *Babes in Arms*! However, they were wedded to a story about teenagers putting on a show at a summer camp that has defeated modern performance – *Babes in Arms* has recently been performed in London's Regent's Park, but is seldom revived in America. So this recording, which restores the original orchestrations played by a splendid band, is all the more welcome. The production quite rightly puts the emphasis on youth, so although it may not be strong on characterization, save for Judy Kaye's hilarious "Way out west", it's the ensemble, including the vocal quartet JQ and the Bandits, that gives this recording its distinction. The recording has plenty of 'oomph', and the booklet notes are exceptionally informative. At the moment, this is the finest recording available of a Rodgers and Hart musical.   **AE**

New review
The Boys from Syracuse 1997 **New York Cast** (with Rebecca Luker, Davis Gaines, Sarah Uriarte Berry, Michael McGrath, Malcolm Gets and Debbie Gravitte) / **Rob Fisher.**
DRG ℗ 94767 (65 minutes: DDD).

New York's "Encore" series of concert versions of little performed shows follows a pattern created in London with the long-running "Lost Musicals" series. However, New York's concerts are more elaborate, with full orchestra playing, as in this case, original orchestrations. This prime Rodgers and Hart score is complete on this new issue, which is something the two other previous, and now deleted, issues could not claim. The 1950s Goddard Lieberson-produced studio cast was pretty close to complete and Lehman Engel's 1953 musical treatment with Portia Nelson and Jack Cassidy was masterly. The 1963 revival cast had a glorious vibrancy about it and was more theatrical and was the previous recommended issue. All these recordings are now deleted – we are lucky to have this loving reconstruction to replace them.

Shakespeare's *Comedy of Errors* is a wonderful base for a musical comedy as it is as close to farce as the Bard got. The score oozes with wit and, as the introduction says, "If it's good enough for Shakespeare, it's good enough for us". This album exudes fun and there are some fine performances backed by an orchestra which claims centre stage with zest in the orchestral interludes. There are some nice little extras not on previous recordings, such as "Big brother" and more of the dance music. But it's not only the completeness that makes this version shine. Whilst recorded in a studio it still has the energy of a concert performance and a rawness which suits this score so well. The score can boast of standards such as "Falling in love with love" and "This can't be love" and the delights of "Sing for your supper". Great fun and highly recommended. **RSB**

New review
A Connecticut Yankee 1955 Television Cast (with Eddie Albert, Janet Blair and Boris Karloff) / Charles Sandford.
AEI mono ℗ AEICD043 (51 minutes: AAD).

The television broadcast from which this recording was taken was based on the 1943 Broadway revival (and reworking) of Rodgers and Hart's 1927 hit. This was the last project Lorenz Hart worked on and for any lover of this pair's glorious output this recording will be a must. The songs include "My heart stood still", "Thou swell" and a few choruses of the murderously funny "To keep my love alive". But perhaps the joy of this, the only recording so far issued of the score on CD, is the chance to hear so many infrequently aired songs from this supreme song-writing duo. The telling lyric to "Can't you do a friend a favor?" (written for the revival) has Hart opening up us as much about himself as the show's characters. The quality of the singing is variable (this was a live recording) but Eddie Albert and Janet Blair are fine and Boris Karloff singing another of Hart's last thoughtful lyrics in "You always love the same girl" is more than charming. There is a bonus track of Jessie Matthews's simple rendering of "My heart stood still" (which she introduced in England) with just a piano accompaniment. Remastered from a Kinescope recording, this historical recording has a fairly clean vocal sound but a background noise of varying intensity is evident – however, for most, the content will act as its own filter against this imperfection. There is a perfect 'setting in place' booklet-note by sadly missed Stanley Green. **RSB**

New review
Dearest Enemy 1955 Television Cast (with Anne Jeffreys, Robert Sterling, Cyril Ritchard and Cornelia Otis Skinner) / Charles Sandford.
AEI mono ℗ AEICD042 (61 minutes: AAD).

Rodgers and Hart's 1925 *Dearest Enemy* was their first 'book' show, a fact which is as much a piece of American history as the episode of the American Revolution upon which this charming show was based. Tricking a British General and his men so the local lads could get the upper hand was far from the bloodthirsty tale it could have been and love did, of course, raise its glorious head and win the day. Its television source base has given the opportunity to give the listener some feed-ins and so a storyline is present, although the real point here is the Rodgers and Hart score which is far from well known. Inevitably there are pleasant discoveries for their devotees. The best-known songs are "Here in my arms" and "Bye and bye", but the cheery marching song "Cheerio" should set your feet tapping and "You must be old enough to love" should make you giggle. Reprises are frequent and there is a wonderfully humorous performance by Cyril Ritchard (listen to "Sweet Peter") and a knowing one by Cornelia Otis Skinner. Four bonus tracks include two by Helen Ford, the original Betty, a contemporary vocal selection and a strange oddity – Alec Templeton's live rendering of the improbable "Mozart meets Rodgers and Hart" with a built-in echo. Remastered from a Kinescope recording, this historical recording has a clean sound. For a live recording the quality of singing is fine although some stray voices appear in the background of one of the musical tracks.   **RSB**

New review
The Girl Friend 1986 **Colchester Mercury Theatre** (with Barbara King, Mark Hutchinson, Jill Pert, John Gower) **/ Martin Yates.**
TER Ⓕ CDTER1148 (63 minutes: DDD).

Early Rodgers and Hart has attracted little attention from the record companies, despite the evident attraction of their songs from the period 1925-31. *The Girl Friend*, one of their few shows to be staged in London, enjoyed an even longer run here than on Broadway with 421 performances. Sandy Wilson paid an affectionate tribute to its title-song when he composed his title-tune for *The Boy Friend*, whilst "Blue room" came to epitomize the London social scene of the 1920s, as Anthony Powell described in a chapter from his novels *Dance to the Music of Time*, where two bands on either side of a Mayfair Square are playing "Blue room" and "Mountain greenery" (here an interpolation from *The Garrick Gaieties*). Other hands also contributed to *The Girl Friend*, though Rodgers and Hart surely composed the Act 1 finale and finaletto to Act 2 that were a common feature of musical comedy at that time. Although this present recording emanates from a stage production, the cast, and in particular the orchestra, often sound inadequately prepared. The closely-miked balance does them few favours. So this has to be a stop-gap recommendation until something better comes along.   **AE**

New review
On Your Toes 1983 **Broadway Cast** (with Natalia Makarova, George S. Irving, Dina Merrill, George de la Pena, Christine Andreas and Lara Teeter) **/ John Mauceri.**
TER Ⓕ CDTER1063 (74 minutes: ADD).

This 1936 Rodgers and Hart masterpiece was given a glorious, near-perfect revival in 1983 when it was a hit again both on Broadway and in the West End. There had, however, been another revival back in 1954 hot on the heels of a rediscovered and successful *Pal Joey* – but it was not the right moment. Even so, it was recorded and is available on CD (mono) with a distinctively winning performance by Elaine Stritch (singing an interpolated "You took advantage of me"). It is a fine alternative but does not quite come up to TER's beautiful theatrical version with its original 1930s arrangements (far more enjoyable than the brash 1950s, even if a little thinner) and sound (one longs for Stritch but this is almost made up for with Christine Andreas). Included in the TER issue are the two major ballets (a previous TER issue under the same number had these in a shorter form) which George Balanchine choreographed originally and which were excitingly reconstructed here. The score is top-notch Rodgers and Hart ("There's a small hotel") with Rodgers excelling in his first real outing into scoring ballet – seven years later with *Oklahoma!* ballet became an accepted part of the musical stage – here it was a remarkable breakthrough. This was a dance show – from the vaudeville opener "Two a day for Keith" to the great "Slaughter on Tenth Avenue" finale telling of the son of vaudevillians who tries not to be in showbusiness but ends up – guess where. This recording gives the dance feel from tap to balletic grace – so put on your dancing pumps. There is also a gangster and a murder on the recording for your pleasure. Any self-respecting lover of the musical stage should not be without this in his or her collection (just listen to Hart's lyric for "It's got to be love" to get the picture).   **RSB**

Pal Joey 1950 **Studio Cast** (with Vivienne Segal, Harold Lang, Barbara Ashley, Beverly Fite, Kenneth Remo and Jo Hurt) **/ Lehman Engel.**
Columbia mono Ⓜ CK04364 (44 minutes: AAD).
Pal Joey 1995 **Broadway Cast** (with Patti LuPone, Peter Gallagher and Bebe Neuwirth) **/ Rob Fisher.**
DRG Ⓕ 94763 (61 minutes: DDD).

Pal Joey is generally regarded as Rodgers and Hart's most revivable show, and it's certainly the most recorded. It tells a tough story, in a consistently (and honestly) cynical tone, and it was in that respect a departure. The paradox is that, ahead of its time or not, the team's supposed masterpiece is actually second-rate Rodgers and Hart. At least, it's second-rate Hart; Rodgers seems to enjoy this excursion into the brash and sleazy, and he does it with a conviction that seems especially pungent considering that his more wholesome partnership with Hammerstein was only three years away. But Hart could only sing in his own voice; given his first sustained opportunity to write closely to plot and character and handed a subject and a *milieu* that he knew intimately, he couldn't reinvent himself. When he resorts to forced rhymes and jokes it's far more damaging than in his earlier, looser shows; while his unique bittersweet grace has little scope. That said, these discs between them offer much to enjoy. The original 1940 production went unrecorded, robbing us of the chance to hear Gene Kelly in his one great stage role, but its leading lady Vivienne Segal was enlisted for the studio version ten years later. Hailing from operetta, she sounds at first blush too genteel for Joey's erotic protectress; soon, however, the contrast of style and substance makes its own effect. By turns kittenish and forthright, she doesn't miss a nuance or a *double entendre*; she's the lady *and* the tramp (and she was Hart's own favourite performer). Harold Lang, a hoofer cast as a hoofer, has rather a featureless voice, but there is something to be said for rendering Joey, at once street-smart and naïve, as a blank slate. The other performers are mostly unknown outside this recording, and sound it. Ted Royal's orchestrations are heavy-handed; fine for the deliberately exaggerated brassiness of "That terrific rainbow", the ultimate awful floor-show number, but oppressive elsewhere.

DRG's preservation of a New York concert performance restores the original orchestrations by Hans Spialek and they are a revelation, full of piquant punctuation and, as conductor Rob Fisher observes, remarkably swinging for Broadway 1940. There's some wonderful pixilated brass in the out-chorus of "Rainbow"; Joey's dream ballet might as well never have been recorded before; and the bump-and-grind interludes in "Flower garden" are delightful. Authenticity rules in other departments as well. The gangster Lowell has his songs back (usually they're appropriated by Joey or the girls) and, unlike his predecessor on Columbia, he sounds like a gangster. A pity he doesn't sound like a gangster who can sing. Daisy Prince does a lot with the pretty unrewarding role of the *ingénue*. We still don't have a definitive Joey; maybe he too is underwritten. Frank Sinatra in the 1957 movie would have been the best, had he been allowed to sing the authentic score rather than selections from the Rodgers and Hart songbook. Peter Gallagher doesn't live up to all the claims made for him in the blurb, but he has an unusual sort-of-haunting voice and some presence. He's at his best in the title-song, Joey's peak of self-assurance, and he also gets to sing the very revealing (of both Joey and Hart) "I'm talking to my pal" ("I can't be sure of girls/I'm not at home with men/I'm winding up with me again") cut from the original production. Patti LuPone doesn't waste much charm on Vera, and her enunciation – though not as tortured as in *Anything Goes* – can still be peculiar, but she points the lyrics freshly, especially in "Bewitched", and she doesn't have to cheat on the notes. *Pal Joey* here comes closer than ever before to the show it's cracked up to be.   **RC**

Dawn Upshaw sings Rodgers and Hart   Dawn Upshaw, Audra McDonald, David Garrison; Fred Hersch (pf); Orchestra of St Luke's / Eric Stern.
Nonesuch Ⓔ 7559-79406-2 (53 minutes: DDD).
Songs from Simple Simon, Garrick Gaieties, Too Many Girls, The Boys from Syracuse, By Jupiter, Jumbo, A Connecticut Yankee, I Married an Angel, Pal Joey, Spring is Here, Higher and Higher, Heads Up!, Ever Green.

Dawn Upshaw's first music-theatre recital ("I wish it so" – see Singers) daringly combined songs of Bernstein, Blitzstein, Sondheim and Weill into a compelling entity that united critical enthusiasm and won the 1995 *Gramophone* Award for Music Theatre. There is perhaps less of the daring about this follow-up offering, in so far as it concentrates entirely on the proven appeal of Rodgers and Hart. Yet the result is every bit as compelling. The poetic beauty of Hart's lyrics and the exquisite charm of Rodgers's melodies guarantee that these songs are gems indeed. I expected that I would miss the original theatre orchestrations, but the arrangements here are imaginative, ever apt – more consistently so, perhaps, than in Upshaw's earlier recital – ranging from tenderly expressive to jazzy and upbeat. Upshaw brings out the range and depth of Hart's tender poetry in numbers like "Little girl blue" from *Jumbo*, where her performance has a great variety of expression. Upshaw's delivery throughout is of a superb clarity, expressed simply and in a totally non-operatic way. The occasional contributions of supporting artists add greatly to the dramatic effect.   **AML**

Also available:

Lido Lady (1927 London Cast) – see **Kern:** Show Boat
Pal Joey (1952 Broadway Cast) EMI Angel ZDM7 64696-2
Pal Joey (1980 London Cast) TER CDTER1005

Richard Rodgers

Oscar Hammerstein II   1895-1960 USA – see also separate entry

After parting company with Hart, Rodgers's new collaborator on *Oklahoma!* was Oscar
Hammerstein II – together they set about transforming the shape of American musical theatre
with a series of immensely successful shows that wove songs into the fabric of the play: *Carousel*
(1945), *South Pacific* (1949), *The King and I* (1951) and *The Sound of Music* (1959) being their
most enduringly popular works. After Hammerstein died, Rodgers continued working, writing
the lyrics of *No Strings* (1962) and teaming up with Stephen Sondheim for *Do I Hear a Waltz?*
(1965), Martin Charnin for *Two By Two* (1970) and Sheldon Harnick for *Rex* (1976). Rodgers
also wrote instrumental works including *Nursery Ballet* (1938) and the incidental music for
Victory at Sea (1952).

Allegro 1947 **Broadway Cast** (with John Battles, Lisa Kirk, Roberta Jonay, Muriel O'Malley,
    William Ching and Gloria Wills) **/ Salvatore dell' Isola**.
    RCA Victor mono Ⓜ 07863 52758-2 (34 minutes: ADD).

Allegro was the show that Oscar Hammerstein always wanted to take a second shot at. It was
a brave, experimental piece unlike the previous shows Rodgers and Hammerstein had
written – or were to write in subsequent years – originally conceived as an allegory taking
its doctor hero from birth to death. In the event, the show stopped roughly half way, ending
when Joe returns to home in a rural small town, turning his back on the shallow, meaningless
values of big city life. One of only two Rodgers and Hammerstein original subjects (the other
was *Me and Juliet*), *Allegro* offered advances in score, structure and staging that were at least
ten years ahead of their time. Luckily, the score was substantially covered on record. The hit
was "The gentleman is a dope" but "So far", "A fellow needs a girl" and "You are never
away" are fine songs too. The original cast led by John Battles and featuring Lisa Kirk are
excellent, and the recording, from the last years of the 78 era, comes up well in RCA's careful
transfer.   **MPK**

Broadway Julie Andrews sings the Music of Richard Rodgers. **Julie Andrews; London
    Musicians Orchestra / Ian Fraser**.
    Philips Ⓟ 442 603-2 (66 minutes: DDD).
    Songs from The Sound of Music, The King and I, Babes in Arms, No Strings, The Boys from
    Syracuse, A Connecticut Yankee, Higher and Higher, Spring is Here, Pal Joey, Carousel,
    South Pacific, Do I Hear a Waltz?, State Fair and Oklahoma!.

That crystal-clear soprano might have deteriorated slightly around the edges, but Julie
Andrews remains one of the class acts of musical theatre. Crucially, the impeccable diction
remains unaltered, as does her ability to sing a song the way it was written. Rather than
attempting to ignore the inevitable effect of the passage of time on such a voice, she skilfully
uses newly discovered textures to find new meanings in a collection which represents the
cream of Richard Rodgers's work. Assisted by superb orchestrations from Angela Morley,
Eddie Karam, Bill Byers, Bob Florence and Ian Fraser, Andrews takes each of these familiar
standards and turns them into a complete story. She swings cynically through "I wish I were
in love again", takes a grand tour of some great musical waltz tunes in a medley which unites,
among others, "Do I hear a waltz?" with "A wonderful guy" and "This nearly was mine", and,
naturally, revisits the scene of one of her greatest triumphs with mature performances of "The
sound of music" and "Edelweiss". But perhaps the real treats here are the more intimate
ballads. Her lower register has developed a darker, husky quality which she uses to great
emotional effect on "My funny Valentine" and "Nobody told me". "It never entered my
mind" segues into "Spring is here" – and never has melancholy sounded so beguiling.

Rodgers & Hammerstein | **R**

Concluding an album of treasures is a down-tempo but highly positive rendition of "A cock-eyed optimist". Great stuff. **PF**

Carousel 1945 **Broadway Cast** (with John Raitt, Jan Clayton, Jean Darling, Christine Johnson, Eric Mattson, Murvyn Vye and Connie Baxter) / **Joseph Littau.**
MCA mono Ⓜ MCAD10799 (55 minutes: AAD).

Carousel 1956 **Film Cast** (with Gordon MacRae, Shirley Jones, Cameron Mitchell, Barbara Ruick, Claramae Turner and Robert Rounseville) / **Alfred Newman.**
EMI Angel Ⓜ ZDM7 64692-2 (51 minutes: ADD).

Carousel 1993 **London Cast** (with Katrina Murphy, Joanna Riding, Michael Hayden, Meg Johnson, Clive Rowe and Phil Daniels) / **Martin Yates.**
First Night Ⓜ OCRCD6042 (80 minutes: DDD).

Certain songs – not necessarily the most famous ones – in the first two Rodgers and Hammerstein musicals sound so right, so sure-footed and inevitable, that it's hard to believe that somebody actually sat down and wrote them. They're like modern folk-songs. Were the first night audiences at *Oklahoma!* surprised by "I cain't say no" and "Many a new day" or those at *Carousel* by "When the children are asleep" or "What's the use of wond'rin'?", or even the throwaway "Stonecutters cut it on stone"? Did they immediately accept them as among the good and necessary things in life? And what did they make of "The Carousel waltz", a tune – or a series of tunes – that the world should never have had to do without? Coming out of nowhere, it remains the greatest opening any musical has ever had, and the sound is only the half of it. Against that music is played out the first meeting of the mill-girl Julie Jordan and the barker Billy Bigelow in the fairground that – rather surprisingly, since we never return there – gives the show its name. But then the music and the tableaux set it up so compellingly that we don't have to.

"The Carousel waltz" virtually ensures that any recording of this show will at least start off sounding great, and it would be a very weird reading of the score that didn't have the listener close to tears by the end. The MCA original comes through on both counts; it was recorded as a collection of 78s, so some things get shortened, especially the main love-ballad "If I loved you" which is a whole long scene in the script. Only one song gets left out completely – "Geraniums in the winder", the charming lament of the temporarily broken-hearted Enoch Snow – and the CD throws in three alternate takes, including an extended version of the "Waltz". John Raitt's round, youthful baritone heads up a cast of singer's singers; even Murvyn Vye, as the ragamuffin villain Jigger, sports a polished bass voice – he actually sounds rather elderly. You have to supply some of the drama for yourself, even in Raitt's delivery of Billy's famous "Soliloquy", but nobody actually gets in its way.

The film soundtrack leads off with a semi-symphonic "Waltz": the Alfred Newman sound. There is a lack of contrast in the voices; the delightful Barbara Ruick, who plays Carrie, sounds as if she could have sung Julie at least as well as Shirley Jones, who actually does. "When the children are asleep", Ruick's duet with the earnest Robert Rounseville, is the highlight, not least for the squeak with which she responds to her fisherman-fiancé's plans for an expanding family: "Are you building up to another fleet?". Gordon MacRae, despite his extensive pop experience, is even more of a light-operatic Billy than Raitt. His posthumous demand to be judged by "The highest judge of all" was cut from the film, along with (again) "Geraniums in the winder". The quiet opening of "This was a real nice clambake" and the slow crescendo of its development, as of a gradually approaching crowd, is more spectacularly served here than on any other record. The disc is far more entertaining than the stolid movie that begot it, but much of the score's blood has drained away. There is even some Hollywood bowdlerization; a disillusioned young wife complains in "Stonecutter" of "Not much sleepin' at night" (as opposed to Hammerstein's far more flavourful "God-knows-whattin' all night").

The Royal National Theatre production, recorded by First Night, takes nearly all honours. It starts with a "Waltz" whose successive themes, in William David Brohn's orchestration, are more brilliantly distinguished than ever before. Nicholas Hytner's production began not at the carousel but in the mill where Julie and Carrie work, and the oppressive setting perfectly matched the dark chords of the opening music. On disc, the overwhelming sense of an acted production is preserved. The voices aren't historic; even Joanna Riding's radiant Julie has some trouble on top. What really tells is her sympathetic laughter while Katrina Murphy's Carrie sings "Mr Snow".

Even better is the light and shade that she and Michael Hayden find in the "If I loved you" sequence, with Hammerstein's dialogue coming up triumphantly. As played here, it's the most erotic number in the musical repertoire, with consummation the inevitable sequel. Hayden plays Billy as a Sinatra-like nervously tough street arab, although some of his high notes pierce in the wrong way. He is terribly believable; it's a shame that "The highest judge ..." has been cut, for his performance seems to be leading up to it. Also missing, and more damagingly, is the battle-of-the-sexes chorale that should introduce "June is bustin' out all over" and recur at the start of "What's the use in wond'rin'?". "June ..." has gained a sexy last stanza previously unheard, at least on record, and, far more importantly, the ballet-music has been included, framed by dialogue that captures some, at least, of its emotional impact. Other jewels are the way Meg Johnson begins "You'll never walk alone", as if she's really groping to find words of comfort, and the unprecedented raucous swagger of Phil Daniels's outcast Jigger, so gravelly you can hardly believe he's singing. (But he is.) **RC**

Cinderella 1957 US Television Cast (with Julie Andrews, Jon Cypher, Dorothy Stickney, Howard Lindsay, Ilka Chase, Kaye Ballard, Alice Ghostley and Edith Adams) / **Alfredo Antonini**.
Columbia Ⓜ CK02005 (43 minutes: AAD).
Cinderella 1965 US Television Cast (with Lesley Ann Warren, Stuart Damon, Don Heitgerd, Celeste Holm, Pat Carroll, Barbara Ruick and Jo Van Fleet) / **John Green**.
Sony Broadway Ⓕ SK53538 (51 minutes: ADD).

The earlier and much more successful of two original musicals for television by Richard Rodgers had two productions, one starring Julie Andrews, the other Lesley Ann Warren (it would also be expanded into a pantomime for a season in 1958 at the London Coliseum with Tommy Steele as Buttons). For the second production a song dropped from *South Pacific*, "The loneliness of evening", was added for the Prince. Rodgers's score is a classic, from a classic period, "Do I love you because you're beautiful?" being the big love song, with additional delights in "Ten minutes ago" and "A lovely night". The original, featuring Julie Andrews, is indeed definitive, but there's nothing wrong with the other, newer version. **MPK**

Do I Hear a Waltz? 1965 Broadway Cast (with Elizabeth Allen, Sergio Franchi, Stuart Damon and Carol Bruce) / **Frederick Dvonch**.
Sony Broadway Ⓕ SK48206 (51 minutes: ADD).

Here's an excellent example of a musical show that is, by common consent, dramatically flawed, yet it is always a pleasure to hear on a disc where the performances, musical direction and recording are all tip-top. But there's more to it than that, for the musical numbers in this by all accounts unhappy partnership between the senior composer of the Broadway musical of the 1960s and his junior collaborator, one Stephen Sondheim, have "endured well and gained perspective over the years", to quote the booklet-note. Sondheim once said that the reason for the show's failure "is that it's about a lady who, metaphorically, can't sing". However, the authors had a crack at it. In the story, their leading lady after one disappointment hears the waltz she'd expected to when she fell in love. As the reality dawns on her she sings the title-song, a swirling waltz with the cross rhythms indicating her joyful feelings. I think there is a vulnerability to this character, originally a middle-aged spinster, that Elizabeth Allen was too young to suggest, though she comes close to it in the lovely trio, "Moon in my window", where Carol Bruce and Julienne Marie join her in an expression of love's illusions. Sergio Franchi is the smooth Italian whom she fell for. I suspect that the show's nickname, "Dearth in Venice", was coined after hearing him sing the lugubrious ballad, "Stay", but he gets a better one, "Take the moment", to round off the first act and some taxing *falsetto* in imitation of a shop-keeper in the bargaining number. Apart from the title-song, Rodgers, and particularly Sondheim, are at their wittiest in the ensembles, as in the hilarious description of air travel, "What do we do? We fly!", the self-congratulatory, "Perfectly lovely couple", a sexy tango, "No understand", full of innuendo, and a young couple's duet, "We're gonna be all right", where Sondheim's verses were deemed too sharp for Broadway in 1965. A few summers ago *Do I Hear a Waltz?* was given its British première at the Guildhall School of Music and Drama. Given the current passion for classical tenors and baritones and the wealth of female talent in middle age who say there aren't any suitable parts for them, the door is wide open for this show to have a more permanent foothold in the repertory. **AE**

Flower Drum Song 1958 **Broadway Cast** (with Miyoshi Umeki, Larry Blyden, Juanita Hall, Ed Kenney and Keye Luke) / **Salvatore Dell' Isola**.
Sony Broadway Ⓕ SK53536 (54 minutes: ADD).

Flower Drum Song 1960 **London Cast** (with Yan Shan Tong, Kevin Scott, Ida Shepley, Zed Zakari, George Pastell and Yama Saki) / **Robert Lowe**.
EMI Angel Ⓜ ZDM7 89953-2 (53 minutes: ADD).

Rodgers and Hammerstein's penultimate musical may not have been a great theatrical experience like *The King and I* or *Carousel*, nor did it succeed in breaking new ground like *Oklahoma!* or *Allegro*. *Flower Drum Song* is an exotically flavoured, conventional, old-fashioned musical that happens to be set amongst the thriving Chinese community of San Francisco. The best song, "Love look away", is not given to any of the principals, but to a minor character, hopelessly in love. The score is a rich one, dotted with songs of quality like "You are beautiful", "Sunday", the catchy "Grant Avenue" and the confident "I enjoy being a girl". The British cast cover the score well, but the American original is streets ahead in show business expertise and glamour. These recordings date from the time when the British musical stage had some catching up to do in comparison with its American counterpart. **MPK**

A Grand Night for Singing 1993 **Broadway Cast** (with Victoria Clark, Gregg Edelman, Jason Graae, Alyson Reed and Lynne Wintersteller) / **Fred Wells**.
Varèse Sarabande Spotlight Series Ⓕ VSD5516 (74 minutes: DDD).
Songs from Oklahoma!, Carousel, Allegro, State Fair, Cinderella, The King and I, The Sound of Music, South Pacific, Flower Drum Song, Me and Juliet and Pipe Dream.

Timed to celebrate the fiftieth anniversary of the Richard Rodgers-Oscar Hammerstein partnership, *A Grand Night for Singing* is one of the most pleasant of the staged songwriter-fests. The show focuses on R&H as the romantic architects of middle America. All of the team's scores for theatre, film or television are represented, the songs arranged to form a chronological study of the relationships of the sexes from courtship ("The surrey with the fringe on top") to whatever – mature contentment, presumably – is represented by "I have dreamed". The subtleties of this development must have been more evident to the compilers than to the audience, but there are some entertaining juxtapositions. After boy has rapturously requested girl to let him take her out in the surrey, the two remaining ladies in the cast of five react with the jealous "Stepsisters' lament" from the sparkling TV score to *Cinderella* ("Why would a fella want a girl who's merely lovely?").

The performers blend, weave and solo very nicely but two stand out. Lynne Wintersteller's full, secure voice is heard to particular advantage on "Do I love you because you're beautiful?" (also from *Cinderella*). Jason Graae, who seems to be first in line for the light juvenile spot in compilations like this (or for new recordings of vintage shows), drives a wide-eyed citified "Surrey" ("Two bright sidelights winkin' and blinkin'" he proudly emphasizes) and describes a "Maria" who sounds a lot more appealing here than when she's sketched by that puzzled posse of nuns in *The Sound of Music*. Gregg Edelman, subbing at short notice for an indisposed Martin Vidnovic, sounds strained on some numbers but comes through with a full-throated "Oh, what a beautiful mornin'" and a pulsating "Honey bun", another song it's good to hear sung by a man. The others back him up on that one with harmonized interjections and instrumental noises that suggest the 1940s as re-imagined by Manhattan Transfer. They all sound as if they're having fun which, in this kind of show, is the point. **RC**

The King and I 1951 **Broadway Cast** (with Gertrude Lawrence, Yul Brynner, Doretta Morrow and Larry Douglas) / **Frederick Dvonch**.
MCA Ⓜ MCLD19156 (38 minutes: AAD).
New review
The King and I 1994 **Studio Cast** (with Valerie Masterson, Christopher Lee, Tinuke Olafimihan, Jason Howard, Alec McCowen and Sally Burgess); **National Symphony Orchestra / John Owen Edwards**.
TER Ⓕ CDTER2 1214 (two discs: 116 minutes: DDD).

Because the original Broadway cast LP was issued in 1951, when the length of each number had to be compatible with the 10-inch 78rpm disc format, this first cast recording is on the short side. Anna Leonowens, governess to the children of the King of Siam, was Gertrude Lawrence's last stage role before her untimely death at 54, 18 months into the run of the show. Although the recording is now something of an antique, her performance carries its own peculiar brand of 'star quality', a phrase coined by her confidant Noël Coward to denote an indefinable magic about a performer. Notwithstanding the star's penchant for sliding off a note or two, here we have charm, warmth and exemplary diction, as well the occasional vocal uncertainty engendered in the wake of coming to terms with a new score.

Like their recent *Gramophone* Award-winning *My Fair Lady*, this new TER recording of *The King and I* gives us a much fuller account of the score than we've had before on disc; it contains more than 42 minutes of music and dialogue longer then the most recent recording on Philips (see separate review) with Julie Andrews and Ben Kingsley. The book of *The King and I*, a hefty piece of drama in its own right, is well worth hearing when much of it is spoken (to great effect), as when the King, interrupting a dance between Anna and the British Ambassador, an acquaintance from some way back, unleashes a flash of jealousy by declaiming "dancing after dinner". The Ambassador's response, "we'd better be going in Anna", clearly meant to be heard by the King, not only epitomizes the dignity of his post but sends out a note of caution to Anna. It is timed to perfection by McCowen, Masterson and Lee as the graceful palm-court minuet continues in the background. In her first major role on disc in a musical comedy, Valerie Masterson brings a warmth and humanity to her role as governess to the children of the King of Siam. Her skittish laughter and breath of desire in his company as they polka round that deserted ballroom suggests her growing and glowing attraction to him. She rises magnificently to the challenge of "Shall I tell you what I think of you?", drawing on the full command of her operatic experience to give him 'what for'. The role of the King is far smaller musically speaking, but Christopher Lee suggests more than many the doubts of a monarch's troubled heart in "A puzzlement". Although Jason Howard sounds a trifle mature for Tinuke Olafimihan's Tuptim, their casting on disc as the ill-fated lovers is more successful than has been achieved on other recordings: "We kiss in a shadow", at a slow tempo, is beautifully sung. Sally Burgess as Lady Thiang sings "Something wonderful" with dignity and a breathtaking command of the long phrases of the vocal line. The orchestra, conducted by John Owen Edwards, brings renewed admiration for Rodgers's score, glowingly orchestrated by Robert Russell Bennett. Save for a couple of passages where orchestral detail is slightly blurred by excessive resonance ("A puzzlement" and the filigree wind writing in "The processional"), the pace and execution of all the musical numbers is faultless. I've mentioned how the drama of the piece is enhanced by this recording, but listen too for the elegant string writing in the Act 1 finale where the tune of "Hello young lovers" is decorated with a counterpoint that's the last word in courtly elegance. **AE**

The King and I 1956 **Film Cast** (with Marni Nixon for Deborah Kerr, Yul Brynner, Rita Moreno and Terry Saunders) **/ Alfred Newman**.
EMI Angel Ⓜ ZDM7 64693-2 (46 minutes: AAD).
The King and I 1992 **Studio Cast** (with Julie Andrews, Ben Kingsley, Lea Salonga, Peabo Bryson and Marilyn Horne); **Los Angeles Master Chorale; Hollywood Bowl Orchestra / John Mauceri**.
Philips Ⓟ 438 007-2 (65 minutes: DDD).

Julie Andrews's remarkable performance deepens in perspective and authority as it progresses. She brings a lightness of touch and a degree of seriousness to her role whilst her voice has lost little of its bloom over the years. By a fair margin her supporting cast is the most accomplished of these two recordings, with the conductor John Mauceri bringing out both the gravitas and gaiety of the piece in masterly fashion. My only quibble, given the decision to use the orchestrations of the 1956 film as the basis for the Philips recording, is the omission of the splendid six-and-a-half minute overture that was such a feature of the soundtrack LP. That famous bestseller, enshrining so memorably the role that Yul Brynner made his own, and conducted with such panache by Alfred Newman, has never lost its allure nor its place in the catalogue (even though Hollywood neglected to credit Marni Nixon for her skilful vocal portrayal of Deborah Kerr's Anna, a contribution more clearly delineated than ever on CD). Nevertheless, the skill with which Mauceri's recording has been adapted from the soundtrack sources, including passages of Newman's inimitable underscoring and a charming, previously unrecorded minuet Rodgers composed for the

Ballroom scene, offers a degree of continuity that is very satisfying for home listening, particularly in a relatively heavy 'book' musical like this one. Clearly, therefore, the Philips recording is now first choice for the film version. **AE**

Me and Juliet 1953 **Broadway Cast** (with Isabel Bigley, Bill Hayes, Joan McCracken, Ray Walston, Mark Dawson, Jackie Kelk and The Barbara Carroll Trio) / **Salvatore Dell' Isola**.
RCA Victor mono Ⓜ 09026 61480-2 (41 minutes: ADD).

Me and Juliet is a backstage musical with a difference. The usual clichés of such stories are missing here. The hero and heroine are humble backstage members of a show in the middle of a long Broadway run, and by the end of the evening they still are – except that the hero has been promoted from assistant to full stage manager. Their triumphs are small – the hero and heroine fall in love and the hero faces up to a backstage bully, an electrician. Otherwise in "the first of our plays in which nobody dies"(Hammerstein) nothing much happens. The show is a mosaic of everyday life backstage at an elaborate musical (called, of course, *Me and Juliet*). The score is one of the happiest written by Rodgers and Hammerstein. "No other love" (using music previously aired in the TV score *Victory at Sea*) was the standout ballad. There's plenty of wit to savour – "Intermission talk", "We deserve each other", "That's the way it happens" and "It's me" reveal the adroit and quizzical qualities not often associated with this lyricist.The original cast recording makes you long for a revival of the show. Isabel Bigley and Bill Hayes exude freshness and innocence and Joan McCracken, superb as always, adds point and precision to the comedy numbers. **MPK**

No Strings 1962 **Broadway Cast** (with Diahann Carroll, Richard Kiley, Don Chastain and Bernice Massi) / **Peter Matz**.
EMI Angel Ⓜ ZDM7 64694-2 (49 minutes:ADD).

"All style and no content" was how Variety summed up Richard Rodgers's only stage musical for which he wrote the music and lyrics. The style was provided by the leading lady, the glamorous Diahann Carroll, and the novelty by having the orchestra on stage mingling with the cast during many of Rodgers's own songs, immaculately arranged by Peter Matz and Ralph Burns. But the story was another matter. When *No Strings* was presented at Her Majesty's Theatre in London, Bernard Levin went straight for the jugular: "admirers of the cowardice of the Broadway theatre will be relieved to know ... that the coloured girl and white American do not, in the last scene, go home to Maine, passionate though their love for one another is". Rodgers's lyrics make no mention of the black and white romance at the heart of the story, instead the well-drilled company offer performances of songs that alternate between the wistful, "The sweetest sounds" (his last hit song), and the brassy, "Be my host". The 14-page booklet covering this chapter in Rodgers's career is as fascinating as the show itself, with a photograph of Rodgers and Carroll beaming at each other as they collect their 'Tony' awards. The digital remastering has brought up the analogue original to the highest standards. **AE**

Oklahoma! 1943 **Broadway Cast** (with Alfred Drake, Lee Dixon, Celeste Holm, Joan Roberts and Howard Da Silva) / **Jay Blackton**.
MCA mono Ⓜ MCLD19026 (36 minutes: AAD).
Oklahoma! – excerpts. 1943 **Broadway Cast** (with Alfred Drake, Lee Dixon, Celeste Holm, Joan Roberts and Howard Da Silva) / **Jay Blackton**.
ASV Living Era mono Ⓜ CDAJA5198 (73 minutes: ADD). Disc also includes **Kern:** Show Boat – excerpts. 1932 **Studio Cast** (with Paul Robeson, James Melton, Helen Morgan, Olga Albani and Frank Munn); **Brunswick Concert Orchestra / Victor Young**.
Oklahoma! 1952 **Studio Cast** (with Nelson Eddy, Virginia Haskins, Kaye Ballard, Portia Nelson, Lee Cass, David Atkinson and David Morris) / **Lehman Engel**.
Sony Broadway mono Ⓕ SK53326 (54 minutes: ADD).
Oklahoma! 1955 **Film Cast** (with Gordon MacRae, Shirley Jones, Gene Nelson, Charlotte Greenwood, Rod Steiger and Gloria Grahame) / **Jay Blackton**.
EMI Angel Ⓜ CDP7 46631-2 (42 minutes: ADD).
Oklahoma! 1980 **London Cast** (with John Diedrich, Rosamunde Shelley, Madge Ryan, Mark White, Alfred Molina and Jillian Mack) / **Ray Cook**.
TER Ⓜ CDTEM1208 (55 minutes: AAD).

Between them, these recordings have much to offer, not least for the style of performance they represent. Though *Oklahoma!* broke away from the operetta tradition in so many ways, vocal style wasn't going to change over night. On that first recording, Alfred Drake is a trifle suave for the cowboy Curly, whereas Joan Roberts's Laurey sounds more authentically mid-Western. On the Sony recording, Nelson Eddy – a custodian of the operetta tradition – is just a bit mature for Curly though the voice itself is always pleasingly to the ear. His Laurey, Virginia Haskins, never really matches characterization with voice; Kaye Ballard as the girl who "Cain't say no" offers the best performance on this disc which includes Jud's "Lonely room" and the chorus "It's a scandal, it's an outrage" not found on the other current recordings. The orchestra conducted by Lehman Engel is on terrific form and likewise on the original cast recording and the film soundtrack, both of them conducted by Jay Blackton.

With the risk of repeating what has been said so often, Gordon MacRae and Shirley Jones are the ideal hero and heroine in this largely sunny tale and they have the lungs and good looks that have been partly responsible for the film's enduring appeal. This 1955 stereo soundtrack recording has a high hiss factor, but it can be tolerated in this company whilst reliving musical comedy's finest hour. The other recording of the 1980 London production is a rarity, a live performance recorded from the stage of the Palace Theatre, which is something of an achievement in its own right. It's also worth mentioning for John Diedrich's handsome singing in the role of Curly, the spontaneity of the ensemble and the robust playing of the orchestra.   **AE**

Pipe Dream 1955 Broadway Cast (with Wiliam Johnson, Mike Kellin, G. D. Wallace, Judy
Tyler and Helen Traubel) / **Salvatore Dell'Isola**.
RCA Victor mono Ⓜ 09026 61480-2 (41 minutes: ADD).

The original intended composer for a musical based on John Steinbeck's *Cannery Row* characters was Frank Loesser. Sadly this didn't work out; Rodgers and Hammerstein took up the opportunity but the source material was raunchier than any they had tackled before. The result was a cultural mismatch – Rodgers and Hammerstein writing a musical about a whorehouse, starring a beloved Wagnerian diva as its Madam. Perhaps Rodgers and Hart (of *Pal Joey* vintage) could have pulled it off – but Hammerstein and the team softened and lightened the original to the extent that it was no longer recognizably Steinbeck. In addition, Rodgers was in hospital undergoing surgery during a critical rehearsal period. *Pipe Dream* is thus a failure, but a fascinating one with its own set of fine songs. "The next time it happens", "All at once you love her", "Suzy is a good thing" and "The man I used to be" are top-notch, if neglected Rodgers and Hammerstein. The expertly made original cast album has been successfully transferred to CD and is a touching souvenir of both William Johnson and Judy Tyler, both of whom died young as well as offering a glimpse of Helen Traubel's Madam – surely the decade's most bizarre casting.   **MPK**

New review
Rex 1976 Broadway Cast (with Nicol Williamson, Penny Fuller, Ed Evanko, Glenn Close and
Tom Aldredge) / **Jay Blackton.**
RCA Victor Ⓜ 09026 68933-2 (43 minutes: ADD).

In his comprehensive booklet-note "A Requiem for Rex", Bert Fink of the Rodgers and Hammerstein organization, with almost unbearable agony, details the problems that beset this musical adaptation of the life of King Henry the Eighth which resulted in the shortest run, just 49 performances, of any Richard Rodgers musical since the early 1920s. Yet it is the composer, 72 when the show was produced in 1976, who emerges with his credibility intact over a book and lyrics that are often pious or plain sentimental. When Henry, Nicol Williamson, asks his minstrel to sing his new song, we hear a thrice-repeated melody rising one note higher at the end of each refrain, to rival "Greensleeves" in our affection. It is splendidly sung, too, by Ed Evanko with Nicol Williamson as a musical but surprisingly subdued King. Another melody, "Away from you", a duet for Henry and Anne Boleyn, rated highly in the Rodgers canon by William Lloyd Webber, flows along in a courtly manor befitting a royal couple. Readers will note the appearance of Glenn Close in the small but significant role of Princess Mary, and a couple of supporting voices that sound as though they've strayed in from the era of *A Connecticut Yankee*. The well-upholstered RCA recording affords a lush backdrop to Irwin Kostal's attractive orchestrations with its panoply of brass and choral ensembles. Veteran Jay Blackton conducts.   **AE**

The Song is ... Richard Rodgers and Lorenz Hart with Bing Crosby, Jessie Matthews, Johnny Marvin, Dick Robertson, Stuart Ross and Joe Sargent, Leslie A. Hutchinson, George Baker and Sam Coslow.
ASV Living Era mono Ⓜ CDAJA5041 (50 minutes: AAD).
Songs from America's Sweetheart, A Connecticut Yankee, The Girl Friend, Cochran's Revue of 1930, Peggy-Ann, Heads Up!, Garrick Gaieties, Fifth Avenue Follies, Mississippi, Spring is Here, Evergreen and The Phantom President.
The Rodgers and Hammerstein Songbook with Julie Andrews, Theodore Bikel, Larry Blyden, Barbara Cook, Nelson Eddy, Virginia Haskins, Mary Martin, Patricia Neway, Portia Nelson, Ezio Pinza, Pat Suzuki and William Tabbert.
Sony Broadway mono/stereo Ⓕ SK5331 (77 minutes: ADD).
Songs from Oklahoma!, Carousel, South Pacific, The King and I, Cinderella, Flower Drum Song and The Sound of Music.

These are two very different anthologies devoted, it sometimes seems, to two very different composers; the sweet-and-sour cut-up Richard Rodgers who wrote with Lorenz Hart, and the foursquare music-builder of the same name who collaborated with Oscar Hammerstein II. Both deeply romantic composers (if apparently unromantic men), both in their way restlessly experimental, each side of Rodgers was absolutely right for its own era; and both eras were to a great extent Rodgers's creation. Rodgers and Hart belonged to the age of great songs from throwaway shows, preserved in random recordings by pop musicians. Rodgers and Hammerstein practically invented the well-made musical, born to be an original cast album.

The ASV disc collates generally bouncy renditions of generally bouncy songs. Some are classics like "Thou swell", here an instrumental by Bix Beiderbecke (and his Gang). Others are neglected treasures, like the shockingly jaunty "We'll be the same" (from the movie spoof *America's Sweetheart*, 1931), and two numbers from the ground-breaking *Peggy-Ann* (1926). One of these, "A little birdie told me so", a carefree song about contraception (or, conceivably, abstinence) was denounced by one London critic as unfit for a demure young lady to perform in public, but it's done here by a male vocalist, Johnny Marvin, who doesn't seem to have the faintest idea what he's singing about, so that's all right. Composer-lyricist Sam Coslow puts in a rare crooning appearance in an even rarer song, "Give her a kiss", from a thoroughly obscure but fascinating movie, *The Phantom President* (1932). There are three *bona fide* stars: Jessie Matthews with her celebrated "Dancing on the ceiling" and, better because less skittish, "My heart stood still", in which she has Leslie A. Hutchinson on the piano; Hutch himself intoning "With a song in my heart" with its churchy melody and exquisite verse and a revue number, "The little things you do", so unknown that it isn't even in Hart's collected lyrics; and, sounding startlingly modern in this context, Bing Crosby, vintage 1935, with "It's easy to remember". The nadir of gentility is reached with two medleys by the Light Opera Company: soloists who boom and bray like rejects from the D'Oyly Carte. One of the songs on their roster, "Step on the blues", though accepted here as Rodgers and Hart, is actually the handiwork of Con Conrad, Will Donaldson and Gus Kahn.

"The Rodgers and Hammerstein Songbook" draws on the formidable Columbia catalogue of show albums. They caught the original casts of four shows – *South Pacific, Flower Drum Song, The Sound of Music* and the TV *Cinderella* – and did studio revivals of *Oklahoma!, Carousel* and *The King and I*. So the three less famous shows (and the twice-filmed *State Fair*) are missing. It's the less obvious selections that catch the ear, like Pat Suzuki and Larry Blyden in the very fetching "Sunday" from *Flower Drum Song* or Suzuki's irresistible "I enjoy being a girl", the song that established her and that no other female performer could now get away with (males are another matter). There are three big songs from *South Pacific*: sceptics will give the palm to "There is nothin' like a dame" with its impeccably sweaty ensemble spirit. That makes two immensely enjoyable sexist songs on one disc. Rodgers himself takes the New York Philharmonic through "The Carousel waltz" and it sounds as transporting as ever. **RC**

The Sound of Music 1959 Broadway Cast (with Mary Martin, Theodore Bikel, Patricia Neway and Kurt Kasznar) **/ Frederick Dvonch**.
Sony Broadway Ⓕ SK53537 (56 minutes: ADD).
The Sound of Music 1965 Film Cast (with Julie Andrews, Bill Lee for Christopher Plummer, Margery McKay for Peggy Wood and Charmian Carr) **/ Irwin Kostal**.
RCA Ⓕ 07863 66587-2 (47 minutes: ADD).

The Sound of Music 1988 Studio Cast (with Frederica Von Stade and Håkan Hakegård); May Festival Chorus; Cincinnati Pops Orchestra / Eric Kunzel.
Telarc Ⓕ CD80162 (70 minutes: DDD).

The Broadway opening of *The Sound of Music* followed *Flower Drum Song* within a year, so that instead of their customary two-year gap between shows, Rodgers and Hammerstein ended the decade with two productions on Broadway. This came after what had been for them a relatively lean period below their best form with *Me and Juliet, Pipe Dream* and even *Flower Drum Song*. Then, miraculously, with time running out (Hammerstein died eight months after its première), along came *The Sound of Music*, based on a true story tailor-made for their talents. The show was a hit on Broadway, an even bigger one in the West End and then it became the most successful film of the century!

The original Broadway cast recording wears its years lightly and is invaluable to collectors in giving them the songs of the Countess and Max, the impresario, which were cut from the film, and smaller deletions like the verse to the title-song ("My day in the hills has come to an end"), inappropriate in the new daytime setting. Mary Martin was delightful if, at 46, too mature for the young postulant Maria. When Julie Andrews took the role in the film everything seemed to fall into place, not least as far as this record goes with the exuberant and refreshing musical direction by Irwin Kostal. In "Climb ev'ry mountain" his swift but unrushed tempo, with the singer entering almost informally on the second beat of the bar, takes the starch out of the tune. In 1995, on the 30th anniversary of the film's release, RCA finally got round to reissuing a CD worthy of it with proper notes and in good remastered sound with the numbers in the correct sequence.

Telarc's spectacular digital recording, with an organ entry in the "Processional" that takes the breath away, contains the additional numbers Rodgers composed for the film as well as those that were dropped, making it the only complete version on the market. So much of it is enjoyable, not least the children's group and the playing of the orchestra, that it's a shame to report that Frederica Von Stade is a somewhat staid Maria. A musical, then, that stays very much in Julie Andrews's provenance – the way she phrases each song, or captures the high spirits in one ("The lonely goatherd") or the intimacy of another ("Something good"), remains unique.   **AE**

South Pacific 1949 Broadway Cast (with Ezio Pinza and Mary Martin) / Salvatore Dell'Isola.
Sony Broadway mono Ⓕ SK53327 (56 minutes: ADD).
South Pacific 1958 Film Cast (with Mitzi Gaynor, Giorgio Tozzi for Rossano Brazzi, Bill Lee for John Kerr and Muriel Smith for Juanita Hall) / Alfred Newman.
RCA Ⓜ ND83681 (47 minutes: ADD).
South Pacific 1986 Studio Cast (with Kiri Te Kanawa, José Carreras, Sarah Vaughan and Mandy Patinkin); London Symphony Orchestra / Jonathan Tunick.
Sony Ⓜ MK42205 (61 minutes: DDD).

New review
South Pacific 1997 Studio Cast (with Paige O'Hara, Justino Diaz, Shezwae Powell and Sean McDermott); National Symphony Orchestra / John Owen Edwards.
TER Ⓕ CDTER2 1242 (two discs: 107 minutes: DDD).

Here's an instance where I have to admit to a personal choice. *South Pacific* was the first widescreen film I saw as a boy at the Dominion Cinema in London. It ran there for four-and-a-half years where it was presented in multi-track stereophonic sound and in colour so vivid that the impact it made on this young teenager would likely be the equivalent today of a 'rave'. When I later became acquainted with the Broadway cast LP it seemed hopelessly old-fashioned, lacking any kind of presence, though I would now acknowledge that Ezio Pinza's "This nearly was mine" has never been surpassed. The unseen star of the film and certainly of the soundtrack wasn't any of the players but the conductor, Alfred Newman. His orchestra adapts at the flick of the wrist from one style to another with which this score abounds: swing, operetta, waltz time, vaudeville, and a lush romanticism where Ken Darby and his large chorus add their quintessential Hollywood touch. The singers, with the exception of Mitzi Gaynor, are all ghost voices on screen, but they were coached to sing and perform their songs with such conviction and an exactness of dramatic effect that they become as visual as sound can ever be.

Record companies waited almost 30 years before recording *South Pacific* again. Then Sony lined up Kiri Te Kanawa and José Carreras in what amounted to a follow-up to their coupling on DG's *West Side Story*. But where Bernstein put his firm imprint as conductor on that recording, the *South Pacific* album lacked such leadership, with the singers being left too much to their own devices. Tempos are often uncertain and one spectacular mis-entry from Bloody Mary in "Bali Ha'i" remained unnoticed.

TER's new *South Pacific*, however, commands attention right away, with conductor John Owen Edwards bringing a majestic sweep to a score that takes on a Puccinian grandeur in the overture and run-up to that enchanted evening where Emile de Becque and Nellie Forbush fall in love over a cognac. Edwards's conducting has the prerequisite drive that carries his fine orchestra and excellent chorus through the diverse musical styles with which this score abounds, giving this version a formidable start in the *South Pacific* stakes. TER's complete recording omits two cut songs included as appendices on the Sony Broadway recording – "My girl back home" and "Loneliness of evening" – but is faithful to the published score. This *South Pacific* reminds us of what we've been missing so far on disc: namely the skill with which Rodgers and Hammerstein wove together the two disparate love stories between Emile and Nellie, Cable and Liat. This point is forcibly made in the Second Act where Cable gives vent to racial prejudice in "Carefully taught". The swift rhythmic pattern, that underpins his solo, runs on into Emile's own diatribe against the same ugliness that has pursued him. Their subsequent exchange of dialogue over underscoring, played by the orchestra with the lightest of touches, leads to a magical segue setting up Emile's personal expression of loss, "This nearly was mine". Justino Diaz sings it with touching sincerity and that's the key to his whole performance. It's an outstanding piece of casting. Ironically, since she has sung Nellie on stage, Paige O'Hara sometimes sounds as though she's nearer to portraying the earthy Annie Oakley rather than the shy nurse from Little Rock. On the UK release, Shezwae Powell sings Bloody Mary with a touch and more in the direction of Margarita Prakatan, Clive James's *chanteuse* (Pat Suzuki takes this role on the US release). Sean McDermott's Lieutenant Cable and Emile's children sound a trifle under-characterized in the formidable medium of this Dolby Surround recording. These reservations aside, there's no denying this recording brings us closer to understanding why *South Pacific* won the Pulitzer Prize for best play in 1950. **AE**

New review

Two By Two 1970 Broadway Cast (with Danny Kaye, Harry Goz, Madeline Kahn, Walter Willison, Marilyn Cooper) / **Jay Blackton.**
Sony Broadway Ⓟ SK30338 (53 minutes: ADD).

Richard Rodgers's post-Hammerstein shows have been comparatively neglected. Perhaps the best of them are *No Strings* and *Do I Hear A Waltz?*. *Two By Two*, a version of the story of Noah, based on a Clifford Odets play, brought Danny Kaye back to the Broadway musical for the first time for 29 years. As in *Fiddler on the Roof*, we have a family man haranguing his God while dealing with the terrifying events around him – in this case the flood and the building of the Ark. Alas, Rodgers's score is no match for Bock and Harnick, and Martin Charnin's lyrics often have an awkwardness unlike his later work. If Rodgers's melodic flame burns fitfully, it sometimes gives off a lovely light. After quite a while on auto-pilot, his genius reasserts itself in "Something doesn't happen", "I do not know a day I did not love you", and the catchy title-tune. Danny Kaye sounds as good as any 600-year-old hero could expect to. Madeline Kahn revels in the high soprano fireworks of "The golden ram"; Walter Willison and Tricia O'Neil are an attractive young couple. The recording sounds fresh and there are extensive notes in the well-illustrated booklet. *Two By Two* is agreeable minor, but worthwhile, Rodgers. **MPK**

Also available:
Carousel (1965 Broadway Cast) RCA 6395-2
Carousel (1987 Studio Cast) MCA MCAD6209
Carousel (1993 Studio Cast) Carlton Shows Collection PWKS4144
The Girl Friend (1986 Colchester Cast) TER CDTER1148
The King and I (1964 Studio Cast) Sony Broadway SK53328
The King and I (1977 Broadway Cast) RCA RCD1-2610
The King and I (1994 Studio Cast) Showtime SHOWCD024
The King and I (1996 Broadway Cast) Varèse Sarabande VSD5763
I Remember Mama (1985 Studio Cast) TER CDTER1102
Oklahoma! (1979 Broadway Cast) RCA RCD1-3572
Slaughter on Tenth Avenue, Ghost Town, La Princess Zenobia – ballets. TER CDTER1114
The Sound of Music (1993 Studio Cast) Carlton Shows Collection PWKS4145

South Pacific (1988 London Cast) First Night OCRCD6023
South Pacific (Studio Cast) Carlton Shows Collection PWKS4162
Timeless Songs of Rodgers and Hammerstein Showtime SHOWCD039
A Tribute to Richard Rodgers Music for Pleasure CDDL1287

Sigmund Romberg
1887-1951 Hungary

The composer studied engineering at Bucharest University, and the violin with Richard Heuberger. He found the theatre a stronger draw than a career in engineering, so, first in London, then in New York, as a pianist then a leader of a hotel orchestra, Romberg started writing and attracted the eye of the Shubert Brothers, New York theatrical impresarios. His first success came with *Maytime* (1917). After contributing to many revues and book musicals including *Blossom Time* (1921), which used Schubert melodies, his big breakthrough came with *The Student Prince* (1924) and *The Desert Song* (1926). A succession of shows followed, of which only *The New Moon* (1927) lived up to previous successes. Romberg's last full-length show before his death, *Up in Central Park* (1945), did not have the universal appeal of the three shows which made his name and reputation.

The Desert Song 1927 **London Cast** (with Harry Welchman, Edith Day, Dennis Hoey and
    Sidney Pointer); **Drury Lane Theatre Orchestra / Herman Finck**.
The New Moon 1929 **London Cast** (with Howett Worster, Ben Williams and Evelyn Laye);
    Drury Lane Theatre Orchestra / Herman Finck.
    Pearl mono Ⓕ GEMMCD9100 (69 minutes: ADD). Disc also includes **Stolz:** The Blue
    Train **1927 London Cast**.

London took *The Desert Song* to its heart, the first production ran for 432 performances, and it was revived four times in the next 15 years, with both Edith Day and Harry Welchman returning to their roles as Margot Bonvalet and Pierre Birabeau ("The Red Shadow"). Herman Finck found Romberg a very fussy composer to deal with – he insisted on two harps in the orchestra, though they can't be discerned on these famous records. Oscar Hammerstein himself had suggested Edith Day for the London production of *Rose Marie*, and she stayed on to create *The Desert Song*, with more Hammerstein lyrics, at the same theatre. 'The Queen of Drury Lane' became her billing, and even 70 years later it's easy to understand why. Harry Welchman achieved his greatest success as Pierre, his renditions of "One alone", "The Riff song" and the title duet; his diction and fine baritone voice sound old-fashioned now, but still impressive. Dennis Hoey and Sidney Pointer join in the big "Eastern and Western love" duet with chorus. All heady stuff and never better sung.

    No one seemed to worry about such niceties of period authenticity as a musical set in 1794 that had a tango ("Softly, as in a morning sunrise"), or a waltz ("One kiss"), when *The New Moon* was new in 1928. It didn't have the appeal of Romberg's other shows, French revolutionaries in the New World not having the same glamour as Desert Sheiks or Ruritanian Princes. The songs are great, however, and Evelyn Laye as Marianne Beaunoir made what are perhaps her best records, "One kiss", "Wanting you", "The girl on the prow" and "Lover, come back to me". Beauty, dramatic flair and a fine voice, she had it all. Howett Worster isn't bad either.

    The fill-up on this fine CD is a real bit of musical-comedy history. In 1927, the legendary Lily Elsie, London's first Merry Widow and Dollar Princess, returned to the stage in Robert Stolz's *Mädi*, re-titled *The Blue Train* (just a couple of years after Milhaud's ballet for Diaghilev, *Le train bleu*). A typical story of girl-gets-her-man with divorce ruse, not unlike *The Count of Luxemburg* (in which Elsie had also starred), it has some lovely songs and a strong cast including the young Bobby Howes and the veteran Cicely Debenham. Charming in itself, it is invaluable for the glimpse it affords of one of the great romantic figures of theatre history. **PO'C**

The Student Prince 1989 **Studio Cast** (with Norman Bailey, Marilyn Hill Smith, Diana
    Montague and David Rendall); **Ambrosian Chorus; Philharmonia Orchestra / John Owen
    Edwards**.
    TER Ⓕ CDTER2 1172 (two discs: 100 minutes: DDD).

Sigmund Romberg brought to the Broadway stage a thoroughly central-European style of operetta. It is curious to consider that *The Student Prince* (1924) belongs to the same theatrical season that introduced the Charleston, and even then audiences must have sensed that it was part of a tradition that was due for retirement. Still, the drinking song remains one of the most familiar moments in all musical comedy ("Drink, drink, drink, to eyes that are bright") and to hear it in context on this, the first complete recording, is a special pleasure, for it makes much more impact when appearing as one of several choruses, following the marching song and preceding the, by now intoxicated, students' assertion that "Education should be scientific play, boys".

In the title-role, David Rendall as Karl-Franz is sincere, negotiating the low-lying tessitura without difficulty and singing the serenade, "Overhead the moon is beaming", his part in the *valse grandioso* finale of Act 1 and the "Vision sequence" of Act 3, with right royal fervour. Norman Bailey's Hans Sachs manner is well suited to the one song he gets as "dear old Dr Engel", the Prince's tutor – "Golden days". As the waitress heroine, Marilyn Hill Smith gives what is perhaps her best performance on record, soaring over the chorus, holding a high C for five bars, and joining Rendall in the main love song, "Deep in my heart, dear". Act 1 takes up a whole CD and Acts 2, 3 and 4 mostly involve reprises of the marches, duets and waltzes but include the jaunty "Just we two" for the Prince's bored fiancée and her lover, sung by Diana Montague and Stephen Page. As the leading students, Bonaventura Bottone, Donald Maxwell and Neil Jenkins articulate Dorothy Donnelly's lyrics with admirable clarity. Was the massive success of this show in the USA in the 1920s (when in addition to two years on Broadway, nine touring companies took it on the road) in part due to the appeal of a show which, in the midst of Prohibition, declared: "The old professors prate, boys/That you will flunk because you're drunk/Don't hesitate, boys/In drinking, you with honour graduate."? **PO'C**

Also available

The Desert Song (plus songs from The New Moon and The Student Prince, w. Gordon MacRae)
EMI CDM7 69052-2
The Desert Song (plus songs from The Student Prince, w. Mario Lanza) RCA GD60048

Harold Rome
b. 1908 USA

A former draughtsman and holiday camp officer, Harold Rome came to prominence as author of a revue for amateurs, members of the New York Garment Union called *Pins and Needles* (1937). A further, professional revue, *Call Me Mister* (1946), added to the composer's reputation that was finally made with the 1952 musical *Wish You Were Here*. There followed an adaptation of the Marcel Pagnol story *Fanny* (1954) and a Western musical *Destry Rides Again* (1959), *I Can Get it for You Wholesale* (1962) and versions of *Gone With the Wind – Scarlett* (1970) and *Gone with the Wind* (1972).

I Can Get It for You Wholesale 1962 **Broadway Cast** (with Elliott Gould, Jack Kruschen, Barbra Streisand, Marilyn Cooper, Lillian Roth, Harold Lang and Bambi Linn) **/ Lehman Engel**.
Columbia Ⓜ 474903-2 (53 minutes: ADD).

A surprisingly tough musical version of Jerome Weidman's novel about a ruthless and amoral young entrepreneur's rise and rise in the New York garment trade, as he casually uses his charm to avoid personal responsibility for his actions. Elliott Gould gives a horribly convincing leading performance, backed up by sweet-voiced Marilyn Cooper and veterans Lillian Roth, Jack Kruschen, Harold Lang and Bambi Linn. For collectors, the principal interest in the show lies in the performance of a featured role, that of secretary Miss Marmelstein, by Barbra Streisand, showing the vigour and dynamism that would shoot her to stardom. Harold Rome's score ranges from smoky ballads like "Too soon" and tender love songs "Have I told you lately?" and "Who knows?", to expert dissections of character – "The way things are" and "What's in it for me?". *I Can Get It for You Wholesale* is far from being a comfortable show with its keen searchlight vision picking out social and moral dilemmas and with a hero as big a heel as, say, *Pal Joey*. Yet it is a very good one with a fine score, well captured on the original cast recording. **MPK**

Also available:

Destry Rides Again (1959 Broadway Cast) MCA MCAD11573
Destry Rides Again (1982 London Cast) TER CDTER1034
Pins and Needles (1962 Studio Cast) Columbia CK57380
Scarlett (1970 Japanese Cast) DRG CDSBL13105

Dana P. Rowe

John Dempsey

New review

The Fix 1997 **London Cast** (with Kathryn Evans, John Barrowman, Philip Quast and David
Firth) **/ Colin Welford**.
First Night Records Ⓔ CASTCD62 (67 minutes: DDD).

A high-powered miniature American musical given a season at the Donmar Warehouse with the
financial backing of Cameron Mackintosh. A tale of American politics with a title clue – a fix
to get a president elected and a fix in the arm to keep him going. Luckily the tale is told with a
satirical glance and one of the most adventurous scores heard for a long time. There are also
some excellent performances and the recording has one huge benefit over the show – the sound
balance is controllable. "If I can't be the wife of the President, you can bet your ass, I'll be his
mother", sings the versatile Kathryn Evans – and there you have it – the making of a
President with her, the power behind the throne. It is set in Washington but it could be London
as the spin-doctors and the selling of policy all sounds rather too close for comfort. So if you
don't mind being politically disillusioned, listen closely through this adult contemporary rock
score with its odd glance back to vaudeville and country – the lyrics are intelligent and are
included in the booklet. Having singled out Evans, it seems heartless not to mention the
masterly performances by heart-throb John Barrowman as the son and troubled President (he
goes through a great deal what with sex, drugs and, worst of all, corruption) and Philip Quast,
whose physical as well as vocal presence is tingling. Of the crop of recent shows trying hard for
the sound of today this is by far and away the best – it deserves a greater audience and it is
served well here. And while few melodies linger, the warning does.   **RSB**

Michael Rupert

Jerry Colker

New review

Three Guys Naked From The Waist Down 1985 **Off-Broadway Cast** (with Jerry
Colker, Scott Bakula and John Kassir) **/ Henry Aronson**.
TER Ⓔ CDTER1100 (45 minutes: DDD).

A reappearance of a CD originally issued by Polydor but long deleted. The title indicates the
vulnerability of the three characters who are the sole performers in this intimate musical about three
male stand-up comics who join forces and become television superstars. Unfortunately, the success
and roles they play does not satisfy all of them, and the show ends with one dying, another
remaining a star and the other owning his own comedy club, introducing other young hopefuls –
as the lyrics say – "ain't life a bitch". It's an intense little show with three performers giving all-
stops-out performances. It is also an adult listen for modern comedy seems to need explicit
language to help it on its way – but don't be put off by this, it is in context and character. The score,
which is up-beat while definitely theatrical, explores the stand-up comic routines in clever musical
diversions on different levels from the club to television, as well as going into some in-depth analysis
not only for Kenny, the introverted one who doesn't make it to the end, but also Ted (Scott Bakula,
who actually has gone on to become a TV star) who has a great number in "I don't believe in heroes
anymore". It's a quick-witted show that is refreshingly different and there is a haunting ring of truth
about it. However, underlying the bright façade, there is another dissection of the American dream.
People's needs differ and that is what comes through here in a very interesting way.   **RSB**

Willy Russell

Blood Brothers 1988 London Cast (with Kiki Dee, Warwick Evans, Con O'Neill, Robert Locke and Joanne Zorian) / **Rod Edwards**.
First Night Ⓕ CASTCD17 (58 minutes: DDD).
Blood Brothers 1995 London Cast (with Stephanie Lawrence, Warwick Evans, Paul Crosby, Mark Hutchinson and Joanna Munro) / **Rod Edwards**.
First Night Ⓕ CASTCD49 (61 minutes: DDD).

After initial success with Barbara Dickson in 1983, *Blood Brothers* was revived for a British tour in 1987, culminating in a return to the West End in the summer of 1988, where it has stayed ever since. The revamped version preserved here starred Kiki Dee, best known as a 1970s pop star, as the forceful Mrs Johnstone, whose attempts to preserve her family by selling one of her twins meet with tragedy. Willy Russell's moralistic musical is set against a backdrop of Thatcherite Britain and makes sharp comments about a careless society riven by deep class divisions. Russell wrote book, music and lyrics for the piece and it is highly effective – his music includes several beauiful melodies, especially "Easy terms", in which Mrs Johnstone sings of the decision to give up one of her children, and the ballad "I'm not saying a word", a delightful exploration of a young man's inability to declare his love for a girl. There are also several up-tempo numbers, the joyous "Bright new day" and the altogther darker "Take a letter, Miss Jones". Throughout the show, Mrs Johnstone's obsession with the tragedy of Marilyn Monroe (to whom she was once compared) is used as a parallel for her own life and those of her family. Russell also writes excellent music for the children – "Kids' games" and the solo for Mickey, "Long Sunday afternoon", brilliantly express the concerns and joys of the young. It is a strong cast – Warwick Evans is a menacing narrator, Joanne Zorian perfect as the middle-class Mrs Lyons and Robert Locke ideal as Eddie, the twin that she raises. But the recording belongs to Dee and to Con O'Neill (the other twin Mickey). O'Neill is magnificent in the "Sunday afternoon" solo and in his duets with his twin, while Dee demonstrates real dramatic flair, a perfect Liverpool accent and superb singing. In the finale, "Tell me it's not true", she is deeply moving, while never letting one forget that the narrator has throughout blamed her for the tragedy. Unlike most escapist musicals, *Blood Brothers* is set in a real world where unemployment and difficulty are the order of the day, but presented with a fresh voice and real enthusiasm in this excellent 1988 cast recording.

In its seventh year in London a new recording was made, featuring the cast who had served longest in the show. Stephanie Lawrence, who has given more performances as Mrs Johnstone than any other actress, finally gets a chance to preserve her version. She has undoubted power, but sounds slightly more vulnerable than Kiki Dee. Joanna Munro is superb as Mrs Lyons, while Mark Hutchinson is an excellent Eddie, Warwick Evans reprises his role as the narrator. This is a slightly fuller recording than the definitive 1988 version, including several sequences that were not previously available, and as such it makes an ideal companion.   **RAC**

Also available:
Blood Brothers (1983 London Cast) Castle CLACD270
Blood Brothers (1995 International Cast) First Night CASTCD50

Milton Schafer

Ira Levin

New review
Drat the Cat 1997 Studio Cast (with Susan Egan, Jason Graae, Elaine Stritch and Judy Kaye) / **Todd Ellison**.
Varèse Sarabande Spotlight Series Ⓕ VSD5721 (66 minutes: DDD).

Drat the Cat was an eight-performance flop when it premièred on Broadway back in 1965. From the sound of this studio cast reincarnation its closure was a crime against humanity (yes theatre-goers are human), and the jury (some critics are human too) should be brought back to reconsider their verdict. The score has always held a mystique because Barbra Streisand recorded "He loves me", a tantalizing preview to what now has materialized as a delightfully tuneful and humorous score. It was not only off-stage that a crime was committed, for this full-blown musical comedy is about a jewel thief. It takes place in the 1890s when people still wear jewels large enough to steal and the police are after the cat-burglar thief and a rich young lady wants to help. So who is the 'cat' and who does the chief of detectives fall for? It's a story of crime, adventure and love – who could ask for anything more? Well, there is more. Susan Egan is one of the most exciting talents to arrive on the scene for some time. Whether on Broadway or the voice in a Walt Disney blockbuster, Egan is gifted and this score gives her a wonderful showcase. I liked Jason Graae a lot too. This is no cheap reconstruction, the orchestra sounds like a Broadway orchestra should and the orchestrations are those originally used. Most of the story-line is indicated through song introductions or the songs themselves – so it's something to curl up and purr away to. Be warned – Elaine Stritch ventures into song and if you leave the CD on the player there is a little surprise for you. **RSB**

Harvey Schmidt
b. 1929 USA

Tom Jones
b. 1928 USA

It must be a great burden to any composing team to have written, at the beginning of your career, the longest-running musical of all time. Lyricist Tom Jones and composer Harvey Schmidt met at the University of Texas and went to New York together in 1955 where they created *The Fantasticks* in 1960 – it is now heading for 40 years off-Broadway. There followed *110 in the Shade* (1963) – a version of the play *The Rainmaker* – *I Do! I Do!* (1966), *Celebration* (1969), *Colette* (1970, revised 1982/3), *Philemon* (1973) and *Grovers Corners* (1987), a version of Thornton Wilder's *Our Town*.

The Fantasticks 1960 Off-Broadway Cast (with Kenneth Nelson, Rita Gardner, Jerry Orbach, William Larsen and Hugh Thomas) **/ Julian Stein**.
TER Ⓕ CDTER1099 / Polydor 821 943-2 (49 minutes: AAD).

The longest-running musical comedy in the history of the genre, *The Fantasticks*, heading for a 40-year stint at its tiny off-Broadway theatre home, is unlikely to be superseded by any other musical in our lifetime. Although a film (and a soundtrack recording) is expected any time now, only this album is currently available, with its classic intimacy and original cast, of whom Kenneth Nelson and Jerry Orbach have long since passed on to other things. The show is based on a French play by Edmond Rostand and tells of the obstructions put in the face of romance by two parents who want their children to fall in love with each other. Apart from erecting, dismantling and re-erecting a wall, the fathers engage a travelling showman as *deus ex machina* (Jerry Orbach in commanding form) to speed the action along. Tom Jones and Harvey Schmidt have never surpassed their score for *The Fantasticks* (although they came close with *110 in the Shade*, if you include some of the songs that were cut). "I can see it", "Try to remember", "Soon it's gonna rain" and "They were you" are just a few of the musical highlights. Kenneth Nelson and Rita Gardner make an appealing pair of youngsters, although Gardner at times tends towards shrillness. **MPK**

110 in the Shade 1963 Broadway Cast (with Robert Horton, Inga Swenson and Stephen Douglass) **/ Donald Pippin**.
RCA Victor Ⓜ 81085-2 (52 minutes: ADD).

Although it played briefly in the West End in early 1967 (with Stephen Douglass and Inga Swenson from the Broadway cast), *110 in the Shade* will be better known to many audiences as *The Rainmaker*, N. Richard Nash's play subsequently filmed with Burt Lancaster and Katharine Hepburn. In the musical, Robert Horton, a big television heart-throb from *Wagon Train*, sings his heart out as the con-man who awakens the beauty in the plain Lizzie. He leaves no one in doubt that he'll win her over in his superheated ballad "Melisande", or the townsfolk in his exhortation for rain. Stephen Douglass, a powerful baritone, is another asset in the cast, but it was Inga Swenson as Lizzie, with her combination of dramatic tenderness and lovely singing, who stole the musical in a series of numbers designed to show off her transformation from self-doubting farm girl into radiant beauty. The score's big duet, "A man and a woman", glows in Horton and Swenson's luminous performance. Schmidt and Jones's score, which marked their Broadway début following *The Fantasticks*, was expertly orchestrated by Hershy Kay. The original LP issue now has the addition of an overture, but it's not been so easy to tame the original RCA dynagroove recording, which still at times sounds too close for comfort. **AE**

Also available:
Collette Collage (1993 Studio Cast) Varèse Sarabande VSD5473
The Fantasticks (Japanese Tour Cast) DRG DRGCD19005
I Do! I Do! (1966 Broadway Cast) RCA 1128-2

Claude-Michel Schönberg
b. 1944 France

Alain Boublil
b. 1941 France

Claude-Michel Schönberg began his career as a music producer at a record company. His first show, *La Révolution Française* was staged in 1973 after starting life as a concept LP. His show *Les Misérables* (1980) was seen in its spectacular original editon by Cameron Mackintosh,who interested the Royal Shakespeare Company in mounting it in Britain, where it appeared in 1985. It transferred from the Barbican to the West End, where it has remained ever since. In 1989, Boublil and Schönberg came up with a modern-day version of *Madama Butterfly*, *Miss Saigon*, which has become the longest-running show ever mounted at Theatre Royal Drury Lane. To complete the trilogy, 1996 saw the production of a third show in the West End, *Martin Guerre*.

Les Misérables 1985 London Cast (with Colm Wilkinson, Roger Allam, Patti LuPone, Michael Ball, Alun Armstrong, Sue Jane Tanner, Frances Ruffelle and Rebecca Caine) / **Martin Koch**.
First Night ℗ ENCORECD1 (two discs: 98 minutes: DDD).

Les Misérables 1988 International Studio Cast (with Gary Morris, Philip Quast, Debbie Byrne, Gay Soper, Barry James, Kaho Shimada, Michael Ball, Tracey Shane and Anthony Warlow) / **Martin Koch**.
First Night ℗ MIZCD1 (three discs: 168 minutes: DDD).

Les Misérables 1995 Royal Albert Hall Concert Cast (with Colm Wilkinson, Philip Quast, Ruthie Henshall, Jenny Galloway, Alun Armstrong, Lea Salonga, Michael Ball, Michael Maguire, Judy Kuhn and Anthony Crivello); **Chorus; Royal Philharmonic Orchestra / David Charles Abell**.
First Night ℗ ENCORECD8 (two discs: 142 minutes: DDD).

The Royal Shakespeare Company's stunningly successful adaptation of Victor Hugo's vast novel of French society in the 1830s has been a huge hit all around the world. Its timeless themes of the triumph of good and the senseless loss of life in war and revolution have struck chords wherever it has played. The cast assembled for the original 1985 production, here preserved in a fine recording, has become somewhat legendary. Colm Wilkinson, as Valjean the escaped prisoner made good but haunted by his past, is exceptional. His husky voice conveying strength and sensitivity throughout, he particularly triumphs towards the end as, broken by the desolation around him, he prays for the life of Marius in "Bring him home". Roger Allam as the policeman, Javert, obsessed with bringing Valjean to justice is his equal – powerful and menacing, especially in the haunting "Stars". Patti LuPone is magnificent in the small but pivotal role of the tragic Fantine. Her rendition of the ballad "I dreamed a dream" remains definitive. Alun Armstrong almost steals the recording as the revolting innkeeper Thenardier, managing to be terrifying and funny at the same time in "Master of the house", and he is ably supported by Sue Jane Tanner as his awful wife. This production also brought Michael Ball to stardom, and his strong voice in "Empty chairs at empty tables" demonstrates exactly why. The stirring marching songs such as "Do you hear the people sing?" and "One day more" are further reasons to explore this highly influential and successful modern pop-opera, one of the great examples of the sung-through genre that has come to dominate musical theatre.

A complete recording of the entire score of *Les Misérables* with a cast made up from performers in the various international productions and with a full 72-piece orchestra was made in 1988. Because of the cast's international flavour there are a few strange-sounding accents to be heard, but overall the recording is of high quality and, by virtue of its completeness and the size of the orchestra, is well worth the asking price. Gary Morris is a scorching Valjean, Philip Quast a brilliant Javert (possessing all of Roger Allam's menace, and a far stronger voice), Barry James is less terrifying as Thenardier, but very funny, while Debbie Byrne brings everything to the role of Fantine. Michael Ball reprises his definitive Marius, and Kaho Shimada from the Tokyo production is a fine Eponine. The booklet contains the full libretto of the entire show and an interesting essay by Cameron Mackintosh on the idea behind the recording.

To celebrate the tenth anniversary of the original staging by the Royal Shakespeare Company a special one-night concert at the Royal Albert Hall was organized with several of the original principals taking part. In total there were more than 250 performers accompanied by the Royal Philharmonic Orchestra. The recording of the night's concert may seem unnecessary when there are other recordings of the show available, but this does offer some extra pleasures. Ruthie Henshall is an exceptional Fantine, while Lea Salonga is outstanding as Eponine. Although Colm Wilkinson and Alun Armstrong are not in quite as good voice as their earlier recordings, the live nature of the recording gives more immediacy to their performances, while Michael Ball has probably never sounded better. The recording also features the speeches and the line-up of Valjeans from around the world all singing "Do you hear the people sing?" which is an emotionally charged moment, followed by the whole company reprising "One day more". This is a superb record both of an extraordinary evening and an extraordinary show. **RAC**

Martin Guerre **1995 London Cast** (with Iain Glen, Rebecca Lock, Jérôme Pradon, Matt Rawle, Michael Matus, Ann Emery, Sheila Reid and Julia Sutton) **/ David Charles Abell**.
First Night Ⓕ CASTCD59 (73 minutes: DDD).

The third of the Alain Boublil/Claude-Michel Schönberg musicals offers a favourite French subject – that of a certain Martin Guerre who ostensibly arrives back from war to rejoin his bride and consummate his marriage after some considerable time, only to be exposed as an impostor by the real Martin. The impostor then loses his life. When the show originally opened in July 1996, the first act was diffuse and unfocussed. A revised version with many new lyrics and new songs reopened the show in November of that year and received a much more favourable critical response. It is this version that is the basis for the current original cast recording. As always, the creative team (including a trio of English lyricists) have come up with a stirring and dramatic musical evening. "Working on the land" sets the main theme – the struggle for continued possession of the peasants' strongest asset, the land and the need to prevent it falling into other hands (in this case, preserving a Roman Catholic village from losing territory to nearby Protestants). "Tell me to go" and "Here comes the morning" are as fine as any songs yet written by the team. "Martin Guerre" is a very catchy tune, too. Collectors of the curious will relish a love song, "Louison", sung to his dolly by the village simpleton. The album makes highly enjoyable listening. Iain Glen and Rebecca Lock make a fine pair of lovers. Matt Rawle is suitably clarion-voiced as the real Martin and Sheila Reid, Ann Emery and Julia Sutton are an excellent comic trio as elderly ladies looking back ruefully to a happier, more erotic time – "Sleeping on our own". **MPK**

Miss Saigon **1989 London Cast** (with Simon Bowman, Lea Salonga, Monique Wilson, Isay Alvarez, Dominique Nobles, Jenine Desiderio, Pinky Amador, Ruthie Henshall, Suchitra Sen Sawrattan, Sukhubi Yo, Antoinette Lo, Claudia Cadette and Jonathan Pryce) **/ Martin Koch**.
First Night Ⓕ ENCORECD5 (two discs: 107 minutes: DDD).

Miss Saigon **International Cast** (with various cast members from Toronto, Sydney, New York, London and Los Angeles productions) **/ David Charles Abell**.
First Night Ⓕ KIMCD1 (two discs: 130 minutes: DDD).

This superbly successful reworking of the basic story of *Madama Butterfly* succeeds on all levels. The plot, moved from Japan to Saigon and now placed in the years between 1975 to 1978, makes strong dramatic sense. Kim, a hostess, has a child by a visiting GI, Chris. He eventually returns to Vietnam, bringing his American wife. After meeting her, and realizing there is no longer a place in Chris's life for the mother of his half-Asian child, Kim ensures a better life for her boy at the sacrifice of her own. The music and lyrics of *Miss Saigon* pack just as visceral a punch as Puccini's original. The rich, melodious and varied score has a bunch of affecting songs for Kim – "I still believe", "I'd give my life for you" – and duets with Chris, "The last night of the world" and "Sun and moon". The Engineer, a sort of Mister Fixit, has a number of savage comments on life in "If you want to die in bed" and best of all "The American dream". Richard Maltby's words have a bite and sophistication wholly in keeping with the character and situation. The original London cast recording offers the thrill of the new, with Lea Salonga's Kim hard to beat and a commanding Engineer in Jonathan Pryce. It is unlikely to be superseded. For a lusher treatment with a much larger orchestra and 25 five extra minutes of music the international cast recording has great appeal. It offers excellent, in some cases definitive, performances from cast members chosen from productions in Toronto, Sydney, New York, London and Los Angeles. **MPK**

Arthur Schwartz

1900-1984 USA

A revue writer and occasional, though unsuccessful, book show composer, Arthur Schwartz is better remembered for some of his wonderful songs rather than the shows from which they came. His main collaborators were lyricists Howard Dietz and Dorothy Fields. He worked extensively on both sides of the Atlantic. *The Band Wagon* (1931), written for the Astaires, was a huge hit, and the songs were recycled for a film of the same name 20 years later. *Revenge With Music* (1934) was a fine version of *The Three-Cornered Hat. Between the Devil* (1937) and *Virginia* (1937) were not successful. *Stars in Your Eyes* (1939) had lyrics by Dorothy Fields, whilst Ira Gershwin collaborated on *Park Avenue* (1946). One of the composer's most affecting shows was *A Tree Grows in Brooklyn* (1951) but an attempt to repeat its success for star Shirley Booth with *By the Beautiful Sea* (1954) failed. So did *The Gay Life* (1961) and even a show for box-office proof Mary Martin called *Jennie* (1963) which concluded his Broadway adventures. Schwartz also acted as film producer – both *Night and Day* (1946) and *Cover Girl* (1944) were his. He also wrote fine scores for the films *Thank Your Lucky Stars* (1943, with Frank Loesser), *The Time, the Place and the Girl* (1946, with Leo Robin) and *Dangerous When Wet* (1953, with Johnny Mercer).

The Band Wagon 1953 Film Cast (with Fred Astaire, India Adams for Cyd Charisse, Oscar Levant, Nanette Fabray and Jack Buchanan); **MGM Studio Chorus and Orchestra / Adolph Deutsch**.
EMI Ⓟ CDODEON19 (75 minutes: ADD).

The *Band Wagon* contains some of the most striking visual images in the whole canon of MGM musicals: Astaire, a forgotten Broadway star singing "By myself" as he walks from a railway station, brushed aside by the press in favour of Ava Gardner; his routine to "A shine on your shoes" ending with a kaleidoscopic riot of flags and neon lights flashing from a slot machine; a *pas de deux* with Cyd Charisse to "Dancing in the dark" in a nocturnal Central Park; the white-tie-and-tails soft-shoe with Jack Buchanan to "I guess I'll have to change my plan"; the surrealist "Triplets"; and, as a grand finale, a parody of a Mickey Spillane thriller, the narrative (by an uncredited Alan Jay Lerner) spoken poker-faced by Astaire, "She came at me – in sections". These numbers are some of the best of Schwartz and Dietz around which Betty Comden and Adolph Green, themselves incarnate on screen in the persons of Nanette Fabray and Oscar Levant, wrote a screenplay exploring the themes of showbusiness versus highbrow theatre manifest in Jack Buchanan's manic performance as a producer who, after his musical version of *Faust* flops, repents and leads the company in the picture's one new song, "That's entertainment".

It was the recollection of these images that led me to wonder why I wasn't deriving quite the degree of pleasure from this CD transfer as offered by *Brigadoon* and *Seven Brides for Seven Brothers*. In fact, *The Band Wagon*, though released in the cinema only a year after *Seven Brides*, was recorded before the change from optical monaural to magnetic and stereophonic recording had been made. The sound, with a comparatively high hiss factor, simply lacks the weight and perspective found on the other titles. This will probably not deter those who will want every treasured moment from this screen classic – including substantial material and demonstration tracks that have not before been available. **AE**

The Gay Life 1961 **Broadway Cast** (with Walter Chiari, Barbara Cook, Jules Munchin, Loring Smith and Elizabeth Allen) / **Herbert Greene**.
EMI Angel Ⓜ ZDM7 64763-2 (48 minutes: ADD).

It was the song catalogue of Dietz and Schwartz, topped off with their new number "That's entertainment", that graced the celebrated MGM musical *The Band Wagon* produced in 1953 during a 15-year hiatus in their collaboration. *The Gay Life*, premièred in 1961, has a number of advocates who have hailed it as "the renaissance of Schwartz's high style", and when Barbara Cook promises her intended "Something you never had before" the tingles really do run up the spine. The chief drawback to the elegant proceedings was the Italian star Walter Chiari whose vocal charms are limited. He plays the strenuously heterosexual hero of the tale (making the title misleading), whose philandering adventures in turn-of-the-century Vienna were the basis of Arthur Schnitzler's comedy *Anatol*, from which the musical took its cue. Whereas the original had a touch of continental cynicism in its attitude towards sex, *The Gay Life* clung to the mythic idea of old Vienna, contriving a wholly happy end to the sweet and sour original. In this sumptuous recording *The Gay Life* comes over as one of Broadway's final flings at elegance. **AE**

A Tree Grows in Brooklyn 1951 **Broadway Cast** (with Shirley Booth, Johnny Johnston, Marcia Van Dyke and Nathaniel Frey) / **Max Goberman**.
Sony Broadway mono Ⓔ SK48014 (51 minutes: ADD).

The New York Times described the score for this 1951 musical comedy as "the richest Arthur Schwartz has written in years". The overture, where one vibrant tune after another tumbles out, has one thinking this must have been the number-one musical of its time, deserving of much wider attention. The story, based on that favourite period of the Broadway musical, turn-of-the-century New York, embraces elements of such contemporary shows as *Street Scene* and *Carousel* – once again a hero returns from the dead for his daughter's graduation. Between the scenes that focussed on the tragic affair between Johnny and Katie and her attempts to keep the family together, there was deadpan comedienne Shirley Booth stealing the show as an amoral aunt reminiscing about her late husband in a show-stopper, "He had refinement", or dancing the polka in an invigorating ensemble. Whether a piece where sentiment flows in abundance across the stage could now be revived may be questionable but with this record we can just sit back and enjoy a captivating score vividly performed by the original cast. The recording in cleanly focused mono sound breathes the very spirit of Broadway in its heyday. **AE**

Also available:
By the Beautiful Sea (1954 Broadway Cast) EMI Angel ZDM7 64889-2
Jennie (1963 Broadway Cast) RCA 09026 60819-2

Stephen Schwartz
b. 1948 USA

Composer and lyricist Stephen Schwartz was born in New York and studied piano and composition at the Juilliard School. He graduated with a degree in drama from Carnegie Mellon University before working for a short time as a record producer. His first Broadway success came with the rock musical *Godspell* (1971) – the show's album, produced by Schwartz, won two Grammy Awards. He followed *Godspell* with *Pippin* (1972), *The Magic Show* (1974) and *The Baker's Wife* (1978). As a lyricist he collaborated on Leonard Bernstein's *Mass* (1971); more recently he has worked with Alan Menken on Disney's *Pocahontas* (1995) and *The Hunchback of Notre Dame* (1996).

The Baker's Wife 1990 **London Cast** (with Alun Armstrong, Sharon Lee Hill, Drue Williams, Jill Martin, James Villiers, George Raistrick and Myra Sands) / **Gareth Valentine**.
TER Ⓕ CDTER2 1175 (two discs: 83 minutes: DDD).

The Baker's Wife has one of the most unfortunate histories in musical theatre. Stephen Schwartz's adaptation of the Pagnol film *La femme du boulanger* had a troubled road tour in America in 1976, closing before it reached Broadway. Trevor Nunn's attempt to present the show in a revised version in London in 1990, with his wife Sharon Lee Hill in the title role, also ended in commercial failure.

But listening to the score in TER's excellent two-disc presentation causes one to wonder just why the show failed, for it is filled with beautiful melody and a great deal of charm. The opening "Chanson", which becomes a recurring theme, is delightful, sung with grace and power by the excellent Jill Martin. This leads into a nicely observed comic piece about the in-fighting of the villagers, as they describe how happy their lives would be "If it wasn't for you". The songs for the leading characters are all of exceptional quality – Aimable sings the joyous "Merci, Madame" and the bitter "If I have to live alone". Genevieve has three outstanding numbers all of which have been recorded in recent years on solo discs – "Gifts of love", "Where is the warmth?" and the oft-heard but still stunning "Meadowlark". Dominic has one major solo, the muscular "Proud lady", as well as the lovely "Endless delights" duet with Genevieve. The recording contains all the music from the show and some dialogue as well. Alun Armstrong is superb as the Baker, Aimable, performing his role with relish and great sympathy. Sharon Lee Hill's voice is a little shrill, and she is more controlled in the duets than the solos, but does contrast well with Armstrong's northern gruffness. Drue Williams, as the lover Dominic, is suitably full of youthful masculinity and pride. Hopefully *The Baker's Wife* will one day find its audience on stage, but for now one can enjoy the "endless delights" that this lovely score offers via this fine recording. **RAC**

Godspell 1993 **Studio Cast** (with Elizabeth Sastre, Samantha Shaw, John Barrowman, Paul Manuel, Ruthie Henshall, Claire Burt, Jacqueline Dankworth, Clive Rowe, Glyn Kerslake and Darren Day) **/ Stephen Schwartz**.
  TER Ⓕ CDTER1204 (56 minutes: DDD).
Godspell 1994 **Studio Cast** (with Carl Wayne, Nick Curtis, Linda Hibberd, Jacqui Perkins, Paul Jones, Fiona Hendley, Jess Conrad and Dave Willetts).
  Carlton Shows Collection Ⓑ PWKS4220 (50 minutes: DDD). Disc also includes songs from **Lloyd Webber:** Jesus Christ Superstar.

One of the first religious rock operas, *Godspell* is based on the Gospel According to St Matthew, and has achieved great and lasting popularity. Schwartz's infectious score draws on a number of familiar traditional hymns – the words of "Day by day", one of the show's best-loved hits, actually date from the thirteenth century. The 1993 studio cast recording returns to the show's original 1971 four-man band arrangements, which gives these gifted performers a rare opportunity in these over-orchestrated times to let their excellent voices soar above the music. As Jesus, Darren Day reveals the pleasing, wholesome vocal presence which has led to considerable success in British musicals (indeed, he is more than a little reminiscent of Cliff Richard), particularly on "Save the people" and "Beautiful city". John Barrowman, a veteran of *Sunset Boulevard*, brings some lustre to the gospel-style "We beseech thee". Glyn Kerslake delivers a rousing "Prepare ye the way of the Lord" and Clive Rowe as Buckminster Fuller raps mightily into the blues number "Light of the world". Paul Manuel's tenor turns the familiar "All good gifts" into a lilting, moving ballad. Ruthie Henshall is breathy and torchy on "Turn back old man", while Jacqueline Dankworth is exceptional as Sartre. Her musical heritage is quite obvious as she works "Day by day" into a glorious, swinging anthem. British musical theatre has few genuine old-fashioned stars at the moment, but if there is any justice, one day composers will write shows specifically for the likes of Henshall and Dankworth.

From Carlton's Shows Collection we have a budget-priced package of hits from both *Godspell* and *Jesus Christ Superstar*. The quality of this series is inconsistent, but here Carl Wayne delivers an impeccable "Prepare ye" and Linda Hibberd an intense, highly powered "Day by day". Paul Jones, Fiona Hendley and Dave Willetts add the weight of their experience to the numbers from *Jesus Christ Superstar*. Hendley is particularly affecting on "I don't know how to love him". **PF**

Also available:
Godspell (1971 Broadway Cast) Arista ARCD8304
Godspell (1973 Film Cast) Arista ARCD8337

Richard M. Sherman
b. 1928 USA

Robert B. Sherman
b. 1925 USA

Brothers and songwriting team, the Shermans were born in New York and began working at the Walt Disney studios from 1959. Early Disney films featuring their songs include *The Parent Trap*

(1961), *Summer Magic* (1963) and *The Sword in the Stone* (1963). Their score for *Mary Poppins* (1964) won an Academy Award whilst "Chim-chim-cheree" picked up another for Best Song. Other popular Disney films were *The Jungle Book* (1967), *Chitty Chitty Bang Bang* (1968) and *Bedknobs and Broomsticks* (1971). On Broadway they collaborated on the show *Over Here!* (1974).

The Jungle Book 1967 **Film Cast** (with Phil Harris, George Sanders, Sterling Holloway, Louis Prima and Sebastian Cabot) **/ George Bruns**.
Walt Disney Records ⓕ WDR70400-2 (37 minutes: ADD). Additional music and songs by Terry Gilkyson and George Bruns.

Disney's mega-hit from 1967 is just one of the perennial family favourites that never seem to lose their charm. It is basically a two-hit score: "Bare necessities" by Terry Gilkyson (who also penned "The moonspinner's song" for Disney a few years earlier) was Oscar-nominated, and "I wanna be like you" by the Sherman brothers, who had previously written Disney's 1964 hit *Mary Poppins*. So the songs come with a good pedigree. The laid-back vocals of Phil Harris as Baloo the bear add much to the overall enjoyment of this album. Surprisingly, perhaps, over half of the score was the work of George Bruns, Disney's in-house composer who wrote a good deal of fine music that the majority of the audience, intent upon the catchy songs, were probably not aware of. His opening overture is an enthusiastic Africa-via-Hollywood number, the kaleidoscopic "Monkey chase" is all swirling strings, while "What cha wanna do?" betrays its 1960s origins, with twangy guitars and percussion. (Incidentally, Bruns also scored *Davy Crockett, The Love Bug* and *Robin Hood*, and garnered Academy Award nominations for his work on *Sleeping Beauty, Babes in Toyland* and *The Sword in the Stone*.) *The Jungle Book*, songs and underscore, is an infectious treat whether you have seen the movie or not.   **JW**

Also available:
The Aristocats (1970 Film Cast) Walt Disney Records WD7425-2
Over Here! (1974 Broadway Cast) Sony Broadway SK32961

David Shire
b. 1937 USA

Richard Maltby Jr.
b. 1937 USA

Wisconsin-born lyricist Richard Maltby Jr. and composer David Shire from Buffalo, New York have collaborated on many songs and a number of musicals which never reached Broadway. They formed the basis of two successful musical revues, *Starting Here, Starting Now* (1977) and *Closer than Ever* (1989). Happily, both *Baby* (1983) and *Big* (1996) did appear on Broadway and proved to be fine both melodically and lyrically. Both lyricist and composer have also pursued separate and successful careers. Maltby has gained renown as director and conceiver of *Ain't Misbehavin'* (1978). He directed the Broadway production of Lloyd Webber's *Song and Dance* and also wrote the lyrics for *Miss Saigon* (1989). Shire is a highly successful composer of film scores including *The Taking of Pelham 1-2-3* (1974), *Farewell, My Lovely* (1975), *The Hindenburg* (1975), *All the President's Men* (1976), *Saturday Night Fever* (1977) and *Return to Oz* (1985).

Baby 1983 **Broadway Cast** (with Liz Callaway, James Congdon, Catherine Cox, Beth Fowler, Todd Graff, Martin Vidnovic, Kirsti Carnahan and Kim Criswell) **/ Peter Howard**.
TER ⓕ CDTER1089 (65 minutes: DDD).

One of the best musicals of the 1980s, *Baby* is about three American campus couples facing impending parenthood. The show examines their loves, hopes, fears and – as one of the pregnancies turns out to be phantom – frustrations. It is immensely refreshing: emotional without gush, witty without cynicism; it likes all its people, and we do too. At least once Richard Maltby's lyrics boldy tread where no musical-theatre song has gone before: "Picture a failing spermatazoan/Not even knowin' where he is goin'/What's that ahead a diaphragm! screw it!/He knows he's dead – my God he slips in through it." He's equally good on human behaviour, as on why children are "Easier to love" than a spouse; although on marriage he isn't as lethally perceptive as Sondheim in *Company* he sounds more personally involved. David Shire, meanwhile, is the first composer since Cy Coleman to combine a warm, spacious theatrical feeling with a contemporary sound. The one out-and-out pop song ("I chose right") goes to the youngest father, who's a musician. The sterile Nick and Pam get "Romance", a thrice-repeated tango, funny and increasingly desperate as they ruefully attempt to spice up the strict sexual regime imposed on them by helpful specialists. The three women celebrate their fertility in "I want it all" and the men celebrate it too in "Fatherhood blues". Both are exhilarating; so is the triple-strength title song, "Baby, baby, baby", a funky pre-natal lullaby (all three have lusciously rhythmic orchestrations by Jonathan Tunick). The cast are uniformly fine, with Catherine Cox and Liz Callaway maybe having the edge. Callaway gets the most spectacular numbers, "The ladies singing their song", a lolloping solo interrupted by horror stories of other women's deliveries, and "The story goes on", a celebration of the chain of life as she feels the first kick. That could be dreadful, but it's done with such tact and warmth that it's very moving. So is the finale: she gives birth and her husband can't find the words to describe it, so the music takes over. That's what a musical is for. **RC**

Big 1996 **Broadway Cast** (with Daniel Jenkins, Patrick Levis, Crista Moore and Lori Aine Bennett).
Universal Ⓕ UD53009 (66 minutes: DDD).

Big is an adaptation of the 1988 film comedy that starred Tom Hanks and finds collaborators Richard Maltby Jr. and David Shire on top form. A young boy, Josh, wishes to be big – and becomes grown-up in size but not in mental attitude. Eventually he finds a way to resume his childhood. There's an enormously touching song for the boy's mother (who believes her son has been kidnapped), "Stop time", and the confused adult that the boy has become has "Stars, stars, stars" and "I want to go home". Other joys include "Dancing all the time" for his new girlfriend Susan, and "I want to know", sung by his younger self. This is a beautiful score matched by words which range from the touching to the very funny. This distinguished original cast recording contains some fine performances – Crista Moore as the increasingly bewildered girl friend, Barbara Walsh as Josh's forlorn mother, with Daniel Jenkins and Patrick Levis as the older and younger Josh. One of the most attractive original cast albums of recent years. **MPK**

Starting Here, Starting Now 1977 **Off-Broadway Cast** (with Loni Ackerman, Margery Cohen and George Lee Andrews) **/ Robert W. Preston**.
RCA Ⓕ 2360-2 (56 minutes: ADD).
Starting Here, Starting Now 1995 **London Cast** (with Clare Burt, Michael Cantwell and Samantha Shaw) **/ Caroline Humphris**.
TER Ⓕ CDTER1200 (79 minutes: DDD).

For years, David Shire and Richard Maltby Jr. were the most talented writing team never to have a show on Broadway. They now have two – *Baby* and *Big* – neither commercially successful. They have been luckier off-Broadway with *Starting Here, Starting Now* and *Closer Than Ever* (1989), two anthology musicals unlike any others. Both are song-cycles about, as we used to say, 'relationships', the former drawing most of its material from the partners' earlier projects, either aborted or not widely seen.

Whatever was wrong with those shows, it can't have been their scores. Shire writes warm, surging melodies that maintain the traditions of show music while expanding its horizons. "Autumn", deriving from a college musical of *Cyrano*, is a delicate ballad that got on to an early Barbra Streisand album. "Watching the big parade go by", "I hear bells" and "Song of me" are cast in various moods of wistful celebration; "One step" is a traditional production number raised to a higher power of wit; "A little bit off" is a cunning, odd-metered ballad; "Pleased with myself" is an irresistible celebration, overflowing with musicality. Maltby supplies them all with words at once well-crafted and good-natured, and there are a few numbers that are lyrical *tours de force*: "Crossword puzzle" is exceptionally funny, "I don't remember Christmas" is believably desperate, and "Flair" actually finds a new subject: being trapped in plodding reality while yearning for elegant or passionate release. These are generous songs; the authors' achievement has been to rescue the art of romantic affirmation from the Broadway machine-grinders and give it back to intelligent people. They could be the modern Rodgers and Hart.

The original three-person cast from the Manhattan Theater Club give the material a high-polish, high-energy workout, with some especially rich vocal harmonies (a Maltby-Shire trademark). George Lee Andrews is a very supple baritone, forceful and thoughtful; Margery Cohen is sweet and kooky; Loni Ackerman can be needlessly strident, but her blazing guns are perfectly aimed as the lovelorn genius of "Crossword puzzle". The London version, nearly 20 years later, has four extra numbers of which three are good. The trio aren't always on top of the idiom, but they're spirited, sharp and upfront with the neuroses. Samantha Shaw's "A little bit off" is right on and her "Autumn" comes loaded with mellow fruitfulness.   **RC**

Also available:
Closer Than Ever (1989 Broadway Cast) RCA 60399-2

Lucy Simon

The Secret Garden 1991 **Broadway Cast** (with Mandy Patinkin, Rebecca Luker, Daisy
    Egan, Robert Westenberg, Alison Fraser and John Cameron Mitchell) **/ Michael Kosarin**.
    Columbia Ⓟ CK48817 (77 minutes: DDD).

Of a number of adaptations of Frances Hodgson Burnett's classic children's story this is by far the most satisfying. A quality cast recording with plenty of linking dialogue sequences is emphasised by a superb set of performances. Lucy (sister of Carly) Simon's music is quite delightful, although her occasional foray into Eastern mysticism is unwelcome. Marsha Norman manages to keep her lyrics from becoming over-cloying, despite the sentimentality of the story. Although the Yorkshire accents sound a little odd in the American mouths, this is a minor consideration against the riches on offer. Mandy Patinkin is at his best here – one of Broadway's most important, yet erratic performers – he is controlled and avoids his usual histrionics, offering a sensitively sung portrayal of the repressed guardian. John Cameron Mitchell is wonderful as the "forest wizard" Dickon, with a full-throated delivery of his two major songs. Rebecca Luker confirms her position as a premier music-theatre soprano with her performance as Lily (the dead wife), maintaining a haunting and utterly beautiful delivery throughout. Alison Fraser manages to combine a sense of fun ("If I had a fine white horse") with genuine inspiration ("Hold on") in the smaller role of the chambermaid Martha. Daisy Egan surmounts the difficult task of making Mary Lennox a child that one can warm to – she never allows her character to become one-dimensional – combining the wonder of youth with a feistiness and maturity that never becomes irritating. The final scene is a guaranteed tear-jerker that confirms this as one of the most pleasing and finely constructed recordings of recent times.   **RAC**

Julian Slade   b. 1930 England

One of Britain's prominent post-war composers, Julian Slade wrote his first shows and incidental music for the Bristol Old Vic from 1951. This included many sets of incidental music for Shakespeare plays as well as for *The Duenna*. A production of *The Comedy of Errors* with Slade's music was transmitted by the BBC in 1954, but it was the same year's *Salad Days*, a joyously artless musical comedy, that would make his name and reputation. It proved to be the longest-running show of the 1950s. There followed *Free as Air* (1957), *Hooray for Daisy* (1959) and *Follow That Girl* (1960). A number of further shows followed, culminating in what may be Slade's masterpiece, *Trelawny* (1972). A version of J. M. Barrie's *Dear Brutus* awaits a production.

Salad Days 1994 **40th Anniversary Cast Recording** (with Janie Dee, Simon Green, Prunella
    Scales, Leslie Phillips, Tony Slattery, Willie Rushton, Roy Hudd, Valerie Masterson, John
    Warner, Josephine Tewson, Timothy West, Samuel West, Sara Crowe and Lynda Baron);
    Jonathan Cohen, Mark Dorrell (pfs); **Stan Bourke** (drums); **Steven McManus** (bass); **London
    Voices**.
    EMI Ⓟ CDC5 55200-2 (62 minutes: DDD).
Salad Days 1976 **London Cast Recording** (with Christina Matthews, Adam Bareham,
    Elizabeth Seal and Sheila Steafel) **/ Neil Rhoden**.
    TER Ⓟ CDTER1018 (48 minutes: ADD).

Slade **S**

Star-studded yes, and each cast member of this 40th anniversary recording not only enters into the spirit of this perenially fresh musical comedy but offers a vividly characterized performance that contributes much to the enjoyment of this recording produced for BBC Radio and released on CD with abridged dialogue. *Salad Days* broke all musical theatre box office records in the 1950s, running for 2,282 performances. The show was revived in 1976 with most of that cast reassembled on the TER recording and in the summer of 1996 it returned once more to the Vaudeville Theatre from which First Night Records issued a CD of four numbers (listed below). TER's recording was for some time the only one in stereo but there were two drawbacks: the tricked-out arrangements, and more seriously the wayward singing of the heroine. On EMI the two-piano arrangements are brilliantly played by Messrs Cohen and Dorrell with percussion and bass as originally conceived. The immaculate balance within this small ensemble and in the wider context of the cast and choral group catches the team spirit and intimacy of this piece to perfection as demonstrated in the sparkling overture, one of several sequences recorded for the first time. The youthful sounding London Voices capture the period elocution to a tee whilst making light of some tricky and occasionally awkward corners amongst the Slade/Reynolds lyrics. Simon Green and Janie Dee are well suited as the graduates, their dialogue having a touch of unexpected irony. The book of *Salad Days*, essentially a series of revue sketches through which runs the tale of Jane and Tim looking for a job, permits the ensemble to play a number of characters who reflect the middle class mores of the early 1950s. Like a Lowry painting, the simplicity of Julian Slade's music makes *Salad Days* unique. In "We said we wouldn't look back" and in particular Jane's solo, "The time of my life", in which she looks back at the month that's been, he's created a little masterpiece where the nostalgia of the words that explain the show's title ("Look at the weather and look at me/We're both in a summery haze/We're young and we're green as the leaf on the tree/For these our are salad days"), are as quintessentially English as the tune that adorns them. **AE**

Also available:
Salad Days (1996 London Cast – CD single) First Night SCORECD43

Stephen Sondheim

Born in New York, Sondheim attended the same school as Oscar Hammerstein II's son, and he was encouraged by Hammerstein to write musicals – four before he was 21. After musical studies at Williams College, Massachusetts he took composition lessons from Milton Babbitt. Working in television during the 1950s he also wrote a musical, *Saturday Night* (which was not produced until 1997 in London), and contributed incidental music to Broadway plays. Leonard Bernstein asked him to be lyricist for *West Side Story* (1957), and he followed this success with the lyrics for Jule Styne's *Gypsy* (1959). *A Funny Thing Happened on the Way to the Forum* (1962) was Sondheim's first successful work as both lyricist and composer, although his subsequent show, *Anyone Can Whistle* (1964), was a failure. In 1970 he began an 11-year partnership with director Hal Prince – together they staged a series of innovative shows that departed radically from the Rodgers and Hammerstein model of integrating songs into the dramatic structure. *Company* (1970) used songs to comment on the drama; *Follies* (1971) utilized pastiche to portray the musings of a group of disaffected variety artists; *A Little Night Music* (1972), a series of monologues written entirely in triple time, included the hit "Send in the clowns". *Pacific Overtures* (1976), the operatic *Sweeney Todd, the Demon Barber of Fleet Street* (1979) and the chronologically reversed *Merrily We Roll Along* (1981) were the other Sondheim/Prince productions. Sondheim won a Pulitzer Prize in 1984 for *Sunday in the Park with George*. His innovative approach has continued with recent productions, *Into the Woods* (1991), *Assassins* (1992) and *Passion* (1994).

Anyone Can Whistle 1964 **Broadway Cast** (with Angela Lansbury, Lee Remick, Harry Guardino, Arnold Soboloff and James Frawley) **/ Herbert Greene**.
Columbia Ⓜ CK02480 (57 minutes: ADD).

Anyone Can Whistle 1995 **Carnegie Hall Concert Cast** (narrated by Angela Lansbury, with Scott Bakula, Madeline Kahn, Bernadette Peters, Joan Barber and Mary Bentley-LaMar) **/ Paul Gemignani.**
Columbia Ⓕ CK67224 (77 minutes: DDD).

For a nine-performance flop, *Anyone Can Whistle* has shown amazing strength. Goddard Lieberson's act of faith in recording the show in the first place produced a classic that captured Angela Lansbury, Harry Guardino and Lee Remick in their stage-singing débuts, supported by an excellent team. The music and lyrics crackle with brilliance and passion. Can anyone think of a more deeply touching ballad than the title-song? "There won't be trumpets" cut, but recorded anyway, is also highly appealing, and Lansbury has several witty numbers that she delivers with élan. The dance music has all the Western appeal of a film score by Jerome Moross. No wonder the whole show glows so freshly in the 1995 benefit concert staged for charity and featuring as narrator Miss Lansbury (unhappily the only surviving principal cast member). This also has the benefit of restoring another witty cut number, "There's always a woman", as well as including the full dances and underscoring. With Madeline Kahn as the overbearing mayoress, Bernadette Peters as heroine Nurse Fay and Scott Bakula as Hapgood the hero, here is the fullest account of the score yet. Of course, the star performances make the original 1964 recording essential as well. **MPK**

Assassins **1991 New York Cast** (with William Parry, Terrence Mann, Jonathan Hadary, Annie Golden, Victor Garber and Patrick Cassidy) **/ Paul Gemignani**. RCA Victor Ⓕ RD60737 (57 minutes: DDD).

This unsettling musical play about the assassins of American presidents has lost nothing in its impact or topicality in the half-dozen years since it was produced for a limited season at the Playwrights Horizon in New York and then at the Donmar in London for a sell-out run. The score is a remarkable example of Sondheim at his most dramatic and pungent, drawing on many sources from Sousa and Copland to the 'pop' musical idioms of the 1960s and 1970s. The book is equally forceful, especially in the climactic scene on the sixth floor of the Texas Book Depository in Dallas, in which Lee Harvey Oswald is joined by the other presidential assassins, who encourage him to shoot President Kennedy to be envied and for lasting fame. An outstanding cast leave the listener with the disturbing pay-off "everybody's got a right to their dreams". The recording projects the drama with uncommon vividness creating atmosphere with no loss of audibility. **AE**

New review
At the Movies with Alet Oury, Guy Haines, Jane Krakowski, Jennifer Simard, Jolie Jenkins, Bryan Batt, Danny Burstein, James Hindman, Christiane Noll, Cassidy Ladden, Robert Randle, Jim Ryan, Kevin Pariseau, Alec Timerman, Susan Egan, Gary Beach, Liz Callaway; ensemble / [a]Tom Fay, [b]Brad Ellis.
Varèse Sarabande Spotlight Series Ⓕ VSD5805 (65 minutes: DDD).
Songs and instrumental pieces from Dick Tracey[a], Singing Out Loud[a], A Little Night Music[a], The Bird Cage[a], Evening Primrose[a], Reds[a] and Stavisky[b].

A Celebration **1996 Los Angeles Cast** (with Joely Fisher, Tim Curry, Glynis Johns, David, Patrick and Shaun Cassidy); **orchestra / Peter Matz, Gerald Sternbach**.
Varèse Sarabande Spotlight Series Ⓕ VSD2-5820 (two discs: 125 minutes: DDD). Recorded at a performance in the James A. Doolittle Theatre, Hollywood during March 1996.

There always seems to be room in the world for just one more Sondheim anthology, or two. When a selection of even his most familiar songs lends itself to so many interpretive permutations it seems likely that the collector's mission will never be complete.

"Sondheim at the Movies" is a welcome, well-performed and interesting miscellany of his film work, including four show-stoppers he wrote for *Dick Tracy* (1990) and the main love theme for *Reds* (1981). But perhaps the most delightful songs here come from a little-remembered television musical, *Evening Primrose*, produced for ABC in 1967. "If you can find me, I'm here" has echoes of "Could I leave you?" from *Follies*; "I remember" is the kind of poignant gem which is Sondheim's stock-in-trade. There's ample evidence, too, of his facility for pastiche: "Sand", from an unfilmed project, *Singing Out Loud*, is a bull's eye burlesque of a bluesy old torch song, while "It takes all kinds", written for *The Bird Cage* (1996), is a wince-inducing take on those life-affirming disco anthems of the 1970s.

The live revue "Sondheim: A Celebration" follows the tried-and-tested all-star gala format and as such it can hardly fail, although it certainly stumbles on a couple of occasions. A swing interpretation of "The ballad of Sweeney Todd" almost works, but purists be warned: the throbbing, driven menace of the original is sacrificed to comedy which simply doesn't come over on disc. Nancy Dussault murders "Getting married today" and Tim Curry's woeful Shirley Bassey-ish stab at "Losing my mind" means that we are still waiting for a male artist to do justice to that mini-masterpiece. But others shine. Jane Carr and Roger Rees offer a delicious "Invocation to the gods and instructions to the audience", and who could resist Susan Johnson's worldy-wise "Who's that woman?" or Tia Riebling's "The miller's son"? Not to mention Glynis Johns, rolling back the years in silvery voice with "Send in the clowns" and reminding us a quarter of a century on that she was the most affecting of all Sondheim's Desirées.   **PF**

Company   1970 Broadway Cast (with Dean Jones, Barbara Barrie, George Coe, John Cunningham, Teri Ralston, Charles Kimbrough, Donna McKechnie, Charles Braswell, Susan Browning, Steve Elmore, Beth Howland, Pamela Myers, Merle Louise and Elaine Stritch) / **Harold Hastings**.
Columbia Ⓜ CK03550 (55 minutes: ADD).

Company   1995 London Cast (with Adrian Lester, Rebecca Front, Clive Rowe, Clare Burt, Gareth Snook, Liza Sadovy, Teddy Kempner, Sophie Thompson, Michael Simkins, Sheila Gish, Paul Bentley, Anna Francolini, Kiran Hocking and Hannah James) / **Paddy Cunneen**.
First Night Ⓕ CASTCD57 (57 minutes: DDD).

A quarter of a century separates these two recordings of Sondheim's first, masterly concept show which distributes an abundance of musical riches fairly and squarely among a truly ensemble cast. After such a gap, few shows would emerge completely free from the whiff of mothballs. But if anything, Sondheim's wry and acerbic commentary on the mores, angst, neuroses and pressures of the single, urban (specifically, Manhattan) life has gained in currency with the years. On one level, *Company* is a revue in which each character has the opportunity to make a series of observations and recommendations on the status of Robert, the central character, who, despite being surrounded by friends (some married) and girlfriends, is essentially lonely and bemused by his situation, and what he ought to do. In doing so, they also shed light on their own condition. The variety of the musical numbers is almost infinite, each one able to stand alone as a statement on friendship, marriage, hope, fear, or whatever other subject is under consideration.

Both these recordings offer ample evidence of the continued relevance of one of Sondheim's finest works. The sheer, abrasive quality of the original Broadway cast recording has lost nothing with the passage of time. Dean Jones brings a fraught and slightly bitter quality to Robert, at its most effective on "Side by side". As Marta, Pamela Myers really brings to life "Another hundred people", Sondheim's evocation of the magnetic allure of a city which draws people in to work and play 24 hours a day. But the jewel in the crown is surely Elaine Stritch's Joanna. Much-married, sharp as a knife, acidic and self-knowing but ultimately kind, it is difficult to imagine any other actress bringing such scorching irony to the devastating attack on "The ladies who lunch". In comparison, Sam Mendes's 1995 London revival is more introspective, the voices of the other characters chattering and echoing in and around Robert's head, driving him to the cautiously optimistic conclusion that "Being alive" is probably more important than fretting about whether or not one person can make you happy. Adrian Lester is in silken voice as an almost painfully sensitive Robert, for whom Sondheim restores a number dropped from the original production, "Marry me a little". Sophie Thompson is also outstanding, her Amy rigid with hysteria on her wedding morning ("Getting married today"). But overdoing the Manhattan rasp, Sheila Gish falls short of the impossible standard set by Stritch's Joanna. "The ladies who lunch" is the only slight disappointment in an otherwise faultlessly fresh record of a highly successful revival.   **PF**

Follies   1971 Broadway Cast (with Alexis Smith, Gene Nelson, Dorothy Collins, John McMartin, Yvonne de Carlo, Arnold Moss, Michael Bartlett, Fifi d'Orsay, Ethel Shutta, Mary McCarty, Harvey Evans, Kurt Peterson, Virginia Sandifur and Marti Rolph) / **Harold Hastings**.
EMI Angel Ⓜ ZDM7 64666-2 (50 minutes: ADD).

Follies   1985 Avery Fisher Hall Concert (with Licia Albanese, Carol Burnett, Liz Callaway, Betty Comden, Barbara Cook, Adolph Green, André Gregory, George Hearn, Howard McGillin, Erie Mills, Liliane Montevecchi, Phyllis Newman, Mandy Patinkin, Daisy Prince, Lee Remick, Arthur Rubin, Elaine Stritch and Jim Walton) / **Paul Gemignani**.
RCA Ⓕ BD87128 (two discs: 83 minutes: DDD). Also includes music from the film *Stavisky* (1974).

Follies 1987 **London Cast** (with Diana Rigg, Julia McKenzie, Daniel Massey, David Healy, Lynda Baron, Pearl Carr, Teddy Johnson, Maria Charles, Margaret Courtenay, Adele Leigh, Leonard Sachs, Dolores Gray, Paul Bentley, Gillian Bevan, Evan Pappas, Deborah Poplett and Simon Green) / **Martin Koch**.
First Night Ⓜ OCRCD6019 (75 minutes: DDD).

Between them, these three recordings of Sondheim's haunting study of the need to make your peace with the past in order to face the future offer an extraordinary array of Hollywood, Broadway and West End stars. Certainly, there are more treasures than can be detailed here. Each deserves closer attention for that reason alone. Nostalgia isn't what it used to be, as the two middle-aged former Follies girls (Sally and Phyllis) and their husbands (Buddy and Ben) come face to face with the ghosts of their young selves, forced to account for the disappointments, delusions and follies of the past during the course of a reunion. The drama is played out against a backdrop of a gathering of ageing Follies stars at a party held to celebrate their former glories one more time before the theatre is pulled down to make room for a car park. One by one, they parade their old vanities and aspirations in a running commentary on the distorting effect of time on the way the central characters perceive their own past. This is achieved in a series of pastiches of vaudeville numbers in which Sondheim skilfully evokes the glamour of a vanished age of entertainment while exposing the raw reality beneath the brightness and glitter.

The 1971 Broadway cast recording was irritatingly truncated in order to fit on a single LP. Many of the show numbers are either omitted altogether or so brutally abbreviated as to be pointless. For example, Yvonne de Carlo's "I'm still here" should have been a *tour de force* but loses all continuity. Nevertheless, some of the numbers survive with their dignity intact and the relationships of the central couples retain a bitter quality which was lacking in subsequent productions. Witness Alexis Smith as Phyllis: her lacerating attack on her husband, "Could I leave you?", has never been bettered.

In 1985, an astonishing cast was assembled at the Avery Fisher Hall in New York for a concert performance of the complete score. Mercifully taped, the recording preserves the electric excitement of the occasion right from the moment a string of musical legends make their way onto the stage. As Buddy, Mandy Patinkin gives his two vaudeville numbers, "The right girl" and "Buddy's blues", an edgy, frenetic quality unmatched by others in the role. Barbara Cook delivers an exemplary "Losing my mind", Lee Remick is an acid Phyllis and George Hearn turns "Live, laugh, love" into a powerful vignette of a nervous breakdown. Two performers must be singled out from a stellar supporting cast: Carol Burnett for a skilfully low-key "I'm still here", and Elaine Stritch whose palpably thrilling "Broadway baby" practically hijacks the whole two-disc set.

Despite an almost equally lustrous cast, and Julia McKenzie's definitive Sally, the 1987 London cast recording inevitably sounds a mite flat in comparison. But it has its own rewards. Typically, Sondheim updated the score for the production, so there are new songs for Ben ("Make the most of your music" replaces "Live, laugh, love") and Phyllis ("Ah, but underneath" – delivered with scathing self-awareness by Diana Rigg – replaces "The story of Lucy and Jessie"); and there's a new version of "Loveland", the Busby Berkeley number which leads into the individual Follies numbers of the leading quartet. Dolores Gray brings some welcome old-fashioned glamour to Carlotta's "I'm still here", but Margaret Courtenay's "Broadway baby" is no match for Stritch. **PF**

A Funny Thing Happened on the Way to the Forum 1962 **Broadway Cast** (with Zero Mostel, John Carradine, Jack Gilford and David Burns) / **Harold Hastings**.
EMI Angel Ⓜ ZDM7 64770-2 (44 minutes: ADD).
A Funny Thing Happened on the Way to the Forum 1963 **London Cast** (with Frankie Howerd, Kenneth Connor, 'Monsewer' Eddie Gray and Jon Pertwee) / **Alyn Ainsworth**.
EMI Angel Ⓜ ZDM7 65070-2 (45 minutes: ADD).

Forum, to shorten its title to workable usage, marked Stephen Sondheim's début as a composer after his lyrics alone had graced *West Side Story* and *Gypsy*. It was based on the Roman comedies of Plautus with an archetypal clever slave, Pseudolus, providing comic opportunities for two very different comedians, Zero Mostel on Broadway and Frankie Howerd in the West End. Compared with Howerd's unbuttoned performance, Mostel and his company have always seemed to me to be a rather sober lot, though this may be coloured both by having seen Howerd and his merry men on the stage and for a fondness for the English variety tradition from where several of the London cast members emanated. The rewards of Sondheim's words and music, deft, delightful and daft, are given full measure by each company, with the London conductor Alyn Ainsworth favouring brisker speeds. Both recordings are good, but the Broadway version has a more ample acoustic. **AE**

Into the Woods 1987 **Broadway Cast** (with Bernadette Peters, Joanna Gleason, Chip Zien, Tom Aldredge and Robert Westenberg) **/ Paul Gemignani**.
RCA Victor Ⓕ RD86796 (69 minutes: DDD).
Into the Woods 1990 **London Cast** (with Julia McKenzie, Imelda Staunton, Patsy Rowlands, Clive Carter, Nicholas Parsons, Eunice Gayson, Ann Howard, Ian Bartholomew, Jacqueline Dankworth, Mark Tinkler and John Rogan) **/ Peter Stanger**.
RCA Victor Ⓕ RD60752 (72 minutes: DDD).

Stephen Sondheim's masterpiece, and much the finest of his three shows with James Lapine as librettist and director, *Into the Woods* grows and grows on you (like Jack's beanstalk). The score interweaves musical and verbal motifs, delectably underlined in Jonathan Tunick's orchestrations, as cunningly and hauntingly as the book juggles the four fairy-tales – three authentic and one invented – that make up the action. The first act, with the propulsive title tune jingling through it, is composed in various shades of jauntiness, erupting briefly in teasing melodic shards. The music, like the story, becomes deeper and more sumptuous in Act 2. The show handles fissionable material – parents and children, growing up, knowledge and innocence, social responsibility and upheaval – with the lightest touch; and when it turns didactic at the end ("Careful the things you say, children will listen") it has earned the right. The audience has travelled with the characters on a learning expedition, a fierce as well as amusing journey with a few casualties. Death is not exactly unheard-of in a musical – Rodgers and Hammerstein practically made it a convention – but usually we're softened up for it; the death of the King in *The King and I* is signalled several scenes off. But the death of the Baker's Wife at the hands – or more strictly the feet – of the vengeful Giant comes literally out of a clear sky, just as it might in real life. It may be the bravest narrative development in any musical, abruptly killing off the most vivacious and sympathetic character in the piece.

It certainly seemed that way when Joanna Gleason played the Baker's Wife in New York: a funny, quizzical, sexy and pragmatic woman who had just enjoyed a brief encounter – half pleasing, half hurtful – with the Prince of her dreams (her long-range infatuation with Cinderella's spouse is one of the recurring musical strands, intertwined as it is with the Prince's narcissistic view of the situation, that most repays attention). This show may offer more good acting roles than any other musical, and in a terrific cast Gleason is *prima inter pares*. Bernadette Peters's performance of the Witch (alias Destiny) is not as flamboyantly witty as it became later in the run but is still a treat, from the opening rhythmic monologue (strictly a rap, but a rap in which the syllables fall in the right place and the rhymes rhyme) to the doom and disgust of her departing aria, "The last midnight". Robert Westenberg is a Wolf with a blues soul, Kim Crosby and Danielle Ferland make contrasting *enfants terribles* of Cinderella and Red Riding Hood, and Chip Zien passes effortlessly from rib-tickling to heart-warming as the Baker. He assumes the moral and emotional burden of the show in its two most potent numbers: "No more", about fathers, sons, and the hopeless hope of a carefree life, and "No one is alone", about communal solidarity and its obverse, the human propensity for ganging-up. Some people have found the show's second act – what happens after happily ever after – unnecessary, or gratuitously grim. But it gives the show its point, and these last songs are among the most profoundly moving in any musical.

The London production CD offers a clutch of good performances, as intelligent as the competition but less idiomatic. The characters may be timeless and stateless, but they are still infused with Sondheim's New York wit: a matter of timing rather than accent. The Baker's Wife is again the stand-out; Imelda Staunton offering a caressing young mother from the London suburbs in place of Gleason's coruscating Bronx *Hausfrau*. As strong and delightful a combination of actress and singer as exists on the British stage, Staunton has a wonderful line in incredulous stifled laughter. Julia McKenzie as the Witch overdoes the doddery, but rises to a thrilling "Last midnight". She also takes full advantage of a new song, "Our little world", the Witch's attempt to play the protective mother with Rapunzel while wielding the comb ("Something we can share – hair"). Ian Bartholomew is a touching Baker, if without Zien's comic panache. Jacqui Dankworth is a Cinderella more warmly and arrestingly voiced than her predecessor though less sharply characterized, Clive Carter is liltingly snobbish as her Prince and Tessa Burbridge is as determinedly bratty a Red Riding Hood as ever quickened the pulse of a wolf. To split a few hairs: the New York recording is more show-wise but less theatrical, the London version running to blood-curdling sound effects befitting a musical in which giants walk the earth (and finally come crashing down onto it). **RC**

A Little Night Music 1973 Broadway Cast (with Glynis Johns, Len Cariou, Hermione Gingold, Victoria Mallory, Laurence Guittard, Patricia Elliott and Mark Lambert) / **Harold Hastings**.
Columbia Ⓜ CK32265 (58 minutes: ADD).

A Little Night Music 1975 London Cast (with Jean Simmons, Hermione Gingold, Maria Aitken, Veronica Page, Terry Mitchell, Diana Langton, Joss Ackland and David Kernan) / **Ray Cook**.
RCA Victor Ⓜ GD85090 (59 minutes: ADD).

New review
A Little Night Music 1990 Studio Cast (with Sian Phillips, Bonaventura Bottone, Eric Flynn, Maria Friedman, Susan Hampshire, Jason Howard, Janis Kelly, Megan Kelly and Elisabeth Welch) / **John Owen Edwards**.
TER Ⓕ CDTER1179 (71 minutes: DDD).

A Little Night Music 1995 London Cast (with Judi Dench, Laurence Guittard, Sian Phillips, Patricia Hodge, Lambert Wilson, Joanna Riding and Issy van Randwyck) / **Harold Hastings**.
Tring Ⓕ TRING001 (74 minutes: DDD).

Perhaps Sondheim's most enduringly popular musical, this wry, non-judgemental observation of the vanities, delusions and doubts which emerge as a network of relationships is exposed over a country weekend, has been well-served by its various revivals. Based on Ingmar Bergman's film, *Smiles of a Summer Night*, the plot puts the protagonists through a maze of discoveries and revelations, watched and commented on by a quintet of Lieder singers.

Like its successors, the original Broadway cast has many merits, although the later productions draw more heavily on the darker forces at work within Sondheim's exploration of the many facets of passion. Glynis Johns is a silvery voiced, brittle Desirée who delivers a poignant, restrained "Send in the clowns". Len Cariou (a future Sweeney Todd) is outstanding as Fredrik, whilst Hermione Gingold makes a fruity meal of the ageing courtesan, Madame Armfeldt, lamenting the lack of dignity with which the modern generation treats its "Liaisons". Laurence Guittard, who would play Fredrik in London two decades later, generates some fire with the unsympathetic role of the Count, but Patricia Elliott is less satsifactory in the under-developed part of the Countess.

The subsequent London production contains some subtle improvements on the Broadway original. Ray Cook's light touch on the musical direction gives the performers – particularly the all-important Lieder singers – greater freedom to soar through Sondheim's delicate web of waltzes. Gingold reprises her Madame Armfeldt, while Jean Simmons is a waspish, rather grand Desirée, striking sparks off Joss Ackland's crusty Fredrik. Maria Aitken uncovers the dark, masochistic streak which keeps the Countess tied to her errant, brutal husband (David Kernan). Some of the younger roles, like Veronica Page as the sweet-voiced and naïve child bride Anne and Terry Mitchell's earnest stepson Fredrik, are most appealing; but the highlight is Diane Langton's pert, pragmatic maid, Petra. "The Miller's son" is a minor Sondheim masterpiece, half frantic jig, half yearning ode to romantic dreams: Langton's energy and attack are alone enough to recommend this recording.

The TER studio recording uses John Owen Edwards's pared-down chamber orchestration from a 1989 Chichester revival, featuring a string quintet, a woodwind quintet, harp, piano and celesta plus a percussionist. If some of the original richness is necessarily sacrificed, the accomplished cast gives full vent to some of Sondheim's most deceptively lacerating lyrics. Elisabeth Welch is inspired casting as Madame Armfeldt, vague but all there when it comes to penetrating observation. Maria Friedman, probably the leading British

Sondheim interpreter of our time, soars gloriously as Petra in "A weekend in the country" and "The Miller's son". Sian Phillips's Desirée is by turns imperious and exasperated, well-matched by Eric Flynn's resonant Fredrick, but she lacks the basic human warmth which Judi Dench was to bring to the role. Susan Hampshire, who actually played the Countess in Chichester, is deceptively languid, barely concealing a nice irony beneath her world weariness in "Every day a little death".

The most recent, and probably the best, incarnation is the Royal National Theatre's 1995 production, directed by Sean Mathias, who replaced the frills and elegance of its predecessors with an expectant, brooding spareness which exposed the cyclical, multi-layered nature of the intertwined relationships. Much has been said of Sondheim's ability to write complex, rounded roles for women, a gift which is well-rewarded by these performances. Judi Dench's world-weary, sanguine Desirée is half-amused, half-sickened by the vulgarity of her own life as a touring actress. "The glamorous life" is enhanced by extra lyrics imported from the otherwise lamentable 1978 film version. More of a *diseuse* than a singer, Dench rescues "Send in the clowns" from 20 years of easy listening hell and restores it to its rightful place as a searing, cracked assessment of the agonies two adults can put each other through. Joanna Riding's rather shrill Anne aside, there are many other jewels in this recording. Patricia Hodge's Countess delivers an aching "Every day a little death" as well as a restored number, "My husband, the pig" – a beautiful study of knowing self-bitterness and resignation. Sian Phillips exorcises Gingold's ghost with an austere, stately and ultimately moving performance as Madame Armfeldt. In such company the men are somewhat outshone, although Laurence Guittard makes a dignified if bemused Fredrik, comically playing up the frustrations of the denied husband ("Now"). Overall, the most cohesive recording of an intriguing work. **PF**

Marry Me a Little 1981 Broadway Cast (with Suzanne Henry and Craig Lucas) / **E. Martin Perry**.
RCA Ⓕ 7142-2 (53 minutes: ADD).

The music and lyrics of Stephen Sondheim have so far been anthologized on stage at least five times. Of these, only *Marry Me a Little* places the songs in some sort of context: in this case that of two New Yorkers living in separate flats with identical layouts – that enables them to occupy the same space on stage without ever meeting. Craig Lucas, who developed the show with Norman Rene was appearing in *Sweeney Todd* at the time. All of the songs were cut-outs or discards or songs written for unproduced shows, but, due to this show, some have now become famous in their own right. Craig Lucas and Suzanne Henry have a great time and so will you. "Can that boy foxtrot?", "Uptown, downtown", "Happily ever after", "Who could be blue?" and the rest of the score prove yet again that Sondheim's discards are better than many that others retain. Richly melodic, these miniature character studies prove that the art of great songwriting is still with us. **MPK**

Merrily We Roll Along 1993 Leicester Haymarket Cast (with Michael Cantwell, Maria Friedman, Evan Pappas, Jacqueline Dankworth and Louise Gold) / **Julian Kelly**.
TER Ⓕ CDTER1225 (75 minutes: DDD).
Merrily We Roll Along 1994 Off-Broadway Cast (with Anne Bobby, Malcolm Gets, Michele Pawk and Adam Heller) / **Michael Rafter**.
Varèse Sarabande Spotlight Series Ⓕ VSD5548 (75 minutes: DDD).

A definitive recording of the original 1981 production of Stephen Sondheim and George Furth's superb time-reversal musical *Merrily We Roll Along*, complete with the full orchestrations, was made by RCA but is not currently available. Here we have two recordings with more intimate orchestrations and the revisions made in the 1990s, used on both sides of the Atlantic. The score is one of Sondheim's finest and most moving achievements. "Old friends", "Good thing going" and "Not a day goes by" have taken their place as standards. "Opening doors" and "Franklin Shepard Inc." are brilliant, plot-advancing achievements. "Bobby and Jackie and Jack" is a brilliant piece of irony. As to the two recordings here, by and large the American version offers some voices which seem stronger than their British equivalents, but the Leicester cast offer throughout the more searing and charismatic performances. Either would make a fine complement to the original cast recording. **MPK**

Pacific Overtures 1987 English National Opera Cast (with Richard Angas, Leon Berger, Christopher Booth-Jones, Edward Byles, John Cashmore, Gordon Christie, Ian Comboy, Terry Jenkins, John Kitchiner, Simon Masterton-Smith, Harry Nicoll, Malcolm Rivers, Eric Roberts, Michael Sadler, Paul Strathearn and Alan Woodrow) / **James Holmes**.
TER Ⓕ CDTER2 1152 (two discs: 118 minutes: DDD).

This show is in some ways the most extraordinary musical ever done on Broadway: a stylized but full-blooded account of the enforced 'opening up' of Japan to American and other commercial interests in the second half of the nineteenth century. Not only did the show focus uncompromisingly on poltical history, it told its story by adapting some of the traditional forms of Japanese theatre, including an all-male cast. A kabuki musical? The commercial risks it took made it seem like a hara-kiri musical. It wasn't a hit but it was a triumph. Score and staging grew more Westernized as the evening, and the colonizing, proceeded: form and subject perfectly matched. Director Harold Prince's fascination with political conflict fused with his commitment to theatrical excitement to produce his finest work.

Prince's dramatic intelligence, and his visual flair, were much missed in the ENO's valiant attempt at the show. It was more arid than one had remembered, more of a history lesson: even a schools broadcast. That flavour obviously carries over in the recording, which includes the dialogue. One wouldn't want to hear it very often, but it's nice to have – for the record, so to speak – and Richard Angas's narrator gets it off to a trenchant start. The music announces itself at the beginning with a long and mournful threnody on flute, followed by an unsparing assault on traditional percussion. That mixture of force and delicacy is at the heart of the score, and it's admirably brought out by James Holmes. Some of Sondheim's loveliest writing is here, from the spare and extremely beautiful "There is no other way", the most exotic song in the show, to the English sailors's barcarolle "Pretty lady", taking in *en route* the soaring, floating "Poems" in which odd meters work out satisfyingly even; and the terrified and terrifying outcry of "Four black dragons". The score is also Sondheim's greatest feat of sustained irony. This is a piece that never has to raise its voice to make a devastating point. The unblushing demonstration of imperialist *Realpolitik* in "Please hello" puts most self-conscious 'political' theatre to shame. "Chrysanthemum tea", in which, for the good of the country, the Shogun's mother lulls her vacillating son everlastingly to sleep, is black high comedy, exhilaratingly rhymed. "Someone in a tree", which juggles with youth and age, past and present, memory and forgetfulness, historical process and individual perception, is literally incomparable, in its ambition and in its feeling: merciless, compassionate and – as it hurtles to its conclusion on a rising repeated vamp – almost unbearably exciting.   **RC**

New review
Passion 1994 Broadway Cast (with Donna Murphy, Jere Shea, Marin Mazzie, Gregg Edelman, Tom Aldredge) / **Paul Gemignani**.
EMI Angel Ⓕ CDQ72 555251-2 (57 minutes: DDD).
Passion 1996 London Cast (with Michael Ball, Maria Friedman, Helen Hobson, Paul Bentley and Hugh Ross) / **Mark W. Dorrell**.
First Night Ⓕ CASTCD61 (75 minutes: DDD).

Passion may just be Stephen Sondheim's finest work for the theatre. It is certainly his most iridescent, luminously beautiful score, perfumed with the magic of Ravel and Rachmaninov, a sustained rhapsody in words and music. It has been suggested that the show might also be called *Obsession*. A plain, frail invalid, Fosca, wronged in marriage, is now living on a remote Northern Italian military station. When Giorgio, a handsome, recently arrived officer shows her kindness, she responds with an intense devotion that finally overpowers the soldier's affection for Clara, his beautiful married mistress who is back in Rome. There are no songs as such, but many sections can stand on their own. These include "So much happiness", a lovely duet for Giorgio and his mistress, Fosca's deeply moving confession "Loving you" and the letter Fosca dictates to Giorgio, "I wish I did not love you". The show is blessed with two superlative recordings – Sondheim always brings out the best in his interpreters. Apparently the playing time didn't allow for the inclusion of the Christmas song or Giorgio's additional solo added for London. There's little if anything to choose between the two pairs of leads. Michael Ball has the richer, fuller voice and is matched in subtlety and beauty of tone by Maria Friedman; Donna Murphy is wonderful and Jere Shea is a younger but no less convincing Giorgio. There's more spoken dialogue on the

English issue, which derives from concert performances in 1997 and features the 1996 London cast. The Broadway version alone has notes, pictures and the lyrics.   **MPK**

Sondheim: A Musical Tribute 1973 **Broadway Cast** (with George Lee Andrews, Larry Blyden, Susan Browning, Dorothy Collins, Angela Lansbury, John McMartin, Chita Rivera, Mary McCarty, Nancy Walker and Stephen Sondheim) **/ Paul Gemignani**.
RCA Victor Ⓕ 60515-2 (two discs: 106 minutes: AAD).
Songs from Do I Hear a Waltz?, Gypsy, West Side Story, Follies, Company, Evening Primrose, A Little Night Music, A Funny Thing Happened on the Way to the Forum, Anyone Can Whistle and Saturday Night.

Side By Side By Sondheim 1976 **London Cast** (with Millicent Martin, Julia McKenzie and David Kernan) **/ Tim Higgs and Stuart Pedlar**.
RCA Victor Ⓜ GD81851 (two discs: 92 minutes: ADD).
Songs from A Funny Thing Happened on the Way to the Forum, Company, A Little Night Music, Evening Primrose, Follies, The Seven Per Cent Solution, Anyone Can Whistle, Pacific Overtures, Do I Hear a Waltz?, West Side Story, The Mad Show and Gypsy.

A Stephen Sondheim Evening 1983 **New York Cast** (with Angela Lansbury, Liz Callaway, Cris Groenendaal, Bob Gunton, George Hearn, Steven Jacob, Judy Kaye and Victoria Mallory) **/ Paul Gemignani**.
RCA Victor Ⓕ 09026 61174-2 (82 minutes: ADD).
Songs from The Frogs, Saturday Night, Pacific Overtures, Company, Anyone Can Whistle, A Funny Thing Happened on the Way to the Forum, Follies, A Little Night Music, Sweeney Todd and Merrily We Roll Along.

No other current songwriter has been anthologized as often as Stephen Sondheim. The process seems to have begun in 1973 with *A Musical Tribute*, a New York concert made into an album by RCA which boasted a cast of some 50 alumni of Sondheim musicals and a full orchestra playing the original orchestrations. Much of his best work still lay ahead, but they were still able to mount an impressive programme. "Love is in the air" was the original opening number for *A Funny Thing Happened on the Way to the Forum*; as such it was a disaster and had to be replaced by "Comedy tonight", but it is a charming song and its performance here by Larry Blyden and Susan Browning brings an audible sigh of content from the house. Dorothy Collins and John McMartin, from the original cast of *Follies*, revive some of its numbers; *Saturday Night*, Sondheim's first full score – never produced – is uncorked to reveal a very tender ballad, "So many people". Several songs are reprised by their originators: Angela Lansbury gets the biggest ovation, and proceeds to justify it with a dazzling "Me and my town", the opening song from *Anyone Can Whistle*. Finally, Sondheim himself sings and plays "Anyone can whistle", after which eveybody sings "Side by side".

Lack of an orchestra, and of an audience, make *Side By Side By Sondheim* less of a delight on disc than it was on stage. The twin-piano accompaniment gives it, over so long a programme, a dry conservatory air, but the cast offer plenty of pleasures. Millicent Martin does fine versions of "Send in the clowns" and "I'm still here" and takes possession of two showpiece rarities: the lubricious "I never do anything twice" and the hilarious Jobim parody (music by Mary Rodgers) "The boy from ..." which gives her beloved brand of puzzled Cockney a nice outing ("Each time when I say he's the end/'e giggles a lot with 'is friend"). David Kernan, when not apparently bemused by the beauty of his own voice, sings with exemplary sensitivity to verbal and musical nuance: a tingling "I remember" and a viperishly effective gay version of "Could I leave you?". Julia McKenzie, who was the stand-out on stage, strangely comes across least well; her famously plaintive "Broadway baby" loses much of its effect. But she unites brilliantly with Martin on "Can that boy fox-trot" (cut from *Follies*; written as a solo, but great as a randy female duet) and on "If mama was married" where they make a terrific pair of venomous juveniles; and with Kernan on the great morning-after duet, "Barcelona". Martin and Kernan mesh similarly well for "You must meet my wife", his rhapsody punctured by her acid; and all three make "Pretty lady" even more yearningly lovely than it was in *Pacific Overtures*.

Material from *Saturday Night* (1954) bulks large in *A Stephen Sondheim Evening*, which was a concert at New York's Whitney Museum. Here are the title-song, buffed up with a poker-faced "Hail Brooklyn!" choral prelude; a gently satiric number called "Isn't it?" for a young lady out of her depth; and "What more do I need?", a gloriously tuneful rhythm ballad in the warm tradition of Arthur Schwartz or Burton Lane. Indeed *Saturday Night* seems to have more readily extractable songs than any Sondheim show before *Merrily We Roll Along*; it's ironic that of his two most accessible scores one was never staged and the other flopped. *Merrily's* great ballad "Not a day goes by" is here, in its darker version, well sung by Victoria Mallory. The entire cast is first-rate and includes, most unusually, three strong men, all well served by Sondheim's two musicalizations of the classics. Cris Groenendaal leads "There's something about a war", a Miles Gloriosus song cut from *Forum* and just as hilariously sanguinary as the more economical "Bring me my bride" which replaced it. Bob Gunton does a slightly extended version of the delicious "Pretty little picture" and leads off with the "Invocation" to the gods – "You who look down on actors/(And who doesn't?)" and "Instructions to the audience" from the little-known score for Aristophanes's *The Frogs*. George Hearn reinstates *Forum's* "The house of Marcus Lycus", and sings Sondheim's exquisite, house-stilling setting of Shakespeare's "Fear no more", which was also in *The Frogs*. Angela Lansbury makes a 'surprise appearance' to sing "Send in the clowns", accompanied by the composer. The producer, Paul Lazarus, made a conscious effort to emphasize what he calls "Sondheim's most romantic, most openhearted side", and it's rewarding.   **RC**

New review

Sondheim etc. Live at Carnegie Hall. Bernadette Peters / Marvin Laird.
EMI Angel Ⓔ CDC8 55870-2 (50 minutes: ADD).

Carnegie Hall is an inspiration to performers and over the years a number of classic recordings have been born there. This may not be a classic but it comes very close to it. A small quibble is that this is just part of Miss Peters's concert (mainly the second act) and, as the title indicates, it homes in on one person's work – and my guess is that the full concert would have brought a finer balance, as the three non-Sondheim tracks are tremendous (two being "Time heals everything" and "Raining in my heart" which she introduced in *Mack and Mabel* and *Dames at Sea*). I can think of no other actress who can lay the claim to be a 'Broadway baby' as rightly as this powerhouse of a performer and it is this Sondheim song that starts the album off in the now accepted slower-building, all-stops-out ending version (thanks to Julia McKenzie). With rather nice introductions, that do not lack humour, the album is a thoughtful excursion through gold-plated theatre songs by an assured professional. Peters can be cute in a gloriously self-send-up way, wicked and outrageous (witness "Making love alone" by Marilyn Miller and Cheryl Hardwick). But it is to Sondheim that the album is dedicated and she is an ideal Sondheim performer, as she understands lyrics and lets an audience understand them too. She tells us she was touring at 14 in Sondheim and Styne's *Gypsy* as one of the kids and she went on to star in *Sunday in the Park* and *Into the Woods*. Her choice of numbers is not at all obvious and this is another strength of an album which gets more intense as it continues. A great performer on top form with one of the best solo albums released for some time.   **RSB**

New review

Sondheim Songbook Julie Wilson; William Roy (pf).
DRG Ⓔ CDSL5206 (44 minutes: ADD).
Songs from Follies, Merrily We Roll Along, A Funny Thing Happened on the Way to the Forum, Sweeney Todd, Company, The Seven Per Cent Solution, Anyone Can Whistle and A Little Night Music.

The passing years have darkened and lowered Julie Wilson's once intimate nightclub delivery to a far more granular, throaty bass which, if anything, enhances her deft skills with a lyric. Many would consider her more of a *diseuse* these days but in her mid-seventies she still devotes a great deal of her time and energy to her own vocal training. Her dramatic treatment of these Sondheim standards gives a useful insight into her latter-day success as the virtual doyenne of the New York cabaret scene. "Send in the clowns" is meat and drink to her, as is the anthemic "I'm still here" which she performs with a matter-of-fact defiance, stripping it of the glitzier associations which it has acquired through some *Follies* revivals. It's hard to imagine a drier interpretation of "Can that boy fox-trot", the discarded number from *Follies* which has taken on a life of its own in Sondheim revue. Wilson's arch "I never do anything twice", originally from the soundtrack of *The Seven Per Cent Solution*, milks every *double entendre* mercilessly. If the medleys, which include "With so little to be sure of", "Beautiful girls" and "Losing my mind", sound a little rushed and cluttered, there is still much to admire in Wilson's refreshing lack of artifice and utter commitment to lyrical clarity.   **PF**

Sunday in the Park With George 1984 **Broadway Cast** (with Mandy Patinkin and Bernadette Peters) / **Paul Gemignani**.
RCA Victor Ⓔ RD85042 (69 minutes: ADD).

"Finishing the hat", in *Sunday in the Park With George*, is one of the finest and most unusual songs Stephen Sondheim has written. It's sung by George, loosely based on the pointillist painter Seurat, as he works on his latest canvas just after his mistress Dot (aha!) has walked out on him. He sings partly about her, partly about himself, partly about everybody else ("They have never understood/And no reason that they should"), but mainly about the work of painting itself, the prosaic compulsion to get the job done. This concentration on art-as-process, as opposed to the artist's glamorous or miserable private life, is extremely rare in drama. When George, finished, announces "Look, I made a hat/Where there never was a hat", it's pardonable to hear the composer exulting in having written a song on a subject that might have seemed totally impossible.

Though ostensibly very visual (its sets, inspired by the more-or-less eponymous painting, invariably win awards) the show is more satisfying on disc than in the theatre. The inwardness of the piece suits the medium and this recording, produced by Thomas Z. Shepard, has exceptional aural presence. The music, in chamber-styled orchestrations by Michael Starobin, is as haunting as it's inventive. Mandy Patinkin's plangent intensity is ideal for George; he's more controlled, more humorously self-aware, than in his later work. Bernadette Peters's Dot is one of the best performances ever given in a musical: vivacious, touching, making point after point with minimum fuss and maximum wit. In Act 2, playing her own 98-year-old daughter (don't ask), she gives a commandingly gentle rendition of "Children and art", the song that by main force ties together the show's themes, as exemplified in the twin destinies, or the twin creativities, of its protagonists. Peters also stirringly sings "Move on", a mixture of eleven o'clock pep-talk (with disconcerting echoes of "You'll never walk alone") and shrewd observation: "Stop worrying if your vision/Is new/Let others make that decision/They usually do". In the theatre *Sunday in the Park* is easier to respect than to love; in sound alone, its celebration of all kinds of beauty comes powerfully through. **RC**

Sweeney Todd 1979 **Broadway Cast** (with Angela Lansbury, Len Cariou, Victor Garber, Merle Louise, Sarah Rice, Ken Jennings, Joaquin Romaguera, Jack Eric Williams and Edmund Lyndeck) / **Paul Gemignani**.
RCA Victor Ⓔ 3379-2 (two discs: 101 minutes: AAD).

From the first spine-chilling factory whistle to the gruesome finale as Sweeney Todd and Mrs Lovett rise ashen from their graves, Sondheim's operetta is a *grand guignol* revenger's tragi-comedy in which justice is virtually the sole victor. This version remains the only commercially available recording although the show did reach London, briefly, in 1980 and, a good deal more successfully, in 1993 at the National Theatre with Julia McKenzie and Alun Armstrong (followed by Denis Quilley) in the lead roles. Despite the grim and relentless progress of the demon barber Todd (here played by Len Cariou) in his quest for revenge, assisted by his razors ("My friends") and the pragmatic, resourceful Mrs Lovett (Angela Lansbury), Sondheim's richly textured score contains passages of exceptional beauty. The main beneficiaries are the young lovers, Anthony Hope (Victor Garber) and Todd's daughter Johanna (Sarah Rice), in the songs "Johanna" and "Kiss me", and simple Tobias (Ken Jennings), whose "Not while I'm around" unwittingly alerts Mrs Lovett to the threat which he represents. There is also a great deal of robust music-hall comedy at which Lansbury excels, particularly in "The worst pies in London" and "A little priest", where she hits upon a novel way to dispose of Todd's victims, and "God, that's good" in which the denizens of Mrs Lovett's pie shop consume the fruits of Todd's labours unaware of what they are actually eating. But all the while the undertow is dragging the plot to its inevitable conclusion, a fact which Sondheim never lets us forget. The terrifying factory whistle (used to punctuate each throat-slitting) and the oft-repeated "Ballad of Sweeney Todd" act as *leitmotifs* throughout. Although an expensive import into the UK, this double CD has the rare merit of being an almost complete record of the show (much of the dialogue is included) and includes a libretto. Perhaps the most thrilling of all Sondheim's work to date. Essential listening. **PF**

Also available:

Celebration at Carnegie Hall RCA 09026 61484-2

Company (1972 London Cast) Sony SMK53496

Company (1995 Broadway Cast) EMI PRMFCD2
Putting it Together (1993 Broadway Cast) RCA 09026 61729-2
Unsung Sondheim Varèse Sarabande VSD5433

Charles Strouse
b. 1928 USA

Lee Adams
b. 1924 USA

New Yorker Strouse was writing songs at the age of 12, and later studied at the Eastman School of Music and the Berkshire Music Center where he was taught by various teachers including Aaron Copland, Nadia Boulanger and David Diamond. Working as a rehearsal pianist on Broadway, Strouse began collaborating with lyricist Lee Adams, a native of Mansfield Ohio who had previously studied journalism at Ohio State University. Together they contributed songs for off-Broadway revues including *Catch a Star* (1955) and *Ben Bagley's Shoestring Revue* (1956); and in London, *Fresh Airs* (1956). Strouse and Adams wrote their first full-length score in 1960, *Bye Bye Birdie*, which won a Tony Award and was filmed in 1963 (starring Dick Van Dyke and Ann-Margret). A belated and unsuccessful sequel, *Bring Back Birdie*, followed in 1981. Strouse continued working with Adams on several shows including *All American* (1962), *Golden Boy* (1964) and *Applause* (1970), before writing the book and music for *Six* (1971). Subsequently, he collaborated with other lyricists, most successfully with Martin Charnin on *Annie* (1977) – which ran for 2,377 performances in New York and was filmed in 1982. Strouse also wrote music for several films, such as *Bonnie and Clyde* (1967) and *The Night They Raided Minsky's* (1968).

All American 1962 Broadway Cast (with Ray Bolger and Eileen Herlie) / **John Morris**.
   Sony Broadway Ⓔ SK48216 (45 minutes: ADD).

All American was Strouse and Adams's second Broadway show following their début with the hit *Bye Bye Birdie*. A very disappointing run of 80 performances was put down to a clash of generations when Joshua Logan the director, then a senior figure in Broadway history, "came in and sat on our birthday cake" to quote Mel Brooks. But Gerald Boardman, in his book *American Musical Theatre*, lays the blame on Brooks's "inept book" whilst praising the Strouse/Adams score as comparable to *Bye Bye Birdie*. The score has a similar appeal to *Birdie*, though there's a noticeable falling away in inspiration toward the end. One of its most attractive moments, a duet between the visiting Russian professor, Ray Bolger, and the Dean of the American university, Eileen Herlie, has a melody as poetic as a scene from Chekhov. Herlie, alas, finds Strouse's melodies uncomfortably high for her range, something underlined by the piquant orchestration in her duets. Bolger's "I'm fascinating", a soft shoe with tap mirroring his "Once in love with Amy" routine, doesn't have the melodic pull of that ballad from *Where's Charley?*. As in *Bye Bye Birdie*, the composer and lyricist are consistently sucessful in the ensembles for the young. **AE**

Bye Bye Birdie 1960 Broadway Cast (with Chita Rivera, Dick Van Dyke, Kay Medford, Paul Lynde and Susan Watson) / **Elliot Lawrence**.
   Columbia Ⓜ CK02025 (46 minutes: AAD).

By the end of the 1950s, as the clocks were winding down for many of Broadway's major figures, *Bye Bye Birdie* brought much fresh talent to the scene as well as being the first American show to celebrate rock 'n' roll as the new driving force in popular music. The composer Charles Strouse and lyricist Lee Adams went on to write other shows together and Strouse, the more workaholic of the two, later wrote the lucrative *Annie*, but none of their future collaborations captured the innate buoyancy of their writing that found an ideal outlet in *Bye Bye Birdie*. Conrad Birdie was a teenage idol about to be drafted in to the US Army, as had recently happened to Elvis Presley, but the show was less to do with him than his manager, a harrassed graduate, Dick Van Dyke, and his girlfriend and secretary, Chita Rivera. The score opens with "An English teacher" (a characteristic Strouse tune with a strong propulsive bass line) in which Rose (Rivera) disapproves of the developments in Albert (Van Dyke's) career. Each has one show-stopper, "Put on a happy face" for him and "Spanish rose" for her – although the latter's lyric may be dated, the performance rekindles memories of Rivera's sensational "America" in *West Side Story* two years earlier. The older generation express their disapproval of the Birdie phenomenon in the Charleston rhythm of "Kids", whilst "A lot of livin' to do" gives Birdie a rhythmic platform to match his gyrations on stage. When *Bye Bye Birdie* was presented in London in 1961, Birdie was sung by a genuine rock 'n' roller, Marty Wilde; that recording, with Chita Rivera again, has many admirers and should be made available. In the meantime, this one with its spacious employment of stereo is a thoroughly enjoyable listen.   **AE**

Dance a Little Closer 1983 Broadway Cast (with Len Cariou, Liz Robertson and George Rose) / Peter Howard.
TER Ⓕ CDTER1174 (64 minutes: AAD).

Composer Charles Strouse and librettist-lyricist Alan Jay Lerner teamed up at a time when each had had a string of flops (Strouse was to have more; this was Lerner's last show). They pooled their bad luck on *Dance a Little Closer*, which lasted only one performance. But they also pooled their talent, and the show contains some of the best latter-day work done by either man.

The show concerns the reappearance of a long-lost love in a world on the verge of catastrophe, and it inspired what may be Strouse's most romantic score. The title-tune is hauntingly evocative, and there are other ballads – "There's always one you can't forget", "Anyone who loves" – that in the past would have had a future. There is also the Strouse who made invigorating use of pop and jazz sounds in *Bye Bye Birdie* and *Golden Boy*: the first song here is "It never would've worked", a cynical account of past *amours* done by the leading man with a female backing trio and set to a comparatively contemporary beat. It's a brisk tune for which Lerner wrote an ambitiously racy lyric – maybe too ambitious, too frank. Lerner seems at home with the love-songs but self-consciously outspoken about 'issues', sexual or political. But there are still lyrics that crackle, at least intermittently, and one that's a show-piece: "Mad" in which the hero gets all his (and, one suspects, his author's?) pet gripes off his chest, while tacitly admitting that what really incenses him is his lost lady. Len Cariou, an especially fine actor-singer, gives this number everything he has, and manages a gnarled tenderness on his other material. Liz Robertson seems too nice to be a gold-digging adventuress, but she does the sweeter of the sweet-and-sour songs just fine.   **RC**

Golden Boy 1964 Broadway Cast (with Sammy Davis Jr., Kenneth Tobey, Paula Wayne, Terrin Miles, Johnny Brown, Billy Daniels and Jaime Rogers) / Elliot Lawrence.
EMI Angel Ⓜ ZDM5 65024-2 (48 minutes: ADD).

Originally a play by Clifford Odets and subsequently a film (with William Holden as a violinist who boxed to earn money), *Golden Boy* became a long-running musical starring Sammy Davis Jr. who appeared in the show both on Broadway and in London. Charles Strouse and Lee Adams came up with a fine, workmanlike score and Sammy Davis gave it the force of his considerable personality. While this Broadway recording is highly recommendable be warned that it does not include the song subsequently added to the score for London (and which served for the title of Davis's autobiography), "Yes I can", which was subsequently recorded by the star for another label. Despite what you might expect, the show gives ample opportunity to other cast members to impress with some fine songs. Veteran Billy Daniels gives "While the city sleeps" the velvet touch and Paula Wayne is impressive in "Lorna's here", "I want to be with you" and "Golden boy". Sammy Davis is on top form in the witty "Don't forget 127th Street" as well as in "This is the life", "Night song", "Colourful", "Gimme some", "Can't you see it?" and "No more". *Golden Boy* is a neglected score, well worth investigating.   **MPK**

Nick and Nora 1991 Broadway Cast (with Barry Bostwick, Joanna Gleason, Christine Baranski, Chris Sarandon and Remak Ramsay) / Martin Yates.
TER Ⓕ CDTER1191 (59 minutes: DDD).

Three genres are combined in *Nick and Nora*: detective story, screwball romance and period pastiche. Nick and Nora Castle are the wisecracking, Martini-quaffing, married sleuths of the 1930s, created by Dashiell Hammett and embodied – in *The Thin Man* and a string of subsequent movies – by William Powell and Myrna Loy. The show is as much about their relationship as about their crime-busting activities. Composer Charles Strouse and lyricist Richard Maltby Jr. have written a succession of more or less charming numbers for them: Nick's "Look who's alone now", when Nora goes off investigating without him; Nora's "Let's go home", when the independent life palls; their closing paean to an idealized "Married life"; their opening "Is there anything better than dancing?", when the shades of Nick and Nora seem to collide in mid-air with those of Fred and Ginger; and, best of all, a banteringly erotic duet called "As long as you're happy". Barry Bostwick, conscientiously crooning, and Joanna Gleason, aerated and enchanting, make a dream Art Deco couple.

Listening to them, it's difficult to understand why the show flopped (it did, spectacularly) – except that the songs do seem to add up to more points of rest than a thriller can well afford. However, the CD is confessedly not an authentic representation of the score as heard in the theatre. There, the numbers were fragmented in the service of the murder-mystery narrative. Even the plot numbers have apparently been rewritten for recording, and some of them are very impressive. Particularly inventive is "Men" which offers flashbacks, and also includes a spurned woman's memorable avowal, "I dream of sex in bed with springs". Others, even more elaborate, don't make much sense out of context, so one is happy to fall back on *divertissements*: a straightforward Carmen Miranda spoof called "Boom chicka boom", and the confession of an actress hoping to crash the big time with her first song-and-dance role, "Everybody wants to do a musical". (It's piquant that the performer here, Christine Baranski, was making her own musical début. She puts it over better than the lady she's playing: "My high C may sometimes shriek/Still I hit it twice last week".) Jonathan Tunick supplies his customarily classy orchestrations, with a mournful saxophone prominent behind Nick in his torchier moments. Sometimes, though, he falls back on himself: as he score's it, Maltby and Strouse's "Class" sounds a lot like Maltby and Shire's "Patterns" (from *Baby*). **RC**

New review
Nightingale 1982 London Cast (with Andrew Shore, Gordon Sandison, Sarah Brightman, Susannah Fellows, Dinah Harris and Jill Pert) / **David Firman.**
TER Ⓕ CDTER2 1031 (82 minutes: DDD)

Hans Andersen's fairy tale of the nightingale who was invited to sing at the court of the Emperor of China has served a number of composers well, including Charles Strouse who in his through-sung score opened up new territory for listeners familiar only with his engaging Broadway scores for *Bye Bye Birdie* and *Annie*. This recording emanates from a stage production given at the Lyric, Hammersmith in 1982 when Sarah Brightman sang the coloratura role of the nightingale. Strouse's libretto gets off to an unfortunate start with the chorus unfolding a "tapestry of China" in pidgin English. Thereafter there are plenty of plusses along the way. I enjoyed the number for the Chambermaid to a syncopated accompaniment, "Why am I so happy?", the banter of two lively Peacocks, Dinah Harris and Jill Pert; a witty rhumba for two of the Emperor's Aides; the lively choral ensemble where the people have had enough of the stuffy court atmosphere ("must get out of the palace ..."); and the chorus of peasants who quickly grow weary of the mechanical replacement nightingale ("when you wind her up this china bird/there's no meaning to the minor third"). Where Strouse falls just short of his intention to give us something truly memorable is at the finale ("China happy country"), where the music makes the appropriate gestures without finding the memorable melodic germ that made, say, the closing pages of *Candide* so commanding. **AE**

Also available:
Annie (1977 Broadway Cast) Columbia CK34712
Annie (1982 Film Cast) Columbia 467608-2
Bring Back Birdie (1981 Broadway Cast) Varèse Sarabande VSD5440
Bye Bye Birdie (1963 Film Cast) RCA 1081-2
Bye Bye Birdie (1995 Broadway Cast) RCA 09026 68356-2
It's a Bird, It's a Plane, It's Superman (1966 Broadway Cast) Sony Broadway SK48207
You're Never Fully Dressed Without a Smile (Jason Graae) Varèse Sarabande VSD5711

Leslie Stuart
1864-1928 England

Born Thomas Augustine Barrett in Southport, Lancashire, he wrote minstrel-style songs under the pseudonyms Lester Barrett then Leslie Stuart whilst working as organist at Salford Cathedral. In 1895, Stuart went to London where he contributed songs to the musical comedies *An Artist's Model* and *The Shop Girl*. Stuart's imitation minstrel songs were performed by leading blackface performer Eugene Stratton, an American singer and dancer who had settled in London, and together they had hits with songs like "Is yer mammie always wid yer?" (1896), "The cake walk" and "Lily of Laguna" (1898). Their partnership continued until Stratton's retirement in 1915. In the meantime, Stuart penned his first full-length score, *Florodora* (1899), which ran for a respectable 455 performances in London, but became a huge success in New York in 1900. *Florodora* was cited by many American composers including Jerome Kern, George Gershwin and Richard Rodgers as a youthful influence on their own careers. Later Stuart musical comedies were less successful, and he spent much of his time and energy pursuing his passion for horse-racing (also shared with Stratton).

Florodora 1900 Lyric Theatre Cast (with Ada Reeve, Kate Cutler, Louis Bradfield, Sydney Barraclough, Evie Greene and the Florodora Girls); **Leslie Stuart, Paul Rubens, Landon Ronald** (pfs).
Opal mono Ⓜ OPALCD9835 (50 minutes: AAD). Disc also includes piano solos by Leslie Stuart.

Florodora was a huge success on both sides of the Atlantic at the start of the century. It took its title from an imaginary Philippine island and the perfume manufactured there. The show's big hit was the rhythmically ingenious "Tell me, pretty maiden", sung by a double-sextet of fashionably dressed young men and women. Such was the show's success that in October 1900 it became the first from which extensive extracts were recorded by the infant recording process. Here those dozen numbers and a few other early recordings from the show are transferred to CD. The results are certainly not for the faint-hearted. A few singers and piano accompanist, crowding round a recording horn and rushing through numbers to complete them within the duration of a 7" record, could give little idea of the show's true appeal. Moreover, the CD transfers inevitably suffer from surface noise and varying recording levels, and the documentation has been carelessly edited. Yet for anyone interested in the history of musical theatre or the recording medium this is a landmark issue, preserving music from a show that has otherwise been allowed to slip unjustly into oblivion. It allows us to hear the voices of various leading performers of the time and offers accompaniments that are mostly by the show's co-composers, Leslie Stuart and Paul Rubens. Stuart was one of the most distinguished British popular song composers of the time, and his solo piano performances of five of his independent songs (including "Little Dolly Daydream") make welcome fillers. **AML**

Grant Sturiale

Barry Harman

New review
Olympus On My Mind 1986 American Cast (with Joyce DeWitt, Martin Vidnovic, Susan Powell, Nancy Johnson, Frank Kopyc and Jason Graae) / Grant Sturiale.
TER Ⓕ CDTER1131 (47 minutes: DDD).

It's ancient Greece with gods impersonating humans and having a good time in so doing. There's a touch of those boys from Syracuse in the earth-bound plot and when the gods do their human impersonations and sample human delights it comes close to Cole Porter's *Out of This World* – but then that was based (loosely) on the same Amphitryon legend. Not that this matters, for it's a good tale, and this version not only tells it well but is accompanied by a tuneful score and pleasant, and often witty, lyrics. It's also good to hear the likes of Martin Vidnovic and Jason Graae in excellent form, giving good reason as to why they have gone on to greater success. With the storyline so strong, a score that is more than just respectable and naturally flowing humour complementing it, I wonder why a running gag was added. Playing the fourth member of the chorus (the other three are male) is sexy ex-showgirl Delores (played with vocal force by Joyce DeWitt), who, we are told, is only in the cast because she is the wife of Murray the Furrier who has backed the show. Delores shows off her husband's furs on stage but little other talent than what the furs cover. She even gets to sing a 'star is born' number with the rest of the cast playing second fiddle while leaving the plot boiling. Strange indeed – but I have to admit that it made me laugh. A naughty at times, god-like romp which improves with every play. **RSB**

Jule Styne

1905-1994 England

Although born in London, Styne's family settled in Chicago in 1914 where he made his performing début as a pianist with the Chicago Symphony Orchestra. After winning a scholarship to the Chicago College of Music, he performed in and arranged for dance bands, and had a hit song with "Sunday" in 1926. In 1940 he moved to Hollywood where he collaborated with lyricist Sammy Cahn and others, including Frank Loesser and E. Y. Harburg. Film scores include *Anchors Aweigh* (1945), *It Happened in Brooklyn* (1947), *Romance on the High Seas* (1948) and *My Sister Eileen* (1955). With Cahn, Styne wrote his first Broadway show, *High Button Shoes*, in 1947. *Gentlemen Prefer Blondes* (1949), originally starring Carol Channing, ran for 749 performances and was filmed in 1953 with Marilyn Monroe and Jane Russell. The show was revised for a revival in 1974, again with Channing in the lead role, under the new title *Lorelei*. Other notable shows include *Bells Are Ringing* (1956), with book and lyrics by Betty Comden and Adolph Green, which was written for and starred Judy Holliday; *Gypsy* (1959), a vehicle for Ethel Merman, with lyrics by Stephen Sondheim; and *Funny Girl* (1964), with lyrics by Bob Merrill, which was a hit for newcomer Barbra Streisand (although the London run was curtailed because the star was pregnant).

Bells Are Ringing 1956 **Broadway Cast** (with Judy Holliday, Sydney Chaplin, Eddie Lawrence, Pat Wilkes, George S. Irving and Jean Stapleton) **/ Milton Rosenstock**. Columbia Ⓜ CK02006 (48 minutes: AAD).

A classic musical by Broadway veterans Jule Styne, Betty Comden and Adolph Green, *Bells Are Ringing* was a *tour de force* for a former colleague of the lyricists, comedy actress and film star Judy Holliday. We may not have answering services today, but the idea of a telephonist acting as a good influence on her many clients was a clever one, and gave the show's star many fine comic opportunities. There was also a funny sub-plot about a betting ring disguised as a record company (in America betting by phone was illegal). With a score that included "The party's over" and "Just in time" the show was to achieve almost 1,000 performances. The score had quality in depth – and a wonderful eleven o'clock number in "I'm going back" for Judy Holliday, who went on to make a film of the production with Dean Martin as co-star (it was to be her last film). The original production had many more songs than the film (which added a couple of new ones). The cast album captures Miss Holliday at her brilliant and at times poignant best in one of the very few recordings she was to make. No one sang "The party's over" as memorably as she did. **MPK**

Do Re Mi 1961 **Broadway Cast** (with Phil Silvers, Nancy Walker, Patti Karr, Ray Kirchner, Nancy Dussault and Frank Derbas) **/ Lehman Engel**. RCA Victor Ⓜ 09026 61994-2 (50 minutes: ADD).

A tough, no-nonsense musical about shady dealings in the jukebox industry with a completely unheroic hero, *Do Re Mi* produced one out-and-out hit in "Make someone happy", created by John Reardon. The quality score also included "It's legitimate", the passionate "Cry like the wind" for new star Nancy Dussault, and "Adventure" for Phil Silvers and Nancy Walker – as two of life's little losers. Silvers had two star turns – "The late, late show" and a self-revelatory "All of my life". *Do Re Mi* may not be Styne's best show – that was *Gypsy*, with *Funny Girl* a close second – but it's certainly a good one and the cast recording captures some fine performances. **MPK**

Funny Girl 1964 **Broadway Cast** (with Barbra Streisand, Sydney Chaplin, Kay Medford and Danny Meehan) **/ Milton Rosenstock**. EMI Angel Ⓜ ZDM7 64661-2 (52 minutes: ADD).
Funny Girl 1968 **Film Cast** (with Barbra Streisand and Omar Sharif) **/ Walter Scharf**. Columbia Ⓜ 462545-2 (48 minutes: ADD).

To listen sequentially to the Broadway and Hollywood albums of *Funny Girl* is to realize how the Streisand legend had cemented in four years. The show leaves a fair amount of room for other people. Sydney Chaplin, a leading man with a scratchy voice but some charm, gets to do a couple of duets with the star, one of them the jaunty "I want to be seen with you" (one suspects that his solos vanished on the road). Kay Medford, of the lugubrious poker-voice, makes a magnificently deprecatory Mama Brice, a performance she repeated in London. There are fine songs in the stage version that moviegoers never knew: "Cornet man", a tribute to early jazz with which Streisand-Brice tears up her local music hall on her first engagement, and two momentous ballads placed back-to-back near the end of the show: the unearthly "Who are you now" and the undeviatingly magnificent "The music that makes me dance", the second-best tune of Styne's career (the best was "Time after time" from the 1947 film *It Happened in Brooklyn*). Another of Styne's finest and most unusual melodies, "Absent-minded me", was one of *Funny Girl*'s many pre-Broadway casualties, although Streisand preserved it on her "People" album.

The film retains quite a lot, including Medford, whose singing is now down to one contemplative chorus of "If a girl isn't pretty", which she does charmingly. Omar Sharif also sings pleasantly in the one number he has. As is the way with soundtrack recordings, it sounds more polished, studied and elaborated than the stage original, but less alive. Styne and Merrill also wrote some new songs, "Roller skate rag" which is negligible, "The Swan", a ballet spoof far superior to the original's "Rat-a-tat-tat", and a pleasantly meditative title-song. The conventions of screen bios being different from those of the stage, there are a couple of authentic Brice songs. One, "I'd rather be blue" (by Fred Fisher and Fanny's husband Billy Rose), is absolutely sweet, with Streisand in shy vein cherishing all the 1920s slang (anachronistic for this picture, but never mind); the other – replacing "The music that makes me dance" – is of course "My man", one of the great bad songs, shorn of its melodramatic verse ("he beats me too") but with the singer turning up the heat to compensate.

On both discs, Streisand's sense of musical-dramatic architecture, and her detailed exploration of a lyric, are phenomenal. Those who liked her best when she really was a funny girl (and, because of it, a touching one) singing Broadway repertoire will prefer the show. Those who worship the subsequent star, the movie queen and the diva, will go for the film: she isn't singing rock yet, but the attitude is in place. Fanny Brice, as great a torch-singer as she was a comedienne, would never have emoted like that. **RC**

New review

Gentlemen Prefer Blondes 1949 Broadway Cast (with Carol Channing, Yvonne Adair, Jack McCauley, Eric Brotherson and George S. Irving) / **Milton Rosenstock.**
Sony Broadway mono Ⓕ SK48013 (51 minutes: AAD).

Julie Styne's and Leo Robins's jolly 1920s musical was a successful reworking of Anita Loos's comic novel about amoral golddigger Lorelei Lee. This was the show that made Carol Channing a star. Its two hit songs "A little girl from Little Rock" and "Diamonds are a girl's best friend", plus "Bye bye baby" were carried over into the film, starring Marilyn Monroe and Jane Russell, which otherwise virtually jettisoned the stage score in typical Hollywood fashion. The original cast recording shows how much had been lost. "I love what I'm doing", "Just a kiss apart", "It's delightful down in Chile", "You say you care" and "Mamie is Mimi"are vintage Styne, and the lyrics are witty, stylish and fun. The show ends on a delightful period note, "Keeping cool with Coolidge". Here's Channing in her prime, before she descended into self-parody, with a supporting cast of attractive performers. The mono recording has a vintage Broadway feeling that is totally appropriate. **MPK**

New review

Gypsy 1959 Broadway Cast (with Ethel Merman, Jack Klugman, Sandra Church, Jacqueline Mayro, Karen Moore, Lane Bradbury and Paul Wallace) / **Milton Rosenstock.**
Columbia Ⓜ CK32607 (48 minutes: AAD).

Gypsy 1973 London Cast (with Angela Lansbury, Bonnie Langford, Helen Raye, Barrie Ingham, Zan Charisse, Debbie Bowen, Andrew Norman, Valerie Walsh, Kelly Wilson and Judy Cannon) / **Richard Leonard**.
RCA Victor Ⓜ 60571-2 (52 minutes: ADD).

Ostensibly the story of the rise of striptease legend Gypsy Rose Lee, but in fact concentrating on the personality of her archetypal stage mother, *Gypsy* is one of the great Broadway musicals of all time, representing the finest achievement of veteran stage and screen composer Jule Styne and a significant staging post in the career of lyricist Stephen Sondheim, soon to be established as a major composer in his own right. The original cast album is one of the finest ever made. From the raucous excitement of the pit band in the most thrilling Broadway overture ever, through to the lacerating honesty of Merman's final number, "Rose's turn", the show represents Broadway at its most compelling. Every song presents a new facet of the characters – "Some people" and "Everything's coming up roses" reveal the mother's driving and indomitable ambition for her daughters, and they respond in kind – "If mama was married" is a cynical look at their show business life. The rest of the largely unknown cast is excellent. Paul Wallace's touching "All I need is the girl" is just one of many highlights. In the absence of this version, the London edition, 14 years later, would take pride of place. Angela Lansbury gives a triumphant performance as a slightly more intelligent, but no less driven, no less overpowering Rose and there's the definitive, horrifyingly competent child star, Bonnie Langford's Baby June. "You gotta have a gimmick" for a trio of tired strippers is as good here as on the Broadway cast album. In the end, however, Broadway pizazz just wins over London élan and brio – but only just. **MPK**

Hallelujah, Baby! 1967 **Broadway Cast** (with Leslie Uggams, Robert Hooks, Allen Case and Lillian Hayman) **/ Buster Davis.**
Sony Broadway Ⓔ SK48218 (48 minutes: ADD).

The book of *Hallelujah, Baby!* follows a similar line to *Love Life*: the principal actors never age though the story round them advances 60 years – years here that chronicle the fortunes of a group of black entertainers. It seems that the show ran into an inordinate amount of trouble during production, but this CD preserves a set of uncommonly fine performances sensationally well recorded. Leslie Uggams, another winner in composer Jule Styne's line-up of leading ladies, is the girl looking for her destiny alongside the two men in her life. An introspective trio, "Talking to yourself", brings the three of them together as they try to sort out their feelings for each other and the greater cause of black rights. It's a rare moment of calm in a clamorous score that misses some of the opportunities for variety given the differing styles in music over the period. The cast often give more than their material offers, no one more so than Lillian Hayman, a quintessential black mama who wonders where her daughter's talent came from in the number "I don't know where she got it". Peter Matz's orchestrations are as much of an attraction as Styne's music, beginning with an overture that carries all the expectancy of a great show to come. Although *Hallelujah, Baby!* isn't another *Gypsy* or *Funny Girl* it was the best of Styne's last group of Broadway shows, apart from *Bar Mitzvah Boy*, his West End collaboration with Don Black. **AE**

New review
Overtures, Volumes 1 and 2. **National Symphony Orchestra / Jack Everly.**
TER VIP Series Ⓔ CDVIR8318/9 (two discs, only available separately: 60 and 51 minutes: DDD).
CDVIR8318, "Everything's Coming Up Roses" – Gypsy, High Button Shoes, Gentlemen Prefer Blondes, Two On the Aisle, Hazel Flagg, Bells Are Ringing, Do-Re-Mi, Subways Are for Sleeping, Funny Girl, Fade Out-Fade In, Hallelujah Baby!, Sugar. *CDVIR8319, "I'm the Greatest Star!"* – Funny Girl, Darling of the Day, Look to the Lilies, Bells Are Ringing, One Night Stand, Arturo Ui, Say Darling, Gypsy, Funny Girl, Bells Are Ringing.

The orchestral sound of Jule Styne's shows was nothing if not brash. Where that brashness was supported by strong melody the result was several outstandingly successful shows (*Gentlemen Prefer Blondes, Bells Are Ringing, Gypsy* and *Funny Girl*) and some outstanding hit songs ("Diamonds are a girl's best friend", "Long before I knew you", "The party's over", Everything's coming up roses", "People" and "Don't rain on my parade"). Elsewhere there seems to have been all too little behind the brashness, and Styne suffered his share of shows that achieved no more than short runs. Yet this imaginative collection serves splendidly to give a potted account of the output of one of Broadway's major creators of the post-War period, and there are times when one does indeed sense an unjustly neglected score. Such, for instance, would seem to be *Darling of the Day*, a rather less brash than usual score for a piece that starred Vincent Price as a painter thought to be dead, and earned Patricia Routledge a Tony award. Its Overture, moreover, demonstrates the huge amount of trouble taken by conductor Jack Everly to restore performance material for some of the tracks. Since we are given both the theatre and film overtures for *Bells Are Ringing, Gypsy* and *Funny Girl*, there is enough of Styne's major numbers to balance the less familiar and ensure all his admirers rewarding listening. **AML**

Also available:
Bar Mitzvah Boy (1978 London Cast) Sony SMK53498
Gentlemen Prefer Blondes (1995 Broadway Cast) DRG DRGCD94762
Gypsy (1990 Broadway Cast) Nonesuch 79239-2
One Night Stand (1980 Broadway Cast) Original Cast OCR9366
Prettybelle (1971 Broadway Cast) Varèse Sarabande VSD5439
Some Like it Hot (1992 London Cast) First Night OCRCD6028

Sir Arthur Sullivan
1842-1900 England

William Schwenck Gilbert
1836-1911 England

London-born Arthur Sullivan was educated at the Chapel Royal, the Royal College of Music and Leipzig Conservatory. He headed for a career in serious music – and through his life he attempted to return to it, especially at the behest of Queen Victoria. But the public preferred his comic operas to such elevated opuses as *The Golden Legend*. His first collaboration with the acerbic-tongued William S. Gilbert was the short comic masterpiece *Trial By Jury* (1875). There quickly followed *The Sorcerer* (1877), *HMS Pinafore* (1878) *The Pirates of Penzance* (1880), *Iolanthe* (1882), *Princess Ida* (1884), *The Mikado* (1885), *Ruddigore* (1887), *The Yeomen of the Guard* (1888) and *The Gondoliers* (1889). After this incredible run of success, the partnership was dissolved over the price of a carpet. Although they came together again for *Utopia Limited* (1893) and *The Grand Duke* (1896) the magic was gone. Both wrote forgettable pieces with other collaborators, but their enduring work was done together. Their works are the most important, most enjoyable, most revivable shows of the nineteenth century – and the most influential.

The Gondoliers David Fieldsend (ten) Marco Palmieri; **Alan Oke** (bar) Giuseppe Palmieri; **Lesley Echo Ross** (sop) Gianetta; **Regina Hanley** (sop) Tessa; **Richard Suart** (bar) Duke of Plaza-Toro; **Jill Pert** (contr) Duchess of Plaza-Toro; **Elizabeth Woollett** (sop) Casilda; **Philip Creasy** (bar) Luiz; **D'Oyly Carte Opera Chorus and Orchestra / John Pryce-Jones**.
TER Ⓔ CDTER2 1187 (two discs: 109 minutes: DDD). Disc also includes *Overture di ballo*.

With its Venetian setting and an appropriately sunny score, *The Gondoliers* has always been on everyone's shortlist of G&S favourites. It is the most consistently joyous and tuneful score of Sullivan's maturity, not only in the shorter numbers but in a divine opening sequence lasting some 20 minutes and a superbly developed Act 1 finale. This 1991 TER recording by the revived D'Oyly Carte Opera Company admirably reflects all the virtues in a performance of lively tempos and lightness of touch under the baton of John Pryce-Jones. John Rath is an especially agreeable Don Alhambra, giving "I stole the prince" and "There lived a king" real depth and character. Jill Pert is a slightly light-voiced but imposing Duchess of Plaza-Toro, while Richard Suart contributes to the role of the Duke the sort of fine characterization and admirably clear articulation that has made him the leading performer of Gilbert and Sullivan patter roles of the present day. The team of principals is led by an appropriately young quartet of lovers, who put across such numbers as "Take a pair of sparkling eyes" and the quartet "In a contemplative fashion" with agreeable freshness. This *Gondoliers* is by far the most modern available and should suit all but those who demand Gilbert's complete dialogue, for which they must go to the 1961 D'Oyly Carte recording on Decca's London label (see below). TER include a delightful bonus in the form of Sullivan's 1870 *Overture di ballo*, complete with a section that Sullivan later excised. **AML**

The Grand Duke John Reed (bar) Grand Duke Rudolph; **Meston Reid** (ten) Ernest Dummkopf; **Kenneth Sandford** (bar) Ludwig; **Michael Rayner** (bar) Dr Tannhauser; **John Ayldon** (bass) Prince of Monte Carlo; **Jon Ellison** (bar) Ben Hashbaz; **James Conroy-Ward** (ten) Herald; **Barbara Lilley** (sop) Princess of Monte Carlo; **Lyndsie Holland** (contr) Baroness von Krakenfeldt; **Julia Goss** (sop) Julia Jellicoe; **Jane Metcalfe** (mez) Lisa; **Patricia Leonard** (contr) Elsa; **Anne Egglestone** (sop) Gretchen; **Beti Lloyd-Jones** (mez) Bertha; **Glynis Prendergast** (sop) Olga; **D'Oyly Carte Opera Chorus; Royal Philharmonic Orchestra / Royston Nash;** [a]**Philharmonia Orchestra / Sir Charles Mackerras**.
London Ⓜ 436 813-2LM2 (two discs: 119 minutes: ADD/[a]DDD). Disc also includes *Henry VIII* – March and Graceful Dance. *Overture di Ballo*[a].

The Grand Duke was the last Gilbert and Sullivan comic opera and the least successful. The blame has generally been placed more at the door of the librettist for a somewhat weak and contrived plot about a theatrical company who seek to take over power from a European Grand Duke. Though Sullivan, too, was well below his best, anybody who loves this composer's work should seize the opportunity given by this 1976 recording to sample a score that possesses some typical Sullivan delights. There are attractive dance melodies and, in "When you find you're a broken-down critter", a comic song reminiscent of the "Nightmare song" in *Iolanthe*. This is sung by John Reed, who with fellow D'Oyly Carte stalwarts Kenneth Sandford and Michael Rayner turns in a typically reliable performance. Not all the voices in the D'Oyly Carte company of the time were of the best, though, and one of the most attractive numbers – the "Roulette song" – suffers in this respect. On the other hand, Meston Reid brings an especially attractive tenor voice to the role of theatrical manager Ernest Dummkopf, and Jane Metcalfe is no less charming as the company's comedienne Lisa. Perhaps the score's musical highlight is the dramatic and touching Act 2 solo, "Broken ev'ry promise plighted", for the troupe's leading lady Julia Jellicoe, and this is most expressively sung here by Julia Goss. The inclusion of some of Sullivan's most charming orchestral music as a filler adds to the appeal of the set.   **AML**

HMS Pinafore **Richard Suart** (bar) Sir Joseph Porter; **Felicity Palmer** (mez) Little Buttercup; **Rebecca Evans** (sop) Josephine; **Thomas Allen** (bar) Captain Corcoran; **Michael Schade** (ten) Ralph Rackstraw; **Donald Adams** (bass) Dick Deadeye; **Richard Van Allan** (bass) Bill Bobstay; **Valerie Seymour** (sop) Hebe; **Welsh National Opera Chorus and Orchestra / Sir Charles Mackerras**.
Telarc Ⓟ CD80374 (74 minutes: DDD).

Of all the Gilbert and Sullivan comic operas, *HMS Pinafore* perhaps has the most uncomplicated appeal, with its comic situations, its unpretentious and attractive score, a cast of likeable characters (even including Dick Deadeye), and a popular catch-phrase in "What never?". This 1994 Telarc recording captures the work to perfection. Right from the overture, with its deliciously shaped *andante* section, this is inspired music making. Mackerras keeps the music bubbling along throughout, yet without ever a hint of rushing. The lighter numbers such as "Never mind the why and wherefore" gladden the heart, and yet he also gives full weight to the tender moments, caressing every detail of Sullivan's masterly orchestration. Felicity Palmer's Little Buttercup oozes plumpness and pleasure, while Thomas Allen's Captain Corcoran provides a superb serenade, "Fair moon to thee I sing". Rebecca Evans's Josephine may be a shade lacking in colour, but she pairs up agreeably with Michael Schade, whose Ralph Rackstraw is a particularly elegant characterization. Not least, Richard Suart's Sir Joseph Porter provides as stylish a demonstration of patter singing as one will find on disc, and Donald Adams's Dick Deadeye has a freshness belying his 40-odd years singing the role. Committed choral singing and splendidly clear sound contribute to a recording that is sheer delight from first note to last. The fact that the score is absolutely complete on a single disc is merely an extra bonus, and only those who demand Gilbert's complete dialogue need look elsewhere to London's 1959 D'Oyly Carte recording (see "Also available" below).   **AML**

Iolanthe **Regina Hanley** (mez) Iolanthe; **Philip Blake-Jones** (bar) Strephon; **Jill Pert** (contr) Queen of the Fairies; **Elizabeth Woollett** (sop) Phyllis; **Richard Suart** (bar) Lord Chancellor; **Lawrence Richard** (bass) Earl of Mountararat; **Philip Creasy** (ten) Earl Tolloller; **John Rath** (bass) Private Willis; **D'Oyly Carte Opera Chorus and Orchestra / John Pryce-Jones**.
TER Ⓟ CDTER2 1188 (two discs: 100 minutes: DDD). Also includes *Thespis* – ballet music.

Iolanthe is one of the most roundly enjoyable of the Gilbert and Sullivan works, with a well-constructed and humorous libretto and a score that admirably balances the light and dainty music for the fairies against the rousing music for the peers. This 1991 recording by the revived D'Oyly Carte Opera Company makes a most attractive recommendation, with Sullivan's delicate scoring coming through with especial clarity. In the hands of John Pryce-Jones the whole score trips along in sprightly fashion, with a lightness of touch missing from some earlier versions. The team of singers offers some delightfully fresh-voiced young performers in the lighter roles, and there are rich contributions from John Rath with his imposingly shaped sentry's song and Jill Pert as an imposing Queen of Fairies. Not least there is the Lord Chancellor of Richard Suart, who manages to combine impeccably clear articulation with first-rate characterization in an outstanding "Nightmare song". This recording has the added interest of the only recording of a song for Strephon cut shortly after the 1882 premiere and an intriguing bonus in some recently rediscovered ballet music for the lost G&S work *Thespis*. Only if the dialogue is essential need one consider the 1960 London recording (see "Also available" below). **AML**

The Mikado Donald Adams (bass) The Mikado; **Anthony Rolfe Johnson** (ten) Nanki-Poo; **Richard Suart** (bass) Ko-Ko; **Richard Van Allan** (bass) Pooh-Bah; **Nicholas Folwell** (bar) Pish-Tush; **Marie McLaughlin** (sop) Yum-Yum; **Anne Howells** (mez) Pitti-Sing; **Janice Watson** (sop) Peep-Bo; **Felicity Palmer** (sop) Katisha; **Welsh National Opera Chorus and Orchestra / Sir Charles Mackerras**.
Telarc Ⓕ CD80284 (79 minutes: DDD).

The Mikado has always been the most widely enjoyed of Gilbert and Sullivan's works, appreciated for the satire of its decidedly anglicized Japanese setting and for a range of comic characters that has made the work most readily exportable. To accommodate the work on a single CD, Telarc have had to dispense with the overture (which was anyway put together by one of Sullivan's assistants) and make a couple of minor snips. Unless that is a drawback, this 1991 recording offers a clear recommendation. Sir Charles Mackerras's love of Sullivan's music has been an enduring feature of his long career, and he brings out not only the delicacies of Sullivan's scoring but also many points of humorous detail such as the 'short, sharp shock' in the trio "I am so proud" and the chilling orchestral shriek in "The criminal cried". His generally brisk tempos are applied to sparkling effect, though he gives Richard Suart space to produce his usual finely tuned performance as Ko-Ko. Anthony Rolfe Johnson shades his voice to delicious effect as Nanki-Poo, and Marie McLaughlin is a charming Yum-Yum, without stealing the female honours away from Anne Howells's ravishing Pitti-Sing or Felicity Palmer's formidably imposing Katisha. Richard Van Allan is an appropriately pompous Pooh-Bah, while Donald Adams brings to the title-role over 30 years' experience in the part and a well-practiced and blood-curdling laugh. For an alternative *Mikado*, the 1962 Sadler's Wells version on the Classics for Pleasure label (see "Also available" below) still has much to offer, with an refreshingly individual Ko-Ko in Clive Revill. **AML**

Patience Elsie Morison (sop) Patience; **George Baker** (bar) Bunthorne; **John Cameron** (bar) Grosvenor; **Marjorie Thomas** (contr) Lady Angela; **Heather Harper** (sop) Lady Ella; **Elizabeth Harwood** (sop) Lady Saphir; **Monica Sinclair** (contr) Lady Jane; **John Shaw** (bar) Colonel Calverley; **Trevor Anthony** (bar) Major Murgatroyd; **Alexander Young** (ten) Duke of Dunstable; **Glyndebourne Festival Chorus; Pro Arte Orchestra / Sir Malcolm Sargent**.
EMI Ⓜ CMS7 64406-2 (two discs: 113 minutes: ADD). Disc also includes *Irish Symphony*.

Patience was a satire on the aesthetic movement, of which Oscar Wilde was a prominent member. Rather as with *Iolanthe*, it offers an attractive contrast between the pastel shades of the music for the aesthetes and the rousing military music for the dragoon guards. Unless one insists on the most modern recorded sound, EMI's 1962 recording provides a fine recommendation, being one of the best in the so-called 'Glyndebourne' series under Sir Malcolm Sargent. The Glyndebourne Festival Chorus provides a most imposing set of love-sick maidens and dragoons, and Sargent's love of the music shows through in the fine shaping of the score, the concerted items being especially telling. The singers were chosen from the leading British singers of the time, with Elsie Morison's Patience and John Cameron's Grosvenor just two examples of the well-characterized and finely sung performances. Especially worthy of favourable mention is the Bunthorne of George Baker, who when well into his seventies was still the sprightliest and most expressive singer of the patter songs around. What additionally gives this version the edge over other versions is the inclusion of Sullivan's delightfully lyrical symphony – a most generous and enjoyable fill-up. The 1961 London recording (see "Also available" below) is the only one to include Gilbert's dialogue. **AML**

The Pirates of Penzance Donald Adams (bass) Pirate King; **John Mark Ainsley** (ten) Frederic; **Richard Suart** (bar) Major-General Stanley; **Rebecca Evans** (sop) Mabel; **Nicholas Folwell** (bar) Samuel; **Richard Van Allan** (bass) Police Sergeant; **Gillian Knight** (mez) Ruth; **Jenevora Williams** (mez) Kate; **Julie Gossage** (mez) Edith; **Welsh National Opera Chorus and Orchestra / Sir Charles Mackerras**.
Telarc Ⓕ CD80353 (78 minutes: DDD).

The Pirates of Penzance is one of the more immediately enjoyable of G&S works. The notion of a maiden mistakenly apprenticed to a pirate (instead of a pilot) and forced to stay until her 21st birthday (which, because she was born on leap-year-day, is in her eighties) has always appealed. The music is no less immediately accessible in such numbers as the coloratura waltz "Poor wandering one", the Major General's song, and the numbers for the comic policemen. This recording is not quite complete, with the overture and a couple of minor passages sacrificed in the interest of getting it all on one well-filled CD. But, under the loving direction of Sir Charles Mackerras, this version has a sparkle missing from its predecessors. Singing, orchestral playing and choral work alike are of a particularly high standard, with the double choruses especially joyous affairs. Among the principals, Donald Adams, Gillian Knight and Richard Suart all have experience as members of the D'Oyly Carte Opera Company and know this repertory intimately, and they are ably supported by hand-picked principals, notably John Mark Ainsley as a well-characterised and elegantly sung Frederic, Richard Van Allan as a superb Sergeant of Police, and Rebecca Evans as a tender Mabel. If you want the work complete and with dialogue, London's 1968 recording (see "Also available" below) still comes up extremely well. **AML**

Princess Ida   **Kenneth Sandford** (bar) King Hildebrand; **Philip Potter** (ten) Hilarion; **David Palmer** (ten) Cyril; **Jeffrey Skitch** (bar) Florian; **John Reed** (bar) King Gama; **Donald Adams** (bass) Arac; **Anthony Raffell** (bar) Guron; **George Cook** (bass) Scynthius; **Elizabeth Harwood** (sop) Princess Ida; **Christine Palmer** (contr) Lady Blanche; **Ann Hood** (sop) Lady Psyche; **Valerie Masterson** (sop) Melissa; **D'Oyly Carte Opera Chorus; Royal Philharmonic Orchestra / Sir Malcolm Sargent**; [a]**Philharmonia Orchestra / Sir Charles Mackerras**.
London Ⓜ 436 810-2LM2 (two discs: 129 minutes: ADD/[a]DDD). Disc also includes *Pineapple Poll*[a].

Princess Ida deals somewhat uneasily with the subject of feminism and has never been among the most popular of Gilbert and Sullivan's works. Sullivan composed it whilst in considerable pain, and the results lack his usual ebullience whilst containing some delightful numbers with almost chamber-like textures. For this 1965 recording Decca reinforced the D'Oyly Carte Opera Company of the time with two major imports. Sir Malcolm Sargent was one, and he offers a broadly lyrical, somewhat over-spacious, interpretation, emphasizing the work's charm and the dramatic nature of the music for the title character. For this role, Decca imported the soprano Elizabeth Harwood, and she sings quite ravishingly, producing an especially beautiful sound in "The world is but a broken toy". From the regular D'Oyly Carte company, Kenneth Sandford and John Reed play the rival kings Hildebrand and Gama with typical reliability, the latter bringing an appropriately croaky voice to the role of the disagreeable King Gama. Philip Potter, David Palmer and Jeffrey Skitch make a well-balanced and agreeably voiced trio of male friends, their sequence of lighthearted numbers as they raid Princess Ida's castle in Act 2 proving predictably engaging. Supporting roles are well taken by Donald Adams as the leader of Gama's war-mongering sons, Valerie Masterson early in her career, and Christine Palmer as the formidable Lady Blanche, though sadly deprived of her solo "Come, mighty must!". If both work and performance lack some sparkle, there is compensation in the generous fill-up of the effervescent *Pineapple Poll* ballet score, which Charles Mackerras compiled from Sullivan's melodies. **AML**

Ruddigore   **Marilyn Hill Smith** (sop) Rose Maybud; **Gordon Sandison** (bar) Sir Ruthven Murgatroyd; **Joan Davies** (sop) Dame Hannah; **Alexandra Hann** (sop) Zorah; **Linda Ormiston** (mez) Mad Margaret; **John Ayldon** (bass) Old Adam; **David Hillman** (ten) Richard Dauntless; **Harold Innocent** (bar) Sir Despard Murgatroyd; **Thomas Lawlor** (bar) Sir Roderick Murgatroyd; **New Sadler's Wells Opera Chorus and Orchestra / Simon Phipps**.
TER Ⓕ CDTER2 1128 (two discs: 89 minutes: DDD).

If *Ruddigore* has never been considered in the front rank of G&S works, it has its delightful moments in the nautical music for Richard Dauntless, the charming contributions of the chorus of bridesmaids, the imposing "When the night wind howls" for Sir Roderick Murgatroyd and his family ghosts, and the zany numbers for Sir Despard Murgatroyd and his companion Mad Margaret. The work was subjected to cuts and changes after its first performance and again when it was taken into the repertory of the D'Oyly Carte Opera Company in the 1920s – long after the deaths of its creators. For this 1986 centenary performance the New Sadler's Wells Opera Company restored music from the autograph score, making this a more complete and authentic version than any other. It is well cast, too, with Joan Davies a rich contralto Dame Hannah, Linda Ormiston a richly characterized Mad Margaret, Marilyn Hill Smith a delightfully pert Rose Maybud, David Hillman an elegant Richard, and Harold Innocent a delightfully lugubrious Sir Despard. This is certainly the most readily recommendable *Ruddigore*, though the 1962 London recording (see "Also available" below) may appeal for the addition of the one-act operetta *Cox and Box* as an attractive fill-up. **AML**

The Sorcerer Donald Adams (bass) Sir Marmaduke Pointdextre; **David Palmer** (ten) Alexis; **Alan Styler** (bar) Dr Daly; **Stanley Riley** (bass) Notary; **John Reed** (bar); John Wellington Wells; **Christine Palmer** (contr) Lady Sangazure; **Valerie Masterson** (sop) Aline; **Jean Allister** (mez) Mrs Partlet; **Ann Hood** (sop) Constance; **D'Oyly Carte Opera Chorus; Royal Philharmonic Orchestra / Isidore Godfrey**.
London Ⓜ 436 807-2LM2 (two discs: 123 minutes: ADD). Disc also includes *The Zoo*.

The Sorcerer tells of the topsy-turvy results that occur from a whole village being mistakenly administered a love potion. It is the earliest full-length G&S work to survive, and it shows the collaborators' inspiration not yet at fullest throttle. Yet in the character of the village sorcerer John Wellington Wells the piece possesses one of Gilbert's most attractively etched characters, and for him Sullivan provided some fine patter music, which is excellently done here by John Reed. The principal tenor and soprano also have some readily appealing numbers, with Alexis taken by David Palmer (elegant in the waltz song "It is not love") and Aline sweetly sung by Valerie Masterson (delightful in "Oh, happy young heart"). Other principal roles are the village vicar Dr Daly – engagingly sung by Alan Styler – and the elderly Lady Sangazure and Sir Marmaduke, whose splendid minuet is done by Christine Palmer and the ever-reliable Donald Adams. With the D'Oyly Carte Opera Company's long-time musical director Isidore Godfrey sustaining a buoyant performance, this 1966 recording does the work full justice. The Sullivan one-acter *The Zoo* (without Gilbert) is rather spoilt by intrusive sound effects and a pretentious and unnecessary narration; but it makes an intriguing novelty filler. **AML**

Utopia Limited Kenneth Sandford (bar) King Paramount; **John Reed** (bar) Scaphio; **John Ayldon** (bass) Phantis; **Jon Ellison** (bar) Tarara; **Michael Buchan** (bar) Calynx; **James Conroy-Ward** (ten) Lord Dramaleigh; **Meston Reid** (ten) Captain FitzBattleaxe; **John Broad** (bass) Captain Corcoran; **Michael Rayner** (bar) Mr Goldbury; **Colin Wright** (ten) Sir Bailey Barre; **David Porter** (bar) Mr Blushington; **Pamela Field** (sop) Princess Zora; **Julia Goss** (sop) Princess Kalyba; **Lyndsie Holland** (contr) Lady Sophy; **Rosalind Griffiths** (sop) Phylla; **D'Oyly Carte Opera Chorus; Royal Philharmonic Orchestra / Royston Nash**.
London Ⓜ 436 816-2LM2 (two discs: 139 minutes: ADD). Also includes *Imperial March*. Overtures – *Macbeth*; *Marmion*. *Victoria and Merrie England* – Suite No. 1.

The notes accompanying this 1975 recording remind us that *Utopia Limited* was the most extravagantly mounted of all the Gilbert and Sullivan collaborations. Far from satirizing a single British institution, Gilbert this time had a go at the Establishment in general. But sheer size of cast and opulence of staging could not save a work that showed that the spark between the partners now flickered spasmodically. Yet, if overall there is little of the old fluency, there is much that is well worth hearing. Sullivan's scoring is as delicate as ever, and there is some graceful drawing-room music and some suitably charming passages for the languorous island maidens. The major successes include a delightful duet for the young Princesses Nekaya and Kalyba, the leading tenor's Act 2 aria, "A tenor, all singers above", and the scene in which Utopian King Paramount and his advisors perform a take-off of a minstrel show. This was a particular hit of the original production, and for this recording the effect has been highlighted by the inclusion of a few lines of dialogue. The work is well performed by the D'Oyly Carte company, and the recording should certainly be heard by G&S fans – not least for the bonus of some 35 minutes of Sullivan's independent orchestral music. **AML**

The Yeomen of the Guard Gareth Rhys-Davies (bar) Sir Richard Cholmondeley; **Neill Archer** (ten) Colonel Fayrfax; **Donald Adams** (bass) Sergeant Meryll; **Richard Suart** (bar) Jack Point; **Donald Maxwell** (bass) Shadbolt; **Alwyn Mellor** (sop) Elsie; **Pamela Helen Stephens** (mez) Phoebe; **Felicity Palmer** (contr) Dame Carruthers; **Clare O'Neill** (sop) Kate.

Trial By Jury Rebecca Evans (sop) Plaintiff; **Barry Banks** (ten) Defendant; **Richard Suart** (bar) Judge; **Peter Savidge** (bar) Counsel; **Gareth Rhys-Davies** (bar) Foreman; **Welsh National Opera Chorus and Orchestra / Sir Charles Mackerras**.

Telarc Ⓕ CD80284 (two discs: 121 minutes: DDD).

Between them, *The Yeomen of the Guard* and *Trial By Jury* contain all that is best in Sullivan's music for the theatre. In the former, there is some of his more serious and ambitious writing, with an imposing overture, a solemn funeral march and genuine emotion in the tale of the love-wracked jester. In the latter, Sullivan is at his most consistently light-hearted and engaging. All of this is brought out in this 1995 coupling. Sir Charles Mackerras paces the music impeccably, and he has assured contributions from such stalwart performers as Donald Adams, Felicity Palmer and Richard Suart. The last-named may be a light voiced Learned Judge; but in *The Yeomen* it is his performance that stands out above all. His handling of some snatches of dialogue is masterly, and his singing of "Oh, a private buffoon" displays impeccable clarity of diction and a marvellous way with Gilbert's lines. In *The Yeomen of the Guard* Neill Archer and Alwyn Mellor make an admirable romantic couple as Fairfax and Elsie, while Pamela Helen Stephens and Barry Banks provide able support in the two works. The 1992 Philips recording of *The Yeomen of the Guard* includes Gilbert's dialogue in sensibly abridged form, while London's 1964 D'Oyly Carte coupling of the same two works (see "Also available" below) still has much to offer. **AML**

Also available:

The Gondoliers (D'Oyly Carte/Godfrey) London 425 177-2LM2

The Gondoliers (Glyndebourne/Sargent) EMI CMS7 64394-2

The Gondoliers/Trial by Jury (1927 D'Oyly Carte/Norris) Pearl GEMMCDS9961

HMS Pinafore (D'Oyly Carte/Godfrey) London 414 283-2LM2

HMS Pinafore (New Sadler's Wells/Phipps) TER CDTER2 1150

HMS Pinafore/The Mikado (1930 D'Oyly Carte/Sargent) Happy Days CDHD253/4

HMS Pinafore/Trial by Jury (Glyndebourne/Sargent) EMI CMS7 64397-2

Iolanthe (D'Oyly Carte/Pryce-Jones) London 414 145-2LM2

Iolanthe (Glyndebourne/Sargent) EMI CMS7 64400-2

The Mikado (D'Oyly Carte/Nash) London 425 190-2LM2

The Mikado (D'Oyly Carte/Pryce-Jones) TER CDTER2 1178

The Mikado/Iolanthe (Sadler's Wells/Faris) Classics for Pleasure CD-CFP4730

Patience (D'Oyly Carte/Edwards) TER CDTER2 1213

Patience (D'Oyly Carte/Godfrey) London 425 193-2LM2

Patience/The Gondoliers (1930 D'Oyly Carte/Sargent) Arabesque Z8095-2

The Pirates of Penzance (D'Oyly Carte/Godfrey) London 425 196-2LM2

The Pirates of Penzance (D'Oyly Carte/Pryce-Jones) TER CDTER2 1177

The Pirates of Penzance (Glyndebourne/Sargent) EMI CMS7 64409-2

The Pirates of Penzance/Ruddigore (1929 D'Oyly Carte/Sargent) Happy Days CDHD255/6

Ruddigore/Cox and Box (D'Oyly Carte/Godfrey) London 417 355-2LM2

Ruddigore (Glyndebourne/Sargent) EMI CMS7 64412-2

The Yeomen of the Guard (ASMF/Marriner) Philips 438 138-2PH2

The Yeomen of the Guard (D'Oyly Carte/Edwards) TER CDTER2 1195

The Yeomen of the Guard (Glyndebourne/Sargent) EMI CMS7 64415-2

The Yeomen of the Guard/Trial By Jury (D'Oyly Carte/Godfrey/Sargent) London 417 358-2LM2

Bernard J. Taylor

Wuthering Heights 1991 Studio Cast (with Lesley Garrett, Dave Willetts, Bonnie Langford, Clive Carter, James Staddon and Sharon Campbell); **Cantorum Choir; Philharmonia Orchestra / Nic Raine**.

Silva Screen Ⓕ SONGCD904 (64 minutes: DDD).

Not the Cliff Richard vehicle, but a 1991 work by Bernard Taylor which has yet to see the light of day as a stage production. Despite its enduring fascination as a source of inspiration for screenwriters, composers and songwriters, Emily Brontë's masterwork is a tricky subject for a musical. Do you go for the Gothic undercurrents or emphasize the intense drama of the romance at the core of the story? Inevitably, perhaps, both Taylor and, by all accounts, the new Cliff Richard production fall between the two stools. As a lyricist, Taylor is no Tim Rice: collectors of mundane rhyming couplets will have a field day with this text. But his lush score does encompass a variety of textures, from the stirring choral work in the Act 1 finale to the cracking pace of "The Gypsy waltz", and is carried along by a momentum which, within its limitations, certainly suggests the driving forces of nature at work in the book. There is a particularly pleasing duet between Cathy and Nellie Dean, "One rules my heart", in which Cathy expresses the dilemma presented by her unbreakable bond with Heathcliff. Of course, Taylor is helped considerably by the exuberance of an expert cast and the playing of the Philharmonia. Certainly, Dave Willetts is a more convincing prospect as Heathcliff than Cliff Richard, and here he interprets the role with a variation on the mixture of pathos and vengeful bitterness he brought to *The Phantom of the Opera* ("Let her live", "I will have my vengeance" and "Heathcliff's lament"). Lesley Garrett as Cathy runs the gamut of an emotional series of ballads ("He's gone" and "I belong to the Earth" for example) with utter conviction. Was there ever a more enthusiastic or committed performer? There is also able support from Bonnie Langford as Isabella and Sharon Campbell as Nellie Dean. A polished curiosity for collectors.   **PF**

Also available:
Nosferatu the Vampire (1994 Studio Cast) Dress Circle NVDC2
Success (1995 Studio Cast) First Stage DCSC1

Harry Tierney
1890-1965 USA

After studying at the Virgil School of Music in New York, and touring as a concert pianist, Tierney worked in music publishing as staff pianist and composer. He contributed songs for revues, including four editions of the popular *Ziegfeld Follies*, and wrote his own complete show, *Irene* (1919), which became Broadway's longest-running show with 670 performances. The London run began in 1920 and clocked-up 399 performances. *Irene* made a star of Edith Day, for whom Tierney had conceived the songs. It was filmed in 1940 and revived – albeit with a much-altered score – in 1973. His 1927 show, *Rio Rita*, was one of the first Broadway shows to be made into a movie in 1929. Encouraged by its success, Tierney moved to Hollywood where he wrote songs for films, but was unable to recapture the popularity of *Rita*.

Rio Rita – see Collections: **Lilac Time**

Pete Townshend
b. 1945 England

Founder member of the rock group The Who, Peter Dennis Blandford Townshend was born in London the son of a professional saxophonist. He played banjo with trumpet-player John Entwistle in trad-jazz groups while at school. Together with Roger Daltrey and Keith Moon, they formed The Who. Townshend wrote the band's early hits, "My generation" (1965), "Substitute" (1966) and "Pictures of Lily" (1967). Their 1967 album, "The Who Sell Out", contained a 'mini-opera' entitled "Rael", which proved to be a prelude to a much more ambitious undertaking, the full-length rock-opera *Tommy* (1969). The work was performed by the band on tour and was first staged in 1973. Ken Russell's film version, starring Daltrey, Tina Turner and Elton John, appeared in 1975, and the show was revived on Broadway in 1994, for which Townshend contributed a new song, "I believe my own eyes". Townshend planned another rock opera, *Lifehouse*, which was shelved, although songs originally written for it found their way into *Quadrophenia* (1973 – filmed in 1979). He returned to the rock-opera format with *Psychoderelict* (1993).

Tommy 1993 Broadway Cast (with Michael Cerveris, Marcia Mitzman, Jonathan Dokuchitz, Cheryl Freeman, Donnie Kehr, Paul Kandel, Anthony Barille, Bill Buell and Sherie Scott) **/ Joseph Church**.
RCA Victor Ⓕ 09026 61874-2 (two discs: 94 minutes: DDD). Additional music by John Entwistle and Keith Moon.

The ongoing evolution of what is, perhaps, the definitive rock opera is one of the most satisfying stories in modern musical theatre. From concept album (1969), to film (1975), to concert performances (throughout the 1970s), to a West End production (relatively unsuccessful, in 1979) and finally to rebirth as an outstanding Broadway and West End production in the mid-1990s, *Tommy* has simply grown in stature rather than been marooned in its own time like so many other works in this genre. Pete Townshend's guitar-driven score contains many passages of rare beauty, not least Tommy's *leitmotif* ("See me, feel me"), and his lyrics have a poetic eloquence which, frankly, makes some of the more populist modern shows pale in comparison. This is the recording of the 1993 production which took Broadway by storm, with a revised book and a barrage of special effects. Masterfully produced by George Martin, the work has a momentum and coherence which are not always achieved in the limited time available for cast recordings. As Tommy, the boy struck deaf, dumb and blind by childhood trauma, who finds his metier and remedy as the "Pinball Wizard", Michael Cerveris heads up a passionate, highly talented ensemble. Equally impressive are Marcia Mitzman as Mrs Walker, who is by turns puzzled ("Do you think it's alright?") and angered ("Smash the mirror") by her child's condition, and Jonathan Dokuchitz as Mr Walker. As the Gypsy, Cheryl Freeman delivers a sultry, grinding "Acid Queen" and there is good support from Paul Kandel as the vile abuser Uncle Ernie ("Fiddle about" and "Tommy's holiday camp"). Ignore the strange 'London' accents of some of the cast and play it loud. Outstanding. **PF**

Also available:
Psychoderelict (1993 Studio Cast) Atlantic 7567 82494-2
Tommy (1975 Film Cast) Polydor 841 121-2
Tommy (Orchestral version, with the LSO) Essential ESSCD029

Jimmy Van Heusen

1913-1990 USA

Edward Chester Babcock was born in New York and composed both for Broadway and Hollywood. He wrote primarily with lyricists Johnny Burke and Sammy Cahn. Bing Crosby and Frank Sinatra introduced many of the hits that streamed from their pens. "It's the dreamer in me" was his first big success (music by Jimmy Dorsey). A Broadway musical *Swingin' the Dream* (1939) followed (lyricist Eddie de Lange). At Paramount Studios he contributed to the Bing Crosby-Bob Hope *Road* series of films. In 1953 it was back to Broadway for *Carnival in Flanders* ("Here's that rainy day" was a hit – the show wasn't). He contributed songs to many of Frank Sinatra's groundbreaking concept albums and in 1954, when Burke fell ill, teamed up with Sammy Cahn. *Three Coins in the Fountain* (1954), *The Tender Trap* (1955) and the complete score of *Robin and the Seven Hoods* (1964) were further Hollywood successes. In 1965 with *Skyscraper* and 1966's *Walking Happy*,Van Heusen visited Broadway for the last time.

Skyscraper 1965 Broadway Cast (with Julie Harris, Peter L. Marshall, Dick O'Neill, Rex Everhart, Charles Nelson Reilly and Nancy Cushman) **/ John Lesko**.
EMI Angel Ⓜ ZDM7 65132-2 (39 minutes: ADD).

Skyscraper is an adaptation of Elmer Rice's successful play *Dream Girl*. "Julie Harris sings" exulted the *New York Herald Tribune* – indeed she had already done so in a screen version of *I Am a Camera*, and a play about marathon dance contests. In the event she proved ideal casting for the feisty role of Georgina, a daydreamer and antique dealer who stands out against the redevelopment of the land on which her house stands. By the end of the show she has married the idealistic architect (Peter L. Marshall) involved with the development. The score was by two of Frank Sinatra's favourite writers, Sammy Cahn and Jimmy Van Heusen, and included some fine songs that sounded as if they had been written for him to sing (and indeed he did). "Everybody

has the right to be wrong" and "I'll only miss her when I think of her" have graduated to an·
independent existence and are typical of the loose-limbed charm of the score. Neglected joys
include "Opposites", Miss Harris's throaty duet with Marshall, and a paean to urban
conservation, "Save that building". The show ran into trouble during full-price previews when a
prominent columnist for the Hearst chain, Dorothy Kilgallen, reviewed the show. As it turned,
out she died in her sleep five days before the show opened. **MPK**

Walking Happy 1966 **Broadway Cast** (with Norman Wisdom, Louise Troy, George Rose, Ed
Bakey, Gordon Dilworth, Lucille Benson, Jane Laughlin, Gretchen van Aken and Sharon
Dierking) **/ Herbert Grossman**.
EMI Angel Ⓜ ZDM7 65133-2 (50 minutes: ADD).

It's always been a mystery that no one has yet been able to bring this musical version of the
perennially popular Harold Brighouse comedy *Hobson's Choice* to London. Perhaps other
commitments prevented the original star, Norman Wisdom, taking the show to London. In
the original play, of course, it is the strong-willed Maggie Hobson that is the principal
character, moulding a shy bootmaker (Will, Wisdom's character) into a husband to be proud
of. With Wisdom as star the emphasis obviously changed – he has seven numbers to the five
in which Louise Troy's Maggie participates. The Cahn/Van Heusen score is a success on many
counts. The songs have charm, immediate appeal and a feeling for the show's period and
location (1880s Lancashire). There's even a clog dance. Troy exudes strength and vulnerability
in "Where was I?" and Wisdom makes the most of his opportunities to exhibit pathos and
charm in "What makes it happen?" and "I don't think I'm in love". The title song (originally
written for an unproduced Fred Astaire film) is irresistible. This is one of the few American
musicals with an English setting that's free of embarrassing mistakes – and it has a fine
musical score, too. **MPK**

Harry Warren
1893-1981 USA

Al Dubin
1891-1945 Switzerland

Born Salvatore Guaragna of Italian parents in Brooklyn, Harry Warren was a self-taught
musician who sang in his local church choir. He began his professional career as a pianist for
silent films at the Vitagraph studios, and had his first hit song, "Rose of the Rio Grande", in
1920 (lyrics by Edgar Leslie). Warren became assistant director of Vitagraph before being
offered a job as a song-plugger for a music publisher. After his song "Home in Pasadena"
(1923 – again with Leslie) was a hit, he became increasingly successful as a songwriter. "I love
my baby, my baby loves me" was another hit in 1926. In 1928 he moved to Remick Music
Corporation, where he teamed up with lyricist Mort Dixon, scoring a hit with "Nagasaki".
Warner Brothers bought the Remick company, precipitating a move to Hollywood for
Warren, where his first assignment was to write six new songs for the film version of Rodgers
and Hart's *Spring is Here* (1930). After working on Broadway for a time, Warren was hired to
collaborate on a ground-breaking new movie which was to feature innovative musical
sequences choreographed by newcomer Busby Berkeley. The result, *42nd Street* (1933), was a
conspicuous success for both men. Warren's songs, including "You're getting to be a habit
with me" and "Shuffle off to Buffalo" were written with lyricist Al Dubin.

Born in Zurich, Dubin arrived in America in 1893, where, like Warren, he was eventually
to find work in song-publishing. Their songwriting partnership flourished during a series of
glorious Depression-era musicals in which their refreshing and witty songs were set off by
Berkeley's sometimes surreal, occasionally outrageous, but always unique visual style. Their
second collaboration, *Gold Diggers of 1933*, for example, opened with Ginger Rogers dressed
as a coin singing "We're in the money". For five years, Dubin and Warren produced a string
of hit songs, including "Keep young and beautiful" (from *Roman Scandals*, 1933), "Boulevard
of broken dreams" (*Moulin Rouge*, 1934), "I only have eyes for you" (*Dames*, 1934) and the
epic "Lullaby of Broadway" (*Gold Diggers of 1935*). But by the end of the decade, Dubin was
exhausted by the demands of Hollywood and Warren began working with other lyricists,
including Johnny Mercer and Mack Gordon (1904-59). In the early 1940s, Gordon and
Warren produced "Chattanooga choo choo" (from *Sun Valley Serenade*, 1941) and "I've got

a gal in Kalamazoo" (*Orchestra Wives*, 1942) among others. In 1946, Warren worked with Mercer on *The Harvey Girls*, for which he wrote the Oscar-winning "On the Atchison, Topeka and the Santa Fe". Warren continued writing songs in the 1950s – "That's amore" for Dean Martin in *The Caddy* (1953) – but suffered a failure with his only Broadway venture, *Shangri-La* (1956). His last film song was the theme for *Satan Never Sleeps* (1962).

The Harvey Girls 1946 **Film Cast** (with Judy Garland, Ray Bolger, Virginia O'Brien and Kenny Baker); **MGM Studio Chorus and Orchestra / Lennie Hayton**.
EMI mono/stereo Ⓔ CDODEON11 (74 minutes: ADD).

The Harvey Girls was a lavish production starring Judy Garland as a waitress for Fred Harvey's chain of restaurants which followed the railroad westward into the heart of America. Composer Harry Warren thought that lyricist Johnny Mercer was the right collaborator for this piece of Americana – Alistair Cooke once described Mercer's lyrics "as little bits of Mark Twain". The *pièce de résistance* of their score was that infectious nine-minute production number "On the Atchison, Topeka and the Santa Fe" which won the Academy Award for best song of 1946; beginning on barroom piano it builds into an ebullient ensemble of singing and dancing that somewhat overshadows the other songs, which are mainly in a plaintive mood. Amongst these are "My intuition" and "In the valley", both beautifully sung by Judy Garland and a trio, "It's a great big world", where she is joined by Virgina O'Brien and Marion Doenges, one of several singers who dubbed for the dancer Cyd Charisse. The inventive "The train must be fed", a witty semi-*parlando* ensemble for the waitresses, is an inventive composition that foreshadows later musical developments. The sound varies throughout but not enough to undermine this joyous concoction.   **AE**

Lullaby of Broadway The Best of Busby Berkeley at Warner Bros. **Original Film Casts** (with Ginger Rogers, Ruby Keeler, Joan Blondell, Winifred Shaw and Dick Powell).
EMI mono Ⓔ CDODEON8 (two discs: 152 minutes: ADD). *Songs from* 42nd Street, Gold Diggers of 1933, Footlight Parade, Wonder Bar, Fashions of 1934, Dames, Gold Diggers of 1935, In Caliente, Gold Diggers of 1937 and Hollywood Hotel.
The Busby Berkeley Album with Judy Blazer, Debbie Shapiro Gravitte, Ann Morrison, Jane Sylvester, Nancy Long, Brent Barrett, Guy Stroman, Stan Chandler, Larry Raben and David Engel; **London Sinfonietta Chorus and Orchestra / John McGlinn**.
EMI Angel Ⓔ CDC5 55189-2 (70 minutes: DDD).
Songs from Gold Diggers of 1933, Gold Diggers of 1935, 42nd Street and Dames.

Those familiar with the stage show *42nd Street* will be delighted to encounter so many of its songs on these two sets, for they were composed by Harry Warren, an unsung hero of the Hollywood musical whose name in this context should be indelibly linked with Busby Berkeley, the wayward genius who now has film students pouring over his every shot in "The shadow waltz". The two-disc set of original soundtracks of his production numbers takes the widest view of the director's work and includes some numbers by composers other than Warren, notably "Hooray for Hollywood" by Richard Whiting and Johnny Mercer with the distinctive Benny Goodman Orchestra in terrific form. The sound on the first disc requires some degree of toleration but with "I only have eyes for you", the one notable Warren absentee on John McGlinn's recording, things improve rapidly. The singers are a mixed bunch: Keeler, Powell, Blondell and even Ginger Rogers once separated from their screen image are often a liability. Much more agreeable are the lesser names of Etta Moten in Warren's "Remember my forgotten man" from *Gold Diggers of 1933*, Verree Teasdale in "Spin a little web of dreams" by Sammy Fain and Irving Kahal, and Judy Canova in "The lady in red" by Allie Wrubel. Amongst the other titles there is one masterpiece, "Lullaby of Broadway" (written for *Gold Diggers of 1935*), plus "42nd Street" and "Dames" in outstanding arrangements by Warner's veteran MD, Ray Heindorf, and the delightful "Shuffle off to Buffalo", all by Warren.

John McGlinn's 1994 studio recording concentrates exclusively on his songs. This is an immensely enjoyable recording, conceived on the grandest scale with enormous forces marshalled into pin-point precision by McGlinn and producer Simon Woods. They and the remarkable London Sinfonietta, (John Wallace leading trumpets, John Harle, saxophones and Marcia Crayford, violins) have succeeded in recreating the original Warner Brothers Orchestra sound with that distinctive sweet violin tone and vibrant brass in big-band style that was the studio's hallmark right through to *The Music Man* in 1962. McGlinn's vocal line-up don't put a foot wrong either, with Brent Barrett especially successful in the Dick Powell numbers. Extraordinary to think that for one of them, "Pettin' in the park", Berkeley conceived a scene in which a dwarf, playing a baby, eludes pursuers on roller-skates by leaping from his pram and skating off! **AE**

Lullaby of Broadway The Music of Harry Warren. With **Al Jolson, Bing Crosby, Winifred Shaw, Andrews Sisters, Al Bowlly, Carmen Miranda, Cyril Grantham, Nat Gonella, Dick Powell** and **Frances Langford**.
Flapper mono Ⓜ PASTCD9795 (69 minutes: ADD). Recorded 1924-48.
Songs from Crazy Quilt, The Laugh Parade, Gold Diggers of 1933, Gold Diggers of 1935, Gold Diggers of 1937, Garden of the Moon, That Night in Rio, 42nd Street, Melody for Two, Roman Scandals, Hard to Get, Going Places, Dames, Go into Your Dance, Broadway Gondolier, Weekend in Havana, Moulin Rouge, 20 Million Sweethearts and Footlight Parade.

The Song is ... Harry Warren with **Julia Sanderson, Frank Crumit, Elsie Carlisle, Frances Day, Denny Dennis, Boswell Sisters, Bing Crosby, Al Bowlly, Harry Roy, Andrews Sisters, Mills Brothers, Carmen Miranda, Frances Langford** and **Dick Haymes**.
ASV Living Era mono Ⓜ CDAJA5139 (76 minutes: ADD). Recorded 1931-42.
Songs from Gold Diggers of 1933, Gold Diggers of 1935, Artists and Models of 1927, Crazy Quilt, The Laugh Parade, Roman Scandals, 42nd Street, 20 Million Sweethearts, Dames, Broadway Gondolier, Melody for Two, Garden of the Moon, Going Places, Hard to Get, That Night in Rio, Sun Valley Serenade, Orchestra Wives and Hello, 1942.

Stop anyone in the queue at your local film society, and I doubt if many people would hesitate to name the choreographer who did the dances for all the great 1930s and 1940s Hollywood films like the *Gold Diggers* series, *42nd Street* (1933) and *Dames* (1934) – Busby Berkeley. Ask them who wrote the music and only the connoisseurs will be able to tell you the name of Harry Warren. Yet he probably composed as many standards as his contemporaries, Gershwin and Porter.

It is a sign of how popular these great numbers were that these two rival CDs, taking their material from dance-band and vocal 78s of the 1930s, only duplicate two items – both discs include the Andrews Sisters singing "Love is where you find it" from *Garden of the Moon* (1938) and Carmen Miranda in "I yi yi" from *That Night in Rio* (1941). The songs are generally much better sung on disc than they were in the movies, but of course the arrangements are completely different, ranging from close-harmony versions of "You're getting to be a habit with me" by the Four Musketeers and "Jeepers creepers" by the Mills Brothers (on ASV) and the same songs done by Bing Crosby and Nat Gonella on the Flapper disc. Rarities include Julia Sanderson and Frank Crumit in "Would you like to take a walk?" (ASV), Frances Langford in "Boulevard of broken dreams" (Flapper) and "Serenade in blue" (ASV). The ASV disc has the Dorsey Brothers Orchestra in numbers from *42nd Street* (with vocals by the Boswell Sisters), while Flapper fields Jack Hylton and his orchestra with vocals by Pat O'Malley. Once you've got one record, you'll want the other. **PO'C**

Kurt Weill
1900-1950 Germany

Kurt Weill's career divided neatly into two halves: his career in opera in Germany and his Broadway and film scores. The composer of *Die Dreigroschenoper* (1928) and *Happy-End* (1929) in Germany wrote *My Kingdom for a Cow* (1935), produced in London but moved to America, where a stream of works resulted in a Broadway idiom which bore little if any relation to that the composer had employed in Germany. *Johnny Johnson* (1936) was followed by *Knickerbocker Holiday* (1938) and a show for Gertrude Lawrence, *Lady in the Dark* (1941). Mary Martin was the star of *One Touch of Venus* (1943). In 1945 he had a failure with *The Firebrand of Florence*, the story of Benvenuto Cellini. The often-revived *Street Scene* came in 1947, *Love Life* in 1948 and, finally, *Lost in the Stars* (1949). He had married singer Lotte Lenya in Berlin in 1926, and she settled in the USA with him. Lenya did much to popularize Weill's work after his death, starring in Marc Blitzstein's English-language adaptation of *The Threepenny Opera* (1953), and recording and performing his work.

Berlin and American Theatre Songs Lotte Lenya, with various artists.
Sony Ⓜ MK42658 (72 minutes: ADD). Recorded 1955-8.
Songs from Knickerbocker Holiday, Lady in the Dark, One Touch of Venus, The Firebrand
of Florence, Street Scene, Love Life, Lost in the Stars, Die Dreigroschenoper, Happy End
and Aufstieg und Fall der Stadt Mahagonny.

After her great New York success in the Blitzstein version of *The Threepenny Opera*, Lenya
returned to Germany for the first time since 1933, visited Berlin where she saw Brecht for the last
time before he died, and received his blessing for this famous recording of some of the
Brecht/Weill songs. Was it "epic" enough, she asked him? "Lenya, darling, whatever you do is
epic enough for me", he replied. The German record was a huge success, so three years later
Lenya made what was the first attempt to reinstate some of Weill's American shows. Some of the
Broadway songs really don't suit her; "A boy like you" from *Street Scene* has the wrong sort of
world-weariness, though she does the tenor aria, "Lonely house" with real feeling. She comes
into her own, though, in "Speak low" from *One Touch of Venus*, it is fascinating to compare this
with Weill's own try-out disc of it, and her version of "Green up time" from *Love Life* has an
infectious gaiety about it that is really surprising. The accompaniments are good, but are in
arrangements, not Weill's own orchestrations. **PO'C**

From Berlin to Broadway with **Lotte Lenya, Harald Paulsen, Bertolt Brecht, Carola
Neher, Kurt Gerron, Ernst Busch, Walter Huston, Gertrude Lawrence, Danny Kaye, Mary
Martin** and **Kenny Baker / Maurice Abravanel** and **Theo Mackeben.**
Pearl mono Ⓜ GEMMCDS9189 (two discs: 153 minutes: ADD).
Songs from Die Dreigroschenoper, Happy End, Aufstieg und Fall der Stadt Mahagonny,
Der Silbersee, Knickerbocker Holiday, Lady in the Dark and One Touch of Venus.

New review
From Berlin to Broadway Volume 2. With **Harald Paulsen, Carola Neher, Lys Gauty,
Marianne Oswald, Walter Huston, Danny Kaye, Helen Hayes / Pierre Chagnon, Maurice
Abravanel.**
Pearl mono Ⓜ GEMMCDS9294 (two discs: 140 minutes: ADD).

Although it is unwise for modern performers to try and imitate the styles of actors and singers of the
past, it is very instructive to hear the creators' recordings. Carola Neher, the original Polly in *Die
Dreigroschenoper*, was a fine actress, but no singer. Lotte Lenya in the 1920s and 1930s had a much
higher, thinner voice than the one that became world-famous in the 1950s. Her phrasing and timing
are already recognizable. The selection ends with six songs she recorded with Weill at the piano in
New York in the 1940s, fascinating, transitional performances. These CDs are particularly valuable
for the *Lady in the Dark* and *One Touch of Venus* selections. No one has ever sung "The saga of
Jenny" or "My ship" with better timing or feeling than Gertrude Lawrence, and Mary Martin's
Venus is superb, her ability to invest the Ogden Nash lyrics with subtle overtones a joy. The two songs
from *Knickerbocker Holiday* are Walter Huston's earlier recordings, without the changed, watered-
down lyrics he used later, and all the better for it.
   Continuing the exploration of different performing styles for Weill's songs, the second volume
has the original Mackie from *Die Dreigroschenoper*, Harald Paulsen, singing numbers for other
characters – the *Moritat* ("Mack the Knife"), about himself, and the actress who should have
sung Polly on the first night, Carola Neher, in alternative versions of her songs. Three great
cabaret *chanteuses* from Paris – Damia, Lys Gauty and Marianne Oswald – offer French versions
of some of the Weill-Brecht numbers. From American radio broadcasts in the 1940s comes a
potted version of *Knickerbocker Holiday*, which has two members of the original 1938 cast,
Walter Huston and Jeanne Madden. It gives a fair idea of the strengths and weaknesses of the
show that gave Weill the biggest song hit of his career – "September Song", also heard in an early
version by Frank Sinatra. The sequence ends with private recordings of Weill accompanying
himself in some of the songs from *One Touch of Venus*, though his singing voice leaves everything
to be desired, his intimate delivery is quite captivating. **PO'C**

New review
Johnny Johnson 1996 **Studio Cast** (with Ellen Santaniello, Lynn Torgove, Anne Azéma,
Donald Wilkinson, Richard Lalli, Paul Guttry); **The Otaré Pit Band / Joel Cohen.**
Erato Ⓟ 0630-17870-2 (74 minutes: DDD).

Johnny Johnson was Kurt Weill's first major assignment once he had settled in the USA. The play by Paul Green was written for the Group Theatre, one of the most innovative and prestigious ensembles in New York, where it opened at the 44th Street Theatre in November 1936. The story is a parable about pacifists and warmongers, with the simple but good intentioned 'Everyman' hero, Johnny. The score is remarkable for the way it shows how skilfully Weill adapted his style to a new type of musical theatre without forsaking many of his trademark qualities. Forgotten for many years, of late it has had a number of productions in the USA and Europe. It received an abridged recording in the 1950s (on MGM) which had the splendid Burgess Meredith as Johnny, Evelyn Lear as his girlfriend and Lotte Lenya as the French nurse. This modern studio reading is much longer, and gives a better idea of the play, but the young singers have much more difficulty in achieving the style, partly naïve, partly realistic. This version brings out much more of Weill's orchestration, and among the songs rescued from the cuts Weill made at the time is "Farewell, goodbye", the first of his really American tunes, with a cowboy hopalong rhythm. **PO'C**

New review
Lady in the Dark 1963 Studio Cast (with Risë Stevens, Adolph Green and John Reardon) /
Lehman Engel.
Sony Classical mono/stereo Ⓜ MHK62869 (64 minutes: ADD). Includes excerpts from the show recorded by Danny Kaye in 1941.

The recent Royal National Theatre production raised a great deal of interest in this rarely seen 1941 Broadway show. This 1963 recording is as complete as the time limitations of vinyl would allow and is the best musically. It is also the only one in stereo (the sleeve incorrectly states mono). In addition the mono tracks recorded in 1941 by original cast member Danny Kaye have been added – the part gave him star status and these tracks give good reason why. Risë Stevens is a likeable true-voiced Liza Elliott (the original was Gertrude Lawrence) and Adolph Green is great in what was the Kaye role of Beekman and the Ringmaster. This adult musical looks at the analysis of Liza, the successful editor and unsuccessful love match. In the end, a child-learnt song (the glorious "My ship") provides the clue to the problem. Originally written as a play, most of the score comes out of the dream sequences in which the play's characters take on new roles. The score is top-notch and in this version given the loving Lehman Engel treatment. Weill really came of Broadway age with this one. Beautifully remastered and presented (this is a CD-sized miniature hardback book not a cold plastic jewel case) this is a must for anyone interested in the musical theatre.

Gertrude Lawrence can be heard singing her songs on Pearl's "From Berlin to Broadway" (see separate review above) and her wavering, but masterful performance is the most haunting. She pops up again in an AEI issue taken from a radio broadcast (the quality is variable) which gives long scenes as well some of the score (Ⓜ AEICD003) and supplements the Pearl issue in showing the perfect Liza. AEI are also the issuer of perhaps the most complete version, taken from a 1954 jazzed-up television presentation with Ann Sothern playing Liza (an LP issued at the time by RCA has not, as yet, been reissued on CD). It has also added the same glorious Gertrude Lawrence tracks as the Pearl issue, which is unfortunate for Sothern (Ⓜ AEI CD041). **RSB**

Lost in the Stars 1993 Studio Cast (with Cynthia Clarey, Carol Woods, Gregory Hopkins, Arthur Woodley and Reginald Pindell); New York Concert Chorale; St Luke's Orchestra /
Julius Rudel.
Music Masters Ⓟ 67100-2 (72 minutes: DDD).

Lost in the Stars is subtitled "A musical tragedy" and was adapted by Maxwell Anderson from Alan Paton's novel *Cry, the Beloved Country*. A new departure for Weill, who was experimenting with the use of Greek-style chorus to augment the action, the piece is rather dated now in its attitudes, Paton's novel much sentimentalized by Anderson.

This recording, directed by Julius Rudel (who conducted a production at the New York City Opera in 1959), is very fine, with a fervent performance from Arthur Woodley as the preacher Stephen Kumolo. Cynthia Clarey as his son's lover, Irina, sings "Trouble man" and "Stay well", while Carol Woods launches "Who'll buy?", the most raucous saloon ballad of Weill's American career. The title-song had originally been intended for a never-completed project, *Ulysses Africanus*, that Weill had worked on in the early 1940s. There is another example of Weill reworking his earlier material – the melody of his 1939 setting of Brecht's "Nana's Lied" is used here as a solo for Kumolo, "The little grey house".   **PO'C**

New review

September Songs The Music of Kurt Weill. **Nick Cave, P. J. Harvey, David Johansen, Teresa Stratas, Elvis Costello, Brodsky Quartet, Lotte Lenya, Charlie Haden, The Persuasions, Betty Carter, Mary Margaret O'Hara, Lou Reed, Bertolt Brecht** and **William S. Burroughs.**
Sony Classical Ⓕ SK63046 (69 minutes: DDD).
Songs from One Touch of Venus, Happy End, The Threepenny Opera, The Rise and Fall of the City of Mahagonny, Lost in the Stars and Street Scene.

Largely recorded for the soundtrack of a Larry Weinstein film based around Weill's music, these performances initially startle and ultimately, for the most part, work their way under your skin. Some of them are enduringly haunting. The presence of the voices of Lotte Lenya, sounding astonishingly young and girlish in a 1955 version of "Pirate Jenny", and Brecht, whose 1930 "Mack the Knife" is considerably sharper than Nick Cave's opening track, poses an intriguing challenge for an eclectic mix of artists. Some rise to it with more success than others. I loved David Johansen's jaunty "Alabama Song" with Ellen Shipley's vocals revealing an unexpected sweetness in one of Weill's most familiar melodies. Teresa Stratas, such an important Weill interpreter to begin with, provides extraordinary images of melancholy, despair and anger with the "Youkali Tango" – in which she evokes the majestic suffering of the archetypal *chanteuse réaliste* – and "Surabaya Johnny". Betty Carter's subtle, swirling "Lonely house" is a masterpiece. There are irritations too: "Ballad of the soldier's wife" is, legitimately, a dirge, but P. J. Harvey has neither the vocal nor the dramatic range to bring it to life; Elvis Costello's "Lost in the stars" is similarly short-changed, while Mary Margaret O'Hara's self-indulgent arrangement of "Fürchte dich nicht" is simply awful. Lou Reed mumbling "September Song" could be Lou Reed mumbling just about anything. Overall, though, it's a mesmerizing collection.   **PF**

Stranger Here Myself **Angelina Réaux; William Schimmel** (accordion); **Bill Royle** (perc); **Robert Kapilow** (pf).
Koch International Classics Ⓕ 37087-2 (two discs: 88 minutes: DDD).
Songs from Das Berliner Requiem, Der Silbersee, Die Dreigroschenoper, Love Life, Mahagonny, Lady in the Dark, Happy End, Marie Galante, Street Scene, One Touch of Venus, The Firebrand of Florence and Knickerbocker Holiday.

Stranger Here Myself, the title taken from one of the songs in *One Touch of Venus*, is a one-woman show that Angelina Réaux first performed in 1988 in New York. It's a sort of 'one woman against the world' story that used basic stage props, battered suitcase, bed and chair. Some of the interpretations are only viable within the context of the show, for instance "Alabama song" teetering on parody. Of all the opera singers who have sung Weill's show music in recent years, Réaux is probably the most successful. The quieter she gets, the better she is. "My ship" is good enough to suggest that in the right production she could be a perfect Liza Elliott in *Lady in the Dark*, but she also succeeds admirably in "Nana's Lied", one of Weill's last songs with Brecht, written in 1939. "Is it him, or is it me?" from *Love Life* suits her perfectly.   **PO'C**

Street Scene 1947 **Broadway Cast** (with Anne Jeffreys, Polyna Stoska, Brian Sullivan and Norman Cordon) **/ Maurice Abravanel**.
Columbia mono Ⓜ MK44668 (52 minutes: ADD).
New review

Street Scene 1989 **English National Opera Cast** (with Kristine Ciesinski, Janis Kelly, Bonaventura Bottone, Richard Van Allan); **English National Opera Chorus and Orchestra / Carl Davis.**
TER Ⓕ CDTER2 1185 (two discs: 146 minutes: DDD).

Weill's Broadway opera was the fulfilment of a dream as far as the composer was concerned. Adapted from Elmer Rice's 1929 play about the tenants living in an old New York rooming house, it was received with critical respect at the time, and notched up over 100 performances – not very good for a musical, but splendid for an opera. It was revived by the New York City Opera in the late 1950s, and has gradually entered the repertory of several opera companies in the USA and Europe. The original cast recording was not issued until after the show had closed, but reveals the considerable strengths of Polyna Stoska as Mrs Maurrant (she later was the first Ellen Orford in *Peter Grimes* at the Met). Her singing of "Somehow I could never believe" and "A boy like you" achieves the perfect fusion of drama and sentiment. Brian Sullivan (a Wagnerian tenor with *Lohengrin* in his repertory) does a beautiful "Lonely house", and as father and daughter, Anne Jeffreys and Norman Cordon are totally convincing. All the later recordings of this work have been by opera companies, only this disc of extracts preserves the original Broadway flavour of the piece.

David Pountney's 1989 production of *Street Scene* for Scottish Opera transferred later the same year to the Coliseum, and was the basis for two recordings. John Mauceri, who conducted it in Scotland, recorded the work for Decca with an all-star cast. Carl Davis, who led the work in London, took his stage cast into the studio for TER and the resulting rival sets both have much to offer, but the ENO/TER effort scores in that it is so obviously based on the experience of performing the work on stage. As usually happens, the English singers have difficulty with American accents, but Richard Van Allan's brooding Maurrant, Kristine Ciesinski's sympathetic Anna and the young lovers, Rose and Sam, sung by Janis Kelly and Bonaventura Bottone, all do well by their arias. When Weill was scoring *Street Scene*, the number that gave him the biggest headache was the jitterbug, "Moon-faced, starry-eyed". Weill eventually handed it over to a theatre orchestrator with the words, "I can't lick the hot-licks". On stage it was one of the highlights of the performance, the street swinging away to reveal the New York skyline in the distance and Catherine Zeta Jones and Philip Day giving it the real showbiz feel. **PO'C**

The Threepenny Opera 1954 Off-Broadway Cast (with Lotte Lenya, Jo Sullivan, Charlotte Rae, Beatrice Arthur, Scott Merrill, Gerald Price, Martin Wolfson and George Tyne) / **Samuel Matlowsky**.
TER Ⓕ CDTER1101 (53 minutes: ADD).

New review
The Threepenny Opera 1995 Donmar Warehouse Cast (with Sharon Small, Tara Hugo, Natasha Bain, Tom Hollander, Simon Dormandy and Tom Mannion) / **Gary Yershon**.
TER Ⓕ CDTER1227 (60 minutes: DDD).

Marc Blitzstein had already started his translation of Brecht's lyrics for *Die Dreigroschenoper* before Weill's death in 1950. The following year a concert performance was given which led to this famous production at the Theatre de Lys in Christopher Street, the staging which virtually began the modern interest in Weill's pre-1933 music and which made Lotte Lenya a star in America, something she had never achieved during the 15 years she and Weill had lived there together. Blitzstein's translations have mostly worn fairly well, though obviously such fierce lyrics as the "Tango ballad" had to be kept pretty tame for the 1950s. Scott Merrill is a fine, sexy Mack the Knife, Lenya recreates her Jenny – it was in this version that she first sang the "Pirate song" on stage (as she had in the 1931 Pabst movie), thereby creating a lot of problems for subsequent producers – whether to give it back to Polly, or let both of them sing it! Beatrice Arthur, later of *Golden Girls* fame, is an amusing Lucy. This is the recording that introduced a generation to Weill's songs, so it is a historic document as well as a still-vibrant version of a great score.

The latest English-language version of *Die Dreigroschenoper*, with lyrics by Jeremy Sams, was made for a production of the Brecht-Weill classic directed by Phyllida Lloyd. Many of the singers doubled up as instrumentalists, giving it at least the authenticity of suggesting what Brecht asked for, the impression of a poor theatre doing its best. The vocal styles range from shouting to a sort of pop-jazz crooning, reflecting the futuristic violence that was presented on stage. The only performer with a vocal style that could be called appropriate is Tara Hugo, the Jenny who, in this radical rethink on the work, gets to sing "Mack the Knife", not as a prelude, but to close the first act (the work was presented in two, instead of three acts). A realistic souvenir of this staging, the recording is for *Threepenny* curiosity-seekers only. **PO'C**

Tryout A Series of Private Rehearsal Recordings. **Kurt Weill** and **Ira Gershwin**.
DRG mono Ⓕ DRGCD904 (29 minutes: ADD).
Songs from Where Do We Go from Here? and One Touch of Venus.

The 1945 film *Where Do We Go from Here?* is a piece of fantasy-propaganda, starring Fred MacMurray, who is transported back in time to pioneering America, and at one point on to Columbus's ship. "The Nina, the Pinta, the Santa Maria" was the longest musical sequence and Weill and Ira Gershwin recorded it for the producer to give him an idea of the tempos. Their performance is full of little asides about how the music should go and is one of the very few documents to include Weill's speaking voice. So far, it is the only available recording from this film, one of several that Weill worked on in Hollywood. He loved the movies, but was never happy working in them, the compromises involved telling against his creative spirit.

The songs from *One Touch of Venus* (1943) include two of the soprano solos, which Weill sings very well, "Speak low" and "That's him", sounding remarkably like Lotte Lenya. When he said that all his compositions had Lenya's voice somewhere in the back of his mind, one might add that all her performances evidently had his voice hovering over them. **PO'C**

Weill on Broadway Thomas Hampson, with various singers; **London Sinfonietta Chorus and Orchestra / John McGlinn.**
EMI Ⓕ CDC5 55563-2 (76 minutes: DDD).
Songs from One Touch of Venus, Knickerbocker Holiday, The Firebrand of Florence, Love Life and Johnny Johnson.

New review
Kurt Weill on Broadway Steven Kimbrough (bar); **Cologne Radio Orchestra / Victor Symonette.**
Koch Schwann Ⓕ 314162 (45 minutes: DDD).
Songs from The Firebrand of Florence, Love Life, One Touch of Venus, Knickerbocker Holiday, Johnny Johnson.

Thomas Hampson's disc is a refreshingly unhackneyed selection from Weill's Broadway shows, the first to use his own orchestrations, and concentrating on a show that was an almighty flop, but which contains some great lyrics (by Ira Gershwin) and lovely Weill tunes: *The Firebrand of Florence*. Hampson makes a wonderfully convincing Benvenuto Cellini, heard at the start of the show about to be hanged, and at the end, once again on trial, defending himself successfully. "You're far too near me" is one of those tunes that once you've heard it, won't go away. The songs from *Love Life* are especially fine, "Here I'll stay", "This is the life" and the duet "I remember it well", an Alan Jay Lerner lyric that Lerner later re-adapted for *Gigi*. Hampson ends with Johnny's song from Weill's first American show, *Johnny Johnson*, and hearing it with its cello and sax accompaniment, one might be back in Berlin. John McGlinn and the London Sinfonietta carry the whole thing off with just the right mixture of devotion and bravado.

Coming hot on the heels of Hampson's recital, Steven Kimbrough's selection might seem something of an embarrassment of riches. Five items are common to both discs – in other words, the Weill specialist will want both, but the hesitant collector choosing between the two will want to know that Kimbrough's CD is rather short on time at 45 minutes, whereas Hampson and McGlinn's is 30 minutes longer. Both perform the opening of *Firebrand of Florence*, Hampson's version much fuller, with contributions from chorus and other soloists. Of the songs only on Kimbrough, the greatest rarity is one composed for Weill's first American show, *Johnny Johnson*, called "The Westpointer". The tune is a conflation of the song of Mandalay from *Happy End*, spiced up with part of the chorus of homeless men from Act 1 of *Der Silbersee*. In other words, it's another example of Weill's process of integration, using his European songs in a different, American context. "The Bachelor song" from *Knickerbocker Holiday* is also a first, apparently never having been performed before, although it is in a finished, scored state. Kimbrough sings them all with style, Victor Symonette's conducting is sympathetic, veering a bit more towards opera, whereas McGlinn gets the feeling of the theatre. **PO'C**

New review
Kurt Weill Songbook Julie Wilson; William Roy (pf).
DRG Ⓕ CDSL5207 (57 minutes: ADD).
Songs from One Touch of Venus, Knickerbocker Holiday, Lady in the Dark, Happy End, Street Scene, Love Life, The Firebrand of Florence, The Threepenny Opera and Lost in the Stars.

Many of Weill's songs contain passages of aching, intense melancholy and resignation which provide the singer with high-octane dramatic fuel. They do not rely on a classically beautiful voice, being, if anything, far more effective in the hands of performers with more textured, individual vocal skills who are willing to take risks with the material. In their time, Lotte Lenya, Marianne Faithfull and Ute Lemper have all thrived on this aspect of his work. To that list add Julie Wilson, whose comeback in the mid-1980s stamped her as something of a Weill virtuoso. Here, her ravaged attack brings real, devastating meaning to "Surabaya Johnny". Her growling, *diseuse* treatments of "Barbara Song" and "The Bilbao Song" (performed with obvious relish as a duet with pianist William Roy) are testament to Wilson's expertise as a story-teller. But she is equally at home with a touching torch song like "That's him" from *One Touch of Venus* or that yearning gem, "September Song", and uncovers layers of meaning in the numbers from *Lady in the Dark*, one of Weill's most complex and troubling works, delivering an outstanding, bleakly comic "Saga of Jenny". Her "Trouble man", neatly coupled with "Stay well", presents a wracked vision of a woman hopelessly in thrall to the bane of her life and there's a grim, threatening "Mack the Knife" which will surprise those who are more used to hearing it in its popular, Bobby Darin or Ella Fitzgerald incarnations.   **PF**

Also available:
Lady in the Dark (1952 Radio Cast) AEI AEICD003
Lost in the Stars (1949 Broadway Cast) MCA MCAD10302
Street Scene (Scottish Opera/Mauceri) Decca 433 371-2

Frank Wildhorn

Jekyll and Hyde 1990 Studio Cast (with Linda Eder and Colm Wilkinson) **/ Kim Scharnberg**.
RCA Victor Ⓟ 60416-2 (52 minutes: DDD).
Jekyll and Hyde 1994 Studio Cast (with Anthony Warlow, Linda Eder, Carolee Carmello, Brenda Russell and John Raitt) **/ Steven Cahill**.
Atlantic Ⓟ 82723-2 (two discs: 122 minutes: DDD).

Of several musical treatments of classic Victorian thrillers, Frank Wildhorn's concept musical of Robert Louis Stevenson's *The Strange Case of Dr Jekyll and Mr Hyde* is by far the most successful. It has undergone numerous rewrites and a Broadway production is in the planning stages after a lengthy but very successful tour, although once again rewritten compared to the latest 1994 recording. This two-disc set is impressive and very enjoyable. Wildhorn is adept at creating strong and moving ballads and exciting, dramatic musical moments. Leslie Bricusse's lyrics are fine, although a little trite in places, but the overall effect works well, largely due to a good sense of tension and excellent performances. The story is well told, with large sections of dialogue/recitative, which can sometimes become tiresome in musicals, but here works well, especially with the presence of fine talents such as Brenda Russell and John Raitt adding to the overall class. The three main performers Warlow, Eder and Carmello are all first-rate. Carmello is strong as Lisa Carew, in love with Dr Jekyll, but wooed by Simon Stride (a suitably smug performance by Bill Nolte). In duets with Warlow and Eder (the latter a wonderfully over-the-top number, "In his eyes") and in her solo, "Once upon a dream", she makes the most of Wildhorn's lush melodies. Eder comes from a pop background but flourishes here as the tragic prostitute Lucy, with two major solos – "Someone like you" and "A new life" – showcasing her considerable vocal talents. But all credit has to be handed to the awesome Anthony Warlow, surely one of the finest tenor voices in musical theatre. His dual performance is quite outstanding, the transformation scenes work well, and he delineates the two characters superbly – a serious, well-spoken Dr Jekyll against a frighteningly rough Mr Hyde. His singing throughout is magnificent, especially "This is the moment", which has already become something of a modern classic, recorded by many artists. Although not suitable for staging in this form, as a recording this is an immensely enjoyable piece, one of the best examples of the pop-opera phenomenon.

The original concept recording of Wildhorn's version of the Stevenson classic, with Colm Wilkinson in the title-role and Linda Eder playing both Lucy and Lisa is also available. Several fine songs were not kept for the 1994 recording and are worth hearing, including two duets for Jekyll and Lisa – "Love has come of age" and "We still have time" – and a strong solo for Jekyll,

"Till you came into my life". The two-disc set on Atlantic is clearly more lavish and works rather better, but Wilkinson is good and Eder once again proves that her pop voice is perfectly suited to Wildhorn's dramatic ballad style. **RAC**

Paul Williams

New review

Bugsy Malone 1997 National Youth and Music Theatre Cast / John Pearson.
TER Ⓔ CDTER1246 (45 minutes: DDD).

Alan Parker's 1976 musical film *Bugsy Malone* was a thoroughly enjoyable spoof of the archetypal gangster movie, with custard shoot-outs, slinky *femmes fatales* and energetic chorus lines all contributing to the chaotic sense of fun. Now it has been revamped and filled-out for a 1997 revival by the National Youth and Music Theatre. Aged 10-16 the cast attack Parker's libretto with gusto and there are some nice moments. A new song, "That's why they call him dandy", is sung with impressive confidence by Stuart Piper, while "That's showbusiness" knowingly sends up the personality of the quintessential showgirl. Ten-year-old Leanne Connelly laments her way through a couple of bluesy torch songs, "I'm feeling fine" and "Ordinary fool", with a wisdom way beyond her age. Paul Williams's score, occasionally a tad repetitive, is at its best in these pastiche numbers. Certainly, the thought of a show based around the talents of a company of child performers is not everyone's cup of tea, but these fresh, rounded performances quickly dispel the most patronizing preconceptions. Unpretentious stuff which, on the whole, stays on the right side of cute. **PF**

Also available:
Bugsy Malone (1976 Film Cast) Polydor 831 540-2

Meredith Willson

1902-1984 USA

Iowa-born Willson went to New York to study music aged 16 and became Sousa's principal flautist before joining the New York Philharmonic Orchestra in 1922. He conducted on radio, continued to study and wrote two symphonies, songs and other works, as well as arranging Charlie Chaplin's music for the film *The Great Dictator* (1940). His song "May the good Lord bless and keep you", was written as the theme for Tallulah Bankhead's radio programme, *The Big Show*. On Broadway he wrote *The Music Man* (1957) – which ran for 1,375 performances and was filmed in 1962 – *The Unsinkable Molly Brown* (1960) – filmed 1964 – and *Here's Love* (1963), all of which were successes.

Here's Love 1963 Broadway Cast (with Janis Paige, Craig Stevens and Laurence Naismith) / Elliot Lawrence.
Sony Broadway Ⓜ SK48204 (41 minutes: ADD).

Meredith Willson was the first to admit that he really only had enough songs in his trunk for one Broadway musical, *The Music Man*. When that turned out to be a smash hit commercial pressure was brought to bear on him to compose another show, *The Unsinkable Molly Brown*, which also enjoyed a fair measure of success and was later filmed by MGM. *Here's Love*, based on the 1947 movie *Miracle on 34th Street*, was only half the hit that *Molly Brown* had been, whilst his last show, *1491*, based on Columbus's discovery of the new world never made it to New York. The composer of "76 trombones" is recognizable from the nine-minute opening overture in *Here's Love* depicting Macy's Parade on Thanksgiving Day, in a very festive orchestration by Don Walker. What a pity that the composer wound it up with "Adeste fideles", weakening the impact of what had preceded it. Thereafter the show stands by its performers rather than its songs, with Laurence Naismith as Kris Kringle and Janis Paige as the mother of the little girl whom he befriends. They share a charming duet, "Pine cones and holly berries", whose counter melody, "It's beginning to look a lot like Christmas", has recently enjoyed a revival through the *Home Alone* movies. The songs for the male lead are less appealing and have dated badly in their sentiments. The recording, like all these Sony Broadway transfers, sounds excellent. **AE**

The Music Man 1957 Broadway Cast (with Robert Preston and Barbara Cook) **/ Herbert Greene.**
EMI Angel Ⓜ ZDM7 64663-2 (47 minutes: ADD).

The Music Man 1962 Film Cast (with Robert Preston and Shirley Jones) **/ Ray Heindorf.**
Warner Bros Ⓜ 1459-2 (49 minutes: ADD).

If there was one performance on the Broadway stage that I would most like to have seen it would have been Robert Preston as Professor Harold Hill, the bogus musician with a wily patter who persuades the townfolk of an Iowa community to part with money to fund a boys' band he can't teach. One can, of course, see his performance on screen, but as with certain Broadway stars, Ethel Merman is another, the medium is simply too one-dimensional to capture the spirit behind the personality, something not helped in this movie by the director shooting all the ensembles head-on. The guileless, folksy tale was taken from the composer's own memories of his boyhood in Iowa and no doubt the music, including the celebrated march "76 trombones", was inspired by his time playing flute in Sousa's band. The score draws on other traditions too, ragtime, barber-shop quartet, cake-walk and barn dance amongst them, but the most remarkable feature of Willson's work was his invention of a countrified speech patter, truly original and razor-sharp with which Preston, with his crisp delivery, mesmerized the community and seduced the local librarian. Here both recordings offer delightful performances of great charm and naturalness from Barbara Cook and Shirley Jones soaring heavenward at the conclusion of that memorable duet "Till there was you". The early Capitol stereo sounds better than ever in its EMI CD transfer capturing all the spontaneity of a cast who seem to know they're delivering something special. The soundtrack, masterminded by Warner's MD Ray Heindorf, is also excellent. Some small changes include a partially new song for the heroine, "Being in love", which is presented in the overture with great élan by the large orchestra. Reprises and small touches in Frank Comstock's arrangements, like the ragtime piano illustrating the lowdown atmosphere of the pool room in Preston's "Ya got trouble", just clinch a verdict in its favour.   **AE**

The Unsinkable Molly Brown 1960 Broadway Cast (with Tammy Grimes, Sterling Clark, Bill Starr, Bob Daley, Joseph Sirola, Harve Presnell, Mony Dalmes, Mitchell Gregg, Don Emmons, Mark Ross and Terry Violino) **/ Herbert Greene.**
EMI Angel Ⓜ ZDM7 64761-2 (49 minutes: ADD).

How do you follow up a world-wide success like *The Music Man*? If you are Meredith Willson, its composer/lyricist, the answer is a musical based on the real-life exploits of a legend from the mining West of America. Molly Brown – unsinkable because she survived the sinking of the Titanic – was a part in a lifetime for Tammy Grimes (who lost the role on film to Debbie Reynolds). Willson produced a warm, energetic, gutsy score including rumbustious show-stoppers and touching, intimate numbers, moving effortlessly from Western high jinks to quieter, more restrained songs, all recognizably the work of *The Music Man* (who had served in Sousa's Band). Harve Presnell's rich baritone (school of Howard Keel) makes the most of "I'll never say no", "If I know" and "Leadville Johnny Brown soliloquy", while Grimes growls happily through "I ain't down yet", "Are you sure?" and "I may never fall in love with you". Much of this fine score was cut for the 1964 film (in which Presnell appears) – and it's a sad loss to MGM's soundtrack album.   **MPK**

Sandy Wilson
b. 1924 England

Born in Cheshire, Wilson appeared in and wrote for revues whilst a student at Oxford. In London he contributed to *Slings and Arrows, Oranges and Lemons* (both 1948), *See You Later* (1951) and *See You Again* (1952). In 1953 he wrote *The Boy Friend*, which after initial runs at the Players' and Embassy Theatres, ran for a record-breaking 2,084 performances at Wyndham's Theatre. The New York show, which ran for 485, starred newcomer Julie Andrews. After revivals in 1967 and 1970, it was filmed in 1972 with Twiggy in the leading role. Wilson followed this success with *The Buccaneer* (1955) and *Valmouth* (1958). He contributed songs to later shows including *Pieces of Eight* (1959), *As Dorothy Parker Once Said* (1969) and *Aladdin* (1979).

The Boy Friend 1954 **Broadway Cast** (with Julie Andrews, John Hewer, Eric Berry, Ruth Altman, Millicent Martin and Bob Scheerer) **/ Anton Coppola**.
RCA Victor Ⓜ 60056-2 (41 minutes: ADD).

The Boy Friend 1984 **London Cast** (with Anna Quayle, Derek Waring, Jane Wellman, Simon Green, Peter Bayliss and Paddie O'Neill) **/ Martin Koch**.
TER Ⓕ CDTER1095 (53 minutes: DDD).

It's difficult to over-estimate the impact that Sandy Wilson's attempt to recreate the spirit of 1920s musicals had in the London and New York of the 1950s. It influenced musicians, playwrights, fashion-designers and interior-decorators. People who had never heard of the Charleston started to learn it. Girls had their hair bobbed. Although it had many, many imitators, and the show has seldom been off the stage since, what made it unique was the author's complete knowledge of the period and its musical form, and the fact that it was created simply to entertain and never for a moment descended to coy pastiche. Though many of the songs seemed to refer to specific numbers from 1920s shows, each was original and the show contributed two huge hits to the 1950s: "I could be happy with you" and "A room in Bloomsbury". Although it isn't difficult to see where the ideas originate ("I want to be happy" from *No, No, Nanette* and "A tiny flat in Soho Square" from *Lido Lady*), what makes *The Boy Friend* into such a cast-iron proposition is its sincerity.

The original London cast (recorded by HMV on 78s, and on a 10-inch LP) has never been surpassed. Both these recordings, the glitzier Broadway version and the 1984 London revival suffer from a too-knowing attitude – what makes *The Boy Friend* work is the audience's compliance in joining in the old formula. The cast let people know they're sending up the era at their peril. The RCA version is a historic document as a record of Julie Andrews's first Broadway show, and with its great energy is largely preferable to the TER version. Both benefit from having an orchestra whereas the HMV version (which is no longer available) was with piano and drums only. Perhaps *The Boy Friend* now deserves a complete 'authentic' recording.   **PO'C**

New review

Divorce Me, Darling! 1997 **Chichester Festival Cast** (with Liliane Montevecchi, Ruthie Henshall, Tim Flavin and Andrew Halliday) **/ Richard Balcombe**.
TER Ⓕ CDTER1245 (69 minutes: DDD).

What a pleasure to be able to welcome this CD of *Divorce Me, Darling!* without reservations – a recording as sparkling and joyful as this endearing show demands. Sandy Wilson's 1953 Twenties musical *The Boy Friend* was a huge hit on both sides of the Atlantic. In 1964 he wrote *Divorce Me, Darling!* to show his "perfect young ladies" ten years later. But the formula that had entranced audiences in the 1950s wasn't much to the taste of Swinging London in the 1960s, and the show only ran for 87 nights. It was recorded and the original cast LP, briefly available on cassette in the 1970s, has long been a sought-after collectors' item. The LP only gave a selection of the music. Here it all is, sung with just the correct mixture of period feel and sincerity by the all-star cast.

On stage the veterans like Liliane Montevecchi, Jack Tripp and Joan Savage stole the show, but their comparatively brief appearances on disc, delightful though they are, leave the field clear for the three leading ladies, Ruthie Henshall, Rosemarie Ford and Marti Webb, to show off their voices. Tim Flavin as Bobby proved himself a song-and-dance man in the great tradition, and Simon Butterkiss as the Upper-Class Twit (Sir Freddy ffotherington-ffitch) provides the essential sub-plot romance. Wilson's score has as many memorable songs in it as *The Boy Friend*. My own favourites are "Maisie", the trio for the three French husbands, "Out of step", Wilson's tribute to the spirit of Astaire and Rogers, and the Noël Coward-style "Back where we started". To cap it all Wilson has provided two show-stoppers in the final cabaret scene on board the luxury yacht. First, the Suzy Solidor/Jean Cocteau-influenced "Blondes for danger" in which Montevecchi proves that the art of the music-hall *chanteuse* is alive and well, and then "Swingtime is here to stay", a grand finale that calls for a staging by Busby Berkeley. Grand irony – Berkeley had been approached to stage the show on Broadway in 1965, a saga that belongs to the catalogue of showbiz might-have-beens. *Divorce Me, Darling!* may yet make it to Broadway, but I doubt it will ever be better performed than it is here.   **PO'C**

Valmouth 1959 **London Cast** (with Cleo Laine, Doris Hare, Patsy Rowlands, Fenella Fielding, Barbara Couper, Peter Gilmore, Alan Edwards, Aubrey Woods, Denise Hirst, Betty Hardy and Marcia Ashton) **/ Neville Meale**.
DRG Ⓕ CDDRG13109 (50 minutes: ADD).

Valmouth 1982 **Chichester Festival Cast** (with Bertice Reading, Doris Hare, Cheryl Kennedy, Femi Taylor, Judy Campbell, Fenella Fielding, Jane Wenham, Marcia Ashton, Robert Meadmore, Simon Butterkiss, Mark Wynter and Robert Helpmann) **/ John Owen Edwards**.
TER Ⓕ CDTER1019 (67 minutes: DDD).

The Boy Friend proved to be a hard act to follow, but this adaptation of Ronald Firbank's fantasy novel, set in the spa town of Valmouth, has been widely hailed as Sandy Wilson's masterpiece. Though its decadent atmosphere denied it a wide audience, it has retained its humour and freshness for nearly 40 years. The central role of Mrs Yajnavalkaya was specifically written for Bertice Reading, who created it in October 1958 at the Lyric Theatre, Hammersmith. By the time it transferred to the West End the following spring, her role had been taken over by Cleo Laine, who enjoyed a hit with the most famous song, "Big, best shoes". Fenella Fielding, one of the most original revue actresses of the 1950s and 1960s, had two solos, "Just once more" and "Only a passing phase", in which she proves that the art of the *double* or *treble entendre* wasn't lost in the age of rock 'n' roll. Fielding, Doris Hare as Grannie Tooke and Marcia Ashton as Sister Ecclesia all repeated their original parts in the 1982 Chichester Festival revival, when Bertice Reading returned to the role she had created as the mysterious masseuse.

Both recordings are very fine, enthusiasts will naturally need to have them both, but the thrifty collector must choose between Cleo Laine, with her inimitable, gentler style and Bertice Reading, part little-girl-lost, part grizzly-bear in manner. As it is, *Valmouth* reinforces Sandy Wilson's position as the only real successor to Noël Coward as the ultimate British sophisticated musical creator.   **PO'C**

Jim Wise

Dames at Sea 1969 **Broadway Cast** (with David Christmas, Steve Elmore, Tamara Long, Joseph R. Sicari, Sally Stark and Bernadette Peters) **/ Richard J. Leonard**.
Sony Broadway Ⓕ SK48214 (52 minutes: ADD).

Dames at Sea 1989 **UK Touring Cast** (with Brian Cant, Josephine Blake and Sandra Dickinson) **/ Malcolm Newton**.
TER Ⓕ CDTER1169 (57 minutes: ADD).

When a parody musical is good, it's often very good. *Dames at Sea* casts a beady eye on those wonderful Warner Brothers musicals of the 1930s (*42nd Street, Dames, Gold Diggers* and such) with their lavish choreography by Busby Berkeley and usually starring Ruby Keeler and Dick Powell with wisecracking Joan Blondell, Ginger Rogers, or Una Merkel. It also aims a deft kick at the Fred and Ginger naval extravaganza *Follow the Fleet*. The real joke is that it does all of this with a cast numbered in single figures. As a result, wit and style substitute for large-scale resources. The songs have a welcome familiarity about them. "Choo-choo honeymoon", "Singapore Sue", "That mister man of mine", "Broadway baby" and best of all "Raining in my heart", are pastiches of the highest order – enjoyable not just because of their similarity to others, but interesting songs in their own right. There are currently two good available recordings, even if the fine original cast, a breakthrough for Bernadette Peters, is a natural first choice. She has reliable support from Tamara Long, David Christmas and Steve Elmore. But don't overlook a fine souvenir of a British 1989 touring production with Brian Cant, Josephine Blake and Sandra Dickinson who miss none of the satirical and melodic points. Either way *Dames at Sea* should be in any collection.   **MPK**

Maury Yeston

A composer whose talents span classical and popular music, Maury Yeston's Cello Concerto was premièred by Yo-Yo Ma. The successful concept album *Goya* was released in Spanish and English and featured Plácido Domingo and Gloria Estefan. Barbra Streisand had a world hit with Yeston's song "Till I loved You". His musicals are *Nine* (1983), based on Fellini's 1962 film *Otto e Mezzo*, *Phantom* (1990), an alternative to the Lloyd Webber version of the same subject,

Titanic (1997) and *Grand Hotel* (1989), where he added songs to the Forrest and Wright score (see under Forrest and Wright).

Nine 1982 Broadway Cast (with Raul Julia, Karen Akers, Shelly Burch, Taina Elg, Lilianne Montevecchi, Kathi Moss and Anita Morris) / **Wally Harper**.
Columbia Ⓕ CK38325 (68 minutes: DDD).

Yeston's absorbing and unusual score for the musical version of the 1962 Fellini movie *Otto e Mezzo* is beautifully preserved on this original cast recording. From the extraordinary overture sung by the 21 women in the life of movie director Guido Contini (played by Raul Julia), the attention is commanded and held. Julia is a strong presence – demanding, flirtatious and obviously under great stress as he is pulled in all directions by the women surrounding him. His wife, sung by husky-voiced Karen Akers, is resigned to his obsessions ("My husband makes movies"), but cannot cope with his adultery, angrily rejecting him in "Be on your own". Anita Morris as the mistress delivers an erotically charged performance with "A call from the Vatican", and later also rejects Guido in the haunting "Simple". Lilianne Montevecchi brings all her French flair to the big production number, "Folies Bergères", while Kathi Moss as the lustful nun teaching the young Guido the ways of the flesh is equally delightful. Yeston's music has a strong European flavour, drawing on French, Italian and Spanish influences. The lyrics are uniformly excellent – the women's songs striking the perfect chord throughout – and although the final acceptance that he has to grow up (Guido is lectured by his eight-year-old self in "Getting tall") might be a little simplistic, this is a minor criticism of a modern musical that strives to offer something different, and succeeds admirably in all departments.
 A two-disc TER set (see below), based on a charity concert staged at the Royal Festival Hall in 1992, and with a cast featuring Jonathan Pryce, Ann Crumb, Meg Johnson, Lilianne Montevecchi and Elaine Paige, is the most complete available version of the show, but it lacks the authority and style of the original. **RAC**

Phantom 1992 US Cast (with Richard White, Glory Crampton, Jack Dabdoub, Paul Schoeffler and Meg Bussert) / **Jonathan Tunick**.
RCA Victor Ⓕ 09026 61660-2 (58 minutes: DDD).

Gaston Leroux's novel has proved, literally, a haunting source of inspiration for composer and filmmakers. Alas for the also-rans, Andrew Lloyd Webber's 1986 extravaganza is now widely accepted as the definitive musical treatment of this ultimately tragic tale of the disfigured being who lurks in the caverns beneath the Paris Opera, his life briefly given new meaning when he hears the beautiful but untrained voice of a young singer and resolves to make her a star. Too bad, then, that this charming operetta is unlikely to be staged much further afield than than Houston, Seattle or San Bernardino, where it was performed and developed throughout 1991 and 1992. Ignoring the potential for *grand guignol* horror, Maury Yeston's score focuses instead on the Phantom's growing passion for Christine and the inevitable final tragedy. Richard White sings the title-role with the dignity which is essential if the audience is to feel any compassion for him. We do. The part of Christine, better developed than Lloyd Webber's, is also beautifully sung by Glory Crampton, particularly in a moving finale, a reprise of "You are music". Between them, they evoke memories of Nelson Eddy and Jeanette MacDonald at their best. The competition medley ("The bistro") is a delightful Lehár-style pastiche, then, in one bound, we are transported to a good old-fashioned Broadway duet, "Who could ever have dreamed up you?", between Crampton and Paul Schoeffler's Count. As a bonus, there's a wickedly comic performance from Meg Bussert as the bitchy owner/resident prima donna of the Opera whose soprano has seen better days ("This place is mine"). **PF**

New review
Titanic 1997 Broadway Cast / Kevin Stites.
RCA Victor Ⓕ 09026 68834-2 (73 minutes: DDD).

Despite a mixed critical reception, Maury Yeston's bold attempt to evoke a disaster which, more than 80 years on, still grips popular imagination, did not quite suffer the desperate fate of its subject. On one level, the story is simple: arrogant ambition thwarted by human error with catastrophic consequences. Yeston's considerable achievement, however, is a multi-textured score which, rather than relying on the high drama of the central tragedy, builds layers of context, social and musical, through which the Titanic's maiden voyage becomes a metaphor for the doomed aspirations and hopes of its passengers. Contemporary musical references are plentiful: British folk tunes and hymns, ragtime, Gilbert and Sullivan, a hint of Elgar and Strauss, all cleverly used to indicate the social status of the characters. But there is also a soaring, cohesive quality which makes this a musical to meet the expectations of a late-twentieth century audience, helped by the lush playing of a decent-sized orchestra.

On CD there is an intimacy about this ensemble piece more reminiscent of a chamber opera than a blockbusting musical. Curiously, too, the score tends to underplay the two dramatic highpoints of the story, the collision itself and the sinking. And those expecting a handful of show stoppers *à la* the same composer's *Nine* or *Grand Hotel* will be disappointed, although there is a touching duet between Isidor and Ida Straus as they resolve to meet their fate together ("Still"). But repeated listening pays dividends. There are some truly haunting passages and romantic musical dialogues: "In every age", for example, which embodies the dream of the ship's architect and, at the end, its futility; or "No moon" which becomes the insistent theme for the ship's collision course with the iceberg. It's too early to tell where *Titanic* will ultimately sit in the panoply of grand musicals, but on this evidence it's certainly more than a fleeting curiosity. **PF**

Also available:
Nine (1991 Australian Cast) TER CDTER1190
Nine (1992 London Concert Cast) TER CDTER2 1193

Vincent Youmans

1898-1946 USA

Originally a piano salesman, music-roll maker and song-plugger, Youmans began composing while in the navy in World War I. One of his tunes, "Hallelujah" was turned into a popular march by Sousa. He published his first song, "The country cousin" in 1920, and with Paul Lannin wrote his first show, *Two Little Girls in Blue* in 1921. Both this and *The Wildflower* (1923) were successes, leading to his biggest hit show, *No, No, Nanette* (1925), which included the song "Tea for two", written with Irving Caesar, a hit not only in America and Britain but right across Europe. The show was filmed in 1930 with most of Youmans's music replaced, and revived on Broadway in 1971, featuring veteran performer Ruby Keeler, and in London in 1973. 1927's *Hit the Deck* (which featured his old navy tune, "Hallelujah", with added lyrics) was his last successful show, although many of his individual songs became recognized standards. He moved to Hollywood in 1933 to write the music for *Flying Down to Rio* – including the song "Orchids in the moonlight". In 1934 the onset of tuberculosis forced him into premature retirement.

No, No, Nanette 1971 **Broadway Cast** (with Ruby Keeler, Jack Gilford, Bobby Van, Helen
  Gallagher, Susan Watson, Patsy Kelly, Roger Rathburn, Loni Zoe Ackerman, K. C.
  Townsend and Pat Lysinger) **/ Buster Davis**.
  Columbia Ⓜ CK30563 (54 minutes: ADD).
No, No, Nanette 1973 **London Cast** (with Anna Neagle, Tony Britton, Anne Rogers, Teddy
  Green, Thora Hird, Barbara Brown, Peter Gale, Anita Graham, Elaine Holland and Jenny
  Wren) **/ Grant Hossack**.
  Sony West End Ⓜ SMK66173 (51 minutes: ADD).

The revival in the 1970s of one of the most enduring and attractive musical comedies of the 1920s turned out to be a lavish affair – with Busby Berkeley nominally credited for the dances and a glitteringly no-expense-spared production, with casts of both sides of the Atlantic replete with stars from the past – Ruby Keeler headed the cast in New York and Anna Neagle in London. Youmans's wonderful score glows anew in its bright new setting. "Tea for two", "I want to be happy", "Take a little one-step", "You can dance" and "Too many rings around Rose" show what a loss the musical stage sustained when the composer succumbed to the ill health that eventually led to his death decades later. Neither recording is for followers of authenticity. The orchestrations are bang-up-to-date 1970s with no concessions to the sound of the 1920s. The vocal performances of Keeler and Neagle have equally poignant charm: both were primarily dancers. The strong surrounding casts include strong, charming voices – particularly the team of Peter Gale and Barbara Brown. In the final analysis, you will probably choose the dancing lady you prefer, and the recording that contains her. **MPK**

Also available:
Songs of Vincent Youmans, Vols 1 & 2. Arabesque Z6692/70

Collections

Broadway Bound New Writers for the Musical Theatre. **Guy Haines, Jason Graae, Liz Callaway, Sarah Jessica Parker, Matthew Broderick, Sally Mayes** and **Michael Rupert** (sngrs) / **Todd Ellison**. Varèse Sarabande Spotlight Series Ⓕ VSD5676 (58 minutes: DDD).
Songs from **Ross:** Little Pinks. The Times. **Cummins:** The Little Prince. **Cohen:** No Way to Treat a Lady. **D. Bernstein/Markell:** Showing Off. Gotham. **Cavallari:** The Game. **Hoffman/Campbell:** The Tenants of 3R. **Sklar/Beguelin:** Lady Chatterley's Lover. **Abel/Steffan:** Camille. *Songs by* Chapman, Blumenthal and Greenberg/ Lawrence.

This is one of the most important recordings for the future of musical theatre, a compilation of songs by some of the younger talents currently working their way towards fame and fortune on the Great White Way. Brad Ross, Douglas J. Cohen, Douglas Bernstein and the others may not be household names but their talents are evident in this compilation. The two tracks from *No Way to Treat a Lady* are outstanding. Cohen is clearly a writer with a great future – well-crafted lyrics combined with great musicality, assisted by excellent performances from Liz Callaway and Jason Graae. The range of projects is interesting, including musical versions of *Les Liaisons Dangereuses* (two fascinating songs are featured here from *The Game*, whose lyricist, Amy Powers, worked briefly on Lloyd Webber's *Sunset Boulevard*), *Lady Chatterley's Lover* and *The Little Prince*. There are some quaintly old-fashioned songs, such as "Let's get domestic", performed by Matthew Broderick and Sarah Jessica Parker, and the up-tempo "Kicks" from *Little Pinks* by Brad Ross. Ross is featured again with his "Watching the show" from *The Times*, performed by the ever-reliable Michael Rupert, a great lyric by Joe Keenan about the development of a critic. For classic ballads look no further than "When the rain comes", sung by Andrea Burns. The comic song is happily assured, with writers such as Alan Chapman's very funny "Everybody wants to be Sondheim" and Douglas Bernstein's "Ninas". The latter is a well-written list song celebrating the work of cartoonist Al Hirschfeld (his daughter's name is inserted on all his cartoons). Or listen to Tammy Minoff singing of the charms of Joshua Noveck – from another Bernstein project, *Showing Off*. According to producer Bruce Kimmel's introduction, hundreds of songs were submitted for this project. The high quality and enjoyable result is really encouraging for the future of Broadway and musical theatre. **RAC**

New review

The First Torch Singers, Volume 1: The 1920s. With **Fanny Brice, Helen Morgan, Ruth Etting, Libby Holman, Sophie Tucker, Belle Baker, Lee Morse, Kate Smith, Annette Hanshaw, Frances Williams** and **Eva Taylor**.
Take Two mono Ⓜ TT407CD (61 minutes: AAD).
Songs from **Yvain:** Ziegfeld Follies of 1921. **Rose and Dixon:** My Man. **Kern:** Show Boat, Sweet Adeline. **Kahn:** Whoopee. **Gilbert:** Frozen Justice. **Youmans:** Great Day. **Sizemore:** Song of Love. **Bryan:** Footlights and Fools. **Goodwin:** Untamed. **McHugh:** Blackbirds of 1928. **Harburg:** Applause. **Rainger:** The Little Show. *Songs by* Gershwin, DeRose, Cottier, Etting, Fiorito.

Many of the performers on this excellent compilation were not torch singers *per se*, but all of them included torch material in their repertoires as a matter of course. Helen Morgan, Ruth Etting and Libby Holman were, of course, definitive torch singers while Fanny Brice, the great vaudeville comedienne, virtually created the genre on Broadway when she introduced the English lyrics of the French chanson "Mon homme" in the *Ziegfeld Follies of 1921*. The recording here was made in 1927 and preserves all of the pathos and suffering which Brice wrung from the song. It's a far cry from the full-throated Streisand approach! It's also interesting to compare Etting's low-key version of "Love me or leave me" (Donaldson/Kahn) with Doris Day's rendition in the superior biopic of the same name. They are very distant cousins but demonstrate how a fine torch song will always adapt to a new age. Morgan's three towering achievements were her portrayal of Julie in *Show Boat*, her creation of the title-role in Kern's follow-up, *Sweet Adeline*, and her performance in Rouben Mamoulian's 1929 film of backstage burlesque life, *Applause*. Seventy years after *Show Boat* opened, she is still the model by which any Julie is judged. Here, "Can't help lovin' dat man" and "Don't ever leave me" (from *Sweet Adeline*) are sung with typical tremulous plaintiveness. Elsewhere, Sophie Tucker ("The man I love") and Kate Smith ("Maybe who knows") bring their more robust vocal qualities to songs which are commonly treated with more wistful restraint. Less well-remembered but equally appealing are singers like Belle Baker, Lee Morse and Eva Taylor. As always with Take Two, the digital mastering is first-class.   **PF**

For Me and My Gal 1942 **Film Cast** (with Judy Garland, Gene Kelly, George Murphy, Lucille Norman and Ben Blue); **MGM Studio Chorus and Orchestra / Georgie Stoll**.
EMI mono/stereo Ⓕ CDODEON12 (75 minutes: ADD).

For Me and My Gal, which has no connection with Noel Gay's *Me and My Girl*, was an unashamed tribute to Uncle Sam, designed to cash in on the patriotic fervour sweeping America in 1942 after its entry into the Second World War. But it was the first global encounter of the century that provided the peg on which to hang a dozen and more songs of the period, most of which fell to Garland and Gene Kelly, making his début in a Metro musical directed by Busby Berkeley. The juxtaposition of Garland's deep, sweet voice with Kelly's high, light voice in such songs as "When you wore a tulip" and "For me and my girl" was later recalled by Pauline Kael this way: "their duets have a plaintive richness ... there was a vulnerability both Gene and Judy brought out in each other and which neither had with anyone else". Some tolerance of the variable soundtrack sources should be mentioned.   **AE**

Forbidden Broadway Cast performances from 1982-4 (with Bill Carmichael, Nora Mae Lyng, Chloe Webb, Gerard Alessandrini and Fred Barton) **/ Fred Barton**.
DRG Ⓕ CDSBL12585 (40 minutes: ADD).
Forbidden Broadway 2 Cast performances from 1985-6, 1990-1 (with Michael McGrath, Toni Dibuono, Gerard Alessandrini, Roxie Lucas, Philip George, Linda Strasser, Karen Murphy, John Freedson, Kevin Ligon, Dorothy Kiara and William Selby) **/ Philip Fortenberry**.
DRG Ⓕ 12599 (65 minutes: ADD).
Forbidden Broadway 3 Cast performances from 1985-93 (with Gerard Alessandrini, Susanne Blakeslee, Dorothy Kiara, Herndon Lackey, Barbara Walsh, Brad Oscar, Craig Wells, Nora Mae Lyng, Roxie Lucas and Carol Channing) **/ Brad Ellis**.
DRG Ⓕ 12609 (71 minutes: ADD).

A late-night revue show, the original inspiration of Gerard Alessandrini, that has become something of a phenomenon in off-Broadway theatre. If you have not been parodied by the *Forbidden Broadway* team you have not really arrived. This is an extraordinary turn around for a show which originally was constructed by those frustrated because they could not get jobs in Broadway shows! But such is the brilliance of these parodies that one can easily understand why this should have happened. Using the original songs, Alessandrini and his cohorts rewrite the lyrics and invent different situations for the stars that send them up with a lot of affection, and occasional spite. In this first selection of goodies from the team, you can hear the cast of the Broadway *Pirates of Penzance* wondering just what Linda Ronstadt is doing in a musical, Angela Lansbury bewailing her fate in an unsuccessful revival of *Mame*, and Patti LuPone complaining about Streisand purchasing the film rights for *Evita*. These parodies are obviously tied to Broadway in the early 1980s, but some of the others are timeless – Lyng and Webb are especially wonderful as duelling divas Merman and Martin, while Webb as Carol Channing *still* playing in *Hello, Dolly!* is equally relevant in the mid-1990s! The small cast of performers are excellent, brilliantly impersonating a whole host of Broadway stars, each and every one good enough to be performing on Broadway in their own right. Fred Barton's arrangements and piano playing are a wonder – cleverly conceived and as much a part of the parody as the very funny lyrics. Barton is even given his own solo spot as an audition pianist "Sick of playing their songs". There are a lot of in-jokes and one has to be a dedicated Broadway watcher to understand them all, but no matter, every listener will find this a thoroughly enjoyable and funny recording.
    The second in the series has the parody team at their very best: parodies of Sondheim (*Into the Words*), and the invasion of British musicals (*Phantom of the Musicals* and a magnificent extended sequence on *Les Misérables*) are highlights, as are the send-ups of the stars – Patti

LuPone, George Hearn, Liza Minnelli, Elaine Stritch ("The ladies who screech") and Mandy Patinkin all come under the merciless scrutiny of the *Forbidden Broadway* team. Perfect piano accompaniment by Philip Fortenberry makes for a follow-up disc that betters the original.

A third parody disc might be considered to be dangerous – would the joke wear thin? Happily, this too succeeds superbly. It is clear that musical theatre is wide open to such an approach and Carol Channing's guest appearance amidst a host of her imitators in the opening number, proves that the format can still work beautifully if it is well written. Targetted in this issue are *Grim Hotel, Mess of the Spider Woman, Mug Brothers* and *Tommy*. Barbra Streisand is imitated twice by different performers for both of her Broadway albums, while Topol, Michael Crawford, Julie Andrews ("I couldn't hit the note") and (once again) Merman and Martin are all included. Perhaps over an hour is too long for a disc of this nature, but selectively played it is once again a joyously funny experience for all lovers of music theatre. **RAC**

Front Row Centre The Broadway Gold Box 1935-88. **Original Cast Recordings**.
MCA mono/stereo Ⓟ MCAD4 11353 (four discs: 300 minutes: AAD).
Songs from **Rodgers:** Oklahoma!. Higher and Higher. A Connecticut Yankee. Carousel. The King and I. On Your Toes. **Gershwin:** Porgy and Bess. Girl Crazy. **Schwartz:** At Home Abroad. **Rome:** Pins and Needles. Call Me Mister. Destry Rides Again. **McHugh:** Streets of Paris. **Porter:** Leave it to Me. Panama Hattie. Mexican Hayride. Something for the Boys. Anything Goes. **Kern:** The Girl from Utah. Roberta. **Donaldson:** Whoopee. **Fain:** Sons o' Fun. Ankles Aweigh. **Duke:** Banjo Eyes. **Berlin:** This is the Army. Annie Get Your Gun. Call Me Madam. **Weill:** One Touch of Venus. Knickerbocker Holiday. Lost in the Stars. Lady in the Dark. **Bizet:** Carmen Jones. **Arlen:** Bloomer Girl. **Wright/Forrest:** Song of Norway. **Charig:** Follow the Girls. **Bernstein:** On the Town. Wonderful Town. **Romberg:** Up in Central Park. **Siegmeister** (arr): Sing Out, Sweet Land. **Scott:** Lute Song. **Whiting:** Take a Chance. **Martin:** Look Ma, I'm Dancin'!. High Spirits. **Loesser:** Where's Charley?. Guys and Dolls. **Dolan:** Texas, Lil' Darlin'. **Gould:** Arms and the Girl. **Moross:** The Golden Apple. **Young:** Seventh Heaven. **Selden:** The Amazing Adele. **Bock:** Mr Wonderful. **Barer:** Once Upon a Mattress. **Barnes:** The Billy Barnes Revue. **Herman:** Parade. Mack and Mabel. **Burke:** Donnybrook. **Styne:** Fade Out – Fade In. **Leigh:** Man of La Mancha. **Merrill:** Henry, Sweet Henry. **Previn:** Coco. **Strouse:** Applause. **Wilson:** The Boy Friend. **Lloyd Webber:** Jesus Christ Superstar. Evita. **MacDermot:** Two Gentlemen from Verona. **Hall:** The Best Little Whorehouse in Texas. **Swados:** Doonsbury. **Miller:** Big River. **Gay:** Me and My Girl. **Herrmann:** Romance, Romance.

A four-disc treasury of musical riches containing rare cuts and material previously not available on CD as well as a number of classic recordings from the MCA archives. MCA control all the American Decca recordings and, as they arguably established the tradition of the music theatre cast recording in 1943 with the issue of selections from *Oklahoma!*, such a selection is bound to be of importance. The pieces have been chosen carefully to represent the stars and shows at their best and are presented in chronological order of issue, except for the first track on Volume 1 (the *Oklahoma!* finale) and the last on Volume 4 ("There's no business like show business" fittingly enough). The remastering of the early recordings is exceptional – listen to Millie Weitz from the original *Pins and Needles* in "Nobody makes a pass at me", recorded in 1938 and sounding as fresh as Streisand's version from 1963. The three selections from *Oklahoma!* are alternate takes previously not issued, as is Muriel Smith's recording of "Dat's love" from *Carmen Jones*. Ethel Merman, the queen of the Decca cast recording, is well represented, including several selections from her "Songs She Made Famous" album and the host of star names includes Gertrude Lawrence, Ray Bolger, Walter Huston, Burl Ives, Mary Martin, Pearl Bailey, Dolores Gray (in two wonderful songs from *Destry Rides Again*), Katharine Hepburn (the title-song from *Coco*) and Lauren Bacall. Accompanied by a sumptuous booklet with superb notes by Max Preeo, this is one of the most successful box sets ever issued concerning music theatre – a perfectly balanced, beautifully presented collection of the rare and the familiar. **RAC**

A Gala Concert for Hal Prince 1995 **Munich Philharmonic Cast** (with Teri Bibb, Len Cariou, Kelli James Chase, Robert DuSold, Debbie Shapiro Gravitte, David Michael Johnson, Ria Jones, Patricia Nessy, Kenneth Nichols and Dave Willetts); **Munich Radio Orchestra / Charles Prince.**
First Night Ⓟ DOCRCD2 (two discs: 105 minutes: DDD).

Songs from The Phantom of the Opera, Evita, West Side Story, Cabaret, Follies, Kiss of the Spider Woman, Fiddler on the Roof, Sweeney Todd, Show Boat, She Loves Me, Candide, A Little Night Music, Company, Pacific Overtures and A Funny Thing Happened on the Way to the Forum.

Although this celebration of Harold Prince's career wasn't held on either Broadway or in London's West End, where he has been a major figure as both producer and director for the past 40 years, no one should pass over this pair of CDs thinking they may be short-changed in some way. The music ranges from the lush Novello-like strains of "All I ask of you" to the pastiche of the past, *Follies*. As a bonus this concert from Munich offers some performances that are as good as any on disc, with the *Phantom* duet, sung by Robert DuSold and Teri Bibb, unlikely to be surpassed. Individually they turn in some other fine performances, with Bibb singing the "Ice-cream" song from *She Loves Me* (one to rank alongside the original by Barbara Cook), and Robert DuSold with "Beautiful girls" from *Follies*, which must be a joy for any man to perform. "Ol' man river", a song with a much longer recorded tradition, resonates in a way I've not heard before in Kenneth Nichols's deeply impressive interpretation (he has been singing the role in Prince's production of *Show Boat*, now in its second year on Broadway). Other performances that make the ears prick up include Debbie Shapiro Gravitte's "Cabaret", again vying with Dame Judi Dench's original West End Sally Bowles, and from *Sweeney Todd*, "Not while I'm around", a ballad that I'd always considered small fry until I heard this version by Dave Willetts. There are perhaps two disappointments: a "Glitter and be gay" (from *Candide*) that goes over the top in the heat of the moment and, alas, the bewitching "Kiss of the Spider Woman".

The CDs get off to a good start with an overture arranged by William David Brohn which reminds us of the extent of Prince's work, going back to *The Pajama Game* and *Damn Yankees* with, *en route*, snatches of such diverse scores as *On the Twentieth Century*, *Fiddler on the Roof* and *Merrily We Roll Along*. The Munich Radio Orchestra, under Hal Prince's son Charles, contribute a characterful account of the *Candide* Overture and "Night Waltz" from *A Little Night Music*. The deft pay-off, "Side by side" (from *Company*), is a charming conclusion to a great entertainment. **AE**

New review

Great Theatre Songs With **Al Jolson, Fred Astaire, Paul Robeson, Binnie Hale, Mary Ellis, Peggy Wood, Gertrude Lawrence, Jessie Matthews, Dorothy Dickson, Alfred Drake** and **Patricia Burke.**
Happy Days Ⓜ 75605-52284-2 (79 minutes: ADD). Recorded 1925-45.

Songs from Sinbad, Lady, Be Good!, Peggy-Ann, Will-O-the-Whispers, Show Boat, This Year of Grace, Bitter Sweet, Evergreen, For the Love of Mike, The Cat and the Fiddle, Music in the Air, As Thousands Cheer, Nymph Errant, Anything Goes, Jill Darling, Glamorous Night, Me and My Girl, Lights Up, Lady in the Dark, Oklahoma!, The Lisbon Story, Perchance to Dream.

This is a splendid introduction to the great musical comedy stars of the 1920s and 1930s, and some of their most famous songs. Of course here are Gershwin (Al Jolson in "Swanee", the Astaires in "Lady, be good!"), Kern (Robeson's 1932 "Ol' man river" and three contrasted leading ladies, Binnie Hale in "Who?", Mary Ellis's beautifully articulated "I've told every little star" and Peggy Wood's haughty "She didn't say yes"), and even Weill (Gertie Lawrence's "Saga of Jenny"). Rodgers and Hart and Rodgers and Hammerstein are represented by two of Rodgers's London hits – "Dancing on the ceiling" sung by Jessie Matthews and "Tree in the park" sung by Dorothy Dickson, while Alfred Drake's original "Surrey with a fringe on top" is the latest Broadway item on offer. Coward, Novello, Ellis and Gay are here to represent the West End, with the nowadays comparatively rare songs from *The Lisbon Story* sung by Patricia Burke and Vincent Tildsley's Mastersingers. The singing ranges from quavery, old-fashioned light opera style to jazz-influenced, all-out showbiz (Ethel Waters in "Heat wave"). For anyone who wonders why people are interested in listening to old records this would provide a ready-made answer. **PO'C**

I Wants to Be a Actor Lady and other hits from early musical comedies. **Cincinnati University Singers and Theatre Orchestra / Earl Rivers.**
New World Ⓟ 80221-2 (45 minutes: ADD).
Songs from **Operti:** The Black Crook. **Cohan:** Little Johnny Jones. **Rice:** Evangeline, Conrad the Corsair. **Von Tilzer:** In Dahomey. **Luders:** The Prince of Pilsen. **Kern:** The Earl and the Girl. **Englander:** The Passing Show. **Morse:** Wang. **Gaunt:** A Trip to Chinatown. **De Koven:** Robin Hood. **Emmet:** Fritz, Our German Cousin. **Herbert:** Babes in Toyland.

This fascinating collection was first issued in 1978 and is thus one of the earlier attempts to recreate the American shows of yesteryear in modern sound. Indeed, there is a fascinating link with more recent collections in the presence of a young Kim Criswell, heard here in a delicious Victor Herbert number and in Jerome Kern's earliest hit "How'd you like to spoon with me?". The collection spans the period from 1866 to 1905, and its most familiar number is probably George M. Cohan's "Yankee Doodle boy". Other items rise gloriously from the pages of books on the history of American popular song – May Irwin's boisterous "Bully Song", the lilting waltz "The bowery" from the landmark *A Trip to Chinatown*, plus a number from turn-of-the-century operetta *The Prince of Pilsen* that found clear echos in Sigmund Romberg's *The Student Prince*. Other items will be new even to students of the genre, but the whole collection not only provides a fascinating glimpse of early American musical theatre but is performed with flair and distinction by soloists, chorus and orchestra alike. It all makes hugely enjoyable listening. **AML**

Invade My Privacy 1993 **London Cast** (with Jacqueline Dankworth, Lucy Dixon, Michelle Fine, Tina Jones and Howard Samuels) **/ Dave Brown.**
TER Ⓟ CDTER1202 (73 minutes: DDD).

Howard Samuels devised and performs in this revue show based on the writing of London-based New Yorker Fran Landesman. She may not be a well-known name, but her lyrics to two Tommy Wolf tunes have become modern classics – "Spring can really hang you up the most" and "The ballad of the sad young men". Both are included, although it would have been more effective if they were performed as solos rather than pieces for the whole company. Despite this, the recording, running at well over an hour, works well with its mix of poetry and songs. Miss Landesman's way with words is fascinating uncompromising, tough, often hilariously funny, but also bleak and depressing. She is not a writer of tender, cloying sentiment, and occasionally one thirsts for a big romantic ballad, but there is something refreshing about a piece that completely eschews such feelings and instead offers contemplation of such diverse subjects as "Shoes", "A Brontosaurus named Bert", and "Doner kebabs". There is also a mini-opera based on *Sunset Boulevard* that predates Lloyd Webber's rather more lush interpretation of the classic movie. The cast, supported by a small band, is excellent. Jacqueline Dankworth (daughter of Cleo Laine) shines in both the songs and poetry, Tina Jones is magnificent in the *Sunset* piece and hysterical in the deadpan "If they can't take a joke". Howard Samuels has a clear love of the material throwing himself into his songs with total commitment and fire. Landesman offers a quirky and very different perspective on everyday life – it is well worth investigating her world via this interesting and unusual recording. **RAC**

New review
Jelly Roll 1996 **Off-Broadway Cast** (with Vernel Bagneris) **/ Morten Gunnar Larsen** (pf).
GBH Records Ⓟ BCD400 (72 minutes: DDD).

Jelly Roll Morton claimed he invented jazz and died believing he had not received the adoration he deserved. The life story of Jelly Roll, who was a Creole brought up in New Orleans, is fascinating as a history of the early days of jazz, the times and the progress of the black (or Creole) performer. This 'musical' should not to be mistaken for Broadway's *Jelly's Last Jam* of a few seasons ago, which adapted Jelly Roll's songs and tended to concentrate upon his unpleasant side; this one-man show keeps fairly on the straight and narrow using the unadulterated originals – and they sound just fine as they are (a few other composers do get a look in). Vernel Bagneris, who plays Jelly Roll, narrates and sings the songs – he also 'created' the show. It was a performance which earned him an Obie award and a string of others for his creation. However, the back-bone of this entertaining love-in is the glorious jazz piano playing of Morten Gunnar Larsen.

A must for the jazz collector and anyone with rhythm in their jellied bones, the songs are as well sung as they are played and there are some beauties here including the well-known "Ballin the Jack", "Tiger Rag" and the fun "Animule Dance". However, if you like your musicals with more than just a piano accompaniment and a solo performance the simplicity of this will not satisfy you. Bagneris can also be heard on the original cast recording of *The Life*.   **RSB**

Jolson 1995 **London Cast** (with Brian Conley, John Bennett, Sally Ann Triplett, John Conroy, Brian Greene, Craig Stevenson and Chrissy Roberts) **/ John Evans**.
First Night Ⓕ CASTCD56 (57 minutes: DDD).

A live recording from the Victoria Palace Theatre, London in 1996, this recording is a souvenir of the remarkable impersonation of one of Broadway's greatest showmen, Al Jolson by Brian Conley. There are 24 songs, and Conley's Jolson has the lion's share of them. It's another of the biographical concerts that Britain's audiences are so fond of. The first half or so of the show whizzes through a more-or-less accurate survey of the main events in the subject's life (in this case, for instance, Jolson is restricted to one wife, Ruby, who stays with him rather longer than accuracy demands) and then abandons all to allow the star to present a concert of his hits. The show won the Olivier Award for Best Musical for 1996 – and deserves it if only for the energy and commitment expended by the cast led by the tireless Conley.   **MPK**

Lilac Time (Schubert, arr. Berté and Clutsam) 1923 **London Cast** (with Clara Butterworth, Percy Heming and Courtice Pounds) **/ Clarence Raybould**.
Rio Rita (Tierney) 1930 **London Cast** (with Jose Collins and Claude Flemming) **/ John Heuvel**.
A Southern Maid (Fraser-Simson/Novello) 1920 **London Cast** (with Edith Day and Geoffrey Guyther) **/ Merlin Morgan**.
Pearl mono Ⓜ GEMMCD9115 (66 minutes: AAD).

Prime billing in this collection goes to the selection from *Lilac Time*, the World War I portrayal of Schubert on stage with a score arranged from his own melodies. It was greatly popular and doubtless still has its adherents. Yet it is perhaps the least attractive of the selections here, with a trio of quasi-operatic principals, heard through the crackle that Pearl prefers to leave the listener to filter out, laying a decidedly heavy hand on the whole thing. Far better all round is the selection from *Rio Rita*, an unashamedly escapist and altogether less pretentious piece, set on the Rio Grande. It is full of stirring numbers such as the "March of the Rangers" and delightfully lighthearted and romantic ones like "Following the sun around". The cast is led with elegance and style by sweet-voiced 1920s leading lady Edith Day, who had earlier starred in the same composer's *Irene*. In much the same escapist vein is *A Southern Maid*, the immediate successor to *The Maid of the Mountains* at Daly's Theatre, London, with another gypsyish leading role for the glamorous Jose Collins. The numbers that enchant here are by the young Ivor Novello and, as with the *Rio Rita* excerpts, they should attract any lover of escapist twentieth-century operetta.   **AML**

Lost in Boston, Volumes 1-3. With **Liz Callaway, Gregg Edelman, Jonathan Freeman, Jason Graae, Debbie Shapiro Gravitte, Harry Groener, Guy Haines, Judy Kaye, Liz Larsen, Emily Loesser, Rebecca Luker, Karen Mason, Sally Mayes, Michelle Nicastro, Lynnette Perry, Ron Raines, Michael Rupert, Lynne Wintersteller** and **Karen Ziemba** (sngrs) **/ James Stenborg, Tom Fay**.
Varèse Sarabande Spotlight Series Ⓕ VSD5475/5485/5563 (three discs, only available separately: 48, 47 and 43 minutes: DDD).
VSD5475 – Songs cut from **Holmes:** The Mystery of Edwin Drood. **Schmidt:** 110 in the Shade. **Bock:** Fiorello! Fiddler on the Roof. **Rodgers:** The King and I. **Bernstein:** West Side Story. **Kander:** Chicago. The Happy Time. **Flaherty:** Once On This Island. **Bacharach:** Promises, Promises. **Charlap:** Peter Pan. **Porter:** Silk Stockings. **Berlin:** Annie Get Your Gun. *VSD5485 – Songs cut from* **Schmidt:** I Do! I Do!. The Fantasticks. **Bacharach:** Promises, Promises. **Weill:** Street Scene. **Bock:** Fiddler on the Roof. The Rothschilds. The

Apple Tree. **Bernstein:** On the Town. **Strouse:** Applause. **Forrest/Wright:** Grand Hotel.
Kander: The Act. *VSD5563 – Songs cut from* **Styne:** Gypsy. **Loesser:** Guys and Dolls.
Where's Charley?. **Martin:** Meet Me in St Louis. **Coleman:** Seesaw. Sweet Charity. **Willson:**
The Music Man. **Schmidt:** 110 in the Shade. **Bock:** She Loves Me. **Strouse:** Bye Bye Birdie.
Rodgers: Flower Drum Song. Oklahoma!. **Sondheim:** Merrily We Roll Along. **Flaherty:**
Once On This Island.

A collection, spread over three volumes, of songs that were cut from well-known musicals
either in preview or in out-of-town tryouts. Although cut songs are often reused by
composers in other shows, this selection is based on songs that are tied musically and
lyrically to the scores from which they were cut. Sometimes strains of the music reappear in
the same score, but substantially these are songs that would not have a life outside of their
shows. On the first disc, Sally Mayes features strongly in the early selections – appearing in
one duet and two solos cut from *110 in the Shade*, her Texan drawl perfect for the gentle
"Sweetriver" and the up-tempo "Flibbertigibbet". Liz Callaway delivers a crystal-clear
rendition of the bittersweet "Where do I go from here?", cut from *Fiorello!*. There is a
fascinating recreation of an Act 1 trio cut from *The King and I* in which Judy Kaye, delivering
a brilliant Anna, despairs at how long she has been "Waiting". A sweet song removed from
Fiddler on the Roof, another delinquent's song from *West Side Story* and the agent's song
from *Chicago* (the character and the song were cut) are all worthy of examination. From
more modern pieces, the two songs from *The Mystery of Edwin Drood* are good (the
"Evensong" duet is especially lovely), while Lilias White's rendition of "Come down from the
tree" from *Once on This Island* is a delight. Probably the two songs that will be of most
interest are Cole Porter's "Let's make it a night", one of a dozen songs cut from *Silk
Stockings*, and "Take it in your stride", which Ethel Merman decided not to sing in *Annie Get
Your Gun* – here Liz Larsen gives a bravura performance of a rhythmically complex Irving
Berlin number. Steven Suskin's liner notes are amusing and informative, the perfect
accompaniment to the disc.

Fourteen more songs that shows lost along the way to their final incarnations appear on the
second disc. In many ways a superior presentation altogether, Suskin's entertaining liner notes
are far more detailed, opening with a discussion of why songs are cut, using four songs from *I Do!
I Do!* as examples. Karen Ziemba, star of the 1996 Broadway revival, is featured on one of the
selections, which are all very strong. Other highlights are "Italy in Technicolor", written for
Street Scene and "Say when" (brilliantly performed by Kaye Ballard), one of two female comic
numbers for *On the Town*.

The series continues to improve with a further 16 selections on the third disc. Peter Filichia
now provides the liner-notes, opening with a fascinating insight into the construction of
"Rose's turn" through the song "Mama's talkin' soft" removed from *Gypsy*. Highlights are
Lynne Wintersteller's rendition of "Pink taffeta sample, size 10" cut from *Sweet Charity*, the
duet "When I go out walkin' with my baby" conceived for the show that would become
Oklahoma!, and used in the 1996 Broadway production of *State Fair*, and two bittersweet up-
tempo numbers from *Seesaw* (fun performances from Debbie Shapiro Gravitte and
Michelle Nicastro). **RAC**

New review

Lost in Boston, Volume 4. **Klea Blackhurst, Brent Barrett, Michael Rupert, Jane Krakowski,
Sal Viviano, Ron Raines, Guy Haines, Karen Morrow, Melba Joyce, Jason Graae, Eydie
Alyson, Reece Holland, Jani Neuman, David Romano, Gerry McIntyre, Obba Babatunde,
Dee Hoty, Crista Moore, Danny Burstein, Alet Oury, Rupert Holmes (sngrs); instrumental
ensemble / Brad Ellis.**
Varèse Sarabande Spotlight Series Ⓟ VSD5768 (61 minutes: DDD).
Songs cut from **A. Schwartz:** By the Beautiful Sea. **S. Schwartz:** Pippin. **Styne:** Sugar.
Schmidt: 110 in the Shade. **Goldenberg:** Ballroom. **Coleman:** Sweet Charity. **Schafer:** Drat!
The Cat!. **Menken:** Little Shop of Horrors. **Arlen:** Jamaica. **Hall:** The Best Little
Whorehouse in Texas. **Shire:** Big. **Anderson:** Goldilocks. **Carnelia:** Working.

There's a modern vogue for the 'director's cut' approach to musical recordings, presented in their
authentic entirety, complete with discarded and replaced numbers. That's fine for the archivist, but
the excellent "Lost in Boston" series of discs takes the more accessible approach of raiding the

vaults for songs which were ultimately 'lost' from the final scores for a multitude of reasons that rarely had anything to do with their quality and presenting them in compilation form, with concise accompanying notes. The wonder is that there is apparently a limitless treasure-trove of these lost numbers.

The fourth volume kicks off with the rollicking "Thirty weeks of heaven" from the little-remembered 1954 Dorothy Fields/Arthur Schwartz show *By the Beautiful Sea*. A vibrant assessment of the minstrel's life, delivered with great verve by Brent Barrett and the Merman-esque Klea Blackhurst. Previous volumes have focused on numbers cut from the all-time greats. *Little Shop of Horrors* (Ashman and Menken), *Pippin* (Stephen Schwartz) or *Ballroom* (Bergman, Bergman and Goldenberg) are not in the same enduring league, but cut songs from these shows still have much to offer in terms of great tunes, acerbic lyrics and good old-fashioned *joie de vivre*. "Gimme a raincheck" was replaced by "The rhythm of life" in *Sweet Charity* but still sounds like a showstopper on its own merits, as sung here by Melba Joyce. Another highlight, albeit a sad one, is Karen Morrow's rendition of "Who gave you permission?", a bitter paean to loss and bereavement from *Ballroom*. Lushly orchestrated throughout by Brad Ellis and Larry Moore, these numbers might have been lost from their original shows, but thanks to the "Lost in Boston" team, they have been given a life of their own. **PF**

Music from the New York Stage, 1890-1920 – Volume 1 (1890-1908); Volume 2 (1908-13); Volume 3 (1913-17); Volume 4 (1917-20). **Original Casts.**

Pearl mono Ⓜ GEMMCDS9050/2, GEMMCDS9053/5, GEMMCDS9056/8 and GEMMCDS9059/61 (four three-disc sets: 231, 230, 214 and 208 minutes: AAD).

This wondrous 15-hour collection is claimed to include "virtually every extant original cast recording" from shows produced in New York from 1890 to 1920. In the fact that it is totally unselective lies part of its charm. Whereas shows that one wrongly imagines must have been recorded (Herbert's *The Red Mill* or *Mademoiselle Modiste*, for instance) are missing, there are deeply weird items such as German dialect scenes by Weber and Fields and an appalling yodelling and teeth-clicking number by Al H. Wilson that leave one astonished at what Americans listened to in those days. But there are numbers here from shows such as Kerker's *The Belle of New York*, Herbert's *The Fortune Teller* and Friml's *The Firefly*, as well as from British shows such as *The Geisha*, *Florodora*, *Three Little Maids* and *Tonight's the Night*. From the early days certain voices – George M. Cohan, Chauncey Alcott, May Irwin, Marie Cahill, Bert Williams – rise gloriously above the primitive conditions and surface noise of the infant recording industry. By Volume 4 there is greater assurance from the performers as well as greater familiarity about the numbers – lengthy excerpts from Kern's *Oh, Boy!*, Eddie Cantor and Fanny Brice in *The Ziegfeld Follies*, Al Jolson in *Sinbad* (including "Swanee") and Edith Day in *Irene*. This is not a collection for the faint-hearted; but for the lover of musical theatre history it is a treasure-trove. There are fascinating discoveries at every turn. **AML**

`New review`

Musical Winners   1996 International Musical Concert Casts (with Claire Moore, Denis Quilley, Clive Carter, Joanna Riding and John Barrowman).

Columbus Records Ⓔ CD81569/70 (two discs: 59 and 51 minutes: DDD).
CD8159 – Enter the Guardsman. The Three Musketeers. Red, Red, Rose. *CD81570* – Best Songs.

The venue for this competition is Denmark which is surprising as the four new musicals previewed here are either British or American and the other shows represented by single songs on the second CD are all sung in English. The two separate discs do not indicate who won but for me the outright winner would be *Enter the Guardsman* – which coincidentally is the only show to have received, as yet, a commercial showing. This is the second of the 20-minute sections we are given on the "Musical Winners" CD which also showcases a new musical version of *The Three Musketeers* and a Robbie Burns outing called *Red, Red Rose*. The first sounds very workmanlike and can boast of a score by the talented George Stiles who will hopefully one day find success. "Lilacs", sung by Claire Moore, is a fine number and the whole certainly deserves a wider audience. *Enter the Guardsman* is, however, far more tantalizing as it is an entire section with dialogue that we hear with excellent performances by such seasoned performers as Denis Quilley, Clive Carter, Claire Moore and Joanna Riding – 20 minutes is just long enough to get the marvellous title-song and three other above average numbers. *Red, Red Rose* sags terribly after the middle section.

The second CD is a mixed bag of songs with no details as to which shows they represent, but it does end with an eight-minute medley from a new version of *Peter Pan* which sounds fun and seems to be a Danish audience-pleaser, judging from their applause. The "Musical Winners" album is recommended mainly for its central section.   **RSB**

Noël/Cole Let's Do It! 1994 Chichester Festival Production (with Liz Robertson, Louise Gold, David Kernan, Robin Ray, Peter Greenwell and Pat Kirkwood).
Silva Screen Ⓕ SONGCD910 (66 minutes: DDD).
Songs from Operette, Out of This World, Tonight at 8.30, Kiss Me Kate, Leave it to Me, Sigh No More, Anything Goes, Private Lives, Conversation Piece, Bitter Sweet, Nymph Errant, Red, Hot and Blue!, Ace of Clubs, Fifty Million Frenchmen, The New Yorkers, Panama Hattie, Set to Music, Sail Away, Words and Music, Cavalcade, Waiting in the Wings and Seven Lively Arts.

There is always a demand for sophisticated revues based around the work of much-loved composers, and the words and music of Noël Coward and Cole Porter are a gift to a group of artists of this calibre. David Kernan, who might be described as a doyen of this type of entertainment (he is a veteran of *Side By Side By Sondheim* and *Kern Goes to Hollywood*), compiled and starred in this production. The result is an elegant sparring session between two of the wittiest songwriters in the history of musical theatre. It's an even contest, of course, but the chief delight is the intelligent, instinctive reading which these performers bring to a collection of evergreen standards. There are a number of cleverly combined medleys: for example, Kernan gives a sublime "London pride" (Coward), matched by Liz Robertson and Louise Gold as they duet on "I happen to like New York". Robertson and Gold go on to deliver a gently swinging "Twentieth-century blues". There is also a delicate combination of Coward waltzes: "Someday I'll find you", "I'll follow my secret heart" and "I'll see you again". But the emphasis is generally on the comic. Gold, a regular participant in Ian Marshall Fisher's annual season of 'lost' musicals concerts at the Barbican in London, is a particularly gifted comedienne, as her rendition of "The physician" clearly demonstrates. She is more than a match for the memory of Gertrude Lawrence. Other treats include a couple of numbers from Pat Kirkwood (Coward's "Chase me Charlie" and Porter's "You're the top"), and Kernan wringing every nuance from Coward's "Nina", which includes the line, "She cursed Cole Porter, too". Tastefully and expertly performed, this revue would suit anyone who likes their nostalgia laced with a touch of acid.   **PF**

Original Cast! 1891-1994 Broadway Casts.
Metropolitan Opera Guild mono/stereo Ⓕ Met801/11CD (22 discs, available in two-disc sets as below).
Met801CD, "The Early Years: 1891-1929" (two discs: 145 minutes: ADD) – with Ethel Levey, Noble Sissle, Dennis King, Evelyn Herbert, Libby Holman and Helen Morgan. *Met802CD, "The Thirties"* (two discs: 142 minutes: ADD) – with Ruth Etting, Gertrude Lawrence, Clifton Webb, Todd Duncan, Olive Stanton and Hollace Shaw. *Met803CD, "The Forties, Part 1"* (two discs: 138 minutes: ADD) – with Shirley Ross, Ethel Merman, Danny Kaye, Alfred Drake, Mary Martin and John Raitt. *Met 804CD, "The Forties, Part 2"* (two discs: 140 minutes: ADD) – with Pearl Bailey, Brian Sullivan, Ella Logan, Patricia Morison, Alfred Drake and Inez Matthews. *Met805CD, "The Fifties, Part 1"* (two discs: 140 minutes: ADD) – with Boris Karloff, Stubby Kaye, Vivian Blaine, Rufus Smith, Vivienne Segal and Walter Slezak. *Met806CD, "The Fifties, Part 2"* (two discs: 143 minutes: ADD) – with Gwen Verdon, Sammy Davis Jr., Barbara Cook, Robert Preston, Dolores Gray and Rosetta LeNoire. *Met807CD, "The Sixties, Part 1"* (two discs: 148 minutes: ADD) – with Anthony Perkins, Tammy Grimes, Kaye Ballard, Elaine Stritch, Diahann Carroll and Richard Kiley. *Met808CD, "The Sixties, Part 2"* (two discs: 144 minutes: ADD) – with Lee Remick, Liza Minnelli, Robert Goulet, Bill Hinnant, Angela Lansbury and Paul Hecht. *Met809CD, "The Seventies"* (two discs: 144 minutes: ADD) – with Shelley Winters, Len Cariou, Lauren Bacall, Dale Soules, Bernadette Peters and Georgia Brown. *Met810CD, "Completing the Century: 1980-94"*

(two discs: 140 minutes: ADD) – with Jim Dale, Gregory Hines, George Hearn, Mandy Patinkin, Patti LuPone and Shirley Verrett. *Met811CD, "Visitors from Abroad: 1900-94"* (two discs: 138 minutes: ADD) – with Jack Buchanan, Julie Andrews, Elizabeth Seal, Anthony Newley, Danielle Darrieux and Thandi Zulu.

This 22-CD survey of the Broadway musical is the brainchild of Paul Gruber of the Metropolitan Opera Guild, the august publishing and educational wing of the New York Met. Each two-disc set comes with a handsome 90-page booklet with full-page photographs, most of them unfamiliar, from the 500 or so productions covered. Although much of the material will be familiar to the enthusiast, each disc has at least one or two major rarities that amount to a collector's feast.

Many of the items appearing on the first set (1891-1929) are the same as those found on Pearl's 12-disc anthology "Music from the New York Stage" (see separate review), but even here there are some different items such as Irving Berlin singing his own "Oh, how I hate to get up in the morning" from *Yip-Yip-Yaphank* (1918). From the 1920s, on the second CD, Helen Morgan's "Don't ever leave me" from Kern's *Sweet Adeline* (1929) and Irene Bordoni in "Let's misbehave" by Cole Porter (from *Paris*, 1928) are particularly valuable. In the 1930s, it is wonderful to hear Gertrude Lawrence singing "Exactly like you" from *The International Revue* (1930), as well as the expected hits from the Astaires, Ethel Waters and Tamara singing Kern's "Smoke gets in your eyes". There is also a very rare live recording of Gershwin himself conducting the opening moments of *Porgy and Bess* (1935), with Abbie Mitchell's original "Summertime". Olive Stanton's "Nickle under the foot" from Blitzstein's *The Cradle Will Rock* (1937) contrasts with "Sing me a song of social significance" – a direct Blitzstein parody from *Pins and Needles*.

It doesn't take much historical knowledge to pinpoint the 1940s and 1950s as the richest era of all on Broadway. The first 1940s volume has such rarities as Danny Kaye in "Farming" from Porter's *Let's Face It* (1941), Eddie Cantor and June Clyde in "We're having a baby (my baby and me)" from *Banjo Eyes* (1941), and the whole sequence ends with Kern's last song, "Nobody else but me", from the 1946 revival of *Show Boat*. Volume 2 of the 1940s includes original casts of *Annie Get Your Gun, Street Scene, Finian's Rainbow, High Button Shoes* and *Brigadoon* – all put on within a year (1946-7)! Even in this rich era there is room for some less well-known items, such as Elaine Stritch singing "Civilization Song" from *Angel in the Wings* (1947) and Danny Scholl describing "The big movie show in the sky" from *Texas Li'l Darlin'* (1949). Carol Channing sings the decade out with "Diamonds are a girl's best friend" from *Gentlemen Prefer Blondes* (which opened in December, 1949). The early 1950s are heralded by Ethel Merman in *Call Me Madam* (1950), and passes by way of such curiosities as Nanette Fabray in *Make a Wish* (1951), via Jack Cassidy in *Wish You Were Here* (1952), to arrive at Don Ameche and Hildegard Neff in *Silk Stockings* (1955), Cole Porter's last Broadway musical. The late 1950s and early 1960s saw the original cast album become something of a specialized industry, so inevitably, with the choice being much greater, there are perhaps more things that one would question as missing, but no one could doubt the importance of – to name but four peaks – Barbara Cook singing "Glitter and be gay" from Bernstein's *Candide* (1956), Ellen Hanley's rendition of "When did I fall in love?" from *Fiorello* (1959), Alfred Drake in "To look upon my love" from *Kean* (1961) and Mary Martin in Arthur Schwartz's *Jennie* (1963) explaining what she'll do "Before I kiss the world goodbye".

The later era saw the Broadway show lose some of its home-grown pizzazz, and the emergence of a new European style which has prompted the publishers to add the coda "Visitors from Abroad". This begins with the *Florodora* Girls in "Tell me pretty maiden" in 1900, has two very rare USA Gertrude Lawrence tracks ("Poor little rich girl" and "A cup of coffee, a sandwich and you"), and is inevitably dominated throughout the second disc by Lloyd Webber, the whole enterprise ending with Betty Buckley's version of "With one look" from *Sunset Boulevard*.

With its annotations, illustrations, and glorious mixture of the great, the familiar and the rare, this edition is not only a pleasure to look at and listen to, but would make a wonderful tool for anyone attempting to teach the history of 20th-century American musical theatre.   **PO'C**

New review
Play On! 1997 Broadway Cast (with Carl Anderson, Yvette Carson, Andre DeShields, Cheryl Freeman, Lawrence Hamilton, Larry Marshall and Tonya Pinkins) **/ Luther Henderson.**
Varèse Sarabande Spotlight Series Ⓟ VSD5837 (67 minutes: DDD).

A 'new' musical based on an intriguing idea of setting Duke Ellington's songs to a 1940s Harlem (a perfect excuse for Cotton Club settings) telling of Shakespeare's *Twelfth Night*. The cross-dressing is dealt with cleverly: the plot concerns a young lady trying to be accepted into a man's world of writing songs – a very free adaptation indeed. Not that the recording gives much indication to that, for what we hear is more a review of Ellington's work done in a jazzy up-beat way which this talented black cast perform with vitality and sheer joy – it's as much a tribute to the black performers of the past as to the songs. The show flopped on Broadway but could easily resurface in London at any time. The reason for its flop status would certainly not be the tried-and-tested score, with such standards as "Take the 'A' train", "Mood indigo", "Don't get around much any more" and "I'm beginning to see the light", and there are some terrific lesser-known songs. There are 19 tracks, making this an attractive celebration of Ellington's work, though it's a pity that the booklet does not give a better plot summary showing how the songs went with the new story (it just mentions various episodes and characters in a wide-brush explanation, perhaps indicating that the book was indeed the problem with the show). If you like these songwriter compilations you won't be disappointed.

RSB

Return to the Forbidden Planet 1989 London Cast (with John Ashby, Matthew Devitt, Kate Edgar, Nicky Furre, Allison Harding, Anthony Hunt, Christian Roberts, Kraig Thornber, Tim Barron, Ben Fox, Jane Karen and Patrick Moore) / **Kate Edgar**.
Virgin Ⓕ CDV2631 (69 minutes: DDD).

This live recording from the Cambridge Theatre, London, captures all the exuberance of what is cheekily described as "Shakespeare's forgotten rock and roll masterpiece". That is to say, a musical version of the cult 1956 Sci-Fi picture *Forbidden Planet*, itself based on the story of *The Tempest*. There are 42 rock 'n' roll classics performed with professionalism by the entire cast who are actors, singers and multi-instrumentalists of a high order. The songs are well chosen to suit the characters to whom they apply – thus "Rocket man" applies to Robby the Robot and "Monster mash" is a natural for the creature summoned up from the psyche. A raucous delight for the young in heart and strong in ear. Incidentally, the team followed this up with a version of the Scottish play entitled *From a Jack to a King* which didn't prove as popular. **MPK**

Shakespeare on Broadway Studio Cast (with Jason Graae, Lynnette Perry, Crista Moore, Sean McDermott, Melba Joyce, Rupert Holmes, Karen Ziemba and Debbie Shapiro Gravitte) / **Tom Fay**.
Varèse Sarabande Spotlight Series Ⓕ VSD5622 (58 minutes: DDD).
Songs from **Porter:** Kiss Me, Kate. **Valenti:** Oh, Brother!. **Adler:** Music Is. **Rodgers:** The Boys from Syracuse. **Sondheim:** The Frogs. **Lunden:** Another Midsummer Night. **Hester/Apolinar:** Your Own Thing. **Jones:** Rockabye Hamlet. **Holmes:** Twelfth Night. **Van Heusen:** Swingin' the Dream. **Kimmel:** The Comedy of Errors. **Bernstein:** West Side Story. **Loesser:** Red, Hot and Blue.

The proud sub-title of this interesting collection is "The Bard as musicalized, dramatized and bowdlerized by ...". Several great musicals have been written based on the works of Shakespeare and "Brush up your Shakespeare" runs as a theme through the recording, surfacing with three different lyrics – Jonathan Freeman, Guy Haines and Harry Groener have great fun with these. But Shakespeare has equally inspired some disasters and flops, and it is the recordings of songs from these shows that make the most fascinating listening. For instance, two songs are included from *Rockabye Hamlet* – a rock musical directed by Gower Champion that lasted a week on Broadway. The songs are not great, but the liner-notes conjure up all sorts of images for musical fans (apparently there was a number for Hamlet and his mother entitled "Shall we dance?", while Ophelia strangled herself with her microphone cord). Other rare gems on this disc are "Should I speak of loving you?" from the unrecorded Richard Adler score of *Music Is* (an adaptation of *Twelfth Night*) nicely sung by Marcia Mitzman, and Crista Moore's rendition of "It's Love ... I think" from a contemporary musical setting of *A Midsummer Night's Dream*. In fact, it is the rarities that constitute the best part of the disc. The familiar material is less interesting – "Tonight" from *West Side Story* is disappointing, while Ron Raines's version of Sondheim's "Fear no more" is not as strong as

George Hearn's recording. That aside, the fascination of much of this material makes it worthwhile listening. **RAC**

The Shakespeare Revue 1995 **London Cast** (with Susie Blake, Martin Connor, Janie Dee, Christopher Luscombe and Malcolm McKee).
TER Ⓕ CDTEM2 1237 (two discs: 110 mintes: DDD).
Songs by Porter, Coward, Wilson, Fragson, Bratton, Pritchett, Edwards, Oddie, Zwar, Sondheim, Stiles, King, McKee, Keane, More, Slade and Stamper.

Benefiting immeasurably from the presence of a live, evidently enraptured audience, this recording of the RSC's *Shakespeare Revue* is a delight from start to finish. Not only does it mix tried, tested and evergreen material from the likes of Coward, Porter, Priestly, Sandy Wilson and Julian Slade (not forgetting the Bard himself) with the modern wit of Victoria Wood, Sondheim, Dillie Keane and various Footlight talents, but it boasts a cast of consummate revue performers. It is virtually impossible, and certainly invidious, to single out particular items from a galaxy of treats. But Susie Blake's turn as an ageing actress living on past triumphs ("Which witch?"), Janie Dee as "The heroine the opera class forgot" (Cleopatra as Verdi might have presented her), Malcolm McKee's wistful "Teach me, dear creature" (Slade's setting of Shakespeare's words) and any of the Company numbers are all high spots. The spoken pieces, too, are priceless. Anecdotes compiled by Derek Nimmo, Victoria Wood's wicked take on an amateur director of *Hamlet* ("Giving notes") and a reading of Richmal Crompton's "William and the lost tourist" trip effortlessly off the players' tongues. With the magical setting of various Shakespearian farewells to McKee's music at the end, the temptation is to go back to the beginning and play it through all over again. This is revue at its acerbic, generous and affectionate best. **PF**

Summer Holiday – songs from the musical (with Darren Day).
RCA Victor Ⓕ 74321-45616-2 (50 minutes: DDD).

While Cliff Richard was showing his nasty side in *Heathcliff*, the nice Darren Day was impersonating the younger Cliff in a show based on the film *Summer Holiday*. It's not a bad impersonation and through 19 tracks there are often moments when it's just like listening to a Cliff compilation by the man himself. The film score has been supplemented with other Cliff hits dating back to the early rock "Move it" and the Peter Pan of English pop songs, "Living doll". Giving this CD a seal of approval, Cliff makes a guest appearance helping out with many of the backing vocals and Hank Marvin, from Cliff's backing group The Shadows, plays lead guitar on some (he is also composer of many of the tracks). As a show, it is a star vehicle for the talented Day who is building his own set of devotees, and while this is not strictly an original cast recording it shows what the musical high spirits on this holiday to the Mediterranean sun was like. This is high spirits without the lager louts; clean thoughts and clean living all the way – and it's good clean fun to listen to. However, it must reflect upon the music of today when a new generation wants to share their parents' youthful exuberance. Good for a party! **RSB**

Swingtime Canteen 1997 **Studio Cast** (with Ruth Williamson, Amy Elizabeth Jones, Penny Ayn Mass, Kelli Macquire and Marcy McGuigan) **/ David Wolfson**.
Papa Ⓕ HF9798 (56 minutes: DDD).

It's 1944 in wartime London and an all-girl band from Hollywood, headed by MGM star Marian Ames, are beginning a tour of troop camps. Part of the first concert (to which we are invited) is to be broadcast. The interplay between the girls is nice and the plot is not too demanding – although quite a lot happens as the concert proceeds. And, yes there are happy endings. Not that any of this will worry the listener, for the plot has stayed firmly in the theatre and there is no original score to dissect. The CD is, therefore, little more than a compilation of songs of the period. This is pleasant enough and the performances are fine, but there is not too much authenticity and with so many of these songs available on other compilations by contemporary artists with original arrangements the comparison does not always hold up. Maxene Andrews (yes, she of the Andrews Sisters) introduces this 50th anniversary tribute to the end of the Second World War (sadly, she died soon after being involved in one of its productions). Guests on the recording are some of the girls who have been in various productions, such as Alison Fraser and Emily Loesser. I found the sequence when "Sing, sing, sing" gets interrupted by an air raid and two First World War songs a little hard to take. It is difficult to see many buying this for any other reason than as a memory of what was no doubt a very pleasant little show.   **RSB**

That's Entertainment! The Ultimate Anthology of MGM Musicals. **Original Film Casts** (with Judy Garland, Mickey Rooney, Fred Astaire, Gene Kelly, Frank Sinatra, Lena Horne, Ann Miller, Joan Crawford and Maurice Chevalier).
Rhino mono/stereo Ⓟ 72182 (six discs: ADD). Highlights available on EMI CDODEON21.

MGM came into its own as a studio for musicals in the 1940s. Although this anthology, based on the three compilation films *That's Entertainment!*, parts 1, 2 and 3, runs from *The Broadway Melody of 1929* to *Gigi* in 1958, the 1940s emerges easily with the most numbers.

RKO had Astaire and Rodgers, with Berlin, Kern, Gershwin and Porter to write for them. Over at Warner Bros., Harry Warren provided a great stream of unforgettable songs for Busby Berkeley and his team. Paramount had Jeannette MacDonald and Maurice Chevalier, although MGM eventually poached them for Ernst Lubitsch's film of *The Merry Widow*, transformed out of all recognition (Lehár had other things on his mind in 1934), and here is Chevalier in a snatch of "Girls, girls, girls". But from the early days the revelation is Joan Crawford, solid of tone and with clear diction, in a song by Louis Alter and Jo Trent, "Gotta feelin' for you" from *The Hollywood Revue of 1929*. Because of the format of the *That's Entertainment!* films, there are some infuriating cuts: for example, three versions of "Singin' in the rain" splash in and out of each other. Although Allan Jones's dubbing for the voice of Stanley Morner (later known as Dennis Morgan) in "A pretty girl is like a melody" from *The Great Ziegfeld* (1936) is impressive, from the 1930s it's Groucho Marx who takes the prize with 'Yip' Harburg and Harold Arlen's "Lydia the tattooed lady" from 1939's *A Day at the Circus*.

From the 1940s, all sorts of famous Judy Garland performances are obvious choices, with a handful of surprises, "I'm an Indian, too" from her never-completed film of *Annie Get Your Gun*; Kern's "Who?" from the biopic *Till the Clouds Roll By* (1946), and the extraordinary "Mr Monotony" cut from the final version of *Easter Parade* (1948). Rarities include Lena Horne singing Porter's "Just one of those things" from *Jubilee*, interpolated into the film of *Panama Hattie* (1942), Ethel Waters in *Cairo* (1942) singing "Buds won't bud" and the unusual sight (well, one has to imagine it on CD) of Clark Gable in *Idiot's Delight* singing "Puttin' on the ritz".

From the later era, Ava Gardner (with her own voice) in *Show Boat* (1951), Dolores Gray in *Designing Woman* (performing a modern version of the old Ethel Waters success "There'll be some changes made") are both outstanding, but it takes the old-timer Astaire to make the greatest impact in one of Cole Porter's last songs, "All of you" from the 1957 film of *Silk Stockings*.

EMI in the UK have given us a single disc of highlights, but the comprehensive six-disc set from Rhino in the USA is beautifully presented, with a 96-page booklet illustrated in colour with many stills and posters. The effect is a little schizophrenic as one jumps from decade to decade and film to film, but it's a charming salute to the old studio that gave us not only *The Wizard of Oz* but also *Dangerous When Wet*.   **PO'C**

Thoroughly Modern Millie 1967 **Film Cast** (with Julie Andrews and Carol Channing) **/** **André Previn.**
MCA Ⓜ MCAD10662 (36 minutes: AAD).

At the end of 1965 Julie Andrews had the world at her feet – she and John Wayne were America's favourite film stars and she was sought after for virtually every film musical being planned in the wake of the phenomenal success of *Mary Poppins* and *The Sound of Music*. *Thoroughly Modern Millie* went on to become the biggest grossing film in the history of Universal Pictures, with Julie's delicious recording of the film's newly composed title-song going round the world. However, it was a picture over which she came to have misgivings when producer Ross Hunter turned a charming tale into a roadshow blockbuster that went way over the top in its extravagances. Nevertheless, in a role that was specifically designed for her sweet nature, our star didn't disappoint, giving winning performances of some authentic 1920s standards in 'spiffing' arrangements by André Previn. Some new songs were provided by Sammy Cahn and James Van Heusen, while Elmer Bernstein won an Oscar for his original score (not represented on this disc). Alas, the MCA recording doesn't sound very well in this transfer, bringing back memories of those horrid-sounding boxed-in soundtracks of yesteryear. **AE**

Unsung Musicals Volumes 1[a] and 2[b]. with **Christine Baranski, Jodi Benson, Liz Callaway, Jonathan Freeman, Davis Gaines, Jason Graae, Debbie Shapiro Gravitte, Harry Groener, Judy Kuhn, Rebecca Luker, Sally Mayes, Lynette Perry** and **Michael Rupert / **[a]**Tony Fay,** [b]**Lanny Meyers.**
Varèse Sarabande Spotlight Series Ⓟ VSD5462/5564 (two discs, only available separately: 52 and 58 minutes: DDD).
VSD5462 – *Songs from* **Hamlisch:** Smile. **Schmidt:** The Bone Room. **Brush:** The First. **Larsen:** The Vamp. **Lawrence:** La Strada. **Karr:** We Take the Town. **Shire:** How Do You Do, I Love You. **Coleman:** Welcome to the Club. **Rosenthal:** Sherry!. **Schafer:** Drat, the Cat!. **Yeston:** One, Two, Three, Four, Five. VSD5564 – *Songs from* **Valenti:** Honky Tonk Nights. **Schmidt:** Roadside. **Strouse:** A Broadway Musical. **Leonard:** The Yearling. **Van Heusen:** Carnival in Flanders. **Bergersen:** Carib Song. **Styne:** The Red Shoes. **Skloff:** Arthur, the Musical. **Dolan:** Foxy. **Bernstein:** Merlin. **Holmes:** The Phantom of the Opera.

Commercial failure is not a register of poor quality, as these excellent compilations prove. Reborn on the first disc are 15 songs from 11 ill-fated musical projects. The earliest is 1955's *The Vamp*, a vehicle for Carol Channing, although the song "Ragtime Romeo" was sung by one of the other performers in the show. The selection runs through a variety of flops and non-starters, including songs from musical versions of *La Strada* and *The Man Who Came to Dinner*, as well as *We Take the Town*, based on the life of Pancho Villa (a favourite role of Robert Preston's according to Ken Mandelbaum's excellent liner-notes). Of particular note are three songs from the 1986 Broadway flop about a beauty pageant, *Smile*, by Marvin Hamlisch and Howard Ashman: Lynette Perry is crystal-clear in the anthem "In our hands', Harry Groener a suitably smug MC in the title-track, while Jodi Benson, reprising the role she played in the show, is outstanding in the dramatic "Disneyland". Christine Baranski and Jonathan Freeman have fun with the title-song from *Sherry!*; Sally Mayes shines in two songs from Cy Coleman's *Welcome to the Club* (one a duet with Michael Rupert), and the selection ends with "New words" by Maury Yeston, beautifully sung by Liz Callaway.
A further collection culled from previously unrecorded shows, the second disc may not be quite as enjoyable as the first, but it is still worthwhile. The earliest example here is 1945's *Carib Song*, the most recent Jule Styne's last Broadway show, 1993's *The Red Shoes*. For both discs, producer Bruce Kimmell has assembled an excellent cast of bright talents to bring the songs to life. The songs are re-orchestrated and not as they were for the original shows (the gender of the singer is often altered), but these are nevertheless an important addition to any collection, offering fine but unfamiliar show songs that would otherwise not have been recorded. **RAC**

New review
Unsung Musicals, Volume 3. **Danny Burstein, James Hindman, Judy Malloy, Jennifer Simard, Alec Timmerman, Christianne Tisdale, Tammy Minoff, Patrick Levis, Sal Viviano, Glory Crampton, Jason Graae, Brent Barrett, Alet Oury, Diana Canova, Melissa Hart, Guy Haines, Patricia Ben Peterson, Kristine Fraelich, Jolie Jenkins, Jason Workman, Debbie Gravitte, Harry Groener; ensemble / Lanny Meyers.**
Varèse Sarabande Spotlight Series Ⓟ VSD5769 (53 minutes: DDD).
Songs from **S. Schwartz:** Personals. **M. Rodgers:** Freaky Friday. **Legrand:** A Christmas Carol. **Raposo:** A Wonderful Life. **C. Hall:** To Whom it May Concern. **Hamlisch:** Smile. **Waldman:** Here's Where I Belong. **Adler:** A Mother's Kisses. **H. Schmidt:** The Bone Room. **Freeman:** Lovely Ladies, Kind Gentlemen. **Larson:** Brownstone. **Sheffer:** Diamonds. **Menken:** Babe. **Oliver:** Murder at the Vanities.

Do we really need another selection of ballads, novelty numbers and singalong dance tunes from shows which were either unproduced, entirely unsuccessful or have existed solely in the commercial neverland of out-of-town tours? Largely due to the enthusiasm and commitment of the teams which put together compilations like the "Unsung Musicals" series, the answer is a qualified "yes". The most vibrant performance can't rescue some of these offerings from mediocrity, however pleasant, but if even the most doomed musical can throw up a touching gem like "Simple words" from *Lovely Ladies, Kind Gentlemen*, supply will continue to meet demand for the forseeable future. Other highlights include "Penny by penny" from the 1981 Harnick/Legrand version of *A Christmas Carol*, and two numbers from lyricist Harnick's 1991 collaboration with composer Joe Raposo, a musical adaptation of the classic film *A Wonderful Life*, of which "In a state" is a toe-tapping Charleston to rival anything in *The Boyfriend*. There's also a delicious homage to Carmen Miranda in "Maria's Song" from *Smile*, a 1986 show with music by Marvin Hamlisch. With decent booklet-notes for the connoisseur, this series is proof that shows don't necessarily fail because of their musical shortcomings. **PF**

Ziegfeld Follies 1946 **Film Cast** (with Fred Astaire, Virginia O'Brien, James Melton, Lena Horne, Avon Long, Judy Garland and Kathryn Grayson) **/ Lennie Hayton**.
EMI Ⓕ CDODEON3 (71 minutes: ADD).

Ziegfeld Follies was a curate's egg of a movie designed to showcase MGM's star roster of 1944, though the troubled film took two years to reach the screen. Lena Horne sings one of the film's new songs, "Love" by Hugh Martin and Ralph Blane with a lyric that rings as true today as it did then, Avon Long whistles and sings Gershwin's "Liza" (one of four numbers on this disc that were filmed but ended up on the cutting-room floor) with two pianos adding a distinctive touch to the arrangement, and Astaire chants Harry Warren's exquisite ballad "This heart of mine". It's interesting to hear in the Ziegfeld tribute, "Bring on the beautiful girls", that quintessential show business euphoria that Sondheim tapped for the same purpose in his *Follies*. Lennie Hayton conducts a wonderfully elaborate ballet on the British hit "Limehouse blues", a piece that he was to conduct in *Star!* for Julie Andrews many years later. This is the film that may now best be remembered for bringing together Astaire and Kelly in their one joint appearance to sing the Gershwin's "The babbitt and the bromide", a rather wearying song concerning two boring acquaintances. As I said – good in parts! **AE**

Singers:

Thomas Allen and Valerie Masterson

If I Loved You Love Duets from the Musicals. **Valerie Masterson**, **Thomas Allen**, with the **Philharmonia Orchestra / John Owen Edwards**.
TER Ⓕ CDVIR8317 (60 minutes: DDD).
Songs from **Lloyd Webber:** The Phantom of the Opera. **Loewe:** Brigadoon. **Berlin:** Annie Get Your Gun. **Wilson:** The Music Man. **Loesser:** Guys and Dolls. **Rodgers:** Oklahoma!. The King and I. Carousel. South Pacific. **Bernstein:** West Side Story. **Kern:** Show Boat. **Friml/Stothart:** Rose Marie.

Too often, when performing songs from the shows, opera singers fall into the trap of being led by the music, to the detriment of the all-important lyric. The result can be pedestrian and uninspired. That is not the case with this lush selection of love duets, skilfully rendered by Allen and Masterson. Every word is clear, every lyric impeccably phrased. Particularly successful are the Richard Rodgers numbers from *Oklahoma!, The King and I, Carousel* and *South Pacific*. The duo bring an essential lightness of touch to "People will say we're in love" and "If I loved you", serving the lyric and the tune equally, telling the story and creating fully rounded characters. On "Tonight" they succeed in evoking the doomed, youthful optimism of *West Side Story*'s Maria and Tony where others, notably Te Kanawa and Carreras, merely sound earthbound and stately. They are equally at home with "They say it's wonderful", that delicate moment of realization for Annie Oakley and Frank Butler in Berlin's *Annie Get Your Gun*. There is a brief visit to the land of operetta with "Indian love call" from *Rose Marie* and a swelling, richly romantic reading of Kern's "Make believe" from *Show Boat*. Bearing in mind that *The Phantom of the Opera* is, in part, the tale of a *bona fide* opera singer, there is a nicely authentic version of "All I ask of you", the collection's sole nod in the direction of more contemporary material. Perfect stuff for those who like their standards sung with a bit of extra depth.   **PF**

Fred Astaire

Top Hat, White Tie and Tails Fred Astaire, with various artists.
Saville mono Ⓜ CDSVL184 (58 minutes: ADD). Recorded 1933-6.
Songs from **Berlin:** Top Hat. Follow the Fleet. **Porter:** The Gay Divorce. **Youmans:** Flying Down to Rio. **Kern:** Swing Time. **Astaire:** I'm building up to an awful let down.

This collection begins with two mementos of Astaire's final stage appearance in London and New York in *The Gay Divorce* singing "Night and day" and the gently understated "After you who", and concludes with five numbers from *Swing Time*, Kern's screen masterpiece. Leo Reisman's orchestra provide the straighter-laced accompaniments here, with Johnny Green, his piano and orchestra taking over for *Follow the Fleet*. At this point the CD really comes into its own with the marked improvement in sound highlighting both Astaire's unique style in ballad and swing numbers and the more imaginative arrangements that take advantage of Kern's high romantic style and initial venture into swing. Green's effortless piano work, which he recreated 50 years later in "The Gershwin Festival" at the Barbican in 1987, the tap rhythms, and to cite one instance, Fred's graceful and tender declaration to Ginger that he will never dance again in the neglected "Never gonna dance", bring this CD to an exhilarating finish.   **AE**

Josephine Baker

Star of Les Folies Bergère Josephine Baker with various bands.
ASV Living Era mono Ⓜ CDAJA5239 (71 minutes: AAD). Recorded 1926-44.
Songs by Scotto, Alamby, Waller, Orefice, Porter, Misraki and Brown.

Josephine Baker took Paris by storm in 1925 when she was 19 years old, and 50 years later she celebrated her anniversary with a show in which she was starring when she died. The first woman of American birth ever to be honoured with a 21-gun salute State Funeral (at the Madeleine), she has become a legendary figure, as a symbol of the art-deco 1920s, as a Black icon and as an example of sheer bravery and perseverance. Her initial fame was as a dancer, in particular with her versions of the Charleston (dancing on a mirror), the Black Bottom and the Conga, sometimes dressed in nothing but a string of rhinestone-encrusted bananas. As her career progressed she took to singing, and was equally successful, even if her voice and style remained on the dance-band side of pure jazz. One this selection of her discs made for Columbia in the 1930s she can be heard singing in English and French, songs from her repertory which took her all over the world. She starred in Buenos Aires and Budapest, Cuba and Copenhagen, before returning to become the first Black girl (and, as it happened, the last) to star in an edition of the *Ziegfeld Follies*. The cover of this CD misspells (as do many people) the name of the theatre in which she starred in the rue Bergère – it's the Folies Bergère, not Bergères. Among the less familiar numbers are Mayotte Alamby's "Madiana" and Orefice's "La Conga Blicoti" in both of which she is accompanied by the Lecuona Cuban Boys, two very early songs from the time of her first Paris seasons, "Sleepy time gal" and "Then I'll be happy", and a beautiful song by Bay, Reale and Grant – "Mon rêve c'était vous".   **PO'C**

Laurie Beecham

No One Is Alone Laurie Beechman, with orchestra / Lanny Meyers.
Varèse Sarabande Spotlight Series Ⓕ VSD05623 (67 minutes: DDD).
Songs from **Menken:** Kicks: The Showgirl Musical, The Hunchback of Notre Dame, A Christmas Carol. **Sondheim:** Company, Into the Woods. **Schwartz:** Godspell. **Rodgers:** The

Sound of Music, Carousel. **Brel:** Jacques Brel is Alive and Well and Living in Paris. **Loewe:** Brigadoon. **Smalls:** The Wiz. **Lane:** On a Clear Day You Can See Forever. **Krieger:** Dreamgirls. **Bernstein:** Candide, West Side Story.

Subtitled "Songs of Hope and Inspiration from Broadway", this album is clearly a celebration of Laurie Beechman's tenacity in the face of ill health. A mixture of ballads and up-tempo anthems like "These are the good times" (from *Kicks: The Showgirl Musical*) and "Beautiful city" (from *Godspell*) is well-handled and Lanny Meyers's pleasing modern arrangements of some well-worn standards add considerable zest. There's a touching vulnerability in Beechman's voice which finds new nuances in Sondheim's "Being alive" and "No one is alone" and is perfect for a small Bernstein medley ("Make our garden grow" and "One hand, one heart", a duet with Sam Harris). But as Alan Menken's booklet-notes suggest, she's quite capable of letting rip on occasion. This makes for a tumultuous climax to "Climb every mountain" and the most overblown treatment of "You'll never walk alone" this side of Patti Labelle. Rousing stuff to be sure, but Beechman is probably at her most effective on Menken's numbers, the aforementioned "These are the good times", the gentle "Someday" from Disney's *Hunchback of Notre Dame* and the irredeemably sentimental "God bless us every one" from *A Christmas Carol*. There's also a powerhouse rendition of "I am changing", the life-affirming anthem from *Dreamgirls*.   **PF**

Betty Buckley

Children Will Listen Betty Buckley, with various artists / Kenny Werner.
   Sterling Ⓕ S1001-2 (54 minutes: DDD).
   Songs from **Sondheim:** Into the Woods, Sweeney Todd, Evening Primrose, Sunday in the Park With George, Company, Merrily We Roll Along. **Styne:** Peter Pan. **Lloyd Webber:** Song and Dance, Cats. **Gore:** Carrie. **Schwartz:** The Baker's Wife. **Schönberg:** Miss Saigon.

Betty Buckley's performance as Norma Desmond in Lloyd Webber's *Sunset Boulevard* has brought her great acclaim across the world, but on Broadway she was already a well-known name having won a Tony award for her performance as Grizabella in *Cats*, as well as appearing in many other shows and concerts. Her 1993 solo disc "Children Will Listen" reprises some of her great roles as well as featuring other music theatre favourites. But the material is presented in a totally fresh setting, with a great emphasis on percussion, using unusual arrangements and combinations of songs. Unlike many singers who slavishly refuse to tamper with Sondheim's work, Buckley is refreshingly unafraid to try something different. How many singers would dare take *Company*'s morose and masculine "Sorry, grateful" and add a rhumba rhythm and a female perspective? Or combine "Children and art" and "Stay with me" (respectively from *Sunday in the Park* and *Into the Woods*) into an eerily haunting piece, leading into a song that will whet the appetite of all lovers of flop musicals? *Carrie* has become a household word amongst music theatre *aficionados* as one of the all-time great failures. In the short-lived Broadway production, Buckley played Carrie's fanatical mother, and here reprises her solo "When there's no one". As *Carrie* was not commercially recorded, collectors will look upon this inclusion as making the disc worthy of purchase. But it is only one of many good things. Buckley's voice is unusual – husky and intense – often falling away almost to a murmur, and only occasionally sweeping upwards with the power she displayed in her performance as Norma. She is exultant in "Unexpected Song" from *Song and Dance*, contemplative in Sondheim's "I remember", and emotionally charged in "Meadowlark" from *The Baker's Wife*, a show which she claims Stephen Schwartz wrote for her, although she lost the role to Patti LuPone. The selection closes predictably with "Memory", but in a new arrangement by Michel Colombier, this rather hackneyed song is reborn, as are all the other offerings on this excellent and very unusual disc.   **RAC**

Barbara Cook

Live from London Barbara Cook, with various artists / Wally Harper.
   DRG Ⓕ 91430 (67 minutes: DDD).
   Songs from **Menken:** Beauty and the Beast. **Styne:** Peter Pan. **Sondheim:** Follies. *Songs by* Harper, Berlin, Williams, Arlen, McBroom, Bucchino, Schwartz/Dietz, Bourke, Bernie/Casey/Pinkard, Allen/Callen/Malamet, Rodgers and Leonard.

In the 1950s and 1960s, Barbara Cook was the *ingénue* to beat all *ingénues* – her performances in both successes (*The Music Man, She Loves Me*) and failures (*Flahooley, The Gay Life*) are legendary. Her crystal-clear soprano and fresh-faced beauty was her trademark, but with changing times became a curse, and by the late 1960s she was struggling to find work in the very different environment of a Broadway dominated by shows such as *Hair* and *Company*. By the late 1970s, however, she had firmly re-established herself as a concert performer, her remarkable presence, still magnificent voice and extraordinary ability to interpret a lyric making her much in demand. This live recording from her concert appearance at Sadler's Wells in July 1994 is a perfect example of the talent that has allowed her career to flourish anew. The song choice is excellent – a marvellous balance of the classic and the modern, the familiar and the unusual. She opens with a lovely blend of the two – conductor Wally Harper's own "Sing a song with me", blended with Irving Berlin's "Let me sing and I'm happy". This is followed by another example – "Beauty and the beast" from the Disney movie, leading into "Never never land" from Jule Styne's *Peter Pan*. Her renditions of the classics are object lessons – Arlen's "Come rain or come shine" sung with total conviction, swinging versions of "I'm beginning to see the light" and "Sweet Georgia Brown", a beautiful medley of "I see your face before me" and "Change partners". Of the modern songs, one cannot help but be moved by her interpretations of two Amanda McBroom songs, "Ship in a bottle" (accompanied by solo piano) and "Errol Flynn", and by the inspirational "Love don't need a reason". It is the ease with which she moves between so many styles that is so impressive and makes for thoroughly enjoyable listening. Cook was 66 years old when this recording was made and she sounds fresher and more lively than many performers half her age, her commitment to the songs is total and this comes across throughout this recording. **RAC**

Marlene Dietrich

New review
Marlene Marlene Dietrich with various artists.
  MCI Ⓜ MCCD178 (54 minutes: AAD). Recorded 1939-63.
The Marlene Dietrich Album Marlene Dietrich with various artists.
  Sony Ⓜ MDK47254 (61 minutes: AAD). Recorded 1952-9.

Although today she is remembered equally as a singer and an actress, it's surprising how many of Dietrich's films didn't give her an opportunity to sing. "Marlene", the MCI disc, gathers some of her most famous records made in Hollywood in the late 1930s and 1940s, the brash songs from *Destry Rides Again* ("You've got that look" and "The boys in the backroom"), the sultry "I've been in love before" from *Seven Sinners* and the film which was unusual in examining the lives of Berliners after the war, *A Foreign Affair* (with "Illusions" and "Black market"). All these songs were written for Dietrich by her colleague from pre-Hitler Berlin, Frederick Hollaender. The CD includes her very last song from a Hollywood movie, "I may never go home any more" from *Witness for the Prosecution*, and her earliest recordings with Burt Bacharach, *Another Spring, Another Love* and the rock 'n' roll *Near you*.

Sony's portrait begins with her cabaret act at the Café de Paris, recorded in 1954, has some numbers from a later live performance in Rio, and some very rare recordings from the 1950s, including two never issued at the time, "Baubles, bangles and beads" and – as a tribute to her friend Mae West – "A guy what takes his time". Though Dietrich's singing was limited to a very small range, her ability to put over a song and to invest the lyrics with layers of innuendo, made her one of the most influential singers of the twentieth century. Perhaps the biggest curiosity of all is on the MCI record – her version of the theme music from *Tom Jones*, the 1963 Tony Richardson movie – "If he swing by the string". As Jean Cocteau memorably described her, with a name that begins with a caress and ends with a whiplash. **PO'C**

New review
Marlene A Tribute to Dietrich. **Sian Phillips / Kevin Amos.**
  Playback Ⓕ PLMARCD1 (46 minutes: DDD).

Sian Phillips proved to be more than just a talented actress when she played the legendary Marlene Dietrich in Pam Gems's play, and almost performed the impossible by becoming the living image of this sex goddess in both looks and voice. Of course, on stage there was the help of carbon-copy wigs, make-up, costumes and lighting to create the deception. But, on disc we have no illusions, simply Miss Phillips impersonating a voice in songs associated with her. It is still a remarkable performance. The disc follows the pattern of the play with the first set of songs being those sung in her dressing room – some introduced with a comment or two – as she prepares for the concert which takes up much of the second act. These set the scene of her arrival in Hollywood and her thoughts on Europe and Hitler's Germany, with seven songs which go a little behind the legend. The public view follows with eight more songs as performed in the 'concert', a reconstruction of those which delighted audiences back in the 1960s. The latter section has an echo and an 'audience' who respond to the songs with polite canned applause that only reacts to the performance with anything close to sincerity after the political "Where have all the flowers gone?" – it's a pity is wasn't recorded live. The backing throughout is just piano, violin and bass and is thin compared with the Bacharach-conducted concert orchestras heard on the original Dietrich recordings. Those having seen the show will need little persuasion to purchase this memory of a theatrical treat. Others may well be a little more critical, for the illusion is only partial.   **RSB**

Deanna Durbin

Deanna Durbin Deanna Durbin, with various artists.
    Flapper mono Ⓜ PASTCD9781 (60 minutes: ADD).
    Songs from First Love, Three Smart Girls Grow Up, Spring Parade, 100 Men and a Girl, Nice Girl?, It's A Date and Mad About Music.
Her Greatest Recordings, 1936-1944. **Deanna Durbin**, with various artists.
    ASV Living Era mono Ⓜ CDAJA 5149 (76 minutes: ADD).
    Songs from Three Smart Girls, 100 Men and a Girl, Mad About Music, That Certain Age, Three Smart Girls Grow Up, First Love, It's a Date, Spring Parade, Nice Girl?, The Big Show of 1916, Mlle Modiste, The Chocolate Soldier and Can't Help Singing.

Despite her relatively brief film career (13 years), Deanna Durbin is still regarded with extraordinary reverence and affection. Her roles were all variations on the same theme – a well-meaning, busy little miss, rushing around fixing the problems of the other characters who, on occasion, was allowed to mature into a romantic *ingénue*, but was always ready to burst into an aria, a bit of light operatic trilling or a saccharine ballad, as circumstances required. Her clear, bell-like coloratura garnered her an immense fan club and record sales to match. With her wholesome, pretty looks, it was a winning combination. Durbin retired in 1949, aged just 28, depriving her audience of the chance to see if her pleasant, light soprano would mature into something more resonant and substantial. Never mind. Many would still regard any hint of adverse criticism as sacrilege. Both of these charming collections offer a wide range of the arias and traditional folk songs which were her hallmark. Flapper and Living Era should be commended on their pioneering work in bringing the work of artists from the pre-stereophonic age of recording to CD, often returning to the original acetates for their sources.
    The Flapper selection contains Durbin's sweet renditions of both the Bach and Schubert settings for "Ave Maria", a mature (considering she was only 18) rendition of Puccini's "One fine day" from *First Love*, the first film in which she was allowed an adult kiss, Arditi's "Il bacio" and several pleasant ballads such as Kern's "It's foolish but it's fun" and Foster's "The old folks at home". There's also a rather sentimental "Loch Lomond" from *It's A Date* (1940). There is some overlap with the Living Era selection, which includes a brace of traditional American show tunes such as Golden's melancholy standard "Poor butterfly", the perky "It's foolish but it's fun", "Can't help singing" and Berlin's rousing "God bless America". Either of these offerings would make a useful introduction to the work of one of the silver screen's most treasured song birds.   **PF**

Ruth Etting and Helen Morgan

`New review`
More Than You Know Ruth Etting and Helen Morgan.
    Box Office mono Ⓔ ENBO-CD15/95 (76 minutes: ADD). Recorded 1929-37.
    Songs from **Youmans:** Great Day. **Donaldson:** The Great Ziegfeld. **Coslow:** It's Love Again.

McHugh: Banjo On My Knee. **Revel:** Head Over Heels, Wake Up and Live. **Kahn:** A Day at the Races. **Freed:** Midnight Frolic. **Kern:** Sweet Adeline. **Heyman:** Three's a Crowd. **Washington:** Frankie & Johnny. **Gorney:** Marie Galante. **Wrubel:** Sweet Music. **Warren:** Go Into Your Dance. **Alter:** Dizzy Dames. *Songs by* Levinson, Lewis, Whitcup, Teesor, Hill, Ahlert.

These recordings made between 1929 and 1937 represent the peak years of the relatively short careers of two of the most important Broadway stars of their time. Both were Ziegfeld protégées. Etting's light soprano was at its most effective in revue and she went on to become the first major American female radio performer as well as a prolific recording artist. Morgan's performance as Julie in *Show Boat* has attained legendary status and she also made a number of memorable film appearances before succumbing to a chronic addiction to brandy. Vocally, they are an interesting contrast and here we have the chance to compare their respective renditions of "More than you know". With a lighter touch and an infectious warmth which could border on being baby-voiced, Etting was the clear forerunner of the song stylists who would follow in her tracks. She didn't just sing about tragedy, and her treatment of material such as Coslow's "It's love again" and McHugh's "There's something in the air" is highly appealing. Morgan, also a soprano, was perhaps less versatile as a singer, but who could resist the frailty of her lamentations and pleas on "Mean to me" or "Why was I born?", in themselves enough to conjure the classic image of the torch singer perched on a piano, wringing a silk scarf through her hands? This selection includes several numbers from her film appearances – "Song of a dreamer" from *Marie Galante* is particularly poignant – but features neither of her signature songs from *Show Boat*. **PF**

Marianne Faithfull

Twentieth Century Blues Marianne Faithfull, with **Paul Trueblood** (pf).
RCA Victor Reverso Ⓟ 74321 38656-2 (54 minutes: DDD).
Songs from **Weill:** Aufstieg und Fall der Stadt Mahagonny, Die Dreigroschenoper, Happy End, Johnny Johnson. *Songs* Complainte de la Seine, The ballad of the soldier's wife. **Hollaender:** A Foreign Affair, The Blue Angel. **Warren:** Moulin Rouge. **Coward:** Cavalcade.

The great Parisian *chanteuse* Damia – the first French singer to record "Mack the knife" – was once asked how she had managed to sustain her career and her individual voice. "Try smoking two packs of Gauloises every day for 30 years", she replied. Marianne Faithfull had a lovely voice, pure and true, in the 1960s, the days of *Tears gone by*. Her roller-coaster career – chronicled in her harrowing autobiography and recently in numerous interviews – has left her with a raucous, extraordinarily haunting voice, with a rich palette of colours. It's a case of low, lower and lowest, but she has grown so much as an artist that she invests every song with original nuances.

Her Weill interpretations will offend purists, but on their own terms they work very well. I heard her sing this group early in 1996 at the Jazz Café in London, when hundreds of young people stood shoulder to shoulder and cheered her. Like other storm survivors she attracts the alternative music-theatre crowd. She has recorded "Boulevard of broken dreams" (from *Moulin Rouge*) before, on her "Broken English" album, and it has become a sort of theme song, with its lament, 'the joys that you find here you borrow – they're never yours for long it seems'. She sometimes yells a word, but her voice is still firm, and although one might classify her as a *diseuse*, her musicianship and dramatic sense are always present. Though the album credits Eisler as the composer of "The ballad of the Soldier's wife" it is the Weill setting she sings. In evoking the interwar turmoil, she adds two Hollaender songs written for Dietrich, "Illusions" from Billy Wilder's *A Foreign Affair* and "Falling in love again" from *The Blue Angel*, and she is the first singer since Dietrich to find a way with them that doesn't jar. I admit that my reaction to Faithfull is tinged with sentimentality born of an admiration for such a resourceful survivor. A couple of young people leaving the Jazz Café after her set asked me if I'd heard her in the 1960s. Of course, I replied, but she's much better now. **PO'C**

Jane Froman

The Star Thru Three Decades Jane Froman, with various artists.

Box Office Recordings mono Ⓟ ENBO-CD10/94 (72 minutes: ADD). Recorded 1930-53.
Songs by Norton, McHugh, Warren, Freed, Berlin, Jacobs, Noble, Gershwin, Tchaikovsky, Washington, David, Loesser, Rome, Arlen, Darby, Mann, Simmons, Malneck, Sigman, Douglas, Drake. *Includes songs from* Seven Days Leave, The Sky's the Limit, Let 'em Eat Cake, Wish You Were Here.

Jane Froman was one of the brightest stars in musical revue on Broadway during the 1930s and 1940s, making her début in the *Ziegfeld Follies of 1934*. Crippled in a plane crash in 1943, she continued her career largely as a radio and recording artist, making spasmodic stage appearances as her health permitted. Her life was ideal fodder for the Hollywood biopic treatment in the 1952 Susan Hayward vehicle *With a Song In My Heart*, with Froman providing her own superior vocals. This selection from Box Office Recordings covers the years 1930 to 1953 but doesn't include any of the numbers from that film. Despite digital remastering, there's still a lot of surface noise on the early recordings, but it's an appealing summary of her talents. While Froman's classically trained contralto might seem staid to the modern ear, there's a languid fluidity to her phrasing and at times she sounds downright sultry, particularly with the lusher orchestrations of the 1950s as provided by Sid Feller and his orchestra. The Loesser/McHugh number, "Can't get out of this mood" (from *Seven Days Leave*) is a case in point. Standards like "I only have eyes for you", "Melancholy baby" (Norton/Burnett) and the McHugh/Dorothy Fields torch song "Lost in a fog" are meat and drink to her, although she is not enough of an actress to get maximum mileage from a Gershwin character piece like "Boy! What love has done to me." "Cling to me" is worth noting as an early effort from Hal David, better known for his 1960s collaborations with Burt Bacharach.   **PF**

Judy Garland

Collectors' Gems from the MGM Films Judy Garland, with Original Film Casts.

EMI mono Ⓟ CDODEON22 (two discs: 151 minutes: ADD).
Songs from Every Sunday, Broadway Melody of 1938, Thoroughbreds Don't Cry, Everybody Sing, Love Finds Andy Hardy, Listen, Darling, Andy Hardy Meets Debutante, Little Nellie Kelly, Life Begins for Andy Hardy, Ziegfeld Girl, Presenting Lily Mars, Thousands Cheer, Till the Clouds Roll By, The Pirate and Annie Get Your Gun.

Judy Garland's reputation as one of the century's greatest entertainers has become something of a cliché, tarnished by the morbid fascination which her long, tortuous decline still exerts over her fans and showbusiness historians. This expertly packaged compilation covers her MGM career, from 1936 to 1949, and includes a number of less familiar songs as well as some unused out-takes from *The Pirate* (1948) and the tracks which Garland laid down for *Annie Get Your Gun* (1950). She never, of course, completed the last mentioned film and her suspension from the picture marked the beginning of the end of her illustrious MGM career. On the overwhelming evidence of this double-CD set, Garland was indeed a unique artist. At the earliest age, she could convey an adult lyric with astonishing maturity. She was equally at home with jazz, swing, a ballad or a novelty number. Her later recordings would continue to demonstrate those abilities with more mature material, but there are treats aplenty here, including a duet with Deanna Durbin ("Opera vs. jazz") from the 1936 short, *Every Sunday*, and her immensely moving "Zing! went the strings of my heart!" from *Listen, Darling* (1938). Many of the selections were the fruit of an enduring professional relationship with Hollywood composer and arranger Roger Edens. From 1943's *Presenting Lily Mars*, there's a glorious 10-minute medley entitled "Where there's music", which includes samples from "St Louis blues", "Don't sit under the apple tree" and "Broadway rhythm". As a whole, the collection benefits from its unfamiliarity (there's nothing from *The Wizard of Oz*, for example, *Meet Me in St Louis* or *Easter Parade*). It is, indeed, an album for collectors which doesn't, for a change, trade on the more sensational aspects of Garland's life. True, the numbers from *Annie Get Your Gun* are a tantalizing glimpse of what might have been: when you know the circumstances in which her efforts came to grief, her rendering of "They say it's wonderful" has a heartbreaking quality. But first and foremost, this is a fine, scholarly celebration of the youthful phase of a fine talent. **PF**

Lesley Garrett

Soprano in Hollywood Lesley Garrett, with **Serenata Voices; BBC Concert Orchestra /**
Paul Bateman.
Silva Classics Ⓕ SILKTVCD2 (56 minutes: DDD). All items arr. Bateman.
Songs from **Rodgers:** Spring is Here. Love Me Tonight. **V. Herbert:** The Only Girl. **N. H.**
Brown: The Kissing Bandit. **Schertzinger:** One Night of Love. **Gershwin:** Goldwyn Follies.
Lady, Be Good!. **Whiting/Harling:** Monte Carlo. **Kern:** Roberta. Cover Girl. **J. Gade:**
Anchors Aweigh. **Romberg:** The New Moon. **Porter:** Kiss Me, Kate. **A. Penn:** Smilin'
Through.

Lesley Garrett's previous CDs have been enormous commercial successes and, for me at least, considerable artistic successes, both for the imagination shown in drawing up the repertoire and for the appeal of Miss Garrett's unaffected, pure singing. As the orchestra played an overblown trailer for the songs included in this latest collection, I wondered if artistic standards had finally fallen. But no. That introduction is a particularly apt setting of the Hollywood context, and when the singing begins criticism is soon stilled. Miss Garrett seems especially well suited to bring out the subtle melodic writing of Victor Herbert and Sigmund Romberg: but she proves no less winning elsewhere, duetting with herself in "Lover" (from *Love Me Tonight*), trilling outrageously (and gloriously) in "Love is where you find it" (from *The Kissing Bandit*), and (with male chorus) evoking a more reflective mood in "One night of love". Nor can I imagine a better encapsulation of the Gershwins' songwriting skills than the sequence of "Love walked in", "The man I love" and "Love is here to stay". This is altogether a glorious selection of songs, and the orchestrations by Paul Bateman are equally imaginative and admirably geared to capturing the mood of the Hollywood musical of the 1930s and 1940s. This is a CD to curl up and surrender to. **AML**

Betty Grable

The Pin-Up Girl Betty Grable, with **Original Film Casts**.
Jasmine mono Ⓜ JASCD103/4 (two discs: 128 minutes: ADD). Recorded 1930-44.
Songs from Whoopee, Student Tour, The Gay Divorcee, The Nitwits, Old Man Rhythm,
Give Me a Sailor, Down Argentine Way, Tin Pan Alley, Moon Over Miami, A Yank in the
RAF, Footlight Serenade, Song of the Islands, Springtime in the Rockies, Coney Island,
Sweet Rosie O'Grady, Pin-Up Girl, Billy Rose's Diamond Horseshoe and The Dolly Sisters.

Servicemen swooned over her, Neil Sedaka later serenaded her, but despite starring in a dozen or so hit musicals for 20th Century-Fox in the 1940s, Betty Grable recorded only "I can't begin to tell you" for commercial release (Columbia DB2646) and that was under the pseudonym Ruth Haag with her husband Harry James directing the band. Like all the songs on this disc, the version presented here has been lifted from the soundtrack of the film (*The Dolly Sisters*, 1944) with fade-ins and -outs tactfully managed by compiler Geoff Milne. In essence the disc offers a profile of the Fox musical of the period, with Alfred Newman in charge of the music and a mixture of traditional tunes and newly composed numbers. Grable herself is heard at her most affecting in "My heart tells me" (*Sweet Rosie O'Grady*, 1943) written by the prolific Harry Warren, whose ballad "The more I see you" (*Billy Rose's Diamond Horseshoe*, 1945) is the outstanding song in the collection. Grable's pre-Fox career is represented by six numbers including "Let's k-nock k-nees" with Edward Everett Horton from *The Gay Divorcee* (1934). Don't expect too much from the transfers, quite clearly the budget hasn't permitted the revelations currently on offer in the Turner Classic Movies series of MGM soundtracks currently available on Rhino in the US and EMI in the UK. However, this is a handy and economical way of collecting Grable memorabilia, well documented by Geoff Milne whose extensive booklet-notes set the Grable phenomenon within the studio politics at Fox and a world at war. **AE**

Debbie Gravitte

The MGM Album Debbie Gravitte, with various artists / Ron Abel.
Varèse Sarabande Spotlight Series Ⓟ VSD5742 (52 minutes: DDD).
Songs from **Arlen:** Summer Stock. **Blane:** Ziegfeld Follies. **Gershwin:** Girl Crazy. **Sedaka:** Where the Boys Are. **Abrey/Drake:** Bathing Beauty. **Berlin:** Easter Parade. **Williams/Donaldson:** Love Me or Leave Me. **Lane:** Royal Wedding. **Kern:** Roberta. **Kalmar:** Three Little Words. **Rodgers:** Jumbo. **A. Schwartz:** The Band Wagon. **R. Strauss:** 2001: A Space Odyssey.

At full throttle, Debbie Gravitte (formerly Shapiro), one of the brightest Broadway stars of recent times, displays more than a touch of Merman or Garland at their American brassiest. When things quieten down a little, there's a hint of Streisand here, a husky reminder of Peggy Lee there. With every note the listener gets the feeling that the music and lyrics are simply in the blood. Any attempt at suppressing them could result in spontaneous combustion. Gravitte is no identikit Broadway belter, though. She brings a classy, natural jazz inflection to Berlin's "I love a piano" and the Kalmar/Ruby standard "Nevertheless (I'm in love with you)". But for most of this glossy set she eschews subtlety for an open-throated attack which is, by and large, exhilarating – for example, there's a tumultuous, swinging version of "Love me or leave me". Gravitte smoulders with an artful degree of camp on the Gershwins' deliciously non-PC "Treat me rough" from *Girl Crazy*, and there is a passionate medley of "Little girl blue" and "My romance". In the company of this material, a jokey vocalese billed as "Theme from 2001" merely sounds contrived. It's the only jarring note in an otherwise glittering selection. **PF**

Libby Holman

Moanin' Low 1927-34. Libby Holman, with various artists.
Take Two mono Ⓜ TT415CD (64 minutes: AAD). Recorded 1927-34.

Libby Holman was the earthiest of a trio of torch singers who dominated American popular song and Broadway revue in the late 1920s. While Helen Morgan and Ruth Etting presented the passive, fragile side of despair, Holman suggested a more aggressive reaction to life's cruelties ("Find me a primitive man" from Porter's *Fifty Million Frenchmen* is hardly the response of a tremulous wallflower!). Her voice was so dark and husky that people who heard her before seeing her expected a black blues singer. All three endured a fair amount of buffeting in their stormy private lives, but Holman attracted particular notoriety when her husband died in mysterious circumstances in 1932. Many suspected her of murder. The scandal effectively ended her Broadway career, although in later years she made a comeback of sorts as a blues and folk singer. Holman's signature tune was "Moanin' low", a Ralph Rainger/Howard Dietz composition which she introduced in *The Little Show*, a 1929 revue. It's featured here twice, as a radio performance and a studio recording. In 1930 the show's successor, *Three's a Crowd*, produced two more scorching Holman torch numbers which bore her indelible stamp: "Body and soul" and "Something to remember you by". Other familiar standards featured here include a world-weary rendition of Porter's "What is this thing called love?" and the Dietz/Schwartz classic "You and the night and the music". Take Two have done an excellent job on the noise reduction for the 20 tracks on this disc, preserving the ominous, throbbing quality of Holman's voice which ensured her cult status as a torch singer long after her brief heyday. **PF**

Lena Horne

Ain't it the Truth Lena Horne at MGM. Lena Horne, with Original Film Casts.
EMI mono/stereo Ⓟ CDODEON32 (70 minutes: ADD).
Songs from Panama Hattie, Cabin in the Sky, Thousands Cheer, Swing Fever, I Dood It, Broadway Rhythm, Two Girls and a Sailor, Ziegfeld Follies, Till the Clouds Roll By, Words and Music, Duchess of Idaho and Meet Me in Las Vegas.

Although Lena Horne also had a separate recording contract with RCA, "Lena Horne at MGM" is a collection of her soundtrack recordings for the studio, which includes three numbers from *Cabin in the Sky* (see also separate review unde Duke) plus solo guest spots from many MGM musicals of the 1940s – so filmed that they could be omitted in prints destined for the American South. "Just one of those things", "Bill" and "The lady is a tramp" are typical of her definitive, assured performances. This CD is a fine survey of a talented and sophisticated singer in her prime.   **MPK**

Al Jolson

New review
Let Me Sing and I'm Happy Al Jolson at Warner Bros. 1926-36. **Al Jolson**, with **Original Film Casts.**
EMI mono Ⓟ CDODEON24 (62 minutes: ADD).
Songs from A Plantation Act, The Jazz Singer, The Singing Fool, Say It With Songs, Mammy, Big Boy, Go Into Your Dance and The Singing Kid.

The name of Al Jolson, like that of Judy Garland whose work is celebrated on a similar collection from the same source (see separate review), still bestrides the entertainment world. This timely release provides the perfect opportunity to reassess the ingredients which make his work so compelling. Producer and archivist Ian Whitcomb has worked wonders with the Vitaphone discs which form the main source of Jolson's recordings, preserving the immediacy of the early film performances delivered live to camera, but resisting the temptation to over-restore. Ironically, by the time he made *The Jazz Singer* in 1927, Jolson's star as the leading vaudevillian of his generation was already waning along with the genre. These recordings serve as an invaluable documentation of a frenetic improvisational talent that the increasingly disciplined world of cinema could barely contain. Sample the patter, for example, between "Dirty hands! Dirty face!" and "Toot, toot, Tootsie!". His speciality was the black-faced minstrel act which reached its apotheosis in the sobbing baritone vibrato of "My mammy". There's a jaunty, up-tempo reading of Irving Berlin's "Blue skies", but Jolson could also handle a gentle, lachrymose ballad like "(Across the breakfast table) I'm looking at you" from *Mammy* (1930). Whitcomb's sympathetic and comprehensive booklet-notes complete a package that skilfully extracts the essence of this irrepressible entertainer.   **PF**

Salena Jones

New review
Making Love Salena Jones in Hollywood. **Salena Jones**, with various artists / **John Pearce.**
TER Ⓜ CDVIR8328 (57 minutes: DDD).
Songs from **Bacharach:** Making Love. **Marchetti:** Love in the Afternoon. **Warren:** An Affair to Remember. **Henley:** Beaches. **Mancini:** Days of Wine and Roses. **Carmichael/Parton:** The Bodyguard. **Kern:** Cover Girl, Music in the Air. **Mandel:** The Sandpiper. **Hudson:** Picnic. **Young:** My Foolish Heart. **North:** Ghost. **Porter:** High Society. **Douglas/Gershwin:** Goldwyn Follies.

Salena Jones has made a welcome return to the London jazz scene during the last couple of years. This eclectic, well-produced set demonstrates why performers of her class are so respected. Never resorting to artifice, she generates a sense of jazz around some popular film songs rather than taking any outrageous liberties with the phrasing or melody. The overall effect is mellow without being bland. The much-loved theme from *An Affair to Remember*, for example, becomes a gently rambling ballad. Given the generally laid back ambience of the disc, there are a couple of surprise choices. "The wind beneath my wings", best known as a Bette Midler power ballad, is reduced to almost spartan simplicity. Dolly Parton's whimsical little piece of heartache, "I will always love you", was given the heavyweight treatment by Whitney Houston in *The Bodyguard* but here, Jones brings it down to more appropriate, intimate proportions. She is on more familiar territory with material like Kern's "Long ago (and far away)", Gershwin's "Love walked in" and the title-track from that atypical 1940s 'womens' picture' *My Foolish Heart*. In all, a sophisticated mix of the standard and the contemporary.   **PF**

Only Love Salena Jones on Broadway. **Salena Jones**, with various artists **/ Paul Sawtell**.
TER Ⓔ CDVIR8327 (63 minutes: DDD).
Songs from **Kander:** Zorba. Flora, the Red Menace. **Hamlisch:** They're Playing Our Song.
Rodgers: The King And I. Evergreen. **Van Heusen:** Skyscraper. **Gershwin:** Crazy for You.
Lady, Be Good!. **Herman:** Mack and Mabel. **Styne:** Funny Girl. **Hague:** Plain and Fancy.
Duke: Cabin in the Sky. **Bricusse:** The Roar of the Greasepaint, the Smell of the Crowd.
Ford: I'm Getting My Act Together and Taking It On the Road.

Jazz interpretations of standards from the shows are not to everybody's taste, but this sophisticated set from the versatile, innovative Salena Jones repays close attention. These are songs for the other side of midnight. Apart from a strikingly swinging "Hello, young lovers" and a shuffling "Embraceable you", the emphasis is on the melancholy aspects of love. Jones's artful phrasing renders a good but little-known torch song, "I only miss him when I think of him" (from *Skyscraper*), into a poignant little story of heartache. Clearly, she is at home with the genre, treating Herman's "Time heals everything" and the Leslie Bricusse/Anthony Newley standard "Who can I turn to?" with the same blend of restrained, wounded dignity and resilience. The intimacy of the recording owes a great deal, also, to Paul Sawtell's stripped-down, minimalist arrangements which allow Jones's voice to take centre stage without force: she brings a new delicacy to the Streisand signature tune "People". The set gives a welcome airing to some less familiar numbers, such as the title-track, "Only love", from Kander and Ebb's scarcely remembered *Zorba*, and "Old friend" from the awkwardly titled *I'm Getting My Act Together ...* . There's plenty of Richard Rodgers and George Gershwin too, concluding with a nifty reading of the tricky "Fascinating rhythm".   **PF**

Danny Kaye

The Very Best of Danny Kaye Danny Kaye, with various artists.
MCA Ⓜ MCLD19049 (60 minutes: AAD).
Songs from **Weill:** Lady in the Dark. **Fine:** The Straw Hat Revue. **Loesser:** Hans Christian Andersen. *Songs by* Smith, Hilliard, Von Tilzer, Morgan, Handy, Kleinsinger, Tibbles and Livingston.

Danny Kaye was a frenetic, multi-faceted performer, at his best on stage in front of a live audience. He was also a very popular, likeable film star whose career reached its apotheosis with the lead role in the Loesser-scored 1952 musical, *Hans Christian Andersen*. Much of Kaye's finest work was achieved in revue and in his one-man show, which drew heavily on material written specifically for him by his wife, composer and lyricist Sylvia Fine. That aspect of his career is well represented in this collection of 20 'golden greats' – the two parts of "Manic depressive presents" were the perfect vehicle for his talents as a mimic. Likewise "Anatole of Paris" and the lachrymose "Molly Malone". Kaye's first appearance in a stage musical was *Lady in the Dark* (1940), when his tongue-twisting rendition of Weill's "Tschaikowsky" stopped the show. Kaye had a pleasant tenor voice and *Hans Christian Andersen* provided him with a brace of hits which confirmed him as one of the screen's most versatile personalities. They are all included in this selection. The best known are probably "The ugly duckling" and "Wonderful Copenhagen". Bringing up the rear are a handful of the novelty numbers which Kaye could probably have performed in his sleep. The story of "Tubby the tuba" retains a comforting charm and for good measure, there are cartoon favourites "The Woody Woodpecker song" and "I taut I taw a puddy-tat".   **PF**

Judy Kaye

Diva by Diva Judy Kaye, with various artists **/ Patrick Brady**.
Varèse Sarabande Spotlight Series Ⓔ VSD5589 (53 minutes: DDD).
Songs from **Berlin:** Call Me Madam. **Rodgers:** South Pacific. The Sound of Music. **Schwartz:** The Baker's Wife. **Duke:** Cabin in the Sky. **Bock:** The Apple Tree. **Lloyd Webber:** Song and Dance. **Forrest/Wright:** Song of Norway. **Loewe:** Camelot. **Fain:** Flahooley. **Leigh:** Man of La Mancha. **Anderson:** Goldilocks. **Sondheim:** Anyone Can Whistle. **Herman:** Hello, Dolly! **Coleman:** Sweet Charity. **Van Heusen:** Carnival in Flanders. **Weill:** Love Life. **Arlen:** House of Flowers.

Judy Kaye is one of those rare performers who is equally at home in the world of musical theatre as in the opera house – as this impeccable showcase of her talents demonstrates. The theme of the disc is a tribute to the legendary ladies of Broadway and offers a chance to hear fresh and lively interpretations of some of the classics of the genre. The first two tracks are slightly off-putting and do not match the quality of the remainder of the disc. But the recording bursts into life with Stephen Schwartz's "Where is the warmth?" from *The Baker's Wife*, a beautiful rendition with a sumptuous orchestration underneath. From that point onwards the listener is in the hands of a singer at the top of her form working with arrangements that are sublime. There is the deeply romantic "I loved you once in silence" from *Camelot*, accompanied by arranger Patrick Brady's superb piano playing. Kaye's operatic skills are on display in Wright and Forrest's flamboyant "Now" (*Song of Norway*). Her wonderful humour is displayed to perfection in "Mr Right" from the rarely heard *Love Life* as Kaye spells out her ideas of the perfect man. If proof were needed that she is a singer who can compete in all departments, she even turns her voice onto a swinging "Taking a chance on love" from *Cabin in the Sky*. This is truly a diva tackling the divas – it is no mean feat to take on such a range of classic songs that are firmly associated with their originators and to provide a wholly satisfying and thoroughly enjoyable result. **RAC**

Gene Kelly

The Best of Gene Kelly Gene Kelly, with **Original Film Casts**.
EMI Ⓟ CDODEON9 (61 minutes: ADD).
Songs from **Brown:** Singin' in the Rain. **Previn:** It's Always Fair Weather. **Loewe:** Brigadoon. **Porter:** Les Girls. The Pirate. **Warren:** Summer Stock. **Gershwin:** An American in Paris.

Between them, Fred Astaire and Gene Kelly raised the art of dancing on the silver screen to the level of genius. If Astaire stands for elfin grace and incredible fleetness of foot, Kelly means athletic, bold, masculine choreography. His signature tune, of course, was the title-track from *Singin' in the Rain* and the image of his joyous umbrella routine in a torrential downpour is one of the most indelible in Hollywood history. Kelly was not in the same league as a singer although his easy, slightly husky timbre makes pleasant listening. This is a tasteful collection of numbers from his great days with MGM. Also from *Singin' in the Rain*, we have two delightful duets, the comic masterpiece "Moses" (with Donald O'Connor) and the delicate, romantic "You are my lucky star" (with Debbie Reynolds), as well as Nacio Herb Brown's largely instrumental, swinging "Broadway ballet". Other much-loved classics come from the Gershwins' *An American in Paris*, including "I got rhythm", "Love is here to stay" and "'S wonderful". Collectors will appreciate less familiar Porter tracks from *Les Girls*, including "You're just too, too!", a duet with the tragically short-lived British comedienne Kay Kendall, and the comic "Blue Danube (why are we here)", performed with Dan Dailey and Michael Kidd in the André Previn-scored *It's Always Fair Weather*. Kelly's understated "Almost like being in love" from *Brigadoon*, later associated with his sometime co-star Judy Garland, is a delight. Garland herself doesn't feature here, although there are numbers from two of their collaborations, *The Pirate* and *Summer Stock*, the last including a duet with Phil Silvers, "Heavenly music". **PF**

Frances Langford

New review
I'm in the Mood for Love Frances Langford, with various artists.
ASV Living Era mono Ⓜ CDAJA5219 (70 minutes: ADD). Recorded 1935-42.
Songs by McHugh, Marks, Porter, Hirsch, Woods, Bassman, Chaplin, Charles, Herbert, Rodgers, Mills, Washington, Styne, Schwartz, Warren, Kern. *Includes songs from* Every Night at Eight, Gay Divorce, Born to Dance, You Never Know, Leave it to Me, The Boys From Syracuse, The Fortune Teller, Show Boat, Pinocchio, Hit Parades of 1937 and 1941, Navy Blues, Weekend in Havana, Orchestra Wives.

Frances Langford's cool and effortless mezzo-soprano delivery and Betty Grable blonde good looks emphatically place her as a 'song stylist, *circa* 1940'. Enduring stardom on the scale of Peggy Lee or Dinah Shore didn't materialize, but Langford was among the classiest of the wartime pop singers, supplementing her radio and recording successes with a handful of notable film appearances, and her contribution to the ascendancy of American popular song was considerable. Her repertoire was largely drawn from Broadway composers (she was a fine Porter interpreter as these renditions of "At long last love and "Get out of town" will testify) and the bank of standards which includes Rodgers and Hart's "Blue moon" and the Ned Washington gem "I'm getting sentimental over you". Living Era have done a fine job of reducing the surface noise on these transfers without sacrificing the definitive period sound. Langford's strong voice and assured way with a lyric have the stamp of the quintessential nightclub performer of her age. There's a notable duet with Bing Crosby ("Gipsy love song" from Victor Herbert's *The Fortune Teller*), evocative of McDonald and Eddy at their peak, and a fresh-sounding rendition of the Oscar winner from *Pinnochio*, "When you wish upon a star". Accompaniment for the bulk of the selection is provided by Victor Young, Harry Sosnik and their respective orchestras, with Jimmy Dorsey putting in an appearance on the Porter tracks from *Every Night at Eight*, the 1935 film in which Langford first came to prominence.   **PF**

Gertrude Lawrence

New review
Gertrude Lawrence and Noël Coward Gertrude Lawrence, Noël Coward with various artists.
Flapper mono Ⓜ PASTCD9715 (67 minutes: ADD). Recorded 1926-36.
Songs by Coward and Gershwin.

Gertrude Lawrence, whose centenary it is in 1998, wasn't really beautiful, she often sang out of tune, and her acting could be mannered, yet she was hailed as one of the most charismatic and glamorous stars on both sides of the Atlantic for nearly 30 years. Though she was always closely associated with Coward in revues and plays, he never composed a musical for her – but Gershwin, Porter, Weill and Rodgers did. This CD includes some of her performances of Coward, including "Mad about the boy", "Someday I'll find you" (in the famous scenes from *Private Lives*) as well as her two great hits from Gershwin's *Oh, Kay* – "Do, do, do" and "Someone to watch over me". Her recordings of Weill's *Lady in the Dark* are on "From Berlin to Broadway" (see separate review) and the original cast of Rodgers's *The King and I* is available on MCA. Even without being able to see her, it is still possible, just listening to her voice, to understand why Coward described her as "kaleidoscopic ... capable of anything and everything".   **PO'C**

Evelyn Laye

Gaiety Girl A Tribute. Evelyn Laye, with various orchestras and conductors.
ASV Living Era mono Ⓜ CDAJA5211 (68 minutes: AAD). Recorded 1923-45.
Songs from **Romberg:** The New Moon. The Night is Young. **Fall:** Madame Pompadour. **Kern:** Blue Eyes. **Noble:** Princess Charming. **Lehár:** Paganini. **Coward:** Bitter Sweet. **Gay:** Lights Up.

Evelyn Laye was London's most glamorous leading lady of the musical theatre between the wars, combining a beautiful appearance with a sweet, clear soprano voice. Her ability to shape phrases to perfection is apparent at once in the excerpts from *The New Moon* that set the tone with a gloriously luxurious 1920s theatrical ambience. This collection ranges through some of the leading stage roles of Miss Laye's career, which included starring with Richard Tauber in Lehár's *Paganini* and ended up with her final appearance as a musical leading lady in Oscar Straus's *Three Waltzes*. Songs heard along the way include such favourites as "I'll see you again" and "You've done something to my heart", and the collection also presents some of her roles from films such as *The Night is Young*, featuring "When I grow too old to dream". There is another Evelyn Laye compilation in Pearl's Flapper series (PASTCD9717) that is less well compiled than this, and ASV has also done a much better job of eliminating surface noise. This is altogether a splendid souvenir of Miss Laye's artistry.   **AML**

Beatrice Lillie

The Unique! The Incomparable! **Beatrice Lillie**, with various artists.
Flapper mono Ⓜ PASTCD7054 (70 minutes: ADD). Recorded 1934-9.
Songs from **Weigall:** Charlot's Revue of 1926. **Youmans:** Oh, Please. **Gideon:** Please. **Rodgers:** She's My Baby. **Schwartz:** Flying Colours. At Home Abroad. **Coward:** Set to Music. **Caples:** New Faces of 1934.

Noël Coward once described a Beatrice Lillie first-night: "She came on, grabbed the audience by the scruff of its neck and shook it into an adoring frenzy." Lillie was one of the most anarchic and original performers to emerge from the heyday of revue in London during the First World War. Though she appeared in various musicals and films, she inevitably turned them into 'An Evening with Beatrice Lillie'.

These recordings from the 1930s include some of her most famous numbers, even though several of them (Coward's "Mad about the boy", "The party's over" and "Three white feathers") were created by others. Without knowing the context, it's a bit difficult to understand "A baby's best friend" by Rodgers and Hart (from *She's My Baby*), but Lillie's accents and timing are never in doubt. The layers of double meaning she finds in "There are fairies at the bottom of our garden" and "I'm a campfire girl" would make the curate blush. **PO'C**

Marie Lloyd

A Little of What You Fancy **Marie Lloyd**, with various artists.
Pearl mono Ⓜ GEMMCD9097 (78 minutes: ADD). Recorded 1903-39.
Songs by Le Brunn, Powell, Scott, Collins, Mayo and others.

Though she only appeared in a few musical productions, pantomimes at Drury Lane, a revue at the Tivoli and a musical comedy called *The ABC Girl* in which she was "Flossie the Frivolous", Marie Lloyd herself inspired at least three productions, and has entered the communal memory as the modern equivalent of Nell Gwynn.

Her recording career was sporadic, but this momentous CD gathers every known recording by her, as well as several by her sisters and daughter, who kept Marie Lloyd's memory alive for 30 years or more after her death. For Londoners, Marie Lloyd embodied a set of "Victorian values" that some people choose to forget. Racy, saucy, witty, she sang of the pleasures of the town and portrayed to perfection what was meant by the 'Naughty nineties'. The titles of her songs at once suggest the thin line she always trod – "Actions speak louder than words", "Every little movement has a meaning of its own" and the song that gives the disc its title and has entered the language, "A little of what you fancy does you good" (written in 1915 by Fred Leigh and George Arthurs). Without being able to see Marie Lloyd's long blonde hair, buck-toothed grin or the wink that could add meaning to the most innocent-sounding lyrics, one can still gather a great deal from her voice.

The excellent booklet has all the words, so despite crackle and hiss one can gauge the extent of her ability, whether in Cockney songs like her trilogy "The Coster's wedding", "The Coster girl in Paris" and "The Coster's christening", or carrying-off a *grande-dame* accent ("The three ages of woman"), country-yokel brogue ("Something on his mind"), or a bit of *parlez-vous* ("The tale of a skirt"), and the voice of a London cabbie in "The Piccadilly Trot" ("I knew the Haymarket when there was hay – not chaff"). T. S. Eliot wrote that Marie Lloyd had "a capacity for expressing the soul of the people – she left her audience not so much hilarious as happy." **PO'C**

Patti LuPone

Live! **Patti LuPone**, with various artists / **John McDaniel**.
RCA Victor Ⓔ 09026 617970-2 (two discs: 95 minutes: DDD).
Songs from **Porter:** Anything Goes. Aladdin. **Weill:** One Touch of Venus. Lost in the Stars. Lady in the Dark. Happy End. **Berlin:** Annie Get Your Gun. **Sondheim:** Company. **Lloyd Webber:** Evita. **Waldman:** The Robber Bridegroom. **Schwartz:** The Baker's Wife. **Bart:** Oliver!. **Blitzstein:** The Cradle Will Rock. **Schönberg:** Les Misérables. *Songs by* Dennis and Adair, Strayhorn, Kramer, Monaco and Jolson, Burke, Telson, Russell and Gold.

Patti LuPone had spent several years away from musical theatre working on an American television series when she was cast as Norma Desmond for Andrew Lloyd Webber's *Sunset Boulevard*. To say farewell to Los Angeles, she played a short concert run at the Westwood Playhouse, which has been preserved on this two-disc set. The first half is a mixture of some of LuPone's favourites, covering both pop and theatre. There are fine versions of Kurt Weill's "I'm a stranger here myself" and "It never was you" which neatly convey her feelings of nervousness at returning to live theatre. She displays fine comic flair with "Everything happens to me", and some nice comments on motherhood with the tender Al Jolson number "Dirty hands! dirty face!" and the raucous "And his rocking horse ran away". Her somewhat poor diction does not help with a patter number like "Come to the supermarket in old Peking", but her dramatic flair is perfect for "Being alive" from *Company*'s Act 1 finale. The second half of the show is based on LuPone's theatrical career introduced by James Taylor's "Looking for love on Broadway", followed by "Don't cry for me, Argentina" which she introduced to Broadway audiences in her Tony award-winning performance. Her early roles allow us to hear the beautiful "Sleepy man" from *The Robber Bridegroom*, and she introduces "Meadowlark" from *The Baker's Wife* with an hilarious description of that show's troubled road tour. Marc Blitzstein's "Nickel under your foot" from *The Cradle Will Rock* is another interesting inclusion before the familiar numbers from her West End and Broadway successes in the late 1980s. The disc ends with another successful Kurt Weill number, "Lost in the stars", which includes Norma's closing speech from *Sunset Boulevard*. This is a powerful and effective ending, all the more poignant because of the subsequent problems that LuPone experienced with the show. LuPone's diction is occasionally poor and her voice does not always move up the register smoothly, but she has a presence and quality that few others possess in modern musical theatre and this enjoyable and varied set showcases her considerable talents. **RAC**

Jeanette MacDonald and Nelson Eddy

When I'm Calling You Jeanette MacDonald, Nelson Eddy, with various artists.
ASV Living Era mono Ⓜ CDAJA5124 (75 minutes: AAD). Recorded 1929-41.
Songs from **Friml:** Rose Marie. **Schertzinger:** The Love Parade. **Whiting:** Monte Carlo. One Hour With You. **Herbert:** Naughty Marietta. **Posford:** Balalaika. **Rodgers:** Love Me Tonight. **Lehár:** The Merry Widow. **Bizet:** Carmen. **Gounod:** Roméo et Juliette. **Romberg:** Maytime. Girl of the Golden West. The New Moon.

The partnership of Jeanette MacDonald and Nelson Eddy was one of the most glamorous show-business pairings of all time, and for many it epitomizes the glamour of the romantic Hollywood film operetta of the late 1930s. This generous collection includes most of the obvious numbers from the films they made together, including three items each from *Naughty Marietta, Rose Marie* and *The New Moon*, which were the three major stage adaptations with which they are above all associated. In addition there are solo numbers such as "Beyond the blue horizon", "One hour with you" and "Isn't it romantic?" from the films that MacDonald made during the significant career she enjoyed before she teamed up with Eddy. More of a surprise, perhaps, is the inclusion of Eddy alone in the Toreador's song from *Carmen*, confirming that the couple's appeal lay in their musical ability as much as their celluloid charm. The collection is attractively and intelligently compiled in the manner typical of ASV's Living Era series. **AML**

Mary Martin

The Decca Years, 1938-46. Mary Martin, with various artists.
Koch mono Ⓔ 37906-2 (45 minutes: ADD).
Songs from **Porter:** Jubilee. Paris. Leave it to Me. Anything Goes. Wake Up and Dream. Du Barry Was a Lady. **Berlin:** Louisiana Purchase. **Monaco/Schertzinger:** Rhythm on the River. Kiss the Boys Goodbye. **Gershwin:** The French Doll. **Styne:** Follow the Boys. **R. Scott:** Lute Song. *Songs by* Padilla, Mercer and Von Tilzer.

Mary Martin was a Broadway star for nearly 30 years. She created the roles of Maria von Trapp in *The Sound of Music* and, in *South Pacific*, Nellie Forbush, and was the first star to whom

Lerner and Loewe played their songs for *My Fair Lady*, a role she turned down commenting, "Those dear boys have lost their talent". In 1966, I recall her cartwheeling across the stage of the Drury Lane Theatre in *Hello, Dolly!*, giving an effervescent performance in a lacklustre production. It was Cole Porter who first gave her a break when he asked her to sing "My heart belongs to daddy", one of five of his songs, ranging from the wistful "Why shouldn't I?" to that rumba and swing cocktail, "Katie went to Haiti".

Indeed, it is the songs as much as the singer that make these old 78rpm discs worth collecting in this format. Though Martin starred in few flops, one of them, *Lute Song*, which ran for 142 performances in 1946, produced a pretty ballad in "Mountain high, valley low". Other numbers come from her Hollywood years at Paramount where, with Bing Crosby and lyricist-composer Johnny Mercer, she teamed up for "The waiter and the porter and the upstairs maid" and appeared in other 'swing' musicals, mostly by Victor Schertzinger, a composer-producer at Paramount. It was the studio's resident songwriting team of Monaco and Burke who gave her the uninhibited "Ain't it a shame about Mame?", where the star seizes a much-needed opportunity to drop her all too respectable image. The Koch team have been able to secure good masters for this compilation with the result that these transfers faithfully mirror the original 78s.   **AE**

Ethel Merman

New review
An Earful of Merman Ethel Merman, with various artists.
Conifer Ⓜ CMSCD1015 (76 minutes: ADD). Recorded 1931-40.
Songs from **Donaldson:** An Earful of Music. **Green:** Roaming. **Berlin:** Alexander's Ragtime Band. **Arlen:** Strike Me Pink. **N. H. Brown:** Take A Chance. **Porter:** Anything Goes. Red Hot and Blue. Dubarry was a Lady. Panama Hattie. **Revel:** We're Not Dressing. The Big Broadcast of 1936. **Hollaender:** Anything Goes. **Pokrass:** Happy Landing. **A. Schwartz:** Stars in Your Eyes.

This handy compilation covers most of Merman's first decade in showbusiness. As well as mementoes of her stage and screen appearances there are some studio recordings of songs she didn't introduce, including mellow renditions of Berlin's "How deep is the ocean?" and Arlen's "I gotta right to sing the blues". For, and in spite of Porter's quip that Merman reminded him of a brass band going by, she could move an audience with more than mere volume, as her all too rare appearances on stage proved. Merman had an extraordinary instinct for the pulse and beat of a lyric and knew how to make the words come alive. Her recording of "I get a kick out of you", with a fractional pause before the key noun in the title reminds us that this was a song about unrequited love. Likewise her version of "Make it another old-fashioned please", is no tear-jerker but a reminder of the truly pickled. Not all her songs are in the Porter class, the composer with whom she shared a seven-show partnership. But amongst the less familiar are two fine Arthur Schwartz numbers, "This is it", where the star adds a number of extended ohhhs to the refrain and a sad ballad, "I'll pay the check", with an eloquent Dorothy Fields lyric which the star puts over with great feeling. The recordings, including three lifted from the soundtrack of Fox's 1938 extravaganza *Alexander's Ragtime Band*, sound remarkably robust.   **AE**

I Get a Kick Out of You Ethel Merman, with various artists.
Flapper mono Ⓜ PASTCD7056 (68 minutes: ADD). Recorded 1934-43.
Songs from **Porter:** Anything Goes. Red, Hot and Blue!. Panama Hattie. Something for the Boys. **Revel:** The Big Broadcast. **Schwartz:** Stars in Your Eyes. *Songs by* Arlen, Berlin and others.

Ethel Merman was one of the great interpretive geniuses of twentieth-century musical theatre. Her style seemed deceptively simple: go out there and sock it to them. But listening to these early recordings, concentrating on Cole Porter numbers but also including some songs by Arlen, Berlin, Schwartz and others, it immediately becomes clear that she was possessed of a great voice and personality, to which she added the most delightful, subtle phrasing and a range of colours in her tone and accents. Her use of speech-mixed-with-song and her ability to vary the rhythm within words to add to the tension, and cap the whole thing with one of her great searing notes like some great jazz trumpeter, would be instructive as an example of how to sing a song for a musician of any persuasion. "You're the top", "I get a kick out of you", "It's de-lovely", "Ridin' high", "Hey, good lookin'" and "Make it another old-fashioned, please" were all written for her by Cole Porter and no one has ever sung them better. Among the lesser-known songs are "Eadie was a lady" by Whiting, Brown and De Sylva, "A lady needs a change" by Schwartz and Fields and Arlen's "You're a builder-upper". **PO'C**

Jessye Norman

With a Song in My Heart Jessye Norman with the **Boston Pops Orchestra / John Williams**. Philips ℗ 412 625-2 (37 minutes: DDD).
Songs from **Rodgers:** The Boys from Syracuse, I Married an Angel, Spring is Here. **Porter:** Rosalie, Can-Can, Mexican Hayride. **Kern:** You Were Never Lovelier, Music in the Air, Very Warm for May. **Arlen:** House of Flowers. **Gershwin:** Goldwyn Follies.

The debate about whether or not opera singers should cross over to popular music continues to rage. This 1984 selection of standards from Jessye Norman makes an interesting comparison with similar recitals from Kiri Te Kanawa and, more recently, Lesley Garrett. Norman sets about her task with brio, but there is no disguising that in some cases the richness of her elegant *bel canto* is simply too much for lyrics and melodies which demand a nimbler touch. Harold Arlen's "The sleepin' bee", for example, with words by Truman Capote, or Cole Porter's "I love Paris". She is more at home when able to let rip with the grandiose emotions expressed by Jerome Kern's "The song is you" or the title-track, a Rodgers and Hart classic from a long-forgotten 1929 musical, *Spring is Here*. From the same writers, "Falling in love with love", originally introduced by soprano Muriel Angelus, is here over-embellished. Likewise "Spring is here", not, confusingly, from the show of that name, but from a later effort, *I Married an Angel*. The force of Norman's interpretations is well-matched by the lush performance of the Boston Pops under the expert direction of John Williams. The overall result is rather like a rich gateau: filling and technically perfect, but not necessarily fulfilling for the soul. Norman lacks the torch singer's touch so essential to bring "In the still of the night" or "All the things you are" to life. A valiant effort, nevertheless. **PF**

Elaine Paige

Encore Elaine Paige, with various artists.
WEA ℗ 0630 10476-2 (53 minutes: DDD).
Songs from **Lloyd Webber:** Sunset Boulevard. Cats. Evita. Jesus Christ Superstar. **Andersson/Ulvaeus:** Chess. **Schönberg:** Les Misérables. **Dumont/Monnot:** Piaf.

This compilation neatly sums up the career to date of a performer whose status as First Lady of British Musical Theatre is pretty much cast in stone. Only *Anything Goes* is missing. The *Piaf* numbers and show-piece ballads from *Sunset Boulevard* demonstrate just how far Paige has come since *Evita* – represented here by a live 1993 recording of "Don't cry for me, Argentina" – made her a star. Always a belter, Paige's versatility, coupled with a genuine talent for subtle lyric interpretation, has now triumphed over an earlier tendency to sound strident. *Piaf* and *Sunset* aside, highlights include her popular hits, "Memory" (*Cats*) and "I know him so well", the duet from *Chess* which she took to the top of the charts with Barbara Dickson. The selection falters only when it strays into hits-from-the-shows territory: there's an undistinguished version of "I don't know how to love him" and superfluous readings of "On my own" and "I dreamed a dream" from *Les Misérables*, a show with which Paige has never been closely associated. An artist of Paige's standing should really be permitted an occasional deviation from the obvious. Time, surely, to tackle some Sondheim. **PF**

Piaf **Elaine Paige**, with **Anonymous orchestra / Del Newman, Laurie Holloway, Mike Moran**.
WEA Ⓕ 4509 94641-2 (38 minutes: DDD).
Songs by Monnot, Dumont, Louiguy, Villard, Bouqet and Emer, arranged by Del Newman
and Mike Moran.

Elaine Paige's 1993 performance as the great French *chanteuse* Edith Piaf was a watershed in a
career which, *Anything Goes* aside, was previously founded on her status as doyenne of the
Rice/Lloyd Webber *oeuvres*. Armed with a sheaf of songs hitherto indelibly associated with
Piaf, she soared above Pam Gems's flawed chamber play in a role which stretched her combined
acting and singing talents to new limits. She didn't fall short of the challenge. Few singers have
been able to loosen the stranglehold which Piaf continues to exert on her repertoire. Here,
eschewing imitation, Paige clearly respects the legend but ultimately seizes the material for
herself, without being tempted to indulge in misplaced histrionics. The result is a powerful but
controlled and mature reading of some of the great French chansons. With new arrangements
by Del Newman and Mike Moran, most are sung in English, or a mixture of French and
English (with new lyrics by Pam Gems, Adrian Mitchell, Hal Shaper and Norman Newell), but
retain the all-important narrative element. Most effective are Monnot's "Hymne à l'amour"
and "Les amants d'un jour", the tragic tale of the suicide of two young lovers as told by a hard-
bitten but sympathetic *concierge*. There's an authentically vulgar rendition of "C'est à
Hambourg" (Dumont) and a highly-charged "La belle histoire d'amour". Best of all, though,
Paige sings three numbers entirely in French, and with complete conviction, including Piaf's
signature tunes "La vie en rose" (Monnot) and "Non, je ne regrette rien". A rousing finale of
"L'accordéoniste" may not banish Piaf's ghost entirely, but certainly sends it from the room for
the duration. **PF**

Romance and the Stage **Elaine Paige**, with the **New World Philharmonia Orchestra /**
Peter Matz.
RCA Ⓕ 74321 13615-2 (54 minutes: DDD).
Songs from **Berlin:** Annie Get Your Gun. **Hupfeld:** Everybody's Welcome. **Bricusse:** The
Roar of the Greasepaint – The Smell of the Crowd. **Rose:** Great Day. **Coleman:** City of
Angels. **Coward:** Words and Music. **Porter:** A Swell Party. **Forrest/Wright:** Kismet. **Styne:**
Bells Are Ringing. **Gershwin:** Rosalie. **Kern:** Roberta. **Weill:** Knickerbocker Holiday.
Loesser: The Most Happy Fella.

Singing standards is an art in itself. The basic rule is to sing the song as the composer
intended. The difficulty is bringing something new to a number that has been performed
by so many great exponents before. Of course, it's quite possible to embellish and take
liberties as long as you preserve the spirit and heart of the original. And that's exactly what Elaine
Paige achieves with this carefully chosen selection of torch songs and ballads. It's fair to say that
she has always been recognized as a hearty belter. But, as her career has developed, Paige has
discovered more subtle vocal qualities which have helped to establish a considerable reputation as
an interpreter of lyrics with a knack for artful phrasing. Her first professional job was in the
chorus of *The Roar of the Greasepaint – The Smell of the Crowd* (1965) and she revisits that show
for a swooping, jazzy "Feeling good". One of the delights of this selection is that, like "Feeling
good", it includes several less well-known numbers which complement the more familiar
evergreens. So, we have "With every breath I take", a splendid modern torch song from *City of
Angels*, set between an early Broadway example, "More than you know" and Coward's classic
study of mature infatuation, "Mad about the boy". There's an interesting reading of Weill's
"September song", billed as a tribute to Lotte Lenya, although Paige wisely avoids any attempt
at imitation, opting instead for a considerate, understated and straightforward approach. Apart
from a rather middle-of-the-road "Smoke gets in your eyes" (*Roberta*), this is a skilfully
performed set of songs, rounded off unexpectedly with Loesser's delightful paean to summer love
from *The Most Happy Fella*, "Song of a summer night". **PF**

Stages **Elaine Paige,** with various artists.
WEA Ⓜ 2292-40228-2 (44 minutes: DDD).
Songs from **Lloyd Webber:** Cats. Evita. Jesus Christ Superstar. **Yeston:** Nine. **Sondheim:** A
Little Night Music. Follies. **Oliver:** Blondel. **MacDermot:** Hair. **Hamlisch:** A Chorus Line.
Krieger: Dreamgirls. **Strouse:** Annie.

Cinema **Elaine Paige,** with various artists.
WEA Ⓜ 2292-40511-2 (44 minutes: DDD).
Songs from **Legrand:** The Thomas Crown Affair. **Gore:** Fame. **Desautels:** Eyes of Laura Mars. **Davis:** Champions. **Goffin:** Mahogany. **Nitzsche:** An Officer and a Gentleman. **North:** Unchained. **Batt:** Watership Down. **Bacharach:** Alfie. **Vangelis:** Missing. **Hamlisch:** The Way We Were. **McBroom:** The Rose.

Hard on the success of *Evita* and her rapid elevation to First Lady of British Musical Theatre status, Elaine Paige embarked on a parallel career as a recording artist and concert performer with equally impressive results. Subsequent efforts have been as diverse as an album of Queen songs and a Christmas selection, but it was "Stages" (1983) and "Cinema" (1984) which first brought her to the attention of a wider listening audience. Admirers of Paige's more recent work as Piaf and Norma Desmond may not find Tony Visconti's pop arrangements of some of the great modern musical standards to their taste. And on occasion, Paige herself surrenders to the temptation to turn a subtle lyric into an overwrought power ballad which the likes of Celine Dion would envy. Even so, as the harbingers of fine work to come, both of these collections make useful listening. Naturally, on "Stages", *Evita* is well represented with the Lloyd Webber-produced "Don't cry for me, Argentina" and the mistress's song from the show, "Another suitcase in another hall". Paige's biggest solo hit to date, "Memory" from *Cats*, opens up the album and, frankly, knocks the Streisand version into a cocked hat. There are good, up-tempo versions of "What I did for love" (*A Chorus Line*) and "One night only" (*Dreamgirls*) which demonstrate Paige's emotional power, one of the gifts which has garnered her such a large popular following beyond the musical stage. Alas, her early attempts at Sondheim are not so successful. True, she is not helped by the ghastly arrangements of two of his finest ballads "Send in the clowns" (which includes a Wurlitzer!) and "Losing my mind" (overkill time, again).

For the "Cinema" selection, Paige turns to some of the best-known theme songs from the silver screen, generally with great effect. There's a swirling, jazzy "The windmills of your mind" (Legrand, Bergman and Bergman) and a moving "Missing" (Vangelis, Rice). Most of these numbers were clearly chosen to give Paige ample room to show off her powerhouse voice and she is at her best and most controlled on "Out here on my own" (*Fame*) and "Sometimes", a beautiful, driving Norman Newell/Carl Davis number from *Champions*. Again, she gives Streisand a run for her money, this time with "The prisoner", the theme from *Eyes of Laura Mars*, although she can't really wrest "The way we were" from Streisand's clutches. Both these albums are enhanced by complete song texts and by Paige's jocular, self-penned liner notes which reveal a distinctly down-to-earth side to her stellar persona. **PF**

Mandy Patinkin

Dress Casual **Mandy Patinkin,** with **Anonymous orchestra / Paul Gemignani**.
Sony Ⓜ MK45998 (73 minutes: DDD).
Songs from **Sondheim:** Evening Primrose, Company, Into the Woods. **Woods:** The Jolson Story. **Weill:** Lady in the Dark. **Schwartz:** Between the Devil, Flying Colours. **Carroll:** Oh Look! **Rodgers:** Pal Joey. **Willson:** The Music Man. **Berlin:** Easter Parade, Alexander's Ragtime Band, Follow the Fleet. **Leiber:** Dancin'. **Warren:** The Harvey Girls.

Experiment **Mandy Patinkin,** with **Anonymous orchestra / Eric Stern**.
Nonesuch Ⓟ 75599-79330-2 (46 minutes: DDD).
Songs from **Hupfeld:** Everybody's Welcome. **Kern:** You Were Never Lovelier. **Menken:** Little Shop of Horrors. **Sondheim:** Company, Saturday Night, Merrily We Roll Along, Follies. **Bernstein:** West Side Story. **Waller:** Ain't Misbehavin'. **Schönberg:** Les Misérables. **Rodgers:** Babes in Arms. **Porter:** Nymph Errant. **Lane:** Finian's Rainbow. **Warren:** Billy Rose's Diamond Horseshoe.

One of musical theatre's most interesting performers, Mandy Patinkin has tackled a wide variety of roles, from Che in *Evita* to George in *Sunday in the Park with George*. Always dedicated and uncompromising, his solo albums reflect his intensity and individuality. His manner can come across as pretentious in the extreme and on "Dress Casual", there are moments of histrionic behaviour which are unsettling: his exhausting rendition of Schwartz and Dietz's "Triplets", for example, is irritating rather than impressive. But the failures are far outweighed by the successes. Outstanding are two central medleys. *Pal Joey* is a familiar Rodgers and Hart piece, and Patinkin offers an excellent selection interspersed with dialogue to recreate Joey's story – it is a highly effective piece of theatricality. But it is the suite of four songs from Stephen Sondheim's TV movie *Evening Primrose* that constitutes the most important work on the album. For this, Patinkin is joined by Bernadette Peters (his *Sunday in the Park* co-star) who plays Ella, trapped in a department store, waiting to be freed by the poet Charles. Two of the songs find their first recording here outside of the original production – "If you can find me I'm here" and "When". Combined with the two better-known songs from the piece, one gets a sense of Sondheim's writing in the late 1960s – the period shortly before his greatest creative period of *Company, Follies* and *Night Music. Company* provides two further selections – fine performances of "Sorry, grateful" and "Being alive". With the help of top-flight arrangers and a brilliant conductor in Paul Gemignani, Patinkin offers a selection that is stimulating and, despite an occasional lapse when his enthusiasm gets the better of his artistry, is of exceptional quality.

Unlike previous albums which feature solo songs and medleys, "Experiment" (taking its title and inspiration from the Cole Porter song from *Nymph Errant*) offers 18 songs in a seamless journey across time and musical form. There is barely a break between the songs and most run straight from one into the other. Patinkin is at his most restrained here, there are none of the histrionics with which he is associated, and what he creates is a quite beautiful showcase of his considerable talents. The song choice is interesting. Always associated with the work of Stephen Sondheim, Patinkin sings some of his lesser-known numbers – "Someone is waiting" from *Company*, as well as a cut song from that show, "Multitudes of Amys". "Good thing going" from *Merrily We Roll Along*, "So many people" from his unproduced 1954 musical *Saturday Night* and a brilliant and moving rendition of "The road you didn't take" from the Broadway version of *Follies*. Predictably, there are classic songs from the 1930s and 1940s – a period for which Patinkin, for all his modernity, seems to have a strong affinity. His versions of "Where or when" and "As time goes by" are delightful, and he sings "I'm old-fashioned" with total conviction. There is a superb intro to Fats Waller's "Jitterbug waltz" with an authentic recreation of the sound of an old 78 being played. Patinkin effortlessly introduces the very modern with two songs from *Les Misérables* as well as Harry Chapin's classic pop song "Taxi". The overall effect of the CD is one of gentleness, far from his usual excitable self – instead it offers a reflective and slow side to the performer, and although some may find it lacking in sufficient up-tempo numbers, it is a superb and very cleverly constructed selection, with excellent and innovative arrangements. **RAC**

Dick Powell

The Man from 42nd Street Dick Powell, with various artists.
Flapper mono Ⓜ PASTCD7079 (65 minutes: ADD). Recorded 1933-39.
Songs from **Whiting:** Varsity Show. Hollywood Hotel. **Berlin:** On the Avenue. **Warren:** The Singing Marine. Broadway Gondolier. Gold Diggers of 1935. 20 Million Sweethearts. **Wrubel:** Flirtation Walk. **Fain:** Footlight Parade. **Kahn:** Thanks a Million.

Dick Powell was a gift to Warner Brothers Studios in their bid to cheer up the nation during the 1930s Depression. Relentlessly cheery and optimistic, if there was a gloomy song to be sung, it went to one of the other characters. He had a good clear voice which, wedded to his angelic, clean-cut good looks, made him into a respectable matinée idol, with none of the menace of his non-singing contemporaries, Gable, Cooper and Cagney. The songs featured here are wonderful: how many other stars got to create so many standards? Even if you've never seen the films from which they come, "Lulu's back in town" (*Varsity Show*), "I've got my love to keep me warm" (*On the Avenue*), "I'll string along with you" (*20 Million Sweethearts*) and the others conjure up the era perfectly. **PO'C**

Barbra Streisand

The Broadway Album Barbra Streisand, with various artists.
Columbia Ⓕ CD86322 (48 minutes: DDD).
Songs from **Sondheim:** Sunday in the Park With George, Sweeney Todd, Company, A Little Night Music. **Rodgers:** Carousel, The King and I. **Bernstein:** West Side Story. **Loesser:** Guys and Dolls. **Kern:** Show Boat. **Gershwin:** Porgy and Bess.

Back to Broadway Barbra Streisand, with various artists.
Columbia Ⓕ 473880-2 (50 minutes: DDD).
Songs from **Rodgers:** South Pacific. **Sondheim:** Anyone Can Whistle, Into the Woods, Sunday in the Park With George. **Lloyd Webber:** The Phantom of the Opera. Sunset Boulevard. **Weill:** One Touch of Venus. **Bernstein:** West Side Story. **Loesser:** Guys and Dolls. **Gershwin:** Lady, Be Good!

Eight years separate these albums but the second (1993) is essentially a continuation of the first (1985). Any Streisand project is an Event with no expense spared. No orchestration is so precious, no lyric so appropriate that it can't be rewritten or tinkered with to suit her abundant talents. Sondheim, who features largely in both collections, clearly thinks so, having updated the lyrics of some of his most memorable songs ("Send in the clowns" and "Putting it together", for example) to tie in with what is essentially a highly personalized Streisand journey through historic Broadway. A pair of concept albums, in fact. Bad news if you are a purist who likes their standards sung as they were written. But you ignore this woman at your peril. With the finest resources at her disposal, to say nothing of her extraordinary vocal range, she is able to take risks in phrasing and modulation of which other singers can only dream. Ironically, Alan and Marilyn Bergman's sleeve-notes for the "Broadway Album" declare that Streisand is at home on the Broadway musical stage. Her disliking for live performance is well known and she hasn't acted on stage since *Funny Girl* (1964). The Streisand personality is so dominant that it is unlikely she could ever have played most of the roles for which these songs were written. But on her own terms, she is a consummate stylist and interpreter, so, with each number or medley, what we get is the story as told by Streisand. The effect is luxurious, expensive, occasionally overpowering and sometimes intensely moving. The highlights of the "Broadway Album" are surely a marvellously restrained "Send in the clowns", all the more breathtaking for the vocal gymnastics which have gone before, a tasteful medley of numbers from *The King and I* ("I have dreamed", "We kiss in a shadow" and "Something wonderful"), a yearning "If I loved you" (*Carousel*) and "Not while I'm around" from *Sweeney Todd*. This is Streisand at her best. Her tendency to self-indulgence is exposed by the embarrassing *ad libbing* around "Adelaide's lament" which finds her resorting to the mannerisms of her early 1970s screwball film roles. Linking "Pretty woman" with "The ladies who lunch" probably seemed a good idea at the time, but the two numbers are not logically related and Streisand completely misses the scathing rawness essential to the latter.

If anything, "Back to Broadway" is more satisfying. There are good, modern arrangements of "Speak low" (*One Touch of Venus*) and "The man I love". "Music of the night" becomes a duet with *Phantom*'s original star, Michael Crawford, accompanied by the London Symphony Orchestra, and Johnny Mathis guests on a medley from *West Side Story* ("I have a love" and "One hand, one heart"). Lloyd Webber chose Streisand to make the first commercial recordings of numbers from *Sunset Boulevard*, both of which appear in this collection: "As if we never said goodbye" and "With one look". There's an overwrought "I've never been in love before" and a quirky "Luck be a lady" (*Guys and Dolls*). Best of all, though, are a thoughtfully executed, moving "Children will listen" (*Into the Woods*) and "Move on" (*Sunday in the Park With George*), with which Streisand signs off. **PF**

Kiri Te Kanawa

Kiri on Broadway Kiri Te Kanawa, with the **London Voices; London Symphony Orchestra / John Mauceri: Nelson Riddle and his orchestra: Utah Symphony Orchestra / Julius Rudel; Leonard Bernstein**.
Decca Ⓕ 440 280-2 (59 minutes: DDD).
Songs from **Loewe:** My Fair Lady. **Weill:** One Touch of Venus. **Rodgers:** Too Many Girls, Carousel, The Sound of Music. **Porter:** Kiss Me, Kate. **Bernstein:** West Side Story.

In the vanguard of the trend for classical singers to embrace the world of the popular musical, Kiri Te Kanawa's considerable efforts have garnered her new admirers and snooty knuckle raps from more reactionary quarters in almost equal measure. There is no doubt, however, that she has an ear for the stately show tune. This is a compilation of various outings including studio cast recordings of *West Side Story* (conducted by Bernstein himself) and *My Fair Lady*, and an album made and arranged by Nelson Riddle. Frankly, she is not a convincing Eliza Doolittle (dreadful Cockney accent, for a start), but her lush reading of "I could have danced all night" has probably not been equalled by any legitimate stage actress with the exception of Julie Andrews. Likewise, she is rather mature for *West Side Story*'s Maria, but brings a certain dignity to "Tonight" and "One hand, one heart". Dame Kiri's album of standards made under the auspices of Nelson Riddle was criticized by some for being too syrupy, but these selections – "Speak low", "I didn't know what time it was" and "So in love" – demonstrate impeccable timing and a fluency with the lyrics which other operatic performers would be hard pressed to match. For a rousing lifting of the spirits, too, it would be difficult to beat her skilful, inspirational versions of two anthems, "You'll never walk alone" and "Climb ev'ry mountain", which many lesser artists on both sides of the musical spectrum have managed to render hackneyed.   **PF**

Dawn Upshaw

I Wish It So Dawn Upshaw, with **Anonymous orchestra / Eric Stern**.
Nonesuch Ⓟ 7559-79345-2 (45 minutes: DDD).
Songs from **Blitzstein:** Juno, No for an Answer, Reuben, Reuben. **Bernstein:** West Side Story, Candide, The Madwoman of Central Park West. **Sondheim:** Anyone Can Whistle, Saturday Night, The Girls of Summer, Merrily We Roll Along, Evening Primrose. **Weill:** One Touch of Venus, Lady in the Dark, Lost in the Stars.

Music theatre recordings by opera stars are often viewed with suspicion by devotees of the genre. Crispness, clarity and quality of voice are usually evident, but often the necessary acting and character are sadly missing. It is refreshing to hear Dawn Upshaw's triumphant first solo foray into this world. Eschewing the well-known and familiar, the song choice is fascinating, concentrating on four Broadway composers whose trademark is the art of dramatic song writing. There are a few trademark songs – "I feel pretty" from *West Side Story*, accompanied by two pianos, and a magnificent "Glitter and be gay" from *Candide* that surely challenges almost every other recording. But on the whole, the songs are not the standard Broadway canon. Certainly her choice of Sondheim material is far from the norm – the songs come from one show that never made it to Broadway, two flops, an obscure TV movie and an advertising song for a play. All are brilliantly executed and the disc contains the first fully orchestrated recording of "What more do I need?" from *Saturday Night*. The Weill is more familiar, but once again performed with a clarity and character that is very exciting – she matches Mary Martin for coy suggestiveness with "That's him" and Gertrude Lawrence for intelligence and wit on a beautifully edited version of "The saga of Jenny". But the revelation of the disc is the work of Marc Blitzstein, the least known of the four composers. His haunting and beautiful melodies, delicately sung by a wistful Upshaw, are quite superb and encourage a greater investigation into the work of this sadly neglected writer. Simply put, this is an essential addition to any collection of theatre recordings – a brilliant and unusual selection performed with great style and finesse.
RAC

Elisabeth Welch

New review
The Irving Berlin Songbook Elisabeth Welch; orchestra / Gordon Langford.
TER VIP Series Ⓟ CDVIR8305 (38 minutes: DDD). Recorded 1987.
Songs from Follow the Fleet, 1923 Music Box Revue, Louisiana Purchase, Blue Skies, Ziegfeld Follies, Annie Get Your Gun, Easter Parade, As Thousands Cheer and Holiday Inn.

The Jerome Kern Songbook Elisabeth Welch; orchestra / Gordon Langford.

TER VIP Series Ⓔ CDVIR8310 (53 minutes: DDD). Recorded 1989.

Songs from Sweet Adeline, Show Boat, Roberta, The Cat and the Fiddle, Music in the Air, High, Wide and Handsome, Cover Girl and Very Warm for May.

Elisabeth Welch began her career in black musical comedies and revues in New York, appeared in Cole Porter's *The New Yorkers* in 1931, and achieved her greatest acclaim in London shows from Porter's *Nymph Errant* in 1933, through Novello's *Glamorous Night* and *Arc de Triomphe*, to Stephen Schwartz's *Pippin* in 1973. In her eighties she attracted renewed attention as a great survivor from between-the-wars days. In these two recordings it is clear enough that Welch's voice is a shadow of what it once was; but what has not diminished one iota is the sheer artistry with which she harnesses those diminished resources and puts over these songs. Berlin's and Kern's songs repay the conversational approach that Welch necessarily adopts, and the intimate effect is heightened by Gordon Langford's restrained accompaniments. Not the least endearing aspect of these collections is that Welch knows this repertory in such depth that she is able to mix the more obvious items with others much less so. Songs such as Berlin's "When I lost you" and "Say it isn't so" and Kern's "Can I forget you?" and 'The song is you" invite especial affection for their tenderness. But there is comedy, too, in Berlin's "Snookey Ookums"; and Welch shows she can swing it when she wants to, as in Berlin's "Shaking the blues away" from the 1927 *Ziegfeld Follies*. It is unrealistic to single out favourites from this collection. Better by far to sit back and soak up all Welch's timeless artistry. **AML**

In Concert, at the Donmar Warehouse, 1986. Elisabeth Welch, with various artists.

First Night Ⓜ OCRCD6016 (47 minutes: DDD).

Songs by Schwartz, Carmichael, Rodgers, Gershwin, Goodwin, Chase, Porter, Hupfeld, Kern, Piaf, Herman, Kahn, Henderson. *Songs from* Pippin, The New Yorkers, Nymph Errant, Blackbirds of 1928, Casablanca, La Cage aux Folles and Roberta.

Elisabeth Welch was approaching 80 when, her status as one of the most enduring and loved cabaret artists long since assured, she gleefully took London by storm once more with her one woman show in 1986. Fortunately, those live performances were captured by the enterprising First Night Records. Few performers would expect to demonstrate this degree of vocal prowess or sheer stage presence at such an advanced age. Kicking off with "No time at all", a song she first performed as Berthe in Schwartz's *Pippin*, she tells the story of an extraordinary career which spans seven decades. There is plenty of light relief, with "Solomon" (her signature tune from *Nymph Errant*), "To keep my love alive" and "When I get you alone tonight" interspersed with nostalgia (Piaf's "La vie en rose" which Welch intoduced to London after the war, and "Bye bye blackbird" which recalls her stage début in New York revue during the 1920s. While she doesn't neglect modern shows (there's a touching "Song on the sand" from *La Cage aux Folles*), Welch's gift for interpreting the standards is sublime. From the prostitute's street cry, "Love for sale" (Porter) to Gershwin's great torch song, "The man I love", or Kern's "Smoke gets in your eyes", her characterization is absolutely convincing, her phrasing perfect. The ease with which she generates a mutual warmth with her audience is consummate. Marvellous, indeed. **PF**

New review

This Thing Called Love Elisabeth Welch, with various artists / Jonathan Cohen.

TER Ⓜ CDVIR8309 (48 minutes: DDD).

Songs by Porter, Heyman, McHugh, Swan, McCartney, Gershwin, Greenwell, Styne, Jacobs, Gensler, Coward, Sondheim, Weill, Mancini, Schwartz. *Includes songs from* Wake up and Dream, Blackbirds of 1928, Bells are Ringing, High Society, Follies, Lady in the Dark, Three's a Crowd, Conversation Piece, Breakfast at Tiffany's.

'Survivor' is one of the most over-used tags in showbusiness carrying, as it does, melodramatic connotations of odds overcome and dark personal tragedy. Elisabeth Welch has been a survivor in the most joyful sense. In a career spanning an incredible six decades, she perfected the art of singing verse in an intimate, deceptively easy manner. She was still doing it well into her eighties, as this delightful 1989 set of standards amply proves. Age failed to dent her ability to hit the notes or her impeccable, instinctive phrasing. From Porter's title-track through Swan's "When your lover has gone" to Coward's tremulous little paean "I'll follow my secret heart", Welch treats the vicissitudes of love and romance with a mixture of understated poignancy and sanguine realism. Her lightness of touch on the Gershwins' "Boy! What love has done to me" and a mid-tempo "I love you truly" is equally effective on Sondheim's "Losing my mind", a song more usually belted out with a deal of anguish. And she bridges the gap between "Porgy" from her first Broadway show (*Blackbirds of 1928*) and the Lennon/McCartney classic of modern melancholy "Yesterday" seamlessly. An artist for all ages. **PF**

Mae West

New review
I'm No Angel Mae West, with **Original Film Casts**.
Jasmine mono Ⓜ JASCD102 (69 minutes: ADD). Recorded 1933-6.
Songs from My Little Chickadee, She Done Him Wrong, I'm No Angel, Belle of the Nineties, Goin' to Town, Klondike Annie, Go West, Young Man and Every Day's a Holiday.

This collection begins with six commercial recordings made for Brunswick in the early 1930s followed by a selection of numbers from the soundtracks of her movies of the same period, including scenes from *I'm No Angel* (1933) with Cary Grant on the receiving end of her familiar sexual innuendos. In *Belle of the Nineties* (1934) she had the inestimable backing of the Duke Ellington orchestra, and in *Goin' to Town* (1934) she turns up in a duet version of Saint-Saëns's "Softly awakes my heart". Though many of the songs are in a 'Frankie and Johnny' idiom, this collection, like the Betty Grable disc on the same label (see separate review), affords a generous look at one of the unique entertainers of this century. **AE**

Dave Willetts

On and Off Stage Dave Willetts, with the **Philharmonia Orchestra / Paul Bateman**.
Silva Screen Ⓔ SONGCD902 (55 minutes: DDD).
Songs from **Loesser:** Guys and Dolls. **Schönberg:** Les Misérables. **Ward:** Penny Millionaire. **Lloyd Webber:** The Phantom of the Opera. **Yeston:** Nine. **Herman:** La Cage aux Folles. **McBroom:** The Rose. *Songs by*: Tozzi, Andrew, Benson, Hammond, Goldsmith and Diamond.

Dave Willetts came from obscurity to star as Jean Valjean in *Les Misérables* and went on to succeed Michael Crawford in *The Phantom of the Opera*. This carefully chosen selection of show tunes and pop numbers offers clear evidence of Willetts's gifts as an interpreter of lyrics. He never resorts to mere belting and unlike some of his contemporaries, he is prepared to take risks. There are two numbers from *Nine*, for example, which were originally intended for the female voice and which Willetts treats with great subtlety. He also rescues "I am what I am" (*La Cage aux Folles*) from its exile in third-rate cabaret and restores its reputation as a moving, life-affirming ballad. "The Rose" has lured many performers onto the rocks of histrionic indulgence; here Willetts shows admirable restraint in a medley which links it to Neil Diamond's "Hello again". As you would expect, both of Willetts's most successful shows to date are represented here: "Bring him home" is one of the less frequently heard standards from *Les Mis*; Lesley Garrett guests on "The phantom of the opera", and with "Music of the night" from the same show, Willetts provides confirmation that he was a worthy successor to Crawford – perhaps even more gifted vocally. Although the lesser quality of some of the pop numbers is exposed alongside classics such as "Luck be a lady" (*Guys and Dolls*), Willetts treats them all with the same vocal ease and good taste, equally at home with a George Benson dance tune or the grander ballads of Lloyd Webber. The booklet-notes emphasize the effort which went into making this album a cut above other show-tune collections. **PF**

Gary Wilmot

The Album Gary Wilmot, with the **London Symphony Orchestra / Mike Batt**.
 Carlton Shows Collection ℗ 30360 0009-2 (55 minutes: DDD).
 Songs from **Loesser:** Guys and Dolls. **Arlen:** The Wizard of Oz. **Rodgers:** South Pacific.
 Lerner: Gigi. **Bart:** Oliver!. **Bizet:** Carmen Jones. **Lloyd Webber:** Sunset Boulevard.

Gary Wilmot's amiable personality and abundant talents as a song-and-dance man have
transferred from the small screen to musical theatre with considerable success. Here, he is
clearly at home with the up-tempo numbers from *The Wizard of Oz* ("We're off to see the
wizard" and "If I only had a brain"), *Oliver!* ("Consider yourself" and "Who will buy?"), and
Gigi ("The night they invented champagne") as well as romantic ballads like "Younger than
Springtime" and "Bali Ha'i" from *South Pacific*. Wilmot scored a personal triumph as Joe in
the first ever London production of *Carmen Jones*. He confidently reprises two numbers from
the show: "Stan' up an' fight" and "Beat out dat rhythm on a drum". These are the high spots
of the collection, together with a soaring rendition of "Sunset Boulevard" which allows him
to give full rein to his powerful voice. Elsewhere, there are some notable duets: *Blood Brothers*
star Barbara Dickson guests on two numbers, "I've never been in love before" (*Guys and
Dolls*) and, most effectively, "Who will buy?". There is also an appearance by Lionel Bart
himself on a boisterous rendition of "Consider yourself". Wilmot easily holds his own in such
exalted company, but all are occasionally let down by the persistent easy listening feel of Mike
Batt's arrangements. "Who will buy?" is well served by a gentle folk treatment, but the
glutinous setting of "Over the rainbow" amply demonstrates why some standards would
benefit from a good long rest.   **PF**

Record companies and distributors

Entries are listed as follows: **Record company** or **Label** – UK Distributor.

Arista BMG Conifer
ASV ASV/Select
Atlantic WEA
Belart PolyGram
Capitol EMI
Carlton Shows
  Collection Carlton
Classics for Pleasure
  EMI
Chrysalis EMI
Columbia Sony
Conifer BMG Conifer
Decca PolyGram
DG PolyGram
Deram PolyGram
Dreamworks
  Universal
DRG New Note

EMI EMI
Epic Sony
Erato Warner Classics
First Night Pinnacle
Flapper Pinnacle
Fox Arista (BMG)
Geffen Universal
GNP Crescendo ZYX
  Productions
GRP New Note
Happy Days BMG
  Conifer
Island PolyGram
Jasmine BMG
  Conifer
Koch Koch
  International
London PolyGram

MCA Universal
MCI MCI
Mercury PolyGram
Milan BMG Conifer
Music for Pleasure
  EMI
Music Masters
  Nimbus
New World Harmonia
  Mundi
Nonesuch Warner
  Classics
Opal (Pavilion)
  Harmonia Mundi
Pearl (Pavilion)
  Harmonia Mundi
Philips PolyGram
Polydor PolyGram

RCA BMG Conifer
Savile BMG Conifer
Silva Screen Silva
  Productions
Sony Sony
Sterling Priory
Telarc BMG Conifer
TER MCI (UK) / JAY
  (USA)
Tring Tring
Varèse Sarabande
  Pinnacle
Virgin EMI
Walt Disney Records
  Buena Vista Home
  Entertainment
Warner Bros WEA
WEA WEA

Record company and distributor addresses

A&M Records
136-140 New Kings Road, London SW6 4LZ.
(www.amrecords.com)
Telephone 0171-705 4343 Fax 0171-731 460

AEI
Sherwood House, 13624 Sherman Way, Suite 222,
Van Nuys, CA91405-2844, USA
Telephone 818 904 9741

Arista Records (UK)
Cavendish House, 423 New Kings Road,
London SW6 4RM.
Telephone 0171-973 8040 Fax 0171-373 9324

Arista Records (USA)
6 West 57th Street, New York, NY 10019, USA.
(www.aristarec.com)
Telephone 212 489 7400 Fax 212 489 7400

ASV
1 Beaumont Avenue, London W14 9LP.
Telephone 0171-381 8747 Fax 0171-385 2653

BMG Conifer/RCA
Bedford House, 69-79 Fulham High Street,
London SW6 3JW.
Telephone 0171-973 0011 Fax 0171-371 9571

BMG (UK Distribution)
Lyng Lane, West Bromwich, West Midlands,
B70 7ST Telephone 0121 500 5545 Fax 0121 553 6880

BMG (USA)
1540 Broadway, New York, NY 10036-4098, USA.
(www.classicalmus.com)
Telephone 212 930 4000 Fax 212 930 4263

Buena Vista Home Entertainment
Beaumont House, Kensington Village, Avonmore
Road, London W14 8TS. Telephone 0171-605 2400
Fax 0171-605 2795

Carlton Records
The Waterfront, Elstree Road, Elstree,
Herts WD6 3BS. Telephone 0181-207 6207
Fax 0181-207 5789

The Complete Record Co
12 Pepys Court, 84 The Chase, London SW4 0NF
Telephone 0171-498 9666 Fax 0171-498 1828

DRG Records
130 West 57th Street, New York, NY 10019, USA
Telephone 212 265 4050

East West Records
Electric Lighting Station, 28 Kensington Church
Street, London W8 4EP. (www.eastwest.co.uk)
Telephone 0171-938 2181
Fax 0171-937 6645

EMI Records
(Customer Services) EMI House, 43 Brook Green,
London W6 7EF
Telephone 0171-605 5000 Fax 0171-605 5050

EMI
(Sales and Distribution Centre) Hermes Close,
Tachbrook Park, Leamington Spa, Warwickshire
CV34 6RP Telephone 01926 888 888 Fax 0181-479 5992

First Night
2-3 Fitzroy Mews, London W1P 5DQ
Telephone 0171-383 7767 Fax 0171-383 3020

Geffen
(www.geffen.com)

GNP Crescendo
Suite 4A, 8400 Sunset Boulevard, Los Angeles,
California CA 90403, USA.
(www.gnpcrescendo.com)
Telephone 213 656 2614 Fax 213 656 0693

GRP Records

555 West 57th Street, New York, NY 10019, USA.
(www.mca.com/grp) **Telephone** 212 245 7033

Harmonia Mundi (UK)

19-21 Nile Street, London N1 7LL
Telephone 0171-253 0863 **Fax** 0171-253 3237

Harmonia Mundi (USA)

2037 Granville Avenue, Los Angeles,
CA 90025-6103, USA. (harmoniamundi.com)
Telephone 310 478 1311 **Fax** 310 996 1366

Jasmine

Hasmick Promotions Ltd., Unit 8, Forest Hill
Trading Estate, Perry Vale, London SE23 2LX.
Telephone 0181-291 6777 **Fax** 0181-291 0081

JAY Records

Allegro Corporations, 14134 NE Airport Way,
Portland, Oregon 97230, USA.
Telephone 503 257 8480 **Fax** 503 257 9061

Koch International UK

Charlotte House, 87 Little Ealing Lane, London W5
4EH. **Telephone** 0181-832 1800 **Fax** 0181-832 1813

Koch International USA

2 Tri-Harbour Court, Port Washington, New York,
NY 11050-4617, USA. (www.kochint.com)
Telephone 516 484 1000 **Fax** 516 484 4746

London Records

(www.decca.com/london)

MCA

(www.mca.com/music.html) – see also Universal

MCI Presents

76 Dean Street, London W1V 5HA.
Telephone 0171-396 8899 **Fax** 0171-396 8903

Mercury

PO Box 1425, Chancellor's House, 72 Chancellor's
Road, Hammersmith, London W6 9QB
Telephone 0181-910 5678 **Fax** 0181-741 1616

Metropolitan Opera Guild

70 Lincoln Center Plaza, New York NY10023.

New Note

– see Pinnacle

New World Records

710 Seventh Avenue, New York, NY10036-1596.
Telephone 212 302 0460 **Fax** 212 944 1922

Pavilion Records

Sparrows Green, Wadhurst, East Sussex TN5 6SJ.
Telephone 01892 783591 **Fax** 01892 784156

Philips

(www.philclas.polygram.nl)

Pinnacle Records

Electron House, Cray Avenue, St Mary Cray,
Orpington, Kent BR5 3RJ
Telephone 01689 873144 **Fax** 01689 878269

Polydor

Black Lion House, 72-80 Black Lion Lane,
Hammersmith, London W6 9BE.
Telephone 0181-910 4800 **Fax** 0181 910 4801

PolyGram Classics and Jazz (UK)

22 St Peter's Square, London W6 9NW
Telephone 0181-910 5000 **Fax** 0181-748 4104

PolyGram Classics and Jazz (USA)

Worldwide Plaza, 825 Eighth Ave., New York,
NY 10019, USA
Telephone 212 333 8000 **Fax** 212 333 8118

PolyGram Record Operations

PO Box 36, Clyde Works, Grove Road, Romford,
Essex RM6 4QR
Telephone 0181-590 6044 **Fax** 0181-597 1011

Priory Records

Unit 9b, Upper Wingbury Courtyard, Wingrave,
Buckinghamshire, HP22 4LW.
Telephone 01296 68255 **Fax** 01296 682275-

Razor & Tie

214 Sullivan Street, Suite 4A, New York NY10012,
USA.(www.razorandtie.com)

Rhino Records

10635 Santa Monica Boulevard, Los Angeles,
CA 90025, USA. (www.rhino.com)
Telephone 310 474 4778 **Fax** 310 441 6578

Select Music and Video Distributors

34a Holmethorpe Avenue, Holmethorpe Estate,
Redhill, Surrey RH1 2NN.
Telephone 01737 760020 **Fax** 01737 766 316

Silva Productions Ltd.

No. 3 Prowse Place, London NW1 9PH.
(www.silvanet.demon.co.uk)
Telephone 0171-428 5500 **Fax** 0171-482 2385

Sony Music Entertainment (UK)

10 Great Marlborough Street, London W1V 2LP
Telephone 0171-911 8200 **Fax** 0171-911 8600

Sony Music Entertainment (USA)

550 Madison Avenue, New York, NY 10022, USA.
(www.sonyclassical.com)
Telephone 212 833 8000 **Fax** 212 833 8659

Sony Music Operations

Rabans Lane, Aylesbury, Buckinghamshire
HP19 3RT **Telephone** 01296 395 151 **Fax** 01296 395 551

Telarc

23307 Commerce Park Road, Cleveland,
OH 44122, USA. (www.dmn.com/telarc)
Telephone 216 464 2313

TER (That's Entertainment)

107 Kentish Town Road, London NW1 8PB.
(www.dircon.co.uk/TER)
Telephone 0171-485 9593 **Fax** 0171-485 2282

Tring International

Triangle Business Park, Wendover Road, Aylesbury,
Bucks HP22 5BL.
Telephone 01296 615800 **Fax** 01296 614250

Universal Music (UK)

5-7 Mandeville Place, London W1M 5LB.
(www.universalmusic.co.uk)
Telephone 0171-535 3500 **Fax** 0171-535 3700

Universal Music (USA)

70 Universal City Plaza, Universal City, California
CA 91608, USA.
(www.univstudios.com/music.html)
Telephone 818 777 4018 **Fax** 818 397 8726

Varèse Sarabande Records Inc.

11846 Ventura Boulevard, Suite 130, Studio
City,CA 91604, USA. (www.varesesarabande.com)
Telephone 818 753 4143 **Fax** 818 753 7596

Virgin Records

Kensal House, 553-579 Harrow Road,
London W10 4RH. (www.vmg.co.uk)
Telephone 0181-964 6000 **Fax** 0181-964 6073/0386

Walt Disney Records
3 Queen Caroline Street, Hammersmith,
(www.disney.com/DisneyRecords)
London W6 9PE. **Telephone** 0181-222 1000

Warner Music (Distribution)
PO Box 59, Alperton, Middlesex HA0 1FJ
Telephone 0181-998 8844 **Fax** 0181-998 3429

WEA/Warner Music (UK)
The Warner Building, 28 Kensington
Church Street, London W8 4BP.

(www.warnermusic.co.uk)
Telephone 0171-937 8844 **Fax** 0171-937 6645

WEA (USA)
111 North Hollywood Way, Burbank, CA 91505,
USA. (www.warnerbros.com)
Telephone 818 843 6311

ZYX Records
Unit 11, Cambridge Court, 210 Shepherds Bush
Road, Hammersmith W6 7NL
Telephone 0171 371 6969

Dealers and mail order services

UK

Backtrack
The Old Grammar School, Rye, East Sussex
TN31 7JP **Telephone** 01797 222777

Dress Circle
57/59 Monmouth Street, Upper
St Martin's Lane, london WC2H 9DG.
(www.dresscircle.co.uk)
Telephone 0171-240 2227/836 8279
Fax 0171-379 8540

EMS Imports
18 Kings Park, Primrose Hill, King's Langley,
Herts WD4 8ST **Telephone** 01923 267060
Fax 01923 260078

Farringdons Records
64-72 Leadenhall Market, London EC3V 1LT
Telephone 0171-623 9605

Farringdons Records
Royal Festival Hall, South Bank Centre, London
SE1 8XX **Telephone** 0171-620 0198

HMV
150 Oxford Street, London W1N 0DJ
Telephone 0171-631 3423

HMV
363 Oxford Street, London W1R 2BJ
Telephone 0171-629 1240

Movie Boulevard Ltd.
3 Cherry Tree Walk, Leeds LS2 7EB
Telephone 0113 242 2888 **Fax** 0113 243 8840

Rare Discs
18 Bloomsbury Street, London WC1B 3QA
Telephone 0171-4580 3516
Fax 0171-788 3809

Soundtrack Deletions
"Hillside House", 1 Woodstock Road, Strood,
Rochester, Kent.
Telephone 01634 711053 **Fax** 01634 294 176

Soundtracks Direct
No. 3 Prowse Place, London NW1 9PH.
Telephone 0171-428 5500 **Fax** 0171-482 2385
e-mail info@silvascreen.co.uk

Tower Records
1 Piccadilly Circus, London W1R 8TR
Telephone 0171-439 2500 Mail Order –
Telephone 0171-287 1510 **Fax** 0171-434 2766

Tower Records
62-64 Kensington High Street, London W8 4PL
Telephone 0171-938 3511

Virgin Megastore
14-16 Oxford Street, London W1R 1DD
Telephone 0171-491 8582

Virgin Megastore
527 Oxford Street, London W1R 7DD
Telephone 0171-580 5822/0171-631 1234

Information on the major retailers who stock shows
and soundtracks, and the location of your nearest
local branch, can be obtained by contacting the
following:

HMV	**Telephone** 0171-439 2112
Music and Video Club	**Telephone** 0181-424 0101
Tower Records	**Telephone** 0171-938 3625
Virgin/Our Price	**Telephone** 0181-400 4000
WH Smith	**Telephone** 01793 616161

In addition, the *Gramophone Blue riband* dealer
scheme contains comprehensive listings of
specialist classical UK record dealers, many of
whom also stock show recordings and soundtracks

USA

All Music Services
530 14th Street, No. 9, San Francisco, CA94103.
Telephone 415 864 8222 **Fax** 415 864 7222

Footlight Records
113 East 12th Street, New York, NY1003
Telephone 212 533 1572 (www.footlight.com)

Nathan Muchnick Inc.
1725 Chestnut Street, Philadelphia, PA19103.
Telephone 800 373 9873

STAR (SoundTrack Album Retailers)
PO Box 487, New Holland, PA17557, USA
Telephone 717 656 0121

Reference books and magazines

Applause

The Applause Building, 68 Long Acre, London
WC2E 9JQ. **Telephone** 0171-312 8051

Fax 0171-312 8090

Happy Talk

The Rodgers and Hammerstein Organization, 1633
Broadway, Suite 3801, New York NY10019-6746.

London Musical Shows on Record, 1889-1989

Gramophone Publications Ltd., 135 Greenford
Road, Sudbury Hill, Harrow, Middlesex HA1 3YD.
Telephone 0181-422 4562 **Fax** 0181-869 8400

Masquerade

32 Woodhill Road, Aberdeen AB2 4JW, Scotland.
Telephone/Fax 01224 313113

Musical Stages

PO Box 8365, London W14 0GL.
Telephone/Fax 0171-603 2221

NODA National News

National Operatic and Dramatic Association,
1 Crestfield Street, London WC1H 8AU.
Telephone 0171-837 5655 **Fax** 0171-833 0609

R.E.D. Soundtracks Catalogue

Retail Entertainment Data Publishing Ltd., Paulton
House, 8 Shepherdess Walk, London N1 7LB
Telephone 0171-566 8216 **Fax** 0171-566 8259

Show Music

Box 466, East Haddam, CT06423-0466, USA.

Tele-Tunes

Mike Preston Music, The Glengarry, Thornton
Grove, Morecambe, Lancs LA4 5PU.
Telephone 01524 421172 **Fax** 01524 421172

The Theatre List

The Society of London Theatre, Bedford Chambers,
The Piazza, Covent Garden, London WC2E 8HQ.
Telephone 0171-836 0971 **Fax** 0171-497 2543

Words and Music

84 Wellmeadow Road, Glasgow G43 1JZ, Scotland.

Index

End credits:

Once again the Editor is indebted to his
contributors for their hard work and
unfailing enthusiasm in the face of
unreasonable deadlines, and especially to
Michael Kennedy for his advice and
support. He would also like to extend his
thanks to all his colleagues in the Editorial
department at *Gramophone* for their
invaluable assistance, cheerfully given. Any
errors in the text are entirely the
responsibility of the Editor.

NAIM AUDIO FRANCHISED DEALERS

LONDON
Billy Vee Sound Systems, 248 Lee High Road, Lewisham SE13 — 0181 318 5755
The Cornflake Shop, 37 Windmill Street, W1 — 0171 631 0472
Grahams Hi-Fi, Canonbury Yard, 190a New North Road, N1 — 0171 226 5500
Thomas Heintz, 35 Moscow Road Queensway, W2 — 0171 229 2077
Hi-Fi Experience, 227 Tottenham Court Road, W1 — 0171 580 3535
Musical Images, 18 Monmouth Street, Covent Garden, WC2 — 0171 497 1346
O'Brian Hi-Fi, 60 Durham Road, Wimbledon, SW20 — 0181 946 1528
Oranges and Lemons, 61-63 Webbs Road, SW11 — 0171 924 2040
Studio 99, 79-81 Fairfax Road, NW6 — 0171 624 8855
Martin-Kleiser Ltd, 109 Chiswick High Road, W4 — 0181 400 5555

NEAR LONDON
Audio T, 173-75 London Road, Camberley, Surrey — 01276 685597
Audio T, 159a Chase Side, Enfield, Middlesex — 0181 367 3132
Infidelity, 9 High Street, Hampton Wick, Kingston-upon-Thames, Surrey — 0181 943 3530
Musical Images, 45 High Street, Hounslow, Middlesex — 0181 569 5802
The Sound Gallery, 65 Castle Street, High Wycombe, Buckinghamshire — 01494 531682
Spaldings, 352-354 Lower Addiscombe Road, Croydon, Surrey — 0181 654 1231
Uxbridge Audio, 278 High Street, Uxbridge, Middlesex — 01895 465444

SOUTH
Audio Designs, 26 High Street, East Grinstead, W Sussex — 01342 314569
Audio T, 4 Feathers lane, Basingstoke, Hampshire — 01256 324311
Audio T, 4 Queens Walk, Broad Street Mall, Reading, Berkshire — 01189 585463
Jeffries Hi-Fi, 69 London Road, Brighton, E Sussex — 01273 609431
Jeffries Hi-Fi, 4 Albert Parade, Green Street, Eastbourne, E Sussex — 01323 731336
Jeffries Hi-Fi, 29 London Road, Portsmouth, Hampshire — 01705 663604
Phase 3 Hi-Fi, 213-215 Tarring Road, Worthing, West Sussex — 01903 245577
Phonography, 2 Star Lane, Ringwood, Hampshire — 01425 461230
Salisbury Hi-Fi, 15 Catherine Street, Salisbury, Wiltshire — 01722 322169
Soundcraft, 40 High Street, Ashford, Kent — 01233 624441

EAST
The Audio File, 27 Hockerill Street, Bishops Stortford, Herts — 01279 506576
The Audio File, 41 Victoria Road, Cambridge — 01223 368305
Basically Sound, The Old School, School Road, Bracon Ash, Norwich, Norfolk — 01508 570829
Rayleigh Hi-Fi, 216 Moulsham Street, Chelmsford, Essex — 01245 265245
Rayleigh Hi-Fi, 44A High Street, Rayleigh, Essex — 01268 779762
Rayleigh Hi-Fi, 132/4 London Road, Southend-on-Sea, Essex — 01702 435255
Rayleigh Hi-Fi, Dansk World of Furniture, Lakeside Park, W Thurrock, Essex — 01708 680551

WEST
Audio Excellence, 65 Park Street, Bristol — 0117 926 4975
Audio Excellence, 156 Sidwell Street, Exeter, Devon — 01392 491194
Audio Excellence, 58 Bristol Road, Gloucester — 01452 300046
Audio T, 40-42 Albion Street, Cheltenham, Gloucestershire — 01242 583960
Audio T, 60 Fleet Street, Swindon, Wiltshire — 01793 538222
Mike Manning Audio, 54 Bridge Street, Taunton, Somerset — 01823 326688
Mike Manning Audio, 110 Middle Street, Yeovil, Somerset — 01935 479361
Radfords, 12 James Street West, Bath — 01225 446245
Radfords, 10-12 Gloucester Road, Bristol — 0117 944 1010
Radfords, 28 Cowick Street, St Thomas, Exeter, Devon — 01392 218895
Radfords, 107 Cornwall Street, Plymouth, Devon — 01752 226012

MIDLANDS
Castle Sound & Vision, 48-50 Maid Marian Way, Nottingham — 0115 958 4404
Creative Audio, 9 Dogpole, Shrewsbury, Shropshire — 01743 241924
Cymbiosis, 6 Hotel Street, Leicester — 0116 262 3754
English Audio, 37 Whitecross Road, Hereford — 01452 355081
Griffin Audio, 94 Bristol Street, Birmingham — 0121 692 1359
Hi-Fi Company, 42 Cowgate, Peterborough, Cambridgeshire — 01733 341755
Listen Inn, 32 Gold Street, Northampton — 01604 37871
New Audio Frontiers, 43 Granby Street, Loughborough, Leicestershire — 01509 264002
Overture, 3 Church Lane, Banbury, Oxfordshire — 01295 272158
Radfords, 6 South Parade, Summertown, Oxford — 01865 511241
Sevenoaks Hi-Fi, 29-31 Peters Street, Bedford — 01234 272779
Sevenoaks Sound & Vision, 12 Queensway Arches, 222 Livery Street, Birmingham — 0121 233 2977
Sound Academy, 152a High Street, Bloxwick, West Midland — 01922 473499
Sound & Vision, Independence House, Trinity Street, Worcester — 01905 619059

NORTH
Acoustica, 17 Hoole Road, Chester, Cheshire — 01244 344227
Audio Counsel, 14 Stockport Road, Cheadle, Cheshire — 0161 428 7887
Audio Counsel, 12 Shaw Road, Oldham, Lancashire — 0161 633 2602
Audio Excellence, 86-90 Boughton, Chester, Cheshire — 01244 345576
Audio Excellence, 131 Friargate, Preston, Lancashire — 01772 253057
Audio Images, 284 Glossop Road Sheffield, South Yorkshire — 0114 273 7893
Better Hi-Fi, 16 Cook Street, Liverpool 2, Merseyside — 0151 227 5007
Doug Brady Hi-Fi, Kingsway Studios, Kingsway North, Warrington, Cheshire — 01925 828009
Hale Hi-Fi, 2 Bold Street, Hale Road, Altrincham, Cheshire — 0161 929 0834
Image Hi-Fi, 8-10 St Annes Street, Headingly, Leeds, Yorkshire — 0113 278 9374
Lintone Audio, 8 The Arcade, Metro Centre, Gateshead, Tyne and Wear, — 0191 460 0999
Lintone Audio, 7-11 Pak Lane, Gateshead 8, Tyne and Wear — 0191 477 4167
Peter Martin Hi-Fi Showrooms, 12A West Street, Congleton, Cheshire — 01260 280017
Moorgate Acoustics, 184 Fitzwilliam Street, Sheffield, South Yorkshire — 0114 275 6048
The Sound Organisation, 2B Gillygate, York — 01904 627108
Zen Audio, 35 George Street, Hull, North Humberside — 01482 587397

WALES
Audio Excellence, 134 Crwys Road,Cardiff, South Glamorgan — 01222 228565
Audio Excellence, 9 High Street, Swansea, West Glamorgan — 01792 474608

SCOTLAND
Loud and Clear Ltd, 520 St Vincent Street, Glasgow — 0141 221 0221
Russ Andrews High Fidelity Ltd, 34 Northumberland Street, Edinburgh — 0131 557 1672
Music Mill, Bonnington Mill Business Centre, 72 Newhaven Road Edinburgh — 0131 555 3963
River Hi-Fi, 28 Church Crescent, Dumfries — 01387 267048
Robert Richie, 102-106 Murray Street, Montrose, Tayside — 01674 673765
Stereo Stereo, 278 St Vincent Street, Glasgow — 0141 248 4079

NORTHERN IRELAND
Lyric Hi-Fi, 163 Stranmillis Road, Belfast — 01232 381296

Naim products are distributed in the USA by Naim Audio North America Inc
2702 West Touhy Avenue, Chicago IL 60645 USA Tel 773 338 6262 Fax 733 338 6202